Archangels and Angels

Embracing Guidance from Guardian Angels, Metatron, Michael, Raphael, Uriel, and the Mysteries of Angel Numbers

© Copyright 2024 - All rights reserved.

The contents of this book may not be reproduced, duplicated, or transmitted without direct written permission from the author.

Under no circumstances will any legal responsibility or blame be held against the publisher for any reparation, damages, or monetary loss due to the information herein, either directly or indirectly.

Legal Notice:

This book is copyright protected. This is only for personal use. You cannot amend, distribute, sell, use, quote, or paraphrase any part or the content within this book without the consent of the author.

Disclaimer Notice:

Please note the information contained within this document is for educational and entertainment purposes only. Every attempt has been made to provide accurate, up-to-date, and reliable, complete information. No warranties of any kind are expressed or implied. Readers acknowledge that the author is not engaging in the rendering of legal, financial, medical, or professional advice. The content of this book has been derived from various sources. Please consult a licensed professional before attempting any techniques outlined in this book.

By reading this document, the reader agrees that under no circumstances is the author responsible for any losses, direct or indirect, which are incurred as a result of the use of the information contained within this document, including, but not limited to, —errors, omissions, or inaccuracies.

Your Free Gift
(only available for a limited time)

Thanks for getting this book! If you want to learn more about various spirituality topics, then join Mari Silva's community and get a free guided meditation MP3 for awakening your third eye. This guided meditation mp3 is designed to open and strengthen ones third eye so you can experience a higher state of consciousness. Simply visit the link below the image to get started.

https://spiritualityspot.com/meditation

Or, Scan the QR code!

Table of Contents

PART 1: GUARDIAN ANGELS 1
    INTRODUCTION 2
    CHAPTER 1: WHAT ARE GUARDIAN ANGELS? 4
    CHAPTER 2: TAPPING INTO YOUR HIGHER SELF 11
    CHAPTER 3: COMMUNICATING WITH YOUR GUARDIAN ANGEL 24
    CHAPTER 4: WORKING WITH THE ARCHANGELS 37
    CHAPTER 5: FINDING YOUR SPIRIT GUIDE 50
    CHAPTER 6: FOLLOWING YOUR ANIMAL GUIDE 59
    CHAPTER 7: CALLING UPON ANCESTORS AND DEPARTED LOVED ONES 67
    CHAPTER 8: CONNECTING WITH ASCENDED MASTERS 74
    CHAPTER 9: WORKING WITH GODS AND GODDESSES 82
    CONCLUSION 88
PART 2: METATRON 90
    INTRODUCTION 91
    CHAPTER 1: WHO IS ARCHANGEL METATRON? 93
    CHAPTER 2: ASCENSION WITH METATRON 104
    CHAPTER 3: RECOGNIZING METATRON'S PRESENCE 115
    CHAPTER 4: METATRON'S CUBE 125
    CHAPTER 5: PILLAR OF LIGHT MEDITATION 136
    CHAPTER 6: ANGELIC REIKI AND HEALING 146
    CHAPTER 7: CRYSTALS TO CONNECT WITH METATRON 158

CHAPTER 8: CORD CUTTING AND SHIELDING 171
CHAPTER 9: DAILY MEDITATIONS 181
BONUS: CORRESPONDENCES SHEET 191
CONCLUSION 200
PART 3: ARCHANGEL MICHAEL 202
INTRODUCTION 203
CHAPTER 1: WHO IS ARCHANGEL MICHAEL? 205
CHAPTER 2: HOW TO CALL UPON ARCHANGEL MICHAEL 215
CHAPTER 3: SIGNS THAT ARCHANGEL MICHAEL IS PRESENT 225
CHAPTER 4: REQUESTING PROTECTION 233
CHAPTER 5: REQUESTING HEALING 244
CHAPTER 6: BANISHING NEGATIVE ENERGY 254
CHAPTER 7: CRYSTALS TO CONNECT WITH ARCHANGEL MICHAEL 264
CHAPTER 8: HERBS AND ESSENTIAL OILS OF ARCHANGEL MICHAEL 274
CHAPTER 9: DAILY RITUALS 284
BONUS: CORRESPONDENCES SHEET 294
CONCLUSION 302
PART 4: ARCHANGEL RAPHAEL 304
INTRODUCTION 305
CHAPTER 1: WHO IS ARCHANGEL RAPHAEL? 307
CHAPTER 2: WHEN AND HOW TO CALL UPON ARCHANGEL RAPHAEL 315
CHAPTER 3: SIGNS THAT ARCHANGEL RAPHAEL IS PRESENT 326
CHAPTER 4: HEALING NEGATIVE THOUGHTS AND EMOTIONS 334
CHAPTER 5: HEALING RELATIONSHIPS AND MARRIAGES 345
CHAPTER 6: HEALING THE PHYSICAL BODY 355
CHAPTER 7: ANGELIC REIKI 365
CHAPTER 8: HEALING FOR HEALERS 376
CHAPTER 9: CREATIVE RITUALS 383
CONCLUSION 391
CORRESPONDENCES SHEET 393
PART 5: ARCHANGEL URIEL 395
INTRODUCTION 396
CHAPTER 1: WHO IS ARCHANGEL URIEL? 398

CHAPTER 2: INVOKING ARCHANGEL URIEL 408
CHAPTER 3: SIGNS OF URIEL'S PRESENCE.. 418
CHAPTER 4: CREATING ANGELIC SACRED SPACE........................... 429
CHAPTER 5: SOLAR CHAKRA MEDITATION.. 439
CHAPTER 6: FIRE-IN-PALM MEDITATION 449
CHAPTER 7: DREAMWORK 458
CHAPTER 8: CRYSTALS AND CANDLES 468
CHAPTER 9: DAILY RITUALS AND EXERCISES................................ 480
BONUS: CORRESPONDENCES SHEET 488
CONCLUSION 490

PART 6: ANGEL NUMBERS 492
INTRODUCTION 493
CHAPTER 1: WHAT ARE ANGEL NUMBERS? 495
CHAPTER 2: NUMEROLOGY 101... 505
CHAPTER 3: ANGEL NUMBERS INTERPRETED 515
CHAPTER 4: OTHER SIGNS OF ANGELIC PRESENCE 524
CHAPTER 5: ANGELIC SYMBOLS AND SIGILS 534
CHAPTER 6: SYNCHRONICITY, DIVINE TIMING, AND COINCIDENCE... 545
CHAPTER 7: ANGELIC CORRESPONDENCES 555
CHAPTER 8: THE LAW OF ATTRACTION... 568
CHAPTER 9: DAILY MEDITATIONS 578
CONCLUSION 589

HERE'S ANOTHER BOOK BY MARI SILVA THAT YOU MIGHT LIKE... 591
YOUR FREE GIFT (ONLY AVAILABLE FOR A LIMITED TIME) 592
REFERENCES 593
IMAGE SOURCES 615

Part 1: Guardian Angels

Discovering How to Connect with Spirit Guides, Angels, Departed Loved Ones, Archangels, Spirit Animals, Ancestors, and Other Helpers

Introduction

Guardian angels are waiting for you to find them. They are standing by to hear you call to them and to respond instantly. The reason why they are not responding is because you are not calling. And you are not calling because you are unaware of their presence. This book aims to dispel the darkness of unawareness and bring you the light of knowledge and acceptance.

Written in easy-to-understand languages and filled with detailed and easy-to-follow instructions and hands-on methods, this book on guardian angels is great for beginners taking shaky steps toward their goal. This book will help you firm up the shakiness brought on by initial doubts that prevent you from moving forward. It supports you until you find steady feet on strong ground so you can move forward to higher planes of consciousness.

This book covers all kinds of guardian angels who can come to your aid, from those who can protect you from harm, keep obstacles at bay, and give you materialistic benefits right up to those who can help you with ascension and enlightenment. This book covers a comprehensive list of guardian angels and instructions on reaching out to them and seeking their help and counsel.

For example, if you need protection, call out to Archangel Michael. If you seek wealth and prosperity, seek Goddess Lakshmi, and so forth. The book is not religious in any way. It is spiritual, dipping into all cultures and religions and taking the best each offers you. You will find connections between guardian angels, colors, symbols, and much more.

Every chapter in this book is filled with angel-seeking and soothing words of knowledge and light. You will be guided to open your heart, mind, and soul to receive the abundance your guardian angels are waiting to shower on you and your loved ones. Read slowly, savoring every word, soaking in the beauty of guardian angels and their powers, and knowing that the lessons taught in this book can help you feel the presence of the angels in your life.

A word of caution before you begin reading the book. Please note that the instructions given in this book are not intended to replace professional medical advice in any way whatsoever. Before trying out any practical exercises mentioned in this book, including meditation, rituals, and other exercises, please speak to a qualified medical practitioner and/or psychiatrist and let them know you are doing this. They will guide you in case of contraindications.

Go on, turn the page, read – and to remind you once again – read *slowly*, savoring every word this book contains, leading you to your guardian angels.

Chapter 1: What Are Guardian Angels?

The concept of guardian angels and helper spirits is found in nearly all spiritual belief systems and religions of the world. These guardian angels are supernatural beings assigned by the divine world for the welfare of human beings on Earth. They are found everywhere.

St. Augustine speaks of guardian angels and angels as follows,

"Angels are spirits created by God. However, if they are simply spirits, they are not angels. If they are sent to do His bidding, the spirits become angels. God makes spirits angels by commanding them to do his bidding or order."

References to guardian angels can be found in the Bible.[1]

Many ancient texts, including the Old Testament, reference to guardian angels. Every religion has its own version of guardian angels. Let's look at a few.

Guardian Angels in Christianity

One of the first references to angels happens immediately after the fall of man (when Adam ate the forbidden fruit). A biblical verse goes like this, *"He drove the man out of His garden. He then placed the cherub along with a flaming sword to guard the tree of life."* Although the word "angel" is not used here, the definition of angel explained above makes the cherub one of them. God commanded the cherub to guard the Tree of Life. So, the first angel was created not for human beings but against them so they could not enter the Garden of Eden without His approval.

Another reference to angels comes when God sends "messengers" to warn Lot and his family about the impending destruction of Sodom. When Lot refused to leave, the "messengers" forced him out of the city, thus saving him, as commanded by God.

In the Gospels, Jesus calls his followers to respect every small and humble being in deference to the creature's guardian angel appointed by God to watch over it. God works His miracles through His guardian angels, protecting and providing for every form of life on Earth.

In Christianity, every person is assigned a guardian angel who stays with them right from the time of their birth until their death. Multiple saints and men of God from ancient and medieval times maintained the existence of guardian angels who live within His grace. These men of the church, like Saint Augustine and Tertullian, Saint Jerome, Saint John Chrysostom, and others, encouraged Christians to connect with their guardian angels.

Further, from the 17th century, the popularity of guardian angels increased considerably in the realm of Christianity, and Pope Paul V introduced the Festival of Guardian Angels to the Christian calendar. These angels found representation in all sacred events and among popular devotion and faith images. These angels were depicted as protectors, protecting everyone, especially children, from harm. Some pertinent points about guardian angels in Christianity follow.

The presence and existence of guardian angels are affirmed by the Gospels and Scriptures, supported by numerous examples and stories. The Catechism teaches followers to feel the presence of their guardian angels from their childhood and trust them.

Angels were created in thousands by the Divine Will in a single moment. After that moment, He did not manifest any more angels, and since then, the original angels have existed for eternity.

A structural hierarchy exists among the angels, and conditions must be met before becoming a *guardian angel*. The position and function of each angel are different, and not all of them are destined to become guardian angels. Some are called upon to take a test, and if they pass, they become guardian angels.

A guardian angel is assigned to every newborn child to remain with the person through their human life until death and beyond.

Every Christian has one and only one guardian angel who cannot be given away, shared, or sold. The primary function of this guardian angel is to guide people. He cannot interfere with their free will, cannot decide for them, and cannot impose choices on them. Those are theirs to make.

But your guardian angel is always by your side, trying his best to suggest a good way of life, avoid pitfalls, show you the right path, and light up your path to heaven. Christians believe that their guardian angel, most of all, helps them to be good people and faithful Christians. Guardian angels never abandon you, come what may.

Guardian Angels in Judaism

In the Old Testament, God is described as sitting in His heavenly court surrounded by spiritual beings who worship Him and do His bidding on Earth. All their actions are of, by, and through Him. The Hebrew word for angel is "malach" or "messenger."

According to Judaism, at every mitzvah (good deed or religious commandment/precept), angels are created who protect and shield followers from harm. Sometimes, God sends an angel as an emissary to help or guide you. After your death, these angels (created through belief work) testify for you in His heavenly court. It is important to remember that Judaism holds that an angel only acts as His emissary, nothing more and nothing less.

The four archangels, namely Michael, Gabriel, Uriel, and Raphael, find abundant references in Judaism. The archangels will be discussed in detail later on in the chapter. While only these four archangels find a hallowed place in ancient scriptures, many more angels appear in later antiquity. It was an angel who stopped Abraham from sacrificing his son. Another angel wrestled Jacob, and an angel of death too.

The Jews believe angels are subordinate beings and act in alignment with God's will. There are many other angel connections in Jewish liturgy, including:

- The famous Kedushah Prayer is believed to have been written from prophetic visions in which angels sang these verses.
- Wearing white on Yom Kippur reflects the belief that on that day of fasting and repentance, the Jews are like angels who rise above bodily needs.

Guardian Angels in Islam

Followers of Islam start their prayers with the acknowledgment of guardian angels, although no prayers are dedicated to them. Muslims recite Hadith and Quran verses that speak of guardian angels.

The quintessential Islamic greeting "Assalamu alaikum" translates to "Peace be upon you." Muslims say this phrase often by looking at their left and right shoulders because they believe that guardian angels referred to as "Kiraman Katibin," reside there. They believe it is appropriate and correct to acknowledge their presence in your life and are therefore included in their daily rituals.

This belief in guardian angels is rooted in various verses in the Quran, such as the following:

"Behold the two guardian angels assigned to learn every man's doings and actions, residing on his left and right side. Not a single word or act is left unnoticed by these appointed sentinels who are ever ready to take note of everything the man does or says."

The "Kiraman Katibin" angelic team works together to record every detail of the man's life to whom God has assigned them. The recordings are very detailed and include every feeling, thought, action, and word. The guardian angel on the right shoulder records the morally good aspects of the man, while the angel on the left shoulder records his bad choices and wrongdoings.

When the world ends, the " Kiraman Katibin" guardian angels will present the records of every human being they have worked with right through the history of humankind. God will send the men and women to heaven or hell, depending on the records of the guardian angels.

Another Quranic verse about guardian angels goes like this,

"For every person in this world, there are guardian angels going before and after him, protecting and guarding the man according to Allah's command."

Therefore, according to Islam, there are guardian angels for protection, too.

Hadiths (prophetic traditions written by Islamic scholars) also reference guardian angels. One such hadith by the scholar Muhammad al-Bukhari goes like this,

"Angels take turns around you. Some of them come by night, and some by day. All of them assemble during the Fajr (pre-dawn) and Asr (pre-evening) prayers. At night, they ascend heavenwards to meet Allah, who asks (even though He knows more), 'How have you left my beloved servants?' They answer, 'Just as we found them. Praying!"

This hadith carries the message of the importance of prayer and the significance of guardian angels, both of which, according to Islam, help followers get closer to God. Guardian angels protect and pray for their assigned people and deliver messages to God.

Who Are Archangels?

There is also a hierarchical structure among angels, and archangels are at the top of the ladder. They are high-ranking angels created by the Divine Will to offer wisdom to human beings so that we can deepen our connection with Him and the universe He created. There are seven archangels referenced in various scriptures. These seven are Michael, Raphael, Gabriel, Jophiel, Ariel, Azrael, and Chamuel.

Every archangel has a specific role to play in the grand scheme of the cosmos, and each of their names also has a different and specific meaning and significance. Let's look at the seven archangels a little more in detail.

Michael - His name means *"He who is as God."* Aligned with warrior-like attitudes such as bravery, justice, and strength, Michael is here to protect humans. Michael is the most powerful and well-known archangel. He is the angel you call for help in moments of crisis. His wise guidance will help and protect you in your weakest moments. He is often depicted as a glimmer of blue light.

Raphael - His name translates to *"God heals,"* and as his name suggests, he is responsible for healing physical and emotional issues and ailments. Doctors and other medical practitioners seek Raphael's help whenever they need assistance. You can call him when you or someone you know is sick and needs healing which can come in the form of a miracle or a solution to restore the affected person's well-being. Raphael is depicted as a glimmer of green light.

Gabriel - Gabriel means *"God is my strength."* He is the angel of communication and the messenger of God. People working in the field of communication consider Gabriel their patron, although he excels at helping teachers, artists, and writers too. If you have trouble expressing or communicating your thoughts and feelings, seek Archangel Gabriel's help. He is associated with the color white.

Jophiel - His name translates to *"beauty of God."* His primary function is to make you see the beauty in God's creation and to redirect your perception to God's love in all that you see. Jophiel is the one you should call when you are stuck in a rut of negativity. He can guide you, shift your perspective, and redirect your life toward love. His color is yellow. Yellow should remind you that you need to change your perspective to find what you seek.

Ariel - Ariel means "Lion of God," and his job is to protect the Earth, her resources, and the life forms that inhabit Earth. He is the patron of environmental activists, animal lovers, and all things associated with Mother Earth and her resources. He is associated with the color purple.

Azrael - His name means *"whom God helps."* Azrael's main role is to help the suffering and the diseases transition smoothly into the spiritual realm, and for this reason, he is also known as the Angel of Death. If you are facing a lot of losses and deaths, call Archangel Azrael to ease the pain and reduce the losses. However, "death" need not be taken in the literal sense. Job changes, moving home, doing things in a new way by discarding the old, starting a new relationship, etc., are also situations where Azrael can help. Azrael's color is indigo.

Chamuel - Chamuel translates to *"he who sees God."* His responsibility is to bring peace to the world. He is created with the power to bring order even in the most chaotic situations. If drama and conflict surround you, call upon Archangel Chamuel to restore peace and harmony. He is associated with the color pink.

Four of these seven archangels have more importance than the other three, which will be discussed in a later chapter dedicated to archangels.

In summary, regardless of the religion, guardian angels are spiritual beings and higher-order angels assigned to each person by the divine to help them through their lives. Most importantly, for all people seeking help from all corners of the cosmos, guardian angels come in many forms. They could be tangible in the form of other wiser and more experienced humans. Or they could be a product of your subconscious mind as you seek a respite from life's burdens and challenges.

Regardless of their form and regardless of which religion or belief system you follow, what matters the most is the keenness or your desire to resonate with them and find ways to reach out and take what they have to offer. And even more important is to be open to having experiences related to guardian angels. It could be an unreasonable expectation if you lock your heart and mind and expect supernatural beings to knock on your door. Keep your heart and mind open to the magic of guardian angels, and you will be able to harvest the advantages of these wonderful beings.

Chapter 2: Tapping into Your Higher Self

Communicating with the invisible, spiritual realms requires you to be prepared with theoretical knowledge *and practice*. You need to know where and how you can access these realms. You need to know the elements that can help you tap into your higher self, one that is usually dormant until you make an effort to awaken it. Four of the most important elements that help you access the invisible realm are the spiritual body, the higher self, the chakra system, and the aura body. Let's look at these three individually and understand how they work.

The chakra system can help you connect with the invisible realm.[2]

The Spiritual Body

Jill Willard – a powerful Intuitive and a leader in the practice of meditation – says that the human body is composed of four distinct parts: the physical, emotional, mental, and emotional. Three of these four parts are seemingly tangible, but each body contributes 25% to your wholeness. Your body's physical, emotional, and mental aspects are clear, and most people know them and have experienced them and their effects on their lives. Thus, it's worth discussing the spiritual body.

So, what is the spiritual body? It is that which connects you to all the things in this cosmos, including the Earth and beyond, God (or the Divine Will), and your higher self. The spiritual body protects and guides you from a source outside and beyond the five-sense world you know and experience daily. The spiritual body connects you to everything in this external source, spirits, angels, divine beings, and everything outside the physical realm.

Many people are unaware of the existence of the spiritual body, a facet of life that has nothing to do with the religion you follow or the culture to which you belong. The spiritual body is an element that tells you that no one in this world is alone. Everyone is interconnected, and it takes more than just one physical body and its mental and emotional aspects to create and sustain life in the universe.

When your spiritual body is balanced, you feel calm and fearless and can work without anything limiting you. You get the fortitude and support to concretize your ideas in the physical realm. You know for certain that there are realms that are way beyond what the average human being can access. With repeated practice of knowing and understanding your spiritual body, you can access the invisible realm where guardian angels reside.

The Higher Self

In most spiritual discussions and talks, you come across words like, "Connect with your highest self to achieve peace, calm, and self-actualize." But what is this higher self? Can it be described? And how can it help you to achieve all that it promises?

The higher self is that part of you that goes beyond your physical body. It inspires, guides, and teaches you through your instincts and insights. Your higher self is well aware of your secret dreams and goals.

However, most people do not really try to connect with this part of themselves because, first, many are unaware of its existence, and those who know it either doubt it or find it difficult and tricky to connect with it.

In the language of psychology, the higher self is an inner guidance connected with the cosmos and separate from your physical, emotional, and mental personality. It is also not your ego, even though it can advise you about your ego. The higher self connects the material world to the mystical, invisible world. Your higher self is part of you, although it operates at a higher vibrational frequency than your physical body.

Your physical body is the current human life that you are living, whereas the higher self is the spiritual component that has seen and lived multiple lives. A life without any connection to the higher self is limited to the physical realms. Such lives are easily swayed by the temporary, feeble aspects of the physical world that lack authentic, sustaining inner strength and power. When you connect with your higher self, you get multiple benefits, including:

- Regardless of what is happening in your physical life, you feel fulfilled, and your life feels magical.
- Your life events are more purposeful, and you don't resent any of the experiences you face.
- You know and accept that pain is not an obstacle but an opportunity for growth and development.
- You feel supported, connected, and empowered.

The Chakra System

Chakra is a Sanskrit word meaning "*disk*" or "*wheel.*" According to the ancient Indian Yoga system, chakras or wheels of energy reside in strategic places aligned with the spine. These wheels of energy cannot be seen but felt, and their power can be invoked to connect with the invisible realm. The healing energy in these chakras forms your body's vital life force, which keeps the body active, strong, healthy, and powerful.

The chakras hold the energy of your feelings, thoughts, past memories, experiences, and future insights. How do these chakras help your well-being and your ability to connect with your guardian angels?

First, your body, mind, and spirit are all interconnected. Therefore, an imbalance in any of these three aspects will impact your entire being. You may have heard of many cases where physicians could not find a physiological reason for someone's illness, yet that disease existed in the body. In such cases, the root cause could be something in the mind or spirit. For example, a woman who has lost her beloved husband can get acute stomach pain or heartburn that may never have a physiological cause. Her physical ailment is rooted in the grief of her broken mind and spirit that she has yet to overcome.

There are seven main chakras, the first at the base of the spine and the last on the crown of the head. Each chakra is associated with different parts of your physical, mental, emotional, and spiritual body. The chakras have to be balanced and energy flow in them unblocked for optimal benefits. Let's briefly look at each of these seven vortexes of power and energy and how they help you to maintain your equilibrium.

The root chakra: Located at the base of the spine, the root chakra (or the Muladhara in Sanskrit) is connected to your basic survival needs, such as food, sleep, shelter, and other basic materialistic needs. When this root is unbalanced and/or the energy flow is blocked, you experience existential fears, and when balanced, you feel safe, secure, and stable.

The sacral chakra: Located two inches below the navel, this energy vortex (Svadhishthana in Sanskrit) is responsible for the reproductive organs, including the testes and the ovaries. Your sexual energy is stored here, and therefore, it is connected with all your relationships. When the sacral chakra is out of balance, you tend to overindulge or under indulge in your sexual endeavors. When the energy flow is unblocked, you tend to have harmonious, happy relationships.

The navel chakra: Located at the navel, this chakra (Manipura in Sanskrit) is the seat of the digestive fire and deals with the functions of the adrenal glands and the pancreas. A person with an unbalanced navel chakra tends to be overly domineering or completely powerless. A balanced navel chakra is a source of enthusiasm leading to empowerment and the ability to achieve your goals. The navel chakra is also called the solar plexus.

The above three chakras represent the physical realms. The four chakras discussed below are associated with the mental and spiritual realms.

The heart chakra: Located in the center of the chest, the heart chakra (Anahata in Sanskrit) is associated with love and connection. It also bridges the upper spiritual chakras and the lower physical energy vortexes. An unbalanced heart chakra manifests in the form of excessive possessiveness and/or an unreasonable desire for constant attention. A balanced heart chakra translates to the start of experiencing an expanded consciousness.

The throat chakra: Located at the center of the throat, this energy vortex (Vishuddha in Sanskrit) is associated with communication and expression, specifically with that of truth and authenticity. When this chakra is blocked, you tend to have difficulty communicating and expressing yourself. This chakra is an excellent source to connect with our authenticity and purity when opened and balanced.

The third eye chakra: Located between the eyebrows, this chakra (Agnya in Sanskrit) is the seat of the mind and the center of your intuition. A blocked or unbalanced third eye chakra prevents you from connecting with your higher self, while a balanced, free-flowing status allows you to control your mind and, through it, your body.

The crown chakra: Located at the top of your head, the crown chakra (Sahasrara in Sanskrit) is the center of enlightenment and the bridge connecting you to your higher self. It is the seat of your soul.

Importantly, the chakras' alignment must be taken step-by-step and gradually. It is impossible to awaken or unblock the Sahasrara without caring for the lower chakras. You have to start with the lower chakras, get your physical body in order, and then move up to the higher energy vortexes until you reach the crown chakra, which, when opened, will give you limitless access to the invisible realm, the seat of divine beings including your guardian angels.

The Aura

Every living thing in this world has an aura, the invisible spiritual field surrounding the body. There are seven layers in this aura body, each of which relates to different elements of your physical, mental, emotional, and spiritual health. The seven colors of the aura body and their connotations are as follows:

- **Red** - The red aural layer represents being energetic, well-grounded, and having a strong will.

- **Orange** - Orange aura stands for being adventurous, considerate, and thoughtful.
- **Yellow** - Stands for being friendly, creative, and relaxed.
- **Green** - Stands for being nurturing, having good social skills, and communication.
- **Blue** - Stands for freethinking, being a spiritual seeker, and being intuitive.
- **Indigo** - Represents being gentle, curious, and spiritually connected.
- **Violet** - Stands for independence, wisdom, and intellect.

The intensity of the colors of these seven layers describes the depth and complexity of the various traits. Your higher self can be felt, experienced, and even seen in your aura, and it appears like a radiant point of light about three feet above the top of your head. So, when you learn to experience your aura by connecting with it and cleansing it regularly, you will be able to tap into your higher self, the one that knows your true purpose, your past, present, and future, your potential, and your strengths and weaknesses.

How to Access the Intangible Systems

So, how do you connect with and strengthen these four intangible elements that play a pivotal role in your effort to connect with your guardian angels? Before you try any of the recommendations below, the first thing to know and accept is that your higher self is not in some unreachable realm. It is part of you; it has been - and will always be - part of you. To harness their power, you must only deepen your connection with these spiritual aspects.

The more you connect with your spiritual identities, the easier it is to accept and take advantage of the power of your spiritual experiences. The most common ways are meditation, visualization, and breathwork, designed to decrease the distance between your physical and spiritual identities. Let's look at each of them in a bit of detail.

Create a Sacred Space

A sacred space is where you can discover yourself repeatedly. It is a dedicated space in your home where you can do all your spiritual work, including meditation, breathwork, etc. Even if you are not yet a spiritually inclined person, a sacred space can be your quiet getaway from the noise and the hustle-bustle of daily life.

Creating a sacred space can be as simple as having a chair in a favorite spot in your home where you can sit and mull things quietly. Alternatively, it can be a space where you can light a candle, place the image or idol of your deity (if you have one), burn some incense, place a couple of crystals to keep out negativity and attract positivity, etc.

Your sacred space can also be a home for your favorite memorabilia you have collected over your lifetime. The foundation of a sacred space is that you should feel at peace and utterly comfortable in that area.

Breathwork

Breathwork involves conscious breathing techniques that help you bypass the mind to enter higher states of consciousness and awareness. Breathwork gives your brain's cognitive function something to focus on so that you can bypass the mental body and go into the spiritual, invisible realm.

There are different forms of breathwork, each with its own set of rules and unique purpose based on which you get varying effects. Breathwork techniques help you become aware of your thoughts, feelings, and memories. Here are some pointers to create your own sacred space:

First, decide what is "sacred" for you. Avoid trends and what others are doing. Ask yourself and find authentic answers aligned with your lifestyle and needs. Do you need your space to do meditation, yoga, or simply an undisturbed spot to read? If you have picked up this book, you are looking for a spiritual connection. In that case, you already know what you need your sacred space for.

Next, find a spot in your home that can become your sacred space. While an entire room is nice, you don't need one. A small corner in your home is enough. It can be the top of your dresser, a small table in your reading room, or a sunroom. Some people have their sacred space right in the middle of their living room, and you can choose one that suits you best.

Once you have found your space, create an altar. Find personal, meaningful items for your altar. For example, some people may have little miniature idols passed on from their parents or grandparents. It could be something you bought while on a trip to your favorite place of worship. It could be a gift from someone special who loves and cares for you. It could be an item that lifted you from your lowest point in life.

Place all these items neatly on a tray or a table, depending on the size of your space. Candles and incense make a lot of sense too. Lighting a candle and/or burning incense before your meditation or breathwork session sets the right mood.

Your sacred place is ready! Remember, there are no hard and fast rules to creating this space. You can do what drives and motivates you. But usually, the items mentioned above are part of any sacred space. So, now it's time to get down to how you can tap into your higher self.

Meditation

Meditation is the easiest lesson to learn but not as easy to practice. Without disciplined regularity, mastering meditation will not happen. When you meditate, you deliberately cut out all external noises and turn inward to find those elements that help you connect with the spiritual realm. It could be your aura, spiritual body, or chakras. Meditation can help quieten the noise around and within you so that you can tap into your higher self. Here is a simple meditation exercise for you to get started.

Sit in your sacred space. You will need about 10 minutes initially. As you keep practicing, you can increase the duration. Make sure all distracting elements are turned off and kept away from you.

Sit with your back erect but not too stiff. You should be relaxed and comfortable. Take a couple of deep breaths for enhanced relaxation.

Now, notice your thoughts consciously. Avoid trying to control your mind. Your mind's job is to think; therefore, trying to stop it would be counterproductive for your needs. Just be aware of each thought as it comes and goes. Suppose the first thought that you noticed was how you felt when your partner rejected you. Notice your body's reaction to this thought. Did you feel your body stiffen? Did tears come to your eyes? Did anger arise? Just observe all this without reacting or responding to them, and you will notice that thought has passed and another has taken its place.

Try and notice as many thoughts as you can. Observe every thought taking root in your mind, becoming powerful, causing reactions and responses in you, and then going away into oblivion. The same thought could return, and you merely repeat the above process for each thought.

It seems like a simple process, and yet it can be a challenge to do it. The most important thing is not to be impatient and/or unkind to yourself. Until now, your mind did as it pleased and without your awareness. Now, you are trying to become aware of your mind. Any change will have resistance, and fighting that resistance is the key to seeing what is behind the wall. Just embrace everything that comes with your thoughts, including your thoughts themselves.

As you practice this day after day, diligently and unfailingly, you will notice that you can sit for longer without becoming affected by the reactions and responses created by these thoughts. You learn to allow them without resistance, and your mind slows down enough to see each thought more clearly and impactfully than before. Thoughts do not disturb you anymore. On the contrary, they give you deep insights into the workings of your mind.

The deeper you go into your mind, the closer you go toward your higher self.

Chakra Meditation with Visualization

Use these steps to meditate successfully on your seven chakras and feel the energy in each of them flow freely throughout your body and mind.

As usual for any form of meditation, make sure you have at least 10-15 minutes of undisturbed time. You can use your sacred space or any other place that suits you. Sit comfortably, ensuring electronic notifications are all switched off.

You can do the chakra meditation while either standing up or sitting down. Close your eyes, take a few breaths to ground yourself, and then focus on the seven chakras, starting with the root chakra. If you are sitting on a chair, ensure your feet are firmly placed on the ground. Your body must be connected to the earth.

Root chakra - Bring your focus to the base of your spine. Imagine a red disc or wheel of light spinning at the root chakra's location. Imagine this red light connecting your body firmly to the earth through your feet. As you breathe in, visualize drawing positive vibes from the earth into your root chakra. As you breathe out, visualize sending off all negative vibes from your body into the earth. When you feel satisfied, move to the sacral chakra.

Sacral chakra – Focus on the point two inches below your navel, where the sacral chakra is located. Imagine a bright orange disc or wheel spinning in that location. As you breathe in, visualize energy being drawn from the ocean into your body. As you breathe out, visualize all the negative energy leaving your body to be absorbed into the mighty ocean. Keep focusing on the sacral chakra until you feel cleansed of all negative emotions.

Remember, the red disc of the root chakra is still spinning even if your attention is not on it. Now visualize a tube of red light from there reaching up to the navel and connecting itself to the orange disc.

Navel chakra - Focus on the solar plexus imagining a yellow ball of fire spinning at the location. As you breathe in, visualize the fire burning away all the blocks and negativity from your body. You can visualize the smoke from the burned negativity finding its way to your nostrils and leaving your system as you exhale. Visualize the tube of orange and red moving up and connecting itself to the solar plexus's yellow ball of fire.

Heart chakra - As you move up to the heart chakra, visualize a disc of green light spinning at the center of your chest, the location of the Anahata. As you breathe in, visualize love filling up the green disc. Imagine this love permeating every part of your body. As you breathe out, visualize hate, resentment, jealousy, and all other emotions opposing your love and compassion for yourself being exhaled out of your system. Finally, imagine the red-orange-yellow tube from the chakras beneath rising up to connect itself with the green disc of the heart chakra.

Throat chakra - As you move up to the throat chakra, move your head around in a circle (5 counts anticlockwise and 5 counts clockwise) to relax the neck area. Focus on the area of your throat, imaging a blue disc spinning there, empowering you to identify and stand by your authenticity.

Visualizing the blue light emerging out of your ears also helps you be a good listener. Imagine the power of written and vocal communication entering your system as you breathe in and visualize all the blockages of communication leaving your system as you exhale. Imagine that tube mixed with the red, orange, yellow, and green of the previous four chakras rising up and connecting itself to the blue of your throat chakra.

Third eye chakra - Meditating on the third eye expands your mind and helps deepen your connection with your intuition. Meditating on the 6th important chakra helps you break limiting barriers that prevent you from connecting with your higher self. Focus on the space between your eyebrows and visualize a disc of indigo spinning there. Just focus gently on this space allowing all the thoughts to come and go.

Visualize your thoughts escaping into the black nothingness, leaving you peaceful and calm. Try and capture the glimpses of light coming from the innermost being of your soul between these thoughts. Keep your breath steady and smooth as you visualize the tube mixed with six colors rising to the third eye and connecting itself with the indigo.

Crown chakra - This energy vortex will help you tap into your higher self. Imagine a thousand-petalled lotus at this vortex. Invite this flower to open itself to you. Visualize a purple or violet column of light on top of your head. Visualize this violet column of light moving down toward your body and up toward the sky with every inhalation and exhalation.

This violet column of light is the Divine consciousness. Next, visualize that tube connecting all the six previous chakras rising up to connect with the thousand-petalled lotus. Visualize the petals opening up and giving you access to all the cosmic energy. Imagine your entire being filled with this limitless cosmic energy.

The trick with chakras is that the energy of all seven of them has to be unified before you can harness the power of the 6th and 7th chakras, two of the most useful energy centers to connect with your higher self through which you can access the invisible, spiritual realm. So, randomly picking one chakra to meditate on may help you deal with the elements connected with the chosen energy vortex, even if compromised.

For a complete, wholesome makeover in your energy field, it is vital that you start from the root chakra and successively move up until the seven colors combine and burst into the white light beyond the crown chakra, the energy center with direct access to the realm of your guardian angels.

Journaling

Journaling is also an easy and effective way to connect with your higher self. Writing down your thoughts and feelings gives you an objective perspective without attachment. Consequently, you find ideas and solutions to hidden problems.

Journaling helps you reach deep into your consciousness and find your deepest desires and dreams. It helps you connect with your authenticity and your true purpose as the external layers of thoughts and complexity of the outside world are peeled away slowly but surely through journaling. Here are some prompts for your journey to your higher self:

- **Who am I?** - The answers to this question can start with something as simple as your name, occupation, and address. Slowly include what you think is your personality, your responses to various stimuli, and how you handle happiness, sadness, anger, etc.
- **What are your desires?**
- **What are the three biggest lessons you have learned in your life until now?** How will you apply those lessons in your current life?
- **What are the desires you have yet to fulfill?** After writing them down, see if those desires look as desirable as before. Do you want to change them? If yes, how?
- **What takes up most of your time and energy?** Are they aligned with your dreams?
- **If all your desires are fulfilled, what plans do you have for your life?** What's left?
- **If you could eliminate all kinds of fear, including the fear of death, what would be the first thing you would do?**
- **What gives you unconditional joy?** Why?

Use the above prompts to start your journey into journaling. The more you write, the more you need to dig deep into your mind, and the closer you will get to your higher self.

Working with Crystals

Crystals have been formed on and under the Earth's surface over millions of years. Every crystal has a unique molecular formation holding the vibrations captured over the million years they took to transform into their present state. Crystals hold ancient energy and wisdom existing from prehistoric times.

Ancient wise men understood and appreciated the power of crystals used for thousands of years for their medicinal and healing properties. Being drawn to a particular crystal is not limited to its physical beauty but also to its vibrational frequency, which may match yours.

Crystals serve different psychological, physiological, and spiritual purposes, including but not limited to the following:

- Amethyst is used to get rid of bad habits
- Kyanite is great for deep emotional healing
- Clear quartz helps you restore balance and harmony in your life

And some crystals help you tap into your higher self. You can hold them in your hand as you meditate or put them on the altar in your sacred space. Here are some crystals which are great for increased spiritual vitality:

- **Clear quartz** is a soul cleanser and improves clarity. It helps you clear your thoughts and connect with your true life purpose. It is also great to enhance the power of your intention and to manifest your desires. It is a highly useful crystal for all types of healing, including physical, mental, and spiritual ailments.
- **Lapis lazuli** is a stone for vision and wisdom. It helps stimulate your mind's higher and deeper faculties to enhance spiritual experiences. It promotes self-expression as it empowers you to confront your inner truths.
- **Labradorite** has strong connections with the spiritual realm. It helps you raise your consciousness and boost your intuitive powers and psychic abilities.
- **Kyanite** is an excellent crystal for dealing with resentment and anger, especially those that confuse and confound you and prevent you from connecting with your true inner self. It amplifies high-frequency energies to heighten your psychic and intuitive powers.
- **Amethyst** is great to use in third-eye meditation. It offers the power of spiritual awakening while soothing emotional and mental disturbances.

To summarize, tapping into your higher self plays an important role in connecting with your guardian angels. The more you dig deep into your psyche to connect with your higher self, the one with direct access to the ultimate cosmic truth, the easier it will be to access the power and guidance of your guardian angels. These invisible, spiritual beings are waiting for your connection to help and guide you as much as you want to reach out to them.

Chapter 3: Communicating with Your Guardian Angel

The previous chapter dealt with tapping into your higher self to connect with the invisible, spiritual realm where the guardian angels usually reside. This chapter deals with communicating with your guardian angels, identifying and interpreting the signs they send you, and following their guidance.

Guardian angels are divine, spiritual beings. They do not use human language for communication and have their own ways of interacting and communicating with you. If you need to understand them, you need to learn their language. The more you connect with your higher self, the more your ability will be to read the subtle signs that your guardian angels are sending you.

Guardian angels constantly communicate with humans, guiding them, teaching them to discern right from wrong, and sending warning signals. They use various types of signals to connect with people. It is easy to miss these signals in the hustle and bustle of your daily life. Sometimes, you see the signals but don't understand the signs because your higher self-connection is weak and may even trivialize them.

Guardian angels can send warning signs to humans.[3]

Guardian angels can also use your inner voice to guide you. Often, you get so lost in your daily life that you don't see danger signs. Guardian angels can send you warnings by speaking to you as your inner voice. You have to remain conscious and stay present to catch these signs and follow their lead.

Sarah was going through a bad phase in life. She lost her job thanks to the economic slowdown and job cuts. Her long-term relationship with Joe had ended recently, and she realized he was cheating on her with his colleague. She was struggling to keep her sanity. Her best friend, Susan, tried to help her as much as she could. But Sarah was drowning in a pool of depression.

One day, Susan decided to introduce her to the concept and belief in guardian angels. It was a long and difficult conversation but worth it.

Susan: *"If you don't get out of your mire of sadness and depression soon, you'll fall into it irretrievably."*

Sarah: *"How can I, Susan? It's so difficult to cope with all this, and I'm so alone."*

Susan: *"None of us is ever alone, Sarah. We always have our guardian angel with us, right from birth until we leave this world. This angel guides us through our lives, lighting our path in times of darkness."*

Sarah: *"What rubbish! If this so-called guardian angel exists, why doesn't she help me now?"*

Susan: *"She is helping you. You choose to ignore her."*

Sarah: *"How can I ignore someone when I don't even know of her existence?"*

Susan: *"Exactly! Now that I've told you about her, can you reach out and seek her help?"*

Sarah: *"How can I reach out if she is not visible?"*

Susan: *"Open your heart and mind to her help, and she will find a way to reach out to you."*

Susan then explained to Sarah how guardian angels work, and with a little bit of persistence, Sarah found her guardian angel, who helped her deal with all her problems by showing her solutions and answers, which Sarah had not been able to see until then. Her life has improved considerably now. She converted her love for embroidery into an income-generating hobby, and she is not only financially independent but has also come to terms with her broken relationship with Joe, moving on to find new love.

There are two parts to this chapter. The first part is how you can reach out and seek answers and guidance from your guardian angels. The second part of this chapter deals with reading the signs your guardian angel is sending out to you.

Communicating with Guardian Angels

Here are some pointers to help you communicate with your guardian angels:

Know Your Guardian Angel's Name

First, learn their names. Yes, you can find out the name of your guardian angel, especially if you are getting closer to your higher self. Remember, the angel is as keen on communicating with you as you are with her. Use these steps to find out the name(s) of your guardian angel:

Sit with your eyes closed in your sacred space. Relax completely, ensuring that all disturbances, including the energies from other people and things, are blocked out. When you are relaxed and ready, ask your higher self the name(s) of your guardian angel. The name will come to you in some way or another. You could get it as a sign (discussed in the next section of this chapter), or the name could be placed seemingly inexplicably in your head. Even if nothing comes to you in your first sitting, try again, and sooner or later, the name of your guardian angel will be revealed to you.

It could be that even after a few sittings, the name is not being given to you. In that case, your guardian angel likely wants you to give her a name. Pick a cherished name, a name that makes you happy and secure. Say the name out loud and see if you feel happy and warm when you say it. Make a note of this name and begin to address your guardian angels by the name you hear or have given them.

Once you have named them, ask them to send you a signal that they are there for you, always. You can ask this question either through meditation, making an entry in your journal, or prayer. Once you have asked the question, keep your eyes peeled for the signs or signals from your guardian angel.

Dedicate a Song to Your Guardian Angel

Dedicate a song to them. Once your first connection with your guardian angel is set, the next thing you need to do is have a calling card for them. There is nothing like a song as a personal dedication to them. Take a favorite song and tell your guardian angel that this is theirs. Whenever you play or sing it, it means that you want to connect with them. The reverse is also true. If you hear the song playing somewhere without you having set it in motion, it could mean your guardian angel is there for your protection and safety.

Write Letters

You can write letters to them. Start with, "My dear guardian angel..." and proceed to write whatever is bothering you. This works well if you are stuck in an uncertain situation and cannot decide which choice is good for you. At such times, write to your guardian angel explaining your predicament and then look out for signs from them to help you make a choice.

Angel Meditation

Angelic meditation helps you communicate with your guardian angel. Use these steps:

- Sit comfortably in your sacred space or any other place that is free of disturbances.
- Turn off the electric lights and light a candle.

- Breathe slowly and deeply for a minute to relax completely, ensuring your entire body is calm and relaxed.
- You can recite a pre-written prayer to your guardian angel during your meditation session.
- Alternatively, you can call their name and speak to them, and you can do so out loud or in your mind.
- Imagine your guardian angel sitting close to you, teaching and guiding you.
- Sit in this state for a few minutes until you are satisfied that you have conveyed your message to your guardian angel.
- Finally, give them your gratitude and open your eyes slowly. Let the candle burn until the end.
- Now, wait for your guardian angel to respond to your prayer.

Visualize Your Guardian Angel

You can easily visualize your guardian angel using a mirror – here are those steps:

Sit comfortably in front of a mirror, opening your heart and mind for the encounter with a heavenly being.

Turn off all artificial lights in the room and light a couple of candles.

1. Close your eyes and breathe deeply and slowly for about 2 minutes until you feel totally relaxed and calm.
2. Send a prayer, asking for guidance to see your guardian angel.
3. Now, open your eyes and look at yourself in the mirror.
4. Notice the calmness and peace on your face and body.
5. Then slowly say, *"You are, I know, my dear guardian angel, always by my side. From the heavenly realm to mine as commanded by Him. You are my protector, my guardian, and my guide. Reveal yourself to me."*

Keep repeating this prayer staring deeply into your eyes in the mirror, ensuring your breathing is relaxed and calm. Look deeper and deeper into your eyes. Slowly, your guardian angel will be revealed to you as a reflection in the mirror. It will start with your aura appearing in the mirror first, and then this aura will change shape to form your angel. Embrace your guardian with an open heart full of love. Send gratitude to Him and thank your angel for appearing before you.

Wait until the form disappears, then blow out the candle and switch on the lights in the room. Sit quietly for a few minutes, absorbing the heavenly feeling of seeing your guardian angel before you return to the human world.

Interpreting the Signs of Guardian Angels

Your guardian angel sends you messages (answers to your questions, guidance, or even warning signals) through different kinds of signs. Let's look in detail at some of these signals:

Angel Numbers

Angel numbers are signs from the spiritual world carrying a message for those who see them. Have you looked at your phone and found that the time reads 1:11 or 2:22, or 3:33? You have just listened to your favorite song that is 2 minutes 22 seconds long while sitting in a cafe. You call for the bill and find the total is $2.22! What are these numbers? Repetitive numbers, usually repeated three or four times, make you stop and look at them with wonder.

In addition to their enchantingly symbolic meaning, these special numbers are also seen as angelic messages sent to people from their spiritual friends. These angelic or special numbers offer insight and wisdom and indicate the path to be taken.

Angel numbers are different from other numbers in numerology because they are not directly connected with your personality. These numbers have nothing to do with your birth charts, astrological and/or zodiac signs, or life path number. Also, they can appear anywhere at any time. They can show up on clocks and watches (as already discussed above), timestamps, receipts, bills, license plates, phone numbers, and other day-to-day elements you encounter daily.

The reason for their appearances in seemingly ordinary objects is that it is a way for the divine will to intentionally show you what you need to know. These numbers can be gentle reminders that there is something greater and bigger than you see and experience, and it is from that One who is running this world. He has your back and will always have it.

The meaning of each of these angel numbers discussed below is very personal and could be interpreted differently depending on the context. For example, for one person, the number 333 could mean that they should follow their instincts, and for someone else, it could mean that they are on the right track. With practice, connecting the angel numbers you see with your current life scenario, you will learn to discern their meanings accurately. It's worth looking at some of these numbers to understand their significance.

Zero - The number zero represents new opportunities and new beginnings. If you see a pattern of zeroes (in threes (000), fours (0000), or a pattern that stands out within a bigger number), then it could mean the start of something new. It could be interpreted that you are at the start of a new cycle or phase in your life. The sighting of this number tells you that you should not be afraid to make bold decisions as it is a time for new opportunities and beginnings.

One - Number one is a powerful symbol and is believed to be the go-ahead message from the spiritual world. Suppose you see a pattern of ones (111 or 1111 or any other unique pattern). In that case, you should quickly make a wish, set an intention, or sow a seed because whatever you do, the cosmos will be aligned with your actions and help you achieve it. Seeing a pattern of number 1 means you are getting the unconditional support of guardian angels and other spiritual beings.

Two - Number two stands for alignment, trust, and balance. Suppose you see a unique pattern of twos (222, 2222, or any other pattern). In that case, it means that your guardian angel is doing everything possible to help you get where you want to go. If you see twos in patterns, then you should try reaching out to someone you trust because He will make the collaboration fruitful.

Three - Three stands for creativity, and if you see the number three in a specific and/or repetitive pattern (333, 3333, or any other pattern), it is time to enhance your unique skills and talent. The appearance of three means the skill you will learn will enhance your value in your current life situation, personally or professionally. Number three is telling you that your creativity is vital.

Four - Number four stands for stability. If you see the number four in repetitive patterns (444, 4444, or any other sequence), then it indicates that you are building a strong structure rooted and grounded so well that it will be a legacy. Seeing number four in angelic patterns means you are navigating through a long-term project that cannot be built on your own. Therefore, sighting number four also means you should not hesitate to ask for assistance from well-intentioned, knowledgeable, and like-minded people.

Five - Seeing the number five in angelic patterns (555 or 5555) could indicate a big shift on the horizon. If you have been trapped, stifled, and caught in a rut, then the sighting of patterned fives means something big is in the offing, and that underground and foundational work toward that end is happening as of now. By showing you fives in a pattern, your guardian angel is telling you that you are on the right path and that patience will give you great rewards.

Six - Contrary to popular religious associations with the number six (666 is referred to as the devil's number!), the angelic number six stands for compassion and support. When you see six in repetitive (666 or 6666) or unique patterns in your vision, it is a gentle reminder that you need self-care and self-compassion. Even if things are not going according to your needs and wants, your guardian angel is sending you a signal to treat yourself with kindness and compassion. Six is a reminder that everything happens for a reason.

Seven - Number seven stands for good fortune. Seeing this number in patterns (777 or 7777) indicates good fortune financially is on its way to you. It could indicate new monetarily lucrative and income-generating opportunities. Number seven exhorts you to explore business ventures outside your comfort zone.

Eight - Eight is one of the most divine numbers in numerology. If you see the number eight in repetition or any other pattern (888, 8888, or any other sequence), it indicates a strong connection to spirituality. It could mean that someone from the afterlife is watching out for you. Eight is also a symbol of infinity, the interconnected, unending loop representing the limitlessness of life and the universe. It indicates that you must not be afraid to dig deep into your intuition and do what you have to do.

Nine - The number nine symbolizes the end of a cycle or chapter in your life. Seeing the number nine in an angelic pattern (999, 9999, or any other pattern) could indicate that a cycle or phase of your life is coming to a meaningful end and that you should be prepared for new beginnings. When you see number nine, it also means it is time to step outside your comfort zone and explore new opportunities, especially now that the previous cycle is coming to an end.

Cloud Formations

Cloud formations and shapes have symbolic meanings in every culture, and the reason for this is that angels and other divine beings use clouds to send messages to humans. Here are some important cloud formations and their significance.

Cumulus clouds - The fluffy, white appearance of cumulus clouds resembling cotton candy and marshmallows signifies hope and innocence. Seen in the sky during springtime, cumulus clouds symbolize new beginnings as well. They can also remind you to stay positive and keep doing what you need to do, and things will certainly fall into place sooner rather than later.

The sight of beautiful cumulus clouds was the first ray of hope that Susan, who was struggling to believe in guardian angels, got from her guardian angel. Her outlook on life changed, and with it came happiness and hope. So, the next time you see cumulus clouds, let them remind you to take a pause from life, enjoy their beauty, and look forward to a hopeful, brighter future. It is a sign from your guardian angel.

Stratus clouds - Stratus clouds block out the sun making the day dull and gloomy signifying impending unpleasant situations. If you feel down on a gray day, thanks to the unhelpful stratus clouds, do an outdoor activity or indulge in your favorite hobby, and you will feel better. Your guardian angel is also telling you to stay low during this time of gloom and despair.

Cirrus clouds - Symbolize change and transition. If you see cirrus clouds during a changing phase in your life, your guardian angel tells you that you are on the right path. Also, cirrus clouds bring happiness and good fortune.

Cumulonimbus clouds - These clouds signify power and strength. They are large, flat-bottomed clouds associated with extreme weather conditions and are harbingers of heavy rains, storms, and even tornadoes. When you see these clouds, your guardian angel may be giving you warnings of an upcoming storm in your life.

Altocumulus clouds - The sightings of these clouds mean something good is on its way to you. They represent balance and harmony and remind you that regardless of what is happening in your life, you must keep your chin up and remain grounded and positive. Good things are on the way.

Lenticular clouds - These cloud formations are bizarre yet beautiful. They signify mystery and magic and appear to hover in the sky like giant saucers. In some cultures, it is believed that angels and spirits live in lenticular clouds. In the world of angels, seeing lenticular clouds could be an indication that something important is about to happen in your life.

Nimbostratus clouds - These low-level, dark, and foreboding clouds signify grief and sadness. They generally precede rain or snow and could also indicate the coming of hope and happiness, even if the current situation involves grief.

Stratocumulus clouds - These horizontal, low, and gray clouds are associated with comfort and security. Often seen in the morning or evening, stratocumulus clouds could bring in a light shower. Feeling fearful and anxious and seeing stratocumulus clouds in the sky could be a sign of comfort and security from your guardian angel.

Cirrostratus clouds - These awe-inspiring clouds signify spirituality and intuition. These delicate, wispy clouds are often mistaken for cirrus clouds. However, cirrostratus clouds are larger, more spread out, thinner, and more uniform in shape than cirrus clouds. When you see cirrostratus clouds, you can be sure that they are a sign of happiness and good fortune from your guardian angel.

Dreams and Visions

The primary difference between dreams and visions is that the latter is manifested in a waking state, while the former is seen when you are asleep. And yet, when people have visions, their five senses are so deeply affected that they are almost unconscious and oblivious to the ordinary happenings around them. Your guardian angel may appear to you while you are talking to someone and give you visions of what will soon transpire.

Visions can be in the form of sparkles of light, hazy (unclear or clear) forms, or absolutely clear pictures and images. These visions often come suddenly and without warning as you go about your daily work. The flashes of light or a glimpse of a glowing figure which resembles an angel may become visible to you. But when you try to look directly at these visions, they can simply disappear.

If you are getting these visions and dreams more than before, your sensitivity to your guardian angel's presence is improving. You could not notice them before, but now you are at least catching glimpses of their form and the vision they are trying to send you.

The same logic holds good for dreams too. If your guardian angel is trying to send you a message through your dreams, then you must pay attention to your dreams and try to interpret them. Start a dream journal and make detailed notes of your dreams every night. The more you connect with your dreams, the easier it will be for you to interpret your guardian angel's messages.

Physical Sensations and Emotions

Quite often, you may have felt a sudden, inexplicable tingling sensation in your body, and quite frequently, you will have dismissed it as something random and unimportant. Now that you know that divine beings from the spiritual realms communicate differently with you, *don't repeat your earlier mistakes.*

The physical sensations could be connected to sudden changes in the temperature or the environment. You may feel warm because it's become inexplicably sunnier, or you could feel cold because there is a sudden nip in the air unexpectedly and without reason or logic.

If you feel this kind of physical sensation, stop and try to understand it better. What did you think before you felt that sensation? Was something worrying you? Or were you wondering how to solve a dilemma? Your guardian angel is always around and already knows your problems.

The angel may not wait for you to seek their help, and they may choose to send you a message without you asking for it. Therefore, you will interpret the sign correctly when you deeply ponder what triggered the sensation. For example, suppose you have had a bad breakup recently, and you are wondering if it is time for you to get over it and move on, and that thought was in your head just before that tingling sensation. It could mean your guardian angel is giving you the go-ahead.

In this way, physical sensations and emotions are used by guardian angels to send you messages.

Feathers

Your guardian angel could use feathers to communicate with you. Suppose you find feathers appearing out of nowhere. In that case, you can safely assume your guardian angel is aware of your situation and there to help you. Feathers are her gift for you. Different colored feathers have different meanings. Here are some examples:

- A white feather signifies a message from your recently deceased loved ones that they are fine and that they are watching over you.
- A brown feather can be interpreted as stability in your domestic life.

- A red feather represents courage, vitality, good fortune, and passion
- A yellow feather reminds you to harness the power of your intelligence and mental acuity
- A green feather is a sign of abundance, fertility, and growth
- An orange feather signifies the power of your sexuality, sensuality, and creativity

Unusual Scents

Guardian angels use scents to send you messages too. Flower scents are the most common way for angels and spirits to communicate with you. If you smell a flower scent when there are no flowers, it could be a message from your guardian angel. Rose scent is specifically powerful because it vibrates at the highest rate among all flower scents. Flower scents have different meanings. Some examples are as follows:

- **Rose** - Encouragement, security, and comfort
- **Mint** - Purity
- **Frankincense** - Spiritual enlightenment
- **Spruce** - Joy
- **Cinnamon** - Peace
- **Grapefruit** - Gratitude

Other scents used include the memorable smell of a loved one, a pet, etc. It could be the scent of your favorite place, hometown, or home. It could be the scent of a food item you love or a dish your mother always prepared to lift your spirits.

Human and Animal Messengers

Your guardian angel may use other human beings and/or animals to send you messages. For example, you could have asked your angel for help or advice concerning some trouble brewing in the office, and as soon as you sit at your desk, your colleague could say something that would be the answer you were seeking all along.

Here's another scenario explaining how guardian angels use animals to communicate with you. Again, suppose you sought help or advice from your guardian angel regarding some issue in your life. And suddenly, you see an animal you feel drawn to without rhyme or reason. You may want to look up the spiritual significance of sighting the animal.

A chapter later on in this book deals with animal guides and helpers.

What are the guardian angels trying to tell you? The answer to this is personal and dependent on what you seek. Often their messages could have the following meanings:

I am with you - Through one of the signs mentioned above, your guardian angel may allay your fears and insecurities. They could tell you that you are not alone, that she is there with you through thick and thin, and that things will be fine.

Be careful - Sometimes, the message could be a warning, and it could ask you to be careful about something. It could be directed at one of your life choices or be a warning about something going wrong soon – something you are not fully focused on.

Communicating with your guardian angel does not have to be only when you need them. You can meditate or visualize their presence at any time. You can talk to them as you would talk to your best friend. You can share your thoughts and ideas with them and let them know everything about your life. It is not that they don't know what is happening in your life. After all, they are by your side right from birth.

Yet, talking to them and telling them everything is a great way to use your free will and align your purpose with the divine will. When you speak to your guardian angel, you acknowledge their presence in your life and show Him your gratitude for this dedicated being in your life, which has happened only because of His command.

Chapter 4: Working with the Archangels

In Greek, the word *"archangel"* translates to *"the chief of angels.* As you already know, archangels belong to the higher ranks and are believed to manage guardian angels. You read about archangels and their roles in brief in an earlier chapter. Many archangels are mentioned in Christianity, Islam, and Judaism. In this book, you will learn more about the four most important archangels and their significance in the spiritual world.

The Almighty God has created the four archangels to be in charge of the four cardinal directions on Earth. This is so the balanced energy of the four archangels in the four directions facilitates humankind to lead a life according to God's will. Uriel is for the north, Michael is for the south, Raphael is for the east, and Gabriel is for the west.

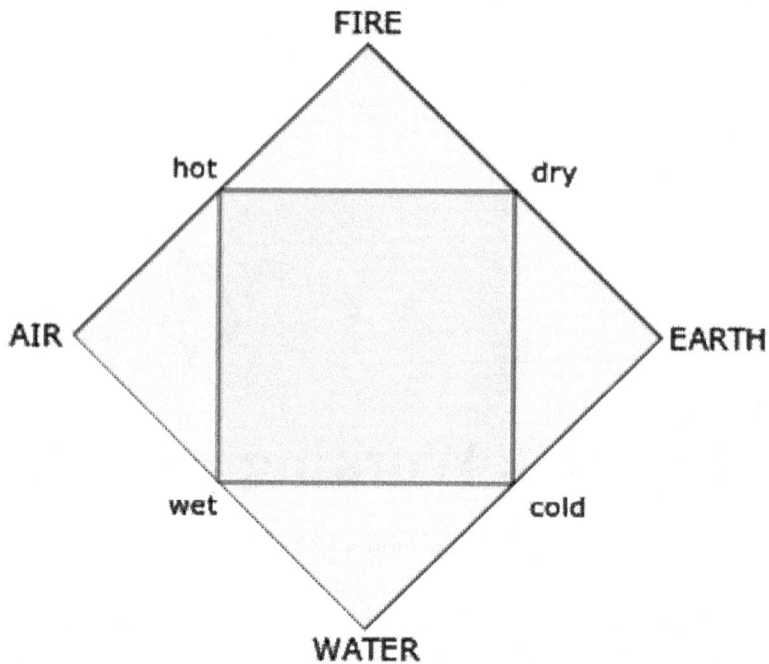

The archangels are in charge of the four elements.[4]

Further, He put each of his four important archangels in charge of the four elements, namely earth, fire, air, and water, as follows:

- Raphael for air
- Michael for fire
- Gabriel for water
- Uriel for earth

Archangel Michael

His name means *"He who is God-like"* and is concerned with truth and justice. As you already know, he is the most important archangel and the epitome of courage, strength, and power. He is the archangel you should reach out to when you feel drained of all energy, and he will help get rid of negative energies in your life. He is the protector of all those who love God.

Michael holds a flaming sword and a shield, both depicting him as a commander. He is sometimes seen holding a set of scales representing him as an angel of justice, delivering that justice swiftly and keenly. Like the element of fire which he governs, Michael helps you burn away your sins to prepare you for the path of spirituality.

Archangel Michael keeps you safe from all kinds of dangers. Call upon him before starting a journey to keep you safe from accidents and mishaps. He is the archangel to call upon when facing a crisis, and he is known to communicate with his seekers boldly. So, in the middle of a crisis (if you have already sought the help of Archangel Michael), you may hear a powerful voice giving you advice, telling you the right thing to do. Sometimes, you may experience a warm, tingling sensation that makes you feel secure and comfortable. Get to recognize this feeling as signifying the presence of this protecting angel by your side.

The colors representing Archangel Michael are royal purple, royal blue, or gold. So, in visions, he may appear as a purple haze, or you could see a blue or gold aura before you hear his words of advice. The presence of Archangel Michael is usually unmistakable. He does not hesitate to make himself and his presence known to seekers.

The primary purpose of Archangel Michael is to help you lead an organized and productive life so that you can fulfill God's purpose. To this end, Michael helps you learn supporting skills and develop your God-given talents.

The crystal of Archangel Michael is sugilite which comes in varied colors ranging from violet to magenta. Sugilite is also known as Luvulite and Royal Azel. Archangel Michael is also associated with amethyst, topaz, and clear quartz. With his sword of truth and scale of justice, he is associated with the throat chakra. Gluttony is one of the worst outcomes of an unbalanced throat chakra, a vice where you only take and do not give. Also, gluttony is manifested in the form of harsh and unkind words. Archangel Michael helps to balance this justice.

Archangel Michael rules over the sun, his weekday is Sunday, the day of relaxation, and his number is 11. Here is a simple prayer to Archangel Michael. Say it when you need his help, and he will reveal himself through his royal purple color and give you the necessary guidance and help.

"Archangel Michael, protect me from the snares of evil, the wickedness in the world. Keep me safe from the evil effects of Satan. I beseech you to ask God on my behalf to cast all negativity into Hell. I pray for clarity and strength to walk the path He has chosen for me."

Archangel Raphael

The meaning of the word Raphael is *"God who heals."* Archangel Raphael is known as the Master Healer and is associated with the heart chakra. When the energy in your heart chakra is free-flowing and balanced, then your life will be filled with love and light.

Seek his help if you are facing obstacles in finding your soulmate because he is the angel of matchmaking. He will balance your heart chakra and help you discover your true love. Like the element of air that he governs, Archangel Raphael helps you to break away from burdens that are holding your soul back. He helps you lighten the soul so that it can rise to meet the divine.

Archangel Raphael shows you the path toward self-healing, and with a healthy body, mind, and spirit, you can do wonders in your life. You can call upon Archangel Raphael for your emotional, mental, and physical healing. The Master Healer often communicates using his signature green light, the light that heals. He is also the patron angel of the sick and all healers, including modern-day physicians, medical practitioners, and conventional alternative healers.

He is also the angel to call upon before embarking on any journey. He ensures smooth travel without delays and problems. He also represents youth. He is depicted as a young man in traveling clothes, holding a staff in his hand and a fish. He is known to have healed a blind man with the help of the fish.

Archangel Raphael's day is Wednesday. He is the ruler of Mercury, and his gemstones are green agate, emerald, and yellow calcite. The scents he uses to connect with you are sandalwood, chamomile, and lemongrass.

He can send you messages through sparks of green light, tingles of warmth or chills, a premonition through dreams, and a sudden love for nature and the outdoors. Here's a little prayer that you can use to seek Archangel Raphael's help.

"Dear Archangel Raphael, watch over our health and protect us from disease and illness. Make me a healthy vessel to carry out His will. Please send me counsel and guidance on love and finding a soulmate. Help my heart to make the right decision."

Archangel Uriel

Uriel translates to *"God's light."* He is the preserver and protector of humanity. He is the angel of insight, information, learning, truth, wisdom, and ideas. He is the patron angel of teachers and students. He is the angel you will call upon when you are stuck for ideas or need a solution for a particularly problematic issue in your life. Like the element earth, which he represents, Gabriel Uriel grounds you to solid reliability that comes with following God's path.

Archangel Uriel is associated with the root chakra, which deals with grounding and stability. Call upon this angel to allay your fears and uncertainties and to help you ground your energy through the root chakra. Archangel Uriel's day is Friday. His colors are orange and/or gold. He is the ruler of the Sun and the symbol of light and the stars.

Archangel Uriel connects with you when you are serving others. He will not hesitate to tell you the truth, no matter how bitter or frightful it is. Knowing the truth is the first step toward making positive changes. He is depicted holding a sword and a book, both of which stand for wisdom.

He communicates in different ways, including sending red sparks of light (red is his color) through dreams and through electricity (because he sparks your mind). If you find your bulb flickering suddenly, then it could mean that Archangel Uriel is showering his blessings on you or sending you a message.

He is associated with number 1, the number of self-growth and learning. So, if you see 111 or 1111, it is an indication of Archangel Uriel's presence. The gemstones associated with the "angel of light" are amber, fire opal, and basalt. Here is a prayer you can use to call upon Archangel Uriel.

"Dear Archangel Uriel, please give me clarity. I'm confused and worried. Light up my path so that I can see into the darkest corners for insights and wisdom. Give me the strength to look the truth in the eye and deal with it without fear or embarrassment."

Archangel Gabriel

Gabriel means *"messenger of God."* Remember, he was the one who brought the message to Mary that she would be blessed to become the mother of Lord Jesus. He works closely with children and childbirth. He is the angel you pray to for safe pregnancies and deliveries, conception, adoption, and parenting. If you face problems while dealing with your children, seek Archangel Gabriel's counsel.

Archangel Gabriel is associated with the crown chakra, the energy center with direct access to the divine realm. The pure white light of Archangel Gabriel will help you connect with divinity through inspiration, clarity of thought, and peaceful joy. This angel will help clear egotism and pride, rendering your soul perfectly pure to embrace divinity in all its glory.

Gabriel is known to help even prophets to gain clarity and vision in their search for truth and closeness with Him. Water, the element which Archangel Gabriel governs, is connected with emotions and thoughts. He helps you deal with your emotions and thoughts to find the truth you seek.

The color of Archangel Gabriel is pure white which stands for honesty, purity, unity, and peace. His symbol is the trumpet, perfectly aligned with his role as the divine messenger. He is the patron of expression and communication-based arts and crafts such as social media, mass media, journalism, clairvoyance, and other methods of truth-seeking and authenticity. He carries a scroll and scepter as he is the patron angel in hand-related arts such as painting, writing, etc.

He communicates with you in different ways. For example, suppose you feel a sudden urge to take action on an idea you have been having for a long time. In that case, it is highly likely that Archangel Gabriel is the motivator behind your action. If you have doubts about your creativity, level of skills, the relevance of your value and contribution to what you are doing, or whether you should follow your passion, seek advice from the messenger of god. He will show you the path leading to the manifestation of your deep passion.

Archangel Gabriel is associated with different crystals, including Moldavite, Citrine, Angelite, and Herkimer Diamond. He is associated with Monday as he is the ruler of the moon. Here is a small prayer you can use to pray to and seek the blessings and advice of Archangel Gabriel.

"Dear Archangel Gabriel, I pray for clarity of thought and the power to express my creativity without fear. Help me find the light to manifest my ideas aligned with His will. Inspire my intuition, help me deepen my connection with my instincts, and help me trust my innate power, His gift to me in this life."

Here is a nighttime Jewish prayer called Krias Shema, which seeks protection from the four archangels.

"Dear God, Almighty, Bless me that Archangel Michael is on my right, Archangel Gabriel is on my left, Archangel Raphael is in front of me, and Archangel Uriel is behind me, all of them keeping me safe. Bless me so that You are always above me."

Zodiac Signs and Archangels

In addition to the four primary archangels discussed above, the 12 zodiac signs are connected with 12 archangels (including the primary four). When you were born on this Earth, the stars and planets were aligned in a particularly unique fashion. When you try to read and interpret the positions of these planets and stars with each other and in relation to your birth, you will get deep insights into your personality and the destiny you are meant to fulfill in your life.

Mainstream media focuses on solar astrology based on your birth month. This aspect gives you only an inkling of your personality and destiny. Traditional astrology is connected to your birth chart or natal chart, which is drawn based on the position of the planets at the precise time of your birth. When read correctly, this natal chart gives you an accurate picture of your personality and the destiny you need to fulfill.

Traditional astrology helps you understand your personality traits, why you behave the way you do, and what corrective measures you can take to lead a more meaningful and purposeful life than before. Learning about your zodiac sign and its corresponding archangel can help you get the right start to delve deep into your natal chart.

This section deals with the 12 archangels associated with the solar astrology-based zodiac signs, which are, in turn, based on the birth month. The twelve zodiac signs are:

Aries

People born between March 21 and April 20 fall under the Aries zodiac sign, whose guardian is Archangel Ariel, the healing angel of nature. People born under the Aries sign are also often nature lovers and selfless human beings. They are full of creative ideas, ably supported by their patron archangel.

Ariel means "Lion (or Lioness) of God," and he protects and preserves wild plant and animal life, especially in the wild. Archangel

Ariel helps you connect deeply with nature and its beauty.

For anything connected with nature, including trying for a job in the environmental science industry or setting up a garden at home, call upon Archangel Ariel for help. He is also the angel who overlooks the fairy world, home to fairies, leprechauns, and elves.

Archangel Ariel is also the angel who can help you reach self-actualization (your full potential). He drives you to dig deep within yourself and discover your true purpose in life – and then helps you find a way to achieve it. He is associated with the color pink and often makes his presence felt by pink light or sparks. Use pink quartz crystal to meditate on her and seek his help.

Taurus

People born between April 21 and May 21 are Taureans, and their governing angel is Archangel Chamuel, also referred to as "the finding angel." He helps you find lost things, and he is the one to reach out to when you are disturbed and want peace and harmony in your life.

His name means *"One who seeks God."* Seeking and finding your own divinity is the ultimate step to discovering peace and harmony within and outside of yourself. You can find Archangel Chamuel and his army of angels hovering over all places of worship. He and his angels carry your prayers to God and return with His responses.

He makes personal and professional relationships work harmoniously and without conflicts. If you want improved relationships in your personal and/or professional life, Archangel Chamuel is the one you should seek. He reveals himself as a streak or ray of pink light. Like their patron angel, Taureans are hardworking and organized, ensuring everything is done in an organized way.

Gemini

People whose birthdays fall between May 22 and June 21 are Geminis, whose governing angel is Archangel Zadkiel, the angel of righteousness, forgiveness, and memory. His memory power is legendary, and he knows for sure that everything comes from and goes into the divine will.

Forgiveness is a vital aspect of personal growth and development. Forgiving yourself facilitates forgiving others and is the first step toward building a compassionate attitude. With the help of Archangel Zadkiel, you can face and deal with troubling memories and hurtful emotions.

When you are able to get over your haunting past, you will find the strength to build a better future for yourself.

Archangel Zadkiel supports those born under the Gemini sign, who, like their patron angel, are great at learning and teaching. Like their angel, most often, you will find Geminis involved in mental pursuits such as research and study. In fact, regardless of your zodiac, you should seek Zadkiel's help for organized study and improved exam results.

Archangel Zadkiel appears in a deep, purplish blue light; his gemstone is lapis lazuli. Seek his help if you want to recall or remember things you have forgotten.

Cancer

Those born between June 22 and July 23 are Cancerians and are governed by Archangel Gabriel, an important archangel who has already been discussed in the section above. Pray to him for strength, and he will deliver.

Cancerians love staying at home. They are nurturing, caring, sensitive, and protective about their homes. Like their patron angel, they are excellent but strict parents who take parenthood seriously. Like Archangel Gabriel, Cancerians are extremely family-oriented.

Leo

People born between July 24 and August 23 fall under the Leo zodiac sign, ruled over by Archangel Raziel, the keeper of mysteries and secrets. Raziel is tasked with being the gatekeeper of supreme knowledge and divine mysteries. He guides each soul to its destiny, helping each soul rise up to meet and merge with the divine because he knows the purpose and the hidden capabilities of each soul.

He is the angel to call upon if you need to disengage confusing and indecipherable thoughts, ideas, and dreams. He will help you sort out these thoughts so that you can move forward. He is the one to seek to deepen your faith because he can reveal all hidden mysteries and truths. Archangel Raziel appears in a rainbow-colored light.

With his rainbow-colored aura, Archangel Raziel is a perfect match for Leo, ruled by the sun, because there is no rainbow without the sun. And without the rainbow, life would be boring. The Leo sign is all about drama and being showy. Like the rainbow, people born under this sign are often the center of attraction.

Virgo

People born between August 24 and September 23 are Virgos, and their guardian angel is Archangel Metatron, the owner and user of the Merkabah, the powerful energy tool shaped from Platonic solids. He uses the Merkabah to clear the lower, negative energies in the world and also to heal. The Virgo sign has a strong connection to healing as well. Like their patron angel, people born under the Virgo sign love to help and serve others through their healing powers.

Call upon Archangel Metatron when your energy is unbalanced and blocked. He will spin his magical Merkabah cube to clear your energy and lift your spirits. Archangel Metatron and Archangel Sandalphon are the only two angels who were once human beings.

In his human birth, Archangel Metatron was Enoch, the one who authored the book on esoteric knowledge, "The Book of Enoch." Archangel Metatron is the "scribe of gods" and a teacher of esoteric teachings. Further, he is the angel to turn to if you are a beginner in the world of spirituality. He will guide you to take baby steps and steady yourself before you dive deep into spirituality.

Libra

Those whose birthdays fall between September 24 and October 23 are Librans and are governed by Archangel Jophiel, the angel of beauty. Like its patron angel, Libra is associated with Venus, who is personified as Aphrodite, the goddess of love and beauty.

Both Archangel Jophiel and the Librans take balance and harmony very seriously. Archangel Jophiel helps restore balance and harmony in any dissonant, conflicting environment. Call upon him when you want to clear your life of unwanted, negative, and havoc-wreaking thoughts and feelings.

Jophiel is also known as the "feng-shui" angel, the one who wants to rearrange your thoughts to create beauty and love. The patron angel of Librans reminds them that beautiful thoughts and feelings bring beauty and love into their lives. Negative thoughts create chaos and problems.

If you want help with your speech, seek his counsel. If you want to uplift yourself spiritually or for self-motivation, Archangel Jophiel is the one to turn to. If you want a relaxing and peaceful environment, call upon this angel of peace and harmony whose energy color is yellow and whose crystal is citrine.

Scorpio

People born between October 24 and November 22 fall under the zodiac sign Scorpio, which is ruled over by Archangel Jeremiel, whose name means *"mercy of God."* He is the angel of emotional problems and helps you deal with your emotions.

His primary function is to guide the souls of recently dead people so that they may seek God's mercy and help them learn and review the lessons life has taught them. He doesn't just deal with dead people. Archangel Jeremiel helps the living to review and relearn lessons from their past mistakes so that they can create better tomorrows.

Call upon Jeremiel when you or someone you know is facing the fear of death. He teaches and shows you that God has better plans for you and that you have to face all fears, including fear of death, because the afterlife is waiting to welcome you. Seek his help to overcome feelings of bitterness and betrayal so that you can learn to build trust again.

Archangel Jeremiel is the perfect angel for Scorpios because this sign guides profound topics like death, grief, pain, and rebirth. People born under this zodiac sign are the deepest-thinking people and often do not hesitate to access the darkest corners of their souls to learn from and clear them of all negativities.

Sagittarius

People born between November 23 and December 22 are Sagittarians who are ruled over by Archangel Raguel, the *"friend of God."* He represents social order, family, and relationships.

His primary function is to heal conflicts, misunderstandings, and arguments so that peace and harmony reign. If you need quarrels resolved or ended, then you should seek Raguel's help. He comes to mediate arguments and helps to find solutions even in disagreements. He helps to enhance cooperation among group and family members.

Also known as the *"angel of fairness,"* he eliminates discrimination and harassment resulting in peace and harmony in the social order. If you feel you are not getting respect for what you do and your position, then you should seek his protection to set your situation right. His symbol is a judge's gavel, and his energy color is white or pale blue.

Like their patron angel, Sagittarians are also driven by the desire to set wrongs right in the world, including poverty, discrimination, lack of human rights, etc. Turn to your archangel and seek his help to achieve your desire. He is perfectly compatible with your drive.

Capricorn

People born between December 23 and January 20 fall under the zodiac sign of Capricorn, ruled over by Archangel Azrael. Called the *"angel of death,"* Azrael helps the souls of deceased people cross over to the other side and helps the grieving survivors deal with the loss of their loved ones. He also helps dead people see their entire life unfolding before them. If you are struggling with the grief of losing someone, seek Archangel Azrael's help and counsel.

Archangel Azrael is perfect for Capricorn because it is believed and known that even as children, people born under this sign exude wisdom way beyond their years. There's an old saying that *"Capricorns are born old."* Further, like their patron angel, Capricorns are fascinated by death and the afterlife. They are not afraid of death but are just curious and fascinated by mortality.

The acceptance of mortality is why Capricorns work so hard in their lives. They know their time is limited here and, therefore, feel driven to finish all the work they need to before their time comes.

Aquarius

People born between January 21 and February 19 are Aquarians governed by Archangel Uriel, one of the four primary angels who have already been discussed earlier in this chapter. Uriel is the most cerebral of all archangels, and therefore, his pairing with Aquarians is perfect. People born under this air sign are known to live in their heads and rarely depend on what their heart is saying.

People born under the Aquarius sign continuously think, leading to innovations and inspired ideas. This relentless thinking makes them highly intellectual too. They are detached, allowing them to view life objectively and make sensible decisions. Archangel Uriel is also known as the "intellectual angel."

Pisces

People born between February 20 and March 20 are the Pisceans ruled over by Archangel Sandalphon, the "Brother" who is tasked with delivering the messages and prayers of human beings to God, working along with Archangel Metatron. He helps to connect with your intuition. He is also connected with sounds and music and often makes his presence felt through your favorite song or music. Like Sandalphon,

Pisces is also associated with music and songs.

Pisces is connected with water, and Archangel Sandalphon is connected with peace; therefore, they are made for each other. In the cycle of zodiac signs, Pisces is the most senior. He has seen the entire life cycle before him and is ready to step into the higher realms of consciousness. Pisces is the sign that is happy to return home to Heaven just as its patron angel is ever ready to take messages and prayers to Heaven.

To end this chapter and this section, it is important to note that although each astrological zodiac sign has dedicated archangels, there are no boundaries or restrictions among the divine creations. You can call upon or access the power and sacredness of any of the 12 archangels to help you, and they will heed your call because He commands them to do so.

Chapter 5: Finding Your Spirit Guide

Angels and archangels are both often referred to as "spirit guides." But spirit guides can be lots of other things as well. This chapter explores various other types of spirit guides that are out there, and you can seek their help and counsel.

So, how do you define *"spirit guide?"* There are many definitions depending on your culture. For example, Africans believe that ancestors become eternal spirits with a passionate interest in the lives of their living descendants. These ancestor guides are on a superior level as compared to living people.

They could be dead parents, grandparents, great-grandparents, and family members (even those who came before them!) The Africans believe that the spirits of dead people form a bridge between the living and the Almighty. The people belonging to ancient African tribes continue to revere their dead ancestors through regular rituals and communicate and interact with them for their help and wise counsel.

The spirits of dead people are believed to form a bridge between the living and the invisible in Africa.⁵

According to Native Americans, spirit guides live in the spiritual world and appear when you call them. Like guardian angels, these spirit guides take note of their wards right from their childhood and stay with them until their last day on Earth, giving them advice and counsel whenever needed. Spirit guides make themselves known to their wards through dreams, visions, music, etc. According to Western spiritualism, a spirit guide is a spiritual being who guides and protects a living person.

Everyone has spirit guides regardless of the religion they follow or the culture they come from. Spirit guides work for everyone, helping people during difficult times, warning them of impending challenges, and guiding them in their daily lives. They are around, always. They can come in different forms and serve different purposes. But they are there for you, to comfort you, and let you know you are alone.

Types of Spirit Guides

Spirit guides come in different forms and shapes, as mentioned above. They could come in the form of a gust of wind that gives you gooseflesh. They could come in the form of animals and plants, gods and goddesses, and even inanimate objects. After all, all things in this cosmos are interconnected and come from the same source, the ultimate divine will.

Trans-Species Spirits Guides

Often, spirit guides manifest themselves in two or more combinations of species. For example, spirit guides can be half-human and half-animal. The animal part could be a wolf, lion, horse, etc. For example, mermaids, half-woman and half-fish; fauns, half-human and half-goat; sphinx, half-human and half-lion; harpies, half-woman and half-bird, etc.

Many trans-species deities in different cultures are also worshiped as spirit guides. For example, Lord Ganesha, the elephant-head god in Hinduism; Anubis, the jackal-headed Egyptian god; Ra, the falcon-head Egyptian god, etc. Most importantly, your spirit guide manifests himself in the form you want to see.

Ancestors as Spirit Guides

Your ancestors, who have a connection through your blood, often come as spirit guides to help you. An ancestral guide could be a deceased relative's spirit, including parents, grandparents, great-grandparents, and even those before them.

Shamans often connect with the ancestors of seekers during shamanic journeys to help them unravel mysteries of the past, the effects of which affect the living. These ancestor spirit guides can lift old curses and heal old illnesses carried forth in the genetic materials of their families so that the present generation is free from those curses and issues. You can also connect with your ancestral guides for their help and counsel.

Spirit Guides as Totems and Animals

Animals are common spirit guides in multiple cultures. Shamans who travel across different planes of consciousness usually have an animal guide to guide them in the world of spirits, ensuring their safety while they are there and making sure they return to the human world unharmed.

Also called spirit animals, these spirit guides have the power and energy of the animal they come from. Native Americans believe that jaguars are ancestors who walk the world of the living as spirit guides. Wolves are commonly seen as spirit guides. Although there is no restriction on the animal that a spirit guide likes to take the shape of, jaguars, wolves, bears, etc., are often believed to be used by them.

Also, spirit animals need not be something as exotic as a jaguar or any other wild animal. It could be a loving pet who has passed on. They can also be your spirit guides. Alternatively, you could be drawn to a dancing peacock in a zoo or a wildlife safari. It could be a deer that appears in your dreams.

Gods and Goddesses as Spirit Guides

Gods and goddesses have been worshiped, and continue to be worshiped, in almost every religion and culture of the world. Multiple male and female deities are spirit guides. Some of them include Lord Ganesh, Athena, Apollo, Kali, Lakshmi, Shiva, Horus, Krishna, and there are many, many more. An entire chapter is dedicated to gods and goddesses later in this book.

Plants as Spirit Guides

Shamans have plant guides as well. The most common psychoactive plant in Shamanism is Ayahuasca, a common vine in Peru. Interestingly, Ayahuasca is known as the *"vine of the soul."* Experienced and wise shamans consume Ayahuasca and feel guided by the plant's spirit to the place where they can find answers to questions they seek, either for themselves or other seekers who come to them for help. Other plants that are taken as spirit guides include San Pedro, a species of cacti, and others.

In addition to psychoactive plants being spirit guides, even normal plants and trees can be your spirit guides, especially those that carry memories for you. Certain plants, flowers, fruit, etc., tend to stimulate your brain toward emotional and mental expansions. These plants are also spirit guides.

Ascended Masters

These masters once lived on Earth and have moved on to the higher realms, either after death or through spiritual awakening. They don't die, nor are they reborn. Their spirits hover around, just waiting for your call so that they can come to your aid. These ascended masters signify the ultimate teachers (called "gurus" in Sanskrit). They are not teachers who teach subjects; they are mentors who help you lead a better life and uplift your soul toward the divine.

Examples of ascended masters include Jesus, Mother Mary, Lord Buddha, Confucius, Kuthumi, and many more. You can find ascended masters in your own culture and religion.

How to Connect with and Summon Your Spirit Guide

Ask

The first step to connecting with your spirit guide is *to ask*. Get into the habit of asking your spirit guide for help. Your spirit guide(s) are always with you and around you. And they may even know that you need help. Yet, the seeker always has to take the first step. The giver usually waits for the request and then gives wholeheartedly. The more you seek, the more connected you will be with your spirit guide.

Ask specifically, not generally. To do this, you must have a list of your needs and desires. This is a seemingly silly but important thing to do too. You need to be very clear about what you seek. What kind of help are you looking for? Be specific with your requests. Only then can the spirit guide respond with specific messages.

For example, don't just say, *"Give me success in my career."* Instead, ask for specific things in your career, such as, *"Give me a promotion (mention the next rank that you seek) so that my income improves."* Don't just say, *"Give me happiness."* Instead, ask how you want happiness to be manifested in your life. For example, *"I would be happy if I could get [mention the person's name] to fall in love with me."*

Seek help specifically and ask for signs from your spirit guide that they have heard you. Once you get the signs, give thanks before you close the session. The gratitude message should also be as if you have already received what you sought. For example:

- "Thank you, my dear spirit guide, for giving me the solutions to my issues in my relationships."
- "Thank you, my dear spirit guide, for showing me how to improve myself to get that promotion I seek."
- "Thank you, my dear spirit guide, for helping me find my soulmate."

Seek Help from the Right Spirit Guides

Seek the guides of the highest truth. This is a critical aspect of summoning spirit guides. Like the human world, the spirit world is inhabited by all kinds of spirits – the good, the bad, and the ugly. This isn't about physical profiles but energy profiles. So, you must call upon the good, kind, and compassionate spirits and keep away from the harmful ones.

Ensure you are psychically protected before summoning spirit guides to prevent the wrong ones from causing you harm. Here are some tips for psychic protection:

Your summoning ritual should ideally take place in your sacred space, discussed in detail in an earlier chapter of this book.

- **First, ground yourself.** There are different ways to do this. Take a bath before the ritual so that your body feels clean and ready.
- **Smudge your sacred space.** Light up one end of a smudge stick (usually made of Sage or Palo Santo) to do this. Wave your hand all over the sacred space, ensuring every nook and cranny gets a waft of smoke from the smudge stick. This method will dispel and keep negative energy out of your sacred space.
- **Meditate for a few minutes** before the ritual to completely calm down and relax. Connect your body to the earth as you sit down for the ritual. Visualize a powerful ray of brown light securing you at your root chakra.

Scrying

Scrying is an ancient tool used for divination and to connect with the spirit world. A crystal ball, a mirror, smoke, or a clear surface of the liquid is used for scrying. People whose visual sense is powerful use scrying to connect with their spirit guides.

Dream Work

Here are some tips for using dreams to contact your spirit guide. Before going to bed, set an intention to meet your spirit guide in your dream.

- Keep a pen and paper near your bed so that you can make notes of your dreams as soon as you get up while it is still fresh in your mind. Create a dream journal recording your dreams and the experiences you had.
- What you need to find is repetitive patterns in your dreams. Re-read the chapter on how guardian angels can communicate with you. Use the lessons in that chapter to find repetitive patterns of numbers, words, symbols, or anything else that stands out in your dreams.

- Relive your dream. If the dream happened in a familiar setting, visit that place and do what you were doing in your dream. For example, if you were walking down a familiar street, take a walk down that street as you did in your dream. You will be amazed at the number of insights you will get from transferring your dream into a real experience.
- Tarot cards. Use your tarot cards to decipher what your spirit guide is telling you. For example, set the intention of understanding your dream and deciphering the message of your spirit guides. Then pull out the cards, place them in one of the many tarot card layouts, and try to interpret the messages the cards give you.

Do this for two weeks, and you will find a pattern emerging from your dreams. Depending on what you sought from your spirit guides, you will likely find your spirit guide's counsel or answer in these patterns.

Experiencing the Presence of and Signs of Spirit Guides

People experience the presence of spirit guides in different ways, including:

Through your inner knowledge: You may just feel or sense your spirit guide's presence. You could "hear" a voice that is audible only to you. The presence is unmistakable even if they are not tangible. Your inner self and/or your instincts simply know they are present.

Light sparks: You suddenly see sparks of light in front of your eyes. These sparks are clear indicators of the presence of your spirit guide.

Free-falling books: Sometimes, they just push a book from the shelf to grab your attention. The book itself could be a message or just to awaken your intuition so that you can read the signs they are sending you.

Free writing: Sometimes, you may feel compelled to pick up a pen and notebook and write something. This could be a way for your spirit guides to send you a message. Don't force yourself to write anything. Just place the pen on the paper and do free writing; just words and phrases are enough to make you understand. Spirit guides do not care about grammar and spelling; they just want you to experience their presence and pass on key messages to you.

Bibliomancy: This is the practice of opening a book (often a spiritual book like the Bible, the Torah, the Gita, the Quran, or any other book that you intuitively pick) and reading a random passage or line from it. Remember, you are doing all this intuitively, which is the way to communicate with spirit guides.

Here are some more important points to remember while you are communicating with your spirit guide:

- **Be fully present,** ensuring you are completely aware and conscious of your surroundings. Being present also includes being aware of the energy within the surroundings. What kind of energy are you radiating into the environment? What kind of energy are you experiencing from the environment? Do you have expectations? Get rid of them. Just do what the present moment is telling you. Feel and be natural.

- **Listen well.** Signs from your spirit guides can also come in the form of sounds. Meditation helps quieten your mind so that you can hear the subtle voices and sounds of your spirit guide as he or she speaks to you. Meditation also helps to slow your energy vibration down to align with the energy vibration of the spiritual world, which makes it easy to connect with your spirit guide.

- **Develop regular spiritual practices.** Spirit beings are not of this world. Therefore, you need to have regular spiritual practices to stay connected with them. They could be simple practices, nothing elaborate. For example, you could draw a tarot card every morning to understand what the day holds for you. Meditate for 10 minutes to enhance your connection with your higher self, the one who has direct access to the spirit world. Attend spiritual gatherings where you meet people who are more experienced than you and who can teach you the way of the spirit world. Learn to use different divination tools, including tarot cards, scrying, oracles, cards, etc.

This chapter ends by discussing gratitude, one of the most important elements of connecting with your spirit guide. Your connection with your spirit guide should always be from a place of gratitude instead of from a place of neediness. The more you are grateful, the more service and love you will get from your spirit guides. They don't need to be paid with money or riches; they want to be included in your life because they are here for you. Acknowledging their presence is the first step toward being grateful. Show them you are grateful for their guidance and love.

Don't say, "*Why haven't you given me what I want?*" Instead, say, *"I am grateful for your presence in my life. Thank you for lighting up my life with your presence. Thank you for offering me solutions and counsel."* When you question their help, there is distrust. When you embrace their offerings, there is trust.

Chapter 6: Following Your Animal Guide

Strictly speaking, an animal guide is not a guardian. Instead, it guides you toward the answers to the questions you ask. Animal guides are usually found in shamanic and astral journeys. In many cultures, animal spirits are spiritual guides who present themselves to help navigate difficult patches in your life. In shamanic journeys, they guide and protect the shamans as they walk through the world of the spirits seeking answers to various questions.

Animals can also be spirit guides.[6]

How to Find Your Animal Guide

As you experience the appearance of your spirit animal, as a beginner, you may find it weird, scary, or even bizarre. Reilly, a novice in spirit world experiences, took time to overcome his fear and uncertainty. He kept dreaming of wolves in the wild and got caught amidst a pack. However, the fear soon turned to something pleasant when he noticed, with each successive dream, that he could get closer to the animals, and one wolf specifically.

With every dream he had, the one that seemed to be drawn to him as he was to it, kept coming closer until one night, he was able to reach out and touch it without fear. The other wolves simply vanished that day. The wolf spoke to him and told him to free himself from the shackles that were holding him back. The wolf, who called herself Rexi, counseled him to use his intelligence and wisdom and live the life he was meant to. So, in this case, the animal guide came in Reilly's dreams. Here are some other ways you can find your spirit animals.

Learn about animal connections in your lineage or culture. Avoid following animal guides simply because they appear more exotic. It cannot really be your animal guide if you don't feel connected to an animal.

For example, for Native Americans, jaguars and wolves often appear as animal guides. However, if you are not a Native American, it is highly unlikely that you will feel a connection to these animals. Do some research within your lineage and find out which animal has a strong connection to your family. Often, this animal will be your animal guide too.

Pay attention to your dreams to see if any animal has repeatedly made an appearance there. Make entries in your dream journal. If you already have a dream journal, look back at your earlier records and see if you have made notes of animal appearances. Otherwise, notice them in your present dreams and make notes. Animal guides often present themselves in your dreams.

Recall your past experiences with animals. Did you have a favorite pet that died, and you missed it so much that you haven't got another pet since? If yes, is this pet appearing in your visions, dreams, or thoughts? It doesn't have to be pets. It could be a chance encounter in the wild while you visit a family or friend in a remote area. Or you suddenly came face to face with an animal while traveling, and you felt an unmistakable connection with this animal.

Ask yourself if you feel drawn to any animal. Meditate on this question. Sit in a quiet, undisturbed place and close your eyes. After your body and mind fully relax, let your intuition guide you to any animal you feel drawn to. Ask yourself what this animal is trying to teach you. If your thought moves to another animal, then move on. Ask the same question to yourself. What is this animal trying to teach you, especially in connection with your spiritual journey and building your inner strength?

Repeat this exercise for as many animals as you want to. Make detailed notes of your intuitive conversations with yourself on each animal. Do this exercise for about a week. Forget about this exercise for a few days and return to your journal after that. See which animal resonates with you the most and what lessons it may be trying to teach you. This animal could be your animal guide.

Some people may find their animal guide quickly, while others could take some time to do so. There is nothing right or wrong about it. The most important thing is to find your animal guide, the one that your heart, mind, and spirit resonate with in perfect harmony. Remember, your animal guide is looking for you as much as you seek it. When the time comes, you will both find each other. Relax, be kind to yourself, and continue your search.

Common Animals as Animal Guides

Here is a list of common animals and their spiritual significance to help you understand how animals can be your guide in the spiritual world.

Bear - The bear is a deeply emotional animal and has a strong connection with the outdoors. The bear stands for courage, strength, and determination. They don't give up, and they don't forget. If your animal guide is a bear or if you feel drawn to a bear, it is likely that you are a natural, strong-willed leader. It also means you have little or no patience with people who cannot keep up with you and, therefore, end up being independent (or lonely, depending on your outlook on life).

Butterfly - The butterfly is an iconic symbol of transformation and new beginnings as it develops into a beautiful butterfly from its struggles as a larva trapped in a cocoon and then as a "creepy" caterpillar doing nothing but eating for days on end. The butterfly demonstrates that everyone will have their day on Earth. You just need to persist, persevere, and work patiently and diligently toward that day when you can break free and soar. If the butterfly is your spirit animal, you will likely be highly adaptable and open to changes and new experiences.

Beaver - The beaver is a hardworking, determined creature associated with family and community. It is known for its uncanny ability to persevere through tough times. If your spirit animal is a beaver, then it is likely that you are also a hardworking, determined person with a lot of stamina and a good head for problem-solving.

Cat - Great instincts, curiosity, and adventure form the core of a cat's personality, not to mention independence and self-confidence. Cats are also the epitome of patience. If your animal guide is a cat, then it is likely that you are also a highly independent, intuitive person and have a powerful sense of self.

Cheetah - The cheetah signifies agility and grace. It is a master of camouflage, and in some cultures, it is a patron of hunters and warriors. If you are drawn to cheetahs, you will likely have a career in athletics or any other performing arts that call for speed and/or grace. The cheetah reminds you never to stop exploring both the external and internal worlds.

Deer - The deer signifies innocence, kindness, and gentleness. Deer are intelligent animals known for their grace. If your spirit animal is a deer, you will likely be kind, intelligent, and considerate. Deers strike a graceful balance between success and gentleness. Personal integrity is paramount for you, both from yourself and others around you, with a deep connection to nature.

Dove - The dove, a bird of optimism and hope, stands for peace and blessings. Doves also represent new beginnings. Doves are gentle and understanding animal guides. They remind you to spread your positivity and embrace tranquility and peace. They can guide you to your soulmate and teach you to cherish your loved ones.

Dolphin - Dolphins are social, playful, and friendly animals. If your animal guide is a dolphin, it is likely that you are also a highly social and friendly person who is ever ready to have a good time. People drawn to dolphins are also known to read people and understand their feelings, just like dolphins, who are very intelligent and compassionate.

Eagle - Eagles stand for vision, freedom, and bravery. If your spirit animal is an eagle, you are also likely to be free-spirited with a strong sense of self and a clear vision for your life.

Elephant - The elephant stands for spiritual understanding, wisdom, determination, and gentleness despite its huge size and strong body and will. It is also known for its intelligence and loyalty. If your spirit animal is an elephant, you could also be an intelligent, strong-willed, and determined individual, along with being a loyal friend who puts others' needs ahead of your own. People who identify with elephants as their animal guides tend to have a powerful sense of power and strength.

Frog - Surprisingly, frogs are popular animal guides, despite their seeming sliminess. They heal emotional and physical wounds. They remind people to check in with themselves, dig up their past trauma, face it, heal themselves, and move on to a better tomorrow. Frogs teach you the uselessness of living in the past and the importance and significance of living in the present.

Fox - The fox is a master of camouflage and detachment. He adapts very well, harnessing the power of his surroundings with his cleverness which some people like to refer to as "sly." Cunning is the middle name of foxes, as they are adept at turning any situation to their advantage. In many cultures, foxes are guides who help people who are lost find their way back. If you find kinship with a fox, then it is likely that you are an artist, writer, or any other creative person.

Horse - The horse stands for passion and drive. Connecting with a horse could make you a highly goal-oriented individual. This majestic animal signifies freedom and endurance too.

Hawk - The hawk is a highly perceptive bird with the capability to see things from all sides. It is also connected with compassion and empathy. The hawk teaches you that you can let your imagination soar even as you keep your hold on reality. People who have hawks as their animal guides are believed to have a deeper and easier connection with the spirit world than others.

Jaguar - The jaguar is a symbol of courage, protection, and temerity. It is associated with decisiveness and powerful intuition. The appearance of this spirit animal is a message from the divine world that you must trust your instincts. If your spirit animal is a jaguar, it is likely that you are always ready for change.

Lion - The lion, the king of beasts, represents courage, strength, and royalty with a natural sense of leadership and authority. People with a lion as their animal guide tend to have careers in leadership roles or study history and/or mythology.

Mouse - The mouse signifies the importance of scrutiny and detail, reminding you not to overlook the seemingly trivial aspects of your life.

Owl - An owl can see what others miss. They go beyond the surface of things, dig deep into everything, and discover hidden treasures. People who have owls as their animal guides tend to be wiser beyond their ears. Such people are referred to as "old souls." The owl also signifies rebirth. They remind you that death is only a side effect of life, a renewal, not the end. If you feel stuck in a rut, the sight of an owl might indicate a time for transition and change.

Peacock - The peacock is a bird of reinvention and awakening. The peacock reminds you that it is never too late for positive change. You could be highly creative and resourceful if you have a peacock as your spirit animal. You have the ability to find innovative solutions to problems.

Possum – A possum stands for resilience and adaptability. You know that possums play dead to escape being killed by their prey. This amazing ability to survive is the reason they are known for their adaptability and resilience. This animal teaches you that playing dead to survive is a useful lesson to learn and master. Since it is a nocturnal creature, possums can help you tap into the darkest corners of your mind so that you swim against the tide and come ashore safe and sound.

Turtle - The hallmarks of a turtle are endurance, patience, and wisdom. If you feel drawn to turtles, it could likely mean that you are determined and patient and value wisdom over cleverness or materialistic intelligence. Also, the turtle teaches you to go slow and steady in life, and this lesson works really well when you feel stuck in a rut. Just remind yourself to take one little step at a time, and soon your goal will be near. The turtle also represents your inward journey toward peace and understanding.

Tiger - Tiger is the epitome of courage and strength. The tiger can easily guide you through your difficult times by helping you find your inner power and strength. If your animal spirit is a tiger, you tend to catch on to some of its confidence and majestic power. You find the strength to continue working with added vim and vigor and the courage to face all challenges fearlessly.

Wolf - The wolf represents freedom, intuition, and intelligence. The wolf reminds you not to forget your primal instincts because they are the oldest of your abilities. Wolves are associated with awareness, family, and communication. So, suppose you are drawn to a wolf. In that case, you are likely to be a family-oriented person who values relationships and friendships. You could also be a great communicator with a wolf as your animal guide.

Working with Your Spirit Animal

Once you have found your animal guide, be open to learning the lesson it is trying to teach you. Here are some tips which will help you:

Find out the symbolic meaning of your spirit animal. Re-read the above section dealing with common animal guides and their spiritual meaning. If your animal guide is not on that list, do some research and gather information regarding the animal and what it stands for: its strengths, weaknesses, and way of life. The more you learn about your guide, the better you will understand its connection to you and the lessons it is trying to teach you.

Do not humanize your animal guide. If you try to deal with your spirit animal the way you would with a human relation or friend, it will silence its unique way of communicating with you and expressing itself. Instead, open your heart and mind and be receptive to their way of expression and communication. Embracing their way of life is the way forward for you. Don't force humanity's way of life on them.

Apply these lessons from your guide's way of life in your life. For example, before taking an important decision, take a step back, and ask yourself how your animal guide would react in this situation. What would be your guide's decision? Talk to your spirit animal and seek advice and counsel. It will send you a message. Follow its advice and let it guide you to the right decision.

Further, think about three important life goals that could be connected with your animal guide; short-term, medium-term, and long-term goals. Apply your animal guide's lessons to these goals and work toward them as your guide would.

Pay attention to the experiences that involve your spirit animal. Whenever you see anything that connects you to your spirit animal, stop for a while and register the experience. You could come across the animal in a poem, book, movie, poster, random conversation, etc. Be aware of these situations and try to understand what your animal guide is trying to convey to you. Whenever you notice these things, ask yourself these questions:

- What are your feelings when you see your spirit animal? Do you feel a sense of foreboding or a sense of joy?
- Is your spirit animal trying to lead you in any particular direction? To do this, notice the way the animal's head is turned or anything else that could convey this meaning.
- Are you at a crossroads in your life? Have you sought help from the spirit world? If yes, what is the help you need? Can the appearance of your spirit animal be the answer to what you seek?

Honor your spirit animal. The more you honor and venerate its presence in your life, the deeper the bond will be. You can place idols of your spirit animal in your home or sacred space. You can wear symbols representing your spirit animal. Most importantly, give gratitude as often as you can.

The last and most important tip about finding and connecting with your animal guide is that you must do what resonates with you the most. Also, some people have one spirit animal right throughout their lives. However, this condition is not mandatory. Many shamans and other healers have more than one spirit animal in their repository.

The one that appears at a particular time is aligned with the specific need of that time. Quite often, a spirit animal may appear just once in a lifetime, help you in one situation, and never come back. The spirit world is dynamic and can change shape and form depending on your needs. So, don't worry if your animal guide changes. It is a perfectly valid thing to happen.

Chapter 7: Calling Upon Ancestors and Departed Loved Ones

As you already know, spirit guides come in different forms. This chapter focuses on departed loved ones, family members, and ancestors who can come as spirit guides in your life. In almost all cultures around the world, family members and loved ones who die automatically become ancestors.

The spirits of your dead relatives find a home in the world of ancestors, and they meet the spirits of other relatives who died before them. The spirits of your ancestors continue to look down on you and can become your guides if you are willing to accept their presence and listen to their advice.

The spirit of your loved ones who have passed away continue to watch over you.⁷

When loved ones pass on, they don't eat at the table, come to the movies with you, play, and laugh with you. You cannot hug them and feel their beating hearts. They don't hold your hand or pat your back. They are not in the form that you knew them when they were living. And yet, they are there, always by our side, waiting to help you in your need.

In many cultures, praying to departed souls is a regular ritual at least once a year. Freshly cooked food is placed on the table for the ancestors. Ancestor spirits are invited for the meal. A few minutes are given for the spirits to sit at the table and taste the food that is served before the living family members partake in the same food.

You can also call upon the spirits of your loved ones and ancestors to seek their guidance and advice. They will become your spirit guides if you ask them.

Connecting with Your Ancestors

Everyone can connect with ancestors and departed loved ones. This ability is not restricted only to the "psychically gifted" people because people are all innately gifted in this regard. In fact, you are likely to have had instances before in your life where the spirits of your ancestors and departed loved ones have spoken to you. Here are a few examples of when the spirit of someone you loved tried to communicate with you. You may likely have brushed it off as a coincidence or something else:

- You may have experienced something strange like a warning before you heard about the sudden death of a loved one or friend
- You may have observed a sign connected with the deceased at his or her funeral
- You may have seen your loved ones in your dream with a specific message you couldn't fathom
- You may have heard the voice of your departed loved ones, which you thought was in your head
- You may have seen something in a faraway location bearing an uncanny resemblance connected with a departed loved one

All these could have been signs from the spirit of the dead person. Because you did not know or were not aware that the spirits of departed loved ones can talk to you, you did not pay attention to these signs. Now that you know, keep your body, mind, and heart open to receiving messages from your loved ones who have moved on from the physical world. Here are some recommendations on how to connect with the spirit of your loved ones:

Create a sacred ritual - Many cultures have detailed rituals to connect with their ancestors regularly. In Hinduism, there are specific days in a year and month called "pitr days" where offerings are made to the ancestors. "Pitr" means ancestors in Sanskrit. In many cultures, offerings are made on the death date, birth date, or other special occasions in honor of ancestors. Here are a few more examples of dedicated ancestor worship from around the world:

- In ancient Mexican and Spanish culture, people worship their ancestors on the "Day of the Dead" or the "Día de Los Muertos" ceremony. They believe that the offerings made to their ancestors help them in their afterlife.
- Ancestor worship is common in the Vodun faith, and Vodun is commonly known as Voodoo in the West. However, there is much more to Voodoo than what is portrayed in popular culture. The people of the Vodun faith believe that the souls of the dead walk the living world on certain days, and it is their duty to honor them.

- In Chinese culture, the Shi ceremony, where a living person impersonates the dead person to whom the ritual is dedicated, is a common way to honor the spirits of ancestors.
- In Cambodia, Pchum Ben is a national holiday, and Pchum Ben is also called Ancestors' Day. On this day, every year, the Cambodians go back seven generations to honor and worship the spirits of their dead ancestors.

If your family already has such a ritual in place, make sure you participate in these ceremonies. Otherwise, you can create your own simple rituals. You could have a small altar with pictures of your departed family members. Lighting a candle for them is enough to let them know you are thinking of them.

Alternatively, you can donate to charity in their honor on their special days. Or simply gather all your family around, cook their favorite dishes, offer them food, and then eat and have a good time reminiscing about their days on earth. You could do this on special occasions or whenever you feel like connecting with them.

Talk to them as you connect with them. For example, as you light a candle in honor of a departed loved one, use their name and say what you want to tell them. Speak to them as if they are still alive and standing next to you. Visualize their response and respond accordingly. Or you can just say a few words of prayers to them.

Seek their help and try to work together on specific family issues. Write down the problem you are facing, and then see how you want to present the problem to your departed loved ones. Keep a pen and paper and write your question. Then wait for a while, and they will guide you to write down the answer to your question. Just be open to receiving their help. Meditation is also a great way to work with your ancestors. Sit quietly in an undisturbed place. Focus on the ancestor you want to call upon and meditate on them. They will make their presence felt and will answer your question too.

Knowing the Presence of Departed Loved Ones and Ancestors

How do departed loved ones make their presence known? Below are some clear signs that you should keep a look out for.

Their presence can be felt. There is a clearly discernible presence in your space. You might be alone in a room. But you know you are not alone. There is someone else there with you. It might be only a feeling. But the feeling is too real and strong to ignore. You can feel their emotions too. Be sensitive to this feeling and acknowledge it.

You can hear a voice. People with powerful auditory senses can hear the voice of their dear departed loved one. Claire lost her mother to cancer last year and is still struggling with the loss. Her mother was a huge pillar of support, and Claire couldn't get over her grief. She took a break from college, but that didn't help at all. In fact, having less to do deepened her grief and loneliness. She didn't have a father to lean on; he had left them a long time ago.

One day, as she lay alone, feeling desolate and lost, she heard her mother's voice, comforting, exhorting, and cajoling her to get on with her life. They had a long conversation where the mother-daughter duo recalled happy times they had experienced together. Her mother's final words were,

"My dear daughter, remember that I'm always by your side. I may not be visible to you as earlier. But I can see and feel you. You can also feel my presence. Reach out to me whenever you need me. But don't stop living your life. You deserve to move ahead and find happiness and love just as I did."

Claire was overcome with emotions after that conversation. But it helped her. She rejoined her college course and completed it with honors. She found a job of her liking, fell in love, got married, and had children. Her mother was always there, giving her help and advice whenever she needed it.

Sometimes, you can feel the touch of your departed loved one. You may feel their hug or embrace, or they may just pat you on the back. Even if this is rare, it happens, especially if you can recognize the touch of the departed person. For example, a wife can feel the hug of her departed husband. A child can feel the embrace of his or her mother.

Often, the spirit of your ancestor can communicate using a fragrance. For example, in the above example of Claire, her mother loved roses. Claire would smell roses even though no rose plants or flowers were nearby. It was her mother's way of telling her that she was close by. Claire would sense this fragrance when she sought her mother during stressful times.

Rarely may your departed loved one make themselves visible to you in their human form, fully or partially. The person could appear to you in their entire form, hale and hearty, and with a smile. Sometimes, you may see a hazy structure of their form. You tend to be most receptive to these images between the dreaming and waking states.

Sometimes, they use material forms to communicate with you. Lights might go off and on without reason. Books could fall off the shelves without anyone touching or moving them. The framed photo of the departed person may keep falling over. All these are ways of making their presence felt or getting your attention.

The spirits of departed loved ones may use symbols to communicate with you. Common symbols include rainbows, birds, flowers, butterflies, or other images that they loved during their lifetime. For example, if your spouse passed away recently and she or he loved butterflies, a butterfly could fly and land on your shoulder, signaling the presence of their spirit nearby.

Ancestor Veneration Ritual for Beginners

The ritual described in this section is specifically designed for beginners who are hoping to reconnect with lost ancestors. It could be that you are doing this for the first time or that your family, somewhere in the midst of modernization, has lost touch with the spirits of your ancestors.

The first thing you need to do before you start the ritual is to get the names of all your ancestors as far back as you can go. Speak to your living elderly relatives and find out the names of their grandparents and great-grandparents, who will all be your ancestors. Make notes of the names of your dead parents, grandparents, and great-grandparents. If someone in your family has a diary of a dead uncle or aunt, read it to learn more about your family. You could also include people who have cared for you during your childhood, including loving governesses, babysitters, home tutors, and others who have passed on.

Make sure you have fasted before the ritual for at least an hour. Next, light a white candle; just a simple candle you have at home will do. Place some unsliced bread and a glass of wine, or any other food that is loved by you and your family, in front of the candle. You can do this alone or include friends and family who want to be part of the ritual.

Settle down in your seat. Take a few deep breaths with your feet flat on the ground and relax. Then, say the following prayer:

"I remember my beloved ancestors and my parents (state the names if they have passed on, or use the last person who has passed on). I remember this is the food they ate. This is the place they lived and breathed. This is the wine they drank."

At this point, read the names of all the ancestors which you have noted. After the name of every ancestor, say a short prayer for their soul, and thank the spirit for their presence in your life. Repeat the above prayer at the end of the list.

When you feel satisfied, tear a piece of the bread, take the wine glass in your hand, thank the spirits for the food and drink, and place it near the candle. Sit quietly for a while, giving the spirits time to take your offerings. After a few minutes, share the bread and wine with whoever is present in the ritual.

Before getting up, thank your ancestor spirits for coming, and give them permission to leave. Let the candle burn itself out. If you gaze long enough into the flame, you may see signs and visions in answer to the questions you seek. There are a number of ways that the spirits of departed loved ones could use to communicate and connect with you. You just need to open your heart and mind and allow the magical miracle to take place and impact your life positively. There is just one small point of discussion before ending this chapter. What is the difference between departed loved ones and ancestors?

Departed loved ones are those with whom you have had contact in your life. Your parents, grandparents, favorite uncles and aunts, cousins, siblings, even close friends, etc., are usually referred to as departed loved ones. Ancestors could go back many generations in your family from either of your parent's sides. They can also help you deal with problems.

Normally, the spirits of your old ancestors are called upon to solve pertinent family issues that have been in the family for years on end. Old ancestors from many generations ago are likely to have information to help you end the misery for future generations. So, you call upon your ancestors in this case. Nothing can stop these spirits from continuously being in your life after you have summoned them once and taken their help. They can become your best friends too.

The spirits of dear departed loved ones help you deal with your personal problems, like how Claire's mother helped her deal with her loss. So, call upon your favorite relative and take their help to improve your life or solve a persistent problem.

Chapter 8: Connecting with Ascended Masters

Ascended Masters can also appear as one's spirit guide. Who are ascended masters? They are enlightened beings, the most evolved in the spiritual hierarchy. They are above even archangels and other spirit guides. They lived a life of the highest virtue, sacrificing all they had during their lifetime for the welfare of others and to realize the ultimate truth.

Examples of ascended masters are Buddha, Jesus, Moses, Melchizedek, Mary, St. Germaine, St. Francis, Yogananda, and many more. Connecting and communicating with ascended masters even once can be a life-changing encounter. While ascended masters can help you in various ways, their primary role in this universe is to help you increase

Buddha is of the ascended masters.[8]

your awareness of the spiritual energy that permeates everything in this world.

Buddha's teachings were based on the fact that each person has the capability to reach Buddhahood – which means each one has the potential to become an ascended master. It is an innately human thing that lies buried deep in your psyche, covered by layers of desire and greed for materialism. The way to overcome these layers is achievable, even if difficult. You have to clear multiple obstacles and make positive but difficult life choices, and to do this relentlessly and long enough to achieve ascended mastership takes multiple rebirths.

The Making of Ascended Masters

Ascended masters themselves had to cross these hurdles and have had thousands of rebirths before achieving their hallowed status in their ultimate lifetime on this Earth. Every rebirth represents spiritual transformations they underwent to learn the deeper secrets of life so that they could ascend the spiritual plane and stay there for eternity, helping humankind. They use the process of self-mastery for spiritual transformation.

With every step of self-mastery, they become increasingly enlightened until they can willingly let go of their body and become a pure soul that ascends into the spiritual realm and becomes an ascended master. So, ascended masters are people like you – facing similar life challenges. What differentiates them from normal human beings is that they choose to express themselves as a pure reflection of Him or the divine will, sidelining baser human tendencies such as greed, desire, anger, fear, etc.

Becoming an ascended master is based on three crucial principles: karma, reincarnation, and ascension. Here, this chapter looks at these three elements in a bit more detail.

Karma - The concept of karma forms the core of Hinduism and Buddhism. But every religion, including Christianity, Judaism, Kabbalistic Jews, Islam, and others, speaks of this concept in some form or other. In the mainstream language of spirituality, karma can be translated as *"you reap what you sow,"* although the karmic concept runs deeper than that. Karma renders you accountable for every action you take and every choice you make.

According to the law of karma, what happens today in your life in the present moment is a result of your actions in the past which could be minutes, days, weeks, months, years, or lifetimes ago. Every "good" deed you do gives you "positive" points, and every "bad" deed gives you "negative" points. The reason for the quotation marks for the words good, bad, positive, and negative is that everything in this world is relative, and what is good today becomes bad tomorrow and vice versa. And thus, the karmic wheel continues.

The trick to increasing the chances of your ascension is to get off the karmic wheel. And the way to get off is to radiate compassion, kindness, and forgiveness at all times, regardless of what is happening with and around you. Ascended masters know that the answers to life's painful questions lie within you and not outside of you. So, whenever they faced challenges in their lives that brought out the negativity in them, they turned inward to face and deal with these negativities without allowing the poison to affect others around them.

These ascended masters dealt with their destructive desires similarly, ensuring no one got hurt. They dealt with their own negativities and used that energy to raise their vibrations for ultimate ascension. These masters know that everyone and everything in this world is interconnected, and negative aspects of life are the challenges and obstacles that help in self-mastery. No one, including yourself, needs to be blamed for anything. It is all the outcome of past actions, and the way off the karmic wheel is to deal with life compassionately and with kindness toward yourself and others around you.

Reincarnation - Karma makes you accountable, while reincarnation allows you to pay off your karmic debts, which, in turn, will help you get off the karmic wheel. Reincarnation or rebirth allows your soul to walk the path of evolution and progress toward enlightenment or ascension. The souls of the ascended masters are not compelled to take rebirth in the human world. They remain in the spiritual realm to teach, heal, and help human beings achieve higher vibrations.

Ascension - Ascension or enlightenment is nothing but the return of your soul to its divine origin. Everyone and everything in this universe has a divine spark that connects them to the ultimate divine or God. The ascension process involves opening your heart and mind to cut through the layers of baser instincts to reach your higher self and reconnect with that divine spark that lies embedded in your soul. Ascension and enlightenment include:

- Awakening of the mind by learning the lessons taught by the challenges and obstacles life throws at you.
- Awakening a new personality, thanks to the lessons learned through the awakening of the mind.
- Awakening of your spiritual energy, thanks to moving up from the baser instincts to higher realms of thinking and consciousness.

As you master the above steps, your soul will slowly but surely awaken until the final ascension and reunion with the ultimate divine.

Ascended Masters and Their Teachings

Buddha - Also known as the Enlightened One, Buddha was born as Prince Siddhartha into a royal family. At the time of his birth, wise sages predicted that he would either be an emperor of the world or a powerful ascetic. His father did not want him to be ascetic, so he made sure his son lived in luxurious comfort, hiding the sufferings and pain of the world from him.

But fate intervened, and Siddhartha left a life of luxury and went in search of the highest spiritual truth. When he found it after years of facing indeterminate obstacles and challenges, he became Buddha, the Enlightened One. He lives in the spiritual world, helping humanity lead a balanced life of "the middle path," a principle he proposed whereby moderation of everything is the key to happiness and reduced desire. He proposed the following four noble truths to achieve Buddhahood that is inherent in each one of us:

- Suffering is an innate aspect of existence
- Desire is the root of suffering
- Suffering can be ended by giving up desire
- And finally, Buddha proposed the eightfold path of how to give up desire. The eightfold path is composed of the following elements: right view, right thought, right speech, right action, right livelihood, right effort, right mindfulness, and right concentration.

Prayer to Buddha - *"Oh, Blessed Buddha, you are the vessel of compassion and bestower of peace. You love unconditionally and are the source of true happiness. Guide me to liberation and enlightenment."*

Babaji - Also known as Mahavatar Babaji or the deathless one, Babaji brought the ancient system of Kriya Yoga into mainstream life, helping thousands of people achieve balance, peace, and harmony in their lives. With his help, you can take yourself closer to the divine. He will guide you to follow God's will and His purpose for you in this lifetime. Babaji can assist you towards a clear commune with God, simplifying your life so that you are free to follow your spirituality, detaching yourself from excessive materialism, and reducing your desires and cravings from causing you harm.

Prayer to Babaji - *"Dear Babaji, I am grateful for your presence in my life. You are my guide and mentor, helping me through the muddling conflicts of life and teaching me ways to overcome the obstacles that stand in my path to reach you. I pray that you hold my hand and light my path during this life and the future life until my pure soul is freed from the karmic wheel."*

El Morya - El Morya was the son of the king of Kashmir, a beautiful kingdom in North India, who became a monk. He lived during the latter half of the 19th century, and he frequented the monasteries and retreats in the mighty Himalayas. He was one of the founding members of the Theosophical Society, established in 1875.

His previous births are believed to have been Abraham, Melchior (one of the three Magi), King Arthur, Thomas Becket, Sir Thomas More, and many more before he became an ascended master in his lifetime as El Morya. You can reach out to him when you need assistance in matters of faith, decision-making, psychic protection, and staying true to your principles and beliefs.

Prayer to El Morya - *"El Morya, you stand by my side at all times. In your name, I tread holy ground. You give me the strength to keep my days happy and holy in God's name. You and I are one. Keep me grounded and humble, and my heart and mind pointed toward Him alone."*

Jesus - Jesus is the one and only Son of God who was sent to earth by Him because of His deep, unfathomable love for humankind. Jesus felt the effects of temptations as ordinary men do. However, Jesus chose to rise above petty temptations and lead his followers to redemption and ascension. Call upon Jesus when you need clear communication with the divine in matters of forgiveness, steering clear of temptation, and healing of all kinds.

Prayer to Jesus - *"Dear Lord Jesus, open my ears so I can hear His word. Open my heart so I can embrace Him into my life. Open my mind so I can see His power. You are my pathway to Him. I beseech you never to abandon me."*

Kuthumi - Master Kuthumi (also spelled Koot Hoomi) lived many lives, including, but not limited to, Pythagoras, Balthazar (one of the three Magi), and St. Francis of Assisi. He was known as a master psychologist and was a big supporter of youth. He was one of the founding members of the Theosophical Society. He is the master you seek when you need to find your life purpose, problem-solving, and focus.

Prayer to Kuthumi - *"Dear Kuthumi, I beseech you to teach me through my own heart the truth I seek. Show me the answers I seek. Show me my life path and my purpose in this lifetime. Heal my physical and mental bodies so I may walk the path destined for me by Him."*

Moses - God called upon Prophet Moses to free the slaves from Egypt and lead them to the Promised Land. Upon God's command, he delivered the Ten Commandments to the Israelites. He is the master you should seek when experiencing diversity and needing a positive outlook. He promotes leadership qualities. Pray to Moses when you need the courage to face people in authority. Seek his help when your faith is shaken for any reason. He will work miracles for you.

Prayer to Moses - *"Dear glorious Moses, be my messenger to Him. Carry my message to Him. Ask Him to deliver me from my suffering. Teach me to stay grounded and faithful to Him and the path He laid for me. Work miracles for me so I may do His bidding in this life and hereafter."*

Melchizedek - His name translates to "king of righteousness." He was the priest of Salem and is mentioned in the Old Testament. He spoke of God being the "creator and deliverer." However, there is no record of his birth and death. He holds the masculine energy of the world, balancing the feminine energy of the Virgin Mary. Reach out to him to correct unpleasant circumstances, purification, psychic protection, and transformations.

Prayer to Melchizedek - *"Glorious St. Melchizedek, help me deal with the unpleasantness in my life bravely and without harm to anyone. Help me meditate on the prophecies you made and fill my life with purity so I may live the life He destined for me."*

St. Francis - St. Francis of Assisi is the patron saint of nature, especially the animal world. Born into a rich family, he served as a soldier and was a prisoner of war. During his time in jail, he received an epiphany from Jesus, exhorting him to set aside his worldly life and follow the spiritual path. Seek his help for your pet and animal needs, finding a career suited to your personality, spiritual devotion, and for your struggles against delinquency.

Prayer to St. Francis - *"Beloved St. Francis, teach me to love where there is hate. Teach me to forgive when I am hurt. Teach me to bring light when there is darkness. Teach me to stay strong in my faith and help me discover my true purpose."*

St. John - St. John is the patron of the sick and their caregivers. He is one of the 12 apostles of Jesus, the Son of God, who came to heal humanity and teach humans compassion and forgiveness. Seek the help of St. John when you are experiencing depression and anxiety. He heals heart ailments and helps you with spiritual dedication.

Prayer to St. John - *"St. John, heal my sickness. Teach me and my caregiver patience so we may pass this difficult phase with minimal difficulty. You are my patron and protector. Accept me as your student and show me the path to a disease-free life."*

Virgin Mary - Mother Mary became an ascended master many years before she took birth again to become the blessed vessel to carry Lord Jesus Christ. Before her birth as Virgin Mary, she lived the life of a nomad and left her tribe to live in a cave to spend her life in solitude and prayer. She became an ascended master in that life only. Seek her help when you need assistance regarding all matters of children, childbirth, and adoption. She is the mother of grace, faith, compassion, and mercy. She is a healer.

Prayer to Mother Mary - *"Dear Blessed Mother Mary, I beseech you to keep my children safe from all kinds of harm. Teach me compassion and kindness so I may transfer your lessons to my beloved children so they may transfer the knowledge to their children until the world is filled with compassionate and kind people, the world that He dreams of."*

Yogananda - Parahamsa Yogananda brought the world of Kriya Yoga from India to the Western world. He taught the Western world to meditate and chant so they may find inner peace and harmony and, in turn, reconnect with their soul. Call upon him to find peace, divine love, and all aspects of yoga that will free you from the burdens of the material world.

Prayer to Yogananda - *"My dear beloved Yogananda guruji, light up my darkness, awaken my soul, and help me find my inner peace so I may live in meaningful joy spreading happiness to my little world."*

You can connect with your chosen ascended masters in three simple ways: meditation and/or channeling your energy to receive their information. The process of meditation has already been discussed in the previous chapters. Here are a few simple steps on how you can use channeling to receive your master's words of wisdom:

1. Find an object through which you want to channel your energy. It could be your journal, Bible or book of your religion, canvas, or anything else you are attached to.
2. Find a quiet, undisturbed spot for the ritual.
3. Close your eyes and set the intention to call your master. Let the intention be simple but powerful. For example, *"I call upon Master Yogananda to come and sit with me now."*
4. Welcome your master and pose your question to him.
5. Use your chosen channel to write down the answers you hear or feel. Write what comes to mind. Remember, your master is speaking to you through your mind.
6. Initially, you may doubt the process. However, as you keep practicing it, you will notice hitherto hidden ideas and thoughts coming to the forefront, and answers are revealed to you.
7. Develop a strong bond with your ascended master to keep the communication strong between the two of you.

And finally, read up a lot about your chosen ascended master(s), learn from their life experiences, and implement what you learn into your life as much as you can. The more you try to mimic the life of your ascended master, the more your energy will align with their vibration. They will definitely respond to your call for help.

Chapter 9: Working with Gods and Goddesses

This final chapter will focus on how to communicate with gods and goddesses who come as guardian angels to help you when you need to call upon them. Here, take a look at some of them with whom you may find a connection.

Find Your Guardian Angel from the Pantheon of Gods and Goddesses

Ganesha - The Hindu elephant god is known by many names, including Ganesha, Ganapati, Vignaharta, and others. He is the god of clearing obstacles. Hindus pray to him before starting any venture, seeking help to deal with potential obstacles in the endeavor. An annual festival in his honor is celebrated with great pomp all over India.

Seek his help to overcome all kinds of obstacles in your life. He may get rid of them or help you to overcome them. Call upon him, and he will come to your aid.

Prayer to Ganesha - *"Lord Ganesha, take care of the challenges in my path so I*

Ganesha, the god of clearing obstacles.[9]

may succeed in my efforts. Give me the strength and courage to overcome struggles and come through unscathed and successfully."

Devi - Devi is a powerful Hindu goddess, believed to be the female aspect of the creator and creation. She is the universal mother. Without her, the divine will would not have been able to create the world. Devi can appear as a nurturing, soft goddess or as an angry one who comes to destroy evil violently if needed.

In every village in India, she is worshiped in some form or other. She has a temple dedicated to her name in the village or town, and the people in that area consider her their family deity and pray to her for all their needs. She provides for them and protects her wards lovingly and unconditionally.

Pray to Devi for purifying your body and mind, getting rid of addictions, finding meaningfulness in your life, and for protection. Call upon her for all kinds of help, from materialistic needs to healing to spiritual uplifting. She will answer your call because she is the divine mother of all creation.

Prayer to Devi - *"Dear Goddess Devi, I pray to you for protection and comfort. Keep me safe from evil. Show me the path of love and help me deal with obstacles and challenges. Always be by my side. Teach me to discern between good and evil, so I may make the right choices."*

Kali - Kali is also a form of Devi. Kali means "black." Her black skin represents the darkness and evil that she has destroyed and consumed to protect her followers and believers. She destroys the strong bonds of materialism that bind people to their karmic wheel, and because of this, people are free to ascend into higher realms of consciousness.

Seek her help if you need to get rid of fear and uncertainties. She is the goddess of death when it comes to dealing with fear. Like a mother who keeps her children safe from danger, Ma Kali (Mother Kali) destroys evil and keeps you safe. Seek her help if you are struggling in the realms of determination, focus, motivation, direction, tenacity, and finding a guiding light in a dark world. She will illuminate your world for you.

Prayer to Goddess Kali - *"Dear Ma Kali, as you destroy the forces of evil for the good of humankind, destroy the negative bonds that bind me to the karmic wheel. Free me from this burden so I may find the path leading to you. Help me keep my levels of determination and focus high. Light up my darkness so I may remove fear from my body, mind, and* *soul."*

Diana - Diana is the goddess of the moon and of hunting. She stands for purity and is sought out by women who want to conceive. Women also seek her out for easy childbirth. Depicted as a tall and beautiful lady, she comes to the aid of all parents. Seek her help for matters regarding the breeding of animals, birthing and pregnancy, infertility issues, etc.

Prayer to Goddess Diana - *"Dear Goddess, keep my children safe from harm. Show me the path to being a healthy parent. Teach me what I need to know to raise my children well."*

Guinevere - Guinevere translates to "white shadow," and she is the Celtic goddess of motherhood, fertility, and love. She brings prosperity and fertility to the Earth. If you need to find your soulmate or true love, reach out to her for help. She helps to get rid of negative emotions like jealousy and desire for revenge. She deals with balance and harmony, ensuring you do not get stuck on the extreme ends of the spectrum.

Prayer to Guinevere (for conception) - *"Dear Goddess Guinevere, my husband and I want to have a child. Bless us so we can have one in your reflection. May he or she be conceived in my womb through your blessing. Grant me this boon."*

For finding your soulmate - *"Dear Goddess Guinevere, I'm lonely and lost in this racing world. Show me the path to my true love, the one who will stay with me (and I with him or her) until death do us part. Help me find my soulmate so we may build a new home together for our children."*

Krishna - Krishna was the reincarnation of Lord Vishnu, who took birth as a human to get rid of adharma (or injustice) and re-establish dharma (justice) on Earth. Every time the world overflows with adharma, Lord Vishnu takes birth (or a human avatar) to re-establish dharma. Krishna is Lord Vishnu's eighth avatar. He is depicted as a romantic, fun-loving person, although he can wield the gavel of justice uncompromisingly when the time comes. He renders joy and happiness to his bhaktas (or followers).

Pray to Lord Krishna for all things concerning romantic love, relationships and friendships, purification, protection, materialistic needs, spiritual awakening, and everything else in between. He is a bestower of blessings, and all he asks for is your unconditional love and surrender to him. He is known by thousands of names, including Krishna, Kanha, Balagopal, Gopal, Venugopal, and many more.

Prayer to Lord Krishna – *"Dear Krishna, you are the ultimate source of this cosmos. Without you, I am nothing. I surrender to you unconditionally. Show me the path I need to take and the work I need to do. I will do your bidding and surrender the outcomes of my work to you."*

Quan Yin - Quan Yin is the Chinese goddess of compassion, protection, and mercy. It is believed that this beautiful deity answers every prayer made to her, and she leaves no prayer unanswered. She loves humankind so much that even after enlightenment, she retained her human form rather than embracing Buddhahood.

In addition to compassion and mercy, she is the goddess of clairvoyance, beauty, musical abilities, femininity, and gentleness. She also teaches self-compassion and has an extra affinity for women and children. When you find yourself floundering in the midst of turmoil, seek her out for stability and groundedness.

Prayer to Quan Yin – *"Dear Goddess Quan Yin, bless me with your powerful compassion and mercy. Teach me to deal with my past mistakes with self-compassion and kindness. Protect my children and show me mercy if I have erred."*

Lakshmi - Lakshmi is the Hindu goddess of wealth and prosperity. Her primary role is to help humankind find income-generating careers to bring in wealth, an important element to human happiness. Seek her out for handsome rewards, especially in the form of material wealth and abundance.

If you find yourself stuck in a rut financially, Goddess Lakshmi is the one you should seek. She is the goddess of abundance, aesthetics, beauty, endurance, food, and balance between spirituality and materialism. She is depicted as a beautiful lady showering gold on her seekers.

Prayer to Goddess Lakshmi – *"Dear Goddess, bless me and my family with abundance. Remain in my home so we may never want for anything. Manifest my desires so my family and I can find the happiness we seek."*

Serapis Bey - Serapis Bey is the Egyptian god of the underworld. His primary role is to discipline people to begin the arduous journey toward ascension physically and spiritually. He motivates his followers to be physically fit and to adopt healthy lifestyles. Seek his help to deal with cravings and addictions, weight-loss and exercise-related stuff, fulfill prophecies, and ascend to higher planes of consciousness.

Prayer to Serapis Bey - *"Dear God of the Underworld, help me stay determined in my journey of physical fitness and healthy lifestyle. Bless me so I may avoid laziness and procrastination. Motivate me to achieve my best through hard work and determination. Protect me from the ills of cravings and undue desires."*

Hercules - The unparalleled hero of Roman-Greek legends, Hercules (Heracles in Greek) is not all masculine and show. He is a guardian angel, too, a warrior who loves humanity. He is known as the guardian of humankind, keeping you safe from perils and dangers. Pray to him for courage, strength, and tenacity.

Odin - Odin is the one-eyed All-Father in the Norse Pagan religion. He has numerous powers and responsibilities assigned to him. His speed and strength are unmatched, and he is also known to control space and time. Seek his help if you want to develop your mental, emotional, and physical strength.

Thor - Thor is the Norse god of thunder. He is the son of Odin, another important deity in Scandinavian mythology. Thor can fight evil spirits, negativity, and even dragons to keep his wards, including men and gods, safe and protected.

Frigga - Frigga is the wife of Odin. She has the power of foresight and also the ability to change the course of destiny. Seek her help when you feel stuck in a rut and want positive changes in your life.

How to Connect with Gods and Goddesses

There are many ways to connect with gods and goddesses, and they are discussed here, starting with the easiest and the most effective way, namely through prayer.

Prayers - Praying to your chosen deity is nothing more complex than talking to him or her. You can pray using scripted prayers or create your own, such as the ones given in the chapter for some of the gods. Praying can be a formal affair, where you sit in front of an altar and follow certain rituals, or informal, where you just sit quietly and speak to your god. Prayers form the foundation of any spiritual practice. Include prayers in your daily routine and embrace the happiness and purpose that seeps into your life from the divine plane.

Meditation - Like all forms of meditation, sit quietly and comfortably in a spot where you will not be disturbed, close your eyes, and meditate on the form of your chosen deity. You can also use a mantra to repeat during the meditation session. This mantra could be a positive affirmation toward a specific purpose or a chant that hails your deity, seeking his or her blessings.

Read - You can read from your favorite holy book to connect with your god. As a Christian, read your favorite passages from the Bible. Take a shloka from the Bhagavad Gita and read it like a mantra. Take a verse from the Koran and read it. Whatever religion you follow, read sacred books of that religion, and you will find yourself getting increasingly closer to your chosen deities. Every poem, hymn, song, verse, or chant which includes God's names can be used for this purpose. Include spiritual reading into your daily prayer routine.

The more seasoned spiritual people use advanced methods of communicating with gods and goddesses. They use journeying into the other worlds or altering their consciousness so that they can be led to the other-worlds to communicate with their chosen deity. For beginners and novices, the three methods mentioned above, particularly prayers, work wonders.

The more you practice communicating with your deities, the stronger your bond will become. Your ability to hear their messages and interpret the signs and signals they send you will improve. Talking to your guardian angels will soon become like talking to your best friend on planet Earth.

Conclusion

To summarize, guardian angels are spiritual beings living in the spiritual realm but with the hope, intention, and God-given role of being humankind's assistants. Archangels are created by God Himself to follow His commands and to help humankind. Every archangel has a specific role to play, although you can reach out to any of them for all kinds of help. The other kinds of spirit guides and guardian angels already want to help you in their own ways; you just need to reach out to them.

Guardian angels and spirit guides can appear in any form and speak to you in a variety of ways. Animal guides come in the form of animals (as the name suggests), and ancestor spirits come to take your offerings and help you deal with family issues. All of this may seem a bit weird at the beginning of your practice, especially since you are still stuck in the five-sensory limited world.

The trick to overcoming the physical world's limitations is to open your heart and mind. The problem with most people is that they are scared to open their hearts for various reasons. Most importantly, the fear of the unknown and the fear of the pain of losing what they already have. Further, people tend to carry their past pain into the future and are scared to be hurt again. And so, they close their hearts and live within the apparent security that "limitations" give them.

You need to find the strength to break these limiting barriers and experience all that you deserve in the physical world and the realms beyond. And for that, you have to open your hearts. Here are a few tips to that end before we end this book:

- **Accept your pain.** *Pain never kills;* it only makes you focus on it so you can find the root of the problem and solve it. Dealing with pain sensibly makes you stronger and better than before.
- **Move out of your comfort zone.** The more you stay in the ease of your comfort zone, the more rigid and inflexible your heart and mind will become. Keep moving out of your comfort zone to build resistance and resilience.
- **Speak to your heart and ask what it wants.** Deal with its fears and show that you care. Your heart will respond in the same way.
- **Identify, engage with, and embrace your dark side as well.** No one is perfect. All people are flawed, and their strengths and weaknesses make each person unique. Accepting your weaknesses is the first step to acknowledging your authenticity. It is easy to accept your strengths. But it is equally important to identify and accept your dark side as well for a wholesome life experience. Your heart will thank you for it and open itself up for new experiences, a key element to going beyond the physical world.

Spend time alone and spend time with others in equal and balanced measures. First, spend time alone to understand yourself and know your uniqueness. What defines you? What gives you joy? What makes you sad? Once you know yourself, then go out into the world and be with people so you can learn from them and complement the gaps in your life in different ways. Engaging with the outside world also allows you to know that the strengths you have taken for granted are gaping holes in the lives of others. Slowly but surely, you'll learn about the wondrous interconnectedness of the universe, and your heart will open wide to accept all things that come in the future.

Engaging with spiritual beings starts from within and ends in a place that brings the entire cosmos to your heart. So, go on, start the wondrous journey toward your guardian angels with an open heart, and your mind and soul will follow.

Part 2: Metatron

Connecting with the Archangel of Empowerment

Introduction

Angels are all around you. They are guiding you, protecting you, and watching over you. Everyone wants to know they aren't alone and that someone out there is watching over them. The idea that these higher beings exist can make you feel safe, and no matter how hard life can get, thinking of angels can provide solace in dark times.

Although millions of angels exist in the world, you can find yourself drawn to just one. Perhaps they heard your prayers and want to help you, or they want to reach out to you to guide you or warn you against danger.

Metatron is one of the most significant angels few people are familiar with, but he is a powerful being who can be very supportive and beneficial to have by your side.

This book begins by introducing the angel Metatron and his origin. It then explains the angelic kingdom so you can better understand his role in their hierarchy. Metatron is also mentioned in many mystical texts, which the book will cover in detail. You will also discover his various attributes and epithets and what they mean. The book will also highlight his different aspects and connection with Enoch.

You may be familiar with the concept of ascension, but do you know what it means? Or how can you achieve it through connecting with Metatron? The book will answer these questions and explain the benefits of this process and how you can recognize when it is happening.

When you reach out to Metatron, he will try to connect with you. However, he won't do this directly. Each angel has their own signs they send to humans to announce their presence. The book will discuss these symbols and recount the personal experiences of some people who managed to connect with the angel.

The following chapter introduces and explains Metatron's Cube and its connection with sacred geometry. The book will then return to the concept of ascension by introducing the Pillar of Light exercise. It will also discuss meditation, its origin, and how to use it to receive Metatron's energy.

The book continues to introduce and explain the concept of Reiki and its origins. You will also learn about angelic Reiki, its principles, and how to use it to develop a deeper connection with Metatron. You will then learn about crystals and how they can heal your body and spirit. Since there are many types of stones, the book will introduce the most common ones, their properties, and which ones work with Metatron.

The last part of the book will focus on cord-cutting and energetic shielding when Metatron is present. It will explain both concepts, their benefits, and how to practice them. Finally, you will learn daily exercises and techniques to strengthen your connection with Metatron.

This book will introduce you to the world of Metatron and provide tips, techniques, and exercises with step-by-step instructions to connect with him. All the information is presented in simple language so beginners can easily understand it.

Transform your life, and let Metatron empower and heal you.

Chapter 1: Who Is Archangel Metatron?

Metatron is often described as one of the most enigmatic Archangels inhabiting the heavenly realm. He is highly praised by Hebrew mythology, yet his origins are shrouded in obscurity. Present in Christian and Jewish mystical traditions, the roles of Metatron have always fascinated those who came across them in their studies or spiritual practices. Besides being seen as the highest-ranking Archangel in Hebrew mythology, Metatron is mostly known as the angel of empowerment. He can help further spiritual elevation and achieve a level of growth that ultimately leads to the ascension of the spirit.

This first chapter introduces this angelic archetype, including the etymology of his name and the origins of the figure. Reading it, you learn about the angelic hierarchy and Metatron's role. You'll also get the opportunity to explore Metatron's different attributes and epithets as viewed by the range of cultures and belief systems in which he appears. Lastly, you'll learn about the long-standing debate of whether Archangel Metatron can be equated with another powerful Archangel, Michael.

The Angelic Kingdom and Hierarchy

The angelic hierarchy.[10]

To understand better who Metatron is, it's necessary to first explore the angelic kingdom as a whole. According to Islam, Christianity, and Judaism, the celestial kingdom has a complex hierarchy system determined by three energetic spheres. The spheres divide the hierarchy into nine different orders and ranks – starting with the beings closest to the divine and ending with the angels closest to people. The hierarchy helps establish and maintain the divine order and balance all creations that need to exist.

The origins of the divine hierarchy concepts are attributed to Pseudo-Dionysius the Areopagite, a 5th-century theologian who spent a copious amount of time studying and deciphering the roles of divine beings. Based on the hierarchy established by Pseudo-Dionysius, the angelic beings are ranked into a clear and beautiful system described below. Each angelic structure highlights the diverse positions and obligations angels play in the celestial kingdom.

Sphere I

This sphere includes the beings closest to the ultimate divine essence – the Thrones, the Cherubim, and Seraphim.

As their name implies (the word "seraph" is translated as "the burning one"), Seraphim are the angels burning with the highest power of the divine. According to some sources, the prophet Isaiah (who visited the celestial realm) described Serahim as tall beings with six wings. Their entire body is covered in light. They use one pair of wings for flying, one to shield their eyes, and one pair to cover their feet. Their roles include honoring and praising the Divine and caring for spiritual nourishment.

The Cherubim are celestial protectors with many faces, including that of an eagle, an ox, a lion, and a man). They have four wings covered with eyes and body parts resembling animal parts. For example, their feet look like the cloven hooves of an ox, while their body is as powerful as a lion's. They are also the guardians of the Garden of Eden and were first described by Ezekiel, who believed that the fallen angels once belonged to the ranks of Cherubim.

The Thrones take care of the celestial throne, thus, are tightly linked to its authority and judicial power. They are responsible for establishing justice in the angelic realm. Besides being the patrons of divine justice, the Thrones are also connected to the Ophanims – also known as *Wheels* in Jewish celestial mythology. In Daniel's visions, the Thrones appear as strange creatures resembling unique wheels that also have other wheels in them.

Sphere II

The second sphere belongs to the governors of all beings. The Dominions, the rulers of the angelic world, occupy the first order. They assign and oversee the duties of all angels, who call them lords (or lordships). They have a humanlike appearance, except for their prominent wings, often depicted shining bright with divine light. The Dominions can be distinguished from other angels by the orb of light shining on top of their swords and scepters.

This sphere also includes the Virtues, the angels who bring miracles. Due to this, they're considered the most influential angelic beings. They help people manifest miracles by providing divine strength. Some of the miracles they manifest include foretelling the future, healing illnesses, and guiding people toward their life's purpose. The Virtues are the first angelic order in direct communication with people. By bestowing them the gift of patience, resilience, humility, and courage, the Virtues assist people in spiritual growth and accepting the power of divine love.

Lastly, there are Powers, the angelic warriors responsible for dispelling evil influences. They fight off malicious spirits threatening the celestial realm and supervise the interactions of celestial beings with all spirits. This way, they maintain the balance and security of all beings in the celestial kingdom. The powers are portrayed as magnificent creatures equipped with weapons, armor, shields, and helmets – a true picture of a heavenly army.

Sphere III

The third sphere of the celestial kingdom is reserved for the Principalities, Archangels, and all the other Angels. The Principalities are closely connected to people; they are the patrons of nations, ethnicities, and institutions. They also supervise lesser angels – they give orders to angels without charges and assign charges to new guardians. However, the Principalities are under the authority of angels from the first two spheres; they receive orders from above and execute them or transmit them to lower angels. In short, they're the messengers of the hierarchy, acting as intermediaries between different spheres. The Principalities are depicted as humans with a scepter in their hands and a crown on their heads.

The next order belongs to the Archangels, the angelic chieftains who look over a group of angels. They're widely known as they can appear to everyone and assist with different tasks, depending on what's needed in any given situation. They can travel between realms, often being present in several worlds simultaneously. Each Archangel has certain specialties. However, they are also divine messengers. The number of recognized Archangels varies from four to nine or more, depending on which belief system you're consulting. Metatron is an Archangel only recognized by some religions.

All the rest of the angels fill the lowest order. These are beings present in people's lives in one form or another. Some angels have guardian roles – they have a human charge assigned to them, and they guide this person from birth to death. The order of Angels is further broken down into smaller categories based on the roles of the angels. For instance, some angels are in charge of nature, while others are tied to emotions. Everything and everyone ever created has an angel. The wisdom of angels in this order is limited to their functions. Even guardians that guide and protect their charges have limited powers. However, your guardian is the closest to you and is more likely to receive your call if you need angelic guidance.

The Role of Metatron in the Angelic Spheres

Now that you've familiarized yourself with the angelic hierarchy system, you can explore Metatron and his celestial role and place in the spheres. Metatron is one of the most powerful beings in the angelic kingdom, so it's no surprise that he has several roles across the spheres. Often called the "Divine Chancellor" or the "Divine Scribe," Metatron is in charge of recording everything happening on Earth. This function ties him to the concept called the "Book of Life," a record listing the names of people worthy of salvation.

Besides recording people's actions (and their consequences), Metatron also carries divine messages to people. He also distributes divine will to angelic beings. Moreover, he establishes communication between the angelic and earthly realms by creating a bridge through divine messages.

Last but not least, Metatron is responsible for aiding the souls of the deceased on their journey toward their final destination. Known as the "Archangel of Death," Metatron ensures that souls find peace in the afterlife. This is what Metatron is most revered for in many traditions and belief systems.

Metatron's Origins

There are references to the origins of Metatron in many mystical texts, including The Zohar, Talmud, and Book of Enoch, to name a few. While the origins of Metatron can only be established based on mystical texts, Hebrew mythology provides a relatively rich source to explain and understand where Archangel Metatron comes from. The Jewish Tanakh describes Metatron as an enigmatic character with the role of a divine messenger. According to this source, Metatron is responsible for transmitting heavenly edicts to both people and angels. He even passes heavenly orders on to other Archangels like Raphael and Gabriel, with whom he communicates daily.

Other sources trace the origins of Metatron back to the day when the Jewish people were led from Egypt to Israel, claiming that it was Metatron who provided the guidance they needed to reach their destination. Interestingly enough, while Metatron isn't mentioned in the New Testament or the Tanakh, Metatron is recognized by some branches of Christianity and Judaism. These belief systems list him under the names of Metator, Metraton, and Mattatron.

The name of Archangel Metatron has unclear roots as well. Different religions assign different etymologies to his name. For example, some assert that Metatron's name is derived from the Greek phrase that translates as "the one behind the throne." While this seems to be a popular definition, it's also the least probable. A far more accepted translation for Metatron's name comes from the Hebrew term that translates as "the guardian of entryways." This is probably because Metatron is mostly known from Hebrew myths, making it more believable that his name also has Hebrew origins. There is also a third possible etymology of Metatron's name. This one comes from the Latin words "*mitator*," which means "explorer of legions," and "*metator*," which is defined as a messenger.

It's also interesting to note that Metatron is one of the two Archangels whose name ends with an "-on," which means "great." The only other Archangel whose name ends with an "-on" is Metatron's brother, Sandalfon. The meaning of the "on" ending is first referenced in the Book of Enoch, a tome later edited in the 1st century B.C. Two centuries later, the Book of Enoch was edited again, which led to different versions of the concepts and participants it describes, including the Archangel Metatron.

In the initial version, Metraton was referred to as one of the most influential beings in the celestial realm – evidenced by the fact he was usually portrayed sitting on the Creator's left. However, later versions claimed that because he sat on the left and the Creator's Son on the right, Metatron represented an opposing force to the Son – equating him with Lucifer, the adversary of the divine. This is also tied to the version that myths claim that Metatron was the oldest of the Archangels; in the third version of the Book of Enoch, Metatron's origins as a human was born. According to this version, the Archangel was a wealthy prophet named Enoch. Precisely because of how many versions of Metatron are in Hebrew mythology and other belief systems, certain branches of Christianity refuse to recognize him as an Archangel. There were just too many different narratives about Metatron, making it challenging to find a cohesive one that fit certain Christian beliefs.

Despite this, he is referenced in many other religions and traditions. The earliest tangible reference comes from the Talmud, a fundamental source of teachings of Rabbinic Judaism. Here, Metatron is portrayed as the most prominent figure in the history of the religion. The Talmud's reference to the angel's role in leading the Israelites from Egypt also allowed Metatron to become a widely known character in Jewish mysticism. Metatron's essence began infiltrating this belief system around the end of the 12th and the beginning of the 13th centuries, when many Kabbalistic theories were born. While these are different from traditional Jewish beliefs, followers still found Metatron to be necessary as they transitioned to the Kabbalistic beliefs. According to these, Metatron (originally referred to as Enoch) is viewed as someone Jews could rely on when they rejected Christ. They turned to Enoch in defiance as he was a human, but they later "converted" him into a higher being. This explains why Kabbalistic beliefs view Metatron as the second most powerful being (after the Creator).

The belief that Metatron was a scribe angel asserts that this angel possesses divine wisdom. Through this wisdom, he can open the doors to cosmic secrets and empower one's spirituality through daily practices. This is illustrated by the image portraying him with eyes all over his being. It's said that he has 365,000 eyes – the number of days in the year multiplied by the totality of his meanings. Some claim that this number also indicates the totality of time. Whereas others believe the numerous eyes symbolize his elevated consciousness. After all, he is known to be clairvoyant and can always predict what is to come.

The Epithets and Attributes of Metatron

The Kabbalah, a form of Jewish mysticism, plays a crucial role in understanding some key attributes of Metatron. Revolving around the Tree of Life concept, this belief system directly ties Metatron to the symbolic representation of the universe's divine structure. The Tree of Life incorporates ten spheres (known as sefirot, or sefirah in singular), all interconnected. The spheres depict different facets of the divine. The highest sefirah, Keter, embodies divine will. It represents the source of all creation and is linked to Metatron. This makes this angel the highest-ranking being in the Kabbalistic belief system. Due to his connection to the divine will, Metatron is also known as "the lesser YHVH." In the Kabbalah, Metatron transmits divine energy through the Tree of Life, allowing it to trickle down to people. While this role seems to lessen Metatron's role in Kabbalistic practices, his influence over the entire celestial hierarchy is undeniable. After all, he is the only angel who can channel divine energy.

One of Metatron's most well-known symbols, the Metatron's Cube, is believed to be modeled after the Tree of Life. However, other Kabbalistic sources claim that Metatron molded this symbol from his own soul, so it is often portrayed as an entity closely connected to the angel floating near him.

Metatron's connection to the divine is also evident in his role as the celestial messenger. He can communicate divine edicts to people and angels because he has access to them. He can also record them and all the information needed to maintain cosmic balance. Metatron is said to record all this information in the "Book of Life," the ultimate source of divine knowledge. Not only is he in close quarters with the divine, but he is also endowed with transformative and healing powers. An example of his powers is seen in his role as the "Highest Angel of Death," which entails guiding souls through the afterlife and ensuring they reach their destination.

Another interesting epithet of Metatron is his role in guarding children – a belief that originates from Metatron's portrayal in Zohar. Here, Metatron is also praised for his role in safely guiding the children of Israel to the Promised Land and across the treacherous desert. Because of this feat, a myth of Metatron guides children in all realms to overcome obstacles they face in life as they transition through the different stages. It is said that parents can call on Metatron to ensure their children's spiritual and academic development and also to help them hone their intuitive abilities. Metatron will hear the parent's inquiries and guide the children toward the right path. Some say that Metatron will also continue to lead children in the heavenly realm should they pass on. Other sources claim that Metatron helps children develop their communication skills and can be particularly helpful for troubled youth struggling with neurodevelopmental disorders. Besides helping children resolve their health and social issues, Metatron can empower parents and those around them, guiding them on the best path to overcome obstacles. Health professionals and scientists working with children also consider Metatron as their patron. Whether he does it on the earth or in the heavenly realm, it's clear that Metatron aims to help children adapt to their environment. He is believed to be a great source of self-esteem, focus, and spiritual awareness for children and adults concerned with children's fates alike.

Metatron's Connection with Enoch

There are many theories about the different aspects of Metatron, including the one that connects him with Enoch – the human incarnation of Metatron. In the Third Book of Enoch, Metatron is clearly identified as Enoch in several parts. For example, Enoch (an ancient patriarch and son of Jared) is given the title "The lesser YHVH" when he describes "the Holy One," referencing him by this name.

Being a righteous man all his life, Enoch was taken to the heavenly realm to appear before the Creator before his death. He walked and talked with the Creator, journeying through the heavenly realms, and eventually transformed into an Archangel. Enoch's transformation from a biblical figure to a celestial being known as Metatron is certainly one of the most intriguing stories surrounding this angel. However, Enoch had to undergo several trials before becoming an angel.

A paragraph illustrates how flames suddenly engulfed Enoch; his veins turned into fire, and his eyes lit up with flashes of lightning as he was elevated by the divine next to his throne of glory. This clearly references Enoch's transformation into Metatron and ascension into the angelic realm. The First Book of Enoch also references Metatron's connection. For instance, it describes the Lord giving an edict to Enoch (addressing him as "The Scribe of Righteousness"). This edict declares to "the Watchers of heaven," who abandoned their duties, gave in to the earthly temptations, and brought great destruction to themselves and those around them on the earth.

Enoch's transformation into Metatron is pivotal in Jewish traditions. It points out that Metatron was once an ordinary human living a mundane life. While this sets him apart from the other Archangels, it's also a testimony to his worthiness to stand close to the divine. He was chosen to stand by the Creator while he was still a human and was allowed to gain a prominent position in the heavenly kingdom after his transformation. Last but not least, Enoch's transformation into an Archangel indicates that people have tremendous potential for spiritual growth. Through spiritual development, everyone can ascend to a higher spiritual plane. Human experiences are necessary for ascension as they teach people many crucial lessons.

Archangel Metatron or Archangel Michael?

While many belief systems clearly distinguish between Archangel Metatron and Archangel Michael, some argue that the two embody the same angelic energy, appearing in different forms. However, historical evidence and mystical texts with several references to the distinct roles of both Archangel Metatron and Archangel Michael indicate that they are not the same figure. For example, in Zohar, in religious traditions and customs, Archangel Metatron is represented by the "Tent of the Congregation," empowering its structure. On the other hand, Michael is embodied by the High Priest, who communicates divine messages to the congregation. For Hebrews, Metatron is a multifaceted being, but he has a distinct role in bringing souls to the presence of the divine, while Archangel Michael has a role in the protection of the soul. He is also more active in combating negativity, while Metatron is known for his peaceful energy. Although there are many similarities between them, they also have different statuses. Archangel Michael is the defender, the "heavenly Prince," as opposed to the "God's scribe," as Archangel Metatron is widely known. Some also claim that because Michael is named in the Bible and Metatron isn't, this also proves that they aren't the same being.

Different roles notwithstanding, Metatron has a unique relationship with Archangel Michael. As another prominent figure in the angelic hierarchy, Archangel Michael serves a role in a divine plan intended for Metatron. Some claim that the transformative powers of Metatron wouldn't be accessible to anyone without the protective guardianship of a warrior Archangel like Michael. Whether this is true or not, several religious and mystical traditions testify to the significant relationship between Archangel Michael and Metatron. One of the parallels between the myths surrounding these two high-ranking celestial beings comes from the stories describing their connection to Enoch. As described in the "Book of Enoch," Enoch was a biblical figure who recorded roles in the angelic hierarchy after visiting the heavenly realm – including the roles he shared and fulfilled in tandem with Archangel Michael.

Moreover, the connection between these two angels is required to maintain the heavenly order. They have ties to the divine essence and do their best to fulfill their roles as intermediaries between the angelic and earth realms and their inhabitants.

Chapter 2: Ascension with Metatron

Given Metatron's connection to Enoch, it's safe to say this celestial being has been through an incredible spiritual transformation when ascending to the heavenly realm. And because of his ascension, Metatron can be a powerful ally for those seeking their spiritual transformation. This chapter will introduce you to the concept of ascension. It analyzes personal ascension, including its steps (abusive past release, raising energy levels and awareness, and others), and how you can achieve them through the connection with Metatron. You'll learn how much time is needed for this procedure and the benefits of completing it. You'll also be given a practical guide (with easy-to-do steps) to achieve personal ascension, along with tips on recognizing whether the process has taken place on physical or spiritual levels.

Personal Ascension

Personal ascension is defined as becoming a newer, better version of oneself. It's a gradual process that starts with slowly increasing self-awareness until you become fully awakened. It's unique (and personal) – a journey you must take by yourself, although you can call on some reinforcements along the way. Because ascension is also confusing and sometimes even painful at first, you need guidance to recognize whether you're on the right path and shift your consciousness toward a better understanding of why and how you need to ascend.

People change all the time. Ascension just makes sure it's for the better. It makes a shift within you, enabling you to manifest positive changes outside as well. It allows you to grow spiritually and personally, discard unwanted ties and release unhealthy thoughts and relationships. It helps you gain insight and self-realization. Sometimes, you get drawn to new ideas and start making new choices that benefit your spiritual journey. You gain a new perspective of the world as a whole and a deeper understanding of how to make it a better place for yourself and those around you.

Here are the basic steps of spiritual awakening and ascension:
1. Encountering darkness after realizing that what you know about your life isn't true.
2. Finding hope when you break through spiritual bonds as you let go of past hurts.
3. Building inquisitiveness – reaching into your intuition for spiritual answers.
4. Facing inner conflict when your spiritual self-confronts your ego self.
5. Experiencing spiritual transformation through higher awareness and raising your vibrations.
6. Spiritual bypassing – unwillingness to delve into and ignore the deeper hurts.
7. Grounding, further raising your energies, and realizing that the only way to move on is to heal from everything – including hurts you haven't explored yet.
8. Opening up to your past and present experiences, bringing awareness to your spiritual needs and desires.
9. Finding and embracing your soul's purpose.
10. Mastering spiritual lessons about enlightenment and becoming the best version of your spiritual self.

Metatron is the Archangel of transformation. If you need help with spiritual development, he is the best guide to call upon. He can teach you how to gain confidence, start your journey of awakening, and recognize the signs that your ascension is upon you. He can accompany you on your journey to discover your own personal and spiritual power. He can help you uncover your power and serve you and this universe's greater good.

You might be wondering why Metatron is your best ally in personal ascension. This Archangel is closely linked to the energy of the solar plexus chakra, your energetic center responsible for strengthening your sense of self. This chakra can be a great source of personal power and self-mastery. Its energy is also linked to co-creative pursuits. Tapping into it will help you build healthy relationships with people around you and connect to higher beings. It allows you to establish boundaries and challenge the divine energy the angels gift you.

Metatron is the source of wisdom that will help you discover and realize your soul's purpose in this life – through spiritual awakening and ascension. All Archangels have specialties – Metatron's is ascension through spiritual empowerment. He can help you empower yourself by bringing forth information you've kept in the depths of your soul. Some of this information might be painful to re-discover, but it's part of a healing process. And when you heal from past traumas, you start living a more fulfilled life. This, in turn, enables you to find your purpose. Regardless of how deep or old your spiritual wounds are, they can affect your spiritual health in the present and future. Some believe that Archangel Metatron can help heal traumas from past lives – traumas so hurtful that they bleed through one's current life.

Whether your practice or beliefs include reaching into past lives or not, when you need to heal distant traumas, if you call on him, Archangel Metatron will help you. He can help you make the connection between past events and current complications in your life. Besides guiding you, Metatron also points you in the direction of personal spirit guides who will work closely with you, empowering your life and spirit and facilitating its ascension to its highest purpose.

Metatron has one of the highest vibrational energies in the universe. If you want to release or remove energetic blocks and heal your energies, the best way to start is to raise your vibrations. And who better to help you boost your vibes than someone who has experienced his own elevation and knows all the benefits of aligning one's vibrations with the highest power?

Metatron is a master channeler of energies. He can help direct your energies toward the right path and harness the power of whoever you find empowerment in. Whether you want to channel the energy of your spirit guides, guardian angels, or your higher self, Archangel Metatron can show you the way.

Metatron is just interested in discovering your soul's hidden desires as you are. Once you establish a connection with him, Metatron will encourage you to get to know your soul. It will also help him learn more about you to provide better guidance in researching your soul and uncovering everything you need to know about it, good or bad. Whatever you find, Metatron will point out that only your overall spiritual personality counts. If you start working on both sides of your soul, the good soon shines through the bad, and you'll have clarity on who your spiritual self is and what you can do for it. Metatron loves to assist in this process because he knows it helps you uncover your soul's characteristics, which is the most critical step in spiritual awakening. The experiences you choose to have and why you chose them from this point on will build a foundation for a self-fulfillment journey that leads to personal ascension.

Archangel Metatron is linked to the higher states of consciousness. By teaching you how to achieve these states one by one, he facilitates spiritual growth and awakening and helps your soul ascend. He can send you the signs you need to unlock your soul for growth and elevate it to higher levels. He will push you forward to become a fully expanded and enlightened conscious version of your spiritual self. Metatron will activate energies that raise your vibration to their fullest power and boost psychic and intuitive development. You will become far more receptive to spiritual messages when you improve your connection with your intuition. Deciphering spiritual messages and aligning your life with their advice is one of the best ways to propel spiritual growth. Besides your solar plexus chakra, Metatron is also associated with your crown chakra. This energetic center oversees and fills all your other chakras with higher energies. As you embrace your intuitive powers, you're opening your crown chakra, allowing Metatron to empower your spiritual being with his energy.

Signs That Your Ascension Is Taking Place

Feeling content for no reason can be a sign of personal ascension.[11]

There are many different indicators of personal ascension. Here are some of the signs that you are arriving at your true nature and have begun your journey toward ascension to the divine:

- You feel your heart opening to others, to all of nature, to yourself; forgiveness and understanding come with ease for yourself and for others
- Raised consciousness and alignment with your conscious self
- A feeling of oneness with the universe and nature
- Developing psychic powers, like telepathy with those around you
- You feel the need to be of service—not in what you do but to do something for others in general
- You feel the freedom that comes with following your path and inner guidance, and you are not constricted by the rules of society
- Trust in the divine – and that everything will work out just fine.
- Seeing beauty in everything and everyone allows your focus on it everything and anything to expand
- Feeling joy and happiness for no apparent reason

- Feeling your authentic self and knowing your soul is the greatest gift you ever received
- Awareness of light – seeing it in nature, other people's souls, etc.
- Feeling lighter – The more you release the old energies that wear you out, the lighter you start to feel
- Awareness of love and other people's soul.
- Ability to let go of judgment and separate your true consciousness from mundane thoughts
- Being able to unconditionally love, accept and forgive yourself and those who hurt you in the past
- Feelings of divine grace – almost as if it would carry you in a state of weightlessness, embracing you with unconditional love and being able to go with the flow
- Gaining the ability to be present – here – now and openly channel peace and awareness in your mind and spirit
- Seeing how your past dissolves behind you, and you cease worrying about your future. You are letting it all go and focusing on being present.
- Taking care of yourself: physically, emotionally, mentally, and spiritually. Loving and honoring yourself
- Recognizing the multidimensionality of your consciousness

Establishing the First Contact

Delving into the practical side of ascension with Metatron, your first step is establishing contact with this Archangel. Here is a simple invocation to make the first call to him:

"*Metatron, I ask you to join me now,*

And request and trust your guidance for my spiritual journey.

I ask you to infuse your wisdom and energy into my being,

So I can ascend and reach my soul's highest potential,

And my journey of expansion and learning will be fruitful.

I ask you to help me to tap into my higher self,

So I can receive the guidance I need to ascend my spirit.

Please join me now and raise my energy with your powers."

Metatron Mantras

Mantras are a combination of words infused with your energy. Your words can have immense power and help manifest your intentions to ascend your soul. Using mantras can also be a great way to invite Archangel Metatron to join you on your ascension journey.

Here are a few mantras you can repeat while calling on Metatron:

I am guided by the magnificent Archangel Metatron today.
I know Metatron is helping me to ascend my spirit.
I am surrounded by the loving energy of Archangel Metatron.
Archangel Metatron is opening my intuition.
I am one with Metatron and the divine energy.
The angelic light of Archangel Metatron courses through me.
I am connected to Metatron's light and angelic essence.
My trusty guide, Archangel Metatron, is ascending my spirit.

Metatron Meditation

The following Metatron meditation will help you establish a deeper connection with this archangel. It will also be a great practice in grounding and working on your intuition.

Instructions:

1. Find a comfortable position at a place where you won't be disturbed. Close your eyes and focus on your breath.
2. Deepen your breathing by gently expanding your abdomen with each inhalation. As you feel your stomach expanding, do your best to release your thoughts.

Meditation can help you establish a connection with Metatron.[12]

3. When your mind is freed of your thoughts, take a deep breath – inhale until your abdomen can't expand anymore.
4. You will feel pressure on your solar plexus chakra – this is the force of your inner power, don't fight it. Take a moment to embrace this and release your breath.
5. Next, feel as if your power begins to rise. Connect to that essence by first focusing on the sensations in your head. This will bring your attention to your crown and third eye chakras.
6. Imagine a purple light coming from your third eye chakra, traveling upwards to your crown chakra, and swirling up to the sky. Feel parts of yourself traveling up with this light higher and higher until you reach the highest plane, the source of universal wisdom.
7. Feel your connection to the universal wisdom and the vastness of the universe. Now imagine a bright star appearing in front of you. As it approaches you, it reaches out to you with a beam of bright energy.
8. As you think about where this energy comes from, you suddenly see Archangel Metatron. Feel free to greet him with the following words:

"Metatron, the brightest of the Archangels.

I am honored to meet you.

Please introduce me to your loving guidance.

My mind is open to receiving your infinite wisdom.

And I am forever grateful for your multidimensional energy.

I ask you to show me the depth of my power

Shine your light on my soul so my purpose becomes clear now.

Thank you, Archangel Metatron."

9. If you have a personal message to send to Archangel Metatron, deliver it now.
10. Imagine Metatron offering you his hand and inviting you to join him under his brightly lit aura. Take a few moments to enjoy the archangel's support.
11. When you're ready, gently open your eyes and let your thought slowly fill your mind again.

Releasing Past with Archangel Metatron

The following deep meditation will clear and align your energy by releasing past energetic influences. It will also bring you closer to Archangel Metatron and his incredibly powerful energy, allowing you to tap into his wisdom. This will help you transform aspects of your life. Practicing this exercise teaches you to cultivate your inner self and share Metatron's unconditional love and angelic energy with those around you. It's an excellent method to deeply purge and release old, unhealthy ties, situations, or relationships from your life.

Instructions:

1. Find a comfortable place to sit, close your eyes, and take a few deep breaths.
2. Imagine a beam of sparkling white light emerging from the earth underneath your feet. See it traveling upwards into your feet, legs, stomach, and back and reaching your arms and, ultimately, your head.
3. Feel how this light fills you with energy and call on Archangel Metatron by chanting his name three times and asking him to join you now. Make this request from your heart. Repeat it if necessary.
4. Take a few deep breaths and imagine how the energy coursing through you becomes even stronger. Imagine expanding it, sending it out as far as it can go - through the universe.
5. Notice how you feel at one with the space you've sent the energy. Feel joined with Metatron's energy. His aura feels like a warm, comfortable blanket.
6. Metatron's energy feels light because he only seeks your highest good. Trust his power, let go and allow your body to absorb his energy.
7. Allow Metatron to explore your energy field to find any troubles or energetic blocks. You can also confide in him about any issues you had with any aspect of your life (if you have conscious knowledge of them).
8. Now imagine Metatron's sparkling bright light reaching all the areas of your life (good or bad) and expanding them, enlightening them with transformative light.

9. Feel your entire body expanding with Metatron's sparkling life, reaching out to your environment. Imagine the energy reaching out to the loved ones you want to protect and empower.
10. Next, channel your attention to your energy. Let the previous image go. Once again, see the universal energy travel up toward your feet and reach every part of your body. You might feel it more intensely now because Metatron is guiding you.
11. As you feel energy reaching different areas of your body, focus on the sensation you feel in each of them. Pay attention to any negative feelings because these can be sources of bad energy.
12. Let the energy swirl around you to ensure it catches all the negativity and unwanted energies in your entire system. As it does, you'll feel lighter, safer, more loved, and happier.
13. When the energy reaches your head, feel how it eliminates any emotional and spiritual debris that doesn't belong there. You have energy with incredibly high vibrations coursing through you now. Allow it to purge all stale and old energy from your life.
14. Imagine a beam of sparkling light reaching into your heart chakra, clearing out past traumas, and releasing everything that hurt your heart and soul.
15. When you can feel only gratitude for all the blessings you've received and none of the resentment that comes with past hurt, you're now free of everything that no longer serves you.
16. Take a deep breath, allow your renewed energy to expand toward the universe, and ask Metatron to continue working with you to reach your highest potential.
17. Thank Metatron for his assistance, and when you are ready, imagine bringing your energy back to you. See it form a bubble of light around you, containing protective energy around you.
18. When you're ready, you can return to your thoughts.

Raising Vibrations

When you work with Archangel Metatron, you're reciting a large dose of high-frequency vibrational ascension. Below, you'll find a quick but powerful exercise to connect you to the energy of Archangel Metatron and clear your energy.

Instructions:

1. After assuming a comfortable position, close your eyes and focus on your breath.
2. As you relax, imagine roots coming out from your feet. They're then developed by a bright light that travels up to your core.
3. The light fills you with energy you can extend – because it *vibrates at a higher frequency.*
4. As you expand the energy, take a couple of deep breaths and ask Archangel Metatron to join you. Allow him to tap into your energetic field and work with you on upgrading it.
5. Feel how he elevates your vibrations and cuts all unwanted ties from your life.
6. You're now filled with even more light and energy that vibrates so highly you never thought it possible. Yet you feel safe because you know that having this energy in you is beneficial for you.
7. Take a few deep breaths and allow Metatron's light to fill your mind, body, and soul. Feel how your energies are bringing you closer to Metatron's. This is a sign that your vibrations are being raised.
8. Imagine the Archangel Metatron creating a protective shield around you, containing your energy and vibrations at a higher level.
9. Slowly let the image go and let your thoughts return to you.

Chapter 3: Recognizing Metatron's Presence

Metatron is watching over you. When you seek his guidance and reach out to him, he will answer your call. For some people, this can happen right away, while for others, it can take some time. However, you have to believe that he will eventually respond. Angels don't usually send direct messages and can't appear to you in their true form because they vibrate at different frequencies. Therefore, they will announce their presence through specific symbols. If you aren't familiar with these signs, you will not notice when an angel is present and miss the messages they are trying to communicate to you.

In this chapter, you will discover the different signs and symbols associated with Metatron so you can recognize the angel's presence.

Colors

Metatron has a colorful aura, and he is associated with white, dark green, pink, blue, and red. Each of these colors has a meaning behind it. Once you learn them, you can decipher the angel's message to you.

White

The color white indicates that tough times are passing.[13]

The color white indicates that you are going through a tough time, but things are about to improve. You may be facing problems in your personal life, like a bad breakup or family issues. Metatron can send you this color as a message of hope to tell you to be patient because good things are coming.

Green

The color green represents healing or truth.[14]

The color green has multiple meanings; it represents healing, honesty, or truth. If Metatron sends you a green color or green flashes of light, it can be a sign that you are about to heal from your pain. It can also signify that the truth you seek is about to be revealed.

Pink

Seeing a pink light might indicate that you've been neglecting yourself.[15]

Seeing a pink color or light indicates you should restore balance in your life and relationships. It can also be a reminder that you have been neglecting yourself. Real empowerment comes from self-love, so you should make yourself a priority. Metatron is telling you to take care of your well-being and the people in your life. Nourishing your relationships can contribute to your personal growth, but you cannot love and support others until you learn to value yourself.

Blue

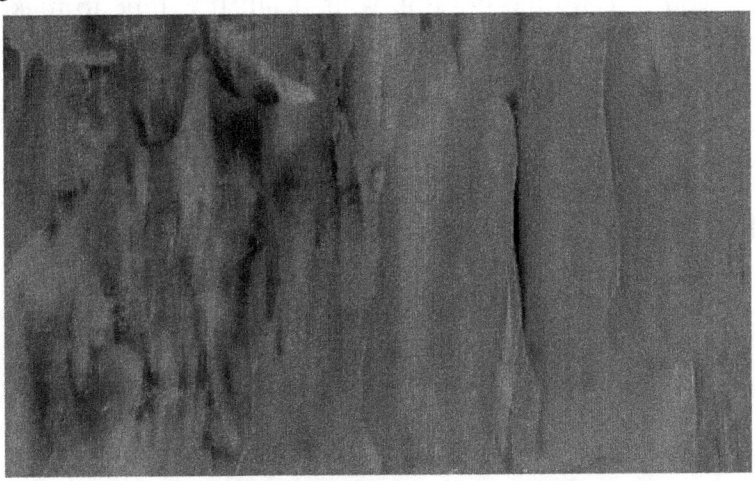

Blue indicates that you have potential.[16]

Blue is associated with motivation and encouragement. When you receive this message, it means you have potential and can achieve your goals, so start working on them right away. It is a sign that you should start believing in your abilities and have the power and courage to show your true self to the world. The angel is trying to tell you not to be afraid to open yourself up because this is the only way you will receive what the universe is ready to give you.

Red

Seeing red can indicate that you're facing stress.[17]

Metatron will send red flashes or colors your way when you face conflict, stress, or anxiety in your daily life. The purpose of this message is to urge you to calm the noise in your head. It is time to make peace with those who hurt you and forget your painful past. You should let go of your guilt and forgive yourself for all your mistakes.

The main purpose of Metatron's signs is to get your attention. He wants to tell you that he is present and has a message for you so his symbols will be loud and clear. You will keep seeing the same color everywhere you go until you notice it and look for its meaning.

For instance, you can keep seeing blue cars every day on your way to work. When you arrive at the office, you see your boss or any of your co-workers wearing a blue suit, and when you get home in the evening, you find your partner bringing you a blue sweater as a gift or your children or pets playing with blue toys. Simply put, the color will take over your life. All these events aren't coincidences; you are receiving a message from your angel.

Dreams

Metatron can come to you in a dream to warn you against an impending danger or let you know he is right here with you. He can appear to you as a white light or in any different form. However, you will be able to recognize him because you are already connected.

Courage

Everyone experiences fear; it is one of the most common emotions in the world. However, this feeling can bring negative thoughts and energies that stop you from reaching your potential and achieving your goals. Metatron will replace your fears with courage and confidence when he is present. You will start believing in your talents, abilities, and skills and seeing yourself differently.

Remember that Metatron's presence is empowering. He will give you the courage to face the unknown when he is near you, and your limitations will no longer control you.

Geometric Patterns

Seeing geometric patterns is a sign of Metatron's presence.[18]

Suppose you keep seeing squares, triangles, circles, 3D objects, or any other shape in random places. In that case, these are all signs of Metatron's presence.

Intuition

Once you reach out to Metatron, look for his messages immediately. Believe that he will eventually respond and start searching for opportunities and meanings in every random event and person you meet. Since angels can't directly communicate with you, they will send you people or specific situations to convey their message.

For instance, you have a job interview tomorrow at a reputable company and are very excited about it. Out of nowhere, your cousin, whom you haven't spoken to in months, calls you. While you are catching up, she tells you about her last job and how her boss ruined her life. She tells you that working in this place is her biggest regret, but she is grateful to get out and put this horrible experience behind her. When you ask her about the company's name, you discover that this is the same place you are having your interview tomorrow.

You are grateful for your cousin's phone call and decide that you will not go to the interview. You probably think that this is a coincidence. However, this is the work of Metatron. He sent your cousin to warn you against going to this interview.

Metatron will reach out to you in different ways, so listen to your intuition and focus on your impulses. You can have the urge to do something or a gut feeling to steer clear of a situation. Your angel is showing you the right path and nudging you toward your destiny. He will put people in your way to inspire you to reach your goals or warn you against things that aren't right for you.

Make Peace with Your Past

Since Metatron has access to the Akashic Records, which contain your memories and past mistakes, he can influence you to deal with your past issues and traumas so you can make peace with them. He will bring all the emotions you are afraid of to the surface so you can face them and deal with them.

These records will be discussed in detail in the coming chapters.

Paintings

In paintings, Metatron is often depicted as a guardian standing next to the tree of life, keeping it safe. He usually wears a pink, green, or blue robe and has golden wings. Randomly seeing this image in paintings or pictures is a sign of his presence.

Processing Emotions

If you have been processing your emotions differently lately, this indicates that Metatron is close to you. In the long run, his presence will inspire you to reach your higher self and learn how to express your emotions properly. This change in your personality will not happen immediately; it will take time, but eventually, you will experience real transformation. Metatron is by your side, pushing you to become the best version of yourself.

Number Eleven

You have probably been told to make a wish at 11:11, as this is a special time. 11:11 indicates that a gateway is open, giving you access to the spiritual world.

The number eleven is associated with Metatron. If you constantly see it in this specific form, 11:11, the angel is present and providing guidance. It can also be a message of validation.

Eleven is also a sign that something amazing is about to happen in your life. You can see it on buses, tickets, your cell phone, or digital clocks. The number also indicates that you are experiencing a spiritual awakening. If you are struggling with a decision, this sign encourages you to take a leap of faith.

Although 11:11 is usually open to many interpretations because each person relates it to something different depending on their own experiences, it is always associated with Metatron and the spiritual world.

When you see this number, pay attention to your life and goals and assess what needs to be done or changed to achieve them. Metatron is by your side, guiding you every step of the way.

It can also be a reassuring sign to remind you that you aren't alone and that Metatron will always be here for you. If you have asked him about ascension, he can send you this number to give you the answers you seek.

Numbers are usually the most common symbols angels use to communicate with human beings.

Scents

When Metatron is near, you will experience strong and unusual scents of spices and herbs, like peppercorns, chilies, or sweet floral smells. You wake up every day smelling an unusual fragrance. It is in your car, on your way to work at your office, and everywhere you go. The scent is taking over your life.

Sounds

Auditory signs are often the easiest to recognize. You may miss colors or scents, but it is impossible not to notice a loud noise. When Metatron is near, you can hear a high-pitched buzzing sound in your left ear. In some cases, you can also hear him speak in a low and soft voice.

Tingling in the Chakras

When Metatron wants to announce his presence or communicate with you, he will activate your seventh chakra (crown chakra), located on top of your head. It is associated with divine communication and spiritual elevation. You will experience higher awareness and spiritual energy revealing the answers you have sought about yourself or the universe.

Thoughts Shifting

Since Metatron is meant to empower you, he can influence you to change your thought pattern. Say you have been having negative thoughts lately, but suddenly, you have the urge to replace them with positive and happy ones. This means the angel is with you and working on eliminating the negativity from your life.

Metatron is the keeper of the universe's records; this gives him insight into the human mind. He knows how people's negative thoughts can impact their lives. He is curious about how they think, and he has seen that positive individuals lead happy and healthy lives while negative ones are miserable and constantly struggle to make healthy and good decisions.

When Metatron is present, he will inspire you to focus on your thoughts and to choose positivity over negativity. He wants to remind you that you are in control of your mind, not the other way around. You have the power to alter your pattern of thoughts so you can think positively and change your life.

Metatron's presence will elevate your consciousness and fill your mind with creative ideas. Your thoughts will inspire and motivate you to make better choices and live your best life. This is a clear sign that Metatron is by your side, guiding you and inspiring you to think positively.

White Light

Metatron can send you flashes of white light to let you know he is here. You will easily notice this sign since the light will be strong and almost blinding. Metatron's vibrational frequency is higher than any other angle, so his fiery presence is always noticeable. He can also manifest in any colors associated with him, like blue, green, and pink.

Personal Experience

Many people have encountered Metatron at one time or another during their lives. The last part of the chapter will narrate the personal experience of a young girl who communicated with the angel.

Elizabeth was connected with Metatron and knew he was her guide. She constantly saw many signs from him; he appeared in her dreams, and she was always drawn to him. One night, Elizabeth was meditating and saw herself standing in front of a cathedral door in heaven. She knew Metatron was on the other side and was nervous. The angel waited for her to enter; he didn't want to rush her. She opened the door, walked in, and sat beside him. Elizabeth didn't say a word because she was overwhelmed by the experience. However, Metatron welcomed her and expressed his joy that she had found him. He explained to her that her negative thoughts weren't her fault and they shouldn't define her. She was strong and had power over her darkness, and he asked her to forgive herself.

Elizabeth hugged Metatron, and she could feel his unconditional love for her. However, she was overwhelmed by her emotions and broke down in tears. The angel comforted her and told her he wasn't going anywhere.

She asked him to show her who she was in a past life, and he complied. In the vision, Metatron was standing behind her. He told her he was always with her in every life she experienced. Metatron explained that he would have her back and constantly watch over her forever. He then took her to an oak tree, and they sat in silence.

In her experience, Metatron didn't have a face. He was a tall light with long hair and wearing a purple robe.

In life, there are no coincidences. If you encounter strange events, don't brush them off because there is always a meaning behind them. Metatron can manifest himself to you in different ways. However, you will never recognize his messages if you don't pay attention.

Understand the meaning behind everything you experience. Suppose you keep smelling a strange scent, seeing the number eleven everywhere you go, or seeing geometric patterns. In that case, this can indicate that Metatron is near you.

You are the only person who can decipher Metatron's signs when he reaches out to you. Although his symbols can have general meanings, the hidden message behind them is personal. For instance, if you feel alone and Metatron sends you the number eleven, he lets you know he is with you. For someone else, the number can provide guidance.

You and your angel share a special bond, so even if the messages can seem strange or unclear to someone else, you will know what they mean.

When you call out for Metatron, keep all your senses open and prepare yourself for all the messages you are about to receive. Metatron can be by your side right now, and you don't even know it, *so stay focused.*

Chapter 4: Metatron's Cube

In many religions and spiritual belief systems, God is credited with having created the entire universe with a unique geometric plan. This is why most people consider geometrical shapes to be sacred and symbolic of some underlying divine message and is how the concept of sacred geometry came into being. If you think about it, the principles of geometry govern the very essence of this universe. The patterns, proportions, frequencies, ratios, and geometric shapes underlie any organic life forms, objects, and phenomena in the universe. Many people revere sacred geometry symbols for this exact reason and try to use them to understand and interpret the divine truths behind all existence. One of these revered shapes is Metatron's cube.

If you're interested in the healing and empowering strength of the Archangel Metatron, you've probably heard of Metatron's cube and how it plays into spiritually connecting with the Archangel. This divine and complex structure is considered one of the most sacred geometric patterns in existence in history. The Archangel Metatron oversees the energy flow in this sacred cube, which encompasses every geometric shape and structure in this universe. Metatron's cube is said to be derived from the ancient structure of the flower of life. It is the perfect blueprint of cosmic creation, an architecture of life that defines the very universe. When you look at Metatron's cube, you'll intuitively feel something alluring about the crisscrossing lines, intersecting circles, and the unique arrangement of each shape. The cube is especially captivating when in 3D, forming a complex geometric structure.

Since you've decided to spiritually connect with the Archangel Metatron, learning about Metatron's cube and how it can help you connect with the revered Archangel is an essential step in the process. Suppose you've already encountered Metatron's cube's beautifully dynamic and complex shape before. In that case, you've probably felt the powerful pull of this hypnotic symbol and wondered what the meaning behind this intricate pattern is. This chapter will help you find that out. Metatron's cube is not just a symbolic shape but has significant spiritual powers that help you connect with the Archangel Metatron more easily. However, to properly harness its power, you must first understand the history and complex dynamics behind this unique shape.

Metatron's Cube and All the Shapes in Creation

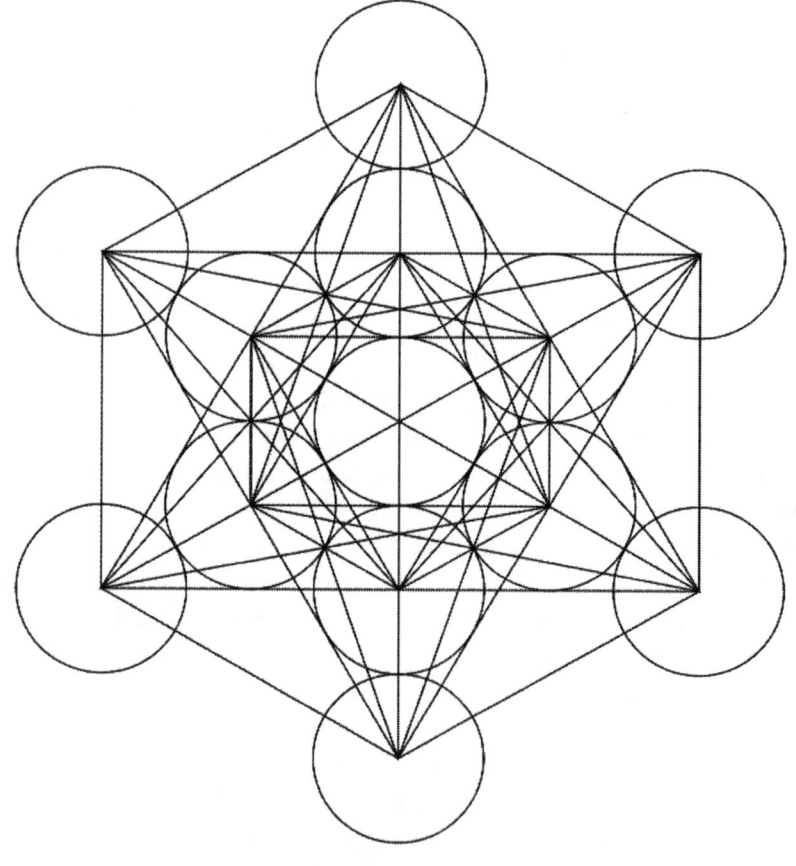

Metatron's cube.[19]

Why is Metatron's cube so special? After all, it's just a combination of shapes! However, if you focus on the shapes present in this combination, you'll notice that it contains every common shape that exists in the universe! These shapes are considered the building blocks of all physical objects, as they appear throughout creation in everything, whether it's crystals or even human DNA. Do you ever ponder how everything in this universe forms a specific shape and how timeless geometric codes like this cube highlight parallels between patterns in flowers, snowflakes, shells, the corneas of eyes, the DNA molecules that make up our genetic material, and the galaxy itself in which our planet resides? The Creator has designed this world around us, and everything in this world point to the unity and connection of the divine mind that created it.

Various interpretations have been postulated from the symbol of Metatron's cube. Some believe that the cube symbolizes how God has created shapes that fit perfectly together throughout creation and how he designed people's souls and bodies to fit together. The cube represents how this universe's reality is three-dimensional; it has so many aspects and perceptions that things are never one-sided or black and white. Within the cube lies the sphere, so while the cube is said to represent your body, the sphere represents the consciousness of the soul within you.

Meaning and Symbolism of Metatron's Cube

Metatron's cube comprises 13 circles of the same size, with 12 lines extending from the circle at the center towards the other 12 circles. This shape is considered a geometric variant of the Fruit of Life symbol, which is also derived from the Flower of Life symbol. The flower of life symbol is considered to hold all the patterns of creation. Consequently, Metatron's cube symbolizes the birth of the universe and how it infinitely expanded in all directions of time and space. Like the leading theory of how the universe came into existence from a single point, Metatron's cube also begins from a single point in the middle of the shape and then expands outwards.

Everything in our universe is believed to have the same fundamental elements and follow the same principle mathematical laws of physics and nature. Anything and everything in this galaxy, whether it's humans, animals, or plants, is composed of the same materials, albeit in very different ways. And, like many uncovered secrets of this universe, the interwoven patterns and shapes of Metatron's cube have multiple layers that are not easily comprehensible by human minds. However, people have tried interpreting some fundamental concepts from this unique pattern. This can be done by considering the cube's shapes and patterns – not just in 2-dimensions – but also by trying to view it in 3D to further explore it.

Many experts argue that Metatron's cube is just a combination of several sacred patterns like the flower or Fruit of Life. These patterns consist of overlapping circles and make up one unified pattern of creative intelligence. Metatron's cube differs from these patterns because it has 78 additional lines that intersect the 13 circles of the Fruit of Life pattern. This results in a complex pattern consisting of five platonic solids and the Merkabah. The platonic solids are a huge part of Metatron's cube's interpretation and will be discussed later. On the other hand, the Merkabah is a star tetrahedron with eight points, similar in design to the Star of David. This shape is often envisioned as a bright ball of light rotating inside the cube's body.

The Merkabah consists of a downward-facing triangle which symbolizes the descending impulse, and another triangle opposite to it, representing the ascending impulse. The downward shape connects to Earth, whereas the upward triangle connects with the central star of the universe. This is why the Merkabah is sometimes considered a bridge between heaven and earth. The word, *Merkabah*, is roughly translated to "a body of light," which is how it's envisioned. It is said to transport you from this plane to a higher dimension and enhances your spiritual consciousness. When you connect with the archangel Metatron, the Merkabah's creative powers are activated, essentially making you realize your true potential. This will help you transcend your spiritual level and reach a higher level of consciousness.

As for the symbolic representation of Metatron's cube, the unique aligning patterns are said to reflect balance and harmony when viewed from the perspective of sacred geometry. When you look closely at the shapes and patterns adorning the symbol, you'll realize how all the shapes are connected regardless of how small or insignificant they seem. The same is the case with our universe; even small things matter and can significantly alter how things turn out in the big picture. You'll also notice how the circles are connected by lines that reflect the harmony of all things. Some people believe that the circles in Metatron's cube represent the feminine, while the lines are associated with masculine aspects. In other cultures, Metatron's cube is said to attract the guidance and blessings of the Archangel Metatron, as he can attract positive forces and dispel negative energies.

The History Behind Metatron's Cube

Where did the symbol of Metatron's cube come from? As you know by now, the Archangel Metatron has been mentioned in many religious texts, including Kabbalistic, Judaism, and Jewish texts. According to Jewish legends, it's believed that the cube was created from the angel's soul. According to the early scriptures, Metatron created this cube from his soul, meant to oversee the balance and natural floor of the universe. Since the cube is linked to all the shapes existing in the universe, it represents all the patterns that create every single thing in nature. Although the exact dates for its creation are unknown, it is believed to be formed sometime between the creation of this world and 1000 years after. It's more than likely that Metatron's cube has its origins rooted in the symbolic tree of life pattern.

The Theory of Sacred Geometry and Its Origins

Metatron's cube is closely related to the notions of sacred geometry, which have existed for thousands of years in numerous religious teachings. The word "Geometry" comprises two Greek words, "Geos" and "Metron," which refer to "earth" and "measure," respectively. So, geometry refers to the study of shapes and mathematical formulas found in nature. The practice of sacred geometry has roots in old civilizations like the Sumerians, Phoenicians, Greeks, Egyptians, and Minoans. This practice was initially considered sacred and therefore restricted to the priesthood. It was believed by followers of sacred geometry that everything in this world is created according to a specific geometric plan and that studying these natural shapes would uncover great mysteries of the universe.

As you know, Metatron's cube contains all of the geometric shapes and patterns in this world, from circles to spirals, to hexagonal shapes. So, the meaning of Metatron's cube, when viewed from a Sacred Geometry perspective, has many layers, depending on the viewer's understanding. Beginners will observe the cube as a two-dimensional object without focusing on the circles and straight lines and what they represent. On the other hand, experts on this subject will view the cube as three-dimensional and observe the five platonic solids in this sacred shape. Individuals who meditate on the cube as a focal point will begin to see it in five dimensions, revealing new shapes and patterns as it moves through the fourth to the fifth dimension. In some cases, Metatron can divulge heavenly secrets or significant guidance.

So, for the people who are skeptical about the beliefs in sacred geometry, and the power and symbolism of Metatron's cube, it's suggested that they focus a bit harder on this unique shape and try to learn the secrets it hides. Sacred geometry is not some concept formed by over-zealous religious people trying to grasp nothing; it is a real concept that stems from observations, research, and scientific study. This study has resulted in numerous advancements in every field, whether architecture, medicine, music, or art. And not only is sacred geometry real, but it also underpins almost everything humans do and seeks.

The Five Platonic Solids – Five Fundamental Elements of the Universe

Metatron's cube is considered to contain five sacred patterns that connect to the five platonic solids. These shapes make up all the matter in this universe. This concept is named after Plato and connected to his "Theory of Everything." The platonic solids include the tetrahedron, hexahedron, octahedron, dodecahedron, and icosahedron. If you focus on the three-dimensional form of Metatron's cube, you'll notice that two of each pattern are present within the symbol. Each shape is connected to different elementals, like Fire, Earth, Air, Spirit/Ether, and Water. These shapes are the only ones with the same edge length, angle, and face size and perfectly fit in a sphere with all points touching the surface. Forming a perfectly balanced and harmonious pattern, these shapes map everything in this world, from your DNA to the galaxies and beyond. The platonic solids are also called the perfect solids because each of these shapes has perfectly symmetrical sides and formation.

1. Star Tetrahedron – Fire

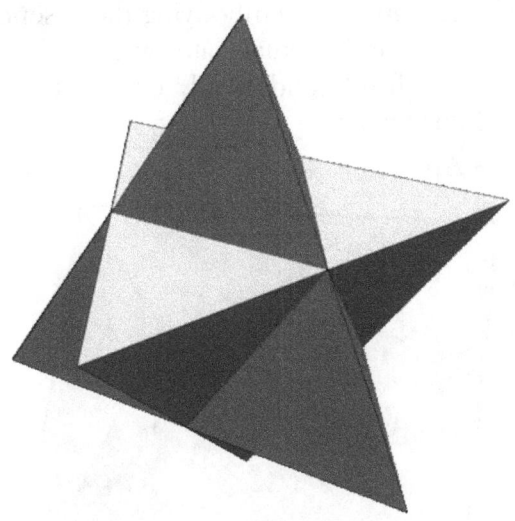

A star tetrahedron represents the element of fire.[20]

The Star Tetrahedron represents the essence of the fire element. It comprises two triangular pyramids and embodies flames' intense and penetrating nature. The precise structure of the shape aligns with the searing heat associated with fire. On the other hand, its symmetrical form symbolizes harmony, balance, stability, and equilibrium.

2. Hexahedron – Earth

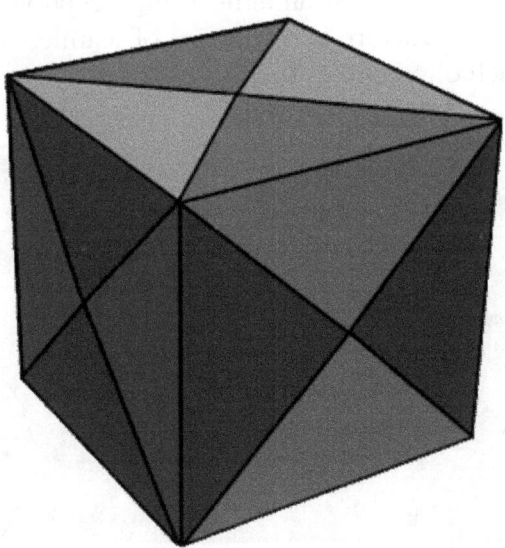

The hexahedron represents the Earth element.[21]

The Hexahedron signifies the element of Earth. It resembles a cube and is defined with straight lines embodying the essence of solidity and firmness, which are fundamental attributes of the Earth. The Hexahedron itself rests firmly and evenly on a flat surface, akin to the grounded nature of this planet.

3. Octahedron – Air

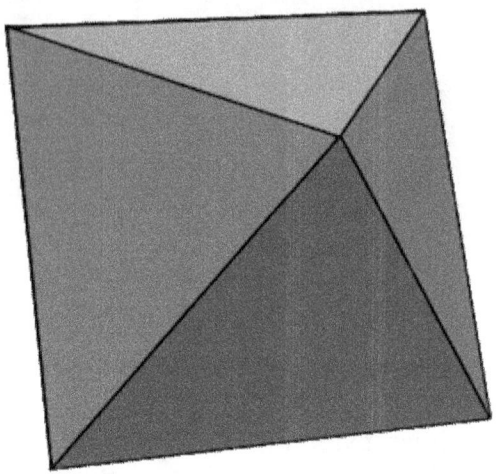

An octahedron represents the element of air.[22]

The Octahedron symbolizes the element of Air. Its sleek form consists of eight equilateral triangles, representing the minute components of air that possess an almost imperceptible smoothness. Just as the Octahedron's structure is composed of seamless triangles, so is the nature of air, which often eludes touch.

4. Icosahedron – Water

The icosahedron is associated with the element of water.[23]

The Icosahedron is closely associated with the element of Water. Composed of 20 equilateral triangles, it stands as the Platonic Solid with the greatest number of faces. Its harmonious and uniform shape is an apt representation of water, which effortlessly slips away when one attempts to grasp it. The Icosahedron's smooth and flowing structure mirrors water's fluidity and elusive nature.

5. Dodecahedron – Ether

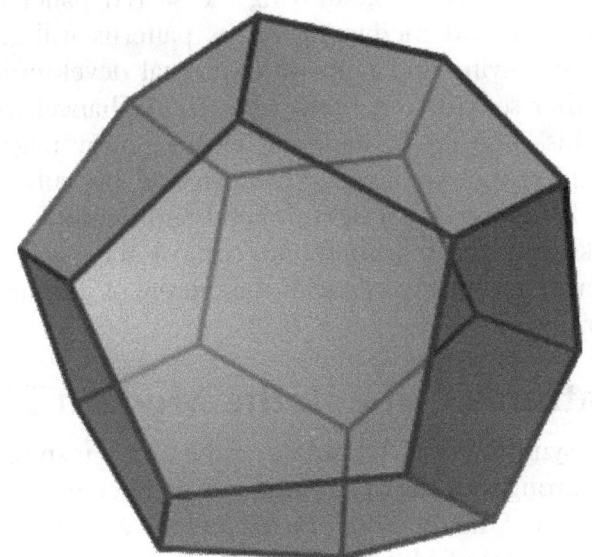

The dodecahedron is associated with the concept of ether.[24]

The Dodecahedron is intricately linked to the concept of ether, a distinct element associated with the celestial realm, sky, or space. Ether is often recognized as the fifth essential element that harmoniously combines with the classical elements of fire, earth, air, and water to form the fundamental components of the universe. As a representation of this ethereal element, the Dodecahedron embodies its unique qualities and serves as a symbol connecting the material and spiritual realms.

Connected with the five essential elements that make up this world, the five platonic solids are considered significant to the creation; thus, the cube becomes a symbol of unity and interconnectedness of the world. When you look at Metatron's cube, you'll notice how all the lines, nodes, and circles are connected with one another. Similarly, notice how everything else will be affected if you pull on one string or node from this shape. This is similar to how this world works and how even little things can make a huge difference.

A Tool for Inspiration and Transformation in Sacred Geometry

So, how, when, and where can you use Metatron's cube to help you? Well, for starters, Metatron's cube is known to inspire and motivate humans, whether it's for personal transformation or anything else. According to ancient scholars, studying the sacred patterns and shapes present in the cube and meditating on its patterns will give you inner knowledge of the divine and help with spiritual development. You can use this to further secure your bond with the Archangel Metatron. You can also use this cube for healing and clearing away negative energies. You can call upon the Archangel Metatron and his cube to clear your energy channels whenever you feel drained and demotivated. Archangel Metatron is known for his ability to control the malleability of the physical universe, and this works with the energy of the universe to heal, teach, and purify you.

Metatron's Cube in the Modern Times

The unique symbol of Metatron's cube has inspired numerous masterpieces throughout history in art and architecture. It's even been used as jewelry and meditation practice. Here are some of the most common modern uses of Metatron's cube:

1. Rituals and Meditation

Metatron's cube is perfect for use in meditation and other spiritual rituals. It can help with creative blocks and find deeper meaning in life. It also helps promote balance and peace in one's life and ward off negative energies. In some cultures, this symbol is hung on doors and windows to keep evil influences away.

2. Balancing Energy

Metatron's cube helps manifest balance and harmony by ensuring that the energy flowing through your body and around you is in proper balance. The symbol can therefore act as a visual focal point that will help you connect with the Archangel Metatron, or it can be used as a concentration tool in meditation, as discussed before. You can place an image of the 2D shape anywhere you like or get a 3D model and put it somewhere in your line of sight.

3. Fashion and Jewelry

Metatron's cube enthusiasts often integrate the symbol into their personal style through tattoos and jewelry. This can include necklace pendants, rings, and charms crafted from materials like silver and gold. Additionally, fashion items like t-shirts, jackets, and dresses featuring prints of the symbol are also available. The cube's symmetrical form lends itself to intricate and captivating tattoo designs, making it popular among those seeking complex body art.

4. Arts and Architecture

The concept of Metatron's cube is exemplified in the masterpiece Trocto, showcased at the Hyperspace Bypass Construction Zone, an art and design studio in California. This artwork serves as a visual representation of the sacred geometry symbol. Furthermore, the symbol finds its place in the design of various religious structures, from tabernacles and altars to temples, mosques, and churches.

Sacred geometry recognizes Metatron's cube as a symbol containing all the shapes and patterns found within the universe, endowing it with significant potency for rituals and meditations. Its profound meaning has influenced art forms and architectural designs. The inherent power of Metatron's cube is believed to foster balance and facilitate healing. Whether worn as jewelry or carried as a talisman, this powerful symbol attracts positive energy that promotes protection and restoration. Suppose you feel a connection to Metatron's cube and find solace in its symbolism. In that case, it's a good idea to integrate the symbol into your life as a source of inspiration.

Chapter 5: Pillar of Light Meditation

This chapter delves deeper into the ascension process, discussing one of its fundamental elements – the initiation of the Pillar of Light exercise. It will provide further information about this meditation, including its significance and how to receive Metatron's energy by activating it. Besides a few meditation exercises regarding the Pillar of Light activation, you'll also learn a couple of concentration exercises designed to help you focus better.

What Is the Pillar of Light?

The pillar of light describes a metaphysical bridge between your conscious (present) self and your soul or higher self. You can visualize the pillar of light as a column surrounding your physical body, using it as the center point to connect to your energy and divine empowerment. The width of this pillar around you depends on your energy levels and ability to manifest it. The more energy you can channel into manifesting the column of light, the stronger it will become, allowing great sources of spiritual light to come into your life. It will also enable you to receive and send

The pillar of light is a bridge between your physical body and your higher self.[25]

spiritual messages when building a connection with your higher self and the divine.

A pillar of light is an ideal communication tool between your physical and metaphysical aspects – which is where Metatron's help comes in handy. He can guide you through the journey of activating the pillar of light and receiving more guidance, wisdom, and inspiration for elevating your spirituality. He can also teach you how to use the pillar of light to enhance your psychic abilities.

The concept of the pillar relies on a connection to the divine consciousness. The column extends from way above your head into the heavenly realm and under your feet into the ground. Energy from both sources can move through it, nurturing your own energies. Once the pillar is activated, it dispels all the lower frequencies, enabling you to further raise your vibrations and reach spiritual enlightenment. You can never establish a meaningful connection to your higher self without a pillar of light. The column acts as a reminder of your spiritual sovereignty – reintroducing your divine nature and activating a deep consciousness.

Fully activating your pillar of light takes a lot of energy and practice. You'll need to channel a lot of light and high-vibrational energy into your energetic body. You must empower your chakras with cleansing energy so they can enable you to radiate your energy toward the higher bodies. However, each time you do this, you are rendering your pillar more powerful until it becomes so potent that you won't need to consciously focus on activating it. Remember that your intention matters the most – as with any other spiritual work. If you truly want to activate your pillar of light, you must channel your energy into manifesting it.

Activating the Pillar of Light

You can do this meditation at any time of the day, which makes it great for those who haven't yet established a schedule for spiritual exercises. That said, finding a regular slot for it is a good idea. This will improve your focus and bring you closer to your goal of spiritual alignment and ascension.

Instructions:
1. The activity is designed to ground and connect you with the Earth and the universe, so it's best done as a standing exercise. Standing makes you plant your feet firmly on the ground. Relax your shoulders just enough to avoid being distracted by uncomfortable

sensations in your body.

2. Close your eyes and focus on something that brings you joy. Smile, and let this smile melt the stress around you – see it drip onto the ground.
3. Imagine your feet sinking into the ground, extending roots that travel into the earth like plant roots seeking nourishment. Feel the roots moving out in all directions, north, south, east, and west, above and below. They connect you to the energy of the universe and divine essence.
4. Feel your energy infuse with the energy harnessed by your roots. Suddenly, a source of light comes up from the ground, travels up the back of your legs, up your spine, and flows into your heart and head.
5. Feel how the energy begins to vibrate inside you, the light illuminating you from the inside out. When you feel that the energy can no longer be continued inside you, imagine it being divided into two powerful streams.
6. Imagine the streams flowing down your arms and radiating out of your palms, surrounding you with golden light. The light infuses your energy with the energy of the earth.
7. Imagine being connected to the divine and the earth simultaneously. You're now a bridge between the heavenly realm and the human one. As you focus on this awareness, you feel your every tissue and cell becoming saturated with the bright light that unites the energy of nature and divine empowerment.
8. Your entire being vibrates with bright light and becomes lighter and lighter. You become aware of your divine energy and let it expand toward the universe.
9. As you let the bright light course through your body, your divine energy becomes rooted in your consciousness.
10. Call on your spiritual guides (including Archangel Metatron) and ask them to help you use the light for a higher good. Ask them to help you bring love and spiritual fulfillment to yourself and others, and thank them for their assistance.
11. Complete the meditation by letting the image of your spiritual allies and the light go. Gently bring awareness back to the present as you open your eyes and let your mind be filled with mundane thoughts.

Short Pillar of Light Activation Practice

Here is an easy-to-do exercise to activate the pillar of light and initiate your ascension journey. While this might not allow you to fully open the pillar right away, with time and practice, you'll be able to do it with just a few simple breaths. In the meantime, this short exercise will help you start mastering the basic steps.

Instructions:

1. Find a comfortable position and relax by taking a few deep breaths. Keep your feet on the ground - preferably do this exercise outside (where you can be closer to nature).
2. Imagine positive energy traveling down the center of your body, leaving you smiling and stress-free.
3. Visualize your feet being grounded into the earth, uniting you with it, like ice melting into water. You can almost feel your feet being absorbed into the soil beneath them.
4. Feel your energy extending into the ground, like a tree growing its roots. Imagine your roots traveling all the way into the core of the planet. See your core connection to your roots but also to a powerful source of light suddenly surrounding you.
5. The light fills you with empowering energy. It travels into your body, down your arms, and fills the space around you with golden light.
6. Imagine yourself being completely saturated by this light. As you inhale, the energy expands your body and the surrounding space. As you exhale, the energy wraps around you like a cocoon.
7. You feel weightless, almost as if you are floating in the heavenly realm. You can feel the clouds around your waist - yet your feet are still connected to the earth.
8. You're now a pillar of light. As you inhale, imagine overflowing your being with bright light, your center becoming illuminated by this light.
9. You're now connected to your divine being - a being of pure consciousness. Now say the following invocation:

    "I am who I am.

    I am now calling upon the presence of the divine,

I am now calling upon the presence of Archangel Metatron.
I am surrounding my ego.
May the divine will become my will."

10. If needed, repeat the invocation twice more. This will help you channel stronger focus and deeper your connection to your spiritual self.
11. Now, you are free of anything that no longer serves you and empowered with your pillar of light – the divine source that will prompt your ascension. Rest in this awareness for as long as you need to, then slowly let your thoughts flow back into your mind.

Pillar of Light Activation Meditation

The following practice will help you experience the activation of light within. It's an exercise that focuses on breathing and improving contention to manifest your desire to activate and channel the energy of your divine light. The meditation will become your source of peace and reminder of your love for your divine existence.

Instructions:

1. Find a comfortable position – sitting or lying down.
2. Take a few deep breaths, and allow your eyes to close naturally. As you feel yourself relaxing, become aware of the sensations near your spine. Imagine a bright energy source emerging from your spine, pulling you upwards.
3. Connect with your breath consciously, beginning with a simple awareness of your breathing. As you breathe in, notice the energy that enters your body.
4. With each breath you take, feel your heart expand, and the energy revitalizes your soul.
5. Repeat the simple "Ahhh" mantra six times. With each repetition, feel the energy vibrating through your body. Continue taking deep, conscious breaths.
6. With each breath, allow your awareness to move toward your heart. Relax and connect to your soul, deeper and deeper.
7. Welcoming your breath, aligning yourself with your awareness of every part of your body until it reaches the top of your head. When it does, allow it to open your crown, welcoming a bright light into it.

8. See this bright light shining upon you, penetrating your head and expanding your inner light. Welcome the light with your heart and every cell of your body. Feel how it fills your cells.
9. Your heart is filled with joy as you see the light slowly seeping outside, embracing your body just as it did with your insides.
10. Imagine this bright light creating a column of light, centering you in the middle of itself. With each breath you take, the column radiates brighter and fills you with more empowering energy.
11. Allow yourself to experience the power of the pillar of light you're in this moment. You can affirm it to yourself by saying:

    "I am a pillar of light."
12. You can start empowering this pillar even more with deep breathwork. Place your thumbs over the nail of your index fingers. The other fingers should be outstretched as your hands rest relaxed on your knees, palms up.
13. Find a steady rhythm for your breath. The goal is to contract your abdomen as you breathe out through your nose while your inhalations remain natural. Speed up your breathing while maintaining the same pattern for 10-15 seconds.
14. Then breathe as fast as you can for about 5 seconds, and feel empowered by the pillar of light.
15. Take a deep breath and hold it for a few seconds. Feel the activation within you. Exhale gently and keep your body still and relaxed.
16. Focus on extending your inner experience. If any thoughts come, allow them to drift in and out and bring your awareness back to your breath, reestablishing the powerful stillness within.
17. Take a gentle deep breath, and be aware of the pillar of light – penetrating and surrounding you. Feel your heart filling with gratitude for this light and the empowerment of your mind, body, and soul.
18. As you breathe in again, bring your awareness to the space around you. Slowly stretch your body as you open your eyes and let your everyday thoughts return.

Improving Your Focus

When trying to master the pillar of light meditation, beginners often have trouble focusing on their intention. Whether due to a lack of experience or because they're overwhelmed by the sudden energy shift in them, some people have trouble concentrating long enough to manifest long-term changes. If you have similar issues, you'll be happy to learn that improving your focus simply takes a little practice. If you can take a few minutes a day to pause your thoughts and quiet your mind, you'll soon discover the strength you need to channel your focus in the right direction. Consider practicing improving your focus as an opportunity to be more present with yourself. It helps raise awareness of what you want to create in your life and what no longer resonates with this goal. It also teaches you that you can take control of your thoughts and actions and use them to connect with spiritual helpers like Metatron and initiate your spiritual growth. This affirmation-based mediation allows you to connect to your inner self. Learning to ground yourself can improve your focus and reaffirm your intention of creating the pillar of light.

Instructions:
1. Start by taking several deep breaths. While you do, focus on an intention of aligning with your divine self.
2. Empty your mind of all thoughts except for your intent. If it wanders in any other direction, shift your focus back to your intention. If you're having difficulties concentrating, focus on the sensations in your body.
3. Call on Archangel Metatron (and any other spiritual guide) to join you and empower you as you take control of your focus.
4. Imagine a ball of light descending from up in the sky, traveling toward you. As it descends, it leaves a trail of bright light behind it – forming a pillar that connects it to the center of the universe.
5. Suddenly, the ball of light stops just above your head. Then it descends further into your crown and travels down to your toes, filling your entire body with light.
6. Feel how your body radiates with light – as an extension of the magnificent pillar of light above you. The pillar of light shines through you and from you. It's filling you with divine power, unconditional love, and the angelic essence of Archangel Metatron.

7. Focus on your breathing, sensing how you are refilled with the angel's energy with each breath. Tap into this energy and use it to boost your vibes and fuel your intention of connecting to your divine self.
8. Your goal is to take control of your divine energy – so you can radiate it toward others. Feel free to keep focusing on this target until you feel that your frequencies are starting to align with the divine frequency. The pillar of light will raise your frequencies so you can accomplish this.
9. As you sit, proclaim these words:

    "I accept myself as I am.

    I am an aspect of the Creator.

    I align every aspect of my being to this truth.

    I know who I am.

    I know what I am.

    I know who my allies are."

10. After each line, stop to take a deep breath and channel your energy toward your intention. Tap into the part of you who knows who you are in a spiritual sense.
11. Sit quietly under the pillar of energy for a few moments. When you feel it's time, slowly return to your thoughts. Enjoy being empowered by the pillar of light and the knowledge of being able to focus on any goal you establish for yourself.

Opening Your Heart

Opening up your heart is another fundamental step in any spiritual work. Whether you want to connect with Metatron or other spiritual guides or facilitate your ascension, you must be open to accepting their energies. The following pillar of light exercise helps activate your true potential by opening your heart and filling it with positive emotions. This enables you to cultivate love, compassion, and sincerity that fills your soul, allowing it to become enlightened and connected to the pillar of light. You can do this as a standalone exercise or perform it before a deeper meditation. Whichever way you use it, remember to practice daily for at least a month before taking a pause. It only takes 5-10 minutes a day. When the month is over, you'll have a much stronger connection to Archangel

Metatron and the divine. It might take you longer in the beginning, but once you master it, it will go much faster.

Instructions:

1. Start in a relaxed standing position. If you haven't performed similar meditations before and have trouble relaxing, do the exercise in a sitting position a couple of times. After a few seated sessions, you can switch to the standing version.
2. As you relax, let your body slowly settle. You might have a subconscious urge to move any parts of your body. This is entirely natural – let your body make any movements it needs to make. It will help reinforce the thought that you're free to do whatever feels comfortable.
3. When you feel relaxed, take a deep breath and imagine a light entering your head.
4. As you do, place your hands in front of your heart in a prayer position. Invite the light to cleanse your ego, starting with your trusting heart and soul.
5. Move your hands toward your sides, lifting your palms toward the sky, in honor of all the spirits and creations in the universe, including Archangel Metatron.
6. As you feel your heart being opened, lift your hands and slowly place them on your head. Imagine your mind being transformed due to all the positivity emanating from your heart and soul.
7. Remove your hands from your head and start lowering them, using them to outline the contours of your body. Focus on channeling the energies that transformed your heart and mind across your entire body, healing it from the inside out.
8. As your body starts to heal, you will feel more connected to the universe and grounded in nature. Repeat the hand movements from step 4 twice more.
9. With your first repetition, focus on aligning your energy with the lights and channeling it toward the space around you. The goal is to cleanse your sacred space and dispel any energy that could close your heart and mind.
10. The second repetition is to extend your newly empowered energies further, creating deeper bonds with the universe and Archangel Metatron.

11. You've opened your heart and activated the pillar of light. You are ready to take the next step toward full activation and delve deeper into your spiritual practice.

Chapter 6: Angelic Reiki and Healing

If you yearn for a deeper connection with the angelic realm, you must always look for different ways to help you connect with the angels. As it turns out, you can connect spiritually with the angelic realm in countless ways. It's almost as if the heavens have opened up and bestowed inspiration, spurred you into action, and implored you to ask for help, guidance, or direction in your life. Among these divine beings, one Archangel has been more gracious than any others and has extended his hand to humans, inviting them to find inspiration, creativity, and profound guidance. Metatron is more receptive to you than any other Archangel you'll encounter.

In the previous chapter, you learned about the transformative power of the pillar of light meditation and how you can use this technique to connect with Archangel Metatron. You tapped into the depths of your soul and tried to unravel the mysteries of the universe or of your own life. Now, it's time to embrace another facet of spiritual connection, one that complements meditation just like two sides of a coin. Reiki is a metamorphic technique that helps you harness the mystical energy flowing through the cosmos to channel it for healing and spiritually opening yourself. Much like meditation, Reiki allows you to tap into the divine frequencies that resonate within and around us. In simple terms, it helps you spiritually connect with angelic beings, such as Metatron.

In this chapter, you'll learn what Reiki is all about and how you can use it to connect with Archangel Metatron. Through this practice, you can open your heart and mind to his divine presence and immerse yourself in a reality where energies and intentions intermingle, and healing seamlessly merges with enlightenment. But that's not all you'll learn. Once you master Reiki symbols and their traditional practice, this chapter will dive into angelic Reiki, which is more centered on connecting with angels, particularly the Archangel Metatron. So, prepare yourself to witness the healing magic of a Reiki session, and get ready to form a transcendent bond with Metatron.

The Basics of Reiki

Reiki therapy is a method of guiding energy throughout the body to encourage healing and mindfulness. The Reiki belief system explains that the practice itself doesn't produce energy or heal anything on its own. Instead, it's a channel for energy, similar to how a garden hose acts as a channel for water. Reiki's roots can be traced back to early 20th century Japan, and this method is defined as a form of energy healing. It is based on the concept that everyone has an invisible life force energy flowing through their bodies at all times. In fact, it's believed that everything in this world comprises energy and is surrounded by energy. By encouraging a healthy flow of this energy through your body, Reiki can work wonders for your spiritual health. This technique is perfect for stress reduction and relaxation but also promotes healing. The principle behind the concept of Reiki is that if a person's life force energy is depleted, imbalanced, or weakened, then they're more likely to get sick or feel stressed, and when it's high and flows freely, they're more capable of being healthy and happy.

This method is considered to be mainly a spiritual practice but is not limited to any religion. The word Reiki itself is composed of two Japanese words, "*Rei*" and "*Ki*," which mean "God's wisdom" and "Life force energy," respectively. So, Reiki actually translates to spiritually guided life force energy. During a Reiki treatment, you'll feel a glowing radiance around you, which will treat not just your body but also your mind, emotions, and spirit. Numerous health benefits come with the practice of Reiki, and although it doesn't necessarily cure diseases, it does promote healing of all kinds, both physical and spiritual. Reiki is usually practiced by a professional Reiki therapist who has done extensive training and acquired the proper knowledge to practice this art form.

Traditionally, Reiki is taught by the sensei (teacher) to their students through attunement, which is basically an initiation ceremony that helps open up the student's energy channels to help improve the flow of energy. Once these channels have been opened, they remain accessible to the practitioner for the rest of their life. Just like meditation, Reiki is also considered a spiritual practice. It is taught at three levels, where practitioners on the first level practice this technique on themselves or others through light touch. Then at the second level, practitioners learn the ability to perform it at a distance, and third-degree or master practitioners are capable of teaching and initiating other people into Reiki.

How It Works

Many people ask, "How exactly does Reiki work?" Well, there's no single answer to this. Most practitioners and Reiki researchers don't have an explanation for the mechanism of action associated with Reiki. However, several theories, though not concrete, provide a rough idea of how this method takes place. One popular theory, which addresses the science behind this process, explains a phenomenon known as the "biofield," which is basically an electromagnetic field that permeates and surrounds every living organism.

Experts say this electromagnetic field extends 15 feet or more from the human body. In fact, there is evidence of energy being present within and around your body all around us. For instance, the heart produces an electric field observed through an ECG, while the brain also produces an electric field, albeit at a much lower level than the heart. All of the body's cells are known to produce positive and negative electric charges, which result in magnetic fields.

So, according to this theory, when Reiki is performed, and the energies of the magnetic fields of two human beings interact, these energies are altered or influenced, you could say. It's believed that the biofield that surrounds every person is what guides their bodily functions. Reiki energy is said to influence said biofield, thus affecting a person's physical and spiritual energy. So, in essence, the practice of this technique gathers and directs the biofield energy to you through thoughts, intentions, and touch.

Some Reiki Techniques

Similar to meditation, there are so many types of Reiki techniques and modalities developed that it becomes difficult to learn and remember all of them. Whether it's for centering purposes, clearing away negative energies, beaming energy, extracting harmful energies, infusing energies, or smoothing and raking the aura, Reiki takes on many forms. Reiki practitioners often use crystals and healing wands to enhance the quality of their practice. However, in essence, Reiki does not rely on any instruments other than the practitioner. A general Reiki session lasts about an hour, and the number of times you take a session depends on your goals. Similarly, the type of Reiki practice you want to perform is also up to you. Some common techniques include:

- **Usui Reiki:** The original form of Reiki, which originated in Japan. This technique involves physical touch to channel the healing energy throughout one's body. It helps promote emotional, spiritual, and physical health.

- **Karuna Reiki:** This technique is comparatively more complex than the traditionally practiced Reiki. It incorporates some additional symbols and movements to address the psychological and emotional aspects of healing. You should practice this method when you're looking to focus on compassion and deep healing.

- **Kundalini Reiki:** This powerful type of Reiki is perfect for spiritual growth and healing, which is what you'll prefer when trying to connect with an Archangel. The Kundalini event is located at the base of the spine, and this technique targets that area to harness this special healing energy.

- **Shamanic Reiki:** This method incorporates shamanic practices into Reiki techniques. The many indigenous spiritual traditions, like connecting with spirit guides or forces of nature, can come in especially handy when you're learning to work with an Archangel.

- **Crystal Reiki:** This technique involves using crystals and gemstones to speed up the healing process, whether spiritual or physical. For this, crystals are placed on or near the body during the reiki session.

- **Tibetan Reiki:** As you can tell from the name, this Reiki technique combines the teachings and methods of Tibetan Buddhism. This includes using mantras, sacred symbols, and rituals to help with the healing process and spiritual transformation.
- **Angelic Reiki:** Angelic Reiki, which will be the focus of this chapter, helps you work with angelic beings and their healing energies. For this, you need to connect with angelic guides to channel their healing energies and guidance.
- **Seichim Reiki:** Seichim Reiki, also called Sekhem or SKHM, is a little-known Egyptian form of Reiki that includes balancing masculine and feminine energy. This method provides deep healing and self-awareness.

Each type and modality offers a unique perspective and can be used for specific purposes. It's best to stick to general and angelic Reiki practices for this journey. Make sure these techniques resonate with you and meet your specific needs.

Reiki Symbols and Their Meanings

The founder of traditional Reiki, Mikao Usui, introduced several symbols to this powerful technique. These symbols are known to be calming and spiritual and have specific meanings that decide when they should be used. What are these symbols used for, you wonder? During Reiki treatments, of course! The practitioner draws these symbols on the receiver's hands, eyes, or in the air. During Reiki training, these symbols are taught and have to be memorized, and are also used during attunement ceremonies. There are four main symbols in designated orders, with a few additional symbols in other Reiki systems. These include:

1. Cho Ku Rei

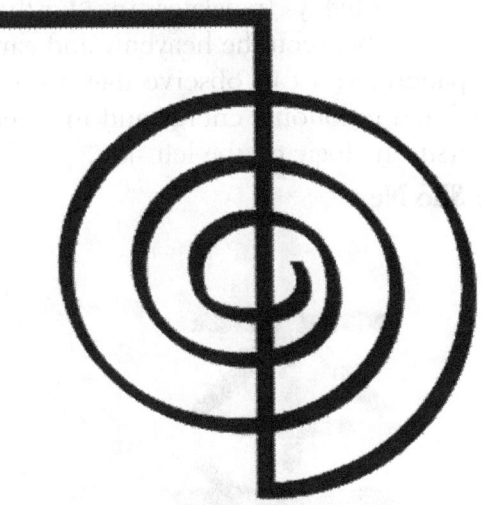

Reiki power symbol.[26]

The top symbol in the Usui Reiki system is the Cho Ku Rei, the power symbol. This symbol helps turn on the switch of the energy flow, drawing the life force power from the upper chakra, going all the way through all seven chakras. It translates to "focusing the energy of the universe here."

2. Sei Hei Ki

Reiki symbol of harmony.[27]

The next Reiki symbol is the Sei Hei Ki, considered the harmony symbol. This symbol roughly translates to "Earth and Sky Meet," highlighting the harmony between the heavenly and earthly energy forces. From its drawing pattern, you can observe that it's also about harmony between the mental and emotional energy and the creativity on the right side of the brain versus the logic on the left side.

3. Hon Sha Ze Sho Nen

Distance healing symbol.[38]

This symbol is considered the most complex and challenging one to draw out of all the Reiki symbols. The Distance Healing symbol translates to "Across past, present, and future." This symbol empowers Reiki healing across these elements of time and space. For instance, this symbol can be used to perform Reiki to help those not in the same space or even in the same time period.

4. Dai Ko Myo

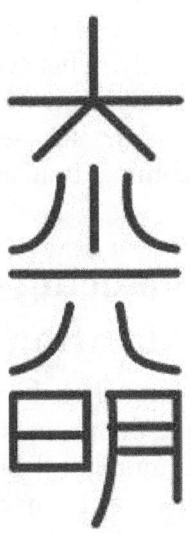

Great shining light symbol.[29]

This is the last of the four main Usui Reiki symbols and is considered to be the Master Symbol. This symbol translates to "The Great Shining Light" because this symbol is all about connecting with the universe's life force energy beyond the restrictions of this world. This symbol is learned in level three or master-level training of Reiki and is considered very sacred to the Reiki system.

5. Raku Symbol

Completion symbol.[30]

The Raku symbol is considered to be the completion or grounding symbol, which helps conclude a session by channeling the energy from the crown to the root of the body. This symbol also helps draw a clear separation between the practitioner and the receiver. Although not part of the four main Reiki symbols, this symbol is considered just as important. It resembles a lightning bolt and is often called the "Fire Serpent."

Angelic Reiki: Enhancing Connection with Metatron

Angelic Reiki is a lot like traditional Reiki in many ways, but it also has significant differences that make the process more specific to its intended purposes. Angelic Reiki is a tranquil and powerful healing modality that works at a soul level and helps you channel guidance from the Angels. Through this technique, you can treat the root causes of any condition and bring about healing and balance in your life. This system of Reiki helps you connect intimately with the angels as they move through you and bring in harmony and guidance from the divine. As you know, all forms of Reiki healing include hand movements that channel the life force energy through the recipient. But where this energy comes from depends on the type of energy healing being practiced. In the case of Angelic Reiki, the abundance of energy is channeled from the angels, specifically, the Archangel Metatron.

What does an Angelic Reiki healing session feel like?

An Angelic Reiki session, much like any traditional Reiki treatment session, should be carried out in calm, tranquil, and dimly lit environments. To practice this technique, find a place where you're comfortable, away from the noise, and where you feel peaceful. Once you're in a nice, relaxed position, close your eyes, and get the Reiki session started. For this, you can either learn all the Angelic Reiki techniques by yourself or get the help of a professional Reiki practitioner. You will feel very deep feelings and physical sensations during an Angelic Reiki session. People have reported feeling:

- Tingling
- Warmth
- Shivering
- Numbness
- Coolness

Benefits of Angelic Reiki

If you've never practiced Angelic Reiki or just Reiki of any kind, you've been missing out on so many benefits. This practice is spiritually healing for you and will strengthen your bond with whatever angel you're trying to connect with. Archangel Metatron is one of the most accessible and helpful Archangels out of all. He will surely help you with any problems you're facing and guide you in the right direction. Some benefits of Angelic Reiki include:

- Enhanced self-healing
- Improved sleep quality
- Pain relief
- Restores chakra balance
- Improved energy levels
- Stress reduction
- Enhanced immune system
- Strengthens intuition and spiritual development
- Eliminates negative energy

What is the difference between Angelic Reiki and Usui Reiki?

In some ways, Usui Reiki, or traditional Reiki practice, is similar to Angelic Reiki, but not exactly the same. Although all systems of Reiki fundamentally have the same purpose, which is providing powerful healing of one's life force energy, Angelic Reiki has significant differences from Usui Reiki, which can include:

1. Source of Energy

In traditional Reiki practice, the energy is manifested and sustained by the practitioner and then channeled through the receiver's body. On the other hand, in Angelic Reiki practice, the energy is purely divine, channeled by the practitioner, and transmitted to the recipient through touch or with sacred symbols.

2. Attunements

During the attunement process, the energy channels are opened by the Reiki Master teacher for traditional Reiki practices. However, for Angelic Reiki, the attunement is done by a specific healing angel assigned to every person. In this case, it should be Metatron who should be called upon for the attunement process.

3. Practitioner's Role

The practitioner's role is considered pretty significant in traditional Reiki practices, as they're responsible for using their intuition and healing abilities to find the areas of the body that need to heal most. On the other hand, Angelic Reiki does not require a practitioner to have an active role in the healing session and only acts as a passive vessel while letting the angel's guidance direct them throughout the process.

Angelic Reiki Healing Session

An Angelic Reiki session will heal spiritually and help you feel connected more closely with the Archangel Metatron. You'll feel the gentle and loving energies of the Archangel and feel at ease by the end of the session. Sticking with a healer is best unless you have proper training in performing a Reiki session. The healer will act as a conduit for the angelic healing energy and play a crucial role in the whole process. Here's a step-by-step explanation of how the process will take place:

- **Preparation:** To prepare for the Reiki session, the practitioner cleanses the room, lights candles, and places crystals near the treatment table or chair. Sometimes, soft music is also preferred.
- **Invocation:** Next, a connection needs to be formed with the Archangel Metatron, which is done by invoking the angel's presence and asking for his guidance. The practitioner usually does this with a silent prayer or a verbal intention.
- **Energy Scanning:** The healer/practitioner then uses their sensitivity, intuition, and psychic abilities to scan the recipient's aura and chakras. They may do this by moving their hands over the recipient's body or through their clairvoyant abilities.
- **Energy Clearing:** The healer then uses the Reiki symbols, the four main ones, and other additional symbols desired to clear the recipient's energy blockages, negative patterns, or stagnant energy.
- **Healing Intuition:** Then the main process of Reiki starts when the healer uses their hands to channel the angelic energy through the recipient's chakras. During the session, the practitioner receives guidance from Metatron and inspires them

to perform this technique perfectly.
- **Chakra Alignment:** Next, the practitioner focuses on balancing and aligning the chakras. This is done by removing any blockages from their chakra points and restoring the free flow of energy.
- **Closing and Grounding:** Towards the end of the session, the healer gradually reduces the flow of healing energy. They guide the recipient into a grounded state, ensuring that the client feels centered, present, and fully integrated with the healing energies they received.

The presence of Metatron in Angelic Reiki amplifies its transformative essence. The healer's profound connection with Metatron's energy infuses the healing session with divine light. Through this connection, messages and insights flow, offering profound healing and guidance. One's chakras align and harmonize, which helps restore balance and vitality to the body. Within this sacred modality, miracles await those who open their hearts to the boundless possibilities of divine love and healing.

Chapter 7: Crystals to Connect with Metatron

As you know by now, angels are essentially beings made of energy, the celestial messengers between mankind and the divine. The Archangels are no exception to this but are significantly distinguishable from other angels. Each archangel has specific crystals and gemstones which resonate with their abilities, energies, and attributes. After all, crystals are composed of the earth's energy and act as conductors or amplifiers. Therefore, they are perfect tools to help you communicate, heal, and become more in tune with the angelic realm. Crystals and gemstones have an invisible frequency that resonates with the energy frequency of specific angels, or in this case, Archangels.

Many consider crystals to be energy stores that enhance spiritual processes like healing, guiding, protecting, grounding, etc. Archangel crystals can be used to absorb the heavenly energy of Archangels and anchor this energy to the earth and you. Of course, working with crystals isn't something mandatory when working with Archangels. However, these crystals improve the whole process of connecting with Archangels significantly, especially Archangel Metatron, who has certain crystals that can encompass his creative guidance perfectly. This chapter will guide you in using crystals when connecting with the Archangel Metatron. You'll learn about using crystals in spiritual processes and connecting with the divine.

The Basics of Crystal Healing

You'll often encounter healing crystals in many spiritual circles because of their apparent magical, metaphysical, and energetically healing properties. In fact, numerous theories explain how crystals can enhance a spiritual process or merely have a placebo effect. One of the most common explanations is that crystals have certain vibrational frequencies aligned with specific outcomes or tangible results in real life.

When you have certain crystals around you whose vibrational frequencies align with your body, soul, or goals, you'll feel an invisible force helping you every step of the way, whether with spiritual healing, angelic communication, or to get divine guidance. And even if you're still skeptical about the efficacy of healing crystals, even if there is no concrete fact proving their properties, they can still play a deeply supportive role in your spirituality and help improve your intuition.

Crystals are associated with certain outcomes like healing, love, protection, clarity, and cleansing, any of which you could be seeking when trying to connect with the archangel Metatron. Plus, crystals can serve as a physical reminder of an intention you're keeping or a goal you're striving towards. For example, you may keep a crystal associated with clarity on your work desk. Even if you don't truly believe in its metaphysical powers, you'll be reminded of your intention whenever you look at it, and automatically work better. Or maybe, you wear a rose quartz necklace to remind yourself to be loving and empathetic to the people around you. Now, whenever you gain sight of this crystal, you'll naturally be more conscious of your behavior with others, try to make it better, and be more compassionate.

Crystals can also help you feel grounded and centered. In this day and age, it's easy to feel scattered and believe you're a mess. Almost everyone gets this feeling of being lost and dissociated because of the sheer number of responsibilities and tasks they have every day. This is where crystal meditation comes in. Certain crystals promote peace, calmness, and serenity and can help bring you back to the center. Finally, crystals are also commonly used for rituals, incantations, and manifestations. They are a popular tool used to try to connect with the divine, especially the Archangels. In fact, almost every Archangel has several crystals they favor.

Benefits of Healing Crystals

The use of healing crystals isn't something that has gained popularity in this century but has been in practice for thousands of years. Back in Egyptian times, these beautiful minerals were used to cleanse and protect against evil spirits. Today, crystals are used for various purposes and have several benefits, some proven by facts, while others are reinforced by experience. These include:

1. Placebo Effect

The placebo effect is the most identifiable result of the effectiveness of using crystals for healing. It is a phenomenon in which people feel a significant improvement in their symptoms after receiving a treatment with little to no therapeutic value. In this case, the placebo effect results from using healing crystals to speed up regular healing processes. It doesn't matter if crystals do, in fact, help the process; a person's belief in this method of treatment is enough to make a difference.

2. Emotional and Physical Healing

Emotional imbalances are common, but did you know you can alleviate these mental pressures and emotional worries with specific crystals? Since crystals are known to carry unique energy, they can help target emotional stresses and help relieve some stress from your mind. On the flip side, these rocks and gemstones are also known for aiding physical healing and providing pain relief. For instance, amethyst can be used to relieve pain, while hematite can be used to improve blood circulation and grounding.

3. Cross-Cultural Significance

Crystal healing has a rich history and an undeniable cultural significance attached to it. This method has been utilized for centuries, whether in traditional medicine or spiritual development; it holds prominence in many cultures. So, even though there are not a lot of scientific facts proving the effectiveness of crystals, their historical prominence should count for something.

4. The Piezoelectric Effect

Suppose you're familiar with the basics of electronics. In that case, you'd know that the piezoelectric effect can also be used to explain vibrational medicine. However, it is mainly used to describe the generation of electricity. This effect basically enables crystals to convert mechanical force into another form of energy like sound, electricity, or light and then amplify it. When this concept is applied to crystal healing, this effect magnifies the energy flow in a person's body or surroundings.

5. Spiritual Communication

Since crystals can amplify and transmit energy, they're commonly used for spiritual communication and to get guidance. Particular crystals have the vibrational frequency to enhance a person's intuition and psychic abilities and help them access higher states of consciousness. They can also be used to balance and align energy chakras in the body. Specific crystals are associated with each chakra and can be used to remove energy blockages and improve energy flow.

The Most Popular Crystals

In the world of spiritual communication, and angelic guidance, there is a vast array of crystals and gemstones that act as powerful energy conduits to help connect with the celestial beings. From the shimmering quartz crystals to the vibrant amethyst and the mysterious obsidian, there's no shortage of crystals to help you commune with the divine. The most popular ones include:

1. Amethyst

Amethyst can quell anxiety.[81]

Amethyst is one of the most popular crystals – and for a good reason. In addition to its vibrant purple hue, and beautiful design, it can quell anxiety and even improve one's sleep quality. Amethyst is said to target the crown chakra, which is located at the top of the head, resulting in a feeling of peace and tranquility for your brain. Although not proven, amethysts are known for their ability to ease headaches and migraines and strengthen intuition. Many people believe that placing an amethyst crystal by your bedside can calm your mind and bring you pleasant dreams.

2. Rose Quartz

Rose quartz is associated with love.[32]

Like its pinkish color, Rose quartz is associated with love and relationships. This crystal is wonderful to keep around if you manifest love or want a new relationship. It can also be useful if you're already on an emotional rollercoaster and don't know how to solve your problems. Rose quartz crystals are known to bring empathy, reconciliation, kindness, and love to those around them. If not needed for any of the reasons above, pink quartz can help bring you a feeling of peace, which is a good enough reason to keep it around.

3. Black Tourmaline

Black tourmaline absorbs negative energy.[33]

The black tourmaline targets the root chakra, which is located at the center of the body. This absorbent crystal can soak up all the negative energies that approach you or are already in your life. This is a grounding crystal that can also be used in many spiritual rituals.

4. Selenite

Selenite can cleanse auras.[34]

Selenite is an aura-cleansing crystal. When you interact with people throughout your day, the energy around you, commonly known as your aura, can get contaminated with other people's negative and positive energy. So, when your aura darkens, it's time to cleanse it of all the negativity it has acquired. Do you ever feel perpetually exhausted for no reason? This may be your body and mind indicating that your aura needs cleansing. And selenite is the perfect crystal for doing so. It can help rejuvenate the auric field around you, clear out the day's bad energy from your essence, and envelop your body in a peaceful energy flow.

5. Citrine

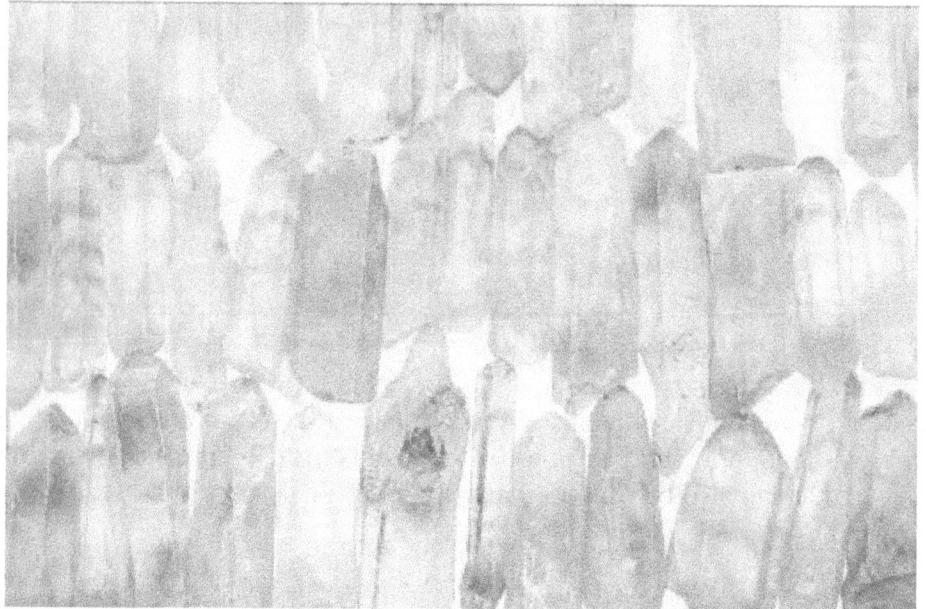

Citrine loosens knotted energy.[35]

Citrine, a bright yellow quartz crystal, is perfect for use when you're feeling stuck in a situation. This crystal focuses on your solar plexus chakra, which is located near your belly, and helps loosen any knotted energy or tension you have. This crystal can also be used when you're feeling nervous and need an extra confidence boost.

6. Jade

Jade is said to bring fortune.[86]

Jade is the crystal you want if you need a little bit of extra luck in your life. This beautiful green crystal is extremely popular because it is said to bring fortune, abundance, and prosperity in both material and social spheres. Jade jewelry is very common, whether it's necklaces, bracelets, or simple jade rings.

7. Clear Quartz

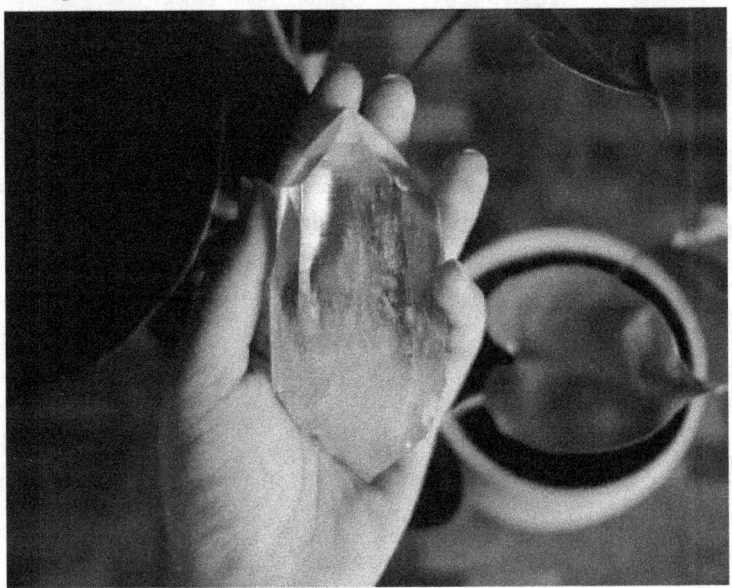

Clear quartz has many healing powers.[87]

If you plan to have a crystal collection, clear quartz is the first crystal you should get. This crystal is considered essential because of its versatile amplifying properties, which is why it's also often called the "master crystal." This crystal supposedly has numerous healing properties, especially in the realm of spirituality and energy work. Clear quartz is renowned for its ability to cleanse and purify the energetic field, dispelling negative energy and promoting a harmonious environment. It also enhances clarity of thought, making it an ideal companion for meditation, manifestation, and spiritual growth.

8. Rhodochrosite

Rhodochrosite aligns with the heart chakra.[88]

Not a very popular crystal but equally beneficial, rhodochrosite is said to help mend a broken heart. Seems like nonsense. This crystal aligns with the heart chakra and carries a gentle yet profound healing energy that can indeed support emotional healing and ease heartache. This crystal is found in varying shades of pink and is usually used as jewelry. This crystal's gentle yet potent vibrations can assist in opening the heart to receive love and joy once more while also encouraging compassion and empathy towards oneself and others.

9. Lapis Lazuli

Lapis lazuli can inspire creativity.[89]

This beautiful blue crystal can hone your creative senses and inspire new and innovative ideas. Whether you're an artist, writer, or engineer, this crystal will help you get your creative wheels turning. This crystal is also known for encouraging clarity and directness, which is especially effective in the workplace. This crystal's energy resonates with the third eye and throat chakras, harmonizing intuition and communication.

10. Chrysocolla

Chrysocolla can aid all chakras.[40]

This crystal is unlike any other in the sense that it aids all of the chakras instead of just being associated with one. As a result, the chrysocolla gemstone can help your body tune into the latent psychic sensibilities of your soul. Your intuitiveness and spiritual awareness are heightened as the gentle energies of chrysocolla flow through your being. With its vibrant shades of green and blue reminiscent of the Earth and the sea, the chrysocolla radiates a harmonious and soothing energy that resonates with all chakras.

Crystals for Metatron Connection

No doubt crystals hold immense power for healing and spiritual growth, as explored in this chapter. However, the purpose of this chapter was to help you learn how you can use these crystals to connect with the Archangel Metatron. The answer to this lies in the use of specific crystals that are associated with Metatron's qualities. When you use these particular crystals to reach out to him, your intentions will be amplified through these stones and help you establish a profound connection with the Archangel.

1. Ruby in Fuchsite

Although a lesser-known crystal, Ruby in Fuchsite holds the captivating energy that resonates with Archangel Metatron. This unique gemstone combines the vibrant red of ruby with the lush green of fuchsite, creating a harmonious union of passion and healing. Ruby in Fuchsite radiates a vibrant energy that ignites the fires of inspiration, creativity, and personal drive. This crystal harmonizes the heart chakra, allowing for the release of emotional blockages and the cultivation of self-love and acceptance. Ruby in Fuchsite also serves as a bridge between the physical and spiritual realms, opening channels for divine guidance and enhancing your connection with the celestial energies of Archangel Metatron.

2. Fluorite

This crystal is a kaleidoscope of vibrant colors, ranging from soothing blues and greens to deep purples. This crystal stimulates mental prowess, enhancing concentration and focus, making it an invaluable aid for meditation and deep contemplation. It encourages spiritual growth, helping you navigate the complexities of your spiritual journey with grace and enlightenment. With fluorite as your companion, you can align with the radiant presence of Archangel Metatron, tapping into divine wisdom and experiencing profound spiritual transformation.

3. Unakite

Unakite, a crystal revered by those seeking to connect with the archangel Metatron, holds a profound energy of balance and harmony within it. Combining pink feldspar, green epidote, and clear quartz, unakite emanates a gentle and transformative vibration that aligns with Metatron's guiding presence. This crystal also enhances psychic abilities and intuition, inviting you to explore the realms of higher consciousness and connect with the wisdom of Archangel Metatron.

4. Rainbow Tourmaline

One of the main crystals associated with the archangel Metatron, the rainbow tourmaline, represents the strength, protection, and growth that the angel provides. This crystal is a must-have if you plan to go through a spiritual journey to connect with Metatron, as it will protect your mind, body, and spirit. You can also use it while meditating by simply cupping it in your palms or placing it close to you since it will calm your mind and allow messages from Metatron to be heard.

5. Moss Agate

This crystal contains pure energy associated with nature and the earth. When you go through a spiritual journey, you must stay grounded during the process so you don't get lost or dissociate. Moss agate has a unique healing energy you can manifest during a meditative session to enhance the quality of your spiritual journey and assist in communicating better with the Archangel Metatron.

6. Garnet

Garnet is another crystal favored by the Archangel Metatron and is, therefore, perfect for any spiritual journey you embark on. It is a powerful stone that empowers you to overcome any kind of situation in life. Like Metatron, this crystal can inspire you to overcome even the toughest battles and live your life with love, drive, and passion. Whether facing personal struggles or seeking to manifest your dreams, Garnet's energy aligns with Metatron's divine essence, offering unwavering support and inspiration.

Crystal Cleansing

Keeping a crystal collection can seem pretty simple at first, but there are other considerations you must make once you have these crystals and plan on using them for spiritual connections. As you already know, crystals carry energy, and just like your aura, this crystal energy can also get contaminated with negativity and energy gaps. This is where crystal cleansing comes in. Similar to how you need to cleanse your aura when it's contaminated, you should cleanse your crystals regularly to ensure they're effective during your spiritual practices. There are many methods to cleanse crystals, from simply washing them with tap water to leaving them in a salt bath.

You should use running water for softer stones or let them soak in the sun or moonlight. Water is believed to be a good neutralizer of negative energy and can wash away the contaminations in just 5 to 10 minutes. Sunlight cleansing works best for warm-colored crystals, while moonlight cleansing works better for colder crystals. The sun/moonlight bath is also required when your crystal starts to look dull and drab. You can also try to cleanse your crystals with quartz or selenite. As you've learned in this chapter, both quartz and selenite can cleanse and purify auras, and crystals are no exceptions to this. Another method of cleansing is through smudging, which can be done with a sage stick, sandalwood, or palo santo to create smoke. Finally, you can also soak your crystals in a saltwater bath to cleanse their energy but don't forget to rinse them with regular water afterward.

In conclusion, crystals have held quite a significance in numerous cultures and spiritual practices. They have an array of unique qualities and amplification powers that can help you communicate with the Archangel Metatron. However, beyond simply working with these crystals, a more powerful way to enhance their energy is to program the Archangel's energy into these crystals. To do this, you simply need to set an intention. Hold the crystal in your hand, take a few deep breaths, and close your eyes. Ask the Archangel Metatron to provide you with his energy, and visualize a vibrant beam of light descending from the sky. Imagine this light going into the crystal and enveloping you. After programming the crystals, make sure to cleanse and recharge them as described in the chapter.

Chapter 8: Cord Cutting and Shielding

This chapter is about cord-cutting and energetic shielding methods when Metatron is present. Besides being provided with the definition of cord-cutting and shielding and an explanation of their significance for healing and transformative purposes, you'll be introduced to various techniques for eliminating unwanted ties from your energies.

What Is Cord Cutting?

Cord cutting involves cutting out negative energy from your life."

Throughout your life, you form ties to energies of different levels. Unlike the cords that tie you to high-frequency vibration with uplifting effects, the cords to lower energies have the opposite effect. They generate negative emotions like guilt, fear, pain, and endless worry. Some of these cords can be attached to your loved ones. Yet instead of filling you with happiness and positivity, they're draining your energy, causing it to vibrate at a lower frequency, which isn't conducive to spiritual growth. This happens because you don't have any boundaries in place. However, because these ties are already attached, you need to sever them before establishing healthy boundaries. This is where the practice of cord-cutting comes in.

Cord cutting is the process of releasing unwanted energies from your mind, body, and soul. It also involves self-cleansing and healing from the negative influences of these unwanted attachments or the wounds caused by their release. Many hesitate to go through the cord-cutting process because they think it will harm their relationships. However, this doesn't have to be the case at all. If the relationship is based on mutual trust and love, releasing the unnecessary burdens will only make it stronger. And it's even more critical to sever cords of unhealthy relationships, places, situations, and items. It can do wonders for those struggling to leave behind addiction or other forms of unhealthy behavior.

Whenever you have a negative thought or feeling about something or someone, you send out a cord to its energy. The more often these thoughts and emotions emerge, the thicker the thread gets. Also, the more frequently you send energies through this cord, the more absorbed you will be in its energy and the harder it will be for you to raise your vibrations. This is why it's recommended to cut the cords regularly. It can prevent low vibrations from taking away your joy and the ability to raise your vibrations and experience spiritual growth.

It's equally critical to shield yourself after you've severed the unwanted cords. This way, you can remain free of them longer, and new ties won't attach to you as easily. Establishing a powerful energetic shield will help you defend yourself from negative influence and experience life without unwanted ties attached to you. You won't have to worry about anything or anyone depleting your energy reserves or lowering your vibrations for a very long time. Calling on Metatron for the cutting and shielding process will increase our chances of successfully severing unwanted ties, raising your vibrations, and establishing a favorable energetic flow. And the more you practice this, the more befits you'll see from it, prompting you to keep up the good work.

A Short Cord Cutting Exercise with Archangel Metatron

While many angels can help you with cord-cutting, the process will only be fully successful if you use your own power to eliminate unwanted influences from your life. And who better to call on when you're trying to raise your energies for this task than Metatron, the Archangel of spiritual transformation and ascension? He is always there waiting for you to ask for his assistance on your spiritual journey. However, he lets you walk your path to fully empower you until you call on him. This is his way of teaching you to explore what you need for spiritual growth. The following exercise will help you tap into Metatron's angelic essence and find empowerment for cord-cutting,

Instructions:

1. Light a candle in the name of Metatron, and sit or stand comfortably. Close your eyes, take a few deep breaths, and call on Archangel Metatron:

    "Please, Archangel Metatron, join my side,

    And help cut all the unwanted cords connected to me."

2. Continue breathing in and out and focus on what's happening in and around you. You might feel a tingling sensation in your body, hear a whooshing sound, or suddenly feel lighter.

3. It's also possible that you won't feel anything at all. This is normal, too, so don't feel obligated to expect a specific outcome or feeling. If you do, this might hold you back in the cord-cutting process. Just embrace any sensations or the lack thereof.

4. Have faith in Metatron's power to guide you through the process. Know whether you sense anything or not, it's working because the Archangel is there to assist you. Perhaps you'll start to feel the effects a few days later. If not, you can always repeat the exercise.

5. You may not feel an immediate effect. It might take days or weeks, but you will definitely start to feel a difference in your energy levels.

6. When you practice this exercise regularly, it will become easier, and the results will come faster. With enough practice, you'll feel healthier and lighter – like a weight has been lifted off your shoulders immediately after the session.

Cord Cutting and Shielding Meditation

Sometimes when you try to cut cords with people, situations, places, or items you strongly connect with, their negative influences will simply re-attach themselves. Even if you channel Archangel Metatron's power to cut unwanted ties, they will return if you don't take measures to shield yourself. This is because you did not address the original issue with the cords. The easiest way to pick up unwanted ties is to be vulnerable due to past hurts. This exercise will help you identify any unwanted cords in your energy field and address why they bring down your energies. As your attention shifts to whatever energy lurking around you that doesn't belong there, you learn why it's critical to healing the underlying issue. You'll also understand how doing it will help prevent them from ever hurting you again.

Instructions:
1. Find a comfortable position and take a few breaths to settle your body and mind. Then recite the following prayer:

   "Archangel Metatron, I ask from my heart and soul for you to join me now,

   So, your love, light, and healing empower me as I cut the cords.

   The ties that bind me to low energies and take me away from spiritual well-being.

   Thank you for hearing my call and supporting me on this task.

   I am now ready to cut the cords and heal the issues they caused.

   Archangel Metatron, I give full permission from my subconscious and conscious mind,

   The depths of my soul and every cell in my body is willing to follow you.

   I am willing to follow your guidance in cutting cords that bind me.

   I invite all the other Archangels, angels, and spiritual guides who wish to join me.

   To assists in this process of cutting cords."

2. It's possible that, despite your declaration, you're still resistant to continuing the process. This is normal, especially if it's your first time doing this. It's not easy to let go of ties you've held onto for so long. However, letting go of all the resistance is crucial for successful cord-cutting. So, the next step is to channel your energy into this intention.
3. To do this, imagine replacing the resistance with light and self-love. You have the tools for this within you. You just have to reaffirm your power to release the resistance. The following affirmation can help with this:

    "With the power of the spirits and angels that join me,

    I release everything that's preventing me from cutting cords.

    I now declare that I know who I am.

    I know my power and my subconscious mind is open to the divine light.

    Now I complete the process of cutting cords, and it will be done forever."
4. Now, you're ready to call your guides closer. Start by invoking Archangel Metatron, asking him to use his power to assist you in cutting the unwanted ties around you. You may wish to say something like:

    "Archangel Metatron, I ask you to step closer and by my side.

    May I be surrounded by your loving energy and angelic power.

    I ask you to intercede if I struggle to complete the process,

    And empower me as I start cutting the cords that bind me."
5. Visualize the Archangel's light uniting with your energy. Suddenly you can see the unwanted ties that no longer serve you. See the light from within you push the cords away, severing them one by one.
6. Next, call for your own power to heal yourself. Visualize your energy by tapping into your higher self and allowing it to transcend your body, seeping outside and enveloping you in a protective shield. This will be useful when transmuting the cords once Metatron has helped you cut the cords around you. You can reach into your higher self and its energies by saying the following:

"I ask my higher self to manifest with its bright flames and with all its light.

I ask you to help my conscious self-transmute the cords that I cut,

So, I can heal from their influence."

7. Call on the divine power of the Creator and ask it to empower your healing. Imagine being surrounded by a bright light that shines like a diamond. You will now be prepared for any wounds caused by the unwanted ties to be separated from your energy body.
8. To reinforce your power of keeping the cords away in the future, tap into a mantra that cultivates positive emotions within you. Whatever you say, do it with conviction and in the *present tense*, like you've already accomplished something. For example, you can say:

"I am now free of unwanted ties."

"I am now safe from negative influences."

"Low vibrations can no longer affect me."

9. After reciting your mantra(s), contemplate your newfound empowerment for as long as you feel necessary.
10. Now it's time to express your gratitude for the divine empowerment and Archangel Metatron's assistance in helping you cut the cords and establishing a shield that will dispel them in the future. You can do this by saying the following words of gratitude:

"Thank you, Archangel Metatron,

And all the other beings that helped me cut the cords,

Heal from their influences and keep them away from me in the future.

I am forever thankful for all these blessings."

11. When you're ready, slowly return to the present. Rejoice in your newfound freedom.
12. If you wish, you can even give yourself a treat for accomplishing this enormous spiritual goal. There is no better way to propel yourself forward in your ascension journey than to do something you enjoy just after you've eliminated the ties that precluded you from enjoying life to the fullest. For example, you can take a walk

in nature, write about your experience in your journal or do whatever your soul desires.

Deep Cord-Cutting Meditation

The following meditation is designed to clear unwanted energetic attachments in your body. It helps eliminate links you have with other people, places, situations, or beliefs. By implementing this cord-cutting exercise into your spiritual practice, you'll clear your subconscious and learn how to call back your power to obtain spiritual freedom. You'll also learn that you don't need to attach yourself to outside energy sources because your biggest source of empowerment comes from within. As you do the exercise, you might feel unexpected emotions bubble up – this is perfectly normal. As you release the cords, remember to be kind to yourself and let the meditation unfold naturally.

Instructions:
1. Settle into a comfortable meditation posture – you can sit cross-legged, lie down, or do whatever feels best for you when doing this exercise. If you choose to lie down, place your hands next to your body, palms up, with the backs of your hands resting on the ground.
2. Take a little time to adjust your posture until you find the perfect place of comfort and ease. If you feel comfortable with it, close your eyes. Deepen your breathing.
3. Feel the cool air entering your body through your nostrils into your lungs. As you exhale, let your whole body soften and relax.
4. On your next inhale, follow your breath as it travels inward and observe whatever sensations are present within you at this moment. Pay attention to the emotions you feel, and let them express themselves fully.
5. Find your way back to that quiet place within you, where nothing can disturb you. Recognize this place as a place of refuge, the spot that's always there, no matter how challenging your life is currently in your outer world.
6. Settle as deeply as you can into this inner stillness. Call upon spiritual improvement by reaching out to Archangel Metatron. Ask him to join you on your cord-cutting journey.

7. Visualize a door that leads to a new environment. Let this door appear fully in your mind's eye – notice its shape, size, and material.
8. Focus on the door handle; see yourself reaching for it and opening the door. Step through the door and close it behind you. Take in the environment that awaits you. It appears to be nighttime, but the landscape before you is illuminated by the bright silvery light of the full moon.
9. Suddenly, Archangel Metatron appears beside you but doesn't interact with you yet. He knows this is your space, and he lets you explore it. Take a moment to observe your environment, allowing every detail to become more vivid and real.
10. The air is warm, and you can feel the sweet fragrance of flowers that bloom at night. In front of you is a still pool of water. Reflected in it is the light of a thousand stars.
11. Walk toward the pool of water, and sit by its edge. You can feel the pull of water and sense its healing qualities.
12. Move your attention to the natural rhythm of your breath. Notice the small pause between your inhale and exhale. With each inhale, imagine drawing in the silvery light of the moon.
13. Allow the light to fill your inner world as it swirls through your entire body. Suddenly you become aware of a bubble of energy around you. This is your energy body. Use your imagination to tune into this subtle energy layer and sense its cocooning you.
14. Now, switch your awareness to the places in your energy body where unhealthy cords might be attached. Sense these cords however they want to appear. For example, they might come across as ropes, branches, vines, or pipes. Sometimes you will feel where these cords are connected to you – you might sense them as hooks, arrows, plugs, anchors, or any connection types. Other times you will not.
15. Approach the cords with curiosity and without judgment. Tap into these energetic attachments and pay attention to whatever you notice in them. If you have trouble identifying or reaching into the cords, ask Metatron to help you.

16. Take a deep breath to yourself, and repeat the following:
    "With Archangel Metatron by my side,
    I reclaim my own energy.
    I release these cords and attachments."
17. Deepen your breath and fill yourself up with even more light. Feel how the light slowly pushes out the unwanted attachments as they start disconnecting from your energy body. You might feel hot or cold, or strong sensations rise up.
18. Continue breathing deeply until all the attachments are removed from your energy body. If you wish, you can imagine yourself reaching for one of the disconnected cords and taking it into your hands.
19. Dip the cord into the healing water in front of you, sealing the connection. Pull on the cord until it stretches and let go, sending it back to where it came from. To ensure you'll be shielded from it in the future, say:
    "Thank you, I release you."
20. Repeat the step above with all the cords you wish to permanently eliminate from your life. When you reach the last one, take a deep breath, exhale, and dip your toes into the water.
21. Feel the warmth of the water nourish your body and slowly lower yourself into it. You feel loved and supported. If you wish, imagine yourself staying back and admiring the blanket of stars and the bright full moon in the sky.
22. Feel yourself being filled with fresh, new energy to replace the void left after the unwanted energies left your body, mind, and soul. As you emerge from the water, you see that your energy body is now clear of any blemishes.
23. Look at Archangel Metatron and soak in his healing and empowering energies, allowing your mind to become still.
24. Feel the shift in your body and mind, and commit to becoming unapologetic with your boundaries in the future. Promise yourself that you'll release and dispel any unhealthy energies should you come in contact with them to protect your precious energy.
25. Thank the energies and Metatron for the blessing of being free of unwanted cords and feeling that you're powerful. When you feel

it's time to leave, look for the door you came in through.

26. Walk through the door, close it behind you, and slowly bring yourself back to the present. Feel the hardness of the surface beneath you and let it bring you back fully.
27. With slow movements and perhaps a sigh, come back to your space by opening your eyes. Be prepared for any energetic influences that might want to reach out to you. It's common for energies to want to attach themselves back to you. However, if you're prepared for them, they won't be able to do you any harm.

Chapter 9: Daily Meditations

The Archangel Metatron has left many doors open for us to connect with him and ask for his guidance. While there are numerous other ways to communicate with the Archangel of inspiration and creativity, meditations take the number one spot when hoping to strengthen your bond with Metatron or ask him for guidance. Meditation is a powerful way to connect with your higher consciousness and reach out to celestial beings for their divine guidance. They help you relax and be mindful of the present moment while also enjoying the peace and tranquility that comes with a true inner connection with the Archangel Metatron. All you have to do is connect through your open heart and ask for help.

Using meditation and tools, you can spiritually develop with Metatron.[42]

Not only are meditative rituals great when asking for help with spiritual development and learning, but also when you need to cleanse your energy and gain inspiration, insight, or confidence about a particular situation in your life. Guided meditation is indeed a very powerful tool for spiritual enlightenment, and angels, specifically archangels, play a major role in meditative sessions. In fact, Metatron is considered to be the master of higher self-meditations and is the best Archangel to call upon when you're meditating for spiritual guidance. When you connect with a celestial being like Metatron, you'll see an improvement in your spirituality as a whole and a difference in your meditating experiences.

While you've gone through the pillar of light meditative sequences, there's still much to uncover regarding Metatron-related meditation practices and rituals. So, this chapter will act as your guide to some daily meditations you can perform to gain spiritual wisdom from none other than the archangel of wisdom. In this chapter, you'll go through several types of meditation practices combined with Metatron's invocation. Whether you want to cleanse your energy with the help of Metatron's light or become aware and mindful through an awareness meditation ritual, this chapter has it all.

Energy Cleansing Meditation

As you've learned throughout the previous chapters, everything in this world consists of energy, whether material objects or living beings. Imagine how many people you meet throughout your day, not just people; you come in contact with different environments and situations where you absorb and exchange energy. This is where your energy can get contaminated and stagnant, negatively affecting your well-being. For instance, have you ever had a day where you were around a fight or some other negative situation and just felt anxious or fatigued for no reason? Maybe the fight wasn't even connected to you, but you still feel as if the negativity of the situation rubbed off on you. Well, this isn't just a feeling, but what happens, which is why cleaning your energy and restoring balance is crucial.

This is where energy-cleansing meditation comes in. You've already learned about other tools that can help with aura cleansing, but there's nothing better than a smooth session of cleansing meditation with Metatron's energy and blessings. The Archangel serves as an invaluable guide through the meditative process, and using his profound wisdom, he can help reach your chakras and provide additional support during the process. Metatron can be called upon before starting the meditative process to adjust your ascension frequency and align your chakras. This will result in the elimination of any energy blockages and imbalances you may have.

Preparation:
1. Before you can invoke the blessings of Archangel Metatron, it's essential to create a suitable meditation space with candles and incense if needed. You can also add the crystals favored by Metatron to aid the process.
2. Next, you need to ground and center yourself on the earth chakra star, which is present beneath your feet.
3. Then, designate the created space for meditation by invoking an ascension column of light, platinum net, and ascension flame from the Archangel Metatron. Ask him to provide the space with high-frequency energy and provide protection.
4. Also, request Metatron to place a golden dome of protection around your meditation space to keep it clear of any negative energies.

Setting Intentions:
5. Now, it's time to sit comfortably in the space you've created and close your eyes. Take a deep breath and visualize yourself journeying to the Archangel Metatron's temple through your higher consciousness.
6. Visualize the temple radiating deep shades of pink and dark green, constructed with sacred geometric shapes. As you approach, imagine the temple doors automatically opening for you.
7. In the center of the temple, visualize Metatron awaiting you with his arms stretched in front of him, and between his arms, the delicate and intricate Metatron's cube is rotating. Let your gaze focus on the cube.
8. Ask the angel to remove all negative energies from your life, and imagine these negative energies as black balls. Envision these balls being sucked from your aura and toward the cube.

Breathwork and Visualization

9. While imagining all the negative energy leaving your aura, your breathing should be slow and stable. Inhale deeply for five seconds, then hold for five and exhale for five seconds to form a rhythmic breathing pattern.
10. Visualize Metatron's cube absorbing all the negativity from your life. Feel the cube spin clockwise while destroying the balls of negative energy.
11. Allow the spinning cube to further expel any excess dark energy from your body and aura. As the negative energy is expelled, you'll start to feel lighter.

Body Scan

12. Do a slow body scan from head to toe to feel any areas of tension, heaviness, or discomfort that might remain.
13. If you still feel any tightness or tension in your body, visualize the cube's cleansing energy moving toward those areas and washing away any impurities.

Grounding and Integration

14. Once you're done with the visualization process, take a few moments to ground yourself and feel the cleansing experience.
15. Express gratitude to Archangel Metatron for his support and guidance.
16. Slowly start returning to your regular state of awareness, moving back from your higher consciousness.
17. Stretch your hands and feet, and feel your body making contact with the ground.
18. Finally, open your eyes, and blow out the candles to conclude the meditative session.

Breath Awareness Meditation

Breath awareness meditation can be done for various reasons, including reducing stress, regulating emotions, improving mindfulness, and enhancing spiritual insight. When done with the invocation of the Archangel Metatron, this meditative technique is also known as Merkaba heart meditation. The process involves certain visualizations that get the body, mind, and spirit in tune with lower and higher vibrations, spinning them into an energy vehicle at the heart center. This technique involves mindful meditation coupled with breathing exercises that align the heart chakra with Metatron's energies and help fill up your body with love.

Preparation
1. Start with finding a quiet, comfortable space where you won't be disturbed.
2. Cleanse the space of any negative energy by smudging or crystal cleansing.
3. Take a relaxed position on the ground or a yoga mat, dim the lights, and close your eyes.
4. Take a moment to invoke the presence of the Archangel Metatron and ask him for guidance and clarity through the meditative session.

Focusing on the Breath

5. Bring your attention to the sensation of your breath as you inhale and exhale slowly.
6. Focus on the natural pattern of your breath without trying to control it.
7. Observe the rise and fall of your abdomen and feel the sensation of your breath passing through your nostrils.

Cultivating Awareness

8. While you're focusing on your breathing, you'll likely get distracted by thoughts, emotions, or sensations. When you do, you should observe them without judgment and bring your focus back to your breathing.
9. Whenever your mind wanders, make sure you bring your attention back to your breath, making it an anchor for your focus.
10. Whatever arises during your awareness session, keep a calm and curious attitude toward it without thinking about it excessively.

Deepening the Practice

11. To deepen the practice, start by placing your hands on top of your chest. Your left hand should be placed first, followed by your right.
12. Exhale deeply, and visualize a brilliant ball of light or energy moving from your heart to all parts of your body until it engulfs you completely.
13. Visualize this loving heart energy flowing into your left hand, moving through the entire left side and into the right side of your body.
14. Allow this light to get brighter and stronger while moving through your body, flowing in a figure-eight pattern (through all eight chakras)
15. As you breathe in, envision yourself in the space between the center of the earth and the sun, with the sun shining its bright light right above you.
16. Then, imagine a beam of loving power shooting from the start of the universe to the end, passing through the center of the galaxy, the center of the earth, and connecting with the center of every atom in the world.
17. Imagine yourself floating, with the sun above your head aligned with your spine and the heart chakra, while the lower energies of the earth should be aligned below your spine.
18. Experience the higher energies of the sun moving into your body as you're drawn upwards. Imagine the light passing through your crown, flowing into your head, face, spinal cord, and every system of your body from top to bottom. At the same time, feel yourself being drawn downwards toward the lower, calm, and cool energies of the earth. This will create a balance of energy, with your body floating in between these two visualizations.

Closing and Integration

19. Feel the love energy flowing through your body as you exhale, and allow this energy to expand naturally until it engulfs your whole body.

20. Envision your body getting larger with the light, expanding until it becomes the size of the whole planet, the solar system, the galaxy, and the whole universe.
21. Feel yourself become one with the universe and realize the vast energy within you. Be mindful of every sensation you're feeling.
22. Continue breathing and visualizing this energy as long as you want while also envisioning Metatron's cube spinning within your heart.
23. With each exhale, breathe out pure love and radiate it to every part of your body, extending it to the universe.

Akashic Records Meditation (Advanced)

Akashic records meditation with Metatron's guidance is the perfect option for people who want to take their meditation game to the next level. This meditation technique is for advanced spiritual practitioners who want to access their Akashic Records and gain more spiritual wisdom to reach a higher state of consciousness. Think of the Akashic Records as a warehouse of information or a cosmic computer that contains all the records of your life. These records contain every feeling, intention, and situation you've had. These records are said to be stored in the etheric plane, and they also contain psychic information about a person's lifetime of experiences. To read and understand the Akashic Records, a person has to rise above their physical form and gain a non-linear, higher-dimensional awareness.

Akashic Records are also sometimes known as the "Book of Life." It holds the vibrational records of everything and everyone that has existed in this universe. These records contain the very lifetimes of all the souls to have existed. The vibrational body of these records is located in the etheric region, everywhere, at all times. These records are continually updated as the world goes on and contain future points of choice and possibilities. As you take a breath, get a thought, set an intention, and make a move, these records keep being updated with your every move, every choice, and every thought. So, how do these records relate to the Archangel Metatron? The powerful Archangel is responsible for encoding and recording everything in the Akashic Records.

Consequently, only Archangel Metatron can help you access these records and improve your spiritual self. Of course, this doesn't mean you'll be able to read about future events or change your future, but you will be able to align your past skills and resources while also healing the present blockages tied to your past. The best way to access these records is through a deep meditative session guided by none other than the Archangel Metatron himself.

Preparation
1. Prepare a suitable meditation space where you'll be away from noise and won't be disturbed.
2. Dim the lights, and light some candles near you. Place a few crystals around your meditation space, like rainbow tourmaline or garnet.
3. Close your eyes, and invoke the presence of the Archangel Metatron. Call upon him, and ask him to surround your space with divine white light.

Visualization and Protection

4. Visualize the angel enlightening your space with brilliant white light, and take a few deep breaths.
5. Imagine you're sitting in this beautiful light and exhale as you let go of any stress, tension, or pain you're feeling.
6. Breathe the pure energy in, and along with it, absorb the positive vibes, love, strength, and relaxation
7. Ask the Archangel to let you access the divine Akashic Records to gain wisdom, knowledge, and clarity.
8. Now, envision a ball of pure energy as big as you; this is where the Akashic records are held. To enter within, you'll need to lift your vibration and achieve a very pure light frequency.
9. Once you've reached the higher consciousness, ask Metatron to guide you into the dimensional understanding of the Akashic Records.

Deepening the Meditative State

10. Now, it's time to deepen the meditative state and visualize deeper. Imagine an elevator of light appears as soon as you enter the ball of light.
11. Visualize yourself stepping into this elevator, and feel the doors close behind you. As the elevator moves upward, feel yourself

moving closer to the divine.

12. Open up your heart and tune into the infinite connections of the divine flowing through you. Feel your mind expanding with the energy flowing all around you. Imagine this energy entering your heart until you feel love, light, and joy wash over you.
13. Once the elevator opens up, step out into the sacred space, and take a deep breath to submerse yourself in the conscious realm of the Akashic Records.
14. For a few moments, take some deep breaths and remain mindful of the present moment. Calmly observe the knowledge encoded in the white light surrounding you. Try to examine the records present in this energy, and notice how every soul is interlaced with each other. Realize the interconnectedness between all things and how individual choices can cause a ripple far and wide.
15. Take a moment to observe your connection to the records, to the universe, and to all that exists.

Exploring the Akashic Records

16. To explore the Akashic records, consider a situation or question you need guidance for or answered. Archangel Metatron will be there to guide you toward the right answer.
17. Ask your question out loud, and let the answer appear in the space in front of you, like being in a magical library. You may envision that Metatron is handing you a book, a scroll, a simple piece of paper, or even a visual where you can explore your life and get the insight you need.
18. Just trust your intuition and the Archangel's guiding hand, and you'll find the solution to your problem.
19. Keep in mind that the Archangel is assisting you; open your heart to the Akash emerging before you, and receive the guidance you need.

Closing and Integration

20. Once you've gotten your answers, or have had a revelation, express your immense gratitude to the Archangel and the Akashic Records. Imagine you're stepping away from the scene and back into the elevator of light.

21. The elevator will gracefully and swiftly take you back, after which you should take a deep breath, lower your frequencies and step out of the glowing white ball of energy.
22. Slowly return your awareness to your physical body. In the next instant, take a moment to write down or record the guidance and answers you received from your spiritual journey. Write every little detail down, including your feelings, impressions, insights, and any unknown symbols or knowledge you've received.
23. Don't wait to note down this information because it can escape your mind soon, similar to how a dream drifts away after you wake up.
24. Although you may not fully understand what you've gained during this session, once you write it down and contemplate it, you're more likely to make sense of the whole thing.

You can gain a wealth of information and knowledge about your soul and psychic consciousness through the dedicated practice of guided meditative sessions from Metatron. As you continue on this journey, don't lose patience with yourself, everyone's journey looks a little different and can take considerable time. You should allow yourself enough time to attune to the frequency of Metatron and hope for the best. Although various forms of meditation serve as effective pathways to connect with Archangel Metatron, the key to a successful session lies in maintaining unwavering faith and belief in the guiding light of Metatron. *Trust that he will provide the necessary assistance and guidance in navigating the challenges you may be facing.*

Bonus: Correspondences Sheet

This chapter provides an easy-to-check reference of all correspondences associated with Archangel Metatron. Feel free to use them when you want to connect or work with this Archangel.

Festivals or Feasts of the Year

Metatron can be celebrated any day or part of the year – although he is the most powerful on Friday night and Saturday morning. In some parts of the world, a festival celebrating Archangel Metatron is held on September 29, the international day of the Archangels.

Colors Associated with Metatron

The typical colors attributed to Metatron are white, black, and rainbow. White symbolizes his angelic purity and his place in the angelic hierarchy. Black is a complementary color to white, indicating Metatron's ability to establish harmony and balance between different aspects of life. The rainbow color alludes to Metatron's colorful aura and is often depicted on the Metatron cube.

Zodiac Signs and Planets

Archangel Metatron is linked to all the zodiac signs because he rules all months and planets. However, he has a particularly strong link to Virgo. He helps this sign establish their path in life and allows this sign to explore their limitations and set boundaries, preventing them from venturing too far away. He might also help Virgos banish low-vibrating energies and motivate them to become more productive – especially when it comes to utilizing the divine blessing they receive.

Angel Numbers

Angel numbers are numeral symbols sent by the angels, communicating their messages. Regularly seeing specific numbers could represent that a particular angel is nearby and wants to talk to you. Metatron, for example, often communicates through the number 11. Most of the time, this number will appear in duplicate. For example, you might see 11:11 on your clock mid-morning, and the same number appears again on a receipt. If it appears several times in a row as a synchronicity, it might be a sign that Metatron is calling you. He often sends this message when trying to bring one's attention to finding life's purpose or a connection you need to make for spiritual growth. He might use it to guide you on your path to ascension or signal that you're ready to awaken your spirituality and elevate it to a higher level.

Symbols and Sigil

Cord

Metatron is often depicted severing ties – a symbol of his ability to guide people through cord-cutting. With the Archangel's help, you can release yourself from unwanted connections and heal from their effects while raising your vibrations.

Brightly Colored Lights

Bright swirls of a colorful aura and colorful lights are often linked to Metatron – with purple and red being the most prevailing colors. Metatron's aura combines his connection to the heavenly realm (manifesting in violet spiritual energy) and his link to the earthly realm (appearing as a red light). Besides these, Metatron's aura might also contain rays of bright pink, white, and dark green.

Crown Chakra

Those working with Metatron often experience a tingling sensation that begins at the crown of the head. This is where the crown chakra is located and where you can receive the most support from Metatron. The crown chakra is the gateway for high-frequency energies you can call on during experiences like the pillar of light meditation and others.

Metatron can help activate this chakra and remove any blockage.

The Solar Plexus Chakra

Besides the crown chakra, Archangel Metatron is also associated with the third, or solar, plexus chakra. Because this energy point is linked to personal power, self-mastery, and sense of self, working with Metatron can help you enhance all these qualities.

Buzzing Noises

If you're sensitive to auditory signals, Metatron often communicates through a high-frequency buzzing noise in your left ear. Besides indicating the Archangel's proximity, this sign is also one of his favorite ways of sending direct messages. Some say that if you listen closely, you can hear his faint voice telling you how to move forward with your goals and life.

Overpowering Scents

Those more sensitive to olfactory signals often associate Archangel Metatron with overpowering aromas that appear out of nowhere. For example, if you're walking on the street and suddenly encounter a floral fragrance with no flowers or people wearing perfumes nearby, this could be a sign of Metatron trying to reach out to you.

Diamond White Light

One of the most common ways Metatron sends his messages is through flashes of white light that shine bright like a diamond. This Archangel's essence is so powerful that it's meant to be a shining light that brings inspiration and motivates your spiritual growth.

The Pillar of Light

Metatron is often visualized as providing empowerment by standing close to a pillar or column of light. Some say that this column appears as a fire that burns with flames so bright it can blind a person if they look at it directly.

The Metatron Cube

The Metatron cube is a symbol associated with sacred geometry. It depicts 13 spheres, which are arranged to form two hexagrams. This unique shape is said to exemplify every power in the universe – from the smallest to the all-consuming ones. It also depicts the energy that connects all things. Because of this symbolism, the Metatron cube is often used as an energetic conductor by those who wish to harness positive energies and banish negative vibes. For the same reason, this object vibrates at very high levels – and can serve as a powerful protection against low-vibrating energies.

The Tree of Life

Archangel Metatron is portrayed as the guardian of the Kabbalistic Tree of Life, presiding on its crown (also known as Kether). In art, Metatron's connection is seen in the images that paint him as a magnificent creature wearing a multicolored robe with several pairs of golden wings. The golden color of the wings is linked to the high aspect of the crown. The robe's different colors (pink, blue, green) speak of Metatron's all-encompassing power as the ruler of the Tree of Life.

Book of Life

Also known as the Akashic Record, the Book of Life is a collection of records of peoples' and angels' actions, indicating who is eligible for spiritual elevation and granted entrance to heaven and who isn't. As the divine scribe, Metatron is often depicted recording good acts in the Book of Life in art.

Metatron's Sigil

Metatron's sigil is a special symbol associated with this Archangel. It's represented by a single letter that combines two letters. It generally resembles the letter "A," except one leg of this letter is formed by the letter "M," which is located on the lower end of this leg and is turned upside down. The sigil is often used to invoke Metatron's guidance, protection, and healing during spiritual work.

Trees, Plants, Herbs, and Oils

Metatron is usually linked to lavender and jasmine, which can be used to attract self-love and obtain tranquility, happiness, beauty, wealth, and luck. Using geranium rose and lime when working with Metatron can improve your health, strengthen your connection to loved ones, and protect yourself from bad luck, misfortune, injuries, and illnesses.

Other trees, herbs, and plants associated with Metatron include almonds, mistletoe, orchids, dill, ylang-ylang, basil, chrysanthemums, wild rose, white rose, lilies, and carnations.

Essential oils to use when working with Metatron are frankincense, benzoin, sandalwood, roman chamomile, myrrh, cedar, vetiver, cypress, patchouli, rose, neroli, juniper, geranium, tangerine, jasmine, and lavender. All these are known for facilitating spiritual elevation and can serve as reminders of the benefits of abandoning materialistic thoughts for a peaceful transition of one's soul.

Crystals and Metals

Diamonds, white crystals, and other stones of empowerment. For the best effects, use a clear crystal to connect the energies of other stones and unite them in high-frequency vibrational energy. Clear quartz is one of the most powerful crystals in the spiritual world. You can imbue it with any intention and use the crystal's vibrations to amplify your intention and manifest it.

Labradorite is another crustal you can use when working with Metatron. It's a stone with incredible protective abilities that can help you block intrusive energies. It's useful for recalling hurtful memories if you want to heal your energy and your ties with your loved ones. You can also benefit from using labradorite when communicating with Metatron to decipher any signals you receive in dreamwork or while journeying.

As their name implies, meteorite metals have a powerful connection to the universe. This also links them to one of the most powerful angelic beings who distributes energies and records happenings in this universe. These metals are often used to represent Metatron in rituals and ceremonies – whether in the piece of metal object that holds other tools or as the main element used for the Metatron cube.

General Associations
Spiritual and Religious Intentions

Metatron can teach you how to enhance your magical abilities and, if necessary, find a magic teacher or coven you can learn from. He empowers people's religious nature, often helping them find enlightenment through religion or discover their life path and gain spiritual knowledge within a religious community. He can also help you uncover and understand karmic paths in life.

Metatron is responsible for being an angelic energy source, the being that gives you "the wings" you need to overcome obstacles, the guide for transcending pain and healing from traumas, the angel that manipulates spiritual paths, the second greatest source of divine power, the lord of the afterlife and heaven, the incarnation of a fully ascended human, a cosmic guardian, the manipulator of the portals between realms. He is also responsible for providing divine assistance, establishing divine authority, banishing negative energies, facilitating reincarnation, empowering with a supreme voice, preventing evil influences from entering heaven, the ultimate power to release unwanted ties, awareness of multidimensionality, granting psychic abilities like teleportation, telekinesis, knowledge projection, spiritual healing, granting immortality to souls.

Metatron is further linked to spell casting and supports those who venture into angelic magic or want to explore resurrection, gain increased strength and stamina for spiritual work, endure hardships for growth, and renew their spirits repeatedly until they reach ascension.

As the divine scribe, Metatron possesses a great deal of cosmic knowledge. He can even erase warnings and remove negative protective sigils and give you strategies for dispelling negativity from one's life.

Metatron is keen on supporting those who work toward goals that benefit everyone around them. He awakens powers, virtues, values, and talents that help people to persevere on this path. He cleanses the body, mind, and spirit, restoring balance and contributing to overall well-being. Working with Metatron sharpens your mind, opens you up to new ideas and visions, and helps you tap into your intuition and sense spiritual communication. He can also help you see your reality more clearly and other people's views without judgment and accept it so you can get along with others.

Qualities he can help you cherish: spiritual growth, connection to the light body, seeking divine union, energetic activation, and ascension.

Due to having firsthand knowledge of the records contained in the Book of Life, Metatron knows how negative thoughts can lead to disproportionate actions and undesirable outcomes. Because of this, he will always encourage people to embrace positive thought processes. He knows these lead to better choices and outcomes – and you can only gain from positive thinking.

Indigo and Crystal Children

While Metatron is the patron of all children who struggle to thrive, he is particularly protective of so-called crystal and indigo children. These children are highly sensitive to energetic shifts and more open to spiritual communication. However, these children are prone to pick up negativity because of their innate connection to the spiritual realm and energies around them. It permeates their energetic bodies, depleting them of their energy and causing emotional, mental, physical, and spiritual imbalances. On a positive note, these children are more likely to pick up clues from spiritual guides early in life. For example, Metatron might appear to them as he feels they need his help to become their best version. Metatron can help them tear down antiquated beliefs and build communities that serve the greater good. He teaches them skills of empowerment and gives them tools such as fearless courage, enabling them to fulfill their life's purposes.

Tarot Cards

The Judgment

The first Tarot card associated with Archangel Metatron is the Judgement. It's a symbol of rising vibrations and embracing a higher level of consciousness – and it's easy to see why it's linked to this angel. If this card comes up, it might indicate that Metatron is suggesting that you're starting your spiritual awakening. Heed his call and act on it by tuning into his higher frequency so you can step into the newer version of yourself.

This card can also carry a message urging you to make a potentially life-altering decision. To make this decision, you must combine your intellect and intuition. If you're at a crossroads, Metatron might be signaling that any choice you make now will have long-lasting effects. He tells you that before making a decision, tap into your higher self and trust whatever you see there.

The Judgment card can also pop up when you're close to a significant stage in your spiritual journey. Perhaps it's time to review and evaluate your past experiences and learn from them. Now that all pieces of the puzzle of your life are finally coming together, it's more important than ever to make a conscious decision. Only this will allow you to heal your wounds and put the past behind you. You will let go of regrets and release any sadness or guilt about past events.

The Fool

The Fool is a card denoting new beginnings, having faith in the future, being inexperienced, not knowing what to expect, having beginner's luck, improvisation, and believing in the universe as the Fool stands at the beginning of his journey and is about to venture into the unknown. On his journey, the Fool will receive guidance from much-treasured sources. Similarly, Archangel Metatron is the treasure holder of angelic wisdom, which he uses to guide souls through life, death, and beyond. This card might indicate that although you might not know where you're going yet, you shouldn't worry because Metatron will be there to guide your spirit.

The card could also be a reminder to keep an open, curious mind and see everything as an exciting opportunity instead of a challenge. Leap into new experiences, and you will soon have personal growth and spiritual development. Experiment with different forms of spiritual work and do your best to learn about your spiritual allies, including Metatron. It will help you connect to his energy and all the other energies around you. Tap into this energy and uncover your fullest potential by letting your heart, mind, and soul be free of burdens and negativity.

The Chariot

The third Tarot card attributed to Archangel Metatron is the Chariot – the symbol of willpower, achievements, self-discipline, and public recognition. If Metatron is sending you this card, it means he saw that you'd overcome a challenging situation and managed to keep your energies in balance. He was glad to observe that you took the time to view the situation from different angles and make a decision based on this. It means you've gained his approval, and he encourages you to enjoy your accomplishment and keep up the good work. If you're yet to overcome a situation, Metatron is signaling you to remain grounded so you can think clearly about what you want to achieve. Maintaining self-control will make it easier to keep up the determination to do whatever it takes to succeed. At the same time, Metatron is cautioning you to be kind to others. Feel free to use this card as a motivation to boost your energy levels to stay true to your priorities. Combining this card with the Metatron cube in spiritual work is believed to help harness the Archangel's ability to warp time and shorten the timeframe you need to manifest your dreams.

The Dreamer

In Angelic Tarot, Metatron is associated with the Dreamer. This card signifies your entrance into a new and exciting stage of life. Metatron might send you this card to tell you that you should believe in yourself, indicating you should have faith in your ability to succeed and take the steps you need to move forward. He might also signal that you should listen to your intuition and be open about the guidance you receive from spiritual sources. As the angel of spiritual transformation, Archangel Metatron will always gladly oversee those embarking on their first spiritual journey. If he sends you the dreamer card, take a leap of faith and follow his signals. It takes strength, courage, confidence, and believing in yourself. It can even be scary, but in the end, it's an exhilarating prospect that activates spiritual growth and ascension. The card might also be Metatron's way of telling you to use faith and courage to combat negative energies of fear and doubt. Put your faith in his divine guidance, and you won't regret it. You'll gain a powerful ally in Metatron and all the knowledge you need to empower your inner guidance and connection to the divine essence.

Other Correspondences

- **Month:** All months
- **The day of the week:** Friday and Saturday
- **The hour of the day:** The hours between sunset on Friday and sunrise on Saturday
- **Season:** Fall
- **Deities:** Ceres, Demeter, Thoth
- **Body parts ruled:** Skeletal system, the spine, stomach, legs, and skin
- **Animals and mythical creatures**: Horse
- **Direction:** Center
- **Element:** Earth

Conclusion

Whether you're a beginner at Angelic Magic or have some experience in the topic and are interested in alternative ways to heal spiritual traumas to become empowered, hopefully, this book gave you enough information to heal, empower and transform yourself. This book sets out something for everyone, from easy-to-do exercises to more advanced spiritual teachings. And most importantly, you had the chance to explore the spiritual, cultural, and religious background of Archangel Metatron, - along with a review of the basic spiritual concepts associated with him.

Those who needed a stepping stone for further exploration of personal ascension had a chapter dedicated to explaining the process and its importance, together with exercises to facilitate this process. In the subsequent chapter, you've learned about the signs Metatron might send you after you've initiated the first contact seeking healing, protection, or guidance to ascend. Meanwhile, those looking to expand their knowledge got to delve deeper into the ascension process by exploring some of the most powerful spiritual tools associated with Metatron.

One of the first spiritual instruments you've learned about was the Metatron cube, a symbol based on sacred geometry often used for energy transfer. As one of the most influential Archangels, Metatron's energy vibrates at incredibly high frequencies. Implementing the Metatron Cube into your practices can help you connect with his energy, regardless of your vibrational levels. As an angel, Metatron is also associated with light (often used to symbolize his power in visualization exercises), so another great tool to connect with him is the Pillar of Light

Meditation.

Due to his immense energy and willingness to share it with those seeking spiritual healing, Archangel Metatron is the perfect ally for energetic healing methods like Reiki. Angelic Reiki is one of the most popular ways of self-healing – and for a good reason. It empowers your energy body to eliminate unwanted disturbances. Crystals vibrating at high frequencies have the same effect because they carry unique healing powers. Moreover, they can be imbued with the intention of healing or banishing negativity, as well as connecting with Metatron, who will further empower you on whatever journey you decide to take.

Those who had trouble eliminating negativity from their lives or experiencing the return of negative influence despite banishing them have likely found the chapter about cord-cutting most helpful. Besides explaining the importance of cutting unwanted ties, the chapter also offered practices for creating an energetic shield that will prevent the unhealthy cords from re-attaching you again. As you've learned, when this exercise is performed in the presence of Metatron, it will have a long-lasting effect. It will also help you heal from the influences of low-energy cords and their sudden release from your energetic body.

Archangel Metatron can be a powerful ally in any spiritual journey. Whatever your goal is for reaching out to him, know that he will always be there to assist you. However, to make the most out of your connection with this angel, you must nurture it – and the best way to do it is through daily practices. Even spending a few minutes a day will work wonders on your spiritual development. And if you have trouble incorporating the celebration of Metatron into your day-to-day schedule, you only need to revisit the correspondence sheet at the end of the book to find the tools to best represent him.

Part 3: Archangel Michael

Connecting with the Angel of the Lord

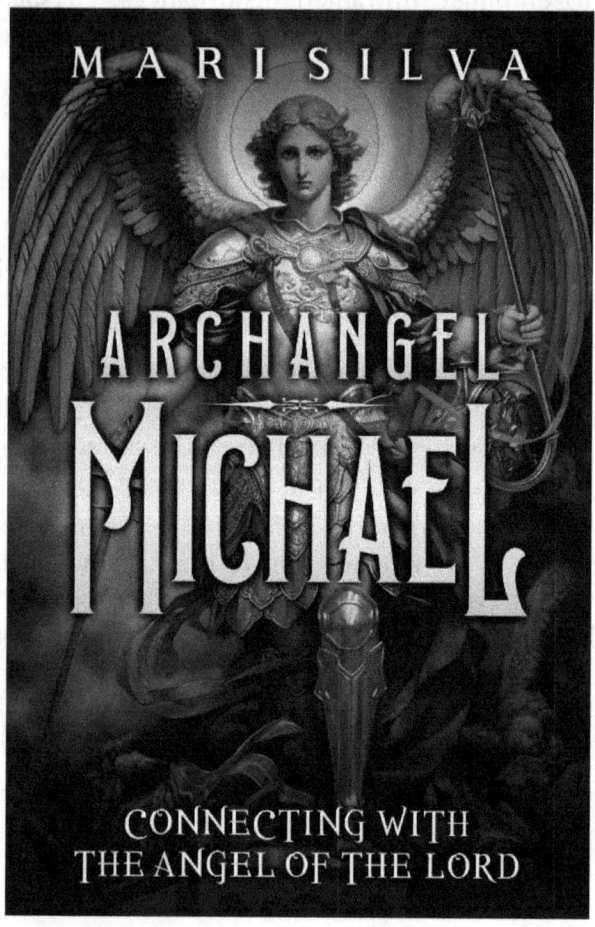

Introduction

As the most powerful of Archangels, Michael can provide an enormous boost to your spirituality. Known as the "Angel of the Lord," Michael stands closer to the creator than any other Archangel. He commands all the other Archangels and an army of other angels. That should tell you exactly how much power he can lend you if needed. Suppose you want to deepen your spirituality and require protection from malicious intentions, cut out toxic influences from your life, expand your self-confidence and faith, and protect your space and your loved ones. In that case, Archangel Michael is the angel to connect with. However, to obtain any or all of this, you'll need to establish and nurture a personal connection with Michael; this is where the information you'll learn from this book will come in handy.

The book offers a comprehensive insight into who Archangel Michael is and the many ways you can communicate with him. To communicate with him efficiently, you must learn to recognize the signs he is sending you and decipher their messages. Once you familiarize yourself with his signs after reading the relevant chapter, you can delve into the specific request you wish to make. The first chapter will provide plenty of beginner-friendly methods for requesting Michael's protection for different occasions, like meditations and rituals. This will be followed by a chapter detailing how to request healing (through prayer, mediation, and harnessing the angel's light) and another chapter on asking for help in banishing negative energy from yourself, space, and others.

The tools you use when communicating with Archangel Michael can enhance your energy, allowing you to tap into his power more efficiently and manifest your intention faster and more accurately. Besides blue light, Michael is also associated with certain crystals (and their vibrations), herbs, and essential oils. Each of these elements carries its own energy, which can empower your own energy and increase the likelihood of manifesting your desires. The relevant chapters will show you which tools to use when requesting Michael's assistance. The last chapter will guide you in nurturing your bond with Archangel Michael through daily rituals, from wearing his colors to daily meditations and Reiki exercises. If you want to learn how to honor Archangel Michael throughout the year and what other tools you might use to call upon him, the bonus chapter will provide you with all his correspondences. It will act as a quick reference guide whenever you need something to use to establish and build a profound connection with Michael.

Archangel Michael is always there in times of distress, ready to take on any challenge and defend those in need – and this is no different with his modern-day followers. Independently of your cultural or religious background, Michael can help you reach spiritual fulfillment. After all, all you need is your willingness to connect with him, an open mind, and the ability to hone your intuition to recognize his messages. Throughout this book, you'll receive plenty of practical guidance for every aspect of working with this Archangel, from taking the first step of calling out to him to honoring him through regular practices. If you're ready to start your journey of building a beautiful and spiritually uplifting lifelong connection with Archangel Michael, continue reading.

Chapter 1: Who Is Archangel Michael?

Knowing that you aren't alone and angels constantly surround you is comforting. God created these heavenly creatures to serve Him and protect and guide humanity. You have probably experienced moments in your life when you felt that someone was watching over you, or you encountered events that were too strange to be considered coincidences. These are the angels at work. They always look out for you, send you messages, or change your direction to put you on the right track.

Archangels are the most powerful angels in Heaven. God entrusts them with significant tasks, and they have the freedom to travel to Earth to follow God's commands and help mankind. They hold the highest position in Heaven and are superior to all other angels.

An icon of Archangel Michael in a cathedral.[48]

The word "archangel" is derived from two Greek words: "arche," which means *ruler,* and "angelos," meaning *messenger.* The word represents their two responsibilities: the ruling of all angels and acting as messengers of God who deliver His messages to mankind. Archangels exist in all religions and spiritual beliefs.

There are four archangels in Islam and Judaism and seven in Christianity. This book will focus on the archangel Michael and in this chapter, you will learn everything about him, how he is represented in all three religions, and the symbols associated with him.

Introducing Archangel Michael

Michael is a leader and one of the main angels in Heaven. He is a strong and brave warrior who always fights on the side of good. He seeks to achieve justice and truth among all of mankind. Michael believes that evil will never prevail as long as people have faith in God. The angels are always on the side of the weak and helpless, protecting and defending them. People often call on Michael to give them the strength and courage to resist temptations, conquer their fears, and protect their hearts against straying from the right path. They also seek his help to heal the sick and ease their pain.

Michael is originally a Hebrew name that means "a gift from God." It is mentioned three times in the Book of Daniel from the Old Testament and once in the Quran. The name can also be spelled as Mikhail, Mikhael, Mikail, and Mikael. He is the only angel mentioned by name in the Quran, Bible, and the Torah.

Archangel Michael in the Bible and the Book of Daniel

Archangel Michael is described in the Book of Daniel as the "chief prince" of Heaven or the "great prince" who protected the people of Israel. He was mentioned without any introduction, and the book doesn't provide much information about him. This indicates that people were already familiar with him and knew who he was. The New Testament also doesn't give any details about Michael. When he was first mentioned, he and Satan were arguing over who would take Prophet Moses's dead body.

The Bible does not mention what Michael looks like, but he is often portrayed as a captain or a warrior. However, angels are often depicted as strong, beautiful, and tall beings. Mankind isn't equipped to see angels in their true form, so they usually appear in human form when they want to communicate directly with people to guide them or warn against impending doom. Therefore, scripture instructs believers to be kind and gracious to strangers since they can be angels in disguise.

Michael will play a big role in the fight against evil at the end of times. The Book of Daniel describes Michael as the protector of people who will rise to lead the angels in a war against Satan and his army of demons. The Book of Revelation tells us there will be a battle in Heaven, and Michael will fight a strong and vicious dragon. Both will have an army of angels by their side, but Michael will be victorious, and he will cast out the dragon from Heaven. The dragon and his army are Satan and his fallen angels.

In the Book of Enoch, Michael threw Satan and other fallen angels out of Heaven at the beginning of time. This wasn't mentioned in the Bible, but it is considered a prophecy of the battle that will take place in the future. Since Michael was able to get rid of Satan once, he will be able to do it again. The Bible states that good will triumph over evil, and Michael will win against Satan and his army.

Only Michael can defeat Satan because he always defends and protects believers from the devil and his demons.

He is also responsible for taking the souls of the dead believers to Heaven, and he will be the one to call on all mankind to come to life for Judgment Day.

Even though Michael isn't human, the church often refers to him as a saint. He is even celebrated and has his own feast, which takes place on September 29th. It is called Michaelmas, and people usually follow certain traditions to honor this day. For instance, they refrain from eating blackberries after the feast because when Michael threw Satan out of Heaven, he fell on a blackberry shrub. Ever since that day, all blackberries turn sour after Michaelmas in memory of Satan landing on them.

There is a misconception among Jehovah's Witnesses that Michael and Jesus Christ are the same person. They argue that since he is the protector of the people of Israel and the Bible also states that the Lord protects the children of Israel, they are the same. Michael is also described as "prince" in the Bible, and many believe this title only fits the son of God, Jesus Christ.

However, Michael is only a prince among the angels; his superiority doesn't extend to human beings. There are also six other archangels, so

Michael isn't unique – unlike Jesus Christ, who is a prophet and the son of God.

Even though Michael is a powerful angel who always aids mankind, the Bible makes it clear that people should only worship God and pray to Him.

There are only a few mentions of Michael in the Bible which makes him one of the most fascinating and mysterious angels.

Archangel Michael in the Quran

In Islam, Michael is spelled as Mikhail or Mikail and is only mentioned once in the Quran:

"Who is an enemy to Allah, and His angels and His messengers, and Gabriel and Michael! Then, lo! Allah (Himself) is an enemy to the disbelievers."

Even though this is the only mention of Michael and Allah didn't provide any other information on him, it is clear from this verse that he is held in high regard as he is mentioned with the Prophets, who are all dear to Allah. No other angel is mentioned in this verse, indicating that Michael and Gabriel are superior to all the other heavenly beings.

In Islam, Michael is responsible for the rain, plants, animals, human beings, and all-natural events. His job is to provide food for the body and the soul. He also appeared to Prophet Muhammad on more than one occasion. It was narrated in a hadith (a saying by Prophet Muhammad) that he once asked Gabriel why he had never seen Michael laugh. Gabriel said that Michael hadn't laughed since Hell was created.

The Quran tells the story of Prophet Muhammad's ascension to Heaven. Before he embarked on this journey, Michael and Gabriel prepared him by purifying his heart. The Prophet also said that both angels were his personal advisers.

Michael also cares about humanity and rewards believers for their kindness and good deeds. He is known for his mercy, and he often prays to God to forgive sinners and protect mosques and other places of worship. He and Gabriel will play a big role on Judgment Day. They will weigh each person's good and evil deeds, determining whether they will end up in Heaven or Hell.

In the Quran, when Allah created Adam, He ordered all angels to bow to Adam, and Gabriel and Michael were the first ones to follow His commands.

Archangel Michael in Spirituality and Other Beliefs

In Hinduism, Michael is described as the "Warrior Prince." He is the leader of the army of the gods and the defender of Dharma (the divine law in Hinduism). Some belief systems consider Michael a symbol of strength and hope rather than a protector and defender. Whether you are religious or not, you can benefit from having Michael in your life.

Nowadays, many people have lost hope, especially in the face of the injustice they face daily. They have given up and accepted that things will never get better. During these hard times, they need to look for something bigger than themselves. Michael became their light in their darkest days and their strength when they felt weak. In all religions and beliefs, Michael is a symbol of goodness, love, courage, dignity, strength, and other qualities people desperately need.

How Archangel Michael Can Help You

People often call on Michael more than any other angel. He can heal the sick, provide spiritual defense, and guide people to find meaning and purpose in their lives. He pushes them to discover who they really are and be loyal to their true selves. He can also raise their inner forces and psychic vibrations.

Michael is the first angel created by God, and he became in charge of dignity, truth, power, and security. He is often depicted with a sword that he uses to protect humanity from the devil.

Call on Michael whenever you struggle with self-esteem issues, lack energy, need direction, lack inspiration, or feel like you're under psychological attack. He can also help people who work in stressful jobs, struggle with nightmares, or have an addiction.

Find Meaning in Your Life

Call on Michael when you lack motivation; he will encourage you to become productive and organized and even find inspiration. Don't worry if you don't have what it takes to achieve your goals and realize your dreams. Michael will put you on the right track so you can acquire the necessary skills and talents to succeed in life and impact the world. He will encourage you to create a routine so you can have a sense of stability in your life and thrive.

Comes Through During Tough Times

Don't hesitate to call on Michael if you are going through a tough time. He will come to your aid right away. Michael is always there for anyone in need. Whatever type of protection or help you require, he can provide it. All you have to do is ask. If you are in a tough situation and can't get through it alone, Michael will give you the strength and courage to overcome anything life throws at you.

Reassurance

Sometimes, you can feel alone, especially when you are about to make a big decision and aren't sure if it's right. Call on Michael, and he will reassure you that you aren't alone and that he is there, listening to you, and is aware of your struggles. He is watching over you and will encourage you to make the best decisions that will benefit you in the future.

Protects Your Energy

Empaths and highly sensitive individuals are easily affected by other people's energies. For instance, you have a friend who complains about everything. When you go out for lunch, they will complain about their job, relationship, the weather, their friends, and even the service at the restaurant. After spending a few hours with them, you return home feeling exhausted and depleted. Negative people are dangerous to empaths. They can drain your energy and make you feel tired and unable to do even the simplest of tasks. If these people are your co-workers and you meet them every day, this can severely damage your mental health.

Archangel Michael has the power to protect your energy from negative people. Every morning before you go to work, call on Michael to provide you with spiritual protection. If you are about to enter a place filled with negativity, ask the Archangel to clear the harmful energies from the place. If you share an office or a home with a negative person, ask him to watch over it and protect it when you are away.

You can even ask him to use his shield to protect you against negativity.

Provides You with Positivity

It is normal to be worried and scared if you are about to make a big decision, like getting married or changing your career. Stepping into the unknown is never easy. Michael will give you the courage to take the necessary risks. When things don't go your way and you lose hope, ask him to increase your positivity and optimism so you can keep going. He will show you that something good can always come out of every situation, even during moments when you feel like there is no hope.

Gives You Courage

There will be moments when you lose your self-esteem and feel scared and discouraged. For instance, your co-worker keeps taking credit for your work, or your boss dismisses all your ideas. Ask Michael to provide you with support and guidance to speak up for yourself and stand your ground. He can prepare you before talking to your boss and give you the confidence to say what is on your mind, even if your voice is shaking.

Michael can also help you with issues you are afraid to tackle, like aspects of your life that need changing or improving. For instance, your partner keeps crossing your boundaries, and you let them because you are afraid that they will leave you if you stand up for yourself. Or, you receive terrible news, feel lost, and struggle to accept it.

Remember that Michael is a warrior who can give you the courage and strength to face the unknown. Call on him to bestow his courage upon you so you feel confident enough to tackle these difficult situations. Michael won't only provide you with guidance, but he will also send you resources, opportunities, and even people who can help you. He will also make the journey easier by walking in front of you to fight battles you can't handle alone.

Protects You from Nightmares

Everyone has nightmares occasionally, but some people have realistic ones that wake them up feeling terrified in the middle of the night. Ask Michael to watch over you while you are sleeping or to scare away the nightmares using his mighty sword.

Your nightmares can stem from your subconscious. Perhaps you are worried about losing your job, or a family member is sick, and you are afraid they might not make it. These thoughts can keep you awake at night, and when you finally go to sleep, you end up having nightmares. If you call on Michael, he will cover you with his wings all night to make you feel comfortable and safe.

Cuts the Energetic Cords

You are connected to everything and everyone around you through invisible energetic chords. These places and people will be part of your life forever. However, there are some relationships that no longer serve you. Your invisible bond will remain intact even when you physically detach yourself from them. Say you broke up with your partner and moved out of the house. If you are hung up on them and can't move on, it's because you are still connected.

Call on Michael; he will cut the energetic chord with his sword and release you from your past relationships.

He Is Always by Your Side

Most people turn to their family and friends whenever they need support. As you grow older, you will realize that people can't always be there for you. This doesn't make them bad friends or family members. They just lead busy lives. Even though they want to be there for you, life can sometimes get in the way.

However, no one is ever really alone. Angels are always around you. Don't be afraid to call on Michael. While everyone in your life is busy, he is always available anytime during the day. In some cases, you won't want anything from Michael. You just need him by your side. Call on him and tell him that you only need to feel his presence to know that everything will be fine eventually.

Symbols Associated with Archangel Michael

Sometimes, Michael will call on you. Perhaps he wants to reach out to you to deliver a message from God, warn you against something, or let you know that he has heard your call and will come to your aid. However, some of the messages he sends aren't straightforward. Each angel has their own symbols that they use to communicate with mankind. Learn Michael's signs so you can instantly tell when he reaches out to you.

The Name Michael

This is one of the easiest signs you can pick up on immediately. If you keep seeing or hearing the name Michael everywhere, this can be the angel trying to tell you something. This will happen through random events that will take place in a short amount of time. You wake up in the morning and check social media, then you see a piece of news about a guy named Michael, but you don't think much of it. While driving to work, you hear a song on the radio by Michel Jackson. You are sitting at the office, and a friend shows you a book she is reading. You accidentally drop it, and it opens on a random page starting with the name Michael. Obviously, these events can't be considered simple coincidences; this is the Archangel trying to get your attention.

Perhaps you are going through a hard time, and Michael wants to let you know he is here for you and everything will work out.

The Color Blue

Archangel Michael is associated with the color blue. It is a common color that you can easily see everywhere. If you keep seeing it more than usual, it is clearly a sign from him. For instance, every day on your way to work, you see four blue cars, you see a blue jay flying by every morning, or you subconsciously wear blue for three days in a row. Pay attention to these messages.

You can also randomly see flashes of blue light when he wants to reach out to you. The light will be very clear and hard to miss since Michael's symbols are rarely subtle.

Feathers

You keep seeing feathers everywhere you go. You find two on your doormat, a friend gives you a necklace with a feather pendant, or you keep seeing large numbers of birds in the sky. This symbol indicates that Michael wants to make you aware of his presence and lets you know he is here for you.

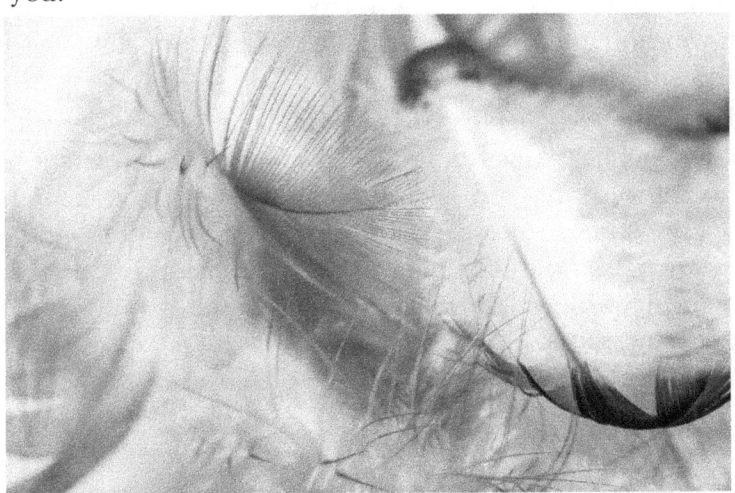

Seeing a feather is a sign from Michael wants you to be aware of his presence."

Déjà Vu

Michael will use déjà vu to get your attention when something that can change your life is about to happen.

The Number Eleven

Michael is associated with the number eleven, and he will often use it to try to communicate with you. Your watch could stop at eleven o'clock, or you might keep seeing the number everywhere you look.

Dreams

Michael or other angels can appear to you in your dreams. These dreams will usually be vivid and comforting. Pay attention to every detail, as they could contain hidden messages from Michael.

Voices

As Michael is never subtle with his messages, he can directly speak to you. Say you are about to cross the street and hear a loud voice telling you to stop. You notice a drunk man driving like a maniac could have hit you if you had crossed the street. Sometimes, the voice can be a whisper. Either way, the message should be obvious, so don't ignore it.

He can also send you a message through other people. For instance, you apply for a job and feel that you will get accepted, so you decide to quit your current job. Suddenly, your sister calls you to chat and, out of nowhere, tells you about her co-worker who quit his job after going to a couple of interviews because he thought he believed he would most likely get accepted in one of them. However, he has been unemployed for six months now and regrets his decision. Upon hearing this story, you decide to stay in your job until you hear from the other company. This is clearly a warning from Michael.

Working with archangels can be intimidating, especially with one as powerful as Michael. Angels are created to support and guide mankind, so dare to call on him, and he will always answer the call. Remember, you are never alone. Michael is by your side, providing guidance and assistance whenever you need him, so never despair. He can reach out to you to help or warn you, so pay attention to the world around you to recognize his messages.

Chapter 2: How to Call Upon Archangel Michael

Archangel Michael can be called upon for various reasons. However, before you determine a specific intention, you first need to learn how to make contact with him. In this chapter, you'll learn about the many ways you can call upon Archangel Michael, from mediation and prayers to free writing and dreamwork and using crystals and astral projection. You'll also find instructions for the best ways to contact him for the first time.

Astral Projection

Astral projection involves leaving one's body and journeying to the astral plane. This approach requires very deep meditation and focus (which takes lots of practice), and it can be a great way to get in touch with archangels. Archangel Michael is the closest archangel to divine power. Working with him can empower your spiritual practices and elevate your spirituality. Using astral projection will help you form a deeper connection with this angelic being. With his help, you'll reach a higher level of consciousness, which will make you more susceptible to the angel's messages.

It is recommended to only practice astral projection when you have mastered more profound meditation techniques. This also involves practicing visualization techniques, as astral traveling often requires you to envision scenarios related to your intent. Having learned visualization and meditation, you can reach a deeper level of consciousness. This is almost like a trance-like state, where your spirit can travel freely, gathering knowledge and wisdom from all the different realms.

Free Writing

The written word has a powerful effect on empowering your spiritual work. It can channel your energy and make it flow in the direction of your intention. Besides healing, writing can also help you manifest positive life changes, especially if you use it to summon Archangel Michael to your side. One way to use writing to contact this angel is journaling.

Free writing requires focus and intention to channel the archangel's energy.[45]

Sharing your thoughts and needs in a journal is a great way to build a personal relationship with Archangel Michael. Another way to write to Michael is free writing. This requires setting an intention and writing down whatever comes to mind without conscious control. You are channeling his energy, so staying focused will take a lot of practice. Just let the angel guide your hands whenever you feel:

- the need to share your deepest aspirations, trepidations, and feelings with someone
- the desire to make positive changes in your life, but you aren't sure where and how to begin this new chapter

- helpless due to being stuck in the past and that you're constantly focusing on thoughts that are interfering with your present
- a lack of resources and opportunities to fulfill any part of your life or to find your life's purpose
- insecure or afraid of a certain situation, person, or the unknown
- hurt by someone close to you
- the need to express your gratitude for everything you have

After writing with your intention, you can look at it and try to decipher it. Depending on your experience, the message might not make sense to you right away. However, when you're ready, you can acknowledge it and use it to your advantage.

Meditation

Regardless of your reason for meditating with Archangel Michael, he will provide you with the clarity you need to find what you're searching for. For that reason alone, meditation is a great way to channel Michael's energy and summon him to your side. He can help you unclog your mind of stressful thoughts, elevate your spirituality, or even clear out your blocked chakras if needed. Simply reaching out to him during a quick daily meditation can be an elevating experience that will allow you to move forward.

There are several ways to meditate with Michael, with morning meditation being the most common one. In the morning, you feel the most relaxed, and it's easier for you to focus on clearing your mind, center yourself, and manifest your intention. You can combine this with a morning prayer or invocation dedicated to Michael.

One of the other ways is chakra meditation. This involves setting the intention of raising your energies in your chakras and channeling them toward connecting with Michael. The chakras are the main energy points of the body. They are connected to the major organs and all the physical, biological, and spiritual processes transpiring in you. Since summoning Michael requires a heightened level of spiritual energy, it's best to focus on your third eye chakra when meditating with him. Opening this chakra directly influences your ability to soothe your body, silence your mind and enhance your psychic abilities. Your third eye chakra is your best tool for tapping into your higher self and acknowledging the presence of angelic guardians. Once you start practicing chakra meditation, you will find it easier to notice the signs Michael sends back to you as an acknowledgment of your newly-established connection.

Positive Affirmations

Just like mantras, positive affirmations enhance the energy of your intention. They also empower your bond with Archangel Michael, even if it's the first time you're reciting them. Besides speaking them out loud, you can also sing them. Remember, angels like music and singing, and Michael is no different. The positive affirmations should be expressed in the present tense and an upbeat tone. Even if something hasn't happened yet, you must believe that it will. The more you do it, the more likely it will happen. For example, you can say:

"I have Archangel Michael's strength by my side, and I know it will help me clear all the hindrances out of my pathway."

Besides empowering you with the knowledge of your strengths, it will also let Michael know that you're thinking about them. He will see this as an invitation to join you on your life journey.

Chanting

Sometimes all you need to do to connect with Archangel Michael is chant his name. Suppose you suddenly find yourself in a tough situation and need urgent help. In that case, you can simply say Michael's name out loud several times. He will listen to you and respond even if you don't notice his response immediately (whether you do or not depends on your experience with spiritual communication and ability to tap into your intuition). Or, you can chant his name to acknowledge your belief that Michael will help you whether you ask for his assistance or not.

Mantras

A mantra is a way to channel your energy into your words. Your words carry unique vibrations. Coupled with an energetic intention, the spoken word can become a powerful tool for delivering vibrations and messages to the universe. Remember, everything has energy, and this energy is alive. You can consciously channel your energy to connect with the energy around you, including angelic essences. You have the extraordinary power to link your energy to thoughts, emotions, and actions and influence the outcomes of your energetic exchanges. You can use the vibrations of your mantras to call on Archangel Michael's energetic force and use it for what you want. For starters, you'll need mantras that help you establish a profound connection with this angel. However, this will require practice, and you'll need to be patient because it won't happen overnight.

Looking at Images

Some people find it useful to look at pictures or other representations of Michael to establish a connection with him. Gazing intently at Michael's likeness can send a powerful message to the angel. It also helps you tap into your higher self. Practicing this method is a way of affirming your connection with Michael without spending too much energy. It's a great strategy for beginners who wish to connect with Archangel Michael.

Using Representations of Michael

You can use items associated with Archangel Michael to summon him. You can place these in your sacred space (altar or shrine) or wherever you need his help the most. You can also carry them with you for added reassurance and protection. For example, you can light a blue candle and place it on your altar. Blue is the color associated with Michael, and his energy is often envisioned as an orb of blue light. You can say a prayer, mantra, or invocation when lighting the candle, or make this step part of your meditation with the angel. Wearing blue clothes when using any method for summoning the angel is also a powerful way to channel them and your intention to establish a connection with them.

Carrying objects representing Archangel Michael is a subtle way of anchoring the angel to you. It channels his energy (and his attention) to you, so you'll always feel protected by him. Tap into your intuition and choose an item that feels right for you. It could be a feather, a coin, or whatever object you feel drawn to when thinking of Michael. It can also be a crystal associated with the angel. Opt for blue or clear stones with high vibrational frequencies. The higher the crystal vibrates, the easier it will be to channel its energy to your intention. Angelite, blue chalcedony, lapis lazuli, and clear quartz are all great choices. Dedicate the chosen item to the angel by saying an affirmation or mantra reassuring you of Michael's presence and willingness to assist you.

Prayer

While many pray to Archangel Michael in times of need, you can also use this method to summon him just to get to know him better or thank him for his blessing and presence. Prayer is an incredibly powerful way to channel spiritual energy, regardless of your religious preferences. Prayer is empowering, opens one's mind, and deters errant thoughts that could hinder one's intention. Simply knowing and believing that Michael is there to hear your prayers can give you emotional resilience and enable you to overcome any obstacle in life. You don't have to face challenges.

You just have to have an open heart to accept Michael's presence, and prayer is a great way to reinforce this knowledge. Through prayer, you can let him know that you appreciate him, which allows him to step into your life. It's like talking to someone who is always there for you when you need them to support you, offer advice, or simply listen.

Calling Out to Archangel Michael

The simplest way to connect with Archangel Michael is to call on him and ask him to join you. You can ask him to accompany you wherever you are or invite him to join you at work or at an event where you might need a little boost. You don't have to ask him for a specific favor, just ask him to join you, and he will come. You can do this when you feel like there's too much negativity around you or when you feel ready to get to know the angel. This method doesn't require much preparation or practice. It can also help you hone your intuition. After making your plea, you'll need to listen to the signs telling you that he has accepted your invitation. Sooner or later, his presence will be known, and it's up to you to learn how to deepen your connection with him.

Inviting Archangel Michael into Your Dreams

Some people find it easier to communicate with supernatural beings through dreams. While angels have no limitations for spiritual communication, people do. Dreams can provide a safe medium for spiritual messages if you aren't sure how to communicate safely in your waking life. So, if you're ready to connect with the angel, invite him to join you in your dreams. You can do this by praying to him, lighting a candle, or doing a quick meditation with him before going to bed. Your subconscious will help you put aside the stress and enable you to interpret angelic messages. You can combine dream work with journaling and record the messages that you receive in your dreams. This way, you'll be able to revisit them and decipher those that didn't make sense at first. You can even ask Archangel Michael questions about himself to learn how he likes communicating and his preferences regarding contact and summoning. Remember that you might not receive answers to all your questions right away. However, they will come eventually, so keep an eye out for them!

Practical Techniques for Connecting with Archangel Michael

Here are several easy strategies for summoning this angel and asking him to join your side:

Archangel Michael Morning Invocation

You can invoke Archangel Michael first thing in the morning if you think you'll have a rough day. He can guide you through the day's challenges, and the two of you can learn more about each other. Here is an invocation you can use to summon Michael:

"I call on you, oh powerful Archangel Michael,

Who was sent by the universe to be by my side.

I ask you with all my heart and power,

For you to bless me with your presence on this day.

Hold my hand and guide me,

May your presence bless my day with strength and courage.

Archangel Michael, surround me now with blessed energy

And remain by the side of your faithful follower

Who I will become now that our connection has been made."

Archangel Michael Meditation

The following meditation will help you make an initial connection with Archangel Michael. You can combine meditative practice with prayers, invocations, or any other way that helps build a powerful bond with this angel.

Instructions:

1. Find a quiet place where you can focus on calling upon Michael. Sit in a chair or with your back to the wall. The goal is to relax your shoulders, all while avoiding slouching or tensing up.
2. Take a few deep breaths to center yourself and start grounding. Visualize your legs taking root, tying you to the ground. You should feel them pulling you towards the earth as your spiritual grounding nears completion.
3. When you feel rooted and secure, you can move on to the next step, visualizing Archangel Michael. If it helps, close your eyes. Conjure up an image of the angel standing in front of you,

surrounded by bright blue light.
4. See his flaming sword, the symbol of his protection, and allow yourself to be reassured by his presence. When you're ready, call out to the angel.
5. You can say whatever comes to mind, greet him, ask him questions, or do anything else you want. Avoid asking favors. The purpose of this exercise is to establish a connection.

Archangel Michael Prayers

The following two prayers are used to call upon Michael. Use the first prayer right after waking up to reestablish and strengthen your connection with him. The other one is an evening prayer you recite when winding down for the day. It can help you express gratitude or ask for signs for the following day.

Morning Prayer:

"May the mighty Archangel Michael be sent to my side,

To guide me, blessing me with his presence.

I am willing to put my faith and trust in you, Michael,

As I know that you can provide me with the strength and courage I need.

May our connection be as bright as your sword light,

To clear all blocks and obstacles that stand in our way."

Evening Prayer:

"I offer my gratitude for your divine guidance Archangel Michael

I have felt your presence today.

I have sensed your strength, trust, and faith in me.

I thank you, Michael, for being by my side."

Walking with Archangel Michael

Walking with Michael is a great way to communicate with him. It's a form of active meditation and involves the same essential elements as regular meditation – finding focus and channeling your mind toward your intention.

Instructions:

1. Walk briskly for ten minutes in a place where you can focus your mind – nature is the best place. Slow to a regular walking pace and continue for about two minutes.

2. Then, think about your intention of talking with Archangel Michael. Send him thoughts of gratitude and love and desire to meet him.
3. Now, envision Michael walking beside you. Thank him for joining you, and tell him whatever comes to mind. Don't ask for favors, and only talk about you or him.
4. Listen to whatever he has to say in response, and thank him for his answer.
5. If you have trouble envisioning him beside you, don't worry. You can still talk to him. He will hear you even if you can't see him just yet.
6. Whatever the outcome, just enjoy your walk. Even if Archangel Michael doesn't appear, he will send you messages sooner or later.

Mantra Repetition

When repeating mantras, it is crucial to do so while focusing on your intention. Since mantras work best when they're personal, try to write your own angel-invoking mantra. That said, here is how to get the best out of using mantras for calling on Archangel Michael.

1. Set the intention. Think about what you want to accomplish. Do you want Michael to contact you in a specific way? Maybe you want to summon him to learn more about him.
2. Whatever you need the angelic mantra for, keep it in mind. You can do this by bringing up an emotion that thinking of the intentions provokes in you. Once you determine the emotions, you'll know which mantra to choose.
3. Go to your sacred space. This can be any space you dedicate for spiritual practice. You can create an altar or shrine or use one regular spot where you feel safe and focused, from your bathroom to a tranquil patch of nature.
4. Settle into a comfortable position, breathe deeply, and allow yourself to relax. When your breath slows down and deepens, your body will release tension, and your mind will stop racing. You will then enter into a light meditative state.
5. Inhale and exhale 5-6 times to fully direct your focus to your intention. With each breath, you will channel more and more energy into your intent until you reach an absolute taste of

calmness and concentration.

6. Now, envision an orb of blue light in front of you. Watch it grow until you see Archangel Michael emerge from it. Think about your desire to connect with him, and he will help you make the connection by extending his energy toward you.

7. Once you sense his energy surrounding you, you will feel a sense of lightness. You can now start chanting your mantra to further empower your bond with the angel. Say it out loud or silently in your mind.

8. After three to five minutes of mantra repetition, you'll see Archangel Michael smiling at you, reassuring you of his presence and protection. You can let the image go and slowly emerge from the meditative state.

9. Repeat the mantras frequently. The more you do so, the stronger your bond with the angel will become. He will be more sensitive to your needs, and you'll find it easier to call on him.

Chapter 3: Signs That Archangel Michael Is Present

This chapter offers a list of signs that Archangel Michael has answered your call. These signs can include seeing feathers or angel numbers, seeing the color blue often, and many others. You'll also find a few personal stories of people who have successfully connected to or "seen" Archangel Michael.

The Most Common Signs of Archangel Michael's Presence

Physical Signs

Physical signs are the most common ways that Archangel Michael will communicate with you. They can also be coupled with other signs that make you feel that the angel is present. Michael likes to take a straightforward approach and leave you an unmistakable sign of his presence. Some signs will be more subtle than others, but if you have already reached out to Michael, you'll only have to rely on your intuition to decipher them. In any case, if you notice one of the following things standing out in some way in your environment, you can be sure that the angel is present:

- **Feathers** – These are the universal calling cards of angels. If you keep finding feathers around you, you'll know that the Archangel is near.

- **Butterflies** – They are a signal of reassurance of Michael's presence.
- **White birds** – Another group of winged creatures that often act as messages to angels. Archangel Michael could be sending them to you to help you feel his love and bring peace to you.
- **Breadcrumbs** – Leaving a trail of breadcrumbs is the angel's way of letting you know you can rely on divine powers.
- **Temperature** – An unmistakable sign of a powerful angel being present is the sudden drop in temperature. This is often followed by an instant feeling of warmth emanating from Michael.

Orbs of Light

If you've called upon Archangel Michael before, you already have his protection. To reassure you of this, he will send you messages in the form of colorful sparks, flashes of blue light, and orbs. If you haven't welcomed him yet and he feels that you're in need of protection or healing, sending you those things can be his way of asking you to let him in. You might see a long streak of light or an orb floating in front of you for a couple of minutes. Or, you might see a flash of light out of nowhere when you're just going about your day. Either way, seeing his light will make you feel warm and loved. You'll know that you're surrounded by Michael's protection, and you will be relying on his guidance from then on.

Seeing orbs or sparks of light indicates that Michael is asking to be let in.⁴⁶

Tones of Blue and Purple

Noticing tones of blue and purple can also indicate Archangel Michael's presence. As a powerful Archangel, Michael is associated with colored light, unlike other, lesser angels whose light is white. This relates to his divine purpose, which is protection. The colors purple and blue are linked to the protective layer of the aura of all living beings. They are also associated with Michael's most well-known qualities, serenity, determination, honesty, and truth. If you suddenly notice these colors pop up around you, you can be certain that Michael is present.

A Warm, Tingling Sensation

There are several reasons you might feel warm or tingly if Michael is present. He has a very powerful essence, and his bold protective instinct is transmitted on higher frequencies. When these frequencies reach you, you'll feel the warmth of his protectiveness wash over you. As a result, you'll feel satisfied and happy. Second, Michael is the Archangel associated with the Sun. He is even depicted with a flaming sword at times. So, if you feel a sudden wave of heat coupled with a positive energy flow, it's a sign that Michael is there to boost your mood and spirits.

Images of Swords, Warriors, or Archangel Michael

If you keep seeing pictures of warriors, swords, or Michael himself, this could also be the angel's way of making his presence known. You might see him in paintings, statues, and other art forms. Some of these might be accompanied by words such as evil and slaying. Swords and warriors are among his correspondences, so these are his signs too. For example, you might see paintings of warriors battling evil. Or, you might encounter this motive in a video game. If any of these appear for no apparent reason, pay attention to them because they might be messages from Archangel Michael.

A Feeling of Uplifting or Grounding Energy

Archangel Michael provides the perfect balance of energies that will uplift you and ground you at the same time. If you feel a sense of security and spiritual improvement, the angel signals that you won't have to worry about having enough strength to overcome your obstacles. It might feel like being wrapped in a protective blanket that also provides resilience and endurance. Or, you might suddenly realize that you can overcome the challenge you're currently facing or about to face. You might also have a sudden moment of clarity, feeling grounded, and having a renewed sense of focus. Either way, you won't miss this energy for sure.

A Sense of Peace

Having an overwhelming sense of peace could also denote the angel's presence. Being a great protector, Michael will offer a comforting presence. Regardless of your situation, you'll feel at peace and sure that everything will turn out all right. This is because having this angel near you wards off negative energies and harmful influences. It's like being embraced by invisible wings. If the sense of peace is also accompanied by love and a surge of positivity that calms your worries and uplifts your hearts, know that Archangel Michael is there to reassure you of his presence, listen to you, and even dry your tears if necessary.

The Name "Michael"

Besides his image, Michael's name can appear as a sign of him being around. If you keep encountering the name Michael wherever you go without any reason for it (it's not your name or any of your loved ones'), this might be the Archangel letting you know that he is by your side. For example, you might encounter several people named Michal (a cashier, a server at a restaurant, a co-worker, etc.), hear or see it in the news, or when browsing the internet. Typically, you'll run into his name several times in one day. The specific ways the name appears might offer clues on what message the angel is trying to send. For example, hearing it in the news could be a warning sign. While running into a co-worker named Michael could be a hint to pay more attention to your work.

Feeling Safe and Protected

Sometimes, the only sign you'll receive from Michael is a feeling of safety. This can come independently of your spiritual work and might even take you by surprise. You just suddenly feel protected and safe for no reason. You don't know why, but you feel nothing can hurt you at the moment. Michael's powerful protective energy will surprise you even if you've requested protection or taken measures to protect yourself from harmful influences. It will give you a sense of direction, and you'll intuitively know how to raise your protective energies. Acknowledging that the feeling of safety means Michael's presence will fill you with confidence for moving forward in life and your ability to manifest the changes you want. You know that nothing will deter you from your goal, no matter how scary the obstacles seemed a couple of minutes ago. Your fear has now diminished because you know he is there with you.

Trust Your Intuition

If this is your first time working with an angel, you're probably still learning to listen to your intuition (especially when receiving and deciphering angelic messages). However, after contacting Michael, you might notice that you can trust your gut feelings more. The presence of Archangel Michael causes a powerful energetic shift around you, raising your vibrations. While this energy is different, and you can't explain why it is, you just know you can trust it.

Hearing Michael's Voice

Another direct way Michael announces his presence is by speaking to you directly. If you've invited him into your life and started hearing a voice that is different from your inner one, that is probably the Archangel's. This is particularly common with beginners who find it easier to receive messages in a more mundane way. The angel lets you know he is there and ready to listen to you by whispering in your ear. Wondering how you can tell that what you hear is his voice and not that of your inner monologue? It's simple. You'll know because it will be much stronger. Some report it is a booming sound that states a message loud and clear. Unlike other angels who send subtle messages through music and other sounds, Archangel Michael will get straight to the point. If you suddenly hear a blunt warning not to proceed with something, listen to it. Michael is warning you that the action can have serious negative consequences and lead you down a path you don't want to go. If you hear a calm voice offering advice, he simply tries to guide you in the right direction. Regardless of how you hear Archangel Michael, know that his message always comes from a place of love. Those with heightened physical abilities like clairaudience will be more susceptible to auditory messages from Michael. Conversely, those with claircognizance will simply know that the voice they hear comes from this angel.

Persistence

Have you lacked determination in the past but now feel the urge to remain persistent in working toward your goals? If you are determined to persist - regardless of how challenging the road might seem - Michael is probably guiding you. Persistence is one of his most admirable traits.

The Urge to Defend

When you come under Archangel Michael's influence, you might feel the need to defend someone from injustice. Let's say you hear that your co-worker is about to be punished for someone else's mistake. Instead of letting it go (because you fear you'll be disciplined, too), you stand up and voice your outrage in the face of that injustice. Archangel Michael has a protective streak a mile long. By passing on some of his qualities, he shows you how you can connect with him. Likewise, you might also have the need to confront your adversaries. This could be something as simple as finally letting the neighbor know that you're not okay with them listening to loud music in the middle of the night. Or, you simply decide to control your biggest deterrents – your own fears. Whether it's fear of a specific situation or the unknown, you'll suddenly be encouraged to take risks and see where things go. By facing your fears, you might encounter new opportunities or learn that you have nothing to fear at all.

A Pull toward Archangel Michael

If you've invited Archangel Michael into your life, you might need to start working with him immediately. If this is the case, this indicates that he has received your call and is ready to build a connection with you. Whether you want to request healing, get a spiritual reading with him, or work with him in any other way that contributes to your spiritual fulfillment, he is willing to participate. Archangel Michael has the power to channel energies and intentions, which ultimately pushes you in the right direction. While he won't force you to do anything (he is a fan of free will), he can help you make better choices. One of his ways of doing this is by making you feel like you're pulled toward a certain type of spiritual work that he can help you explore. This thought might pop up when you tap into your gut feelings. If you've just made the first call to him and haven't asked him for his assistance, he might be telling you that you should. Maybe he is trying to tell you that to work with him, you need to heal from an emotional trauma first, and he is offering to accompany you on this healing journey. If you don't understand why you are feeling an intense pull toward Archangel Michael, look at the bigger picture. Look for other signs as well and ask for more if needed. Asking Michael questions is the best way to build a connection with him, particularly if you feel drawn to him.

Finding Your Life's Purpose

If you've been struggling to find your life's purpose and you've suddenly encountered it recently, you can be sure that it had something to do with Archangel Michael. Michael motivates you to become more productive, so you can have a fulfilled life and attain spiritual enlightenment. He is there to let you know he will help you develop your talents and skills to fulfill your purpose. Whether you've found something that benefits you and your loved ones or your entire community, Michael will certainly support you in your endeavors. He will help you remain determined, organized, and stick to the routine that keeps you in the proper rhythm as you work towards your goals. You can verify this by reaching out to Archangel Michael after you've made the first steps toward fulfilling your life's purpose.

Keeping Relationships Simple

If you have struggled with constant conflicts in one or more of your relationships, Michael can send you a message that will help you resolve the issue. For example, you might receive a message in your dreams or the morning after a fight with your partner before going to bed. Or, you might see a sudden flash of blue light as you're arguing with your employer while demanding a raise. If any of these scenarios are repeated more than once, it can indicate that Archangel Michael wants to guide you in the right direction. He wants you to resolve the conflicts that are complicating your relationships. He knows relationships are only fulfilling when based on simple yet profound emotions, ideas, and values.

Testimonies of People Who Recognized Archangel Michael's Signs

Countless records of people encountering or verifying their successful connection with Archangel Michael exist. Below are some of them.

> *"One morning, I woke up and walked out onto my balcony to get some fresh air while having my first cup of coffee of the day. It was a late spring morning with clear skies, and I was still sleepy. Standing with my cup in my hand, I suddenly noticed something floating in the air in front of me. As it got closer, I realized it was a white feather. When it reached the height of my face, it stopped and just hovered in front of my eyes for a few seconds and then was carried away by a slight breeze. At first, I didn't know where the feather came from because there were no birds in the sky. And even stranger was the way it lingered in front of me. Then I remembered reaching out to Archangel Michael several days before, asking for a sign that he was ready to work with me. I realized the feather was Michael telling me he was here with me now. When the feather kept appearing in other places, too, I knew I'd interpreted the sign correctly."* - Olivia

"I was haunted by a disturbing, heavy presence for several days, and I didn't know where it came from. I didn't think anyone near me would wish me ill will, but I was wrong. Wanting to learn the origin of this negative energy in my life, I asked for Archangel Michael's help. I lit a candle and prayed to him, asking him to send me a sign before going to bed. Michael came into my dreams and let me know it was my best friend poisoning me with his toxic energies. He was envious of my accomplishments and wanted me to fail. Michael came to warn me of him and asked me to pray for my friend. Suddenly, the negative presence no longer controlled me. I will forever be thankful to Michael for pointing this out." - Charlie

"I've struggled with depression most of my life. After losing my mother, I felt so lost. I wanted to be by myself and refused to leave home. I knew this wasn't good for me, so I decided to ask Archangel Michael to help me heal. I have always liked meditation, so I thought this could be the best way to start my healing journey. After praying to Michael, I relaxed my mind and summoned him to my side. Suddenly, I saw a bright blue orb in front of me. At first, I felt scared, but then I heard Michael telling me not to be afraid. The light got closer and eventually enveloped me before connecting with me. I felt as if it started draining negativity from me. When there was no negativity left, the light vanished. I thanked Michael for his help and reemerged from my meditative state. I felt much lighter and knew that I could be happy. From then on, I decided to regularly work with Archangel Michael. Soon after, I started feeling better, and slowly, the smile returned to my face." - Laura

Chapter 4: Requesting Protection

Archangel Michael is a spiritual warrior and leader of the army of angels. He fights against evil, which makes him perfect for guarding against harmful influences. Who better to call upon when you need protection? In this chapter, you'll find several ways to acquire the Archangel's protective shield, including prayers, meditations, amulets, and more.

Archangel Michael is a spiritual warrior.[47]

Protection Charm Infused with Michael's Powers

Carrying a charm or talisman infused with Archangel Michael's powers will always make you feel protected. Whenever you feel that you're in danger, the charm will be there as a reminder of Michael's love and protection. It works best if you first cleanse your body and space of harmful energies.

Ingredients:
- A white candle
- A piece of red fabric – large enough for your talisman
- Bay leaf
- Vinegar
- Dried chili pepper
- Coarse sea salt
- Essential oil associated with Michael
- An image or symbol of Archangel Michael
- A needle
- Red thread
- Scissors
- Safety pin (optional)

Instructions:
1. Take the sea salt into your hands and start walking clockwise. Sprinkle the salt around, making a circle large enough to sit in.
2. Anoint the candle with the essential oil, and light it while calling upon Archangel Michael.
3. Using the needle and thread, make a pouch from the fabric. Put the chili pepper, bay leaf, the representation of Michael, and a pinch of salt inside it, dip the needle into the vinegar, and sew the pouch shut.
4. Imagine a beam of blue light shining down on you, enveloping your body, until it starts radiating too.

5. Then recite the following: *"May this holy flame burn above me, May this holy flame burn below me, May this holy flame burn beside me, May this holy flame burn in front of me, May this holy flame burn behind me, May this whole female burn be within me, My Michael will always be with me."*
6. Snuff out the candle. You can light it again when you wish to invoke Michael's protection again.
7. Secure the pouch inside your clothes or bag with the safety pin if you prefer. If not, just place it there where you need its protective powers.
8. To reinforce the power of Michael's protective fire, take some sea salt and sprinkle it around the entrances of your home, including window sills and back doors.

A Ritual to Call on Archangel Michael for Protection

With the following ritual, you can request Michael's protection and ask him to remove negative energy. Traditionally, this ritual would be performed on a day associated with Archangel Michael. However, you can do it any day you prefer. Before the ritual, cleanse yourself both spiritually and mentally.

Ingredients:
- Tools for cleansing your space and items
- Tools for purifying your body
- A red candle
- Michael-associated oil to amount the candle
- A talisman charged with Michael's protective powers

Instructions:
1. Declutter your space and clean it. Then, light an incense or smudge stick to cleanse it spiritually. Alternatively, you can anoint the entrances with essential oil or sprinkle salt mixed with herbs associated with Archangel Michael.
2. Cleanse your body with a salt bath, and purify your tools with salt, smoke, or any other method you prefer.

3. When you're ready, find a comfortable position, take a deep breath, and focus on invoking Archangel Michael. Chant the following:

   "I call upon your power Archangel Michael
   I acknowledge your strength and courage
   And I offer my gratitude for your presence in my life.
   As you've dominated evil,
   I ask you to help me overpower what threatens me
   Protect me, my space, and my loved ones from evil influences.
   Guard me against anything that can harm me
   Anyone who wishes me ill will.
   I thank you again, Michael."

4. Light the red candle and place it in a safe place. Let it burn down completely, but snuff it out anytime you can't attend to it.
5. When the candle has burned down, bury the remaining wax in the ground. You can do this in your garden, a pot on your windowsill, or in the park.
6. Take the talisman and place it where you need the most protection. If it's your home, put it in your entryway. If it's for you, carry it with you.

A Prayer to Archangel Michael

Praying to Archangel Michael is the most straightforward and surefire way to obtain his protection. It can be used for any occasion and combined with invocations, meditations, or any other strategies you might want to use to petition for Michael's protection.

Instructions:

1. Sit in front of your sacred space. This could be an altar or any place where you feel safe and focused.
2. If you wish, light a candle in the name of Michael. Then, recite the following prayer:

   "I pray to you, Michael, the heavenly prince who defends us in battle,
   Whether it's between the powers of darkness and light,
   Or the battle of spiritual principalities.

I ask you to come to my aid now,

And join a fellow creation made to the creator's likeness.

Help me redeem myself from influences I couldn't ward off,

And fight the battles of the spirit alongside your angels.

I know dark energies are powerless to resist your omnipotent essence,

On the Earth and every other realm in the universe.

You are the slayer of the enemy,

Who transformed into a being of light.

And as you wander among the wicked spirit,

Slay them all, casting them out of the universe.

I ask you to protect me against these impure forces,

Which threaten to deprive my mind and corrupt my heart.

Help me remain free of these energies,

And avoid falling into the trap of lies, resentment, and fear.

I know my obstacles and enemies can be formidable,

But with your help, I can overcome even the craftiest of challenges.

Help set a light of protection around me,

And use your sword to ward away anything that threatens me."

3. Repeat the prayer three times in a row. Only stop to take a deep breath between each repetition.
4. Once you're finished with the prayer, you can state a petition if you have one. If you do, be as specific as you can. For example, if you feel threatened by a specific person, ask Michael to protect you from them.
5. Alternatively, you can meditate for a couple of minutes after your prayer or simply go about your day or night. When you're finished, snuff out the candle.

Visualizing Michael's Shield

This visualization meditation will help you invite Michael's protection into your life. It will help you feel safe and protected as you work on expressing your authentic self. It makes you confident in embracing your light and leaving behind any interference that comes from the external or internal environment.

Instructions:
1. Find a secluded space where you can focus without any distractions. Get comfortable by relaxing your body and mind.
2. Focus on deepening your breathing, and imagine breathing in light energy. Feel how the light enters your body. At the same time, with each exhalation, you release any energy that doesn't belong to you.
3. Once your entire body (all dimensions, physical, mental, and spiritual) is filled with light, you can call on your spiritual helpers. Start with your higher self, as this is where your power lies, and this is what will help you attract and use Michael's shield.
4. Then, ask Archangel Michael and all angels working with him to join you. Close your eyes and visualize Michael's sword floating in front of you, enveloped in an electric blue flame.
5. Feel how the sword's flame is reaching you, permeating your body, and clearing out all layers of your body, first the physical, then the metaphysical (the chakras and aura layers).
6. Then, feel how the flame reaches your emotions, clearing any negative or confusing feelings and emotions that you have picked up from others. Along with the emotions, the flame will eliminate all energies that don't belong to you but are clouding your emotional judgment.
7. Other people's ideas, thoughts, beliefs, and judgments are now released from your mind. Your energies are disentangled from the negative ones threatening it.
8. Now, ask Michael to help you seal your freshly cleansed energy. Visualize the electric blue field surrounding your body.
9. As the light seals your body, imagine yourself reaching out to the sword, placing it in front of your heart to seal your heart chakra. Next, move the sword towards your back, sealing yourself from that side as well.
10. After your front and back, seal your left and right side, then move the sword above your head before going to your feet, protecting the above and beyond space.

11. Imagine being protected by seven swords, one from each direction you sealed your energies and one from within. Take a deep breath and tap into your higher self. Feel how you are empowered by higher frequency energies while the lower ones are unable to enter your energy field.
12. Breathe and allow the alignment of protection to create a shield around you. This is Michael's, and you can call on it anytime you need protection. Whenever you need protection, you just have to imagine it multiplying itself, effectively protecting you from all lower-frequency energies.
13. Let all the images go, and keep breathing deeply for a few minutes. During this time, Michael and the angels working with him will intensify the energy of your protective shield.
14. Emerge from your meditation and go about your day, carrying Michael's shield with you wherever you go.

Archangel Michael Chakra Meditation

With this meditation, you can summon Archangel Michael's powerful energy to protect you from spiritual interference. During this exercise, you'll encounter Michael, who will help you cut unhealthy attachments, allowing you to establish a higher connection with your higher self and the spiritual realm of healing, relaxation, and protection.

Instructions:
1. Find a comfortable and quiet space. If you can, do this outside. If you're meditating inside, leave a window open.
2. Close your eyes and focus on your breathing. Feel how the fresh air enters your body and the stale, warm air leaves it. Continue until you feel relaxed enough to connect to your spiritual self.
3. You'll know you're relaxed when you feel you can let go of any thoughts that pop into your head.
4. Now imagine a beam of light coming from the ceiling, reaching the top of your head, and opening your crown chakra. See how your crown chakra opens up like a beautiful purple flower.
5. As the flower opens, it lets the energies in, and you can see it connecting to the divine spirituality, opening the chakra even more. The light then travels down, cleansing your head, relaxing your muscles, and opening your other chakras.

6. When the light reaches your feet, it continues down to earth, rooting you to the ground. Deep inside, you know that the elevated part of you is now open to receive higher energies.
7. You're now connected to both your physical nature and spiritual truth. As you breathe, visualize being surrounded by a beam of blue light. With each breath you take, the light brightens, and you feel blissfully one with the defender of the spiritual realm, Archangel Michael.
8. Feel Michael's energy floating everywhere around you, flooding your chakras. Imagine him walking towards you, with his hair floating around and his sword by his side.
9. As you're admiring Michael's sword, you see Michael opening his wings, making you feel his protective energy. You feel safe, at home, and incredibly thankful for his presence in your life at that present moment.
10. Look at the field of energy around you. You might see lighter and darker aspects; the latter is what you need protection from. As Michael's power draws the darker aspects front, you know he will protect you from them.
11. Next, Michael takes his sword with both hands and cuts any unwanted ties that threaten your spirit. As the ties are cut, you feel a warm and tingling sensation.
12. After that, repeat the following:

    "From now on, I will be protected from harmful energies.

    Only good energy will be allowed into my auric field.

    I ask you, Michael, that with your sword, shield me from

    Anything that's not attached to me through life and light."
1. See how Michael lifts his sword again, blessing you with it. Breathe out and see Michael looking at you with his eyes full of kindness.
2. You now feel that Michael will always watch over you no matter what. Because of this, you'll be as powerful a warrior as possible. Thank Michael for his blessing. Let the images go, and return your focus to your breathing. You feel lighter, stronger, and cleaner as you open your eyes and breathe deeply.

3. Anytime you need a boost, remember that Michael is there. You can use his protection to fight your battles or help others fight theirs; the choice is yours.

Protective Meditation with Archangel Michael

Here is another mediation for calling upon Archangel Michael's protective powers. This is simple and quick. You can do it even if you only have 10 minutes.

Instructions:
1. After finding a secluded spot, start focusing on your breath. As you do so, imagine letting everything go when you exhale.
2. Release every thought and just focus on the moment. Notice how your breath becomes lighter and set your intention to feel safe and protected.
3. As you continue breathing, feel yourself reaching deeper inside until you feel anchored to your higher self, your soul, and all its desires.
4. Now, call on Archangel Michael, asking for his assistance. Invite him from the highest of the realms to join you.
5. Feel free to imagine his presence as you feel comfortable. This might be a human figure or a blue orb of light floating in front of you.
6. As he arrives, you suddenly feel all the negativity around you leave your presence. With the Archangel by your side, you feel loved and protected.
7. Ask Michael to keep you safe and allow this feeling of safety and security you now feel to accompany you. Ask him to protect you everywhere you go.
8. Archangel Michael will heed your request, granting you a protective shield. This shield will prevent anyone from taking something you aren't willing to give.
9. Basking in Michael's security, protection, and love, enjoy feeling safe in this space and that nothing will affect you. Michael will always be by your side.
10. Thank him for bringing you the feeling of safety and love. Finish your meditation by returning to your physical presence.

Whenever you need to feel safe, ask Michael to step in and remind you that you're safe.

Lighting a Candle for Archangel Michael

Lighting candles for Archangel Michael is another fantastic way of letting him know you need his protection. You can do this before a ritual, prayer, meditation, or any other form of spiritual work. For example, you can light a candle before asking Michael to send you a sign in your dreams. This way, you will be protected while communicating with him. You can use any color you want. However, blue candles are the best for channeling his protective powers. Whereas red ones are best for protection against negative influences during spiritual work.

Blue candles are the best to use to ask for his protection.[48]

Instructions:
1. Before lighting your candle, cleanse it by rubbing it between your hands or in a bowl of salt. This will remove any negative energy it could've picked up before reaching your hands.
2. As you're cleansing the candle, visualize a black or gray light leaving it. As the candle is freed from negative vibes, it becomes lighter in your hand.

3. Now, focus on your intention and channel it towards the candle. While you do this, rub the candle from the ends toward the middle. At this point, you can also use anointing oils (incorporating oils associated with Michael).
4. When infused with your intention, the candle will slowly release your desire as it burns, helping you manifest it. The candle becomes heavier again.
5. Light the candle and say a prayer to Michael. You can also recite a mantra or simply chant Archangel Michael's name nine times. Then ask Michael for his protection.
6. Let the candle burn down completely. However, don't leave it unattended, and always keep it in an area where you can keep an eye on it. Alternatively, you can place it in a dish with a little water at the bottom. This will catch any sparks that might fly. The intensity of the negative power you need protection from depends on whether there are sparks.
7. Whenever you need to leave the candle unattended, snuff it out. Avoid blowing it because this is considered insulting to Archangel Michael. If you need substantial protection, relight the candle each day and repeat the same ritual/prayer/mantra every time. If not, just light it each day until it burns out.
8. When the candle burns out, look at its remains. If they contain dark soot, that means it has trapped negativity, and you won't need to worry about being affected by it anymore.
9. To avoid having to fight off negativity again, don't touch the candle with your hands. Dispose of the wax to make your defenses whole and allow Michael's protection to envelop you.
10. You should now feel protected. If you don't, light another candle, repeat everything, and ask for Archangel Michael's protection.

Chapter 5: Requesting Healing

Amongst other things, Archangel Michael is often associated with healing. As an Archangel, his energies vibrate at higher frequencies, which gives them powerful restorative effects. Their light is healing, and by connecting to it and harnessing it, you can empower your mind, body, and soul and encourage their healing from traumatic events. Some of the methods you'll be introduced to here include meditating with Archangel Michael's light to heal your energy and physical body, blessing water with Michael's energy, and using his symbols for Reiki and other self-healing methods.

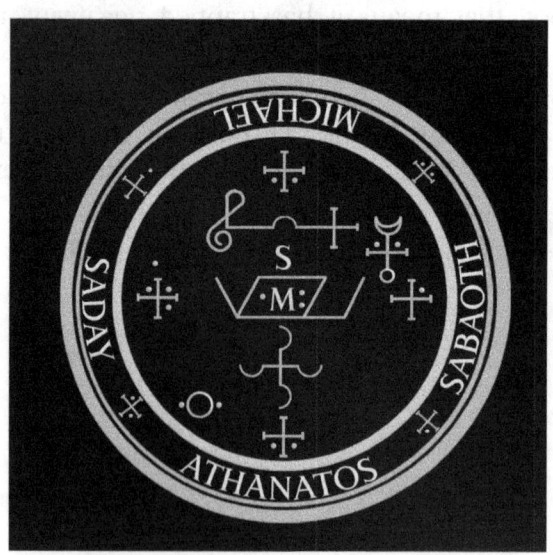

The reiki symbol for Archangel Michael.

Creating Blessed Water with the Energy of Archangel Michael

As he is often associated with water, Archangel Michael can bless the water with his restorative and protective energy. You can use this water to protect yourself from mental, physical, and spiritual influences threatening your health and wellbeing. Here is a great way to ask Michael to bless your water with his energy.

Ingredients:
- 1 cup of spring water
- 1 tablespoons of sea salt
- A bowl
- A jar with a lid

Instructions:
1. Mix all the ingredients in a bowl, and pour them into the jar.
2. Hold the jar up to your chest in front of your heart.
3. Ask Michael to bless the water and infuse it with his divine energy. While you do that, recite the following Prayer to Archangel Michael:

   "Archangel Michael, as you stand before me

   I trust you to protect me wherever I go.

   I ask you to bless this water,

   So, I can use its power to heal myself and my loved ones.

   In the name of the highest good, I ask you now for your blessings.

   Thank you, and I'm looking forward to working with you."

4. Feel how Michael's light empowers the water with love and protection.
5. Sprinkle the water on your body as needed for physical healing. You can also spritz it around you and your space for mental, mental, and spiritual healing.

Using Archangel Michael's Symbol for Reiki and Self-Healing

Archangel Michael's guidance extends beyond infusing with healing light. By building a close relationship with him, you can harness his energy and empower yourself for self-healing. One of the most effective self-healing methods is Reiki, a form of spiritual empowerment in which the person receives restorative energy. This energy unblocks and balances the chakra system and aids in the restoration of the person's physical, emotional, spiritual, and mental health and wellbeing. It's a deep restorative method that heals the inner spirit, allowing it to empower the other aspects of a person's being. Often physical and mental illnesses are caused by the ailments of the soul. The longer this goes unnoticed, the more the spirit will try to get the person's attention by manifesting in the form of illnesses or injuries. Given that the main component in Reiki healing is energy, who better to receive the power from than a powerful being like Archangel Michael. The following Reiki session will help you connect with Archangel Michael to receive his guidance and protection on your self-healing journey.

Instructions:

1. The first step here is asking for Reiki energy. Remember, Michael won't just start showering you with energy. He needs your permission to do that, so make sure to set an intention and make a conscious effort to welcome his light.
2. Prepare the tools you'll be using. This step is optional, as you won't necessarily have to use any if you don't want to. However, beginners might benefit from energy-channeling tools like crystals and symbols. Use the ones associated with Archangel Michael, such as blue crystals, images of swords, feathers, etc.
3. Prepare your body and mind to work with the Archangel's light. He will help you open channels of divine wisdom and help you communicate with the spiritual world during healing sessions. However, for the most profound healing, you must be prepared for his presence.
4. Assume a comfortable position and close your eyes. Focus on channeling your intention of inviting Michael's energy. Think about him sitting in front of you, with his hand extended,

channeling healing energy towards you.

5. He might send you a personal message to guide you in your self-healing journey. If you do not receive a message, don't worry. Just focus on the sensations his energy is evoking in your body.
6. Feel the deep peace and calm in your body and mind. You feel so light, almost as if you could lift off the surface you're currently on. You're filled with love, comfort, and renewed energy.
7. If you wish, recite a prayer to Michael to thank him for his blessings. You can also use this prayer as a reminder of your strength and courage that stems from the knowledge that Michael is always there to guide you.
8. Here is a prayer you can recite to the Archangel Michael:

"I call you to me, Michael,

And I welcome your divine presence.

Please help me discard the worries from my life.

Shine your light and warmth onto me

In any shadows that lurk within my energies.

So that I can heal and have a fertile and productive life

And everything I create is infused with love, happiness, and freedom of all ailments."

9. As you become receptive to Michael's energies, consider all the good it represents. It will boost your confidence in healing yourself and chase away all the emotional burdens hindering your recovery.
10. Remember, love is stronger than any other force. Michael loves you and will always stay close to you if you need him to be. He will help you banish whatever is affecting your energies and reclaim your health and happiness.

Feel free to do whatever you want when receiving Reiki energy empowered by the Archangel Michael. You can sit, lie, and even engage in activities like reading or meditation. The only requirement is to have an open mind and be prepared to receive the healing energy. At one point, you will feel it flowing toward you; make sure not to resist. Healing energy is as powerful as Archangel Michael's and can be overwhelming. Still, do your best to embrace it. The sooner you do, the sooner it can play its role in transforming your health and wellbeing. During or after receiving the energy, you might feel a warm, tingling sensation coursing through your body, a buzzing in your head. It might also happen that you don't feel anything at all. This is entirely normal, too, especially for beginners who aren't receptive yet to the full scope of the energy. Some people also report feeling tired after receiving Reiki. This is a sign that Michael's light has taken its effects and is now empowering you to heal yourself. Healing activates an additional metabolic process, which requires more physical energy, and that can make you tired. Reiki energy can also trigger some unwanted feelings or memories. If this happens to you, just acknowledge them, and let the healing energy sweep them out.

Archangel Michael Healing Meditation for Your Body

Due to his powerful energy and status, Archangel Michael has a highly evolved spiritual essence, capable of restoring spiritual and physical bonds. He will do the same for you if you treat him with respect, honesty, and understanding. It will empower you to heal your physical body from illnesses and injuries.

Instructions:

1. Focus your attention by thinking about what you need assistance with. Are you dealing with a chronic condition or an acute one? Does it affect a specific part of your body or the entire body? The more specific you are when making a request for physical healing, the better.

2. The more Michael knows about your condition, the better. He will be able to channel his energy where you need it the most, and neither of you will waste any time during your healing journey.

3. Michael only works for the highest good. If he feels that you need to learn a certain lesson before healing you (or whomever you want to heal), he won't help you until you've learned it. If you're sure the timing is right, you can proceed.

4. Close your eyes and call upon Archangel Michael. Channel his light and trust in its power to improve your life.

5. Imagine an orb of light blue light in front of your mind's eye. Chant Michael's name three times while gazing into the light to open your energy field.
6. Bring your awareness to the issue you need assistance with and allow the blue light to surround you. As you're enveloped in this blue bubble, you feel that it acts like a shield.
7. Ask Michael to eliminate all the negative energies causing the physical symptoms. You might see him cut unwanted energetic ties with his sword around the affected body part or around your entire body.
8. As he releases you from the unwanted bonds, you might feel your body tense, with your shoulder and back straightening, standing upright like you would be one of Michael's angelic soldiers. This is a sign that you're ready to fight off whatever is ailing your body.
9. Now thank Michael by repeating the following message:

    "Archangel Michael

    I summon you now to guide and shield me on my healing journey.

    To give me strength and confidence that I can find my highest power.

    Send me signs that you have heard my voice

    And that I am protected in your love.

    Thank you for all the blessings you bestowed upon me today."
10. Slowly let the image of Michael and his energy fade and return to the present. Whenever you feel weighed down by your physical symptoms, remember your connection with Michael; he will be there to lift you up and help you overcome your challenges.

Healing Light Meditation with Archangel Michael

By summoning the Archangel's light, you can heal your energy and keep it healthy regardless of your emotional and spiritual challenges. It's a simple yet deep exercise that will help you empower yourself spiritually and be in a better condition to defeat health challenges.

Instructions:
1. Find a secluded place where you won't be disturbed and get comfortable. Close your eyes and deepen your breath. Continue breathing deeply until you feel focused on the present moment.
2. Notice your connection to the surface beneath you. Relax your shoulders and raise your palms up toward the sky as if you're ready to receive whatever blessing you'll receive.
3. When you're ready, close your eyes. Focus on your intention of welcoming Archangel Michael into your space and asking him to heal your energy. Open your mind and heart to receive his energy.
4. Gently and smoothly breathe in through your nose and out through your mouth a few times. Allow your breath to return to its normal rhythms, relax your abdomen and let everything go until your mind is still.
5. Allow your body to feel the energy in and around it. This will help it prepare to receive Michael's healing energy. Then, repeat the following words:

"Across time and space, call upon Archangel Michael To be here with me today.

Michael, I ask you to come with unconditional love

May you also bring your light, peace, and protection

Please help me to remove dark, unhealthy energies

Asst me in cutting out energetic influences that don't benefit my health

Guide me toward my own unique light,

And the unconditional love that resides within me.

Thank you."

6. Take a deep breath and imagine a beautiful aura surrounding you. It has a blue light; feel its energy and allow it to wash over your body. You're held safely within the light.
7. The blue light indicates that Michael is near. Call him closer to you. State what you need from him and remain open to receiving his guidance and blessings. Feel him empowering your aura with his protective light.

8. Michael tells you that you're safe. Use this reassurance to focus on healing instead of worrying about defending yourself from malicious energies. Feel the energy seeping into your body, above and all around you, as they are infused into your aura.
9. Absorb the healing energy and take a few deep breaths to solidify the newly found energized feeling in your body and mind. Think about the unhealthy feelings and energies you no longer want to hold onto.
10. Ask Michael to remove the unwanted energies. Imagine the angel holding a sword above your head, lowering it, and tracing the protective aura around your body. He cuts away the unwanted energetic ties, allowing your body and mind to become stronger.
11. Feel the difference it makes not to have those unwanted energies. As you take a deep breath, you feel lighter and freer. Breathe in Michael's energy. The deeper you connect to his protective energies, the longer its effects will be on your healing.
12. Ask him to bless you with the energy of confidence and wisdom to overcome your health challenges. You can say this out loud or in your mind; Michael will hear you either way.
13. See your blue aura get brighter and brighter as your confidence and wisdom increase. You feel that you'll be supported through your health journey. You'll have Michael as a compass in difficult times, and he will provide you with your strength.
14. Sit and observe the sensation passing through your body. Allow yourself to be confident that you're at the right place at the right time on your journey.
15. Take a few breaths, and if the powerful energy flow you've previously received made your body tense up, relax it. Feel the aura you built with Michael and think about it as a permanent connection to him and all the healing energies of the universe.
16. Thank him for the blessings you've received and for remaining by your side through your health journey. Remember to tap into your aura when you need angelic support in healing, and you'll be immediately connected to Archangel Michael.

Archangel Michael Complete Health Reset Meditation

As the chief of the Archangels and the governor of the Sun, Archangel Michael can empower your healing journey. He can also help you do a complete reset to restore your health and vitality. It's like boosting your immunity, metabolism, mental processes, and spiritual health all at once.

Instructions:
1. Find a comfortable position and close your eyes. Move your focus inward, let go of mundane thoughts and concentrate on your intention.
2. Visualize an orb of light appearing in front of you. That is the light of Archangel Michael. The angel will soon appear in front of you.
3. Take a moment to sense your inner connection with the Archangel. You can do this by focusing on your breath. Think of your breath as your inner spirit. By encouraging it to flow freely, you're creating a connection to the spiritual energies around you.
4. With each breath you release, the spirit within you becomes more connected to the space around you. You're now connected to your inner spirit.
5. Find any unwanted areas in your spirit, and release them when exhaling. Let go of your worries and feel the protective energy of Michael.
6. Now, guide your inner vision towards your inner light, the light of spiritual connection and communication. See it in your body. As your body lights up, it becomes stronger and stronger.
7. Observe Archangel Michael and feel his essence. Pay attention to the sensation in your body or any other signs the Archangel might send you. You might see a light that appears in front of your mind's eye.
8. When you feel connected to Michael, invite his blue aura to come to you. Welcome it as it envelopes you, seeping into your spiritual, mental, and spiritual being. You feel cherished and protected.

9. In Michael's blue light, you're held safely, but you might become aware of any worry or other negative feelings still present. This is normal, don't judge these sensations; just allow them to be. Michael will see them and use his light to cleanse them.
10. Think of your breath as a connection to his light. Think of how every breath you take removes those negative sensations. Once they're gone, Michael's shield will be put in place, preventing them from returning again.
11. Allow your awareness to travel out of your body and into the space around you. Let it go higher and higher until it travels as far as it can go. Enjoy yourself floating in space.
12. The Archangel Michael removes energy blockages within your body, mind, and spirit. He will remind you that when you call upon him, he will come.
13. Allow yourself to fully feel Michael's protection, knowing that it will empower your overall health and wellbeing. Feel the release of this complete energetic renewal.
14. Visualize Michael's blue light shining onto you. He raises his arms and wings, the light of his power beaming onto you, channeling light, love, protection, and restoration.
15. Feel the light filling your entire being. See your chakras shine brighter. Any negative energy trapped in the chakras dissolves, facilitating healing processes in your energetic body.
16. Your body begins to feel free of tension and pain. New healing paths are opening up in your mind and soul. Feel empowered, free, and open to the truth and grace angelic blessings represent.
17. Embrace the gifts you've received. They might be intense, but they are very much needed. Michael placed a shield of protection onto you, your energy feeling surrounded and empowered by his protective and healing energies.
18. Take a moment to think about the messages you've received from Michael and slowly let go of your focus on your intention. Take a few deep breaths to return to your body and become aware of your physical sensations again.

Chapter 6: Banishing Negative Energy

Archangel Michael can be called upon to banish existing negative energies. This chapter is dedicated to practical methods you can use to expel negative energies from your body, mind, and spirit, your environment, your life, and the life of your loved ones. From asking for Michael's help during cleansing rituals to making banishing salt and sigils, there are plenty of ways this Archangel can help you eliminate unwanted influences from and around your energy field.

Cleansing Ritual to Banish Negative Energy

This cleansing ritual will help you banish negative energy from people, items, and your home or office space. It's a deep spiritual cleansing method recommended for first-time energetic sweeping and preparation for major rituals, ceremonies, and festivities. You can also use it when you feel overwhelmed by malicious energies and can't seem to move forward without banishing them.

Ingredients:
- 4 blue or red candles
- A lighter (avoid matches as they're made with sulfur, which is associated with evil spirits)
- Candle holder for each candle

- Incense (optional) – myrrh or frankincense work best for energetic purging

Instructions:

1. Find a place where you won't be disturbed. Turn off your phone. If you're doing this at home and have small children or pets, do this in a room away from them. If you stop the banishing process midway through, it won't work.

2. Focus on setting a strong state of mind so that you can keep going whatever happens. Keep in mind that depending on the strength of the negative energies you're dealing with, they might try to resist, and you have to be stronger than them.

3. Before you can meet Michael, set an intention of asking him to assist you so he knows what you are about to do and so that he can join you. If you wish, you can even pray to him or meditate with him the day before and share your intention and ask for his protection ahead of time.

4. Place the candles at the four corners of your space (depending on the area you want to cleanse). If you're purging your body, place them in the four corners of the space you'll be occupying during the ritual. If a corner has a closed space (like a closet), place a candle as close as possible. Keep the candles away from papers, drafts, curtains, and other safety hazards. The candles might spark due to the influences of the energies you're about to banish.

5. If you're cleansing your home, you'll light the candle nearest to the front door or the door you use most often first. Start with the candle closest to the door if you're cleaning a room. If you're cleansing yourself or an item, start with the one closest to your left or the left of the item you want to purify.

6. If you're using incense, light it before the candles. If not, move on to lighting the candles one by one. When you light the first one, recite the following prayer:

   "Archangel Michael, defend me in this battle

   When I am trying to protect myself against the wickedness,

   And eliminate evil influences from (whatever you're cleansing).

   I pray to you, Oh prince of the angels, by the power of the creator,

Help me banish the evil spirits who seek the ruin of my life and work."

7. Repeat the prayer two more times and call upon Michael, asking for his assistance in banishing the malevolent energies.
8. Moving in a counterclockwise direction, light the second candle. While you do, repeat the prayer from above three times. Generally, you would face toward the outer perimeter of the space because you want to expel negativity. However, if you want to banish negativity that causes disharmony among people in the space, face inward.
9. After each candle you light, repeat the prayer three times and make your request to Archangel Michael. Open a door or window when you reach the last candle and complete the last request.
10. If you're cleansing yourself or another person, you or they should stand as close to the door or window as possible. If you're cleansing an item, move it closer to the opened exit.
11. Making a sweeping gesture outward helps with dispelling the negative energy as quickly as possible. As you do, imagine all these influences as black or gray smoke, leaving the space/person/item you wish to cleanse. Then, say the following:

"In the name of Archangel Michael,

I sweep out all negative energy

and discord from my presence."

12. Repeat the line above nine times while continuing with the sweeping motion. Then, turn around, face inward, and say the following nine times:

"In the name of Archangel Michael,

May the banished energies be replaced,

With the power of angels

And other protective and benevolent spirits.

May Michael guide me in the future,

As I attempt to ward off negative and evil influences.

May this (space/person/item) be filled with divine light."

13. Allow the candles to burn down completely, but don't leave them unattended. Extinguish them whenever you can't stay near them.

Depending on the size of the candles you're using, they can take up to a week to burn down (even more if you're extinguishing them several times a day). Extinguish them only by snuffing them out. Never blow them, as this is insulting to the heavenly fire.

14. When relighting the candles, move again in a counterclockwise direction, saying the prayer from above once for each candle. This will recharge them with your original intentions.
15. After a successful cleansing, you'll notice that the atmosphere around the item, person, or space is lighter. They might have a light aura around them and are easier to use/get along with. You have a sense of peace and wellbeing whenever you're near the person/item/space you've purified.
16. If you don't notice any changes, you might still have some negative energies left over. In this case, you must repeat the ritual. Suppose your work involves regular encounters with evil influences. In that case, it's a good idea to regularly clean your tools, yourself, and your space.

If you can't light a candle in the space you want to purify, you can perform the ritual elsewhere. Writing the name of the unclean space on a piece of paper and under the candles is an excellent alternative to banish unwanted energies. Michael will still know where you want to enact the banishment and will help you do it effectively.

Evocation to Banish Evil

Archangel Michael is the best ally in warding off evil spiritual forces and dispelling them from yourself and your environment. Evil forces always threaten to overcome your soul, but Michael can help you fight them. By building a stronger connection with the Archangel, you'll always be able to keep those negative influences working tirelessly against you in check. This involves regular evocations for banishment. The following prayer is one of the best tools for this purpose.

Instructions:
1. In a secluded area, find a comfortable position and focus on your intention of invoking Archangel Michael to assist you.
2. Take a deep breath, and close your eyes to fully direct your attention to your task. Either aloud or in your mind, call out to Michael. Chant his name several times.

3. When you can see him in front of your mind's eyes, address him with this prayer:

"I welcome you, Archangel Michael, the heavenly host who stands in front of me.

Ready to assist me in my quest to fight the evil forces.

You who valiantly defend me against harm and destruction,

I earnestly entreat you to assist me also

in this painful and perilous conflict I have found myself in against my spiritual foe.

I ask you to join me, Archangel Michael, and allow me to fight courageously

And banish evil spirits, whom you have already overthrown,

and whom I can also completely overcome

Help me triumph over the enemy of my salvation,

May you be with me in all the battles I have yet to fight. "

Creating Banishing Salt

Banishing salt is a great way to spiritually cleanse your living or work environments. It is easy to make from ingredients you might already have in your kitchen pantry or get from a grocery store, and it can absorb any energy you channel into it. For example, you can ask Archangel Michael to enhance your salt recipe, making whatever work you use it for more effective. Most banishing salt recipes require a mixture of herbs (dry or fresh), essential oils, and some form of natural salt. The following recipe uses rosemary, lavender, and sea salt, all of which are known for their spiritually purifying effects.

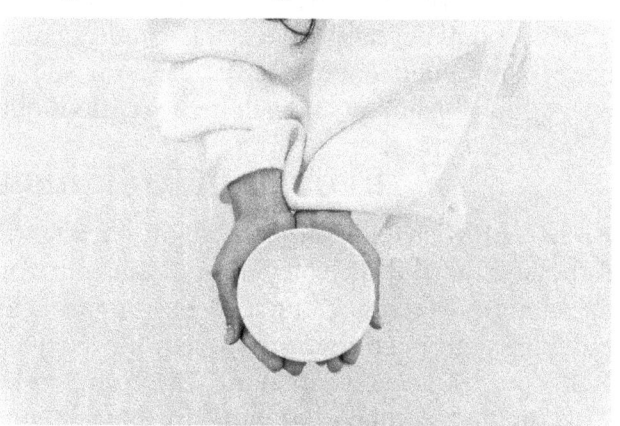

Banishing salt is used to cleanse your work or home.⁴⁹

As one of the world's oldest herbal cleansers, rosemary has been used to banish evil influences for several thousand years. Many cultures used it in combination with spiritual evocations, making it suitable for asking for Michael's assistance too. You can use it to cleanse your mind, body, and spirit, do consecration rituals, and release negative energies. Lavender can be used for similar purposes and to bring you peace, tranquility, happiness, and joy. These emotions empower your energies, allowing them to cleanse your entire being more effectively. Michael's protective powers can give you peace, but they can also amplify the soothing properties of lavender. He can also help you channel the herb's soothing properties for better focus during spiritual work. You can remain vigilant to protect yourself from negative influences and banish any that enter your space as soon as possible. Sea salt has a rejuvenating effect on your mind, body, and spirit. It can also purify your home and items you use for spiritual work. You can use banishing salts to remove unwanted energies from your home, an object, your body, or another person's body (in baths).

Ingredients:
- 1 fresh rosemary sprig (or a tablespoon of dried herb)
- 1 fresh lavender sprig (or a tablespoon of dried herb)
- 1 cup of rock sea salt
- 4 drops of frankincense essential oil
- 1 decorative bowl

Instructions:
1. Put the salt and the essential oil in a decorative bowl, and mix the two.
2. Sprinkle the herbs on top of the mixture but don't combine them.
3. Place the bowl in the area where you want to banish negativity from. Keep it in a safe place, away from children and pets. A great place to put it is a high shelf in the corner of the room.
4. If you want to banish negativity from an object, place the latter into the salt bowl and let it sit there for a while. It's best to do it overnight or eight hours before using the item.
5. When placing the bowl into its designed place, ask Michael to assist you with your intention. Call upon him and address him

with the following prayer:

"Archangel Michael, I ask that you enrich this salt with love and light,

So, I can use it to trap all the negative energy in this space/item/person

And banish it forever. Thank you!"

6. Allow the salt to attract the negative energies for some time. It acts as a magnet for evil, so depending on how much negativity is lurking around, this might take a few days.
7. If necessary, you can repeat the process by preparing a new mixture to trap even more negativity. Alternatively, you can place several small bowls around; this works faster in larger spaces.
8. If you're using salt to banish negativity from your body or another person's body, sprinkle it into the bath water and soak it for at least 30 minutes.
9. When the salt has had time to act, take it and toss it out of your home, along with the negativity. Make sure it leaves your environment to effectively banish unwanted energies.

Creating a Banishing Sigil

The sigil of Archangel Michael is a powerful symbol to use in banishing ceremonies and rituals. As with any sign associated with this angel, the sigil can be used to invoke him, communicate with him directly, and ask for any assistance you need. While plenty of Archangel Michael sigils are available for the best effects, creating one of your own is recommended. It takes some practice but isn't terribly hard to do. And once you master how to make it, you'll have a powerful tool for any ritual or spiritual exercises you might want to include Michael in. For example, you can use it when requesting protection from the Archangel. The sigil infused with Michael's power can be carved into objects and become a talisman for personal protection against evil forces. It can be etched into candles to empower any prayer, meditation, or invocation you use it for. You can draw it on a piece of paper and incorporate it into your work or make a large-scale copy of it and use it as a foundation for a crystal grid empowered by Archangel Michael.

Instructions:

1. Find and prepare (print out) a Rose Wheel symbol, preferably one without any modern additions. You can also draw one by copying one that suits your purposes. You'll also need the letters from the Hebrew version of Michael's name.

The rose wheel symbol.[50]

2. Mark the letters of Michael's name on the Rose Wheel and connect the points going from the first letter to the last (right to left). While you do this, focus on your intention, in this case, banishing negativity.

3. You've now created an Archangel Michael sigil infused with your intention. The next step is to prepare yourself and your space before using the sigil.

4. Take a cleansing bath and purify your space with incense or smudging. Now charge your sign with your energy by holding it close to your body and focusing on your intuition. This will activate it.

5. Next, you can pray, meditate, or simply prepare your sacred space by lighting a candle, placing crystals, or doing anything else you wish before summoning Michael.

6. Call Archangel Michael and ask him to help banish negativity from your life. If you have any questions on how to do it, ask them now. Listen to any messages you receive from the angel.
7. Follow the angel's advice. He will help you banish evil forces.

Deep Spiritual Cleansing with Archangel Michael

This spiritual cleansing and awakening ritual incorporates prayer for calling upon Archangel Michael and the enlightened beings working with him to free you from all negative energetic influences, clearing your aura and chakras from limitations and blockages caused by malicious energies. It can act against both known and unknown influences. For the best effects, repeat it for 21 consecutive days. Each day, you'll ask Archangel Michael to join you as you cleanse yourself from all negativities, and this will strengthen your bond with him.

Instructions:
1. Find a comfortable position in a place where you won't be disturbed for a few minutes. Close your eyes and take deep breaths until you can eliminate all unwanted thoughts from your mind and focus solely on your intuition.
2. Call on Archangel Michael by chanting his name three times aloud. When he arrives, recite the following prayer:

    "I appeal to you, Michael, to calm my fears,
    And eliminate the forces that interfere with my goals and life's purpose.
    I reach into my higher self and close my aura,
    Leaving my energies open to only you, Michael,
    I appeal to you to seal and protect my energies,
    Banishing all negativity from them."

3. Imagine your auric field surrounded by Michael's protective shield. Feel how it repels any energies coming from the outside. Reach into your higher self, and see yourself connecting with Michael's shield.
4. Once your higher self can tap into Michael's shield, bring your awareness to any unwanted energies lurking in your soul. Use your connection to the shield to banish these. See them leaving

your body as a dark cloud, pushed out from the bright light surrounding you.

5. Next, ask Michael to remove all the other unwanted spiritual influences he can detect. Remember, there are often far more negative energies hindering your spiritual growth than you are aware of at any given moment. Fortunately, Michael can remove even these energies.

6. Ask Michael to remove self-imposed limitations too. Then, request that he restores your energetic balance. Imagine him going over your chakras, restoring their functions, balancing your aura, and reinstating your natural psychic defenses.

7. Ask him to remove past influences, present disturbances, and possible future ones too. While he can't protect you from all the negativity you'll encounter in the future, he can banish the ones that have roots in the present.

8. He will infuse you with divine energy and free you from all those ties and associations that no longer serve you. By empowering you with the highest energy, he ensures that your energies will be working for the higher good and the good of your health and wellbeing.

9. Take a few moments to observe the sensations you feel in your body. You might feel warm, light, and happy. You might be elated and tired at the same time. However, you know that you're now free of the remnants of all unwanted energies, and your energy vibrates higher.

10. Through these higher vibrations, you can feel Michael's energy clearer than ever. Thank Michael, and dedicate your future work to honor him for this majestic blessing he has given you. Tell him that he is free to warn and assist you whenever you need spiritual cleansing in the future.

11. Slowly let the image of Michael fade, and your mind be filled with mundane thoughts as you return to the present moment. Take a few moments to feel your renewed energy and spiritual attunement and think about all the good you can do now that you're free of unwanted ties and evil influences.

Chapter 7: Crystals to Connect with Archangel Michael

In this chapter, you will understand what crystals are and how they work. You'll find out how they correspond with the chakra system and how you can use them to improve your overall wellbeing. This chapter also explains how you can use crystals to connect with Archangel Michael and ask for his support and guidance. Finally, you'll know which crystals to use when working with this higher power.

Crystals correspond with the chakra system, and you can use them to connect with Archangel Michael.[51]

What Are Crystals and How Do They Work?

If you're into alternative or holistic healing methods, you've likely heard of crystal healing before. Practitioners believe that when selected and used correctly, crystals can channel the healing energy of the surrounding environment. They can generate positive and revitalizing vibrations and improve your overall mental, emotional, physical, and spiritual state.

Each crystal uniquely impacts the mind, soul, and body, depending on its color and makeup. Each stone emits different vibrations based on its structure and the way that its atoms vibrate and interact with each other. Your body is an electromagnetic structure: energy not only flows throughout it, but it's also radiated and influenced by your thoughts, feelings, and spiritual wellbeing. As long as you don't suffer from an ailment that requires medical intervention, crystals offer an interesting and fun way to channel that energy toward better health.

Approximately 99.9% of all matter is empty space occupied by energy. It is everywhere around us. Inanimate objects like tables, books, phones, and of course, crystals are made of vibrating energy. Everything in the world, including humans and any other living being, has a unique vibrational frequency.

Think of vibrational frequency as a spectrum. People on the lower end are full of negative, unwanted emotions like anxiety and anger. They're often controlled by fear and can't see the positive aspects of life. People on the higher end, on the other hand, emit positivity, love, and compassion. They enjoy peace of mind and always see the cup half full.

Vibrational energies, however, are very volatile. If you have a high vibrational frequency today, this doesn't necessarily mean that you will in a month. Your vibrations fluctuate several times a day because your interactions with others influence them, the content you consume, the events that happen throughout the day, your memories, the news you receive, and so on.

Crystals, unlike humans, have a stable vibrational frequency. Their perfect, fixed, and repetitive geometric structures allow them to maintain their energy. The more stable a vibrational frequency is, the more powerful it is. Since vibrational frequencies can influence the energies around them, you can benefit from using a crystal's stable energy to influence your own.

Even though scientific studies don't back the effectiveness of crystal healing in curing physical ailments, crystals have been used to enhance people's wellbeing for millennia. There are accounts of ancient Egyptians, Greeks, Romans, Indians, and Chinese using crystals to protect themselves in potentially dangerous situations and to treat certain medical ailments. If it worked for past civilizations, then it's not crazy to think that it can help humans today.

Crystals can also help people through the power of color therapy. While there is no scientific evidence that color therapy can cure physical ailments, it can support mental health treatment. Each shade of color radiates rays that have a certain effect on people's bodily responses and, therefore, their behavior. This effect occurs because the sun, the main source of energy on Earth, emits all the colors of the rainbow. While this blend of colors results in white light, it's the only reason so many colors can be seen in the world. Like the sun, Gems have and emit energy and color, which is why they respond to light.

If you use a prism to look at the sun's rays, you'll see infrared and ultraviolet, which are invisible to the naked eye, along with the seven colors of the rainbow. These nine colors are the core energies of the solar system, and the eight planets and Pluto all resonate with them.

Each planet radiates a wavelength of colored light that matches the wavelength of the light emitted from its corresponding crystal. When placed near the body, the crystal absorbs these solar wavelengths and energies and radiates them into the body. This encourages the targeted chakra to become balanced, improving the individual's overall health.

Each color has unique qualities and affects a different aspect of your life. Purple, for instance, has a higher frequency than red. If you look up an image of the chakra system, you'll find that the crown chakra, which is the one with the highest vibrational frequency, is purple. Conversely, the root chakra, which has the lowest vibration, is red.

Each chakra and its corresponding color share vibrational frequencies, so you need to determine the physical, mental, or emotional symptoms you wish to fix or the areas in your life that you want to elevate. This will allow you to determine the responsible chakra and choose a crystal in the color that matches it. For example, if you struggle with self-expression, you might need to restore balance to your throat chakra. In that case, you'll work with sapphires. If you feel unstable in life or are struggling to overcome certain challenges, you should opt for red carnelian, for instance, to activate your root chakra.

There are 114 chakras, or energy centers, in the body. The most important and popular ones are these seven: the Root (Muladhara) Chakra, Sacral (Svadhisthana) Chakra, Solar Plexus (Manipura) Chakra, Heart (Anahata) Chakra, Throat (Visuddha) Chakra, Third Eye (Ajna) Chakra, and Crown (Sahasrara) Chakra. Each one is associated with different organs and spiritual, emotional, mental, and bodily functions.

Since the root chakra has the lowest vibrational frequency, it's associated with the basic elements of life. It is concerned with a person's sense of security and safety. Each chakra represents a deeper aspect of living than the previous one. Blockages or imbalances in the chakras can manifest as emotional dysregulation, mental issues, or physical ailments.

The Crystals to Use for Each Chakra

- **The Root Chakra**: It corresponds with the color red and represents the quality of being grounded and "rooted" in the Earth. It's also associated with a person's sense of safety, security, and survival.

  You can work with crystals like tourmaline, malachite, red carnelian, Smokey quartz, ruby, red tiger's eye, red calcite, hematite, red jasper, red quartz, and garnet.

- **The Sacral Chakra**: It's shown in orange and represents a person's energy or inclination to pursue pleasure, creativity, activity, procreation, and desire.

  It's associated with crystals like orange calcite, amber, tangerine quartz, goldstone, sunstone, bronzite, peach moonstone, orange selenite, and brecciated Jasper.

- **The Solar Plexus Chakra:** Its color is yellow, and it is associated with your confidence, inner wisdom, and assertiveness.

  Opt for crystals like citrine, tiger's eye, yellow jasper, heliodor, bumblebee jasper, rutilated quartz, pyrite, and yellow Aventurine.

- **The Heart Chakra:** Its color is green, and it is responsible for the love you express towards yourself and others.

  To work with the Heart Chakra, you need crystals like malachite, green opal, green aventurine, rhodonite, rose quartz,

pink tourmaline, prehnite, and amazonite.
- **The Throat Chakra:** It is blue and associated with a person's ability to kindly and clearly express their truth.

  Blue calcite, blue kyanite, blue lace agate, celestite, angelite, sodalite, aquamarine, turquoise, and aqua aura quartz are examples of crystals you can use.
- **The Third Eye Chakra:** Its color is indigo, and it's associated with intuition, memory, and imagination.

  Amethyst, lapis lazuli, lepidolite, iolite, labradorite, fluorite, and apatite are among the crystals you can use.
- **The Crown Chakra:** It is violet and associated with your consciousness and spiritual connection and transformation.

  You can work with crystals like moonstone, geode, amethyst, ametrine, clear quartz, howlite, lepidolite, scolecite, charoite, rainbow fluorite, Herkimer diamond, and danburite.

How These Crystals Can Help You Connect with Higher Powers

Thanks to their energetic properties, crystals can help people connect with spiritual realms and higher powers. Their makeup allows them to influence and interact with subdued energies. When you use the right crystals for each aspect of your life and work on balancing all your chakras, you can increase your vibrational frequency.

According to the law of attraction, you attract people and situations that align with your vibrational frequency. To interact with anyone around you, you must both have the same or at least similar frequencies. To connect with the spiritual realm, you must achieve a lighter, clearer, and higher vibrational frequency. This requires you to make several changes to your life, such as eliminating sources of negativity, maintaining a positive outlook, improving your sleep and diet, staying active, nourishing your mind and soul, and engaging in self-care.

While they might not be enough, especially if you're starting at a very low vibrational frequency, crystals can be a good place to start because they're energy amplifiers. As long as you have clear intentions, crystals can make connecting with the spiritual realm easier. However, for this to work, you need to keep your thoughts and feelings aligned with your intentions. If you wish to connect with Archangel Michael, you must clarify this intention at the beginning of your spiritual practice. Make it the focus of your session, know in your heart that it's possible, and keep your thoughts positive. If you feel or think that you won't succeed, this will likely block your manifestation.

Crystals also serve as symbolic representations of higher powers and spiritual entities. They have been incorporated into rituals and presented as offerings since the beginning of time. Each spiritual entity is associated with a crystal that represents the qualities and radiates the energy that they possess. Working with crystals that correspond with Archangel Michael can help you tune into his vibrational frequency and invoke some of his qualities. Crystals are also considered physical representations of the connection you have with higher powers. They help bridge the worldly and spiritual realms, reminding you that this interaction is possible.

How to Connect with Archangel Michael Using Crystals

There isn't a set of rules that you should follow when connecting with archangels or other spiritual entities. Spiritual connections are very personal and intuitive processes. While some tools and practices (such as using crystals) can facilitate the connection, you need to know that the interaction itself is built on your intentions, faith, intuition, beliefs, and alignment.

When working with Archangel Michael, it helps to choose crystals that resonate with his energy and align with your needs. If you can't find a crystal that serves both purposes, you should trust your intuition. Your mind, body, and consciousness know what they need and will lead you to the right choice. If you're unsure what to do, you can work with a crystal that traditionally represents Archangel Michael to invoke his energy and strengths and call on him for guidance.

You should also create a sacred space for your spiritual practices. Dedicate a comfortable and quiet spot in your home for all your connections with Archangel Michael. You can set up an altar or simply decorate a space with images of swords, feathers, scales, or other objects that represent him. Keep your chosen crystal on the altar or near you to facilitate your connection.

Set a clear intention to connect with Archangel Michael. You can practice breathing or other grounding or mindfulness exercises to maintain your focus if you're struggling with intrusive thoughts and feelings. Make sure that your intentions are true and genuine. You can verbally or mindfully state that you wish to connect with Archangel Michael to receive his support, guidance, or protection.

Get in a comfortable position and take a few deep breaths. Close your eyes and only start when you feel centered. Hold your chosen crystal or crystals close to your body. You can bring them close to your heart or third eye chakra to heighten your intuition.

Imagine a sphere of divine light growing around you and blessing you with positive feelings, compassion, and protection. Call on Archangel Michael out loud or in your head, inviting him into your space. Repeat your intention and state the reason you're invoking his presence.

Don't hesitate to repeat your words if you feel you should. Lean into your intuitions and be mentally and emotionally open to receiving any messages, new thoughts, revelations, or sensations during your meditation or prayer. You will likely feel a shift in your surrounding energy once he responds to your efforts. His guidance will likely manifest through your inner wisdom or knowledge.

Express your gratitude towards Archangel Michael once you're done with your spiritual practice. This will show him that you appreciate his guidance and strengthen your connection. Make sure to cleanse your crystal before and after all your spiritual practices using water, salt, sunlight, moonlight, or smudging techniques.

Crystals You Can Use

- **Clear Quartz**: Clear quartz is a multi-purpose, powerful crystal that you can use to charge and cleanse your other stones because it absorbs energy from the sun. Clear quartz is known for its healing properties, as it replenishes one's body and soul. This stone amplifies the energies of other crystals and intensifies people's thoughts and intentions, which enhances manifestation. It also makes it easier to connect with supernatural entities and get in touch with the spiritual realm since it can channel their energy. Carrying around this crystal will help you align with your thoughts and body. It can also bring peace and positive energy to your home if you keep it there.

- **Lapis Lazuli:** This deep blue crystal is speckled with flakes of gold. It's associated with Archangel Michael because of its color and can greatly support your spiritual practice. Working with lapis lazuli can activate your third eye chakra, allowing you to connect with your intuition and higher wisdom. This can make it easier to connect with Archangel Michael and other spiritual entities. Lapis lazuli enhances truthful communication within oneself and in social interactions. Working with this stone boosts an individual's self-awareness and encourages them to be honest and frank.
- **Sugilite:** This stone is very rare, expensive, and difficult to acquire. This mesmerizing stone comes in rich shades of purple. Not only is it beautiful to look at, but it also offers tremendous spiritual support. This makes it one of the most sought-after gemstones in the world. Sugilite helps people reach out to angels and spirit guides and protects against negative situations, thoughts, and feelings. This crystal releases energy blockages in the body, making it easier to attain a balanced chakra system. Working with this crystal gives you the emotional and mental clarity you need to overcome difficulties with ease. It dissipates stress and anxiety and helps you develop peace of mind. Sugilite can help you reap the benefits of your meditation practices, facilitate healing, and bring attention to helpful insights. As it can boost one's awareness of the spiritual realm, sugilite is a very valuable tool for those who wish to engage in astral travel.
- **Amber:** Even though it's a fossilized tree resin and not exactly a crystal, amber is effective in enhancing psychic powers and alleviating anxiety. It also attracts abundance and good fortune. Amber is considered a healing crystal because it encourages the body to regenerate and fosters passion and strength. Its protective and solar energies create a suitable environment for connecting with Archangel Michael, who is also associated with protection and guidance.
- **Golden Topaz:** Like amber, golden topaz is connected to the sun. Working with this shiny yellow crystal will boost your vitality and raise your vibration, creating the ideal environment for connecting with the archangel. This stone is also associated

with confidence, manifestation, and self-empowerment, which allows you to invoke some of the strengths and energies of Archangel Michael. Meditating with this stone can also benefit your physical health as it helps relieve fatigue, indigestion, and the symptoms of arthritis. You can use this stone to manifest prosperity, good fortune, and abundance and support your astral travel efforts.

- **Sapphire:** This vivid blue crystal is associated with Archangel Michael and can open a communication channel with him. Working with this stone allows you to strengthen your intuition and access higher levels of knowledge and wisdom. Sapphire enhances mental clarity and activates the third eye chakra, which allows people to tap into their psychic abilities and become more receptive to otherworldly messages and communications. You can invoke the protective energy of Archangel Michael by working with sapphire to receive his guidance and protect yourself from negative influences. This crystal also helps with verbal and energetic communication and expression, leading to fruitful connections with the angelic realm.

- **Sodalite:** This beautiful blue crystal is characterized by its white streaks. It encourages you to lean into the guidance of your inner compass and even boosts your intuition and psychic abilities. Working with sodalite makes you more spiritually insightful, which deepens your connection with Archangel Michael. This stone can make you a better communicator, improve your focus, and enhance your mental clarity. People who struggle with anxiety and overthinking can benefit from incorporating this crystal into their meditative and spiritual practices. Like sapphire, you can use sodalite to call on Archangel Michael's protective and guiding energy.

- **Apatite:** Apatite comes in several colors, such as blue, yellow, and green. It's known to be the crystal of motivation, inspiration, and manifestation. You can work with this stone to clear your throat chakra and improve your communication and self-expression skills. Apatite is also associated with the third eye chakra, which enhances intuition and psychic abilities. Apatite can help you get in touch with your inner strength and courage, which are some of the qualities that Archangel Michael embodies.

- **Kyanite:** This indigo stone is popular thanks to its high vibration. It also has energy-clearing qualities and corresponds with truth and balance. Kyanite is associated with spiritual connection and transformation, which means that it can help you enhance your communication with higher powers and the spiritual world.

Your intuition is the key to connecting with Archangel Michael or any other higher power. Your intentions need to be sincere and genuine. You should also truly believe in your ability to invoke the Archangel and receive his guidance. While true power comes from within, crystals can support and facilitate your connection by amplifying your intention and refining your vibrational frequency.

Chapter 8: Herbs and Essential Oils of Archangel Michael

This chapter explores what essential oils are and how they work. You'll learn how to use herbs and essential oils to improve your overall wellbeing and balance your chakra system. You'll find out which oils correspond to each chakra and the various techniques you can use to activate your energy centers.

By reading this chapter, you'll understand why essential oils are powerful additions to your spiritual practices. You'll know how to use them to align your vibrational frequencies with those of the spiritual realm. You'll also learn how to use essential oils to work with Archangel Michael and other spiritual entities. Finally, you'll come across a list of essential oils that you can use to connect with the Archangel and learn about their qualities, benefits, and properties.

What Are Essential Oils and How Do They Work?

Essential oils are extracted from leaves, roots, flowers, herbs, and other parts of plants. Pure essential oils capture the entire essence of the plant, resulting in a potent elixir. The compounds in essential oils have strong, energetic vibrations, which is what makes them capable of curing the mind, body, and soul. Depending on the plant from which it was derived, each essential oil has unique healing properties, aromas, purposes, and vibrations.

Essential oils can be used to connect with spirits.[52]

Herbs and essential plants have been used to treat physical ailments for thousands of years. Many people still reach for anise to relieve their cough or chamomile if they're having trouble falling asleep. However, most people don't know that you can use herbs and essential oils to connect with spiritual entities and receive their guidance.

Each essential oil is characterized by certain strengths, qualities, and biological compounds that are associated with certain angelic energies. Just like Sapphire, for example, allows you to invoke some of Archangel Michael's strengths, the energetic frequency in Frankincense allows you to call on him for support. Over millennia of experimenting and examining the qualities of each essential oil, people started associating certain essential oils with specific Archangels.

Essential oils play an extensive role in spiritual practices. From serving as purifying and cleansing oils for your space and body to bridging between the physical and spiritual realms, essential oils are indispensable tools for spiritual growth and development. You can reap the full benefits of your meditations by incorporating aromatherapy into your practice or manifest your desires by setting clear intentions while using them as ointments.

Like crystals, essential oils have constant and stable vibrations. Most of them are characterized by their high vibrational frequencies and their light essence. Using them regularly allows you to influence your vibrations, gradually aligning them with the resonance of the vibrational realm.

Essential Oils and the Chakra System

While you can drink herbs or use tinctures to target certain ailments, you can enhance your overall wellbeing by using essential oils to balance your entire chakra system. Each chakra corresponds with a specific set of essential oils. You can create a schedule that allows you to work on each chakra on its own, starting from the root chakra and working your way up to the crown chakra. You can also determine your needs and areas in life you need to elevate, identify the chakras you need to balance, and work with the corresponding essential oils.

- **The Root Chakra:** Black pepper, vetiver, frankincense, patchouli, cedarwood, spikenard, and sandalwood
- **The Sacral Chakra:** Ylang-ylang, clary sage, orange, jasmine, rosewood, bergamot, neroli, and fennel
- **The Solar Plexus Chakra:** Lemongrass, ginger, clove, cinnamon, coriander, juniper, rosemary, grapefruit, mandarin, and roman chamomile
- **The Heart Chakra:** Rose, melissa, everlasting, eucalyptus, jasmine, yarrow, lemon, and marjoram
- **The Throat Chakra:** Geranium, jasmine, tea tree, peppermint, sage, frankincense, cypress, and clove
- **The Third Eye Chakra:** Palo santo, clary sage, rose, chamomile, bay laurel, carrot seed, jasmine, and geranium
- **The Crown Chakra:** Lotus, helichrysum, sandalwood, spikenard, cedarwood, benzoin, frankincense, and vetiver

Aromatherapy is one of the most effective ways of using essential oils. You can either inhale the aroma from the bottle or add a few drops to a diffuser. Diffusers are great because they purify your space and allow you to inhale the aroma for longer periods. The tiny molecules that you inhale will influence your energy flow and enhance your thoughts and feelings.

You can also use jojoba, coconut, or any other carrier oil to dilute your essential oil before applying it to the targeted chakra center.

Massage your skin in a clockwise direction, close your eyes, and imagine that the chakra is activating and falling into balance. Make sure to test your skin for allergies or sensitivity before using each essential oil.

You can also add a few drops of the selected essential oil to your bath or on your washcloth as you shower. Bring your attention toward the chakra that you're targeting as you relax. Think about the qualities and the aroma of the essential oil and how it's contributing to your general health.

Incorporate essential oils into your regular meditation, visualization, or other mindfulness practices. Choose a comfortable and quiet space to practice, and add a few drops of essential oil to your diffuser. Visualize the chakra in a perfectly balanced, luminous state. Make it the center of your attention throughout the mindfulness session.

You should set a clear intention regardless of the method you choose. Maintain your focus on the chakra with which you are working and avoid engaging with any intrusive thoughts. You can engage in breathwork or grounding techniques before you start your practice to clear your mind and be fully present.

Keep in mind that essential oils alone aren't sufficient to balance your chakras and improve your health. You need to consult with a healthcare professional if you struggle with any medical or mental health issues. Essential oils are most effective when implemented into a holistic treatment program. Prioritize self-care, eat a healthy and balanced diet, get enough quality sleep, exercise regularly, get rid of unhealthy habits, and partake in uplifting activities.

Using Essential Oils to Work with Archangel Michael

You can use essential oils to work with any Archangel you want. To make the most of your practice, you must start by exploring the unique qualities, attributes, and roles of the archangel with whom you wish to connect. Explore their energy and understand what it would feel like to be in their presence.

Archangel Michael is usually portrayed as a defender and a warrior, which means that he's strong, courageous, and powerful. People usually call on him for his protective and supportive energies. Archangel Michael is also the leader of the angels and can help people overcome their fears and challenges. Identifying what Archangel Michael can help you with and the aspects of your life in which he can offer assistance will allow you to establish a meaningful connection.

You should consider the chakras you wish to balance and the qualities of your targeted Archangel when choosing essential oils. In most cases, you'll find a few fulfill both purposes. In that case, you should lean into your intuition when making your final decision. You can alternate between various essential oils and different application methods, but you should focus on a specific intention.

Using essential oils that align with Archangel Michael's qualities and energy will strengthen your connection and facilitate the invocation process. You should generally opt for essential oils that are associated with protection, reassurance, higher consciousness, and purification.

If you wish to establish a relationship with a higher power, you want to make your space as conducive to their presence as possible. Choose a quiet, comfortable, distraction-free space to dedicate to your spiritual endeavors. Cleanse the space by burning or smudging purifying herbs like sage or palo santo. This will help you get rid of negative energies and protect yourself and your space before you enter the spiritual realm. You can set up an altar and decorate the space with objects, crystals, and symbols associated with Archangel Michael to anchor your intention.

You should always start any spiritual practice by setting a clear intention. Get in a comfortable position and practice mindfulness techniques to clear your thoughts. Focus on your desire, close your eyes, and center yourself. Once you're ready, call upon Archangel Michael, either verbally or mentally. Explain that you wish to connect with him and that you're seeking his support, guidance, and protection. Keep your mind and heart open to any signs. Trust that they've successfully received and responded to your request. Trust your intuition and feel the slightest shift in the surrounding energy.

Essential oils can serve as physical and symbolic anchors for your intention. They can help you foster a deeper connection with the archangel. Use a carrier oil to dilute the essential oil before applying it to specific points of your body, such as the heart chakra, your temples, or your inner wrists. You can also rub it in a clockwise direction onto the chakra that you wish to work with. Imagine that a bridge has been formed, connecting you with Archangel Michael. Think about the qualities that you wish to invoke while inhaling the aroma.

Perform a meditation practice that puts your mind and body at ease. This will help you release the mental, physical, and emotional blocks that hinder this connection. Drop your shoulders, relax your jaws, and let go of the tension in your body. Close your eyes and imagine that you're surrounded by protective, supportive, and compassionate energy. This shield of energy glows in blue light, representing the presence of Archangel Michael. Imagine that you inhale some of this energy with each breath you take. Visualize it filling and blessing your body, giving you strength, peace, and wisdom. You can communicate your thoughts and feelings and express your gratitude toward the archangel during the meditation. Keep your mind and heart open to receive any messages that he might deliver.

Praying to the Archangel can facilitate the connection and strengthen your relationship with him. You can either recite prayers out loud or in your head. You can look up prayers dedicated to Archangel Michael or allow your intuition to guide you as you create your own. You can simply express your desires and explain your struggles to the Archangel. Thank him for taking the time to listen, offer his help, and be clear about your intentions. You can also repeat affirmations that embody the protection, courage, strength, and other qualities of the archangel. Make sure you can inhale the aroma of the essential oil throughout your practice.

Express your gratitude after you've completed the practice and slowly bring yourself back to the present moment. Communicate that you're willing to get in touch with him again and consistently work on strengthening your bond. Thoroughly reflect on your spiritual experience and anything unusual you might have noticed. Journal about any messages you received, insights you've made, or thoughts and feelings that surfaced during the practice. Think about how Archangel Michael's presence and guidance resonate with certain aspects of your life.

What steps can you take to incorporate his guidance and insights into your life? What would you change about this practice the next time you connect with the archangel? Is there anything that you haven't gained clarity about?

Essential Oils to Connect with Archangel Michael

Angelica

This essential oil's name is derived from the word "angel" because it has high vibrational frequencies. Incorporating it into your spiritual and meditative practices will give you strength, make you more focused, enhance your stamina and comfort, and allow you to feel grounded. You can use it if you wish to manifest spiritual support, healing, and bravery and ask for Archangel Michael's protection.

Basil

This essential oil is ideal if you wish to balance your chakra system and encourage your mind, body, and soul to fall into alignment. You should use it if you feel like you have fallen out of touch with your environment and reality and need help guiding your attention toward the bigger picture. Working with Basil reminds you of your soul's purpose and spiritual essence. It bridges between mundane and spiritual realities. This oil encourages better self and spiritual awareness, a deeper understanding of physical and otherworldly realities, and intuitive awakening.

Cinnamon

Work with cinnamon essential oil if you're struggling with negative thoughts and feelings. It will help you manifest positivity and happiness and subdue anxiety, stress, and sadness. Use Cinnamon essential oil when you feel like you're less compassionate and giving than usual or haven't been able to express your love and gratitude toward others. Cinnamon oil will deepen your self-compassion and remind you that you're worthy and loved, as well.

Geranium or Rose Geranium

Many people underestimate the importance of acknowledging and comforting their inner child. This part of humans never falters, no matter how old they grow. Growing up, you might have encountered emotionally unsettling experiences that affect you to this day. Mental and emotional issues can keep you stuck in a low vibrational frequency, hindering your ability to effectively engage in spiritual practices and connect with otherworldly entities. You must get in touch with your inner child to resolve any emotional or mental issues caused by your past.

Geranium essential oil can help you connect with your inner child to release any emotional or mental blockages you are dealing with. This oil must be used and handled cautiously because it might trigger heavy emotional responses. Incorporating it into your practices facilitates your ability to call on Archangel Michael for reassurance and comfort. It will also give you insight into potential opportunities and risks you might encounter. The fact that this oil has a subtle, flowery, and sweet aroma is also a plus.

Sandalwood

Sandalwood essential oil can generally assist your spiritual endeavors. It helps you when entering meditative or trance states, which makes it easier to connect with higher energetic vibrations and reach out to your higher self. Sandalwood also encourages understanding and strengthens your bond with the rest of humanity. It allows you to feel present in both physical and spiritual worlds. Sandalwood essential oil also helps create a conducive environment for prayer, rituals, groundwork, and meditation.

Frankincense

This essential oil is a great addition to psychic or spiritual work, especially if you're still a beginner. Frankincense is a protective essential oil that will prevent you from entering mental states or energetic frequencies that you're not ready to deal with yet. It also strips negative energies away from users, allowing them to enhance their spiritual frequency and gradually preparing them for higher and more profound connections. It's naturally aligned with otherworldly matters, making it the go-to aroma for calling for Archangel Michael's help. Frankincense is also effective for expressing your gratitude toward spiritual entities and sending them your prayers. This essential oil leads to better emotional regulation and compassion. It makes you more understanding of others and accepting of your environment.

Myrrh

Myrrh essential oil delves into the inner workings of the soul and the human psyche, where countless emotional and mental challenges exist. Nothing pulls you back as holding onto situations that are out of your control, regrets, and emotional wounds. Working with myrrh, however, gives you the strength you need to move on and forgive yourself and others. It offers the inner peace and sense of calm you need to approach decisions with clarity and untie the knots in your mind, heart, and soul. This essential oil helps you physically relax and unwind, as well. Resting your body is essential if you wish to make material, emotional, mental, and spiritual progress. Like frankincense, myrrh fosters compassion, acceptance, and compassion. Use it in your meditations to facilitate spiritual enlightenment and nurture your psychic abilities.

Orange

This oil revitalizes the mind, spirit, and soul. It makes your heart full and happy. Orange essential oil has an energizing essence that encourages transformation and regeneration. Using it regularly in your aromatherapy can help you overcome your obsessions and fears. Those working in creative and innovative fields can benefit from this aroma because it boosts your imagination and unleashes your creative skills. Orange essential oil also brings the joyful and inspiring presence of Archangel Michael into your daily life.

Rosemary

Reach for essential rosemary oil if you feel lost on your spiritual journey. It can bring your attention to knowledge and insights you have overlooked and will remind you of the very essence of your being. Rosemary keeps you grounded and cognizant that you're ultimately a spiritual being inhabiting a physical body to explore, enjoy, and learn from mundane experiences. It is an all-purpose oil that purifies your body and space and invokes the healing, protective, guiding, and compassionate nature of the angels.

Peppermint

This essential oil can push your spirit toward opportunities for deeper understanding. Working with it, you'll learn to appreciate everything in your life and recognize that everything happens for a purpose. Peppermint teaches you to patiently wait for the truth to unfold. This essential oil has a soothing effect on the mind and body. It keeps negative thoughts at bay while uplifting your overall aura. Peppermint aromatherapy makes you more perceptive and receptive. It makes you more sensitive to angelic messages and connection attempts. Use this oil to improve your self-awareness and alertness, even in your unconscious mental states. This will allow you to expand your knowledge and reflect on the wisdom you acquire from the spiritual realm.

Essential oils are among the most powerful and effective tools you can use to enhance your spiritual practices. You can experience substantial spiritual growth and development if you learn how to carefully select the right essential oils for your needs, set clear intentions for invocation, and use them correctly for their intended purpose. While you can't rely on essential oils to transform your overall health and wellbeing, you can use them to support your holistic self-care routine. Make sure to test for sensitivity and allergies before you apply them to your skin.

Chapter 9: Daily Rituals

Due to their far-reaching power, the abilities of Archangels reach all of humanity and every last individual life. Though Michael isn't a personal guardian angel, he is always available to aid you in any way necessary, regardless of the circumstance. He is a high-frequency being of light and energy, capable of supporting you at any time. However, asking him for help whenever needed and expressing your gratitude for his blessings aren't the only ways to form a connection with him. To build a deeper bond, you must nurture it through daily practices. Remember, he is there to watch over you. But he won't intervene unless he really needs to.

To work with him regularly, you must maintain an active line of communication between the two of you. Even dedicating 5-10 minutes a day to this purpose is enough. You can ask Michael to be with you, sit with you, or accompany you when you're spending time with your friends and family. It doesn't just have to be for healing, guidance, or warding off negative energies either. You can invoke him to keep you and your loved ones company. He is a protector. He will be happy to spend time looking over everyone you ask him to. Through this process, you will develop your connection with him, get to know him better, and hone your intuition to better decipher his messages. This final chapter provides some useful tips and rituals for connecting with Archangel Michael, like prayers, meditations, and wearing items associated with him.

Morning Affirmations with Archangel Michael

Archangel Michael is there to support your experience from the time you wake up until you fall asleep and sometimes even after. However, your mind is freshest and most relaxed right when you wake up after a good night's sleep, so this is the best time to address Michael. You can ask him to bless you with his protective light and love or guide you through your day if you're expecting to run into some challenges.

Here is an affirmation that will help you invoke Michael's energy and feel his presence throughout your day:

"I feel blessed by the Archangel Michael's love and light.

I feel the loving presence of Michael watching over me.

Today, I ask for guidance and the courage to act on it.

I seek harmony and peace to fill my life and to follow me throughout my day.

Today, I ask for guidance in making better choices,

So, I can become and express the best version of myself.

I thank you, Michael, for accompanying me throughout this day."

As you say this affirmation day after day, you'll feel your bond with Archangel Michael growing, getting more formidable, and filled with light. Your intuition will grow, allowing you to gain greater awareness of his presence and trust in the guidance he provides. When you ask him to accompany you, do it with a positive mindset and knowing that he will fully be there. Your mornings might be hectic, but Michael will be there to help. He will ensure that you're filled with serenity and joy and that you know you have the power to take control of the chaos.

Morning Healing with Archangel Michael

One of the main prerequisites of having a healthy mind is having a healthy body. For this, you'll need a good night's sleep to avoid rushing and have a great start to your day. When you wake up, make time for a healthy routine and a ritual dedicated to Archangel Michael. Whether you go for a healthy breakfast or a vitalizing lemon water, you can simply ask the Archangel to bless it for you. Just hold it in front of you, and ask him to purify it. Imagine him cleansing it with his light. This way, you can take advantage of its health benefits even more. It will nourish every cell in your body with positive energy, keeping your health and overall wellbeing in check.

Greeting the Sun

Greeting the sun is another empowering way to invoke Michael's energy, as he is associated with its nurturing warmth.

This is how easy it is to make this your morning ritual:

1. As you rise from your bed, turn towards the window (open it if it's closed and the weather permits). Or better yet, walk outside to your balcony or garden.
2. Look up to the sky (not directly into the sun), and say the following:

    "I greet you, Archangel Michael, the ruler of the magnificent sun.
    The Chief of Archangels and the Prince of Heavenly Army.
    May your light shine on me today,
    As the sun does this morning."
3. Feel the sun's energy permeating through your body.
4. Ask Michael for guidance or protection by sending out a silent request to him or by simply making it your intention for the day.
5. Thank the Archangel and return to your preparation for the day.

Archangel Michael Tea Ritual

What better way to honor Archangel Michael on a Sunday afternoon than with an invigorating cup of tea? You can use flowers or herbs associated with him or any special blend that makes you feel empowered every time you drink it.

Instructions:

1. Make your tea and ask Archangel Michael to bless it.
2. Light incense that makes you feel at peace and grounded. There are ready-made tea blends you can buy, but the ones you make yourself will have a much more powerful effect.
3. Thank Michael in advance for his guidance and blessings.
4. Drinking tea enriched with his light will help you get in touch with your higher self, listen to your intention, and become aware of angelic messages you might receive in the near future.

Daily Grounding Meditation

Take five minutes and do a healing breath meditation with Archangel Michael. He has incredibly restorative effects on your mind, body, and spirit. Whether you need empowerment to heal from a trauma or want to remain healthy, Michael can help you achieve your goals. You can do this at any time of the day.

Instructions:
1. Find a comfortable position in a secluded spot.
2. Have some soft music playing in the background, or enjoy the serenity of silence, whichever you prefer.
3. Ask Archangel Michael to release any energetic blocks you have.
4. Become aware of the sensation of the air going in and out of your nose for five minutes.
5. Any time your mind starts to wander while you're focusing on your breath, simply bring it back to the sensation of cool air going in and warmer air flowing out of your lungs.
6. End the meditation by thanking Michael and bringing yourself back to the room.
7. Enjoy having a clear head as you make or set in motion your plans for the day.

Goal Setting Ritual

The best way to ensure that you'll be able to stick to your goals is to set them while Archangel Michael is guiding you. He can help you set goals that contribute to your life's goals, making it easier to accomplish them regardless of the obstacles you might encounter along the way. Whenever you want to determine short or long-term targets, think of Archangel Michael, and invoke him silently. Whether it's a to-do list for the day or week or landing a promotion, it will be much easier to remain disciplined until you reach the goal if you know that Michael is there to guide and protect you through the process. Alternatively, you can summon him to empower your daily workouts as part of your healing journey.

Guidance Ritual

You'll find the following ritual helpful if you want to receive guidance from Archangel Michael. For example, you can ask him to help you protect yourself and others, release you from fear and unwanted ties, or even discover the truth behind something.

Instructions:

1. Walk for at least 15 minutes, preferably outdoors, where you can be closer to nature. During that time, think about everything you're thankful for in your life. This could be as simple as feeling the sunlight on your cheeks that morning, the smell of fresh air, the chirping of birds, or something as touching as the warm smile of your loved ones.

2. Return home, find a comfortable chair, and sit with your feet touching the ground. Then, close your eyes, and go over the list of blessings that you felt grateful for during your walk.

3. Have a clear picture of these blessings in your mind. Now, set the intention of calling upon Archangel Michael. Ask him for his approval before you proceed. There's a strong chance you will receive advice on changing the course of your thoughts at this point. If you do, listen to it, and act accordingly.

4. When you feel you can proceed, Take a few slow, deep breaths before exhaling slowly. Then, address Michael with the following words:

   "Blessed Archangel Michael

   I am grateful for all the blessings in my life.

   Thank you for your guidance, healing, and love.

   I ask you to join me now, as I need your help again."

5. Pause for a minute. If you've felt the Archangel's supporting presence, you can continue. Otherwise, repeat your request as many times as necessary.

6. Don't worry if you don't receive a response right away. If you've expressed your concern clearly enough, Michael will know how and when to help you. His help might come when you least expect it, so be prepared to receive a message from him at any point throughout the day. For example, if you performed this ritual before going to bed, you might receive a sign from him in

the morning or in your dreams.
7. Finish the ritual by thanking Archangel Michael for his guidance and support.

Heart Chakra Meditation

Chakra meditation doesn't need to be a deep, all-consuming exercise. Simply taking a few minutes to raise your awareness of your chakras and their energy once a day will do wonders in keeping your mind, body, and soul healthy. This will be particularly effective if you do it with Archangel Michael's help.

Instructions:
1. Sit or lie down in a place where you won't be disturbed and bring awareness of your connection to Archangel Michael.
2. Close your eyes, and take a deep breath. Make an *"Aaah"* sound as you release your breath. Repeat until you feel a vibration in the middle of your chest.
3. When you do, you'll know that the energy has touched your heart chakra, the center of compassion and love.
4. Once you feel your heart chakra vibrating at a higher frequency, take three deep breaths and continue saying, *"Aaah,"* as you exhale.
5. At the same time, visualize the energy filling your body through your heart chakra until you feel filled with divine love.
6. Visualize Archangel Michael standing tall in front of you with his flaming blue sword by his side. Once you can feel his presence by your side, forget about your breathing, and start talking to him.
7. Tell Michael everything you want to communicate to him at that moment, even if it's only gratitude for his blessings.
8. When you're done, thank the Archangel for joining you, let his image go, and slowly return to your present.

Wearing Items Associated with Archangel Michael

Michael is often depicted wearing a blue cloak or with his body and sword surrounded by an electric blue flame emanating divine energy. This alludes to Michael's association with the color blue, which you can use to honor him in your daily life. You can wear blue, purple, and red; these colors represent Michael's power, loving protection, and compassion, respectively. As you put on the clothes you'll wear in his honor, invoke his guidance and love. This will be particularly effective if you plan to wear those clothes to do something important, like a job interview. Michael supports your core beliefs, and by being represented through his colors, he will be part of any conversations you have about your values. He won't let intimidation, doubt, and fear hinder you, whether it's coming from you or others. You can also wear talismans and charms, symbolizing Michael's energy.

That said, you do not necessarily have to wear anything associated with Michael to harness the angel's powers. Sometimes, all it takes is to envision them on or around you. For example, when you feel surrounded by negative energy, you can quickly imagine yourself being enveloped by Michael's blue cloak, and you will sense the negativity dissipating.

If you want to ward off negativity and illness from your home, imagine little swords cutting the cord of negativity and chasing away ailments. Everyone and everything inside your home will be protected, and all you did to make that happen was invoke Michael's power for 5-10 minutes a day. Are you struggling with fears or phobias you desperately wish to overcome? Just imagine Michael standing beside you, telling you that you can overcome everything. For example, if you have a fear of public speaking, you can practice speaking while holding a feather and standing in front of the mirror for 5-10 minutes every day. While you do this, just focus on Michael's energy empowering you.

Using Archangel Michael Talismans

If you're looking for a more hands-on daily ritual to honor Archangel Michael, the following one might be right for you. It incorporates gemstones and items associated with this angel. Depending on your purpose, use any of the colors corresponding to Michael, from blue to purple to red. Alternatively, you can use yellow or gold (to represent him as the governor of the sun) or white (to simply invoke universal divine power).

Instructions:
1. Make yourself comfortable, close your eyes, and take the item or items that you've chosen to use into your hands.

2. Take 3-5 slow, deep breaths, and then ask Archangel Michael to join you. If you're using more than one item, repeat this for each one.
3. Focus on the sensations you have when holding the item(s). You might notice a difference in their energies. Or, you might become aware that the angel is with you by feeling a warm, tingling sensation all over your body.
4. If you don't feel any feedback, try again. If nothing happens right away, don't worry. You might receive a message later on that day or the next one.

Thanking Archangel Michael

As part of your daily ritual to honor him, you should take a few minutes to thank Archangel Michael for all his blessings. You don't need to have any specific reason to summon him. You can reach out and thank him for the challenges he helped you overcome. For example, before going to bed, you can say:

"Thank you, Archangel Michael, for keeping me safe today.

Thank you for making me feel protected,

And bring me inner peace at the end of this day."

Imagining Archangel Michael Dispel Evil Influences

Suppose you ever feel troubled by negative energetic influences throughout your day. In that case, you can ask Archangel Michael to help you dispel them. Do this before going to bed; the angel will work for you overnight, allowing you to wake up free of negativity the following day.

Instructions:
1. Light a candle, sit in front of it, and close your eyes.
2. In your mind's eye, imagine Archangel Michael holding his sword, reaching out to you. See him cutting away negativity from your life, giving you the strength and protection you need.
3. Next, picture him catching all that negativity he cut out from your life in a white net, trapping it forever so it would return to your side.
4. Take a deep breath, release it, and you'll feel lighter.

5. Thank Archangel Michael, snuff out the candle, and go to bed.

Ask Archangel Michael for Help

You can ask Archangel Michael for help with anything you struggle with; he will be happy to help you. It's an effective morning or evening ritual for warding off any fears keeping you from living your life to the fullest. Keep in mind that the help might come in unexpected ways (like him staying away and sending encouragement to ensure you can do it on your own), but he will always empower you spiritually.

Instructions:
1. Find a secluded space to address Michael. Invoke him by chanting his name either aloud or silently in your mind.
2. Then, ask him whatever you wish to request. This can be as simple as granting you a safe journey on your vacation or business trip, helping you conduct an emotionally challenging conversion with your loved one, or keeping you and anyone you cherish safe during a storm.
3. Thank Michael for his assistance in advance, and continue with your daily activities.

Journaling with Archangel Michael

Journaling is another highly effective way of maintaining your connection with Archangel Michael. By thinking about what you wish to say, you're already focusing your energies on your bond with him. By writing it down, you're creating a tangible record of your connection to him. While he doesn't need to see your words, they will help you see your progress as your bond develops and you learn to work with him effectively. With enough practice, you might even notice Michael answering you while you're still writing your message, which will establish an active line of communication.

Instructions:
1. Take your journal and find a quiet place where you can focus on what you wish to write. You can pen down any request for resolving problems involving you or someone close to you. Or, you can simply note down what is on your mind. This is an excellent exercise for the night as it helps you organize and calm your thoughts, so they won't bother you during the night.

2. Sit straight, with your shoulders relaxed and your feet planted firmly on the round. This will help you feel grounded and close to nature. There is no faster way to connect to Michael than to the universal energy of nature that courses through all beings.
3. Take a few deep breaths. When you feel your energy settling down and your mind centering around your intention, continue.
4. Ask Archangel Michael to join you and start writing. Make sure to address him as a friend while you write. Don't worry about whether your writing makes sense, is in chronological order, or is grammatically correct. The goal is to clarify any problems you might have and resolve them with Michael's help.
5. Finish your thoughts by thanking Michael for reading your messages. Close your eyes and light a candle. Think about your inquiry, feel free to say anything else you wish Michael to know, and then snuff out the candle flame.
6. As you watch the candle smoke, carry your message to Michael, thank him again, and go to bed. You can be sure you'll hear back from Archangel Michael when the time is right.

Bonus: Correspondences Sheet

This bonus chapter includes all the correspondences associated with Archangel Michael.

The Day of the Week

Given his association with the Sun, Michael's corresponding day of the week is Sunday. This is the day when his powers are the greatest and when it's best to invoke him. Depending on your preferences, you can honor him on Sundays with prayers, meditations, and rituals dedicated to him or any intention he can assist you with. On Sundays, Michael can help you face painful truths, protect yourself from harmful influences and heal yourself through rest and spiritual elevation.

Festivals and Feasts

There are several days of the year associated with Michael. One of the most prominent is Michaelmas, a feast celebrated on the 29th of September in the Western part of the world. This tradition originates from Phrygia, Turkey. The Roman Catholic Church celebrates Archangel Michael on the 8th of May, the day known as the Apparition of St. Michael. According to ancient lore, St. Michael appeared on Mount Gargano in 492. The place has become a medieval pilgrimage site, and the feast of the apparition was born. The Eastern Orthodox Church honors the Archangel as St. Michael on the 8th of November. Meanwhile, the Ethiopian Orthodox Tewahedo Church commemorates this angel on the 12th of each month.

Zodiac Signs

Archangel Michael is the ruler of Leo, the zodiac sign embodying the characteristics of those born under the rule of the Sun. Leos are known for their excellent communication skills and a powerful drive to protect and help those in need. Inspired by Michael, those born under the sign of Leo have no trouble uncovering hidden truths and are in constant pursuit of knowledge that can help them improve themselves. They're always open to new ideas and capable of acknowledging other peoples' beliefs and values, just as Archangel Michael accepts the opinions of anyone willing to work with him. A typical Leo won't judge and demands the same from those around them.

Michael gives Leos an incredible ability to focus and persevere, organize their lives, and use these skills to earn recognition. Because their efforts are often recognized, Leos learn to thrive on success and will always seek to be in the limelight. They are prepared to give the very best of themselves to obtain credit and acclaim. Empowered by Archangel Michael, a Leo will always stand out from the competition. While they often only seek individual success, they will remain generous toward those who helped them.

Michael teaches Leos how to nurture loyalty, love, and compassion, making them warm and sincere individuals who are never afraid to show affection, just as Michael isn't afraid to show love toward his devotees. He also gives Leos self-assurance, allowing them to believe they can overcome any obstacle they face.

In some cases, Leos can be overly proud and egotistical. They might gravitate towards extravagant gestures and showing off their accomplishments before realizing the error of their ways.

Planets

Sun

Out of all the planetary bodies, Archangel Michael is primarily associated with the Sun. In astrology, the Sun determines the most prominent characteristics of each zodiac sign. Under Michael's influence, the Sun helps each sign develop its most basic identity. This forms a person's core identity, the inner place all your personality traits are centered around.

The Sun also determines characteristics like dignity, authority, ambition, resilience towards prejudice, self-awareness, non-conformity, and staying true to your values. To prevent these traits from turning into an overwhelming desire for power, inability to accept other peoples' ideas, lack of will, intolerance towards rules, pride, self-centeredness, and recklessness, Michael (through the Sun) keeps people on the right track. He nurtures people's positive traits, just as the Sun nurtures life on Earth.

Mercury

Mercury is the planet of communication, something at which Archangel Michael excels. He isn't afraid to voice his opinion or stand up for those who can't do the same. Those affected by Mercury can also experience some of Michael's influence when trying to express their desires and their inner world. It also helps develop one's ability to maximize consciousness when learning to discern and correctly interpret reality. Mercury is linked to traits like ingenuity, impartiality, multitasking, adaptability, and the ability to put spiritual exercises into practice. It promotes the union between one's personality and the spiritual realm.

Mars

The red planet, as Mars is known, corresponds to traits like commitment to self-improvement and the ability to overcome obstacles and fears that might hinder your progress and keep you stuck in an undesirable position. These are all characteristics bestowed by Archangel Michael, who ensures you learn how to dissolve everything that stagnates inside and prevents you from becoming the best version of yourself. Under Michael's influence, Mars can bring rapid changes, but it all goes in the right direction. Those affected by this planet often have a sudden urge to start working toward self-realization after fully grasping their present situations and acknowledging that they're stuck. They often switch into a higher gear, empowered by the truth and their ability to nurture their own spiritual strength.

Earth

Due to his ability to nurture life on Earth, Archangel Michael is also associated with it. Representing a symbol of Earth can be a great way of empowering one's connection with nature and the birthplace of humanity.

Angel Number

While Michael can manifest through several numbers, he often gravitates toward the numbers 1, 11, and 1111. Number 1 is incredibly prominent in the world of angels. If Michael is using this number (or combinations of it) to reach out to you, he has a significant message to deliver.

First and foremost, number 1 is linked to the one true self, which you can reach through your intuition. If you're seeing this number, it can indicate that you need to tap into your gut feelings. If you see the number 11, this means you have an elevated spiritual energy. It's a sign that you're receptive to spiritual messages. Messages linked to number 11 are often about the protection of your loved ones. Unlike number 1 (which is linked to your personal intuition), number 11 is more about using your intuition to help others. Some also believe that the number 11 depicts two tall figures, indicating that the Archangel will always stand with you.

If you keep encountering the number 1111, this could also be Michael's way of communicating with you. Never ignore this number because it can hold a message that could change your life. Michael can be incredibly persistent, and if you can't pick up on any other signs he is sending your way, he might start bombarding you with the number 1111 until you have no choice but to notice he is trying to deliver a message.

Another number you'll see when Michael is reaching out to you is 888. This represents Michael's connection to the divine. It's the triplicity of the number 8, the symbol of power, worldly status, and leadership. 888 can be reduced to 6, the number linked to the divine energy of service and another number associated with Archangel Michael. When he sends you the number 888, he reminds you of your responsibilities and the cause-and-effect relationship. He is telling you that every action has consequences. He often sends this number to help you understand the importance of integrity, staying true to your values, and all the steps you need to achieve this. Number 8 is also said to symbolize the divine sword of Archangel Michael. In triplicity, the symbol of the sword embodies the protection you need to live a righteous life, allowing you to grow through your interactions with spiritual power, responsibilities, and decisions, and the lack thereof.

The number 36 might be Michael's way of signaling that you must shift your focus in certain areas of life. If this number appears to you repeatedly, it can be a cue to stop focusing on outside values and to channel your attention to your inner self. Perhaps you're too focused on material possessions and financial gains. Seeing the number 36 can signify that you're ready for a spiritual journey that will make you lose focus on these concerns.

Colors

Archangel Michael is connected to several colors:

- **Blue** – The symbol of his protection, blue is often associated with serenity. It conveys calmness in the middle of chaos, allowing you to overcome obstacles.
- **Gold** – This color represents Michael's power as the Archangels' leader and the Sun's governor. Michael often appears in visions in his majestic form, enveloped in an aura of sparkling golden light.
- **Red** – Michael's association with the color of love alludes to his compassionate nature and ability to teach people how to develop love toward themselves and others and nurture this sentiment.
- **Purple** – Purple combines blue and red, indicating the Archangel's ability to provide loving protection. Purple symbolizes royalty, alluding to Michael's distinguished status among the Archangels.
- **Green** – Michael's abilities are linked to nature, best represented by the color green. Green has a grounding effect, helping to soothe and center one's mind during spiritual work.
- **White** – Michael's magnificent energy is often depicted by the universal angelic color, white. It can be helpful if you don't have a specific intention in mind or when or need all the power Michael can provide.

Symbol, Seal, and Sigil

Archangel Michael is frequently depicted carrying a sword, which has become one of his signature symbols of protection. Devotees often visualize his protective energy through his sword or simply through an orb of light. The sword and the light are either blue or surrounded by blue flame. These two angelic symbols represent Michael's ability to shield and protect you from harmful energies, cut unwanted ties, and free you from falsehood, allowing you to see the truth.

Michael is also attributed to other protection symbols, like the hexagram and pentagram, both of which are used in spiritual and magical work in different religions. Similarly to a shield, a cloak can also be Michael's symbol, especially if it's blue or royal purple. Some also prefer using representations of the sun as Michael's symbol. It depicts the Archangel's nurturing energy, which can come in handy during spiritual healing.

The sigil (also known as the seal of St. Michael) of Archangel Michael is a highly regarded religious emblem among followers of a wide variety of religions. While there are many different versions of the sigil, most devotees agree that it's best used to establish a bond between the Archangel and the person who wants to work with him regularly.

Trees, Plants, Herbs, and Essential Oils

As the Archangel associated with the highest power of angelic healing, Michael has many herbs, flowers, and essential oils in his apothecary. Some corresponding plants for Michael are acacia, angelica, beech, buttercup, blueweed, bay, cedar, hickory, carnation, sunflower, laurel, celandine, lovage, centaury, eyebright, goldenseal, heliotrope, hops, hibiscus, marigold, orange blossoms, peony, oak, rowan, basil, saffron, St. John's wort, sunflower, and tagetes.

To point out a few honorable mentions, basil is linked to Archangel Michael due to their mutual ability to banish negativity. It was once considered a powerful healing herb used by royalty. It can also be used in essential oil form to cleanse spaces and bodies before rituals and prayers dedicated to Michael. Other essential oils corresponding to Michael are orange and frankincense. They, too, can be used as prayer oils, anointments, and spritzers when invoking Michael's power for protection, strength, and peace of mind.

Solar-shaped blooms, flowers with a citrusy scent, and flowers that improve sight also work well when invoking Archangel Michael. As its name implies, the sunflower is one of Michael's correspondences. Using it can be a great way to honor Michael as the governor of the sun. Besides, the sunflower is also said to symbolize trust and faith in spirituality and the divine.

Incenses associated with Archangel Michael are lavender and frankincense. The former has a cleansing and soothing effect on your entire being while cleansing out your energies. The latter promotes calmness and purges the room of negative vibes and energetic influences.

Crystals and Metals

Archangel Michael is mainly associated with purple and blue gemstones, crystals, and stones. The deep purple sugilite has a particularly strong connection to this Archangel. Michael is also linked to topaz, amber, and several yellow, yellowish brown colored crystals, as well as blue stones like aqua aura and turquoise. You can also get great results when invoking Michael with gold and brass metal items. These metals have a high energy signature, just like the angel ruling them. Steel can also be used to summon Michael, as this metal is associated with his immense powers of protection.

Other Associations of Archangel Michael

The hour of the day and night: Michael governs the 1st and 8th hours of the day and the 3rd and 10th hours of the night.

Direction: West

Element: Fire

Tarot card: The Sun

Deities: Helios, Sol, Apollo, Thor, Adonis, Ra, Savitar, Re, and Sekhmet

Animals and mythical creatures: Lion, griffin, wolf, sparrowhawk, and golden butterfly.

Body Parts: The heart and the circulatory system, eyes, spinal column, spleen, upper back, blood.

Chakra system: Heart chakra (Anahata) and crown chakra (Sahasrara).

Spiritual correspondences: Peace, worldly ambition, financial gains, seeking employment, favors gained from others, ability to regain one's youth, acquire good luck and recover something or someone lost. Michael is known to help with business ventures, promotions, establishing mutually satisfying partnerships, and a path toward professional success. He is also linked to health, personal growth and advancement, joy, enlightenment, spiritual prosperity, hope, rational thinking, dispelling negative energies, and resolution of short-term or long problems.

Personal traits and skills: Personal characteristics governed by Archangel Michael are leadership skills, nobility, the ability to establish successful careers, reverence toward the law and rules, being a good role model as a father figure, and in friendships. He is also linked to self-confidence, ego, physical traits, ability to resolve hostile situations, ego, seeking fame, honor, life-bringing energy, spiritual lightness, success, vitality, superiority, virility, power promotion, and pride.

Conclusion

Archangel Michael is known for being a protector and the source of sacred empowerment for angels and people alike. As you've learned from this book, he is the Archangel closest to the divine. However, he is also the governor of the sun, providing nature with his nourishing energy. He protects those who can't speak for themselves and shields those in danger of evil influences. He can help you heal your body and mind by empowering your spirit and overcoming any difficulties you face in life. Whether it's through healing your chakras, bringing you closer to nature, or aligning you with your life's purpose, Michael will elevate your spirits and help you become the best version of yourself.

Suppose this is your first time working with an angelic being. In that case, you'll probably need a little practice establishing a clear communication line with Archangel Michael. After taking the first step and contacting him, you must watch for signs of him. The great thing about Michael is that he is always direct and persistent. With patience, you will eventually recognize his signs.

After that, it will be time to make specific inquiries. Throughout this book, you've received plenty of tips and practical advice for requesting protection, healing, and banishing negative energies. Whether you want to protect yourself, your loved ones, or your possessions from toxic influences, Michael will help you out. You can ask for his assistance during spiritual work or if you simply feel worn down by negative vibes. You can also ask him to dispel all the negativity that already resides in any space, item, or person you want to purify. Negative energies can cause physical, mental, and spiritual distress. By eliminating them with the help of Archangel Michael, you can be sure that they won't return anytime soon. While he can't cure any physical and mental illnesses, Michael can give you strength to allow your mind, body, and soul to heal. Working with Michael can be a superb complementary exercise for any treatment you undergo.

Do you want to form an even stronger bond with Archangel Michael? You can do it by incorporating elements to honor him into your day-to-day life. For example, you can use crystals associated with him to harness his energy. Stones charged with Archangel Michael's energy can be a great source of empowerment to get you through daily challenges. They can also aid you during any spiritual work you dedicate to Michael. Likewise, you can also find power in herbs and essential oils associated with this Archangel, and those are just as easy to incorporate into daily practices.

Even if you don't have items associated with Michael at hand, visualize a symbol associated with him, and he will hear your request. The relevant chapter provided you with a broad range of correspondences linked to this Archangel – feel free to refer to any of them while working with him. Simply wearing adequately colored clothes or addressing him on the day his powers are strongest can make a big difference in your ability to connect with him.

All in all, you've received plenty of advice on how to connect to Archangel Michael. Now it's up to you to begin your journey. Remember, practice makes perfect. You might not be able to decipher any messages you receive from Archangel Michael initially, but this will change over time. As you raise your energies to higher frequencies and become more attuned to your intuition, you'll learn how to get the most out of your connection with him.

Part 4: Archangel Raphael
Connecting with the Angel of Healing

Introduction

There is more to this world than meets the eye. And if you've ever wondered how you can tap into this "more," you will discover that there is no better way than to do so with the help of a celestial being. *But not just any celestial being*. This book is about Archangel Raphael, the Healer of all healers who brings you loving relationships and infinite creativity.

Within these next pages, you will discover the mystical world of Raphael. You will learn that you have barely scratched the surface of how good things can get for you regarding your health, relationships, and creativity.

As you go through each page and chapter, you will learn all about the power you have not taken advantage of until this point in your life. The veil of the celestial world will start to lift, and you will discover all the blessings that have been waiting for you, accessible through a relationship with Archangel Raphael.

Unlike other books on this topic, you will find this one very easy to read and digest. Whether you're a beginner at working with celestial beings or have been working with others other than Raphael, you will find everything you need in this book. It is packed with hands-on instructions and methods broken down step by step so that you never feel lost at any point when connecting with Archangel Raphael.

Are you ready to let Raphael lead you through the depths of your imagination and subconscious to the life you've always wanted regarding health, relationships, and inspiration? This book is definitely the one for you. So, if you are ready to have your life transformed by the emerald green light of Raphael, go ahead and dive into the first chapter.

Chapter 1: Who Is Archangel Raphael?

Who Is Raphael?

A depiction of Archangel Raphael.[63]

Archangel Raphael is known as the Medicine of God. According to the Zohar, this Archangel has one chief task: To heal humanity and the earth itself. "Raphael" means "God heals" or "God has healed," and he's also referred to as the "divine physician" and everyone's guardian angel. Whether your problems are spiritual, mental, physical, or emotional, you can trust Raphael to heal you. This Archangel became known to humanity through the Book of Tobit and the first book of Enoch. Many old and new stories talk about this Archangel's healing powers. After the "father of all nations," Abraham, was circumcised, Archangel Raphael healed him. When Jacob dislocated his hip after wrestling with an angel, Raphael put it back into place.

Raphael, According to Tobit

Tobit was known as a righteous and trustworthy man. Everyone agreed that he always did the right thing. He was devoted to God and did his best to offer others help when he could. He was married to Anna, and they had Tobias, their son. Tobit never strayed from his belief in God. However, that would soon be the reason behind his downfall. For many, his goodness was just too good to be true. Tobit was getting death threats, and on top of that, everything he had was taken from him. That was around the time when most Jews had been captured and being held in Nineveh. The evil King Sennacherib staunchly refused to allow them to pay their respects to those they'd lost and bury them properly. Not many people could stand up to Sennacherib's callousness, but Tobit was one of those who did. He did his best to secretly bury the dead.

One evening, when Tobit was about to have dinner, he was informed of a body that had to be buried. At this point, the man was *fifty*. Regardless, he sprung up and went to help.

According to tradition, handling a dead body meant being defiled, so he couldn't return to his meal. Instead, he spent the night outside his courtyard, sleeping by the wall, where some sparrows were perched; little did he know that this would lead to disaster. While he slept, his face was exposed, and bird droppings got into his eyes. When he woke up, he was blind. No matter who he saw about the condition, no one could cure him. Being blind meant he could no longer make money, and Anna was forced to provide for the family.

With time, Tobit's condition caused him so much shame and feelings of sadness. After eight years, he was so tired of living that way that he prayed for death. Around the same time, someone else was praying for the very same thing. The other prayer was from Raguel's daughter Sara, who had been widowed seven times because Asmodeus the demon kept killing her husband before they could consummate their marriage. God decided to show mercy by sending Raphael to answer Sara's and Tobit's prayers.

As Tobit spent his time waiting for death, he worked to ensure everything was in order before it happened. He had Tobias go to Media for money that a business associate, Gabriel, owed him. That was a dangerous trip, so he instructed Tobias to travel with someone to keep him safe, promising to pay them for their trouble. His traveling companion would be Azarias, a distant relative. Tobias didn't know that Azarias was actually Raphael disguising himself as human. Tobit had no clue, either. He simply wished his son well and sent him on his way.

On the first night of their trip, Tobias and Azarias stopped by the Tigris River to make camp. It was a long trip, so Tobias went to wash in the river, and as he did, he saw a huge fish. Raphael asked Tobias to catch the fish and remove its gallbladder, liver, and heart. They cooked the fish for dinner, and as they ate, Tobias wondered what his travel companion needed the fish's organs for. Azarias claimed that with the liver and heart, he could create smoke that would drive away evil spirits, and the gallbladder could help the blind see again.

They continued the next day, and as they drew closer to their destination, Azarias told Tobias it would be best to stay at Raguel's house. He also suggested that Tobias marry Sara. But of course, he couldn't hide the fact that the woman was thought to bring horrible luck to any man she married. When Tobias learned about her past, he panicked. But Azarias told him it would be fine if he just put the fish liver and heart on an incense burner and let the "lovely" scent send the demon that plagued Sara away. And he was right. When Asmodeus, the husband killer, smelled the incense, it was so rank that he ran and didn't stop until he reached the Northern part of Egypt! As Raphael, Azarias chased after him and bound him so he couldn't cause any more trouble. The next day, Tobias had come out of the bridal chamber alive and kicking – a shock to Sara's dad, Raguel, who had been hard at work the night before, digging what he thought would be Tobias's grave.

For the next 14 days, there was constant celebration. After that, Tobias returned home with his new bride and his strange friend, Azarias, by his side. Azarias had mentioned that fish gallbladder could heal the blind, so Anna told her son to anoint Tobit's eyes with the foul-smelling organ. Tobit's eyes prickled and then teared up, forcing him to rub them hard. As he did, the white film fell off, and he could see again. This was yet another reason to celebrate, and the family thanked Azarias profusely, giving him half of the ten silver talents they brought back from Media.

At this point, Azarias announced his true identity, making Tobias and Tobit quake in their boots! Were they in the presence of an actual Archangel the whole time? They were so scared that they fell to the floor. Raphael comforted them, saying there was no need to be scared. He told them to keep being good men and journal everything they'd experienced. Tobit lived another hundred years before passing away. As for his son Tobias and his daughter-in-law, Sara, they would go on to have six sons and enjoy a beautiful life together, all thanks to Raphael, who continues his healing work to this day.

Raphael, According to Enoch

Raphael appears several times in the Book of Enoch. The Archangels, Michael, Sariel, and Raphael, were watching the Watchers, also called the sons of God in the book of Job, Chapter 1, verse 6. The Watchers were the Nephilim, giants of old who were sons of angels and humans, under the leadership of As'a'el and Semhazah. The giants taught humans about jewelry, cosmetics, war, weapons, astrology, and magic spells – things ruining humanity. So, God asked the Archangels to go and punish them.

Raphael's instructions from God, as recorded in the book of Enoch, Chapter 10, verses 4 to 5, were to "Bind As'a'el; fetter him hand and foot and cast him into darkness; make an opening in the desert... and cast him in. And place upon him jagged and rough rocks, and cover him with darkness and let him abide there for all time, and cover his face that he may not see the light." As you can probably tell, God had had enough of As'a'el. The other Watchers were apprehended by Michael and placed in underground prisons to remain there for seventy generations. At the same time, Gabriel set up the Nephilim to battle each other until they were all dead.

Raphael also interacted with famous Bible characters like Noah and King Solomon. It was Raphael who helped make Noah's ark. Jewish records also say that after the flood had abated, Raphael gave Noah a book of medicine called the Sefer Raziel, which belonged to Angel Raziel. The book mostly had spells but is sadly now lost. As for the great King Solomon, Raphael helped him construct the Great Temple when he faced challenges and prayed to God for assistance. So, God sent the Archangel to Solomon. He went bearing a special ring on which a pentagram was engraved. This ring remains vital in magic, even today, and it's why some refer to Raphael as the angel of magic and miracles. It's also worth noting that the pentagram is an ancient medical symbol. With this ring, Solomon summoned and commanded thousands of demons to serve as laborers and finish the temple's construction.

Raphael in Islam

Also called Israfil, Esraful, or Israfel, this Archangel is highly esteemed in Islam. He's the one who will blow the trumpet of judgment, which he continues to keep close to his lips, awaiting God's instruction. He was created at the dawn of time with four wings and incredible height that let him reach heaven's pillars from Earth. He is also a musical angel who sings songs of praise to God in a thousand languages. He is the go-between for God and the other angels, passing along God's instructions to the hosts of angels. Some insist he had been in touch with the prophet Muhammad even before the encounter with Gabriel.

The Sufi believe in the perfect human, known as the Qutb. This person is said to be similar to Israfil, as they have a heart like his. According to Ath-Tha'labi's narration of Islamic tradition, Rafa'il and Dhu al-Qarnayn (whom some call Alexander the Great) met. The Archangel spoke about the Water of Life or Ayn al-Hayat, and this made Dhu al-Qarnayn crave it, but Khidr, his cousin, was the one who got to drink it.

Raphael in Other Texts

In the Testament of Solomon - a part of the Pseudepigrapha - a demon afflicted a young boy by sucking on his thumb, which made him feel weak and lose weight. To help the boy, Solomon prayed, and Michael was sent as an answer. Michael had a ring meant to capture evil spirits, but this isn't the same as the ring Raphael offered Solomon for the temple's construction. With this ring, Solomon captured Ornias, the spirit plaguing the boy. He grilled Ornias with questions until the demon was forced to summon Beelzebub, who was immediately bound by the ring. After much persuasion, Beelzebub brought every demon to Solomon to quiz all of them. He learned their names, powers, all they knew about astrology and the powerful angels they couldn't stand a chance against. One of the demons was Oropel, who gave people nasty sore throats, but would take off in fright whenever he heard Raphael's name.

The healing effect of Bethesda's pond is Raphael at work. In the Gospel of John, Chapter 5, verses 2 to 4, many people gathered around it with different ailments or ailing relatives and friends, waiting for it to begin moving. The movement was caused by an angel getting into the pond. The first person to get into the water after the angel would be healed of whatever was wrong with them.

In Milton's Paradise Lost, Adam and Eve are warned by Raphael not to defy God's word. He was kind and loving in his delivery. Raphael spoke with Adam at length on all kinds of things. In the end, Raphael warned Adam to be mindful of his interactions with the tempter, Satan, and not to touch the forbidden fruit. Of course, you know how that story played out.

Raphael was one of the angels Abraham conversed with in the Talmud at the oak of Mamre in Hebron. Michael was in the middle, while Gabriel and Raphael were to his left and right, respectively. They all had specific tasks to handle. Gabriel would destroy Sodom, Michael would let Sarah know she'd become the mother to Isaac, and Raphael would help Abraham heal after his circumcision and come to Lot's rescue, too.

According to the Midrash Konen, Raphael was Libbiel once upon a time. Libbiel is Hebrew for "God is my heart." According to this text, before the creation of man, God met with his angels about it. Not all the angels were okay with God's decision. The angels of justice and love okayed God's decision. Still, the angels of peace and truth worried that humans would become dishonest and problematic. In response, God cast the angel of truth to the Earth. Naturally, this upset the other angels, but God responded by telling them, "Truth will spring back out of the earth."

Interestingly, even before the angels voiced their concerns, God only shared the good things about humanity, not the uglier side. The dissenting angels asked, "What is man, that Thou art mindful of him? And the son of man, that Thou visiteth him?"

God responded that all the other creations would be pointless without anyone to appreciate and enjoy them. Some angels went along with God's plan. In contrast, others continued to oppose him, which meant they would bear the consequences of their opposition. These angels would be burned – all except Michael, their leader. The same thing happened to the angels led by Gabriel, who was the only one spared from his group. The third group of angels was under Libbiel's leadership, and he was no fool. He saw what happened to the others and warned his band of angels to do as God commanded. They made it clear to God that He had their full support and that they would watch over the humans and share everything they learned about them. At this point, God renamed Libbiel to Raphael to reflect that he played the role of Rescuer, having saved his angels with his advice. God called him the "Angelic Prince of Healing," in charge of all heavenly and earthly medicines.

Archangel Raphael Imagery, Symbols, and Seals

Raphael is sometimes depicted with a fish. Sometimes, there's a young boy with him, holding the fish. The Archangel could also put on a pilgrim's outfit, and when dressed this way, he may have a gourd or walking staff in his right hand. The fish, pilgrim's outfit, and boy are drawn from the story of Raphael leading Tobias to Media and back home. Usually, the angel's hair is blonde, and sometimes it's a really dark shade of blonde. As a pilgrim, he'll sometimes wear a coat over a tunic that may have a flowing mantle. Raphael always has winged. When he shows up, his light is bright and infused with gold.

Archangel Raphael is often depicted with a young boy holding a fish."

Raphael's color is emerald or moss green. Little wonder since this is the color of harmony and healing and the color of the heart chakra or energy center. Others consider bright green, purple, and gold his colors, too. Of the four classical elements, Raphael corresponds to Earth. The Caduceus is his symbol, which makes sense since he is the Patron of all healers. The sigil of Archangel Raphael has a cross in the middle, with a small circle on top and a slightly larger circle at the bottom. To the left and right of the cross are two vertical lines with small circles on top of each one, and their bottoms are connected by a horizontal line that runs through the bottom of the cross in the middle. To the left and right of this U shape, boxing off the cross, are two small crosses with equal vertical and horizontal lines. Another cross with equal lines rests above the middle traditional Christian cross.

At the bottom of the sigil is another cross with equal vertical and horizontal lines but with a small circle on top. To the left and right of this final cross are two Xs. All of these parts are contained in a circle. Around the circle, you have the words RAPHAEL on top, ADONAY to the right, OTHEOS at the bottom, and AGIOS to the left. Adonay means "Lord" or "Master," Otheos means "God," and Agios means "sacred." Each of these words has a small cross with equidistant lines in between them. Another circle binds these words on the outside.

Now you know all you need to know about who Archangel Raphael is. The question is, when is it okay to call upon him? And how would you even do that? You will learn about all this and more in the next chapter.

Chapter 2: When and How to Call Upon Archangel Raphael

Healing Your Body

No one does a better job than Archangel Raphael when it comes to physical healing. God has blessed him to help you heal in any way you need. Just a touch from Raphael can bring relief and restoration to whatever is out of alignment with your body. As a human, it is only natural that you experience some physical pain occasionally. Raphael, a very compassionate being, has been tasked with bringing you relief. His healing energy is reminiscent of a soothing breeze as it sweeps through your body and removes whatever plagues you.

Many have suffered chronic illnesses and have called upon Archangel Raphael, asking him to intercede on their behalf. Naturally, Raphael swoops in to answer their prayers. More than any physician, he understands what needs to be addressed in the mortal body to bring it back to a flawless state. The beautiful thing about this Archangel is that there is no judgment in his treatment. Not only is he excellent at healing the body of whatever it's going through, but he's also adept at bringing on a state of balance. By calling upon Archangel Raphael, you will experience a sense of wellness you have never known before. This being carries within him a celestial grace that flows into your body, harmonizes all its functions, fixes all that is fractured, and balances all disruptions in the systems within you.

When calling upon Raphael for healing, you must understand that you also have a part to play. For Raphael's healing work to take root, you must surrender to him completely. You must trust that his power can work with your body to create the desired results. It does no good for you to think negatively while calling him for help.

If you think of ill health and negativity, your body picks up on that and draws more bad energy. When you call on Raphael, and he attempts to use his healing energy on you, you will run into a few hiccups that you are responsible for. You must also make the right choices and do the right thing to be a conscious co-creator with Raphael to generate the desired health.

When you're in the presence of Raphael, his healing energy is unmistakable. Learn to tap into that and pay attention to the intuitive nudges you receive. He will use your intuition to communicate how you can improve your condition. You must realize this is a collaborative effort and act like it.

Healing Your Heart

Healing doesn't just occur on a physical level. There are times in life when you need your heart mended. You can reach out to Archangel Raphael to help you with this. The journey of emotional healing is a rhythmic one between light and darkness. It is about understanding that there is pain within your heart and accepting it while at the same time doing your best to stoke the flames of hope in your heart. Raphael can offer you the guidance and solace you need to restore your heart. Archangel Raphael can show you the way to set yourself free emotionally. He has no trouble with you displaying vulnerability, so don't assume that you must meet him in a somber, controlled manner. This Archangel offers the strength needed to battle your shadows and undo the twisted webs of emotions that keep you stuck and bound.

Healing Relationships

Raphael also has the power to heal and restore your relationships. Inevitably, everyone experiences misunderstandings. Sometimes, these misunderstandings can escalate to the point where a previously wonderful relationship is destroyed. However, there is no relationship or connection that Raphael cannot fix. So, call on him if you have a relationship that needs fixing.

Raphael has the power to heal any troubled relationship.[55]

Healing Trauma

Trauma is an unfortunate aspect of being human. Sometimes, it may seem impossible to extricate yourself from the damage caused by traumatic events. However, being a divine being, Archangel Raphael can help you get through whatever trauma you may face. Also, trauma has been known to take away your sense of inner peace and make it impossible for you to feel safe. This impossibility thrives because you have not called upon divine support to help you. Raphael is an excellent inner guide that can keep you at peace amid the storm. If you learn nothing else from this section of the book, remember this: There isn't a thing on earth or anywhere else that Raphael cannot fully and completely heal.

Inspiring Creativity

Sometimes, you find your creative spirit trapped behind an inexplicable block. You do everything conventional knowledge says to shake yourself free of the mud. However, nothing works. Whenever you find yourself in this situation, call on Archangel Raphael. He, more than any other being, can lead you toward a world of infinite creative expression. He possesses the celestial melody that will sing your soul into full creative flow.

Archangel Raphael is known as the celestial muse. He knows how to help you turn your blank canvas into the most vibrant artwork. He knows how to guide your hand so that your empty page is transformed into literary genius. When you seek Raphael's assistance, you learn that creativity is not something you go after on your own. It is not a journey that you must go on alone. By opting to work with the divine, you tap into a realm of great ideas many people are unaware of. As a result, the works you create from this realm are literally out of this world.

So, call on Raphael to help you find your creative flow. Taking you by the hand through your intuition, he'll show you how to release yourself from the prison that is your comfort zone so that you can be at peace with the unknown that houses every creative idea you seek. Also, you can allow his energy to flow through you so you are not forcing things to happen. Instead, you let him flow through you to express divine creativity. In other words, you serve as a channel for divine inspiration. When you experience this flow, time ceases to exist. Not only that, but it also appears as though you could do your work forever. Often, those working with Raphael for inspiration and creativity report that by the time they are done creating their work, it feels like they have nothing to do with it. They were simply along for the ride.

Another thing to consider when it comes to creativity is the balance between taking risks and sticking to convention out of fear. When you find yourself amid this uncertainty, it becomes difficult to flow creatively. You'll notice that fear takes control of your heart and prevents you from exploring the world within you. When your creative work is full of self-doubt and hesitation, it's difficult not to see that. However, Raphael can unfurl his wings and swoop down to your rescue so that you can find the audacious spirit within you. You see, Raphael does not doubt what you can accomplish. He will help you remove the self-doubt and fear that make you hesitant to try new things with your work. He will encourage you to be bold about your writing, painting, or whatever else you do. Proficient at binding demons, Raphael will rope the ones that plague you on the inside and toss them into the abyss, allowing you to tap into the powerful emotions that drive your creativity. Now, do not assume this means you will never be afraid. Raphael will give you the ability to act despite that fear. Therefore, with time, you will realize that fear is nothing to fear when it comes to your creative work.

Helping Pets

It feels painful for both of you when you have an inexplicably ill pet. Naturally, these pets are family to you, so you want them to feel better.

Raphael can help your pet too. You can turn to him to intervene. With his celestial light, he will heal your pet.

The only other thing as heart-wrenching as your being sick is losing them. In times like these, Raphael can act as a beacon that allows your pet to find its way home.

Overcoming Addictions

Addictions can leave you unable to see anything good about yourself. Raphael can offer you the strength to break free of the chains of addiction. As a celestial being, Raphael has a unique point of view on human complexities, particularly when it comes to struggles that appear outside your control. Better than any counselor on earth, Raphael feels the pain you go through and approaches the process of helping you heal with love and zero judgment. Does this imply you should not seek professional mental health therapy? Absolutely not. However, working with Archangel Raphael can help you get where you need to go faster.

Often, addiction can be rooted in trauma, emotional pain, or disconnection from your spiritual self. Raphael can heal the wounds that drive your destructive habits. You see, it is not enough to tell yourself that you will stop being addicted to something. You must address the hidden root causes, and Raphael can expose them to the light so that you can finally do something about them. This Archangel can give you the willpower to push past the temptation to revert to destructive behavior. This is important to know because there will be times when you feel tempted to give in. Raphael will assure you that this does not mean you are a terrible or weak person. He will encourage you through these difficult times to make the right choices.

Raphael offers inspiration and guidance through your intuition. He creates synchronistic events in your life that lead to people who will assist you through your predicament. He lights up the path toward recovery. You don't need to understand exactly how you will arrive at that destination. All you must do is trust Raphael is hard at work to bring you out of the prison of addiction.

On top of that, he can help you restore balance to your life by showing you better habits and practices that you can adopt to replace and totally eliminate your addictions. He can remove all the negative influences that encourage you to indulge in those addictions. When you need to cut off toxic relationships, this Archangel backs you up. He can help you with the resources to move out of negative environments that fuel your addictive behavior. On an energetic level, he can cut the cords that have bound you to places, people, and addictive substances that have ruled and ruined your life. Therefore, it would be best to seek Raphael when struggling with something addictive. The substance or behavior and how strongly attached you are to it do not matter. Raphael can set you on the right path regardless.

Assistance with Travel

Raphael is an excellent travel companion. He offers safety and protection in the air or on the road. You can have him safeguard your travels by ensuring you won't have any delays or accidents. Also, if there are multiple routes to your destination, but you're unsure of which one to take, you can reach out to him and ask him to pick the best one for you. Even in an unfamiliar place, he can guide you.

There are countless situations where people find themselves in travel emergencies, and, calling on Raphael, he came through for them. You should know that no matter how difficult a trip is, he will intervene and make the journey easier for you. All you have to do is ask him.

Summoning Archangel Raphael

Now that you know all the situations where Raphael can help you, how do you get his assistance? You need to summon him. There are several ways you can do that. Look at the following methods, and work with each one until you know what works best and feels right to you.

Prayer

Prayer is a holy bridge that connects you to the divine. When you pray, you craft a space of sacredness within your heart that acts as a sanctuary for your intentions to gain momentum and where they are projected into higher realms. With prayer, you can invite Raphael to your life and ask him to work his magic on you.

Various resources on the internet and other books will recommend specific prayers to use in summoning Raphael. However, there is really no specific template that you must follow. All you have to do is speak from your heart about your desire and believe your prayer has been heard.

Prayer is one of the most effective ways to summon Archangel Raphael.[56]

Meditation and Visualization

Meditation is excellent for summoning Archangel Raphael when you need his help. Visualization involves bringing up specific scenes in your imagination. It will be a part of most of the other methods of summoning Raphael that you'll learn in this book. If you can imagine holding a golf ball in your hand or biting into a lemon, you have visualization skills.

Before you meditate, make you're somewhere free of distractions. Nothing and no one must disturb or interrupt you. You'll need to be in total silence for ten to fifteen minutes. Also, you must put on comfortable clothing.

1. Sit in a posture you can maintain during your meditation.
2. Close your eyes, and allow the world to fade so you tune in to your inner reality.
3. Inhale deeply, exhale slowly, and allow the day's burdens to fly away from you.
4. Notice your weight against the chair or floor, and feel your connection to the earth.
5. Continue breathing deeply until you notice your thoughts are still.
6. If your mind keeps wandering away from your breath, that's fine and nothing to feel frustrated about. Even if it happens a lot, notice that your attention has wandered, and then gently return your focus to your breath. In time, the stillness will come.
7. When your mind feels still, it's time to ask Raphael to come to you. You can state this intention aloud or simply sit with a feeling

of expectancy as if you know now that he will grace you with his presence.

8. As you breathe and wait, imagine a brilliant emerald light with the radiance of a thousand sun-kissed leaves. See it flooding the room and space around you and flowing into your body.
9. Feel the energy of this light as it goes into every cell, awakening every fiber of your being. This is the Archangel's presence, love, light, and healing power. You are now connected to Raphael.

Using Mantras

Mantras are words, sounds, or phrases used to deepen a meditative state or summon celestial beings. While in meditation, you can use mantras to summon Raphael. First, focus on your breath, and when you notice you're still, begin repeating a simple mantra like, *"Raphael, please come to me now."* Your mantra can be whatever you want.

Using Chakras

Your chakras are energy portals that allow life force to flow into you on every level of existence. They also allow energy to flow out of you, affecting your life and even the lives of others around you. You can use these energy centers to summon Raphael.

1. Start by sitting or lying down somewhere comfortable and quiet.
2. Close your eyes, inhale, and exhale a few times as you bring your attention to the present moment and push distracting thoughts away.
3. Bring your attention to your heart chakra, the Anahata. See it as a pulsating, rotating portal of emerald, green energy.
4. In your mind or out loud, repeat Raphael's name. The intention behind this is to draw his presence. While doing this, notice how your heart chakra becomes more active as the light becomes more intense, brilliant, and warm, traveling through your being. This means you have established a connection to Raphael.

Using Reiki

Here's how to work with Reiki to get Archangel Raphael's assistance.

1. Go somewhere without any distractions or noises.
2. Cleanse the space. You can burn incense, light candles, ring a bell, or use any other method to clear out the energy of your workspace.

3. Ground yourself by sitting comfortably, closing your eyes, and focusing on taking deep breaths. As you breathe, imagine roots growing from where you're connected to the floor into the earth.
4. In your mind's eye, see a beam of light from the sky pouring into the top of your head, connecting you with divinity.
5. Set your intention to draw Archangel Raphael's presence to help you during your Reiki session. You can state this intention out loud as an invocation. Invite him to be present and empower your ritual.
6. Place your hands on your body (or that of the person you're trying to help), and in your mind's eye, see healing green light flowing through your hands. Trust that this light belongs to Raphael and that he is now here with you. You'll learn more about Reiki in a later chapter.

Free Writing and Art

Free writing is a way to allow the consciousness of Archangel Raphael to flow through you and get direct insight into whatever situation you're dealing with. You can also allow Raphael to flow through you using art. Here's how to do it:

1. First, find somewhere distraction-free. You'll need to sit at a comfortable desk for this one.
2. Intend to connect with Raphael. Be clear that you want to do this through free writing or art and seek guidance, help, health, or whatever else you need him to help you with.
3. Meditate for a few minutes or until you feel the stillness within you and your mind and body relax. Infuse your body and space with Raphael's light.
4. Open your eyes, hold your pen over your pad (or just sit with the tools of your preferred art medium, whatever that is), and breathe deeply.
5. Let the words or images flow through you. Don't try to think about whether they're actual words, what your handwriting looks like, or why you appear only to be doodling or something. If you're making art, imagine that your hands aren't yours. Instead, see them as Raphael's. Trust that his energy flows through you, and keep your awareness of your connection. It also helps to keep your focus on the paper so you don't get too analytical

about your writing or creating.
6. You can ask a question and wait for your hand to begin writing. It is important to stay open throughout this process.
7. When you're done, thank Raphael. You can read and review what you got after the session and make any additional notes you like that come to mind. If you made art, you could sit with it and meditate on the goal of your practice.

Using Dreams and Astral Projection

Dreams are an excellent way to reach out to Archangel Raphael, making it easier for him to show up in all his glory. Astral projection involves leaving your physical body to explore the astral realms (and other realms) where you can gain knowledge, meet other beings, go places, and so on. Here's how you can have him work with you in your dreams.

1. Begin by setting your intention to connect with Raphael before bed. Be clear about what you'd like him to help you with.
2. Make sure that your room is conducive so that you can sleep well. It must be silent, completely dark (or at least with a nice, relaxing ambiance), and at a comfortable temperature. You can set the mood with some music if you like.
3. Before you drift off to sleep, wind down by meditating. This will clear your mind and keep you focused on your task.
4. As you meditate, envision Raphael's rich emerald green light around you and your room.
5. Say a prayer or make an affirmation to have him present as you go to sleep.
6. Have a pen and dream journal by your bed so you can write down what you remember after waking up.
7. While you drift off to sleep, repeat, *"Thank you, Raphael."*
8. When you wake up, don't move your body. If you do, return to being still as soon as possible, and don't open your eyes.
9. Think of the last thing you saw or what you felt, and this should kickstart the process of remembering what happened.
10. When you've got it all remembered, write keywords to represent each aspect of the dream first and then flesh out each one with details after.

What about astral projection? Here's how to go about it.
1. Set your intention to leave your body and meet Archangel Raphael.
2. Set your alarm for two to three hours before the usual time to get up, then go to bed.
3. When your alarm goes off, turn it off, get out of bed, and drink some water.
4. Take five to thirty minutes to read about astral projection and Archangel Raphael while intending you're going to meet with him in the astral plane.
5. Now, go back to bed, fixing the intention firmly in your mind that you'll leave your body.
6. When you sense you're awake, don't open your eyes or move your body. Instead, just sit up with your astral body and get out. The important thing is not to think too much. You may feel vibrations but don't stick around for those. Instead, leave your body, and get as far away from it as possible.
7. Intend to see Raphael. If he's not already there, you will find him eventually. From there, you can commune with him about whatever you need.
8. As you return to your body, scream one word that summarizes what he was saying (or a short phrase), as this will help you remember what he told you.
9. Don't hurry to get out of bed, open your eyes, or move when you wake up because your astral memories must be allowed to move from your astral mind to your physical one, and you must not interrupt that process. Otherwise, you will forget everything that happened.
10. When you can recall everything (thanks to the phrase or word you yelled out as you reentered your body), you can write it down in your dream journal.

Now that you know how to summon Archangel Raphael, you probably want to know how you can tell that this celestial being is present. The next chapter will teach you the signs that the Divine Healer is with you.

Chapter 3: Signs That Archangel Raphael Is Present

It may seem unlikely that you can interact with beings from other worlds. However, you should not dismiss the fact that you can have a true encounter with Archangel Raphael. But how could you possibly tell when you are in the presence of this wonderful celestial being? You must know the signs that he has arrived and has answered your prayer.

It is important to know that signs aren't only tangible things you can observe with your five senses. Signs of Archangel Raphael's presence can come in infinite ways. However, without exception, you know he is present because of an unmistakable gut feeling. Knowing these signs will comfort you when you experience them. You will have an unshakable faith that whatever you seek Raphael's help for will be a done deal.

Feathers

Many have seen feathers around them as a sign that the Archangel Raphael is present. He has a way of ensuring you spot these feathers at just the right place and time. In other words, a regular feather at any other place or time may not catch your eye or strike your heart. Still, when it is a clear sign from Raphael, you'll know it because, instantly, you will freeze and understand what you're looking at.

Spotting a feather at the right place and time indicates that Raphael is with you.⁵⁷

Someone else seeing that same feather won't even look twice. However, you know better. You know that that feather is celestial. It is important not to take the sign lightly because it symbolizes that you have got Archangel Raphael's attention and that whatever you have brought to him to be handled is being worked on. You may think of these feathers as reminders that you are not alone. You have the hosts of Raphael right by your side, ready to assist you.

A Feathery Message to Samantha

Here's Samantha's encounter with Raphael:

"I had just moved out of a lovely apartment I once shared with my partner, only to downgrade to somewhere in a terrible neighborhood. I was also at a loss about what to do concerning my lower back, which had become a serious problem. I had to sit for extended periods as a writer to create content. This meant I could not write fast enough to make enough money to move somewhere better, and my back's protests had grown from low grumbles to deafening roars of pain.

One day, I watched a YouTube video about reaching out to Archangel Raphael for healing. I thought it couldn't possibly hurt as I was really suffering. So, I said a simple prayer. And then, I forgot all about it and did my best to make the most of my new life. The next day, I walked around my new neighborhood, cautiously watching everyone around me. I realized I was a little too on edge and longed for the days when I could walk care-free.

As I almost broke down in tears, barely keeping it together, I noticed a white feather floating down from above. Right then and there, I stopped in my tracks. As it floated down, I reached out with my palm, and it settled down on it. The moment the feather touched my hand, I felt intense relief. It was as though I had been walking around with a boulder around my shoulders, and someone had suddenly lifted that load off me. I couldn't explain it, but I knew everything would be okay.

For the first time in months, I went to bed comfortably with no back pain. I woke up the next day feeling amazing. Just a couple of weeks later, I got a phone call from a production company that would radically change my life. They bought a TV show that I had been pitching unsuccessfully for the past two years. The company offered me an amount of money that I had never before imagined having. Working with an agent, I decided to ask for more. I did just that, and a week after that, I had more than enough money to move out of that dangerous apartment and into somewhere that was more my speed. I kept that feather as a reminder that angels are real, and if you ask them, they're ready to help you with whatever you need."

Angel Numbers

Have you ever looked at the clock, and a sequence of numbers caught your attention? These numbers show up not just on the clock, but on license plates, in conversations, on price tags, coded serial numbers, and so on. In fact, you may have noticed that you have a penchant for waking up at a particular time every day without an alarm clock.

If you have noticed these numbers popping up often, you may have combed the internet to determine what they mean. You may have found some information claiming these numbers should not be taken seriously. Those who hold this position claim that the numbers you notice are only a result of your reticular activating system, a brain process responsible for helping you find patterns in things. They'll tell you that it's the reason why when you buy a red car, for instance, you suddenly start noticing red cars everywhere.

But you get the sense that there's a lot more to these numbers than what you're being told. The truth is you are right. These numbers aren't ordinary. They are known as angel numbers. They could be repetitive ones like 111, 222, 333, or any other number appearing in threes or fours (or even larger groups). The numbers could be 1010, 411, 414, 717, 8080, etc. It doesn't matter how they show up. What matters is that when they do, you get the sense that the world stops. Whatever thought process you had going on then suddenly becomes irrelevant. You are heavily rooted in the here and now and so grounded that it almost feels as if life is literally a dream or a simulation. You feel this way because the angel Raphael is making his presence known. He is showing you that there are forces and powers beyond physical reality's seeming rigidity and changelessness.

When these numbers show up, you are meant to take advantage of that feeling of unrealness by planting the seed of whatever you desire in your mind. How do you do this? By accepting that no matter how seemingly impossible your desires are, anything under the sun can be accomplished through divine means. And, you have the divine means because you have the support of Raphael and his host of angels. For some people, that's not enough. If this is you, the following section briefly explains the meaning of every number from 0 through 9. Suppose you see number sequences that are a combination of various numbers. In that case, all you have to do is take the meanings of each individual number, and combine them, then apply them to your life.

Numbers and Their Meanings

- **Zero** is the number of infinite potentials. It stands for the divine connections you have. Seeing this number is as if you're being asked to remain in the present. Call your attention and energy from the past and the future and bring them to the here and now. In this moment and space, Raphael advises you to let go of old attachments and allow yourself to move with the flow of divinity, trusting that the unknown is wonderful and will lead you to your highest ideals.
- **One** is the number of divine inspirations. It's about new beginnings and the power of manifestation. When you run into

a number sequence with ones in it, Raphael tells you that you must embrace the strength within and accept your potential to create greatness.

- **Two** is the number of duality. It expresses the concept of partnerships and balance. When you see number two in a number sequence, Raphael asks you to do what you can to encourage harmonious relationships. He also wants you to find harmony within yourself. Number two tells you that you must feed the healthy connections that you have in life and balance your emotions.

- **Three** is the number of creative energy. It is the presence of guidance from above. Whenever a number sequence has a 3, you are asked to acknowledge divinity's presence in your life. Also, you are called to be bold about expressing yourself creatively and living from a place of authenticity. Number three asks you to embrace your unique talents and let go of the doubt that keeps you from fully expressing them so that you can reach new heights.

- **Four** is the number of stability. It represents the idea of being supported. When this number appears in an angel number sequence, Raphael is encouraging you out of uncertainty. He would like you to be more trusting of the universe and its natural rhythms. Four calls you to recognize that you are part of nature, which means you could never be in the wrong place at the wrong time. You must trust that the flow of nature will bring you exactly where you need to go.

- **Five** is the number of freedom change and transformation. When five appears in an angel number sequence, you are asked to be open to future changes. It tells you that you must let go of the old to accept the new miracles you have prayed for and desired for the longest time. Five asks you to be at peace regardless of how chaotic this change may be because, inevitably, it will lead you to where you want to be.

- **Six** is a number that many assume is negative. That is mainly because of the Christian interpretation of the number 666, which is said to be the mark of the evil beast. However, this is not the case when it comes to angel numbers. The number six in an angel number sequence is basically a message asking you to dig below the surface of things so that you can discover the truth of your situation. It calls for destroying and tearing down all illusions that keep you bound to your present, undesirable reality. Six asks you to find the balance point in the confusion and chaos and to reconnect with the divinity that you carry. It reminds you that the light will emerge no matter how dark things may seem.

- **Seven** is a divine number. It represents inner wisdom, intuition, and awakening to your spiritual self. When you see the number 7 in an angelic number sequence, you're called to pay attention to what your soul tells you. Your life is aligned with a divine plan, and you must trust that there is wisdom within you greater than what you are aware of. Seven asks you to trust your intuition and to allow Raphael to show you the way to go.

- **Eight** is the number of success, abundance, and infinite possibilities. Seeing eight in a number sequence means you are being or about to be immensely blessed. It's a sign that everything around you is lining up to favor you in the best way possible. Expect many open doors when this number begins to appear in your life. Expect the unexpected. You know the saying, "It's too good to be true?" Well, you can expect that the good things to come your way will be better than you could have imagined, and they will be true. Remember, you must share the abundance in your life because giving means receiving even more.

- **Nine** is a powerful number representing spiritual alignment, completing things, and finding closure. When nine is in an angel number sequence, Raphael is leading you through the last stages of a situation or the final chapters of a certain book in your life. Nine is the number of endings. Endings are not necessarily bad because they can and do lead to new beginnings. So, when you notice this number, let go of whatever you're dealing with and trust that all things will be reborn. You'll experience a new life cycle, leading to the evolution of your higher self, affecting you positively in every way.

Siobhan's Saving Numbers

Here's Siobhan's story:

"777 has always shown up for as long as I can remember. It's been a guide of sorts. However, when I learned about Archangels, I developed a strong interest in Raphael. The more I learned about this Archangel, the more I saw 777. It reached the point where I could trust that unless I saw 777, I would not act on any major decision I had to make.

One day, I had to make a trip. I had a dream the previous night about my plane crashing. So, when I woke up the next day, I felt some trepidation, but I honestly felt like I had no choice but to go since it was a work trip. I arrived at the airport and saw a truck with the number 777 on its license plate. I felt good seeing the number until I saw what was written on the side of the truck. The words "back home" were boldly staring back at me. Immediately, I asked the driver to take me back.

Later that night, I was watching the news. It turned out that the flight I was supposed to be on wound up crashing just before it could land. More than ever, I am certain that that warning was from Angel Raphael himself. That night, I took a moment to thank Raphael for his protection."

Emerald Green Everywhere

Emerald green contains Raphael's essence. Many people who encountered this Archangel claim that they saw emerald green. Sometimes, it could be a light that isn't detectable by everyone other than the person it's meant for. Other times, something emerald green is in the person's surroundings.

You may have a dream where that color is predominant in the form of light, crystals, or nature. Usually, when you see it, it has a very profound effect on your consciousness. In other words, it affects you mentally and physically. So, it would be best to begin paying attention to emerald green. Not because you're trying to force it to appear, but just to acknowledge that each time you notice it, odds are Raphael is nearby.

Danielle Touched By an Angel

Marshall had been going through a lot since his wife was involved in a car accident. She lay in the hospital for 3 weeks, unconscious, despite the doctor's best efforts. Marshall did all he could to learn ways to help someone regain consciousness. However, he was quickly losing hope.

One day, Marshall stumbled across an article about how someone claimed to have connected with the Archangel Raphael. This person's story inspired him. He decided that he was going to reach out to the Archangel. Marshall was not a praying man. He did not believe in any reality outside of the physical, but he had tried everything at this point. Marshall was more than willing to try praying to this angel. How he saw it, no one was around to judge him for suddenly becoming a believer.

So, he knelt and prayed to Archangel Raphael on behalf of his wife. When he was done, he sat back down, feeling foolish. A few moments later, a nurse he had not seen before entered the room. She smiled at Marshall as she tended to his wife, Danielle. The nurse fluffed her pillow and arranged her body properly in bed. And then she did something Marshall thought was a bit weird. Still smiling at Marshall, the nurse touched Danielle's forehead briefly. And then she placed her hands on Danielle's chest for a few seconds. She turned to Marshall, smiled, and said, "You've been heard."

Then, just as Marshall was about to ask her who she was, the nurse walked out of the room. He noticed an odd flash of green light against the wall just as the nurse headed out the door. This left Marshall baffled. He turned to face his wife, and Danielle opened her eyes for the first time in 21 days.

Disappearing Symptoms

Disappearing symptoms don't always indicate Archangel Raphael's presence. There could be other factors, such as your body naturally healing itself. However, those who have called on Archangel Raphael to help them with their afflictions usually report that they've noticed a reduction in the intensity of their symptoms. Do not be alarmed if you notice this happening when you seek help. It is important to state here that you should always seek out the help of a medical professional in addition to working with Archangel Raphael to confirm that your condition is indeed getting better.

Now that you know all the signs that Archangel Raphael is present and that he's listening, it's time to look at how you can enlist his help to overcome negative thoughts and emotions. Read the next chapter to learn how Raphael can help you take charge of your emotional and mental well-being.

Chapter 4: Healing Negative Thoughts and Emotions

Praying to Archangel Raphael or connecting with him in any other way does not imply you do not need to see a doctor. Raphael can help you with the healing process. Still, it doesn't hurt to do your part and be responsible for your health by going to the hospital when something is wrong with you or a loved one.

Archangel Raphael is known as the Angelic Prince of Healing. He isn't limited to helping with physical health issues but also your emotions, thoughts, and spirit. The question is, why would you need healing on any other level besides the physical one? Do the wounds that can't be seen with your eyes matter? In fact, do they even exist? Yes, they do, and their effects are damaging.

The Effects of Automatic Negative Thoughts

Automatic negative thoughts, also called ANTs, are insidious ideas that enter the mind and take over if left unchecked, leading you to criticize yourself harshly, live a life full of fear, and constantly doubt your abilities. These thoughts make you feel like you're not good enough and that even through blood, sweat, and tears, you just won't succeed. The voice in your head tells you that you don't deserve to be happy, you shouldn't be loved, and that all good things must eventually come to an end - assuming you were ever lucky enough to experience good, to begin with. These thoughts fuel emotions such as sadness, resentment, scorn, anger, pain, and guilt, making it tough for you to live a life full of passion and purpose.

Some studies suggest that intrusive negative thoughts can also affect your health. According to an article titled The Automaticity of Positive and Negative Thinking: A Scoping Review of Mental Habits by Colvin et al., in Cognitive Therapy and Research, thinking negative thoughts, criticizing yourself and others, and constantly worrying about things can lead to terrible mental health. There's also another study in the BMC Public Health by Grobosch et al., 2021, titled Thoughts about health and patient-reported outcomes among people with diabetes mellitus: results from the DiaDec-study, where the researchers discovered that those with diabetes mellitus who had a pattern of negative thinking would wind up having other health issues to contend with.

When you have a constant barrage of negative thoughts and emotions in your head, your body suffers stress too. Your bloodstream gets flooded with cortisol, which spikes your heart rate and blood pressure to concerning levels and causes your muscles to grow tense. These are natural responses to have when dealing with a threat, but when your body cannot turn off these responses, this can cause issues with your cardiovascular health and leave you with a flawed immune system. As for your mental abilities, you'll find it tough to be creative or to find the drive to go after your desires. You'll have a distorted idea of what's real versus what isn't, making it impossible to take practical actions that could change your life. Also, negative thoughts and emotions are the primary drivers of bad habits that keep you captive and make it hard to choose the right thing to elevate your life and uplift your soul. The following are some of the thoughts and emotions Archangel Raphael can you with.

Anxiety

Living with anxiety is like constantly being caught in a storm that refuses to let up. It always feels dark, foreboding, and heavy. People who struggle with anxiety have a difficult time just breathing. Often, situations that shouldn't be a big deal overwhelm individuals who struggle with anxiety. It doesn't matter if your anxiety is about where the bills will come from or a trip you must take. It always feels crippling and has a firm grasp on your heart, putting you in a place of no escape. Anxiety makes it difficult to feel free. It is a relentless emotion when you give in to it.

Archangel Raphael can help you navigate the storms of anxiety. Thanks to his healing power, and soothing presence, you can call on him to shield you from the things that cause you discomfort. Better than that, he can help you find the strength to persevere through whatever you're going through. Say you find yourself on an airplane, and you've always been nervous about flying. You can call on Archangel Raphael to help you manage your anxious emotions. You may notice that the anxiety is still there, but you feel more at peace with it and can just observe it as though it were a guest in your mind. By helping you see anxiety this way, Raphael shows you that you don't have to identify with the emotion just because you feel it. He helps you understand that emotions are transient and they are not your identity.

Ritual for Anxiety

Whenever you feel anxious, you can do this ritual anywhere:

1. Find a quiet place where you won't be distracted or disturbed.
2. Take a moment to ground yourself. Close your eyes, take a few deep breaths, and focus on the present moment.
3. Set your intention to call upon Archangel Raphael. Your intention should be clear. In this case, you want to seek his help to overcome crippling anxiety.
4. In your mind's eye, imagine a brilliant emerald light that surrounds you. Feel this light as it energizes your body from head to toe. Allow the healing light of Archangel Raphael to wash through you.
5. As you breathe in, allow this light to flow into your lungs and spread to every part of your body.
6. As you exhale, imagine your anxiety is a cloud of black energy that emerges through your slightly parted lips with each exhale.
7. As you continue breathing, feel this anxiety in your belly or your chest continuing to fade away with each exhale.
8. At this point, you should feel more at ease and grounded. You should feel an unmistakable sense of calm.
9. Use affirmations to boost the calm and peace you feel within if you want to. You can use a simple affirmation like, *"I am calm now. I am at ease now. "*

10. Take a moment to thank Raphael for helping you and showing up as he always does.
11. Bring your attention back to your breath and allow it to ground you briefly before you open your eyes. Understand that when you leave that space, you will carry Raphael's green, calming light with you.

Once more, it is important to remember that you can use this ritual anytime, anyplace.

Work Stress

You live in a world where it is natural to be stressed out about work. So heavy is the burden of work on your soul that it taints everything you do. You start as a vibrant child, eager to explore life, learn new things, and offer your gifts to the world. At some point, however, life finds a way to weigh you down. The system currently in sway in this world is not conducive to play. It finds a way to take the most enjoyable things about life and make them feel like drudgery. The inevitable result is that you wind up feeling extremely stressed. Even when you return from work, those precious few hours before you have to do it again the next day are tainted by the stress from the office or your business. Unfortunately, most people don't know how to handle this stress effectively, so they take it out on their loved ones, picking up bad habits to feel good.

You can call on Raphael to help you handle stress. He does an excellent job of reminding you of the strength that you carry within you. Also, he can set things up so that you're no longer as stressed as you used to be before you called on him for assistance. Another thing he can do for you is to help you find your love and passion for what you do once more. Usually, when people find a job that aligns with their ideals, it feels like they're not even working. If you are in a situation that needs to change, Raphael can help you deal with this so you can be less stressed about your purpose in life. If you are exactly where you need to be, he can help you change your perspective so that you can begin to appreciate your work.

Ritual for Work Stress

You should perform this ritual either at the start of your day or at the end.

1. Begin by finding somewhere quiet. You will need at least 10 to 15 minutes by yourself.
2. Close your eyes, part your lips slightly, and take a deep inhale through your nose. Exhale gently through your parted lips. As you breathe, allow your body and mind to relax and be rooted in the moment.
3. Now, it's time to invoke the presence of Archangel Raphael. You can do this by saying, "Archangel Raphael, please come to me now with your healing and love. Guide me so I can let go of stress and experience more bliss and peace in life."
4. In your mind, imagine Raphael's brilliant emerald light. See this light as it shimmers around the room, gradually approaching you. Feel it as it wraps itself all around you. You should feel more relaxed and soothed. This light is full of tranquility and peace.
5. As you exhale through your slightly parted lips, allow all the tension and stress you feel in your body and mind to melt away. If you feel like you are bombarded with negative thoughts about work, do not try to fight them. Instead, notice them as you would birds flying outside the window. Understand that the birds will only be there briefly, and allow your negative thoughts to flow away.
6. You can now use affirmations at this point to reaffirm your peace and tranquility. You can simply say, *"I now let go of all the stress I once felt. I now open myself to Raphael's calmness and peace."*
7. Thank the Archangel for showing up and helping you work through the stress.
8. With one last inhale and exhale, gently open your eyes and feel your awareness return to the room. You can now carry a sense of calmness and tranquility into your day.

Regardless of how packed your schedule is for the day or where you are, you can perform this ritual at any point to help you handle stress better than you ever thought possible.

Addiction

Addiction is so powerful that it is difficult even to realize you are an addict. Usually, addicts feel like they are locked away in a cell, and the keys have been tossed into a deep abyss, never to be found again.

Addiction causes you to self-sabotage. You may be addicted to patterns of behavior or substances that bring momentary relief but ultimately wreak havoc on your physical and mental health.

Addiction affects you in every way possible. It has you convinced that there's no option but to give in. It continues to thrive because of the fears you have. Everyone has insecurities, which are the perfect way for addiction to get a hold of you. You may have experienced something traumatic and painful in your past that has led you to your current state of mind. You find yourself helplessly dependent on certain behaviors or substances that drain your life force.

Thankfully, Archangel Raphael can lend his assistance in your recovery efforts. Once more, it is important to state that you must not attempt to deal with your addictions without the help of professionals. Do not assume that just because you've called upon a celestial being, you do not need anyone else's help. Instead, you can consider these professionals as Raphael's helpers and facilitators. He can help set you free.

The great thing about working with an Archangel, especially the Archangel of healing, is that he will illuminate the true sources of your addictive behavior. You see, it is not enough to simply decide to stop doing something. It is difficult to uncover where the drive to engage in these harmful practices comes from, let alone figure out how to address the core issue. But, working with Archangel Raphael, you will experience true, lasting healing. He will not just help you stop the addictive behavior but to heal the emotional wounds and trauma that led to it in the first place. As you recover, Raphael will give you all the strength and assistance you need to go through the treacherous journey of getting back to wholeness.

Ritual for Releasing Addictions

Whether the addictive behavior you are struggling with is binge eating, watching pornography, smoking, or something else, you can use this ritual to call upon Archangel Raphael to help you deal with it.

1. Find somewhere nice and quiet.
2. Light a white candle.
3. Sit or lie down in a comfortable position, and then close your eyes. Part your lips slightly.

4. Inhale through your nose and exhale through your lips. Continue until you feel fully present and focused.
5. Now, imagine the healing emerald light of Raphael flowing down to you from the sky and enveloping you from head to toe.
6. With the light surrounding you, boldly state your intention with sincerity in your heart. You must also completely trust Raphael to help you work on your addiction.
7. In your mind's eye, imagine the addiction you struggle with as a dark, heavy ball of energy that sits right in the middle of your chest. As you inhale, breathe in Raphael's light.
8. As you exhale, breathe out the addiction. Continue this process until you feel the ball getting lighter and lighter in color. The goal is to reach a point where the darkness is gone, and you are full of green, healing light.
9. Now, imagine yourself months or years from the present moment. Imagine that you have not indulged in addictive behavior for years. Feel the gratitude overwhelm you as it occurs to you that you have finally overcome what you once thought you could never beat.
10. Now, affirm the following: *"Archangel Raphael, I thank you. You have set me free, and forever I stay free."*
11. Thank Raphael for helping you to see what's possible and freeing you from the addiction.
12. Take one more inhale through your nose, exhale through your lips, and then gently open your eyes and return to the present.

Phobias

Everyone has a phobia that is difficult to explain, rationalize, or overcome. These fears are uncontrollable and beyond explanation. When faced with a phobia, you feel as if you have been caught in the stickiest web of terror. Raphael can teach you that there is nothing to fear except fear itself.

What exactly are phobias? They come from deep-seated experiences and memories that are the sources of intense traumas. Lacking the ability to deal with the traumatic experience when it happens, your mind pushes those memories into the subconscious, where you don't have to deal with them until you are reminded of that particular phobia. There are theories that some of the phobias that you deal with are not necessarily from your present incarnation but from a previous life. Regardless of the source, denying their powerful, sinister influence is impossible. They make it impossible for you to be truly free and, in debilitating cases, can stop you from accomplishing what you want in life. Phobias can steal your joy and make your days as dark as night.

You do not have to worry about this if you call upon Archangel Raphael to help you process the phobia. He is an excellent choice to help you overcome whatever terrifies you. He shines a light to illuminate that the shadows are not substantial and should not be feared. His loving, green light banishes all the monsters you imagine are on your path. Let's look at a ritual you can use to help you deal with phobias, with Archangel Raphael fighting your battles by your side.

Ritual for Phobias

1. Find somewhere free from distractions. You don't want to be disturbed during this ritual.
2. Light a white candle or a green one to represent the energy of Raphael and healing.
3. Close your eyes, slightly part your lips, inhale through your nose, and exhale through your mouth. Focus on bringing your awareness to the present moment.
4. In your mind's eye, imagine that the candle flame is green. See its light glowing brighter as you breathe. Imagine the green light engulfing you. It feels amazing, warm, soothing, and healing.
5. Now, call Raphael by saying or thinking, *"Raphael, Sweet Raphael, the Greatest Healer of All, I call upon you. I seek your love, protection, and help so that I may master my fear (mention the phobia you want him to help you get over). Please assist me. Set me free from this phobia. Show me how to be brave, strong, and courageous even when it stares me in the face."*
6. Imagine Raphael standing before you, glowing with a beautiful green light. Look into his penetrating yet loving eyes, and allow the power to wash over you.
7. Now, affirm as many times as you'd like, *"I now release every fear and accept love and healing into my life."*

8. Imagine you're faced with whatever you're afraid of and handling the situation with grace, confidence, and boldness with Raphael by your side.
9. Thank the Archangel for supporting and helping you handle your phobia. Trust that he will address it in the best way possible.
10. Take a few more deep breaths to return to the present, open your eyes and put out the candles, or let them burn as you feel gratitude for having handled your phobias.

Sadness, Grief, and Bereavement

Sadness happens to everyone. Sometimes, things won't go as planned. The dreams and goals you'd hoped to have accomplished by a certain time haven't come true yet. You lose something that means a lot to you, or you look around at the state of the world and find the events are appalling and unbelievable, weighing down on your spirit. Either way, this darkness touches one and all, and that's because, as a human being, you're vulnerable. You must remember that there's nothing permanent about sadness. It's like looking at the sky. No matter how hard you try to keep a cloud there, it will get swept away with time.

There is an upside to sadness, as tough as it may be to realize it when you're in its grasp. Sadness is there to teach you that there's something wrong. It shows you that you're carrying pain and that instead of acting like everything is fine, you must take the time to put down the pain and look at it. You must process what hurts you before you rise above it or stop it from defining you. Archangel Raphael can help you with the process of experiencing your sadness and gaining the strength and resilience to overcome the pain.

Grief and bereavement are more intense than sadness. For instance, you may lose someone close to your heart or a key job or relationship. Grief involves other emotions like despair, anger, guilt, and sadness. It's natural and unavoidable when dealing with loss, but sometimes, it can be hard to get out of the feeling of grief. If this is where you're at, know you can have Raphael's assistance. As for bereavement, it is the period after you've lost someone. You're in mourning. It will take as long as it takes, but when it's gotten to the point where you can no longer function even with therapy, divine intervention may just be what you need.

Meditation for Sadness, Grief, and Bereavement

The following is a simple ritual you can do to get Raphael to help you feel better when you're sad or when you need to let go of grief and bereavement.

1. Go somewhere quiet and free of distractions.
2. Light a green or white candle, and place it on a safe surface in front of you.
3. Get a pen and notepad.
4. Sit comfortably and close your eyes. Take some deep, grounding breaths.
5. As you get stiller in your mind, imagine brown roots growing from the bottom of your feet, going into the ground, and anchoring you to the earth's energy. Allow these roots to make you feel more stable and secure.
6. Invoke Archangel Raphael. Just make a simple statement inviting him to your space and letting him know you seek his comfort and assistance through this difficult time.
7. Open your eyes and turn to your journal. Start writing everything about the situation you're dealing with. The intention behind this exercise is to help you release your emotions. Do not be afraid to get it all. No one will read this besides you.
8. When you're done writing, read everything. You may feel the urge to cry if you weren't already doing so during the writing process. Know that tears are fine. You should read what you've written out loud, and as you do, be aware of how much it hurts and how heavy it feels.
9. It's time for you to release the pain. Hold the paper over the candle's flame with a pair of tongs, letting it catch fire. As the paper begins to burn, imagine in your mind's eye that it is everything that has held you down. Then, set it somewhere safe and let it continue burning.
10. Imagine that the smoke is being transformed into an emerald green light. As it rises and dissipates, allow yourself to feel the relief of having poured out your heart and transmuted your

sadness and pain into healing.
11. When the paper is done burning, go ahead and put out the candles.
12. Close your eyes. Imagine you're looking at this beautiful emerald light that is Raphael's signature. Imagine it surrounds you and begins to pour into your heart energy center. As this green light fills your heart, it dissolves and removes all the pain you feel.
13. Picture your heart glowing with green, emerald green light. That means your heart, body, and mind are healed too.
14. Thank Archangel Raphael for infusing your body, mind, and soul with his loving energy that heals and transforms you. You can thank him in your heart or out loud. The wonderful thing about doing this out loud is that you will feel the vibrations of healing and gratitude overwhelm your body.
15. Sit in the stillness as you bask in the emerald green glow from your heart and Raphael. When you are ready, open your eyes, and carry this energy with you throughout the day. You can repeat this ritual whenever you want, as often as you want.

Archangel Raphael can also help you handle troubled relationships. He will be more than happy to help. Dive deeper into this topic in the following chapter.

Chapter 5: Healing Relationships and Marriages

Archangel Raphael is known to be a matchmaker who helps people deepen their connections on a spiritual level. He's not just the master of healing but also of love, which makes sense as love is the energy that powers healing. That is why working with your heart chakra is always a good idea when doing any meditation, spell, or ritual involving healing and Raphael.

Archangel Raphael is known to be summoned to help heal relationships.[58]

Facilitating Marital Unions

In the book of Tobit, Archangel Raphael helped Tobias and Sara with the demon so they could go on to enjoy a long-lasting and happy married life with each other. Now, your relationship may not be suffering because of actual evil entities. Still, the fact remains that when there are troubles between you and your partner, there is some darkness there. You could use the light of Raphael to illuminate the love that still lies between you so that you can recall why you both work so well in the first place. But more than that, if you've been single for quite a while and want someone to call your own, you can reach out to Raphael for assistance. He can set up a situation where you encounter someone meant for you. He isn't a matchmaker for nothing! You can ask for his assistance in finding the right one for you. Here is a simple meditation you can use to get Raphael to help you get the love of your life:

1. Find somewhere comfortable and quiet. Close your eyes, and take some grounding breaths.
2. In your mind's eye, imagine Raphael's green light surrounding you.
3. Now, imagine this green light transforming your space into a lush garden. In your mind, see Archangel Raphael approaching you with his wings stretched out wide.
4. Picture him reaching out to you with both hands, placing one on your chest where your heart is and the other on your head.
5. Imagine that from both his hands, healing, loving green energy flows into you through you.
6. Picture him taking his hands off you and your heart chakra blazing with emerald green light.
7. Imagine that this green light forms a straight line that travels out before you. Notice that in the distance in this large, magnificent garden is another person whose features you can barely make out. Notice that the straight green line of light from your heart flows towards this other person's heart on the other end of the garden.
8. Feel the sensation of being loved and loving someone. This other person on the other side of the garden is your destined partner.
9. Offer your thanks to Raphael.

10. When you are ready, take a few more grounding breaths as you gradually return your awareness to your physical reality and then open your eyes. Whenever you feel alone or wish someone was by your side, simply remember this exercise and let it reassure you that you have already connected to this person. They will be revealed to you at the right time.

Note: You can also use this exercise to strengthen your love for your partner if you're already married or in a relationship. In this case, visualize being in each other's arms and letting the green, loving light flow directly from one heart to the other.

Staying Faithful

Raphael can assist you when you're tempted to stray from your partner. Suppose you ever find yourself in a situation where your desire for someone else is overwhelming, or a third party has made it their mission in life to "get" you. In that case, you can ask Raphael to help you. This Archangel is aware that you are only human. He knows that complexities can arise and cause trouble even when the love is strong between you and your partner. One of the ways that he can help you with this is by getting you to reflect on your thoughts and emotions. He can also help you discover the external influences that make it hard for you to stay committed to your partner. He'll make it easier for you to communicate honestly with your significant other about your struggles. Communication is always key.

You can perform the following ritual to ensure you and your partner remain faithful to each other. For this exercise, you will need an emerald crystal. If you do not have one, use a quartz crystal instead.

1. First, find somewhere quiet where you will not be bothered for the next 10 to 15 minutes.
2. Prepare the space for your ritual using soft lighting and calm music. If you wish, you can incorporate crystals and candles.
3. Sit comfortably, and close your eyes. Take a few deep breaths to ground yourself in the moment.
4. Hold the emerald in your hands. As you breathe, imagine that you are establishing an energetic connection between yourself and the crystal. You can do this by seeing a brilliant emerald light coming out of the crystal flowing all around you and enveloping

your body. Feel the energy of the crystal flow into and through you.

5. Call upon Archangel Raphael. State your intention clearly and boldly by asking him to guide you through your ritual and offer you the energy and state of mind required to remain faithful to your partner. Also, state everything you desire regarding your relationship. All that matters is that you speak from your heart.
6. Imagine that Raphael's energy infuses your partner's heart and yours. Picture this energy forming a bond wrapping itself around you and your partner, bringing you closer together so that you become one. This energy will create loyalty, trust, and love between you.
7. Thank Raphael for his guidance and assistance.
8. Take a few more grounding breaths. Open your eyes when you feel ready. You'll find it helpful to carry the crystal wherever you go.

Navigating Conflict

When you're in a relationship, you'll inevitably butt heads with your partner occasionally. Unfortunately, not everyone has the right skills to navigate conflict successfully, and what should otherwise have been a small issue becomes something blown out of proportion that destroys a formerly beautiful union. When conflicts arise, Raphael can help quarreling partners deal with the situation in a way that allows each person to feel understood. His efforts encourage the love between both parties to grow stronger than ever. He makes it possible for troubling topics to be discussed in a way that allows compassion to flourish.

Often, conflicts can devolve to a point where each person only feels anger and resentment. With Raphael's help, he can give you the patience to hear your partner out and see things through their eyes, allowing more empathy and connection between you two. More than making it easy to talk to your partner, the matchmaking Archangel can also help you find ways in which your seemingly different perspectives intertwine and devise the best fixes that honor what each of you needs from the relationship. In other words, if you want things to always end on a win-win note, you should ask Raphael to intervene before you do anything else. Here is an excellent ritual that you can use to deal with conflict.

1. As always, the first thing you must do is create a sacred space that is quiet and free from distractions and disturbances. Remember, you can set the mood by using soft lighting and ensuring the room is at the right temperature. Some soothing meditation music can also help.
2. Light a green candle. This candle is the representation of the harmony and healing that you seek between yourself and your partner. If you like, you can perform this ritual with your partner, but if they're not willing, you can still perform this on your own, trusting that you will get the results you seek.
3. Invoke Archangel Raphael. You may need to take a few deep, calming breaths while focusing on his emerald green light coming down from the sky and enveloping you.
4. When you feel his presence, you are ready to express your feelings about your partner. First, take each other's hands and hold them gently and lovingly. Express everything, including your frustrations, anger, and all the positive things you love about them. You need to get it all out there. If you are doing this exercise with your partner, they should also express how they feel. In this case, both of you must be respectful during the other's turn to talk. There is a way to communicate grievances without making the other person feel attacked. Be mindful of the words you choose, but speak your truth.
5. If tension is rising, you both must pause and take a few grounding breaths to bring you back to the intention of this ritual, which is to find unity and love once more. When tensions are hard to ignore, you can ask Raphael to intervene by bringing peaceful, calming energy. You can also imagine that the emerald light surrounding you grows in intensity, encouraging you both to be more compassionate and understanding toward each other.
6. When you are done sharing, imagine the emerald light emanating from your hands and flowing to your hearts. Then, picture the green light from each person's heart emanating and beaming towards the other, touching their heart. You are now in a loving, energetic cocoon. This is the melting and coming together point of your spirits, where they become one.
7. Take a few moments to appreciate what you love about each other. You can think about this in your mind, but it would be

more beneficial to say the words aloud so your partner can hear and appreciate you too.
8. If you are performing this ritual alone, you can bring your partner's image to mind while you do it. You can hold their hands in your mind.
9. When you are ready, thank Raphael for assisting you.
10. Take a few calming, grounded breaths, and open your eyes when you are ready. You can hug each other and profess your love to each other. Leave that sacred space with the intention of staying connected, at peace, and in love with your partner.

Restoring Trust and Bringing Back the Spark

Sometimes, you and your partner lose the spark you once had. It could be because you've both been too busy to pay attention to each other, or even worse, you're struggling with the aftermath of infidelity. When it's the latter, it's tough to feel the spark or connection when you no longer trust each other. Is it possible to work through this situation and get things back to how they used to be? You can make things happen if you both want things to work out. Who better to help you navigate this ugly, rough patch in your relationship than Raphael himself?

When you no longer trust each other, Raphael's energy can mend your broken trust. He shows you how you contributed to current affairs and how you can take responsibility for fixing things. He shows you how to forgive and gives you the strength to be open-minded enough to understand each other and see through the issues beneath the surface.

More than anyone else, Raphael knows how important it is to find the spark of true love in a relationship. His efforts are all directed towards getting you in touch with your emotions and doing the same for your partner. This way, you can both remember what it was about each other that had you unable to think of much else in the first place. He guides you without judgment until you both rediscover the joy of being together again. This way, you can get back the romance you lost and feel some hope for your future.

It is possible to restore the trust that you've lost. Here is a great ritual that you can use to bring back the trust and ensure that the spark you had for each other is returned as well.

1. The first thing you must do is create a sacred space. Prepare it as you usually would, but try to make it as romantic as possible this time. You can use white and green flowers, some lovely music, preferably without lyrics, and soft, gentle lighting. Consider using incense or oils that are reminiscent of love and softness. Rose essential oil is an excellent choice.
2. You and your partner should sit facing each other and hold each other's hands. Close your eyes and take a few grounding breaths.
3. Now that you both feel present and grounded, invoke Archangel Raphael's presence. You can each take turns asking him to infuse his healing love into your partnership. You do not have to use specific words. All that matters is you speak from your heart and sincerely.
4. You may both talk about what you've been struggling with regarding trust. Importantly, the main point of this conversation should be reminiscing about the best times you had at the start of the relationship when the spark was still strong. This is where your focus should be.
5. When you're done sharing, spend 5 minutes staring deeply into each other's eyes. You must maintain eye contact. This is not a staring contest but an opportunity to bear your souls. In the spirit of vulnerability, it is easier for Archangel Raphael's energy to flow. Don't be alarmed if either or both of you cry.
6. Profess your love for each other and your commitment to a healthy and successful relationship.
7. When you are ready, you both need to thank Archangel Raphael for his assistance and for helping you rediscover the spark you thought was lost.

Dealing with Trauma from Past Relationships

Raphael can help you work through the trauma you have faced in past relationships. If you have dealt with bad experiences from past relationships, like abuse in any form (physical, mental, emotional, financial, etc.,) betrayal, constant arguments, and so on, you're probably carrying wounds from those relationships. Those wounds will affect how you interact with your present or future partner. Your past will cause you to act in certain ways, interpret things through specific lenses, have unique emotional responses and behaviors, and so on. Logically, you know this is a new, different person. Still, you act in ways meant to keep you from getting hurt again. Sometimes, your choices aren't necessarily the best for the relationship.

Ugliness from your past can make it hard for you to bond with anyone else emotionally, as you keep a part of yourself permanently hidden - usually, the vulnerable part, which you need to share to develop a deeper connection with your partner. You find it hard to trust others, so you retreat behind a wall to avoid getting hurt, but that also keeps you from having a true, loving connection. You approach your interactions with prospective partners cautiously, which can scare them away from you. If you manage to land a relationship, you may find yourself dealing with conflicts, power imbalances, and being iced out as you repeat the patterns from the past because they're now ingrained in your mind. They're a habit.

Another insidious thing about your traumatic past is that it can cause low self-esteem. That can lead you to settle for the bare minimum. At worst, you find yourself dealing with criticism, manipulation, and emotional abuse at the hands of your new partner (who is basically the old one but with a different face). You need help working through the self-limiting beliefs if you want a shot at a healthy relationship where you can be authentic and feel safe. You want to be in a relationship where you can communicate freely without fear. But how can you do this? In addition to therapy, you can ask Raphael to help you.

The trauma that casts a shadow on your relationships can be healed, and Raphael is just the Archangel for the job. He can support you and help you regain your emotional and mental health. He does this by gently leading you to face your wounds and treat them so that you can release the pain and focus on the here and now. He can show you how to trust and be vulnerable once more so that you can return to enjoying love.

As devastating as the effects of trauma are, you can handle them with Archangel Raphael's help. You can do the following ritual to help you heal those wounds.

1. Go somewhere quiet and free from disturbances and distractions.
2. Now, light a white candle. White represents the energy of healing, just like the color green. Still, it also represents the concept of purity and innocence.

3. Lie down, or sit comfortably. Close your eyes. Take deep, grounding breaths, allowing your body and mind to be rooted in the moment.
4. In your mind's eye, imagine a brilliant, soothing emerald light surrounding you. This light comes from Archangel Raphael himself.
5. Invoke Raphael's presence by saying you need him to help you heal. Once more, the words you use for this ritual don't matter as long as you speak from your heart. Remember that your intention for this ritual is to find all the emotional wounds you may not be aware of, bring them to light, and heal them. If you remember certain traumatic experiences as you sit in Raphael's presence, feel free to share them with him. You can break down in tears or be overcome with emotions. Remember, you can share everything because you're safe with him.
6. When you feel ready, thank him for listening to you. Thank Raphael because you know that he will heal not just the trauma you are aware of but the deeper wounds you've been unable to access with your conscious mind.

The Need for Humility

When you reach out to Raphael, you cannot expect him to fix things without you putting in the work. The thing to do is ask him to share insights about how to fix the relationship issues you're facing. There's always some concrete action you can take to show your partner that you still love them and desire to make the relationship work, so listen and watch closely for any messages that come your way after reaching out to Raphael.

Also, you cannot be prideful when contacting Raphael to fix your relationship. After learning that he can help relationships, some people think they can get Raphael to force their partner to come crawling back, apologizing, and putting in all the work on their own. They don't want to have to do anything, but that's not how it works. Don't be like them. You must be humble and be willing to seek forgiveness.

You must put aside whatever notions you have about deserving reparations or anything of the sort and simply forgive your spouse (provided your issues aren't life-threatening, as in the case of abuse, for instance). You must show mercy to help Raphael be even more effective at his work.

Now that you know how Raphael can help you heal your relationships and marriages, you'll discover how you can also draw on his power to heal your body. The next chapter is all about being healed with his loving touch.

Chapter 6: Healing the Physical Body

Archangel Raphael can heal your body. It is important to note that you should not use prayer or meditation as a substitute for seeking medical help. You must understand that working with Archangel Raphael is meant to complement modern forms of treatment. =

Hands-on Healing

Hands-on healing is a healing process that involves channeling the energy meant to heal your body using touch. It is about working with the spiritual connection between one and all. You see, it may look like you are separate from every other person and every other thing around you, but the truth is that everything is connected. Hands-on healing exploits this connection between you and everything else. You are connected to various energies, including healing energies. Therefore, hands-on healing is about the healer and the one to be healed working with these energies. It can help with physical, emotional, and mental well-being. You can work with the healing power of Archangel Raphael to assist you with this particular healing method. Here's how it works.

1. You must first create a sacred space where there will be no distractions and no disturbances. This is important because you do not want to disrupt the flow of healing energy between yourself and the person you will be working with. Make this space conducive for spiritual work by changing the lighting, playing soft

spiritual music without lyrics, lighting candles, lighting incense, and placing crystals around you.

2. Close your eyes, sit or lie down, and take a few deep breaths. Then, intend for Archangel Raphael to join you. You can call upon his presence by verbally asking out loud that he participate in this ritual or by asking him in your mind until you begin to feel his energy flowing in and around you.

3. When you feel ready, put your hands on whatever body part requires healing.

4. In your mind's eye, imagine your hands emanating emerald-green energy. You are working as a conduit for this energy so that Archangel Raphael can allow the light to flow into this person's body and heal them.

5. Keep your hands over the body part. You may notice the differences in temperature, energy flow, magnetism, and vibrations. You need to connect with your intuition as you perform this hands-on healing exercise because it is a very intuitive process.

6. You may receive special messages or insights from Archangel Raphael. Use them to better channel the energy you're working with. For instance, you may realize that the pain you're focused on comes from somewhere else. Raphael might make you inclined to place your hands elsewhere other than where the pain is. This

7. As you continue to work on the body part, you must adopt an attitude of love. Make sure your heart chakra is overflowing with love. Remember, healing is actually rooted in love. So, connect with divinity from a place of love and understand that.

8. When you sense that the session is complete, thank Raphael for being present and offering his help. Tell him that you trust that he will pick up from where you left off and that the healing is already done, even if it doesn't appear that way now. Thank him for offering guidance, insight, love, and energy to transform the body into its original, healthy form. When you are ready, take a last deep, grounding breath, and then gradually let go of your intentions. Trust that Archangel Raphael is on the job.

Gem Water Healing

Did you know you could work with Archangel Raphael's energy and gem water to heal yourself or someone else? Gem water is an elixir made by energetically charging some water with gems. This water can be consumed and applied to the body. It creates the physical reaction and healing that you seek. The water takes on the energetic healing properties of whichever gem you put into it.

Gem water is an elixir that is charged with Raphael's energy for healing.[59]

When you want to work with gem water, you first must figure out what each one is meant to do. Next, ensure that the ones you choose are safe to put in water.

It is important to understand that every gem has a unique energy signature. You don't want to use a gemstone meant to help with digestion to stop a headache. It's not like it wouldn't work. It would be more expedient to go with the more effective option. Here are some gems and what you can use them for:

- **Amethyst** is excellent for alertness, brain, nerves, lungs, intersectional tract, low blood pressure, swellings, bruises, tension release, and pain.
- **Blue apatite** is excellent for healing bone fractures and osteoporosis, improving appetite, and building stronger teeth and healthier joints.

- **Citrine** is excellent for the stomach, digestion, pancreas, and spleen.
- **Dolomite** is a good one to use for pain. It will help you with cramping, metabolic imbalances, heart issues, circulation problems, and cleaning out your blood vessels.
- **Emerald** is excellent for your eyes, gallbladder, heart, and respiratory system. You can also use it to battle inflammation and infections.
- **Green beryl** can eliminate pollutants and toxins. It is excellent for the thyroid gland, bladder, kidney, and autoimmune issues. You can also use this to deal with allergies.
- **Hematite** can be used to improve circulation.
- **Indigolite or blue tourmaline** – both are excellent when it comes to dealing with burns, joint issues, and numbness.
- **Jasper** helps the body feel stronger and more energized thanks to its effects on circulation and temperature regulation.
- **Kabamba** can be used to deal with internal organ inflammation, cases of flu, and colds.
- Use **labradorite** to regulate the menstrual and hormonal cycles.
- **Molokaite** can relieve nausea and constipation and help intestinal health. It is also excellent for healing wounds and boosting the immune system.
- **Nephrite** can detoxify the body, help ear issues, and improve balance.
- **Onyx** can be used for more efficient waste elimination, a stronger immune system, and better hearing.
- **Peridot** can help you deal with detoxification, burning fat, and eliminating warts and fungal infections.
- **Clear quartz** is amazing for healthy nails, hair, and skin. It can also help your nerves, brain, hormones, water balance, and the glands in your body. On top of that, you can use it to amplify the effects of other crystals.
- **Rose quartz** can be used to deal with sexual problems.

- **Smoky quartz** can help with intestinal issues, inflammation, pain in the body, and a weak immune system. You can also use it to improve your nerve health and handle the effects of radiation.
- **Turquoise** is excellent for heartburn, ear infections, and respiratory diseases. If you're dealing with cramps and inflammation, this is an excellent crystal to create your gem water.
- **Green tourmaline** or **verdelite** are excellent for all nervous conditions, detoxification, the reduction of scarring, and better intestinal health.
- **Zoisite** can reduce stress and inflammation.

Creating Healing Gem Water

Now that you know the appropriate gemstones to use, it is time to move on to the process of creating your gem water for healing.

1. Before anything else, you need to cleanse the gemstones and then charge them with your intention. You must put them under the moonlight or in sunlight to cleanse them. You can also bury them in the earth for a night, or you may simply sit with them and use some salt to rubble over them and get rid of the other energies from other people and places that may not serve your purpose. You need to cleanse your gemstones because, in the handling process, other people have touched them and left behind their energies on them. Sometimes, these energies are not necessarily good for you.

2. You now need to charge them with your energy. You will also be infusing these stones with the energy of Archangel Raphael. To do this, sit with them in your hands or around you and close your eyes. Take a few grounding breaths, and then in your mind's eye, envision Archangel Raphael's powerful emerald green light coming down from the sky and going into each crystal to charge it. Imagine that each crystal now has a distinct, green luminosity around it. You have now charged these crystals or the healing power of Archangel Raphael.

3. Prepare your gem water. All you have to do is put the crystals into a glass container filled with water.

4. Enlist Archangel Raphael's help. All you have to do is call on Raphael and ask him to charge the water with his healing power, much like he "troubled" the pool at Bethesda so that people could jump in and get healed. In your mind's eye, see more of his healing green energy infusing into the water from the crystals so it glows with a beautiful emerald green.
5. As you sit with the gem water, be clear about your intentions. You can state them out loud or just ponder them in your mind.
6. Drink or apply the water to the problematic area. When you're drinking gem water, take time to focus on the fact that you are seeking healing. Trust that you will inevitably receive it. This makes it easier for the gem water to flow through you and correct any energetic imbalances. As you drink, envision the green light flowing down your throat and radiating to every part of your body.
7. You can also use your gem water for other things like watering your plants, bathing, misting your skin, etc.
8. When you're done creating, you should thank Archangel Raphael for giving you the energy that will heal you and anyone else using that water.

Crystal Mojo Bags

A mojo bag is a little pouch with special items like crystals, charms, stones, personal effects, herbs, and spices. All of the things in the mojo bag have their own energetic influence, which, when combined together, give you specific results. Since this book is about Archangel Raphael and healing, it will cover healing mojo bags. Sometimes, people call the mojo bag a gris-gris, conjure, or root bag.

There is no wrong or right way to make a mojo bag. So, do not let anyone make you feel like you're not using it right. Consider the instructions in this book as guidelines on what you can do, and go with your intuition if you feel like getting creative. In this case, you are making a crystal mojo bag, so whatever you do, put a crystal in it that will help you accomplish your healing intention. Think of these bags as talismans. You can have the energy of this talisman upon you and around you at all times just by carrying it wherever you go.

When working with these bags to heal yourself or the people around you, you can invoke Archangel Raphael to infuse them with his healing energy. He can also help you choose the right crystal for the job. All you need to do is sit, ground yourself, hold each crystal one at a time, and pay attention to any intuitive nudge you receive from Raphael. Here are instructions for how you can create your own crystal mojo bags.

1. Begin by setting your intention for the bag you'd like to create. In this case, your intention is for healing. Be clear about the sort of healing that you seek from this mojo bag, whether it be physical, mental, emotional, or spiritual. Invoke Archangel Raphael at this point so he can supercharge your intention.

2. Pick your crystals. Choose the one that you sense goes well with Archangel Raphael's energy. Do not rush this process. You shouldn't work with a crystal if you feel unsure about it. Some of the crystals you can work with include clear quartz, rose quartz, malachite, green aventurine, and green emerald.

3. Get the materials you need to create your mojo bag. You'll need a small bit of white or green fabric or a white or green pouch. You'll also need the crystals you chose, a pen, and paper. You can add things that mean something to you or the person you're trying to heal. Herbs and spices that represent the idea of healing to you are fine, too.

4. Prepare the bag. Close your eyes and take some deep, long breaths to ground yourself. In your mind's eye, see Raphael's light coming down from the sky and engulfing you completely. Imagine that this light surrounds all the materials you'll use to create the crystal mojo bag. Feel your hands flowing and pulsing with Raphael's energy. Take a moment to thank Archangel Raphael for giving you his power and assistance.

5. You must cleanse the crystals if you haven't already and then charge them with your intention.

6. As you put them in the bag, say an affirmation about what you want them to do. There is no specific way to state your affirmation. Just make sure that you acknowledge that it is already a done deal. You can also affirm that Raphael's energy charges each crystal and other materials.

7. This step is the personalization process. This is the part where you put personal items in the bag. You can also add other

materials that correspond energetically to your intention. You need to take the pen and paper and write down your intentions, then fold that paper neatly and place it in the bag.

8. Now that you've put all the materials you want in the bag, it is time to seal it with Archangel Raphael's energy. Imagine that the green light circles the bag, powerfully radiating around it, as you seal the bag or tie a security using a string.
9. Once more, call upon Archangel Raphael and tell him what you want the bag to do. Thank him for his assistance as you witness his emerald light working its magic.
10. You can place the bag somewhere safe and sacred. Alternatively, you can carry it around to enjoy its effects all day. You can also leave it under your pillow.
11. It will be necessary to recharge the bag with energy every now and then. Hold it in your hands and invoke Archangel Raphael's presence. State that you want the bag to be recharged with this energy, visualize the emerald green light charging it, and then you're good to go again. If you want to edit your written intention, you can do that before you recharge the bag.

Healing Visualization

Raphael can also help you heal by using visualization. You're already familiar with this, as most of the meditations and rituals here require you to be able to visualize his emerald green light. Visualization is a powerful technique that should never be overlooked. With this particular technique, you will imagine that your body has already received the healing you seek. By placing this in the past, you make it inevitable for your body, mind, and soul to come into alignment with the fact that you have already seen yourself as healed. If you place your healing in the future, the odds of it happening will be slim because it'll always be in the future. Every time tomorrow rolls around, it never does because it becomes today. In other words, the only time is now. By putting something in the past, you ensure that you encourage your subconscious mind to accept that it is already a done deal, making it easier for Archangel Raphael's energies to flow through you and heal you. Here's the process that you need to follow to use visualization to receive your healing:

1. Find somewhere nice and comfortable where you will not be distracted or bothered. Wear comfortable clothing to sit or lie down with ease. Choose a position you can maintain for 10 to 15 minutes.

2. Close your eyes, part your lip slightly, and take a few deep, grounding breaths in through your nose and out of your slightly parted lips. You may notice that the exhales are longer than your inhales. If that's the case, this is fine. If it helps, you can play soothing meditation music to help you focus on the moment. Essential oils can also create the spiritual ambiance required for visualization.

3. Reach out to Archangel Raphael. You can mentally repeat his name over and over until you begin to feel his energy welling up within and around you. Alternatively, you could say, *"Archangel Raphael, I seek your presence. I desire your help. Please come to me right now."* And then, you wait until you begin to feel him unmistakably.

4. Once you sense that you have invoked Raphael, it is time to envision your body healing. For instance, assume you're trying to heal a sprain in your ankle that keeps you from walking properly. In this case, imagine yourself running or walking confidently and powerfully. Imagine yourself walking as though your ankle never hurt a day in your life. Note that you must be in your body during this visualization exercise. In other words, do not look at yourself walking or running as if you are watching yourself in a movie. Instead, take the place of the actor. You should feel each step as you hit the pavement with each foot. You shouldn't be able to see your face; you should only see the parts of your body you would see were you to get up and walk.

5. Use all your senses to take this visualization exercise up a notch. In this example, feel the vibrations reverberating through your body as each foot hits the pavement. You must hear the sounds around you as you walk and notice your breathing as you walk. Using all your imaginative senses will make this feel so real that what feels like some point and time in the future actually feels like it's happening here and now. You'll know you've done this correctly because, by the time you come out of the visualization, you will be shocked to discover that you are still sitting in your

room.

6. As you continue to walk in your imagination, envision this emerald healing light of Archangel Raphael flowing around the problematic area of your body.
7. When you feel ready, gradually return your awareness to the room you're in. Before you open your eyes, affirm that your body has been healed and the changes you seek have been implemented. You may sit in the feeling of being healed for as long as you like, and when you're ready, thank Archangel Raphael for his assistance and open your eyes.

Prayers and Meditation

The subjects of prayer meditation to connect to Archangel Raphael have already been discussed in Chapter 2. However, no details were given on how to ask for his healing. Whether you have chosen to pray to Archangel Raphael or to meditate until you feel his presence, asking him to heal your body is not complicated. If you have chosen the prayer route, you must communicate your desires sincerely.

If you are using meditation to seek healing, all you have to do is bring awareness to the part of your body that requires it. Then, in your mind, envision Archangel Raphael's healing emerald green energy flowing through and around that body part until you feel like the exercise should be brought to a close. At this point, offer your thanks to Archangel Raphael. You can repeat your prayers or meditations as often as you'd like. In addition, it would be helpful to constantly remind yourself whenever you feel like the pain or issue isn't going away. After you do, you must have faith that it is being handled.

In the next chapter, you'll be learning about angelic Reiki. You'll discover how you can work with it to attain whatever you need from Raphael.

Chapter 7: Angelic Reiki

Angelic Reiki is powered by angels who generously offer their guidance and assistance. It involves energy realignment and healing in all ways, physically, emotionally, and mentally. This practice is about developing a stronger connection to angelic dimensions where the Archangels can be found. The difference between traditional Reiki and angelic Reiki is that the angelic version is of a higher dimensional vibration.

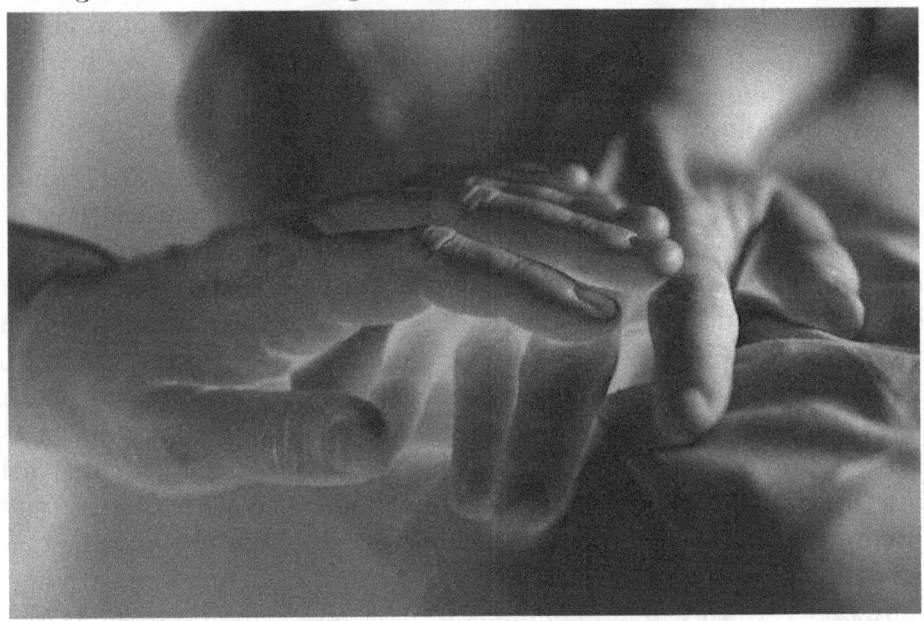

Angelic reiki is powered by the angels.[60]

The Origin of Angelic Reiki

Angelic Reiki was taught to Kevin Core (a Reiki Master) by the Archangel Metatron around 2002, and in 2008, Christine Core took over from Kevin. With Archangel Raphael's guidance and Reiki, you can affect the structure of cells in the body and molecules in everything around you. You can expect changes to occur that will restore harmony and balance to you on an energetic level, and these changes will ripple outward to positively affect your body and life. Angelic Reiki allows you to create a clear route for divine powers to flow freely toward you, especially as you work with the various symbols.

On Attunements

When it comes to angelic Reiki, you'll need to experience various attunements so that you can open up your chakras or energy centers even more, making it easier for you to work with healing energy and to remain in vibrational alignment with the angels as you do your work. You can think of the attunement as an initiation on a cosmic level, granting you access to higher energies. It's a way to become a free-flowing conduit for divinity to act through so you can heal others around you, and when needed, you can heal yourself too. To experience attunement, it's best to work with a Reiki Teacher or Master because you cannot do this alone. These people have years of experience and have been under the tutelage of other Masters, so it only makes sense to make things easier for yourself by letting them help you.

What can you expect to happen during an attunement? The Master will use various methods to harmonize the Reiki frequencies in your energy system. You'll have to work with meditation and specific rituals and experience the direct transmission of divine energy. There's no set way to experience these things because every human has a different energy foundation, and everyone is at different stages when it comes to being prepared for attunement. One thing you can be certain of is that you will be profoundly moved during the process. Your energy blockages will be cleared, and your chakras will be properly aligned for the first time in your life. You'll awaken to the fullness of who you are and discover latent healing powers within you that you can channel as needed.

Before you get a Reiki attunement, look into getting a Reiki Master with a good reputation. Not only should others be able to vouch for their abilities, but you should also be able to align with them easily. Trust is an integral part of the process of attunement. When you've found a great Master, connect with them, and let them know you'd love their assistance with attunement, and they'll let you know what to expect, what you require, and what you'll need to pay. It's best to get all this out of the way before you proceed. Also, you need to be certain that this is something you want because you cannot afford to take it lightly. This is the gateway you will step through to become a powerful healer. Combining this with consciously working with Archangel Raphael's power will make you an unstoppable healing force.

Angelic Reiki Healing Techniques

You'll need to work with certain techniques for this healing modality. One technique involves hand placements, where you must place your hand in certain positions to allow proper energy flow. Your hands may be directly on the body, or they may only hover non - intrusively. Still, they have to match up to the energy centers and channels on the body so that Raphael's angelic healing power can flow and do its thing. Every placement is precise and has a specific role. If you place your hands on or around the crown chakra, for instance, it will help you to feel connected to the spirit realm, clear your mind, and relax. When on the heart energy center, you encourage healing (especially of the emotions), compassion, and deep love. It's also fine to place your hands right over the part of the body experiencing discomfort.

Another technique involves symbols and visualization. You work with specific symbols to draw the divine energy you need to heal yourself or another and use specific visualization exercises to help. The symbols serve as amplifiers of energies and vibrations that facilitate specific intentions. They pull the energy of celestial beings to lend you assistance. When you focus on the visualizations and symbols, and you and the person you're healing intend what you want to accomplish, you make it easier for the healing energy to flow through your hands and create the changes you seek.

The Connection between Raphael and Reiki

Reiki practitioners understand that they are meant to be a channel of the energy Raphael brings. By understanding this, they can get out of the way and not adversely influence the healing process. Raphael can do his work by offering intuitive insight and guidance to the Reiki practitioner and the person to be healed. He helps by revealing the root of the trauma or imbalance causing distress, which is how true healing can be achieved. Usually, the Reiki Master doesn't just work with Raphael alone but with other angelic entities. Think of them as a team of Angelic EMTs, if you will. They can work with ascended masters, other angels, and other beings who specialize in healing certain things to bring you better results. Now it's time to take a look at the various Reiki symbols you can work with.

Cho Ku Rei

Cho Ku Rei is the symbol you use to cleanse and protect, and you can turn it on by drawing it on your palms when you're healing yourself or someone else. You can also draw this symbol on any energy chakra or all of them to increase energy flow, and little wonder, because it's known as the symbol of power. It is said that "Cho Ku Rei" literally translates to "Channel all the Universe's power here and now." Think of this symbol as a prerequisite before you begin your Reiki practice. Like the quartz crystal to other crystals, Cho Ku Rei amplifies the energy of the other Reiki symbols.

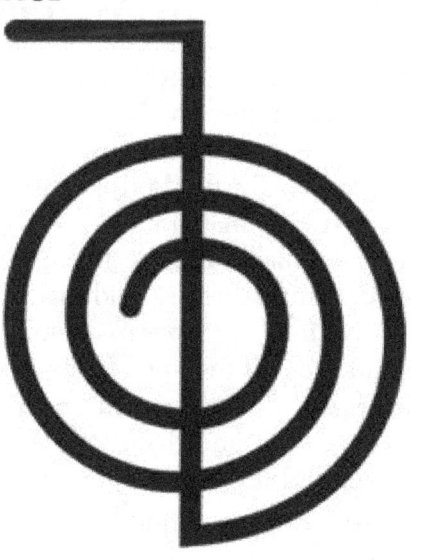

Cho Ku Rei for protection and cleansing.[61]

How to Draw Cho Ku Rei

1. To draw this symbol, draw a line from left to right, then down so it forms an upside-down L.
2. Draw a spiral to the right at the bottom of that L. The outermost part of the spiral should be close to the first horizontal line.
3. Keep drawing the spiral from the outside to the inside until you have three spiraling lines. Do not lift your pen until you connect it to the vertical line in the middle with the smallest spiral.

The horizontal line of this symbol is the connection you're establishing with universal energies. The vertical line is the flow of powerful light from the soul star chakra into all the other centers and channels in the body before terminating in the root chakra. The spiral you draw should create seven intersections with the vertical line, representing the seven major chakras. You must use the same precise directions, no matter which hand you choose. In other words, don't reverse it when you change hands. You can draw this on the main seven chakras (crown, third eye, throat, heart, solar plexus, sacral, and root chakras) and the secondary chakras (feet, knees, hips, shoulders, ears, and eyes). You can also draw on the main organs and on the front and back of the body to ensure protection.

This symbol is excellent for stimulating all your energy centers, fighting fatigue, improving your mood, protecting your energy and physical bodies, removing blocks and bad energies, and so on. You can maximize its power by visualizing Archangel Raphael's green light emanating from the symbol as you draw it.

Sei He Ki

Sei He Ki for harmony.[62]

Sei He Ki is a powerful symbol that brings you harmony, balances your emotions, and heals them. Like the previous symbol, you can activate this one on your chakras and palms. It cleanses and promotes the flow of spiritual energy.

How to Draw Sei He Ki

1. First, draw a line slanted at a 45-degree angle from right to left to draw this symbol.
2. Draw from right to left without lifting your hand to have a slanted letter V.
3. Next, draw from right to left again to have a mirrored N.
4. Draw a short vertical line, and draw a curved line at the bottom with the curve leaning right. When you're done, it should look like you have a slanted letter V with the number 5 at the bottom. This is the first part. You can lift your hand off the paper to draw the next part.
5. Next, you must draw a very short horizontal line above the slanted V, starting from the halfway point and terminating at the top end of the V.
6. Without lifting your hand, draw a larger semicircle encompassing the first sign and the number 5.
7. Lift your hand off the paper, and draw two arches on the larger semicircle beneath the slanted V. The second arch should be higher than the first. When you're done, it should look like you have a small letter m on the larger semicircle.

This symbol will help you connect with divinity so you can easily figure out emotional problems tucked away in your subconscious. You can use it when there's conflict, not by drawing it on the people but discreetly on various areas of the room. This way, the tense environment can be flooded with calmness and peace. You can also use this symbol to assist with addictions and stop intrusive and negative thoughts in their tracks. Use it when you or someone else feels stressed. If it helps, consider Sei He Ki as the window you open when everywhere else feels energetically stuffy.

Hon Sha Ze Sho Nen

This symbol is excellent for healing at a distance. It means "Without past, present, or future." Use this symbol to help you channel Archangel Raphael's healing energy across time and space so that they will receive their miracle no matter where the subject to be healed is. This symbol also transcends time, as you can send it to work on your past, present, or future.

How to Draw Hon Sha Ze Sho Nen

This one will take a bit of practice to master drawing, but you can.

1. First, draw a line from right to left.
2. Draw a line from top to bottom that intersects your horizontal line. You should now have a cross.
3. Imagine there's a circle around the cross. Draw a line from the midpoint of the intersecting lines to the 7 o'clock point.
4. Next, draw a line from the middle of the intersecting lines to the 5 o'clock point.
5. Draw a line from left to right, close to the bottom of the vertical line. Neither point should touch the 7 or 5 o'clock line.
6. Draw a horizontal line from left to right underneath the symbol you've just drawn from steps one through five. Let the line be long enough to act as a table for the top symbol.
7. Next, place your pen or finger on the right side of the 6th line, just above it, so it almost touches the 5 o'clock point of the line from step four. Then draw a line that slants at a 45-degree angle, crossing down through the line from step six and not going beyond the starting point of that line.
8. Draw a short vertical line to the right beneath the seventh line.

Hon Sha Ze Sho Nen for healing.[68]

9. From the top of the vertical line from the previous step, draw a short horizontal line to the right.
10. Now, draw a short line from the endpoint of the previous one downward. If you've done this right, you should have a small, three-sided box with no bottom.
11. Draw a very short horizontal line inside the box from left to right.
12. Underneath the drawing you now have, draw a horizontal line that slants subtly upwards from left to right. Think of it as a table carrying the other signs.
13. Draw another line beneath that starts from the middle of line twelve and slants subtly upward but stops just before the end of line twelve.
14. Draw a vertical line from top to bottom from the middle of line twelve. If you've done this right, you should have what looks like an F.
15. To the left of this "F," draw a vertical line from top to bottom that slants subtly to the right and ends below the bottom of line fourteen.
16. Beneath all the previous drawings, start from the middle and draw a slight curve down and out to the left.
17. Return to the start of line sixteen, and draw another line that curves slightly down and out to the right. If you've done this right, it should look like the roof of a house.
18. Draw a short horizontal line from left to right underneath this roof.
19. Underneath the roof that houses a short horizontal line, start from the end, and draw a horizontal line from left to right, and then without lifting your hand, draw a line down that curves to the left as if it's part of a circle. Let it stop underneath the start of this line so you have what looks like a shark fin.
20. Draw a line that curves down and to the right next to line nineteen.
21. Within the curved line twenty, draw another smaller line that curves down and to the right and is encompassed in line twenty.
22. Finally, draw a line that starts slightly above line twenty but goes down and curves to the left, terminating slightly below the end of line 20.

You can merge Cho Ku Rei, Sei He Ki, and Hon Sha Ze Sho Nen together to allow an even more powerful flow of energy from Raphael to work on your intention.

Working with Reiki and Raphael

1. Go somewhere quiet and conducive for energy work. There should also be no distractions or disturbances.
2. Set your intention for healing, whether for yourself, a loved one, or even a pet.
3. Sit comfortably, close your eyes, and take a few centering breaths while keeping your awareness on your heart chakra.
4. Now, out loud or in your mind, call on Archangel Raphael, and ask him to facilitate the healing process.
5. Open your eyes, and activate the Reiki symbols on your palms, beginning with Cho Ku Rei.
6. Place your hands on the part of the body that needs healing, or you may just let them hover. Suppose the person you want to heal isn't present. In that case, you can activate the Hon Sha Ze Sho Nen Reiki symbol and hold your hands over their photo or some other personal effect.
7. Allow your hands to move where your intuition guides them, envisioning that they burn with Raphael's brilliant, bright emerald green light as you work.
8. While letting the energy flow, you can use healing affirmations in your mind or say them out loud. Continue with this, and let your intuition guide you.
9. When you feel ready, end the session by thanking Archangel Raphael, and then let your energy connection to the angelic realm go.
10. Ground yourself by imagining roots connecting your feet to the earth's core.

Reiki Principles

Reiki has certain guidelines or ethics you should follow to get the best of it. These principles are a strong foundation that makes you more efficient at using your abilities for good. These are the principles, all of them worth remembering.

"For now, I choose not to be angry." Anger is a disruptive force that can cause energy to flow out of alignment, making it hard to experience healing. This emotion must be released by both the Reiki master and the patient receiving treatment. Anger is so powerful that it will cause an imbalance spiritually, mentally, and emotionally. This makes it tough for the healer's touch to channel the healing energy freely to the recipient and tougher still for the recipient to accept the healing power trying to flow through him. So, choosing not to be angry implies you will remain peaceful, calm, and in control of your emotions. It means you recognize where your anger is coming from, but you choose to master it rather than let it consume you. You choose to feel it and then release it. You could do this using breathwork, meditation, journaling, or whatever method feels right.

"For now, I choose not to worry." Worry also does you no good when you're working with Reiki. It is far better to ensure your mind is in the here and now rather than being anxious about a future that may not play out how you fear it will. Worry is natural, sure . . . but too much of it, and you will wreak havoc on your emotions and your mind. In Reiki, everyone working with energy must be present, as healing comes here and now, not later. You worry when you're afraid and untrusting, not sure that life will work out exactly as it should and that everything will be okay. If this is a habit, it will serve you to quit it. Reiki invites you to trust in the universe and its intelligence. Nothing happens that isn't by divine design. When you know this, you no longer feel the need to know what comes next or to control results. You can just focus on living from one moment to the next, which is excellent for encouraging healing.

"For now, I choose to be grateful." Gratitude is a conscious choice to be thankful for all the good in your life. In the attitude of gratitude, you open your eyes to the many blessings and gifts that you get to experience every day. You are thankful because you know there's always something good to be appreciated if you're willing to see it. Practicing gratitude is an excellent way to encourage positive energy flow in every aspect of your life. It's about moving your attention away from what your ego considers "bad" to the abundance of good in your life. This positive energy is necessary for allowing Reiki energy to flow freely and heal you or another. It's also a good idea to express gratitude for the power of Reiki, as this dramatically intensifies the effects of the Reiki master's work.

"For now, I choose honesty." This means that you choose to be transparent and truthful in all your ways. It's about understanding the need for congruence in what you intend, what you actually do, and what you say. It's about ensuring you're never deceiving anyone, not even yourself. In other words, if there are things you must do or changes you must make that would benefit your health and well-being, it's best to face the truth and do something about it. The energy flow will be even more beneficial when you choose to be honest with yourself and work with the truth of your situation rather than pretend it isn't there. As for the Reiki practitioner, he must also practice honesty. He must be upfront with you about the extent of his experience and what you should expect from your sessions with him so that you have the power to make decisions based on accurate information.

"For now, I choose kindness." Kindness is the final cornerstone of Reiki. You must respect all life by demonstrating kindness, compassion, and empathy. Everything that lives deserves compassion and carries undeniable value. It doesn't matter how they look or where they are in life. Reiki masters know it is important to honor the spark of divinity and the breath of life in all things. They know that they must always be about helping people suffer less and heal better. In Reiki, being kind to yourself is also important. Self-compassion is a prerequisite to compassion for others because you cannot give what you don't have. Being kind to yourself means setting clear boundaries, doing what you must to stay healthy, and remaining in harmony as often as possible. Kindness also extends to all other creatures, not just humans. The environment deserves kindness, too. By making this a principle to live by, you make it easier for the healing energy of Reiki to do its work in your life.

Remember that these principles aren't rules per se but are meant to help you work with Reiki more efficiently. You can interpret and embody them in whatever way is most authentic to you. As you do so, you'll experience amazing transformation and growth in your life. Now that you know how to heal others with Archangel Raphael's help, what about healing yourself? In the next chapter, you will learn about healing for healers.

Chapter 8: Healing for Healers

Did you know that Archangel Raphael is the protector and healer of healers? Archangel Raphael is a powerful being who acts as a guardian and supports the people working in the healing arts and medical profession. He is there to offer healing energy, serve as a guide, and assist the healers. So, if you're a doctor, a nurse, or practice Reiki or any of the other healing arts, you can turn to him for help. Usually, during healing, some challenging situations can pop up. When you are faced with something you don't know how to handle, you can ask for his help and know that he will show up.

Challenges Healers Face

If you work in the healing profession, it's not an easy thing, and you should be commended for your selfless service. You must contend with challenges and obstacles along the way. Some of these challenges you may never have witnessed before, or you may be left feeling perplexed about, because, despite your best efforts, your patient is not improving. Here are some challenges you may face while helping others recover.

- **Being physically drained:** This is a real challenge because helping others heal implies you will be expending energy. This energy is not just physical but emotional and spiritual as well. When constantly tending to other people's needs, it is only natural to feel fatigued, exhausted, and, in the worst cases, burned out. This is because you must work long hours and do your best to keep your energy up and light because the unwell person also depends on that to get better. It also doesn't help that sometimes you will face illnesses that appear to be incurable, which can take a toll on your mental health. Sometimes, the illnesses are contagious, and you are at huge risk of contracting them.

- **Being emotionally burnt out:** This is another very real situation that you must face as a healer. You wake up daily and must deal with other people's suffering and pain. Naturally, no one who's going through pain feels great. The emotions are usually in lower vibrations. If you do not know how to take care of your emotional needs, it only makes sense that you will eventually take on your patients' feelings. The problem is that when this happens, you cannot give them the best care because, as mentioned before, part of healing is maintaining a positive, light outlook. When you feel emotionally drained, it affects your own emotional well-being. It makes it difficult to stay resilient in the face of the ugliest of situations.

- **Struggles with self-care and maintaining boundaries:** As a healer, you need to take care of yourself. You can't be in poor health and expect to give your best to someone struggling. It is akin to hanging off of a ledge with someone else and expecting to be able to pull them up when you're also hanging. As a healer, you need to establish clear, healthy boundaries. This is the only way you can truly serve others; therefore, you must find a way to balance your passion for helping others with your desire to care for yourself. This is not an easy thing to do. Still, fortunately, you can call on a certain celestial being whose specialty is assisting those who work as healers.

- **Finding a balance between work and personal life** is another thing you will have to face as a healer. How do you balance your work and your personal life? You are in an extremely demanding profession. Your hours tend to be long and grueling, your schedules anything but regular, and you constantly need to keep yourself open and available in case there's an emergency where you're needed. All of this makes it incredibly difficult for you to give a good amount of attention to the personal relationships you have in your life and other aspirations you may want to fulfill.

- **Emotional resilience:** Part of your job is withstanding the barrage of emotions that would rock anyone else if they had to deal with what you do. You must find ways to handle the challenges that come your way. You will naturally find that stress is just around the corner, waiting to sink its tentacles into your mind and body. Not only that, but you also do a lot of emotional heavy lifting. You not only have to handle your emotions and ensure they're in check, but you also have to help your patients so they do not feel overwhelmed or hopeless about their situations. Therefore, you need to be able to find healthy ways to express and deal with your emotions. Otherwise, you are handling too much emotional stress, which could burn you out to the point where you are no longer useful to anyone and can't even help yourself. These are just some of the challenges that healers face in their profession. Fortunately, there are rituals, meditations, and prayers you can use to help you take care of your emotional, physical, and spiritual health so that you can help others get back to a hundred percent.

Blessed by Green Light Ritual

For this ritual, you will need a green candle, emerald crystal, and a few drops of eucalyptus oil.

Steps:
1. First, ensure you're somewhere quiet and will not be bothered or disturbed for 10 to 15 minutes.
2. Set the green candle on a safe surface before you and light it. Use a candle holder if you have one.
3. Close your eyes and take a few deep, grounding breaths. You should have the emerald crystal in your hands as you breathe.
4. In your mind's eye, imagine that a vibrant green light surrounds you, flowing from the crystal, the candle, and the sky above you. Feel the energy of this light as it wraps itself around you.
5. It is time to affirm that you are protected while healing others. You can say, *"Archangel Raphael, I trust you to keep me safe as I heal others."*
6. Place a drop of eucalyptus oil on your palms and rub them together. Take a whiff of the scent, envisioning streaks of green

light going in through your nostrils into your lungs and spreading out to every bit of your body and soul.
7. Gently bring the crystal up to your heart chakra, and feel their energies merge.
8. Sit for a few minutes and be grateful, trusting that Archangel Raphael will keep you safe throughout your day as you heal others. When you are ready, open your eyes.

Shielding Ritual

For this ritual, you will need palo santo or white sage, a small bowl, and a feather.

Steps:
1. Go to your sacred space and ensure it's free of distractions and disturbances.
2. Light the palo santo or sage, and set it on a heatproof incense burner with a handle. Let it burn, allowing the smoke to move up to the ceiling.
3. With the feather and one hand, fan the smoke so that it moves around your body. If it helps, you can move the incense burner around as you fan the smoke towards you to cleanse your aura. You should move from the top of your head down towards your feet. Be careful when you do this.
4. Imagine the smoke cleansing your auric field so that anything that you've taken on from your work throughout the day is removed from you. Alternatively, you can do this ritual before you go to work. In that case, imagine instead that the smoke is fortifying your aura, keeping it safe, creating a shield that prevents you from taking on other energies and emotions that aren't pure and would bring you down.
5. Now, place the feather into the bowl. That means you have successfully created your auric shield and cleansed your aura.
6. Tell Raphael you would like him to protect you as you do your work and keep your aura as pure as possible. You can repeat this until you start to feel a shift in the energy, indicating that he has heard you.

7. When you are ready, thank Raphael for cleansing and protecting you by setting up your shield. Trust that he has heard you and will do all that you have passed.

The Healing Grid

For this ritual, you will need a set of healing crystals. You can choose clear quartz, rose quartz, amethyst, and emerald. You don't have to use all of them, but you can use a combination. You'll also need an altar or a cloth and a quiet space.

Steps:
1. Set the crystals on your altar or a cloth in your sacred space. Arrange them in a way to form a grid.
2. Pick the largest of your crystals, and let that represent Archangel Raphael himself. This crystal should go in the middle of your grid.
3. Stand before your grid or sit comfortably if you prefer. Close your eyes, part your lips slightly, and take a few centering breaths to bring you into the present moment.
4. In your mind, see healing energy that flows from Archangel Raphael into the crystal you've set in the middle of your grid.
5. Once this crystal in the middle is fully charged with Raphael's emerald energy, see the energy flow to the other crystals in the grid.
6. It is now time to pray to Raphael. Ask him to support you as you go about your healing work. Tell him to guide you whenever you feel lost about what to do to help a patient. Also, ask him to heal you as you inevitably pick up other energies that may bring you down or affect you somehow.
7. Sit in silent meditation with your grid. In your mind's eye, imagine that all the crystals are now connected with an emerald light. This light burns brighter and brighter, then beams directly into your heart chakra. From there, it radiates outwards, spreading into your palms. Feel the energy as it burns in your palms and moves from there to the rest of your body.
8. Thank Raphael for helping you. As the crystals also have their own consciousness, you should thank them for participating in this ritual and assisting you in your good work.

9. When you are ready, open your eyes and return to the present moment. You may now take apart your crystal grid and then cleanse the stones to be ready for use the next time you set up a grid.

The Healer's Prayer

"Dearest Raphael, you are the true healer.
You are my helper; you are my guide.
I seek now your power pure,
Your wisdom, strength, and all your cures.
I asked that you keep me safe,
And in your healing light, I bathe.
Keep me strong and healthy in mind and body,
That your love and grace I may embody.
Through these hands, heal and restore,
That my patients be whole as before.
For answered prayers, I thank you,
Now help me be a vessel true."

The Shielding Prayer

"Raphael, you are power and might.
Fill me now with your beautiful light.
My hands and heart are yours,
To heal all hurts and sores.
May your green energy flow through me,
To restore, to make whole, to make healthy.
Wrap me in your wing's embrace,
So bad energy leaves no trace
Upon my body and soul, by your grace,
As I take on this healing space."

Restoration Meditation

1. Sit somewhere comfortable and quiet.
2. Close your eyes and take a few deep, grounding breaths.
3. Imagine Raphael's light all around you. On each inhale, breathe in the green light. On each exhale, breathe out all the negative, stale energies you have gathered throughout the day. Imagine this energy, stress, and tension as a blackness across your shoulders.
4. With each exhale, move the dark energy from your shoulders down into your heart center and out into the world, where it dissipates.
5. Continue to breathe this way, taking in the green light and exhaling the dark energy until it feels completely clean and clear. You no longer see any darkness hovering around you.
6. It is time to thank Archangel Raphael for relieving you of the burden and negativity you've picked up on throughout your day.
7. When you are ready and completely restored, you may come out of the meditation.

You now know how to work with Archangel Raphael so you can effectively do your job as a healer. The next chapter is about how even musicians, artists, and other creatives can work with this Archangel to improve their work and tap into a constant, endless stream of creativity and inspiration.

Chapter 9: Creative Rituals

This final chapter is for aspiring musicians, artists, and all creative people. Did you know that Archangel Raphael is also connected to creativity? This Archangel not only heals and changes your life, but he can also help you tap into your innate creativity. You can work with him to harness your artistic energies to create work superior to anything else you've ever done before.

Creativity Heals You

The incredible thing about being creative is that you can use the opportunity to heal. As a creative person, you have an inner drive to make and create things. You're not satisfied with simply consuming other people's work. If you do not take your time to create things, it can feel really heavy for you. In fact, many people feel constantly bogged down because they do not habitually express this creativity. They do not realize they would lead much happier lives if they practiced constantly creating.

Raphael Can Inspire You

Archangel Raphael can guide you in finding the root of divine inspiration. He has a way of intuitively nudging you towards the creative ideas that lie within you, untapped and unexpressed. This Archangel can connect to the hearts and minds of various creatives like musicians, writers, artists, and many more. In fact, you can tap into the inspiration and creativity of your innate abilities and the creativity of the greats who have passed on in whatever field of creative expression. In other words, with Archangel Raphael's help, you can channel the creativity of Van Gogh if you are a painter or Sylvia Plath if you are a writer, and so on.

Raphael can act as a conduit so that you can channel their energy into your work, making it something new from something seemingly borrowed.

Eliminate Creative Blocks with Raphael

When you practice invoking Archangel Raphael before you begin any creative work, you will find yourself becoming more and more aligned with his energy, which means that sometimes, you may not even have to invoke him before you start getting a stream of creative ideas. Many can't figure out what to create because they feel uninspired. Imagine having the opposite problem, where you have many ideas and can't wait to start. If only you had enough hands or a clone! This is what Archangel Raphael can do for you.

Archangel Raphael can help release creative blocks."

So, if you've ever had to deal with creative blocks that keep you from expressing your true artistic self, you know how frustrating it can be. That can be incredibly crippling, and if you allow it to continue for long enough, it will get to a point where you feel like you can't do what you really want." You do not need to wait for things to get that bad before restoring the flow of creativity. You can work with Archangel Raphael; he is always more than happy to help you break through any barriers affecting your creativity.

Never Underestimate Rituals

One powerful way to connect with Archangel Raphael's creativity and inspiration is by using rituals. When you make rituals a part of your creative process, you draw in Raphael's energy so that it is infused into your work and drives you to think outside the box. These rituals require elements like essential oils, crystals, candles, and certain colors, all of which should align with the energies of creativity and the Archangel Raphael. As an artist, you have the right to personalize the ritual to resonate with who you are. When you do a ritual, you naturally must set an intention. The process of setting an intention acts as a magnetic force that pulls in the desires you have. In this case, you desire the ability to express yourself creatively and freely.

Teaming Up with Raphael

There's no reason for you to work on your own as an artist. You will find it most productive when you have Archangel Raphael as a partner. As an artist, you will be supported in a way no one else could match. You will feel yourself being divinely inspired. In fact, you will be directly channeling the creative work you have in mind instead of overthinking it. Working with Raphael will be as if you're receiving messages and simply expressing them through your art.

Creativity in Non-Creative Spaces

For some reason, when the subject of creativity is discussed, people only think of it as music, art, dance, etc. However, every aspect of life involves creativity. In other words, you may not think that creativity is involved in the process of, say, doing your taxes. But there's creativity in everything you do.

Whether you're trying to cook a meal or devise a solution to a problem or conflict you're dealing with, you need creativity. You can reach out to Archangel Raphael whenever you feel stumped. It is often a good practice to ask yourself how you can do the things you already do better and faster. Whenever you feel stuck answering these questions, you can easily ask Raphael and trust that you will receive an answer. Humans are here to experience life and to evolve as they do so. Evolution means finding better ways to express who you are. Therefore, creativity is an inherent part of being human, and you have the right to reach out for divine help to discover new and better ways to express your authentic, higher self.

So, do not assume that this chapter is only for artists. It's for everyone. Because, like it or not, you cannot divorce yourself from creativity. Creativity is an inherent part of you and how you express yourself on this planet. If you are curious about how to spark or enhance your inner creativity, these next few rituals will be a great place to start.

Creative Flow Ritual

The purpose of this ritual is to help you be more creative.

1. First, go into your sacred space. It should be free of disturbances and distractions for at least 10 minutes.
2. Light a green candle. This represents the creative power of Archangel Raphael.
3. Close your eyes, and take a few deep, grounding breaths. You should inhale with your nose and exhale through your mouth.
4. When you feel grounded, it's time to invoke Raphael's presence. All you have to do is say: *"Raphael, I seek your help and guidance now. Please inspire me and give life to my creativity with your power."*
5. In your mind's eye, imagine you are in outer space. Imagine that it has a dark, beautiful greenish hue. See yourself surrounded by beautiful vibrant stars, with ones shining a lovely green reminiscent of Raphael's signature color.
6. Now, imagine that all the stars around you begin to emit a powerful, beautiful green luminescent light. Let this light wrap you from head to toe. Feel it pouring in through the top of your head, flowing down to your toes. This light carries new ideas, creative innovations, and wonderful art you can express.
7. Bask in this light for as long as you'd like, allowing it to recharge you. Feel excited as you realize you will soon create fantastic work.
8. When ready, you can open your eyes and thank Archangel Raphael for lending his energy to this ritual.
9. Now, it is time for you to do your creative work, whether writing, painting, or trying to devise a solution to a problem. You need to maintain trust and expectation as you do your work because this will enable the creativity to flow even better than if you had questions about whether the ritual worked.

Creative Block Obliteration Ritual

This ritual is meant to help you eliminate the creative blocks that make it impossible to express yourself creatively.

1. First, get a piece of paper, a green marker, or a pen if you like. You are also going to need a bowl of water.
2. Make you're in your sacred space and that you will not be distracted for the next 15 minutes.
3. Close your eyes. Part your lips. Breathe in through your nose and out through your mouth.
4. When you feel grounded, open your eyes and write down how exactly you feel blocked. Write down all your concerns, including your fears about whether or not you'll be able to create anything. It is important to be as vulnerable as you can. No one else will read this, so be honest with yourself and Archangel Raphael.
5. When you've got everything written down, it is time for you to work with Raphael's light. Hold the paper with both hands and imagine that Raphael's emerald green light begins to surround you.
6. Tell Raphael that you are drawing upon his energy to help you destroy and obliterate the creative blocks that have kept you stuck for a while. It is important to tell him that you truly and completely surrender to him and trust that he will help you easily overcome your obstacles.
7. Take the paper and soak it in the water bowl. This represents that you have released those blocks and that the negative, stale energies holding you back from expressing your creativity are now gone.
8. As you watch the paper dissolve, imagine that you can see the dark cloudy energy of the blocks and that they also dissipate as the paper dissolves into pieces. In your mind's eye, see the dark energy that was once your creative block turning into emerald energy. Imagine this emerald, green energy flowing into your heart, your third eye, and crown chakras.
9. Take some time to think about how you now feel free. Accept that with time, ideas will start to flow again.
10. Thank Raphael for his help.

Sacred Inspiration Ritual

The goal behind this ritual is to allow you to connect directly with divinity to experience its inspiration. It is about connecting your essence with

sacred energy.
1. In your sacred space, surround yourself with things that mean a lot to you regarding your creative work. You can also have crystals, incense, and other objects that matter to you.
2. Light a white or green candle to represent the presence and power of Archangel Raphael.
3. Close your eyes, part your lips slightly, and take a few deep, grounding breaths until you feel fully present.
4. Now, invoke Raphael's presence by saying: *"Raphael, I seek you now. Please open up your source of divine inspiration, and let it flow to me and through me. I yield my body, mind, and spirit to allow the expression of this infinite, divine, sacred creativity."*
5. Continue to breathe deeply, and in your mind's eye, imagine that a golden beam of light comes down from the sky and pierces through the top of your head right through to the soles of your feet. Allow the warm golden light to encompass you. Feel it charging and rejuvenating you. This is a light of divine inspiration that you have acts Raphael to channel through you.
6. As you sit basking in this light, open your mind to the idea of receiving divine guidance.
7. When you feel ready, open your eyes and begin to work on your creative endeavors. Allow the energy of Raphael to flow through you. Let go of the need to be perfect or express things in a particular way along. Instead, trust that you are being divinely led and that every apparent mistake is part of the divine design.
8. When you finish your work, thank Raphael for being with you.

Crafting Your Sigil

You can make your own sigil to assist you in your creative process.
1. The first thing you will do is gather your materials. You'll need markers, pens or colored pencils, a piece of paper, a green candle, and any other thing you have that you can use, like stickers, glitter, and symbols that matter to you.
2. The next thing you must do is get your sacred space ready. As usual, it must be free from distraction so that you can focus.

3. Now, light a green candle. This candle represents Raphael's energy which is going to feel your creativity.
4. Close your eyes, part your lips slightly, take a deep breath through your nose, and exhale through your lips. Continue to breathe this way until you feel centered and calm.
5. Now, invoke Archangel Raphael. You can do this by simply stating that you would like him to show up or by repeatedly calling his name. You can chant it out loud or quietly in your mind.
6. When you sense Raphael's presence, say, *"I seek your help boosting my creativity. I would love to work with your energy to be more expressive in my art."*
7. Now, take some time and infuse your mind with your intention. Think about what it is you hope to accomplish through your creativity. Think about what you want to express using your art. And then, when you figure it out, say aloud what your intention for the sigil is. Your intention could be, "I am now a vessel for divine creativity." Or "I have an abundant stream of creative ideas."
8. You will now design the sigil. First, you must allow your intuition to guide you along the process. In other words, when you put your hand on the paper and begin to write or draw, you should trust that the symbols or shapes you are creating come from a deep, deep place within you. You are divinely inspired. As you draw, imagine emerald green light flowing from your hands into the drawing material and the drawing itself. When you're done, state your intention out loud. You could say, *"With this sigil, I now declare that I have an abundance of creative, divinely inspired ideas. This sigil serves as a reminder to me of this truth."*
9. The next step is to infuse the sigil with your energy. Place the sigil where you can see it, sit down, and stare at it as you meditate. Allow your intention to fuse with it. Imagine that the sigil glows with Raphael's beautiful emerald light. This sigil will now be what you use to manifest your artistic goals.
10. Now that you have energized your sigil, it is time to finalize it. Intend that whenever you look at your sigil, it will become activated. Intend that it will draw creativity out of you with ease and flow when it is active. If you choose, you could have this sigil

laminated or framed and displayed somewhere you can see it every day. You can also make it your phone's wallpaper.
11. At the end of this ritual, you must thank Raphael for giving you his power, support, and guidance throughout the process. Thank him for the inspiration and creativity that is now yours.
12. Finally, it is time to use your sigil. You can look at it whenever you feel like you are blocked or whenever you're about to start some creative work. Whenever you look at it, all you have to do is restate your intention and visualize how you would feel after having created some magnificent work.

Conclusion

You have reached the end of this book – but this is just the start. Once you put everything you have learned into practice, your life will finally transform for the better. You have discovered the profound benefits of developing a relationship with Archangel Raphael. You've learned that he can help you with your relationships, health, or expressing your creativity.

You have learned that the Archangel Raphael is unrivaled when it comes to healing. He can restore the harmony you were born with within your body, mind, and spirit. He can bring back the balance you were used to having as a child before life began to take its toll on you.

In this book, you have learned about various healing modalities, such as working with visualization, meditation, Reiki, and crystal mojo bags. You've also learned to carry Raphael's energy everywhere you go so you never feel drained while helping others heal.

When it comes to relationships, you've discovered that this celestial being has the power to help you mend whatever is broken. As a being full of compassion and love, he can see through to the heart of whatever it is you may be struggling with regarding relationships and fix the problems causing a rift between you and your partner. Also, if you are single, this being is quite an excellent matchmaker and knows exactly who would be a great fit for you. Thanks to Raphael's support, you can go stay in the relationship, regardless of how challenging it is or the kind of trauma you're dealing with from previous ones, knowing full well that you can overcome them and achieve success with your partner.

Regarding creativity, you now know that Raphael can give you access to divine inspiration. You know there is no such thing as creative blocks when your inspiration is divine. You understand that you have unlimited creative potential, and Archangel Raphael's help is just what you need to unlock the door to the greatness you carry within, the one that you and you alone can express.

Raphael is very benevolent and can help you break through the limitations in your mind that keep you from realizing just how creative you are. You can take your creative work to the next level by working with rituals and meditations.

However, you need to understand that it's not enough for you to know how to work with Raphael. You have to take this information and put it to work. That is the only way to take advantage of Raphael's wisdom, guidance, and presence. This is how you achieve results that change your life forever. You must put what you have learned to work so that you can constantly be in alignment with Raphael's healing vibration.

When you practice engaging with Raphael daily, you will find improvements to your health beyond anything you've ever thought possible. Basically, you're going to feel like a kid again!

Finally, you need to understand that you develop your relationship with Raphael not by reading but by approaching him with sincerity and vulnerability. You will have to completely yield to him and trust that he is not only present in your life but that he is actively working to assist you in every way he knows how. All you have to do is open your heart to accept his love, guidance, and healing energy to experience a life touched by divinity.

Correspondences Sheet

The following is a sheet of correspondence that you can use whenever you are trying to come up with creative ways to interact with Archangel Raphael or craft your own meditations, prayers, and rituals.

Day of the week - Wednesday

Hour of the day - 10:00 a.m. to 11:00 a.m.

Feast - February 14, also known as the Feast of Archangel Raphael

Zodiac sign - Virgo, Gemini

Planets - Mercury, Uranus

Angel number - 3

Direction - East

Element - Air

Color - Green

Sigil - The Caduceus

Herbs, oils, plants, and trees - Peppermint, eucalyptus, chamomile, lavender, and rosemary

Crystals - Peridot, green aventurine, malachite, emerald

Metal - Copper, mercury

Animals - Deer, dove, peacock, fish

Tarot card - The Lovers

Musical note - F

Chakra - Heart

Incense – Lavender, frankincense
Planet healing – Earth
Symbolic tool – Healing staff
Astrological house – 6th house (The House of Health and Wellness)
Virtue – Compassion
Sacred geometry – Flower of Life
Metals – Platinum, silver
Season – Spring
Musical instrument – Flute, harp
Body system – Respiratory system
Gemstone essence – Rose quartz
Elemental being – Sylphs (air spirits)
Energy frequency – 528 Hz (the miracle frequency)
Prayer beads – Rose quartz beads or green aventurine beads

Part 5: Archangel Uriel

Connecting with the Angel of Wisdom

Introduction

Have you ever been curious about Archangel Uriel and his powerful gifts? Do you want to become close with one of God's most influential Archangels? If so, this book is for you.

Archangel Uriel is an uplifting figure that fills people with joy and hope. His bright, shining light inspires his followers to see the world positively, even amid challenging times. As one of the four archangels, Uriel is known for his wisdom, creativity, and enlightenment. He is also associated with the element of fire, which represents transformation and passion. Whether you pray to him for guidance or simply feel his presence around you, Archangel Uriel is a powerful force for good in the world.

Worshiped and invoked by many in the Christian faith, Uriel can be called upon to help you in your spiritual journey. He can answer questions that bother you, inspire and help you develop your creative talents, or guide you toward manifesting success in your life. Invoking his presence can bring a sense of peace and balance, allowing you to feel more grounded and connected to the higher realms. Drawing energy from the sun, Uriel is a powerful light and healing source, reminding us of a benevolent divine power. For those looking to deepen their relationship with Archangel Uriel, this book will explain the spiritual and practical tools necessary for invocation.

There are ways to invoke Archangel Uriel and connect with him on a deeper level. But before you do, learn more about him, his energy, and how to create a sacred space for your connection. That's why this book is broken down into nine chapters. This descriptive guide will explore who Archangel Uriel is and examine his characteristics. This book will discuss how to invoke Uriel and recognize signs of his presence. It will also provide step-by-step instructions for creating an angelic sacred space and teach you various meditations, dreamwork techniques, and rituals to connect with Uriel.

This guide includes a bonus correspondence sheet that helps you better understand Uriel's traits and the energies he works with. Through this book, you'll understand what an archangel is, better understand Archangel Uriel, and learn how to create a strong connection with him. The guidance and wisdom he has to offer are sure to make your spiritual journey more rewarding. By reading this book and following the steps, you'll have all the information you need to work with Archangel Uriel. From here, you'll feel His presence in your life and benefit from the power of His light. So, let's get started and learn more about this magnificent archangel!

Chapter 1: Who Is Archangel Uriel?

Out of all the angels in the celestial realms, Archangel Uriel stands out as one of the most powerful and influential figures. He is renowned for his wisdom, justice, and strength across the angelic kingdom. Archangel Uriel plays an important role in communicating between the divine and the humans who call on him. His role is assisting humans and communicating divine messages to us. This chapter aims to explore the origins and characteristics of Archangel Uriel.

The knowledge in this chapter will open your eyes to a world beyond ours and give you a glance into a spiritual place in a deeper and more meaningful way. This chapter will introduce Uriel and explain what an archangel is. It will also explore the etymology of Uriel's name, his role in mysticism, his celestial role, and his close connection to the earthly realm. Lastly, this chapter will conclude by summarizing Uriel's key characteristics and roles in Heaven and on Earth. By the end of this chapter, you will better understand Uriel's place in the celestial realms.

An Introduction to Archangel Uriel

Archangel Uriel first appeared as the angel of wisdom and light in Abrahamic literature. He is one of the seven archangels who stand on the throne of God. Archangel Uriel is also associated with creativity, ideas, and judgment. He is often depicted holding a scroll in his hand, symbolizing knowledge, understanding, and wisdom. If you are seeking inspiration or guidance in your life, calling on Archangel Uriel may be just what you need. With his powerful presence and unwavering commitment to justice and truth, Archangel Uriel exists to help you navigate life's challenges and find your way toward enlightenment.

What Is an Archangel?

Angels are divine beings that play different roles in the spiritual world, but not all angels are created equal. Archangels are known to hold the highest rank in the angelic world and are believed to be powerful and influential beings. Archangels have been mentioned in several religious texts, including Christianity, Judaism, and Islam. This section will explore what an archangel is, its role in the angelic hierarchy system, and its significance in the angelic kingdom.

The Angelic Kingdom

The angelic kingdom is a realm that exists beyond our physical world but can often interact with us. It is a world where divine beings reside, and they are responsible for carrying out different duties. According to most religious texts, the angels were created by God, each having his own role, but they are primarily considered guardians and messengers. The angels' role in the angelic kingdom also includes protecting and guiding humanity, so they work closely with humans to ensure the divine plan is executed.

The Angelic Hierarchy System

Angelic hierarchy.[65]

In the angelic hierarchy system, archangels hold the highest rank. This means they have more power and influence than other angelic beings. They are known to be closest to God, and their purpose is to carry out God's divine will. However, there are different levels of angels, and archangels are just a part of the angelic hierarchy system.

The Divine Archangels

An archangel is a high-ranking angelic being believed to have more power and influence than regular angels. There are several archangels, and they are often associated with specific qualities or attributes. For example, Archangel Michael is the protector, while Archangel Raphael is the healer. Archangel Gabriel is revered in the Christian faith as being the angel who appeared to a young Jewish girl, Mary, with the message that she would become the mother of Jesus.

The Role of Archangels

Archangels play an essential role in the angelic kingdom. They are responsible for carrying out specific tasks that ensure God's divine plan is executed. Archangels are also responsible for helping humans in their mundane life, providing comfort and guidance when needed. They can aid human beings in earthly matters, such as love, career decisions, health issues, and spiritual growth.

The Significance of Archangels

Archangels hold a significant place in various religious texts, myths, and legends. Their significance stems from their status as powerful divine beings that are known to protect and guide humanity and are part of many belief systems, including Christian, Jewish and Islamic religions. They are also considered guardians of virtues such as truth, love, compassion, and wisdom and work with humans to help them achieve spiritual enlightenment and fulfill their life purpose.

Archangels are divine beings that hold a significant place in the angelic kingdom due to their power, influence, and relationship with God. Understanding the role of archangels can give us a better insight into the spiritual realm and help us connect with our spiritual side.

The Etymology of "Uriel" and His Origins

In the world of angels, Archangel Uriel is one of the most fascinating and enigmatic characters. He is associated with wisdom, illumination, and divine light. But where did Uriel come from? What does his name mean? This section will explore the etymology of the name Uriel and the origins of this intriguing archangel.

Meaning

To begin, let's look at the name "Uriel." In Hebrew, "Uriel" means "God is my light." This name is fitting for the archangel, who is the carrier of illumination and divine light. Interestingly, his name is also sometimes spelled "Auriel," and in some medieval texts, it is even spelled "Oriel." Regardless of the spelling, Uriel's name stands for radiance and divine guidance.

Origins

As for Uriel's origins, he is mentioned in several religious texts, including the Torah, the Bible, the Quran, and the Book of Enoch. In Jewish tradition, Uriel is one of the four primary archangels, along with Michael, Gabriel, and Raphael. In Christian tradition, Uriel is considered an archangel, though he is not mentioned in the canonical Bible.

Depictions

Uriel is often depicted as a wise and benevolent angel, offering guidance and illumination to those who seek it. Some stories even credit him as being the angel who warned Noah of the impending flood. He is also said to communicate divine messages to humankind, facilitating spiritual growth and understanding.

Art and Literature

One of the most fascinating aspects of Uriel is the way he is depicted in art and literature. He is shown holding a book in many works, illustrating his role as the angel of wisdom. He is often shown with a flame or a torch, signifying his association with divine light. In some texts, Uriel is even depicted as a warrior battling against evil forces. In modern times, Uriel is still revered by many and has become associated with various New Age beliefs and practices. Some people believe that Uriel can assist with emotional healing and personal transformation and seek his guidance through meditation, prayer, or even angel card readings.

Uriel is a fascinating and influential archangel. His name, which means "God is my light," perfectly represents his role as the carrier of divine guidance and illumination. Though his origins are somewhat mysterious, Uriel is considered a powerful force for good and has been revered by many throughout history. Whether you seek his guidance for spiritual growth or simply appreciate his significance in religious traditions, this enigmatic angel is sure to inspire awe and wonder.

Uriel's Identity According to Mysticism

Mysticism is a philosophy that embraces a vast range of beliefs, practices, and experiences to attain unity with the divine. One of the most intriguing concepts in the realm of mysticism is the angel Uriel. Over the years, Uriel has been the focus of several texts, including the Book of Enoch, the Biblical Apocrypha, and the Apocalypse of Peter, which have all sought to unveil Uriel's true identity. Let's explore these texts and unravel the mystery surrounding Uriel's identity according to mysticism.

Book of Enoch

The Book of Enoch is an ancient Jewish text that narrates the story of Enoch, the great-grandfather of Noah. In chapter XXI of the book, Uriel is described as one of the four archangels created by God. Uriel is said to have been entrusted with the universe's secrets, including the mysteries of the moon and the stars. In addition, Uriel is described as the angel who watches over thunder and terror, making him an angel of judgment. According to the Book of Enoch, Uriel's identity as an archangel makes him one of the highest-ranking angels in heaven.

Biblical Apocrypha

The Biblical Apocrypha also mentions Uriel as an archangel, although with a few variations. In 2 Esdras 4:1, Uriel is described as the angel who has been asked to interpret the vision given to Ezra, a Jewish prophet. Uriel is also called the "angel of repentance," implying his role as an angel of judgment. Nonetheless, Uriel's identity as an archangel remains consistent with the Book of Enoch.

Apocalypse of Peter

A third text that explores Uriel's identity is the Apocalypse of Peter, which is believed to have been written around the third century. In the text, Uriel is not explicitly mentioned but is described as the angel who stands at the gate of heaven, preventing sinners from entering the kingdom of God. This portrayal of Uriel is consistent with his role as an angel of judgment.

These three texts uncover Uriel's identity as an archangel with the power to interpret divine mysteries and exercise judgment. He is a messenger of God, entrusted with secrets known only to Him. Uriel is known as an angel of repentance and an enforcer of divine justice, making him a formidable figure in mysticism.

The mystery surrounding Uriel's identity is answered to a degree in the Book of Enoch, the Biblical Apocrypha, and the Apocalypse of Peter, which all confirm him as a being of divine authority and wisdom. Uriel is a source of fascination and respect in the world of mysticism and remains an enigmatic figure to this day.

Exploring Archangel Uriel's Celestial Role

From ancient times, people have believed in the existence of heavenly beings, archangels, and angels, who are imbued with immense power and divine grace. Uriel is associated with light or fire; some have even revered him as an Angel of Judgment. In this section, we will explore his celestial role and dive into the subtle yet powerful ways in which Uriel guides souls through their life journey.

The Bringer of Light and Wisdom

This divine being is known for shedding light on people's paths, illuminating their minds, and bringing clarity to their thoughts. Uriel is also considered the patron saint of science and education, as he is believed to inspire new ideas and facilitate learning.

The Angel of Repentance and Forgiveness

As the angel of repentance and forgiveness, Uriel is often called upon to help people let go of their past mistakes and find redemption. Uriel is believed to have the power to cleanse people's hearts, guide them toward righteousness, and inspire them to seek forgiveness from the divine. Many people pray to Uriel in times of turmoil, seeking his guidance and grace.

The Protector and Guardian

Archangel Uriel is also said to watch over the gates of the underworld, protecting the souls from harm and defending the realm of the divine. Uriel is believed to work closely with other celestial beings, such as Michael and Gabriel, to protect the realm of the divine from any threats or negative energies.

The Divine Strategist

As the patron saint of science and education, Uriel is often associated with strategic thinking and long-term planning. Uriel is believed to inspire people to think deeply about their decisions, weigh the pros and cons, and consider the long-term impact of their actions. Many people pray to

Uriel for guidance during moments of decision-making, seeking his support and wisdom.

The Angel of Earth and Nature

Finally, Uriel is also revered as the angel of earth and nature. This celestial being is believed to have a deep connection with the earth, and he can communicate with the spirits of nature. Uriel is believed to help people understand the natural world around them, connect with the healing energies of nature, and develop a deep reverence for all living beings.

Archangel Uriel is a powerful yet subtle celestial being who is key in guiding souls through their life journey. As the bringer of light and wisdom, the angel of repentance and forgiveness, the protector and guardian, the divine strategist, and the angel of earth and nature, Uriel holds immense power and grace. Many people worldwide pray to Uriel for guidance, support, and wisdom, believing he holds the key to unlocking their deepest potential and leading them toward righteousness. As we explore Uriel's celestial role, let us open our hearts and minds to the divine grace he generously offers.

Archangel Uriel's Epithets and Attributes

As we strive to understand the infinite and the divine, exploring the essence and characteristics of each archangel is a powerful tool. As the highest-ranking angels, these archangels have been entrusted with particular duties and attributes to help guide us through life's obstacles. Archangel Uriel is one of the most beloved archangels, known for his wisdom, illuminating light, and spiritual guidance. This section will explore Archangel Uriel's epithets and attributes that help us connect with him for personal growth and healing.

Epithets are descriptive terms often accompanying an archangel's name that describes his role or symbolism. Archangel Uriel is also known as the light of God, the angel of wisdom, and the prince of light. His name means the "fire of God" because he embodies divine justice and the sacred fire that purifies the soul. Uriel's attributes are visual symbols representing him, and each symbolizes part of his divine qualities, like his light or wisdom. Here are some of the most commonly used epithets and attributes of Archangel Uriel.

- **Light:** One of Uriel's most significant attributes is light. His light represents the divine illumination of knowledge and

understanding. It is said that His light can assist us in awakening our inner light and growing spiritually.
- **Scroll:** Uriel is often depicted holding a scroll representing divine knowledge and wisdom. He is the guardian of the Book of Knowledge and holds the secrets of spiritual enlightenment.
- **Sun:** The sun is not only a symbol of light but also of power and energy. Uriel's association with the sun represents his powers that provide us with the vital energy of life.
- **Sword:** The sword commonly represents strength, force, and power. As Archangel Uriel is responsible for divine justice, the sword symbolizes his role in protecting and upholding the law.
- **Flame:** Archangel Uriel's flame symbol is one of the most potent symbols in his iconography. The flame represents the purification, illumination, and transformation of our souls.

Archangel Uriel's epithets and attributes signify divine qualities such as wisdom, knowledge, divine light, and justice. Each name and attribute conveys different aspects of his nature and meaning, allowing us to understand and connect with him more profoundly. He is also considered the patron of the arts, channeling intuition and insight and promoting healing and harmony between people. To connect with Archangel Uriel, you can use his visual attributes, recite his prayers, or create a sacred space to meditate and connect with him. Knowing his epithets and attributes helps us feel closer to his protective and guiding presence, initiating a path toward personal growth, healing, and spiritual enlightenment.

Uriel's Close Connection to the Earthly Realm

When it comes to archangels, there is perhaps no other angel more closely linked with the earthly realm than Archangel Uriel. As the angel of wisdom, he is said to preside over the Earth and its elements. His presence is believed to be felt in forests, mountains, and rivers as he watches over the natural world. This section will delve deeper into the significance of Archangel Uriel's connection to the earthly realm and how different cultures worldwide worship him.

The Angel of Wisdom

Archangel Uriel's connection to the earthly realm is rooted in his status as the angel of wisdom. Wisdom is often linked to knowledge of the natural world and the environment around us, so it is no surprise that he is closely associated with the Earth. His name means "God is my light," and he is believed to provide humans with knowledge and understanding of the world and our place in it.

Patron Saint of the Natural World

In many cultures, Archangel Uriel is worshiped as the patron saint of the natural world. In Native American traditions, he is associated with the seasons and the changing of the Earth. In Celtic cultures, he is connected to the elements of air and earth, and in Hinduism, he is worshiped as a teacher of knowledge and wisdom. His influence spans many different cultures and beliefs.

Association with Autumnal Equinox

Another aspect of Archangel Uriel's connection to the earthly realm is his association with the autumnal equinox. This is when day and night are equal in length, and it is believed that Archangel Uriel oversees this transition. He is said to be most present and receptive to worshipers seeking his guidance on this day.

Protector of Humans

In addition to overseeing the natural world, Archangel Uriel is also believed to be a protector of humans. He is called on in times of trouble or despair, as his wisdom and guidance can help us find our way through difficult times. His connection to the earthly realm also means he is closely attuned to human suffering and can offer comfort and strength when needed most.

Archangel Uriel's connection to the earthly realm highlights the importance of respecting and protecting the natural world around us. His role as the angel of wisdom means that he can offer guidance and insight into the environment and all the elements it contains. His influence spans many cultures and traditions, and his association with the autumnal equinox underscores his importance as a protector and guide. Whether seeking guidance in times of trouble or looking to deepen our understanding of the world around us, Archangel Uriel remains a powerful force for good in the world.

Archangel Uriel is also known for his incredible intellect and wisdom. As one of the four archangels, his role in heaven is to assist God in carrying out his divine plan, and he is often referred to as the "light of God" due to his immense knowledge and understanding of the universe. On earth, Archangel Uriel is known for his ability to provide insight and inspiration, helping them see the bigger picture and find meaning in their lives. With his cheerful personality and positive energy, Archangel Uriel is an uplifting presence wherever he goes, always ready to offer guidance and support to those in need. If you are looking for a source of wisdom and inspiration, look no further than this incredible archangel!

Chapter 2: Invoking Archangel Uriel

Invoking Archangel Uriel is an amazing experience that can clear your mind, uplift your spirits, and connect you with the divine. Uriel, known as the angel of wisdom and enlightenment, can bless you with a deeper understanding of yourself and the world around you when you are in his presence. You can call on him for guidance, support, and protection; he will always assist you with your journey. Whether you are facing a difficult challenge or just want to feel more connected to the universe, invoking Archangel Uriel is a powerful way to tap into your inner power and unleash your full potential.

Archangel Uriel, the angel of wisdom.[66]

This chapter will provide an in-depth look at how to successfully invoke Archangel Uriel. It will start by defining the term "invoke" and explain how it works when attempting a connection with angelic figures. It will also discuss the importance of intention and receptiveness in this process and provide several step-by-step exercises, meditations, affirmations, and mantras to help communicate with him. Suggestions for daily exercises that will help develop the ability to sense an angelic presence will be provided as bonus content here.

Definition of Invocation

When invoking something, many different images may come to mind. Some may think of summoning a powerful being from another realm, while others may picture prayer or blessings. In essence, an invocation is an act of calling upon a higher power, whether that be a deity, a force of nature, or even the collective energy of a group of individuals. While the specific practices may vary greatly depending on culture, religion, or belief systems, the underlying idea is universal. By invoking something greater than ourselves, we have access to more power, wisdom, or guidance than we could on our own. So, whether you are a believer or a skeptic, the concept of invocation is something worth exploring and contemplating. Who knows? You may just tap into something truly transformative.

Unraveling the Mysteries Behind Invocation

Invocation as a concept has been around for hundreds of years, but to most people, it remains a mystery. It is a powerful way of calling or praying to a higher being who can unlock the immense potential within us and help us achieve our goals. If you have ever wondered how invocation works, you have come to the right place. This section will explore this fascinating concept and show how it can help you reach your full potential.

At its core, invocation is all about connecting with a higher power. This can be a religious figure or simply an abstract concept like the universe. The idea is that when you can connect with this higher power, you are tapping into a source of energy and strength that you would not ordinarily have access to. This can help you achieve things you might have otherwise considered impossible.

The process of invocation is relatively straightforward. It involves creating a sacred space and performing a ritual of some sort. This can be as simple as lighting a candle and meditating or as complex as performing an elaborate ceremony. The purpose of the ritual is to create a sense of reverence and respect for the higher power you are invoking.

One important thing to remember when undertaking an invocation is that you are not simply asking for a favor. Rather, you are creating a connection and forming a relationship with the higher power you are invoking. This means you must be prepared to give something of yourself in return. This could be as simple as expressing gratitude or as complex as making a sacrifice.

The benefits of invocation are many. For one thing, it can help you overcome fear and self-doubt. When you feel connected to a higher power, you are more likely to feel empowered and capable of achieving your goals. Your invocation can also help you feel a sense of purpose and direction. You will likely stay motivated and focused when you have a clear idea of what you want to achieve.

Whether pursuing a personal goal or seeking spiritual growth, invoking a higher power gives you the boost you need to reach your objectives. By creating a sacred space, performing a ritual, and developing a relationship with the higher power you are invoking, you can unlock immense strength and potential within yourself. So, if you have ever wondered how invocation works, why not give it a try? Who knows what wonders you might achieve?

The Role of Intention and Receptiveness

Have you ever felt a presence around you, but you couldn't put your finger on what or who it was? Many people believe angelic figures surround us every day. Whether you believe in angels or not, something is to be said about the peaceful and uplifting energy surrounding us when we feel connected to these divine beings. The key to invoking angelic figures is through intention and receptiveness. Let's explore the power of intention and receptiveness in invoking angelic figures.

Intention

The first key to invoking angelic figures is intention. Many people pray or meditate with a specific intention, such as guidance, healing, or protection. When you set an intention, you invite angelic figures to align with you and help you reach your goal. A simple way to set your intention is to focus on what you wish to accomplish and then ask your guardian angels or other divine figures for assistance. A clear intention is the first step in creating a strong connection with your guardian angels.

Receptiveness

The second key to invoking angelic figures is receptiveness. When you are receptive, you are open to receiving guidance and support from the universe. This means that you must be open to receiving messages from your angels, even if they come in unconventional ways. Angelic figures may communicate with you through symbols or signs, like seeing the same number repeatedly or noticing a certain flower blooming at a specific time. By remaining open and receptive, you allow yourself to receive guidance and support from your angels in a way that works best for you.

Trust

The third key to invoking angelic figures is trust. Trusting that your angels are always there to guide and protect you can make a huge difference in how you perceive the world around you. By trusting that your angels are working behind the scenes to help you, you can release any fear, worry, or anxiety you may be experiencing. This trust gives you inner peace and serenity that can help you stay grounded and centered in your daily life.

Gratitude

The fourth and final key to invoking angelic figures is gratitude. When you are grateful for the blessings that come your way, both big and small, you open yourself up to receiving even more abundance from the universe. Expressing gratitude for the guidance and support you receive from your angels will help you create a deeper sense of connection with them. Gratitude can also help you shift your focus away from negative thoughts and emotions and instead focus on the positive aspects of your life.

Invoking angelic figures is all about intention, receptiveness, trust, and gratitude. You can create a stronger connection with your angels by setting a clear intention and remaining open and receptive. Trusting that your angels are always there to guide and protect you can help you release fear and worry while expressing gratitude for their help can create a deeper sense of connection. Whether you believe in angels or not, these tips can help you align with the positive energy surrounding you daily.

When Can Archangel Uriel Help?

Archangel Uriel is one of the four main archangels in many spiritual traditions. He represents wisdom, knowledge, and illumination and is often called upon to bring clarity and understanding to difficult situations. Uriel is also known as the *archangel of salvation*, helping individuals and entire communities overcome difficulties and find hope in the most trying times. So, when can Archangel Uriel help you?

Feeling Lost or Unsure of Your Path

When you're feeling lost or uncertain about which path to take to move forward, Archangel Uriel will come to help you. If you are facing a difficult decision about your career, a relationship, or any other area of life, Uriel provides the clarity and guidance you need. By calling upon Uriel, you can connect with your inner wisdom and develop a deeper understanding of your purpose and what steps you need to take to achieve your goals.

Struggling with a Difficult Situation

If you are going through a challenging time, such as a health crisis, financial difficulty, or personal loss, Archangel Uriel will be the one to comfort and support you. He can help you to find peace and hope amid even the most challenging circumstances. You can tap into his divine energy and draw strength from his wisdom and guidance by asking Uriel for assistance.

Feeling Overwhelmed or Stressed

Archangel Uriel can also help when you feel overwhelmed, stressed, or anxious. His presence can bring a sense of calm and peace, helping you to let go of worries and fears and focus on the present. By connecting with Uriel, you can find the strength to face any challenge with grace and ease.

Seeking to Deepen Your Spiritual Connection

Archangel Uriel can be an invaluable guide and mentor for those seeking a greater connection with the divine. He can help you to deepen your spiritual practice, expand your awareness, and connect deeper with your inner wisdom. By working with Uriel, you can build a stronger relationship with the divine and open yourself up to new levels of insight and understanding.

Looking to Heal and Transform

Finally, Archangel Uriel can help when you want to heal and transform on all levels. Whether you are dealing with physical, emotional, or spiritual challenges, Uriel can help you to release negative patterns, beliefs, and emotions and move into a more positive, joyful state of being. By working with Uriel, you can help to transform your life and step into a place of greater love, light, and healing.

Archangel Uriel is a powerful and compassionate ally for anyone needing to overcome challenges, deepen their spiritual connection, and live a more fulfilling life. Whether facing difficult circumstances, seeking greater clarity and understanding, or looking to heal and transform on all levels, Uriel is there to guide and support you. So, if you need his help, simply call on him with an open heart and mind, and trust that he will be there to assist you every step of the way.

Step-by-Step Exercises to Connect with Archangel Uriel

Do you ever feel you need help, guidance, or support from the heavenly realm? Archangels are known to provide just that, especially Archangel Uriel. He is the angel of wisdom, knowledge, and insight, and he can definitely come to your aid. This section will set out three step-by-step exercises to connect with Archangel Uriel: meditations, affirmations, and mantras.

Exercise 1: Meditation

Meditation is a powerful skill to use to connect with the divine. To begin, find a quiet and peaceful space to sit comfortably. Close your eyes and take a few deep breaths. Visualize yourself surrounded by a golden light, protecting you and guiding you. Then, visualize Archangel Uriel standing before you, radiating wisdom and knowledge. Ask him for guidance or clarity on a particular situation, and listen to his response. You may receive messages through thoughts, feelings, or even physical sensations. Finish the meditation by thanking Archangel Uriel for his guidance.

Exercise 2: Affirmations

Affirmations are positive statements that reprogram your subconscious mind. To connect with Archangel Uriel using affirmations, try repeating the following statements each day:

- Archangel Uriel, please guide me toward the path of wisdom and knowledge.
- I am open to receiving guidance and insight from Archangel Uriel.
- Archangel Uriel, please bless me with clarity and understanding in all areas of my life.

Repeat these affirmations in the morning or before bed, or whenever you need extra support.

Exercise 3: Mantras

Mantras are sacred words or phrases that are repeated to create a sense of peace, calm, and harmony. To connect with Archangel Uriel using mantras, try chanting the following at least 108 times:

- Om Anandamayi Namah (I am filled with divine joy)
- Divyatma Prabhu Pragaya Namah (God's light is within me and around me)

Chanting these mantras will unlock your inner wisdom, and you will be receptive to guidance from Archangel Uriel. They invoke Archangel Uriel's energy and clear your mind and bring focus to your thoughts. Repeat the mantra while sitting in a calm, peaceful environment, and visualize Archangel Uriel's energy surrounding you. Using these three exercises, you can deepen your connection with Archangel Uriel and receive his guidance and support whenever needed. Remember to trust the process and have faith that you will receive the necessary messages.

Developing the Ability to Sense an Angelic Presence

Have you ever felt a presence that you couldn't quite explain? Or perhaps you've had an experience that left you feeling uplifted and inspired, even though you couldn't quite put your finger on why. Perhaps you were sensing the presence of an angelic being. Angels are believed to be spiritual beings who exist to help guide and protect us on our journey through life. However, not everyone can sense their presence. This section will explore some techniques to help you develop your ability to sense an angelic presence.

Cultivate a State of Receptivity

One of the keys to sensing the presence of angels is cultivating a state of receptivity. This means opening yourself to subtle sensations and impressions you might normally overlook. To do this, try practicing mindfulness meditation, which involves bringing your attention to the sensations of your body and the present moment. As you become more attuned to your physical and emotional experiences, you may also sense the presence of spiritual beings.

Pay Attention to Your Intuition

Another way to sense the presence of angels is to pay attention to your intuition. Intuition is often described as a "gut feeling" or a sense of knowing that comes from beyond the rational mind. Many people believe that angels communicate with us through our intuition, so it's necessary to develop this faculty. To do this, try journaling about your intuitive hunches and paying attention to any synchronicities or coincidences that occur in your life.

Practice Gratitude

Gratitude is a powerful tool for attracting positive energy and spiritual connections. When we cultivate a sense of gratefulness for the blessings in our lives, we open ourselves up to receiving even more blessings. To practice gratitude, try keeping a gratitude journal where you write down three things you're grateful for daily. You can also make a gratitude altar where you place items that represent things you're thankful for and spend a few moments each day reflecting on them.

Ask for Assistance

Angels are always willing to assist us but won't intervene unless we ask for their help. If you're struggling with a problem or need guidance, try asking your angels for assistance. You can do this through prayer, meditation, or simply speaking aloud as if you're talking to a trusted friend. Be specific about what you need help with, and trust that your angels will come to your aid.

Trust Your Experience

Finally, trust your experience when you sense the presence of angels. Some people may dismiss your experiences as "just your imagination" or "wishful thinking," but only you can know what you sense and feel. Trust that your experiences are valid, even if you can't prove them to others.

Developing your ability to sense the presence of angels can be a powerful ability for navigating life's challenges and connecting with the divine. By cultivating a state of receptivity, paying attention to your intuition, practicing gratitude, asking for assistance, and trusting your experiences, you can become more and more attuned to the subtle energies and spiritual guidance surrounding us all. With time and practice, you may find that you can sense the presence of angels more readily and that your interactions with them bring peace, comfort, and inspiration to your life.

Daily Exercises

Angels are often regarded as celestial beings here to help and protect us. They are said to bring us guidance, inspiration, and support in times of need. While some people may find it easier to sense the presence of angels than others, there are ways to develop your ability to sense them. Here are some daily exercises that can help you to sense an angelic presence.

- **Nature Walks:** Nature is a wonderful way to connect with the energy of angels. Take a walk in nature every day and pay attention to the signs around you. Notice the birds, the trees, the flowers, the wind, and other elements of nature. Be open to receiving messages from your angels through these signs. You may also ask your angels to join you on your walk and guide you along your path.

- **Journaling:** Journaling is an excellent way to connect with the energy of angels and receive their guidance. Write down your thoughts and feelings daily, and invite your angels to communicate with you through your writing. You may also write down any signs or messages you receive from your angels throughout the day.

- **Yoga and Meditation:** Yoga and meditation are both great methods to connect with the energy of angels. Spend some time each day practicing yoga or meditating, and focus on the intention of opening yourself up to the presence of angelic beings. As you practice, ask your angels to join you and provide guidance.

By incorporating these daily exercises into your routine, you can develop your ability to sense an angelic presence. Remember to stay open, receptive, and trusting, and allow the energy of angels to surround you. With practice, you will become more confident in your ability to sense their presence and receive their guidance. Trust that your angels are always with you, guiding you toward your highest good.

Invoking archangels can be a powerful way to connect with the divine and receive guidance. By cultivating a state of receptivity, paying attention to your intuition, practicing gratitude, asking for assistance, and trusting your experiences, you can become more attuned to the subtle energies of these angelic presences. With time and practice, developing a deeper relationship with your angels and accessing their wisdom is possible. Remember to stay open, trusting, and receptive as you explore this realm of spiritual connection. Your angels are here for you, so don't be afraid to seek help when needed. Your journey toward a deeper understanding of angelic guidance will surely bring peace, comfort, and inspiration into your life.

Chapter 3: Signs of Uriel's Presence

Uriel is the Archangel of Wisdom and a messenger between God and people. He delivers his messages to us through signs, symbols, and omens. Although Uriel is known to communicate through various means, his presence can be recognized by certain symbols and signs. To understand better what these signs and symbols are and what they mean, we need a clear understanding of Uriel's role in our lives.

This chapter will provide a general overview of the symbols and signs associated with Uriel's presence while exploring in depth the various aspects of Uriel's role as an Archangel of Wisdom. It'll also look into the personal experiences of people who have come in contact with Uriel and how this practice has affected their perception of life. By the end of the chapter, you should better understand the signs and symbols that indicate Uriel's presence.

Unraveling the Meanings of the Symbols and Depictions of Uriel

Uriel is one of the archangels mentioned in the Jewish, Christian, and Islamic holy books. He is often called the light of God, and his name translates to "God is my light." Over the years, various symbols and depictions of Uriel have emerged, each carrying a unique meaning. This section will take a closer look at some of these symbols and what they signify.

The Flame

Uriel is commonly depicted holding a flaming torch.[67]

The first symbol associated with Uriel is the flame. Uriel holds a flaming torch or sits atop a fiery orb in many illustrations. This flame signifies the light part of his name, *light of God*. The light radiates from him, bringing clarity and illumination to the world. The flame also represents Uriel's passion for aiding humanity in finding its way back to God's divine light.

The Book

Another symbol that is commonly associated with Uriel is a book. In Christian illustrations, he is often depicted carrying an open book or a scroll, representing knowledge given to him by God. The book also symbolizes Uriel's role as a divine teacher, offering enlightenment to those open to it. As the angel of wisdom, Uriel is thought to guide individuals to the truth of God's plan for humanity.

The Scales

The third symbol is the scales. The scales of justice are also associated with Uriel, symbolizing his role as a divine judge. The scales represent the balance and fairness that Uriel is said to bring when passing judgment, ensuring that each decision he makes is just and fair. Those feeling lost or overwhelmed often turn to the energy of Uriel to bring balance to their lives.

Bow and Arrow

Finally, Uriel is often shown holding a bow and arrow. These symbols represent his role in helping people conquer their fears and anxieties. Uriel's energy is said to inspire courage and bravery, the characteristics we need when facing challenging situations. He is also thought to help us tap into our inner strength and stand our ground in the face of adversity.

When we look at these symbols and depictions of Uriel, we see an archangel who represents the light, knowledge, fairness, and courage of God. Uriel's energy can help us find our way back to our true purpose and bring clarity to our lives. By understanding these symbols, we can tap into his energy and allow him to guide us toward finding our true selves. So let us embrace the light of Uriel and allow his energy to guide us toward wisdom, justice, and courage in our lives.

Repetitive Numbers: Signs of Uriel's Presence

Have you ever experienced seeing the same numbers over and over again? Perhaps, you glanced at the clock, and it was 11:11, then later on, you noticed the same numbers on your phone and computer screen? Believe it or not, this could be a sign that Archangel Uriel is trying to communicate with you. Let's dive into repetitive numbers and how it relates to Uriel's presence.

Angel Numbers

Since Uriel is associated with wisdom, he often communicates with us through signs and symbols, including repetitive numbers. Seeing repetitive numbers is a common sign from Uriel, and it is often referred to as "angel numbers" or "divine messages." Each number has a meaning and significance, and paying attention to the numbers shown to you is important. For instance, seeing the number 1111 can represent new beginnings and spiritual awakening. Meanwhile, the number 333 can symbolize growth and progress.

It's not just the individual numbers that are significant but also the *repetition of the numbers*. The more you see the same number repeated, the stronger the message from Uriel is. So, if you keep seeing the number 777, this could suggest that Uriel is acknowledging your spiritual progress and achievement.

Deciphering the Messages

There are a few ways to decipher the messages from Uriel through repetitive numbers. Firstly, take note and remember the numbers that you keep seeing. You can research the meanings of these numbers online or through spiritual guides to understand what they signify. Another approach is to ask a question in your mind, then pay attention to the next set of numbers you see after posing the question. The number could hold the answer to your query.

Seeing repetitive numbers doesn't necessarily have to be a spiritual experience. It could simply be your mind attuning itself to patterns. However, if you do believe in the spiritual significance of seeing repetitive numbers, take the time to appreciate the message being sent to you.

Seeing repetitive numbers indicates that Uriel is trying to communicate with you. Pay attention to the numbers shown to you and their repetition. Take note of the numbers you see and their meanings, and try to understand Uriel's message. Whether it's a message of reassurance or guidance, Uriel's presence can provide a sense of comfort and understanding. So, the next time you see repetitive numbers, take a moment to appreciate the message being sent to you.

Animal Encounters: Signs of Uriel's Presence

When it comes to experiencing the divine, there are many ways to do so. Some of us may meditate and feel a sense of calm or hear a voice inside our heads. Others may feel the presence of someone or something watching over them. For those who believe in the existence of angels, animal encounters can be a clear sign of their presence. Uriel, the archangel of wisdom, is known to communicate using animals to send his messages to people. Here are different signs of Uriel's presence through animal encounters.

- **Birds:** If you look up to the sky and notice a bird circling you, it could be a sign of Uriel's presence. According to spiritual beliefs, birds are messengers of the angelic realm. When you see a bird, watch its behavior. Does it seem to be trying to catch your attention? Does it fly close to you? These could be signs that Uriel is trying to communicate with you, reminding you to trust in your intuition and spiritual path

- **Butterflies**: Butterflies are symbols of transformation and change. If a butterfly lands on you or follows you wherever you go, it could be a sign from Uriel that you need to make some changes in your life. Butterflies can also signify a spiritual awakening, urging you to pursue your passion and purpose in life
- **Owls**: It is said that Uriel often communicates with people through owls. Owls are symbols of wisdom, intuition, and transformation. If you regularly see owls at night or during meditation, Uriel may be guiding you toward a deeper understanding of yourself and the world around you
- **Dogs:** Dogs are known for their loyalty and unconditional love. If you have a dog, pay attention to its behavior. Does it seem to be trying to tell you something? Does it behave differently when you are feeling sad or anxious? Dogs can sense our emotions and may be trying to comfort us or remind us to be kind to ourselves
- **Cats:** Cats are independent animals that seem to have a sixth sense when it comes to energy. If you have a cat, observe its behavior. Does it seem to be attracted to certain people or places? Does it seem to be picking up on negative energy in the house? Cats can help us tune into our intuition and remind us to trust our instincts

Animal encounters can be a sign of Uriel's presence in our lives. Whether it's a bird, a butterfly, an owl, a dog, or a cat, these creatures can communicate with us in ways we may not even realize. By paying attention to their behavior and symbolism, we can receive spiritual guidance from the angelic realm, reminding us to trust in our intuition, pursue our passions, and spread love and kindness wherever we go.

Instincts: Signs of Uriel's Presence

When we feel lost, alone, or unsure of ourselves, we often find comfort in spirituality. We look for guidance and seek the answers to our questions. It can be very comforting to believe that someone is guiding us and watching over us. For many people, that guiding force is Uriel.

Uriel brings answers, insight, and healing into our lives. But how can we know if Uriel is present with us or if it's something else? By learning to recognize the signs of his presence in our lives, we can deepen our connection to him and find more guidance and support.

This section will explore the instincts often associated with Uriel's presence. From intuitive feelings to physical sensations, these signs can help us to feel more connected to Uriel and our higher power and more confident in our spiritual journey.

A Feeling of Warmth and Comfort

When Uriel is present, many people have reported feeling a sense of warmth and comfort. It can feel like being wrapped in a cozy blanket or sitting by a crackling fire. This sensation can occur at any time, but it's often most noticeable when we're feeling lost, scared, or uncertain. If you find yourself suddenly feeling warm and comforted, take a moment to recognize Uriel's presence in your life.

Sudden Insights and Clarity

Uriel is the archangel of wisdom, so it's no surprise that his presence often brings clarity and insight. You may suddenly have a flash of inspiration, a new understanding of a problem, or a realization that helps you see things in a new light. These insights can come to us in many ways, from a sudden urge to write something down to a feeling of certainty about a decision. Pay attention to these moments and see if you can recognize Uriel's hand in them.

A Feeling of Protection

Uriel is also known for his protective energy; many people report feeling safer and more secure when he's near. You may notice that you're less prone to accidents, feel more confident in your abilities, or are more aware of your surroundings. This protective energy can be very comforting, especially during times of difficulty or danger.

A Sense of Peace and Calm

When Uriel is present, many people report feeling a sense of peace and calm. This can be especially helpful during times of stress, anxiety, or worry. You may suddenly feel more centered, more grounded, clearer-headed, or more at ease. This sense of peace can help you to focus on what's important and let go of distractions and worries.

An Intuitive Feeling

Finally, Uriel's presence is often accompanied by a strong intuitive feeling. You may suddenly feel as if you know what to do or have a sense of what's going to happen next. This kind of intuition can be very powerful and can guide you through difficult or confusing situations. If you ever have a strong intuitive feeling, take a moment to consider whether Uriel might be trying to communicate with you.

Uriel's presence can bring comfort, clarity, protection, peace, and intuitive guidance into our lives. By learning to recognize the signs of his presence, we can deepen our connection to this powerful archangel and find more guidance and support along our spiritual journey. Whether you feel a sudden warmth, gain new insights, or just feel a sense of peace, take a moment to acknowledge Uriel's presence in your life and let it guide you toward greater wisdom and light.

Sudden Flashes of Inspiration: Signs of Uriel's Presence

We all know that feeling of sudden inspiration that strikes us out of nowhere. It's that moment when our minds are suddenly filled with an idea, a solution to a problem we've been struggling with, or a newfound sense of purpose. But where does this sudden inspiration come from? Could it be that the archangel Uriel is trying to communicate with us? Here are some signs of Uriel's presence and what they could mean for you.

Dazzling Flashes of Light

One of the most common signs of Uriel's presence is a sudden flash of light, often accompanied by a tingling sensation. This could be a sign that Uriel is trying to guide you toward a new path or help you see things in a new light. Pay attention to any patterns or colors in the flashes of light, as they could hold clues about what Uriel is trying to communicate to you.

A Sense of Inner Peace

When Uriel is near, you may feel a sense of inner peace and serenity that radiates throughout your entire being. This is a sign that Uriel is gently guiding you toward a state of calmness and clarity so that you can receive the messages and insights coming your way with more assurance. If you're feeling overwhelmed or stuck in a rut, call on Uriel to help you find your way back to a state of peace and tranquility.

Synchronicities and Coincidences

Another sign that Uriel is trying to communicate with you is the appearance of synchronicities and coincidences in your life. This could be anything from repeatedly seeing the same numbers or symbols to running into people who share your passions or interests at unexpected times. These synchronicities are often little nudges from Uriel, urging you to pay attention and follow the breadcrumbs to uncover new opportunities or paths meant for you.

A Sense of Heightened Intuition

Uriel is known as the archangel of wisdom and intuition, so it's no surprise that his presence often leads to a heightened sense of intuition and inner knowing. You may find that you're suddenly more attuned to your thoughts and feelings and those of others around you. Trust these intuitive insights, as they could be invaluable in guiding you toward your true purpose or calling.

Inspiration Bursts and Creative Surges

Perhaps the most overt signs of Uriel's presence are the sudden bursts of inspiration and creative energy that come seemingly out of nowhere. You may feel a sudden urge to start a new project, write a book, or learn a new skill. These inspiration bursts are often gifts from Uriel, who is helping you tap into your creative potential and express it in ways that will serve you and others.

The signs of Uriel's presence are varied and nuanced. From flashes of light and inner peace to synchronicities and heightened intuition, Uriel constantly tries to communicate with us and guide us toward our highest good. The key is to remain open, receptive, and trusting of the signs and messages that come your way. Whether you're seeking a new path, a renewed sense of purpose, or simply a deeper connection to yourself and the universe, Uriel is always there, ready, and willing to help you find your way.

Finding Uriel's Presence through Electrical Signs

Known as the Angel of Light, Uriel is the archangel of wisdom and illumination. A lesser-known fact about Uriel is that he is also associated with electrical signs. This section will explore the signs of Uriel's presence and how to recognize them.

Electrical Surges

One of the most common signs believed to be associated with Uriel's presence is electrical surges. You might have experienced your lights flickering or the intensity of the sparkle in your light bulbs increasing. Some people also believe that Uriel sometimes turns off electrical appliances or gadgets to grab your attention.

Feeling the Energy

Another way to recognize Uriel's presence is by paying attention to your energy levels. You might feel a sudden surge of energy or chill, indicating that Uriel is creating a pathway to communicate with you. It is said that during such moments, you might also receive visions or messages from Uriel telepathically or through intuition.

The Power of Numbers

Uriel is also associated with the numerical sequence of 111. If you start seeing 111 frequently or repeatedly, it is believed to be a sign of Uriel's presence. Seeing triple digits or repetitive numbers is also associated with the archangel of forgiveness, unity, and peace.

Unusual Events

Another sign of Uriel's presence is when you experience unusual events that defy your understanding of logic or science. It could be a coincidental meeting with someone familiar or discovering an object you have been searching for. These events might seem insignificant, but they could reveal Uriel's presence and protection to you.

Sensing a Presence

Lastly, you might sense Uriel's presence through your intuition or inner voice. Your gut feeling could signify that Uriel is with you, watching over and guiding you. Trusting this feeling and working on your intuitive abilities can help you connect with Uriel on a deeper level.

Uriel's electrical signs and presence might be challenging to recognize initially, but with time and patience, you will be able to connect with the Angel of Light. Always remember to stay positive, open, and curious about the world around you. Uriel's guidance and wisdom are there to help you navigate your life's purpose with greater clarity and ease. Keep your eyes open to electrical signs and trust the feeling of warmth and positivity that follows!

The Incredible Stories of Uriel's Presence

Millions of people around the world believe in the power of angels. These divine beings are known to bring comfort, protection, guidance, and support to those who believe in them. Among the archangels, Uriel is considered one of the most powerful and loving. Uriel is said to bring messages of hope, healing, and light to humanity. This section will explore the real accounts of personal experiences of Uriel's presence and what people have to say about his impact on their lives.

Healing through a Divine Vision

Many people have experienced some sort of physical, mental, or emotional healing through Uriel's presence. For example, there have been reports of people experiencing visions of Uriel during severe illness or emotional turmoil. These visions have brought comfort and healing, giving people the strength to endure and overcome their challenges. One woman shares that she saw Uriel during a time of deep sorrow and instantly felt a sense of peace and comfort. She believes that Uriel was sent to her as a messenger of hope, reminding her that she was loved and that everything would be OK.

Comfort in Times of Grief

Uriel is also known to help people cope with loss and grief. There have been numerous accounts of people feeling his presence after the death of a loved one. One woman shares that she was struggling to come to terms with the sudden death of her husband. One night, as she had trouble sleeping, she felt a strong presence in her room. She looked up to see Uriel standing there, holding out his hand. She felt an instant sense of peace and comfort, knowing that her husband was in good hands and that Uriel would help her through her grief.

Protection and Guidance

People have also reported feeling Uriel's presence when they were in danger or facing a difficult decision. Uriel is a powerful guardian angel, protecting those who believe in him from harm. One man shares that he was driving late at night on a deserted road when he felt his car suddenly stop. As he got out to check the engine, he felt a strong presence behind him. When he turned around, he saw Uriel standing there, with a look of reassurance on his face. The man felt a sudden sense of safety and knew that Uriel had stopped him to prevent him from being in a potentially dangerous situation.

Signs of Uriel's Presence

Many people have reported seeing signs of Uriel's presence, even if they didn't see him directly. Some people have seen rainbows or clouds in the shape of an angel or have felt a sudden breeze or temperature change. Uriel communicates through signs and symbols, letting people know he is with them and watching over them. One woman shared that she was struggling with a difficult decision and asked for Uriel's guidance. Later that day, she saw a butterfly land on her hand and stay there for minutes. She knew that it was a sign from Uriel telling her to trust her instincts and make the right decision.

These stories of Uriel's presence are truly inspiring and uplifting. Uriel has a powerful impact on the lives of those who believe in him. Whether it is through healing, comfort, protection, or guidance, Uriel is a beacon of hope in a world that often seems dark and scary. So, if you ever feel lost, alone, or afraid, just remember that Uriel is always with you, watching over you and guiding you toward the light.

This chapter has explored the personal accounts of Uriel's presence in people's lives. In times of struggle, sadness, or confusion, Uriel is said to provide healing and comfort to those who call upon him. He is a powerful guardian angel, watching over and protecting his followers from danger. Signs of Uriel's presence have been seen by many, reminding them that they are not alone and that Uriel is always with them. If you ever feel lost or afraid, just remember to call upon Uriel; he will never disappoint you. Believe in Him and His loving guidance; He will lead you toward the light.

Chapter 4: Creating Angelic Sacred Space

Do you feel the presence of angels in your life but don't know how to access their power? Are you seeking a way to honor these spiritual guides and give thanks for their gifts? Creating a sacred space or angelic altar is one way to do this.

By setting up an angelic altar and establishing an intention, you can open the door to angelic blessings, and when you set one up for Uriel, the light of wisdom and protection comes shining through. This chapter will explain how to do it so you can access the energy of Uriel. It will provide practical tools and exercises to help you create an angelic altar that honors the presence of Uriel in your life. The goal is to create a place of peace and protection that allows you to access the divine power and connection with angels. Creating this sacred space and honoring Uriel can open the door to divine blessings.

Creating a Space of Intentional Energy

Angelic altars allow you to connect to a higher power.⁶⁸

A sacred space or angelic altar is a dedicated area where you can connect with a higher power, meditate, or simply find peace and solace. This space is all about intention and energy, where you create an environment that resonates with the person or entity you want to invite into your life. Whether you're religious, spiritual, or just want a peaceful corner of your home to help you relax and unwind, having a sacred space can benefit you in more ways than you can imagine. This section will explore the significance of creating a sacred space, why intention and energy are crucial, and how to make a space that reflects your personality, where you feel free to be you.

Defining Sacred Space

So, what exactly is a sacred space? Simply put, a sacred space is any designated space that holds significance to an individual or community. This could be a room in your home, a corner of a room, a garden or yard, or any space you feel is significant. The most crucial aspect of any sacred space is the intention behind it. Keeping the energy within that space positive and intentional is crucial, ensuring that every object and detail is there for a reason. Whether creating a space to connect with your higher self or inviting angels and spirits into your life, your intention should be crystal clear before you begin.

Significance of Sacred Space

The significance of creating a sacred space lies in the fact that it provides a physical representation of your connection to the divine. It serves as a reminder of the love and light surrounding you and can also be a powerful tool for manifesting positive change in your life. By having a space dedicated to your spirituality, you are sending a message to the universe that you are ready and willing to receive guidance and support on your life's journey. By spending time in your sacred space, you are creating a place for personal reflection where you stay centered and grounded amid the chaos of daily life.

The Importance of Energy

When creating a space, it is essential to remember the importance of energy. The energy within your space should be a reflection of the intention behind it. Consider the objects that will be within your space. They should all have significance and meaning, such as crystals, candles, and other spiritual tools. Also, take time to consider the colors, textures, and materials you are going to put there. Even the scent of your space can affect the energy within it. Experiment with essential oils or burning incense to create an atmosphere that supports your intention.

Creating a sacred space is all about intention and energy. It is an opportunity to connect with your higher self, the universe, or whichever entity you want to invite into your life. By putting in the time and effort to create a sacred space that is unique and personal to you, you are committing to your spiritual growth and well-being. Remember to keep your intention crystal clear, fill your space with items that have personal meaning, and pay attention to the energy within your space. May your sacred space bring peace, love, and light in all you do.

Setting Up an Angelic Altar

Creating a sacred space for angels is a beautiful way to connect with divine beings and seek their help and guidance. It is a physical representation of our intention and desire to invite angels into our lives. While setting up an altar, choose items that resonate with the energy of the angels to help you feel more connected to them. Let's look at some ways and tools for setting up an angelic sacred space.

Choose a Suitable Location

The first step to creating an angelic altar is to choose a suitable location. Select a place that is peaceful, quiet, and free from distractions. The area should be somewhere you can maintain the altar without it being disturbed by kids or pets. A spare bedroom or corner of your living room might be a good option. The location should be one you can easily access and spend time in to nurture the connection between yourself and the angels.

Selecting Angelic Oracle Cards

Angelic oracle cards are perfect tools for communicating with your angels. They offer insight, inspiration, and guidance from the angels. Choose a set to which you feel drawn and invite the angels to help you select the cards that will help you experience their divine presence. Keep the cards in a box or a special place on your altar so that you can use them when needed. When choosing the cards, ensure that they feel that they are aligned with your intention.

Angel Letters

Angel letters are another powerful tool for connecting with the angels. This is where you write letters to your angels and receive answers by channeling messages from divine beings. Begin by explaining your desires, feelings, or concerns, and write them down. Don't edit them. Just let your feelings run free on the paper. Trust the process and listen for the messages that come from the Angels. You can keep these letters in a notebook or a box on your altar.

Scents and Oils

Scents and oils can be an excellent way to create a conducive environment for angelic communication. You can use incense or essential oils like lavender, frankincense, or myrrh. These scents have calming and soothing properties, which can help you relax and connect with the angels at a deeper level. The scent should be gentle enough not to distract you from your intention and should be soothing and uplifting to your senses.

Crystals

Crystals are beautiful tools for enhancing your connection with the angels. Some of the popular crystals used for this purpose include clear quartz, rose quartz, selenite, and amethyst. These crystals have vibrational energies that can help you feel grounded and connected to the divine. Keep them on your altar, and you can even use them for meditation. In addition, you can hold a crystal in your hand and ask for angelic help and guidance.

Incenses/Sage

Burning fragrant sticks or smudging with sage can purify and purify the air in your space, making it more soothing. Frankincense, lavender, and sandalwood are all great options to try out. Frankincense can enhance your spirituality, while lavender is known for its relaxation properties. When using incense, always open a window or door to allow the smoke to escape. A good practice is to recite an angelic prayer or intention as you light the incense and imagine the rising smoke as the bearer of your wishes.

Angels Statues/Pictures

Since the purpose of this space is to welcome angels, it's a great idea to incorporate angelic decor in your Sacred Space. Angel statues, pictures, or other angelic decor items will invite your desired angelic presence. The visual representation of the celestial beings can comfort and inspire you. Take your time to select the items that capture your connection with your guardian angels. Let your intuition guide you in selecting the items to include.

Healing Music

Music is an essential tool that can help you transform your space. Healing music or calming meditative sounds can create a peaceful and serene environment in your angelic space. Depending on your preference, you can use anything from floral to chakra music. One of the best ways to enjoy this music is by using headphones or earbuds. This way, all the distractions around you will be eliminated, and you will be able to focus entirely on connecting with the angels.

Spiritual Books

Placing spiritual books or oracle cards in your sacred space is also said to promote spiritual growth and well-being. You could read from them before meditating or simply keep them close by. Not only do these items offer guidance for you, but they can also make attractive decor. Place them in a decorative basket or box, and they will look great without taking up too much space. Use them as a reminder to keep your thoughts and intentions aligned with the divine.

Setting up an angelic altar can be a beautiful and transformative experience. It is a sacred space that you can use to connect with the angels, seek guidance, receive messages from the divine, and simply sit in serenely. By selecting suitable items for your altar, you set your intentions and invite the angels to communicate with you. With time and practice, you will learn how to create an environment that fosters a deep and meaningful connection with your angels. Trust your intuition, and let the angels guide you through this beautiful journey.

Exercises for Energetic Protection

As spiritual beings, we often experience moments of vulnerability and emotional turmoil, which let negative entities attach themselves to our aura. When invoking Archangel Uriel, we must prepare ourselves and perform exercises for energetic protection so we are safe from any negativity that may compromise our spiritual journey. This section will explore the different exercises for energetic protection that you can perform to channel the mighty archangel and unleash your inner warrior.

Grounding Exercises

Grounding exercises will also help to keep your energy centered and create a strong foundation for spiritual work. Begin by standing with your feet firmly planted on the ground and visualizing roots extending down to the earth's core. These roots will help you feel connected to the earth and allow negative energies to flow freely from your body. You can also try grounding visualizations that involve standing in the middle of a white light that extends down to the ground.

Shielding Exercises

Shielding exercises help to create a layer of protection around your aura, which keeps any negative entities from attaching themselves to your energy. You can use the power of visualization to create a protective shield around you. Picture a ring of light around your aura that is impenetrable. You can also visualize a white light coming down from Archangel Uriel and surrounding you with his protection.

Breathwork Exercises

Breathing exercises help you reach a deep meditative state, necessary when invoking Archangel Uriel. You do this by taking deep breaths in and out, focusing on the air flowing in and out of your body. Inhale deeply through your nose, hold your breath for a few seconds, and then exhale slowly through your mouth. You can also try alternate nostril breathing exercises that help to balance both hemispheres of your brain.

Mantra and Chanting Exercises

Mantras and chants have been used for centuries to enhance spiritual awareness and protection. You can use a simple chant-like "Om" or "Aum," while meditating to create a vibrational sound that protects your aura. You can also try a mantra used to invoke Archangel Uriel, such as "Uriel, I call upon your protection and guidance," while visualizing yourself surrounded by his light.

Relaxation Exercises

Relaxation exercises help calm the mind and body, which is essential when performing spiritual work. You can use relaxation techniques like yoga, meditation, or tai chi, which help you to become still and focused. This calm state of mind allows you to easily connect with Archangel Uriel and receive his guidance. Along with relaxation exercises, you can also try visualizations that involve picturing yourself surrounded by a peaceful landscape.

Unleashing your inner warrior begins with deepening your spiritual practice and ensuring you are protected against negative entities. These exercises for energetic protection when invoking Uriel will help you achieve a heightened spiritual state, where you can unleash your full potential and connect with Archangel Uriel's wisdom and guidance. Remember to practice each exercise frequently and with intention, just as the greatest warriors always prepare themselves for battle. So, let's prepare ourselves to become spiritual warriors and receive the divine love and protection that Archangel Uriel offers us.

Methods for Enhancing Intention and Achieving Better Focus

As we move towards a society that is constantly on the go, being able to focus, be still, and concentrate on the task at hand has become increasingly difficult. You're not alone if you're struggling to get things done or are constantly being sidetracked. However, it doesn't have to be this way. This section will explore effective methods for enhancing intention and achieving better focus.

Clear Your Mind

The first step towards better focus is to clear your mind of all distractions. Start by creating a to-do list and prioritizing it. This will help you focus on the most crucial tasks first and eliminate unnecessary distractions. Also, clear your physical space of anything that could cause a distraction. As the thoughts come in, don't be afraid to acknowledge them, but then let them go and move on. The more you practice this, the easier it will become.

Practice Mindfulness

Mindfulness is the practice of staying present in the moment, focusing entirely on the task at hand. This means you'll need to eliminate distractions from your surroundings and focus solely on one task. Take deep breaths and stay in the moment, enjoying the feeling of getting things done. If your mind starts to wander, refocus it on what you're doing and take another deep breath. A few minutes of mindfulness each day can make a big difference in your focus and productivity.

Take Breaks

It is vital to take regular breaks throughout the day to re-energize and refresh your mind. This can be as simple as taking a quick walk or stepping outside for a bit of fresh air. Taking breaks will help you maintain your focus throughout the day. When you take a break, make sure to stay away from any potential distractions that can take away your focus. To maximize your break, focus on deep breathing, stretching, or doing something that brings you joy. If you feel overwhelmed, take a few moments to notice and accept your feelings.

Set Goals

Setting specific goals can help you stay motivated and focused. Create daily or weekly goals, and ensure they are specific and measurable. Having something to work towards will keep you focused and motivated. The more achievable your goals are, the more likely you are to stay on track and increase your productivity. A great way to ensure you stay on track is by writing down your goals and tracking your progress.

Eliminate Distractions

Identifying the distractions in your life and eliminating them can be a game-changer in terms of focus. This could mean turning off notifications on your phone, closing unnecessary tabs on your computer, or simply avoiding people or activities that distract you. Bring awareness to all the things that are pulling you away from your task, and make a conscious effort to eliminate them.

Break Up Tasks

Breaking up larger tasks into smaller, more manageable chunks can make tackling them easier. This will help you stay focused on the smaller steps that will eventually lead you to complete the task and feel great about yourself for achieving it. From writing a blog post to getting your taxes done, breaking tasks into smaller chunks can help you stay focused and motivated.

Prioritize Sleep

A good night's rest is vital for optimal focus and productivity. Sleep propels us to stay focused, alert, and motivated. That's why prioritizing good, deep, and refreshing sleep is so important to achieve better focus in your daily life. The chemicals in our brains need time to reset and replenish, so ensure you get enough sleep each night. An early bedtime can make all the difference in your focus and productivity the next day.

Exercise Regularly

Regular exercise can have a huge impact on your focus and productivity. Taking just 30 minutes daily to exercise can increase your mental clarity and overall productivity. The aim is to find something you enjoy and can stick with, which will help you stay motivated. Exercise can also be a great outlet for releasing stress and improving your overall well-being.

Drink Water

Drinking enough water throughout the day can help improve focus and clarity. Dehydration can lead to difficulty focusing, so consuming enough water throughout the day is essential. At least two liters per day is the golden rule for staying hydrated and focusing on the point. A water bottle at your desk will help remind you to drink. Remember that caffeinated drinks should be consumed in moderation and only at certain times of the day.

Practice Gratitude

Practicing gratitude can significantly affect your focus and productivity. Focusing on the positives in life helps you to stay motivated and will intensify your sense of achievement. Write down 3-5 things you are grateful for each day, and consider why you appreciate them. Gratitude can be a powerful way to stay focused and motivated.

While staying focused may be challenging in today's busy world, incorporating these ten methods into your daily routine can greatly enhance your intention and focus. Remember to take breaks, practice mindfulness, and prioritize sleep and exercise. With these simple yet effective tips, you'll be well on your way to better focus and productivity.

There's something truly magical about creating your own angelic sacred space. It's where you can feel at peace, connect with your inner spirituality, and find solace amid a busy world. With a few simple tools and a little imagination, you can transform any space into a serene sanctuary that will renew and refresh you. From crystals and candles to sagging and visualization, there are countless ways to enhance the energy of your space and draw in positive vibes. So go ahead and tap into your creative side; your angelic sacred space is waiting for you!

Chapter 5: Solar Chakra Meditation

The Solar Chakra and Archangel Uriel are two powerful forces that can bring balance and positive energy into your life. The Solar Chakra, also known as the Manipura Chakra, is located in the stomach area and is associated with confidence, self-esteem, and personal power. By focusing on this chakra, you tap into your inner strength, and the result is that you'll feel empowered to pursue your dreams. On the other hand, Archangel Uriel is known as the angel of wisdom and enlightenment. He can help you gain clarity and understanding, and his presence can bring a sense of calm and tranquility to your life.

By combining the power of the solar chakra and Archangel Uriel, you can unleash an amazing amount of potential and achieve greater levels of success and happiness. This chapter focuses on the history and etymology of chakras, how to identify imbalances in the solar plexus chakra and step-by-step meditations for activating and balancing the solar plexus chakra while under the guidance of Archangel Uriel. You will also learn what can be achieved by activating this chakra and how Archangel Uriel can help with the process.

The Mystical World of Chakras

Chakra symbols.[69]

Have you ever wondered about the origins of chakras? What do these energy centers signify, and where do they come from? We are all familiar with the buzzword "chakra," but do we truly understand the depth of their significance? In this section, we will take a historical and etymological dive into the mystical world of chakras, which will give us a comprehensive understanding of these pivotal energy systems.

The word "chakra" finds its origin in the Sanskrit language, which means "wheel" or "disc." The earliest mention of chakras dates back to 1500 BCE when the ancient Hindu text, Vedas, describes chakras as a series of energy points, also known as Padma, meaning lotus flower. These energy points were considered vital for the proper flow of energy within the human body.

Dating back to 600 BCE, according to Buddhist and Hindu traditions, seven primary chakras align with the human spine, stretching from the base to the crown of the head. The seven chakras represent different aspects of human life, including spirituality, creativity, personal power, self-expression, love, communication, and intuition.

The concept of chakras entered the Western world in the 1800s through the Theosophical Society, spreading throughout the world through yoga teachers, mystics, scholars, and spiritual teachers. These ancient energy centers were first mentioned in-depth by the renowned psychoanalyst Carl Jung in his writings, where he valued the importance of accessing the subconscious mind and personal transformation through the chakra.

Several countries view chakras as essential to their cultural and spiritual values. Japanese Reiki, for instance, involves treating and clearing spiritual and physical blockages in the chakras using energy healing modalities. Even Chinese traditional medicine has its system of energy centers, known as meridians.

The significance of chakras has gained immense popularity among Western spiritual seekers in recent times, where they are often associated with vibrational frequency, colors, and sound vibrations. Each chakra possesses its own unique element, frequency, and color to balance the chakra system.

Understanding chakras has evolved over the centuries, and our knowledge of their power continues evolving as we learn more about them. Knowing the historical and etymological background of the chakras helps us understand the importance of energy centers within our body and how they can impact our well-being. As we learn and deepen our understanding of these energy centers, we can better align our body, mind, and spirit to live a fulfilling and balanced life.

The Power of Chakras and Their Angelic Associations

In the world of spirituality and metaphysics, there is no more significant concept than the chakras. They are the wheels of energy that connect our physical body and our consciousness. They are said to be the centers of our emotional and spiritual well-being and help balance our energy flows, which affect our emotional health. This section will discuss each chakra's attributes and physical connections, including their angelic associations. Are you ready to unlock the power of your chakras and achieve spiritual balance? Keep reading to find out more.

1. The root chakra, or Muladhara, is the first chakra located at the spine's base. The color associated with this chakra is red, and its attributes are grounding, stability, and security. Archangel Michael is the angelic association of the root chakra, known for his protective qualities. Physical activities such as yoga, walking, or gardening are recommended to balance this chakra.
2. The sacral chakra, or Swadhisthana, is located below the navel and is associated with orange. This chakra is responsible for our sexual energy, creativity, and passion. Archangel Gabriel is the angelic association of the sacral chakra. He is known for his wealth of creativity and inspiration. Balance this chakra with activities such as dancing, painting, or any other creative outlet that resonates with you.

3. The solar plexus chakra, or *Manipura,* is located behind the navel and is associated with yellow. This chakra is responsible for our personal power, confidence, and self-esteem. Archangel Uriel is the angelic association of the solar plexus chakra, known for bringing clarity and purpose into our lives. Try practicing self-care activities such as journaling, meditation, or affirmations to balance this chakra.
4. The heart chakra, Anahata, is located at the center of the chest and is associated with the color green. This chakra is responsible for our love, compassion, and forgiveness. Archangel Chamuel is the angelic association of the Heart chakra, known for its healing properties. To balance this chakra, spend time in nature, practice gratitude, and show kindness to yourself and others.
5. The throat chakra, Vishuddha, is located at the base of the neck and is associated with the color blue. This chakra is responsible for communication, self-expression, and authenticity. Archangel Gabriel is the angelic association of the throat chakra, known for his ability to bring clarity and truth. To balance this chakra, practice singing, public speaking, or any other form of self-expression that speaks to your soul.

The power of chakras and their angelic associations can be life-changing. By acknowledging and understanding each chakra's attributes and physical connections, we can tap into our spiritual energy and unlock our full potential. Take some time to explore each chakra and try different activities that resonate with you. You never know; you just might find the key to unlocking your inner peace and finding your purpose!

Archangel Uriel and the Solar Plexus Chakra

Have you ever wondered about the connection between the Archangels and our chakras? Our chakras are the energy centers in our bodies related to our physical, emotional, and spiritual well-being. Archangels are celestial beings who guide us toward a life full of positivity and love. In this section, we will explore the connection between Archangel Uriel and the solar plexus chakra, the third chakra located in the upper abdomen.

Archangel Uriel is known as the angel of wisdom and enlightenment and is often depicted in association with the sun's power. He embodies the qualities of confidence, courage, and self-esteem. The solar plexus chakra represents our personal power, confidence, and self-worth. When these two entities come together, they create a powerful force that can help us achieve our goals and lead a life full of self-confidence.

The solar plexus chakra is associated with the element of fire, which signifies transformation and change. When we open up this chakra, we let go of old patterns and beliefs and welcome new ideas and possibilities that lead us to our greatest purpose. Archangel Uriel can help us in this process of change and transformation by guiding us toward our inner wisdom and illuminating our path.

If you feel your self-worth has been shaken and your confidence has taken a hit, it could indicate a blocked solar plexus chakra. Archangel Uriel can help you unblock the chakra and give you the strength to move forward. By invoking his presence and repeating affirmations like, "I am confident in my power," we can connect with the angel's energy and heal ourselves.

Moreover, Archangel Uriel can also help us overcome the anxiety and stress often associated with an imbalanced solar plexus chakra. By visualizing a golden light surrounding us and focusing on our breathing, we can invite Archangel Uriel to fill us with his light, which helps to balance our chakra and calm our nerves.

The connection between Archangel Uriel and the solar plexus chakra can help us strengthen our sense of self-worth and lead a life full of purpose and positivity. By including simple practices in our daily routine, we can connect with Archangel Uriel's sound spirit and allow ourselves to receive his divine guidance. Take a moment to connect with your solar plexus chakra, feel the presence of Archangel Uriel, and let him guide you toward your greatest potential.

Identifying Unbalances in the Solar Plexus Chakra

Have you ever felt as if you are stuck in a rut, unable to move forward in life? Do you often struggle with decision-making, lack self-confidence, or experience digestive issues? These may be signs that your Solar Plexus Chakra, which governs personal power and self-esteem, is unbalanced.

This section will discuss identifying the imbalance in this chakra and exploring ways to restore harmony.

- When balanced, the solar plexus chakra helps us feel confident in our abilities, make decisions with ease, and have a sense of purpose. However, when it is unbalanced, it can result in a lack of direction, energy, and self-esteem, amongst other things
- One of the most common signs of an unbalanced solar plexus chakra is a digestive issue related to the stomach and pancreas. This can show up as constipation, diarrhea, acid reflux or indigestion, and a lack of appetite. Additionally, you may experience physical symptoms such as ulcers, infections, and liver or kidney problems
- Another sign of an unbalanced solar plexus chakra is a lack of self-confidence. You may find yourself doubting your abilities or feeling like an imposter. This lack of confidence can prevent you from taking risks, achieving your goals, and pursuing your dreams. You may also find yourself seeking validation from others instead of trusting your judgment
- Decision-making can also be difficult when this chakra is unbalanced. You may find yourself struggling to make even small decisions, like what to eat for dinner or which movie to watch. This indecisiveness can lead to analysis paralysis and prevent you from taking action toward your goals
- Increased stress and anxiety levels can also indicate an unbalanced solar plexus chakra. When this chakra is overactive, it can lead to a constant feeling of stress or anxiety, which can manifest as physical symptoms such as headaches and muscle tension

Identifying imbalances in the solar plexus chakra can help you understand why you may be experiencing certain physical or emotional symptoms. Once you recognize these imbalances, you can take steps to restore balance. Some ways to do this include practicing yoga or meditation, eating a balanced diet, engaging in physical activity, and setting boundaries for yourself. Remember that restoring balance takes time and patience, so be kind to yourself as you start this journey. Dedication and practice can bring harmony and peace back to your solar plexus chakra, helping you live your best life.

Step-by-Step Meditations for Activating and Balancing the Solar Plexus Chakra

Do you often feel overwhelmed, anxious, or insecure? These are common symptoms of a blocked solar plexus chakra, the energy center located in the upper abdomen. This chakra can help you feel confident, empowered, and at peace with yourself when activated and balanced. You can heal this chakra and, again, overall well-being through meditation. In this section, we'll guide you through step-by-step meditations to help you activate and balance your solar plexus chakra for inner peace.

Breathing Meditation

Meditation can start with a simple technique called breathing meditation. It helps you become more aware of your breath and control your thoughts. Sit in a comfortable place, close your eyes, and breathe deeply. Mentally observe your breath and focus your mind on the sensations. Let any thoughts that arise fade away peacefully. Take this time to be mindful and connect with your breath.

Solar Plexus Visualization Meditation

Visualize a bright yellow sun resting within your solar plexus chakra. Close your eyes and focus your attention on the area. Imagine a bright beam of sunlight that flows from the sun in your chakra and spreads throughout your body. Allow the light to transform any negative emotions into positive ones, such as self-confidence, courage, and empowerment. Staying focused on this visualization for a few minutes or until you feel your solar plexus chakra energized is vital.

Chanting Meditation

This chakra is also associated with the sound of "Ram." Chant this sound repeatedly while breathing deeply. As you chant, imagine the vibration moving through your solar plexus and spreading throughout your body. Let the sound fill you with confidence and inner strength. As you chant, your solar plexus chakra will become more balanced.

Affirmation Meditation

Repeat positive affirmations that align with the qualities of the solar plexus chakra. Say things like "I am confident, I am worthy, I am powerful." Feel the energy of the affirmations spreading through your body, filling you with positive energy. Say each phrase confidently and confidently until you feel your solar plexus chakra activated.

Yoga Meditation

Yoga is a great way to balance all the body's chakras, including the solar plexus chakra. Incorporate yoga postures like the Boat Pose, Warrior 1, and Surya Namaskar, which focus on strengthening your core, creating space in the solar plexus region, and activating the energy flow to the chakra.

Meditation is a holistic way to balance, heal, and activate the body's chakras. When you focus on the solar plexus chakra, you can find peace and confidence within yourself. Use these step-by-step meditations to activate and balance your solar plexus chakra to promote overall well-being. As you continue to practice these meditations regularly, you will notice positive changes in your body, mind, and soul. Rejoice in this journey of healing and finding inner peace!

Harness the Power of Your Solar Plexus Chakra

The human body is a complex system of energy centers known as chakras that play a vital role in our physical, emotional, and spiritual well-being. The solar plexus chakra or Manipura Chakra is considered the center of your personal power and self-esteem. This chakra governs your willpower, confidence, and decision-making abilities. It is said that when the solar plexus chakra is balanced, you will feel confident, centered, and self-assured. This section will explore the benefits of activating your solar plexus chakra and how it can lead to success and abundance.

- **Increased Confidence and Willpower:** When your solar plexus chakra is balanced, you will feel a sense of confidence and personal power. You will have the willpower to achieve your goals and the confidence to follow through on them. This will help you make better decisions and live a more fulfilling life

- **Improved Digestion and Metabolism:** The solar plexus chakra is associated with the digestive system, and when it is balanced, it can improve your digestion and metabolism. You will have better assimilation of nutrients and a healthier gut, leading to an overall improvement in your health

- **Personal And Professional Success:** Activating your solar plexus chakra can lead to personal and professional success. You will be able to take charge of your life, make clearer decisions, and act toward reaching your goals. This will lead to a sense of accomplishment, higher productivity, and an overall sense of success

- **Release of Anger and Emotional Healing:** When the solar plexus chakra is balanced, it helps release negative emotions such as anger, resentment, and frustration. This clears the path for emotional healing and can profoundly impact your life. You will feel more peaceful, happy, and balanced
- **Improved Self-Esteem**: One of the main benefits of activating your solar plexus chakra is improved self-esteem. When your chakra is balanced, you will have a strong connection with your inner self, leading to better self-awareness, self-acceptance, and higher self-esteem

The solar plexus chakra is a powerful energy center that can profoundly impact your physical, emotional, and spiritual well-being. By activating this chakra, you can tap into your power and achieve success and abundance in all areas of your life. Developing a daily practice that includes meditation, affirmations, and yoga can help balance your solar plexus chakra and improve confidence, self-esteem, and personal growth. So go ahead and harness the power of your solar plexus chakra today!

How Can Archangel Uriel Help with Activating the Solar Chakra

Archangel Uriel is the perfect helper for activating your Solar Chakra! As one of the seven archangels, Uriel is known for his incredible ability to ignite a sense of peace and enlightenment in those who seek his assistance. Regarding your Solar Chakra, Uriel's powerful energy can help you tap into your inner wisdom and confidence. With his guidance, you can tap into the sun's power that resides within you, unleashing your full potential and inner radiance. Let Archangel Uriel be your guiding light, and watch your Solar Chakra shine brighter than ever!

Along with connecting with Archangel Uriel, there are other things you can do to activate your solar chakra. Eating yellow foods like bananas, pineapples, and squash can help stimulate this chakra. Practicing yoga poses such as the warrior or the sun salutation can also help. In addition, spending time in nature, especially in the sunshine, can boost this energy center.

Connecting with Archangel Uriel can be a powerful way to activate the solar chakra and achieve greater harmony and balance. As you work with the energies of Archangel Uriel and focus on solar chakra activation, you may discover that you have increased energy, motivation, and creativity. Activating this chakra takes time and effort, *so be patient with yourself and continue your practice.* With Archangel Uriel's guidance, you can unlock your true potential and live a more fulfilling life.

Chapter 6: Fire-in-Palm Meditation

If you're a fan of meditation, chances are you've tried various techniques to help you relax and clear your mind. But have you ever heard of the fire-in-palm meditation? This unique practice can help you release stress and negative emotions, leaving you feeling lighter and more focused. Taking just a few minutes out of your day to complete a session of fire-in-palm meditation can make all the difference to your emotional and spiritual well-being. By focusing on your breath and being present in the moment, you can tap into the spiritual realm and draw on a vast well of positive energy for healing and peace of mind.

This section will provide a step-by-step guide to achieving the fire-in-palm meditation. By connecting with Archangel Uriel, you can release any negative energy and achieve emotional healing. This chapter will explore how to find a quiet place for meditation, set an intention, clear your mind, and practice fire-in-palm meditation. Also, ways to take your practice further and ways that will encourage you to reflect on the experience will be looked at. By the time you're done reading, you will have a firm understanding of the fire-in-palm method and how it can be used to achieve emotional healing.

Preparing for Fire-in-Palm Meditation

Meditation can reduce stress.[70]

Many forms of meditation bring relaxation, focus, and inner peace to your life. Fire in palm meditation is an ancient practice that has been used for centuries to clear the mind, reduce stress, and improve overall well-being. To effectively practice fire-in-palm meditation, there are a few steps to take before you start.

Setting Your Intention

Once you have found your quiet place, take some time to connect with your intention for the fire-in-palm meditation. This could be a phrase, word, or feeling you want to focus on during your meditation. It is helpful to write it down on a piece of paper and keep it close by so you can refer to it if you need to during your meditation. Setting an intention will help you to stay focused throughout the practice.

Clearing Your Mind

When preparing for fire-in-palm meditation, clearing your mind of distractions and clutter is essential. You can start by taking a few deep breaths and focusing on your breath. Try to release any thoughts or feelings that may interfere with your practice. Visualize yourself releasing any negative energies or emotions by allowing yourself to be surrounded by love, light, and positivity.

Body Preparation

In fire-in-palm meditation practice, you focus on the palms of your hand. Gently touch your fingertips to your palms, and visualize a flame burning brightly in the center of your palm. The flame serves as a focal point during the meditation, and as you inhale, imagine that you're bringing the flame's energy into your body, and as you exhale, allow it to surround and protect you. You could also do physical exercises like stretching or yoga to prepare your body for meditation before practicing fire in the palm.

Commitment to Consistency

As with any meditation practice, consistency is key in the fire-in-palm practice. This means committing to practice regularly, whether daily, once a week, or twice a month. The frequency of your practice is up to you, but the important thing is to stay committed and consistent. You'll find that the more you practice, the easier it becomes, and the greater the benefits.

Fire-in-palm meditation is a dynamic practice that can help you find peace, reduce stress, and improve your overall well-being. This section has shared some useful tips for preparing yourself for this meditation practice. Remember, finding a quiet place, setting your intention, clearing your mind, and committing to consistency are key. With regular practice, fire-in-palm meditation can help you connect with your inner self and Archangel Uriel and find a sense of calm in your everyday life.

Practicing Fire-in-Palm Meditation

When it comes to palm meditation, it is all about practicing the power of visualization. It is a unique form of meditation to help you focus your mind, increase your intuition, and connect with your inner self. This section will give you a step-by-step guide on how to practice fire-in-palm meditation.

Step 1: Find a Peaceful Place

The first step towards preparing for fire-in-palm is to find a quiet place where you can be alone and undisturbed. This could be a room in your house, an outdoor space, or a designated meditation room. The important thing is to find a peaceful and quiet space where you can be free from distractions. Ensure you're sitting comfortably and the environment is conducive to meditation.

Step 2: Take a Deep Breath

Now that you have found a peaceful place, sit comfortably and take deep breaths. Close your eyes and relax your body. Take long, deep breaths in and out, allowing your body and mind to calm down. Notice how your breathing slows as you become more relaxed. Notice the rise and fall of your chest as you inhale and exhale. Take a few more deep breaths before continuing with your practice.

Step 3: Visualizing the Fire in Your Palms

Once you have relaxed your body and mind, visualize the fire in your palms. Imagine flames burning brightly in the center of both palms and letting the heat spread throughout your body. Visualize the warmth and glow emanating from your palms, and breathe in deeply, feeling the warmth spread throughout your body. Take a few more deep breaths and allow the heat to envelop your entire body. Feel the warmth as it calms your mind and relaxes your muscles.

Step 4: Connecting with Archangel Uriel

Next, you will want to connect with Archangel Uriel. He is associated with the element of fire and can help you connect with your inner self. Say a prayer to Archangel Uriel and ask him to guide you in your meditation. You can light a candle or incense and place it before you to help you connect more closely with the Archangel. The prayer can be as simple or as detailed as you wish.

Step 5: Repeat and Reflect

Continue to visualize the fire in your palms and connect with Archangel Uriel for as long as you like. Take your time and enjoy the process. When you have finished, take a few minutes to reflect on your practice. How did it make you feel? Did any insights or newfound clarity come to you during the meditation? Write your thoughts or feelings in a journal to help you reflect on future meditations.

Finally, take some deep breaths and open your eyes slowly. You should feel more relaxed and at peace. Fire in palm meditation is a potent practice that can help you find inner peace, reduce stress, and improve your overall well-being. With regular practice, you'll soon be able to experience the healing and peace of mind that comes with connecting with Archangel Uriel. Remember to take your time and allow yourself to fully immerse yourself in the experience. You'll develop greater intuition, clarity, and focus on your daily life. So, take a deep breath, light the fire in your palms, and connect with Archangel Uriel.

After the Fire-in-Palm Meditation

Once you have finished your fire-in-palm meditation, take some time to center yourself and get grounded. You may want to drink water or walk outside to help you come back into, and reconnect with, your body. There are a few other things to remember when you come out of your meditation. In this section, we will explore how practicing fire-in-palm meditation can transform your life in three ways.

Reflection and Gratitude

The fire-in-palm meditation is about visualizing a flame, reflecting on your emotions, and practicing gratitude. When you visualize the flame, you also visualize all the things that no longer serve you, such as stress, worry, and negative thoughts. You are then encouraged to release these negative energies and bring positivity by focusing on things you are grateful for. This practice helps you develop a positive mindset and connect with your inner self, which can lead to a happier and more fulfilling life.

Releasing Your Intentions

Another powerful aspect of the fire-in-palm meditation is the ability to release your intentions and offer them to Archangel Uriel. While visualizing the flame, you can focus on what you wish for, whether it's for personal growth, relationships, or career aspirations. By releasing your intentions to the universe, you are creating a positive energy that attracts what you desire. This allows you to manifest your desires and achieve your goals.

Feeling Empowered

The fire-in-palm meditation can also leave you feeling empowered. As you visualize the flame, you are also visualizing the power that comes with it, which will reverberate within you. This practice helps you tap into your inner strength and, together with the help of Uriel, gives you the courage to face challenges and overcome obstacles. Feeling empowered makes you more likely to take action toward what you want in life and achieve success.

In summary, fire-in-palm meditation is a powerful tool that can transform your life in several ways. By practicing this meditation, you can reflect on your emotions and practice gratitude, release your intentions, and feel empowered. These benefits can lead to a happier and more fulfilling life. So, next time you sit down to meditate, try the fire-in-palm meditation and see the positive changes it can bring to your life.

The Art of Grounding

In our busy, fast-paced lives, becoming disconnected from what truly matters is easy. We spend so much time with our heads buried in screens or rushing from one activity to the next that we forget to slow down and connect with the world around us. That's where grounding comes in. Taking the time to be still, breathe, and connect with nature can help us realign with our true selves, gain perspective, and cultivate peace of mind. Grounding is a practice that dates back centuries, but it's just as relevant in today's world as it ever was. Let's explore what grounding is, why it's important, and how you can cultivate your practice of grounding.

What Is Grounding?

Grounding is a natural way of reconnecting with the earth and the present moment. It involves intentionally and mindfully connecting with the physical world around us, whether that's through walking barefoot on grass, taking a walk in the forest, or simply sitting outside and breathing in the fresh air. This practice can help us feel more centered, more rooted, and more connected to our environment.

Why Is Grounding Important?

Grounding can benefit us in many ways, both physically and mentally. Studies have shown that practicing grounding can reduce stress, improve sleep quality, and boost immune function. It can also help us feel more grateful, joyful, and present daily. Plus, it's a simple and accessible practice that anyone can do with no special equipment or training required.

When invoking Archangel Uriel during the fire-in-palm meditation, grounding is important because it helps create a safe and sacred space for you. A grounded presence will ensure you are open and receptive to Archangel Uriel's healing energies. The more grounded you can be, the easier for him to send you his love and healing light.

Cultivating Your Practice of Grounding

The key to grounding is creating an intentional and mindful connection with the physical world around you. The good news is that there are many ways to ground yourself, and you can experiment to find what works best for you. Some popular grounding practices include:

- Walking barefoot on grass, sand, or soil
- Hugging a tree and feeling its energy
- Listening to the sounds of nature – birds, water, wind, etc.
- Sitting or lying on the ground and feeling its support
- Practicing mindfulness meditation and focusing on your breath

Whichever practice you choose, try to make it a regular habit or ritual. Set aside time each day or each week to connect with nature and yourself. Remember, grounding is a practice, and it may take time and effort to find what works for you, but the rewards are well worth it.

Benefits of a Regular Grounding Practice

While grounding can be beneficial in the short term, it has even greater potential when practiced regularly over time. Regularly connecting with nature can bring a sense of well-being and peace into our lives, which can have a ripple effect on all aspects of life. As we ground ourselves more often, we become more aware of our surroundings and more in tune with ourselves. We can experience increased energy, improved mood, and greater clarity of thought. Plus, grounding can help us to better manage our stress levels and cultivate loving relationships with ourselves and others.

- **Reduced Stress and Anxiety**: By connecting with nature regularly, we can become better attuned to ourselves and our environment. This helps us to manage stress in healthy ways and reduce feelings of anxiousness
- **Improved Sleep Quality:** Regular breaks to ground ourselves can help us feel more relaxed before bedtime, resulting in better quality sleep.
- **Boosted Immune Function:** Studies have shown that grounding can help to boost our immune system and reduce inflammation in the body.
- **Increased Mindfulness and Presence**: Regular grounding makes us more mindful of our thoughts and feelings. This makes it easier to be present in the moment and appreciate the beauty of our surroundings.
- **Enhanced Feelings of Gratitude and Joy:** Grounding can help us recognize and appreciate the small things, which can bring more

joy into our lives.

- **Connection with Nature and Community**: As we ground ourselves more often, we open up to the beauty and energy of nature around us. This can lead to stronger connections with ourselves, our environment, and the people in our lives.

Regularly grounding yourself creates a greater sense of peace, stillness, and connection in your life. You'll feel more centered no matter what challenges come your way. Plus, you'll appreciate the beauty and wonder of the world around you.

Grounding is a powerful practice that reconnects us with ourselves, our environment, and the present moment. Whether you're feeling stressed, anxious, or simply seeking a greater sense of peace and stillness, grounding can be a valuable tool. Take time each day to connect with nature, breathe deeply, and feel your feet on the ground. You might be surprised at how much of a difference it can make in your overall well-being.

Taking the Fire in Palm Meditation Further

Fire in palm meditation has its roots in Buddhism and Taoism. It is a simple yet potent practice accessible to anyone who wants to connect with their inner self and awaken their spiritual consciousness. This meditation is especially beneficial for people who are going through a stressful time in their lives and want to find inner peace and clarity. If you've been practicing the fire-in-palm meditation for a while and want to take your practice to the next level, creating a powerful mantra is one way to do so. This section will explore how to create a mantra and how to take your fire-in-palm meditation practice further by practicing with others and growing your spiritual practice.

Creating a Mantra

A mantra is a word or phrase repeated during meditation to focus your mind and help you reach a state of inner peace and relaxation, connect with your subconscious, and unlock your spiritual potential. To create your mantra, start by reflecting on your intentions and goals for your meditation practice. What do you want to achieve? What qualities do you want to cultivate in yourself? Once you clearly sense your intentions, choose a word or phrase that embodies these qualities. Some examples of powerful mantras include "I am peace," "I am love," "I am strength," "I am grateful," and "I am limitless." Repeat your mantra during meditation and notice how it affects your state of mind and overall experience.

Practicing with Others

While the fire-in-palm meditation is typically practiced alone, there are benefits to practicing with others. When you practice with others, you can create a supportive community of like-minded individuals who share your goals and aspirations. You can also learn from each other and deepen your spiritual practice together. To find a community of fire-in-palm meditation practitioners, look for local meditation groups in your area or join online communities. You can also organize your group by inviting friends, family, or colleagues to meditate with you. Set a regular schedule for your group meditation sessions and experiment with different meditation techniques, such as guided meditations, mantra meditations, and visualization meditations.

Growing Your Spiritual Practice

Fire in palm meditation is just one of many spiritual practices that can help you connect with your inner self and awaken your spiritual potential. To take your spiritual practice further, consider exploring other practices such as yoga, mindfulness, tai chi, or qigong. These practices can complement your meditation practice and help you cultivate a deeper sense of balance, harmony, and well-being. You can also explore different aspects of your spirituality, such as exploring different religions, learning about energy healing, or connecting with nature. Remember, spirituality is a personal journey that's unique to each individual. Listen to your intuition, follow your heart as you explore new paths, and deepen your connection with your inner self.

Fire in palm meditation is a powerful practice that can help you connect with your inner self and awaken your spiritual consciousness. By creating a powerful mantra, practicing with others, and exploring other spiritual practices, you can take your fire-in-palm meditation practice to the next level and deepen your overall spiritual practice. Remember, there is no one-size-fits-all approach when it comes to spirituality. Listen to your intuition and follow your heart as you discover new ways to connect with your inner self and the world around you.

Chapter 7: Dreamwork

Are you ready to tap into the guidance of Archangel Uriel through your dreams? Dreamwork is a powerful tool for communicating with angels, and with some intention and practice, you can learn to connect with Archangel Uriel while you sleep. Whether you're looking for insight on a particular issue or seeking to deepen your spiritual awakening, Archangel Uriel can help. Nighttime can be a powerful ground for guidance and growth, so allow yourself to relax and let the wisdom of Archangel Uriel guide you.

Dreams can help you connect with Uriel.[71]

This chapter will introduce you to the concept of dreamwork, provide step-by-step exercises to connect with Archangel Uriel in your dreams and suggest some tips for creating the best environment possible to make the most of your dreamwork. The purpose is to help you gain access to Archangel Uriel's loving and healing energy, making your dreamtime a powerful ally in creating the life of your dreams. By the end of this chapter, you'll be equipped with practical tools and techniques to make the most of your dreamtime.

Defining Dreamwork

Have you ever woken up from a dream feeling like it was trying to tell you something? Dreams have fascinated humans for centuries, and dreamwork has been used as a tool for self-exploration, healing, and problem-solving for years. But what is dreamwork, and how can it help us? To help you understand the power of dreamwork, this section will define it, explore its benefits, and lay out some techniques to start working with your dreams.

What Is Dreamwork?

Dreamwork is the process of analyzing and interpreting dreams to gain a deeper understanding of the self and one's emotions. Through dreamwork, we can unlock our dreams' hidden meanings and symbols to help us navigate life's challenges. Whether you believe that dreams are a window into our subconscious or simply a reflection of our daily experiences, there is no denying the power of dreamwork in helping us to live our best lives. It is essentially the practice of analyzing and understanding the messages within our dreams. These messages can give us insight into our subconscious mind, emotions, desires, and even physical health. It can be done alone, but it's often more effective with the guidance of a therapist or a trained dream facilitator.

Benefits of Dreamwork

So why is dreamwork so beneficial? For starters, dreams can reflect what we're going through in our waking life. By analyzing the patterns and themes in our dreams, we can better understand our inner selves and the challenges we face. Dreams can also offer solutions to problems that we may not have been able to access otherwise. Here are some benefits of dreamwork:

- Gain insight into your subconscious mind and emotions
- Understand recurring themes in your dreams
- Receive creative solutions to problems
- Connect with the spiritual realm
- Heal and overcome trauma

Dreamwork may initially seem intimidating and complicated, but it can be a powerful tool for self-discovery and healing. There isn't a right or wrong way to approach dreamwork, it's based on your dreams, so it's a personal journey that you can tailor to your own needs and preferences. Whether you choose to work with a therapist or explore dreamwork on your own, listening to your dreams can bring a new level of self-knowledge and awareness to your life. So, the next time you wake up from a dream feeling like it's trying to tell you something, don't ignore it. Take the time to explore its meaning and see where it might lead you.

Dreamwork Techniques

Some people believe that their dreams can give insights into their subconscious thoughts and emotions, while others see dreams as a source of creative inspiration. Dreamwork techniques help people explore and understand their dreams, harnessing the power of their subconscious mind. This section will explore some of the most popular dreamwork techniques and how they can help you unlock your inner dreamer.

Dream Journaling

Keeping a dream journal is one of the most effective ways to improve your dream recall and analysis. Writing down your dreams immediately after waking up helps you retain more details and remember your dreams vividly. You can also use your dream journal to reflect on recurring themes or symbols in your dreams, giving you a clear idea of what is going on in your subconscious.

Lucid Dreaming

Lucid dreaming is a state where you become aware that you are dreaming, allowing you to control and manipulate the dream. With practice, you can learn how to induce lucid dreams and use them to explore your inner world. Lucid dreaming can also help you overcome fears or anxieties by facing them in a controlled environment.

Dream Imagery

Dream imagery is a technique that involves visualizing dream symbols and re-imagining them to get more knowledge of yourself. By revisiting a dream and altering certain elements, you can uncover hidden thoughts and emotions that your subconscious mind is trying to communicate. Dream imagery is particularly helpful for working through emotional issues or trauma.

Active Imagination

An active imagination is a method that uses guided meditation or visualization to explore your unconscious. In this practice, you allow your mind to wander freely and follow the images and thoughts that arise. Active imagination encourages you to embrace spontaneity and let go of analytical thinking, promoting a more intuitive and creative approach to exploring your dreams.

Group Dreamwork

Group dreamwork involves sharing your dreams with others and exchanging information and interpretations. By hearing different perspectives on your dreams, you can better understand their meaning and connect with others who share your interests. Group dreamwork can also offer a safe and supportive environment for processing complex emotions or experiences.

Dreamwork techniques are valuable tools for anyone interested in exploring their subconscious and tapping into their inner creativity. By keeping a dream journal, practicing lucid dreaming, using dream imagery or active imagination, and participating in group dreamwork, you can gain new insights into your psyche and understand yourself more deeply.

How Dreams Connect to Angelic Communication

Have you ever had dreams that seem so real that you can't shake the thought of them off when you wake up? Dreams that leave you feeling like there's something more to them than just a mere reflection of your thoughts? Dreams that connect you to a higher power? These dreams could be a way for you to communicate with angels. This section will explore the connection between your dreams and angelic communication and how you can decipher their messages.

Angels often communicate with us through dreams because it's the most natural way to do it. They're pure beings made of light and energy, and they can't communicate with us through the physical realm. Dreams, on the other hand, provide a gateway into the spiritual realm, where angels reside. Our minds are open to receiving messages from the divine when we're asleep, making it an ideal opportunity for angels to communicate with us.

When you have a dream involving angels, pay attention to the dream's details. Notice the messages and symbols that appear. These messages could be literal messages from an angel or hold a hidden meaning that only you can decipher. Angels often use symbols like feathers, rainbows, and numbers to communicate with us, so pay attention to these details in your dreams.

Your intuition is a powerful tool for decoding your dreams. Angels frequently use your intuition to communicate with you. Feeling a sense of peace and comfort during a dream could signify that an angel is reaching out to you. Similarly, if you have a dream that encourages you to explore new opportunities, it could be a way for angels to guide you toward a new direction in life.

One of the key things that angels want to communicate with us is that we're never alone. They're always with us, offering guidance and support whenever we need it. Dreams can be a way to remind us of this fact. If you're feeling overwhelmed with life's challenges, ask the angelic realm for guidance and pay attention to your dreams. You might receive a message that brings you peace and reassurance.

When decoding your dreams, there's no right or wrong way to do it. Everyone's experiences are unique, and it's up to you to find the meaning that resonates with you. However, remember that angels are always here to guide and support us. By paying attention to our dreams and connecting with the angelic realm, we can receive the guidance we need to reach our full potential.

Dreams are a very powerful way to communicate with the angelic realm. Angels often use them because it's a natural way to connect with us on a spiritual level. By paying attention to the messages and symbols in our dreams, we can decipher the hidden messages from angels. Our intuition is a valuable tool for decoding our dreams, and it is important to trust our instincts when understanding the messages. Remember that angels are always here to guide and support us, and our dreams can be a way to receive their messages.

Steps to Connecting with Archangel Uriel Through Dreams

There are many ways to connect with the spiritual world, and Archangel Uriel is one of the most sought-after angels. One of the most powerful ways to connect with him is through your dreams. The dream world, the gateway to our subconscious, can be used to communicate with the spiritual world, and this section will explore the steps you can take to connect with Archangel Uriel.

1. **Set an Intention:** The first step in connecting with Archangel Uriel through dreamwork is to set your intention. Before going to bed, take a few moments to set your intention by simply saying a prayer or setting an intention in your mind. This will help you to be more receptive to his presence in your dreams.

2. **Use Affirmations:** Affirmations are a powerful way to set your subconscious mind into action. Before you go to bed, repeat affirmations such as, "I am open to connecting with Archangel Uriel in my dreams tonight" or "I am ready to receive guidance from Archangel Uriel in my dreams." This will help you align your mind with your intentions. The more frequently you use affirmations, the more likely you will receive guidance from Uriel in your dreams.

3. **Practice Visualization:** Visualization is a powerful tool to help you connect with Archangel Uriel. Before you go to bed, close your eyes, and visualize Archangel Uriel standing before you. Feel his presence and invite him to communicate with you in your dreams. This will set the stage for a powerful dream experience. When you start to drift off to sleep, focus on the visualization you have created and allow yourself to relax in his presence.

4. **Keep a Dream Journal:** As soon as you wake up, write down any dreams you remember. This will help you remember your dreams more vividly and allow you to analyze them later. When you write down your dreams, include any symbols that stood out to you, as they may be a message from Archangel Uriel. Try to write down as much detail about the dream as possible. If you feel something important is missing, take a few moments to meditate and allow yourself to become fully present in the dream.

5. **Interpret Your Dreams:** After writing down your dreams, take some time to interpret their meaning. Ask yourself what the symbols mean, how they make you feel, and if there is a message in the dream that Archangel Uriel may be trying to communicate with you. Interpretations can vary from person to person, so it is crucial to find the meaning that resonates most with you. Some people also like to consult dream dictionaries for additional guidance.

6. **Be Patient and Persistent:** Connecting with Archangel Uriel through your dreams may take time and practice. Remember that not every dream will have a message from him, but that doesn't mean he isn't trying to communicate with you. Be patient and persistent in your efforts to connect with him, and trust that the messages will come to you when the time is right. The more you trust in yourself and the process, the easier it will be to receive Archangel Uriel's guidance.

Connecting with Archangel Uriel through your dreams is a powerful way to receive messages and guidance. By firmly setting your intention, keeping a dream journal, practicing visualization, using affirmations, and being patient and persistent, you can open the door to meaningful communication with Archangel Uriel. Remember, connecting with the spiritual world takes time and practice, so keep at it, and you'll be amazed at the messages and inspiration that come through your dreams.

Using a Dream Journal

Dreams can reveal our deepest fears, desires, and thoughts that we might not even be aware of. Archangel Uriel often uses dreams to communicate messages, so keeping track of your dreams in a dream journal is important. That's why keeping a journal can be an amazing tool for self-discovery, personal growth, and connection with Archangel Uriel. This section will explain the benefits of keeping a dream journal and give you tips on how to start one.

Set a Schedule

The first step to starting a dream journal is to set a schedule. Decide how often you want to write in your journal and how much time you want to dedicate to writing each entry. Choose a time and day that works best for you and stick to it. This will help create the habit of recording your dreams. Once you get into the habit, it will become easier. When you start your dream journal, make sure to include some basic information, like the date and time of the dream, how you felt before you went to bed, and any other information that might be important.

Write Down Your Dreams

Start by recording what stood out most in your dreams: characters, emotions, places, colors, and anything else that stands out to you. Don't forget to include the symbols and messages that Archangel Uriel might be sending you. These can be subtle but very powerful. It's also important to include any feelings or emotions you experienced during the dream. These can give you further insight into the messages that Archangel Uriel is sending you.

Understanding Your Dreams

Dreams can be confusing and fragmented, making it difficult to decipher their meaning. However, by writing your dreams down in a journal, you can identify any emerging patterns and themes. You'll also be able to reflect on particular events or feelings that may have triggered certain dreams. If you have trouble understanding the message of your dream, try writing it down in a story format to help make sense of it. This will also make it easier to identify symbols and themes that appear throughout your dreams.

Record Your Reflections

Once you've written down the details of your dream, take a few moments to think about it. This is a great time to let your intuition free and see what messages you can find within yourself. Ask yourself questions like, "What can I learn from this dream?" and "How does this dream help me make sense of my life right now?" Reflection is a powerful tool for self-discovery and can help you understand any messages that Archangel Uriel sends you.

Don't Overthink It

Dreams can also often be confusing and overwhelming, so it's important not to overthink them but to try to get a balance between introspection and overwhelm. Just record the details of your dream and then let it go. Overthinking can block out any potential messages from Archangel Uriel. So just relax and trust that you'll receive the answers you need. If you're feeling stuck, take a break and return to it later.

By following these steps, you can start to unlock the power of dreamwork and connect with Archangel Uriel in a new way. So, remember to keep an open mind, trust your intuition, and surrender to the messages that come to you in your dreams. With time, patience, and practice, you'll be able to understand the deeper meanings behind the messages that Uriel is sending you.

Benefits of Dream Journaling

Dream journaling is a powerful tool for connecting with Archangel Uriel, but it has several other benefits. Keeping a dream journal can help you become more mindful, better understand your subconscious, and recognize patterns and themes in your dreams. It can also provide clarity and help give you the answers and clarity you're looking for. Here are some of the top benefits that come with dream journaling:

- **Creative Inspiration:** Dreams can serve as a great source of inspiration for writers, artists, and musicians. You can capture and explore those imaginative moments by keeping a dream journal. Who knows, you might even create something beautiful from your dreams.
- **Enhancing Your Memory**: Dreams are often forgotten within minutes of waking up. However, you can store them in your long-term memory by writing them down. This not only improves your ability to remember dreams, but it can also enhance your overall memory skills. The act of recording your dreams can also help you to better remember them.
- **Deeper Self-Reflection:** Our dreams can reveal subconscious thoughts and feelings that we may not be aware of during our waking hours. Writing down these dreams can be a way to open up those inner realms and explore them further. This can help with self-reflection and personal growth. The insights you gain can be incredibly powerful and help give you the answers you want.
- **Better Sleep:** Using a dream journal can help in getting better sleep. Writing down your dreams before bed can help release negative thoughts and feelings from your mind, allowing you to enjoy a peaceful sleep. You can also set intentions for your dreams while journaling, which may help you have more positive and uplifting dreams.

Dream journals can offer many benefits for anyone interested in exploring their inner selves. A dream journal can be an amazing tool for understanding your dreams, finding creative inspiration, improving your memory, deepening your self-reflection, and bettering your sleep. Start your dream journal today and begin unraveling the mysteries of your subconscious mind!

Tips for Connecting with Archangel Uriel through Dreamwork

Archangel Uriel, the angel of wisdom and illumination, is here to help us connect with our inner light and see the truth in our lives. Connecting with him can be a deeply transformative experience. Here are some tips for connecting with Archangel Uriel through dreamwork.

- **Meditate before Bed:** Meditating before bed can also help you to connect with Archangel Uriel in your dreams. Before bed, take a few minutes to meditate and ask Archangel Uriel to guide you in your dreams. This will help to quiet your mind and make it easier to connect with Archangel Uriel.

- **Use Crystals:** Crystals can also be effective tools for connecting with Archangel Uriel through dreamwork. Some crystals associated with Archangel Uriel include amethyst, citrine, and clear quartz. Place these crystals under your pillow or on your nightstand before bed. They can help to amplify your connection with Archangel Uriel in your dreams.

- **Trust Your Intuition:** Trusting your intuition is key to connecting with Archangel Uriel through dreamwork. Pay attention to any gut feelings or hunches you have about your dreams. Archangel Uriel often communicates through our intuition, so it's important to trust it.

Connecting with Archangel Uriel through dreamwork can be a deeply transformative experience. Setting your intention, keeping a dream journal, meditating before bed, using crystals, and trusting your intuition are all tools that can help you to connect with him in your dreams. Remember to be patient and trust the process, and you will soon discover the wisdom and illumination that Archangel Uriel has to offer. This chapter covered the basics of dreamwork and connecting with Archangel Uriel through it. Using the tips outlined in this chapter, you can begin to explore your dreams and connect with Archangel Uriel for answers, guidance, and healing. Happy dreaming!

Chapter 8: Crystals and Candles

Archangel Uriel is known for his association with both crystals and candles. These two elements can be powerful tools for connecting with his energy and seeking guidance. Crystals such as citrine and amber are believed to resonate with Uriel's energy and can be carried or placed on an altar. Similarly, lighting a yellow or gold candle can also invite Uriel's energy into your space. By using these tools and invoking Uriel's presence, you can tap into his wisdom and receive guidance and protection on your path.

Are you ready to tap into the awesome power of crystals and candles? Look no further than this chapter, which has got you covered on both fronts. The first sub-section delves into the fascinating world of crystal energy and how it can be channeled to connect with the Archangel Uriel. From amethyst to rose quartz, there's a crystal for every purpose and intention. The second sub-section explores how candles can communicate with the world beyond, whether to send a message to a loved one or invite positive energy. So, grab your crystals, light a candle, and let Archangel Uriel guide you.

Harnessing the Power of Crystals to Channel Uriel's Energy

Crystals can help you tap into Uriel's guidance."

Uriel is known for being the angel to help us connect with our inner wisdom and bring clarity to our lives. One way to channel Uriel's energy is by using crystals that resonate with his vibration. By harnessing the power of crystals, you can tap into Uriel's vast energy supply and receive guidance and illumination in your life. Whether you choose to use clear quartz, amethyst, citrine, Angelite, or lapis lazuli, each crystal has a unique vibration that calls to the Archangel on an intensely deep level.

Experiment with different crystals and see which ones resonate with you the most. With consistent practice, you'll be able to access Uriel's energy whenever you need it, bringing clarity and illumination into your life. This section will explore the power of crystals to channel Uriel's energy and how you can use them in your spiritual practice.

Hematite

Crystals have been revered for their mystical properties since ancient times, and their power to heal and restore balance to the mind, body, and spirit is growing in popularity more and more today. One such crystal that has been used for centuries is hematite, known for its grounding, protective, and transformative properties. But did you know that hematite can be used to channel the energy of Archangel Uriel? Let's explore the benefits, methods of use, cleansing, and programming techniques associated with using hematite to tap into Uriel's energy.

Benefits

The Archangel Uriel is associated with creativity, wisdom, and spiritual awakenings. According to spiritual traditions, Uriel's energy can help us overcome negative emotional patterns, dispel fear and doubt, assist with decision-making, and access intuition. Hematite, as a grounding and protective crystal, can amplify these effects by absorbing any negative energies we may be carrying and helping to balance our energy centers. By channeling Uriel's energy through hematite, we may experience greater clarity, purpose, and creative potential.

Methods of Use

There are several ways to use hematite to channel Uriel's energy. One popular method is to simply carry a piece of hematite with you throughout the day, either in your pocket, on a necklace or bracelet, or in a pouch. This allows you to stay connected to the crystal's grounding and protective energies while also inviting Uriel's wisdom and inspiration into your life.

Another technique is to meditate with hematite, holding it in your hand or placing it on your third eye or crown chakra. This can help you access Uriel's energy more directly and tune in to your spiritual insights and intuition. Finally, you can use hematite to create a crystal grid or altar, placing it alongside other crystals and symbols reflecting Uriel's energy.

Cleansing and Programming with Uriel's Energy

Like all crystals, hematite should be cleansed and programmed regularly to maintain its energetic integrity. Some methods of cleansing and programming hematite include:

- Cleansing with salt water or moonlight
- Setting intentions through meditation or visualization
- Smudging with sage or other cleansing herbs
- Placing it on a selenite charging plate
- Programming it with specific affirmations or energetic intentions related to Uriel's energy

Hematite is a crystal that carries a lot of force and has many benefits for the mind, body, and spirit. By learning how to use hematite to channel the energy of the Archangel Uriel, you can tap into its transformative power and access greater levels of intuition, creativity, and inspiration. Whether you carry a hematite with you throughout the day, meditate with it, or create a crystal grid, incorporating hematite into your spiritual practice can help you feel more balanced, grounded, and connected to your inner wisdom.

Obsidian

Obsidian is a potent spiritual tool that many cultures have used for centuries. It is a dark volcanic glass with a natural luster, making it highly sought after in jewelry and ornaments. But, perhaps the most impressive use of obsidian is its ability to channel energy. One such energy is Uriel's energy of wisdom and insight. This section will discuss the many benefits of using obsidian to channel Uriel's energy, how it can be used, and how to cleanse and program it.

Benefits

The benefits of using obsidian to channel Uriel's energy are numerous. It can help you gain clarity and insight into complex situations. As the angel of illumination and guidance, Uriel is easily summoned using this crystal and, once with you, bestows his knowledge and wisdom. Another benefit is that obsidian can enhance your intuition, allowing you to make better decisions. Finally, obsidian can help you release negative emotions, such as anger and fear, allowing you to move forward with peace.

Methods of Use

There are several ways to use obsidian to channel Uriel's energy. One popular method is to carry an obsidian stone or wear it as jewelry. This will allow you to have continuous access to Uriel's energy. Another method is to place an obsidian pyramid in your home or office, which can help to clear negative energy and promote positivity. You can also meditate with an obsidian stone, either by holding it or placing it on your third eye chakra, to connect deeply with Uriel's energy.

Cleansing and Programming with Uriel's Energy

Once you have found your obsidian stone that feels right in your hands, it's important to cleanse and program it before you use it. You can soak the stone in saltwater or place it in the sun or moonlight for a few hours to cleanse the stone. To program the stone, set an intention or affirmation for how you want to use it. For example, you can say, "I program this obsidian to help me gain insight and clarity." This will help to focus the energy of Uriel through the obsidian stone.

Connecting with Uriel's Energy

To connect with Uriel's energy, start by finding a quiet space and sitting comfortably in this space. Take several deep breaths and focus on your intention to connect with Uriel. Hold the obsidian stone or place it on your third eye chakra. Visualize a white light surrounding you and the stone. Then, simply allow yourself to receive Uriel's guidance, clarity, and wisdom.

Obsidian is a powerful spiritual tool that can channel Uriel's energy. The benefits of using obsidian to connect with this energy include gaining insight and clarity, enhancing intuition, and releasing negative emotions. There are several methods of use, including carrying or wearing the stone, placing it in your home or office, and meditating with it. To cleanse and program the stone, soak it in saltwater or place it in the sun or moonlight and set an intention for how you want to use it. Overall, using obsidian to channel Uriel's energy can bring peace and enlightenment to your life.

Tiger's Eye

Crystals are natural healers that transmit energy vibrations, and one such crystal is Tiger's Eye. This stunning golden-brown stone has been used for centuries to enhance willpower, courage, and mental clarity. The crystal's powerful vibrations are believed to help us connect with the Archangel Uriel, the angel of wisdom and prosperity.

Benefits

Tiger's Eye is a grounding stone that can bring stability and balance to our lives. It is excellent for dispelling fears and boosting our self-confidence. When we use Tiger's Eye to connect with Uriel, we experience heightened mental clarity and focus. Uriel's energy is known to help us gain deep insights into any situation, and Tiger's Eye can amplify this energy, making it easier for us to channel it. Additionally, this crystal can help us connect with our inner strength, giving us the courage to pursue our goals and dreams.

Methods of Use

There are several ways to use Tiger's Eye to channel Uriel's energy. One of the most effective is to hold the crystal in our hands and focus on the intention of connecting with Uriel. We can also place the stone on our third eye chakra to enhance intuition and inner wisdom. Another way is to wear the crystal as jewelry in the form of a bracelet or necklace, allowing its energy to work on us continuously throughout the day. Lastly, we can also meditate with the crystal, holding it in our hands and focusing on our breath, allowing the crystal's natural vibrations to calm our minds and bodies.

Cleansing and Programming with Uriel's Energy

Cleaning and programming your crystal with Uriel's energy is essential to ensure it works properly. Cleansing the crystal can be done by placing it in a bowl of filtered water and leaving it out in the moonlight or sunlight for a few hours. Programming the crystal can be done by holding it in your hands and reciting a prayer or affirmation, asking Uriel to infuse the crystal with his energy. This step ensures that the crystal's energy is in alignment with our intentions and desires.

Tiger's Eye is a powerful and versatile crystal that can help us connect with Uriel's energy to enhance our spiritual growth and mental clarity. It can bring balance and stability to our lives and give us the courage to pursue our goals and dreams. The use of Tiger's Eye can help us tune in to Uriel's energy, making it easier for us to receive insights and guidance from the angel of wisdom and prosperity. With proper cleansing and programming, Tiger's Eye can become a constant source of comfort and healing, contributing to our overall well-being.

Amber

Have you ever heard of the healing properties of amber? This beautiful golden gemstone formed from the sap of ancient trees is more than just a pretty piece of jewelry. Amber is believed to have incredible healing abilities, and when paired with the powerful energy of Archangel Uriel, it can have a profound effect on your mind, body, and spirit.

Benefits

Amber carries warm, comforting energy to help soothe anxiety, fear, and depression. The stone is also believed to have anti-inflammatory properties, making it useful for various physical ailments, including joint pain, osteoarthritis, and rheumatoid arthritis. In addition, Uriel's energy helps us to let go of negative emotions, boosts our intuition, and promotes clarity of thought. Using amber to channel Uriel's energy, we tap into his wisdom and gain a deeper understanding of ourselves and our path in life.

Methods of Use

There are many ways to use amber to channel Uriel's energy. One of the simplest ways is to wear an amber necklace, bracelet, or earrings. As you wear the stone, you can focus your intention on calling in Uriel's energy, allowing it to flow through the stone and into your body. Another popular method is to meditate with an amber stone. Hold the stone, close your eyes, and focus on your breath. As you inhale, visualize golden light flowing into your body, carrying the energy of Uriel with it. As you exhale, release any negative emotions or thoughts which no longer serve you.

Cleansing and Programming with Uriel's Energy

To enhance the healing powers of your amber, keep it cleansed and programmed with the energy of Uriel at all times. To do this, you can hold the stone in your hand and focus your intention on clearing any negative energy from it. You can also visualize a beam of golden light flowing into the stone, infusing it with Uriel's energy. Once your amber is cleansed, it's time to program it with your intention. Hold the stone in your hand and visualize what you want to manifest in your life. It could be anything from financial abundance to emotional healing. As you visualize your intention, allow Uriel's energy to flow through the stone, amplifying your manifestation power.

Using amber has a powerful effect on your physical, emotional, and spiritual well-being. By wearing amber jewelry, meditating with an amber stone, and cleansing and programming it with the energy of Uriel, you can tap into a powerful source of healing and illumination. Remember that intention is key when using amber to channel Uriel's energy. Set your intention clearly and focus your energy on it with trust and faith. As you practice working with Amber and Uriel's energy, you may find your intuition, inner wisdom, and sense of purpose becoming clearer and stronger, leading you to a more fulfilling and joyful life.

Enhance Your Meditation Experience with Crystals

Welcome to a world of serenity, balance, and peace, where the healing powers of crystals will help you achieve a true state of mindfulness and meditation. This section will explore how you can use crystals to channel Uriel's divine energy to help you unlock your inner self, enhance your meditation experience, and connect with the universe. Whether you are a seasoned meditator or a novice, this will help you explore the power of crystals and tap into Uriel's divine energy using simple yet powerful exercises.

Crystals have been used for spiritual, physical, and emotional healing for centuries. They possess unique vibrational frequencies that can interact with your energy field, helping you to achieve better health, emotional balance, and spiritual growth. The key to unlocking their power during meditation is to choose crystals that resonate with Uriel's energy. Clear quartz, citrine, carnelian, and garnet are all crystals associated with Uriel's energy, and they possess unique properties that can help you connect with his divine energy.

The Basics

To use crystals to meditate with Uriel's energy, start by finding a quiet, safe space where you can meditate without distractions. Sit comfortably with your chosen crystal in your hand, or place it over your heart. Close your eyes, take deep breaths, and visualize Uriel's energy as a golden light entering your body from above. Focus on the crystal's energy, feel its vibrations, and let its energy flow through your body, starting from your head and going right down to your toes. Breathe deeply, release any tension, and let yourself be guided by Uriel's divine energy.

Crystal Grid

Using a crystal grid is another way to connect with Uriel's energy during meditation. This geometric shape is created by placing crystals in a specific pattern on a surface. To create a crystal grid for meditation, start by choosing crystals that correspond to Uriel's energy, such as clear quartz, carnelian, and garnet. Place the crystals in a pattern of your choice, focusing on their placement and intention. Once you have created the grid, sit in front of it and focus on Uriel's energy, visualizing it flowing through the crystals and into your body.

Meditation Necklace

You can use crystals to create a meditation necklace if you want a more attractive meditation exercise. A meditation necklace is made of crystals chosen based on their energy and vibrational frequency. To make the necklace, use crystals that resonate with Uriel's energy, selecting beads of clear quartz, carnelian, and garnet. String them on a cord, focusing on the intention of the necklace to help you connect with Uriel's energy during meditation. Wear the necklace during meditation, allowing the crystals' vibrations to enhance your experience.

The Magic of Candle Work and Uriel's Energy

There's just something about the flicker of a candle that brings a sense of peace and tranquility to a troubled soul. From the soft glow of a birthday candle to the warmth of a candlelit dinner, candles have been used for centuries to create ambiance and set the mood. But did you know that candles can also be used to set intentions, unlock your inner magic, and connect with your spiritual side? This section will explore the world of candle work and the powerful energy of Archangel Uriel.

What Is Candle Work?

Candle work is the practice of using candles to manifest your desires and intentions. Each candle color corresponds with a different intention or energy. For example, green candles are often used for abundance and prosperity, while purple candles are used for spiritual growth and intuition. By lighting a candle with a specific intention, you can focus your energy and bring that intention to fruition.

Combining Candle Work with Uriel's Energy

You can use this combination of a colored candle and Uriel's energy to help with any area of your life, whether career, relationships, or personal growth. But how do you go about combining candle work and Uriel's energy?

Simply light a candle in the color that corresponds with your intention and ask Uriel to be present with you. You can speak your intention aloud or simply hold it in your mind. As you focus on your intention, imagine Uriel's energy surrounding you and providing you with guidance and clarity. Another way to incorporate Uriel's energy into your candle work is by using specific candles that are infused with Uriel's energy. These candles are often charged with crystals and essential oils that correspond with Uriel's energy, making them even more powerful. You can find these candles online or at local metaphysical stores.

Candle Colors and Their Healing Associations

Candles have been used as a form of healing for centuries. They emit a warm glow that has therapeutic effects on the mind, body, and soul. Each candle color represents a unique energy vibration that helps us achieve our desired outcome. Additionally, calling upon an archangel like Uriel can amplify the energy and power of the candle. This section will delve into the associations of different candle colors, their healing properties, and how Uriel can enhance the energy to help us manifest our desires.

- **White Candles:** White candles represent purity and a higher power. They can be used for protection, guidance, and clearing negative influences. To enhance the white candle's energy, call upon Archangel Uriel for guidance and protection.
- **Yellow Candles:** Yellow candles are associated with mental clarity, communication, and self-confidence. They can enhance focus, improve memory, and relieve anxiety. Call Archangel Uriel for mental clarity and guidance to enhance the yellow candle's energy.
- **Green Candles:** Green candles represent abundance, wealth, and prosperity. They can be used to manifest good fortune, health, and wealth. To enhance the green candle's energy, call upon Archangel Uriel for abundance, prosperity, and growth.
- **Blue Candles**: Blue candles represent calm, serenity, and tranquility. They can calm an overactive mind, relieve stress, and promote relaxation. To enhance the blue candle's energy, call upon Archangel Uriel for calm and peace.
- **Red Candles:** Red candles represent passion, strength, and courage. They can attract love, enhance sexuality, and increase vitality. Call upon Archangel Uriel for strength and courage to enhance the red candle's energy.
- **Purple Candles:** Purple candles represent spirituality, meditation, and psychic ability. They can enhance intuition, psychic abilities, and spiritual enlightenment. Call upon Archangel Uriel for spiritual guidance and enlightenment to enhance the purple candle's energy.

- **Black Candles:** Black candles represent protection, banishing, and grounding. They can be used for clearing negativity, protection from malicious energies, and grounding. To enhance the black candle's energy, call upon Archangel Uriel for protection and grounding.

Using candles as a healing tool can be an easy and effective method to manifest our intentions. The energy vibration of each color can help us align with our desires, and calling upon Archangel Uriel can elevate and amplify the energy. Using the practical list of candle colors and their associations, we can be more intentional with our candle selection and create a powerful and transformative healing experience. Remember, working with candles is a form of self-care, and by taking time for ourselves, we can create a more positive and fulfilling life.

Channeling Uriel's Energy with Candle Meditation and Visualization

Do you ever feel emotionally or mentally drained? Do you struggle to remain focused or find inner peace amidst the chaos of daily life? Perhaps it's time to tap into the power of meditation and visualization. By focusing our thoughts and energy, we can connect with the divine and receive the guidance and strength we need. Let's explore the art of candle meditation and visualization exercises, specifically focused on channeling the energy of Archangel Uriel.

1. The first step in candle meditation is to find a quiet, calm space. Sit comfortably on the floor or in a chair with your spine erect and your eyes closed. Take a few deep breaths and focus your thoughts on Uriel. Begin visualizing him before you, glowing with light and wisdom. Allow his energy to envelop you, protecting and guiding you.
2. Next, light a candle in front of you. Watch the flame, focusing your attention solely on its movements. If your mind wanders, gently redirect your thoughts back to the flame. As you watch the fire flicker, visualize Uriel's energy connecting with you, bringing you clarity and insight. You may even wish to recite a mantra like "Uriel, fill me with your wisdom."
3. As you continue to gaze at the candle, visualize Uriel's energy flowing into the flame and then back into you. Imagine the

energy filling up your body, from the crown of your head to the soles of your feet. Feel it cleansing and purifying you, washing away any negativity or doubt. Allow yourself to bask in the warmth and light of Uriel's energy, knowing that you are protected and guided.

4. Imagine yourself surrounded by a golden bubble of light. Picture the bubble growing larger and larger until it encompasses your entire room. Imagine Uriel's energy guiding you, inspiring you, and infusing you with his wisdom inside the bubble. Feel the energy pulsing through you, empowering you to move forward with confidence and clarity.

5. Thank Uriel for his guidance and protection. Visualize his energy lifting you out of your meditation, helping you to feel renewed and refreshed. Affirm to yourself that you are worthy of abundance, joy, and wisdom and that you will continue to channel Uriel's energy as you move through your day.

By practicing candle meditation and visualization exercises, we can tap into Archangel Uriel's power and connect with our inner wisdom. These practices help us to remain calm and centered, even amid life's challenges. Remember to take time for yourself daily, even just a few minutes, to practice these exercises and connect with the divine. You'll be amazed at the clarity and insight that you can gain.

This chapter has explored how crystals and candles can help us channel Archangel Uriel's energy. Using crystals and candles as a form of self-care is a great way to foster positive energy, clarity, and insight. Crystals vibrate at various frequencies, which activate our chakras and bring balance to our energetic field. Candles can enhance our emotional state by promoting relaxation and providing a calming atmosphere. Lastly, candle meditation and visualization exercises can help us connect with Uriel's energy, gaining clarity and insight.

Chapter 9: Daily Rituals and Exercises

Are you looking to connect more deeply with Archangel Uriel? Incorporating daily rituals and exercises into your routine can help establish a strong spiritual connection with this archangel known for his wisdom and guidance. Try setting aside some quiet time each morning to meditate and call upon Archangel Uriel for guidance throughout the day. This chapter will set out step-by-step instructions on creating a daily practice that will help enhance your connection with Archangel Uriel and be simple enough to add to your daily routine. Each section will also detail various exercises, meditations, and affirmations that you can use to re-energize your spiritual connection. By prioritizing these daily rituals, you'll be on your way to building a stronger relationship with this powerful archangel.

Enhancing Creativity through Archangel Uriel

Creativity is a gift, but it's not always easy to tap into. During times of stress or burnout, accessing the creative part of our minds can be even more challenging. However, with the help of Archangel Uriel, we can unlock our imagination and bring our ideas to life. Here's a step-by-step guide for enhancing creativity with the guidance of Archangel Uriel.

Daily Exercises

Daily exercise can allow you to tap into your creativity.[78]

Creating a daily exercise routine can enhance your creativity. Archangel Uriel guides us to focus our energy on the present moment, which helps us relax and focus on the task at hand. One way to do this is through movement. Activities such as yoga, dance, or even a simple walk can help you clear your head and bring inspiration to your projects. You can also try free writing, where you write down your thoughts for a few minutes each day. This will help you identify patterns and themes that may spark new ideas.

Meditations

Archangel Uriel is known for guiding us to our inner wisdom. Meditation is a potent tool to access that wisdom and creativity within ourselves. Begin by sitting silently for a few minutes each day, focusing on your breath and allowing your mind to quiet. As you breathe, imagine a white light surrounding you, inviting Archangel Uriel to join you. You can also try guided meditations specifically designed for creativity. These meditations often take you on a journey to discover new ideas or perspectives.

Affirmations

Affirmations are another powerful way to shift your mindset towards a more positive and creative outlook. Start by choosing three affirmations related to creativity, such as "I am a vessel for divine inspiration" or "My creativity flows effortlessly." Repeat these affirmations to yourself each day, either in meditation or as an intentional thought throughout your day. You can also create vision boards with images and quotes that inspire you.

Access Wisdom and Mental Clarity with Archangel Uriel

Feeling lost, confused, or overwhelmed by life's challenges can take a mental and emotional toll. Fortunately, there are spiritual helpers who we can call for guidance, wisdom, and mental clarity. The guide that this book concentrates on is the Archangel Uriel, the angel of wisdom and illumination. With a little practice, anyone can learn to access Uriel's divine assistance to improve the quality of their lives. Here's a step-by-step guide on accessing the wisdom and mental clarity you need through Archangel Uriel.

Daily Exercises

One of the best ways to access Uriel's wisdom is through daily exercises that help you connect with your intuition and inner guidance. You can easily incorporate these exercises into your daily routine, such as taking 10-15 minutes each morning or night to practice deep breathing and mindfulness meditation, journaling, or simply sitting in silence and letting your thoughts drift.

Meditations

Find a quiet, peaceful place to sit and begin by visualizing the divine light and warmth of Archangel Uriel surrounding you. Focus on your breath and allow any thoughts or emotions to simply pass by like clouds in the sky. As you tune into your breath and the present moment, ask Uriel for guidance, clarity, and wisdom. You may receive a message or impression or simply feel a sense of peace and comfort.

Affirmations

These positive statements can help change your mentality and bring about positive change in your life. Some examples of affirmations you can use to connect with Archangel Uriel include "I am open to receiving divine guidance and wisdom," "I trust that the universe has a plan for me," and "I am filled with peace, love, and clarity."

Nature Walks

Connecting with nature is a great way to access Uriel's wisdom and tap into your intuition. You can take a walk in the park, go hiking, or simply sit outside in your backyard or balcony. As you immerse yourself in the natural beauty around you, ask Uriel for guidance and clarity on any issues or questions. You may find that the answers come more easily than expected.

Healing from Traumas

Whether physical or emotional, trauma can leave deep scars in a person's psyche. They often result in fear, anxiety, and depression – significantly affecting your quality of life. Archangel Uriel's divine guidance can provide a unique path toward healing for people struggling to find a way out of their trauma. Known as the "light of God," Archangel Uriel's healing energy helps release emotional wounds and transform one's life. Here's a step-by-step process to help you heal from trauma with Archangel Uriel.

Daily Exercises

The first step in this journey of self-healing is to take care of your physical health. Start by incorporating daily exercises such as yoga, meditation, or walking into your routine. These activities will bring balance to your mind, body, and spirit, and you will feel relaxed and energized simultaneously. If you prefer intense physical activities like running or weightlifting, go ahead and do those. Whatever you choose to do, be consistent. Physical activity has been shown to lower levels of stress hormones like cortisol and adrenaline, which can trigger anxiety and hyperarousal in traumas.

Meditations

Now that you've incorporated healthy habits into your daily routine, you will move on to meditation. Meditation can help calm the noise in your mind and release negativity. With Archangel Uriel's divine energy, meditations can become a transformative experience that helps you release the toxic energy trapped within you. Start your meditation with deep breaths, inhale through your nose, and exhale through your mouth. Visualize the divine light of Archangel Uriel surrounding you like a warm blanket. You can also visualize yourself in nature, surrounded by trees, rivers, or mountains. This visualization will help you connect with the divine energy and release any pain, fear, or sadness.

Affirmations

The other powerful tool that can help you heal from trauma is affirmations. Words have power, and when you speak them frequently, they become a part of your subconscious thoughts. Affirmations are positive statements you repeatedly say to yourself to remind yourself that you are worthy of love, healing, and happiness. With Archangel Uriel's powerful energy, affirmations become even more potent and effective. Choose positive affirmations that resonate with you, and recite them throughout the day. Examples of affirmations are "I am worthy of love and joy," "I radiate with happiness and positivity," and "I release all the fears and doubts within me."

Seeking Professional Help

While daily exercises, meditation, and affirmations might work wonders for some people, they might not be enough to heal from severe trauma. Remember, it's okay to seek professional help if you feel that you need it. A professional therapist or counselor can help you navigate your emotions and guide you through a healthy path toward healing. Archangel Uriel's energy will always be with you, and seeking professional help will not hinder the process but accelerate it.

Raising Your Vibration

Have you ever felt that everything around you is just slightly off? Maybe you can't shake the feeling of negativity, or you just can't seem to find your happiness. The solution might lie in raising your vibration. When we have a high vibration, we attract more positive experiences, people, and opportunities into our lives. One way to raise your vibration is by working with Archangel Uriel. Here's a step-by-step guide on how to raise your vibration through Archangel Uriel.

Daily Exercises

One way to raise your vibration is through daily exercise that will promote positivity and self-care. For example, you can start or end your day with an uplifting yoga routine or take a meditative walk in nature. When you make time for activities that bring joy to your life, you naturally increase your vibration. The key is prioritizing your happiness and making it a habit to care for your mind, body, and soul.

Meditations

Meditation is a powerful tool for connecting with Archangel Uriel and raising your vibration. Begin by finding a quiet space to sit comfortably and focus on breathing. Once you feel centered, visualize yourself surrounded by a bright, golden light. This light represents Archangel Uriel's uplifting energy. Feel the warmth of his energy and allow it to fill your heart space. When you're ready, silently ask him for guidance and support. Trust that He is always with you, and His energy will help you manifest your highest potential.

Affirmations

Affirmations can help you reprogram your subconscious mind and raise your vibration. You can begin by creating a list of affirmations that resonate with you. Some examples include, "I am deserving of love and happiness," or "I trust the process of my life." Once you have your list, recite these affirmations to yourself every day. You can say them in your head or out loud. The key is to embody the energy of the affirmation and fully believe in its truth.

Self-Reflection

Taking a step back and reflecting on your life occasionally is crucial. Ask yourself what experiences or emotions are holding you back from manifesting your ideal life. Acknowledge them, and then release them with the help of Archangel Uriel. You can do this through a visualization technique. See yourself placing these limiting beliefs in a bubble and surrendering them to Uriel's energy. Trust that he will help transmute these beliefs into positivity and light.

Writing to Archangel Uriel

If you're seeking peace, wisdom, and divine guidance, Archangel Uriel is here to help. This mighty being of light radiates calm, tranquility, and deep insight and can help you overcome obstacles, heal old wounds, and manifest your dreams. One of the powerful ways to connect with Uriel is by putting your thoughts, fears, hopes, and intentions on paper. This way, you can tap into your inner wisdom, release negative energies, and receive powerful messages from the angel realm. Here's a step-by-step guide to show you how to write to Archangel Uriel in a clear, focused, and effective way to receive the guidance and blessings you seek.

Step 1: Prepare Your Space

Before you begin writing, setting the stage for your communication with Archangel Uriel is important. Find a quiet, comfortable space where you won't be disturbed. Light a candle, burn some incense or sage, and play soft music if you like. You can also create an altar or a special place for Uriel by placing crystals, flowers, feathers, or other sacred objects that resonate with you. Take a few deep breaths, center yourself, and ask Archangel Uriel to be with you, guide you, and protect you as you write.

Step 2: State Your Intention

Once you've prepared your space, take a moment to clarify your intention for writing to Archangel Uriel. Do you seek clarity on a specific issue? Do you want to release old patterns, fears, or doubts? Or do you simply want to deepen your connection with the divine? Write your intention clearly and concisely, and let it guide your writing. You can begin with a simple statement, such as "Dear Archangel Uriel, I am writing to you today because..." or "I ask for your guidance on the matter of..."

Step 3: Pour Your Heart Out

Now it's time to let your words flow freely and openly. Don't worry about grammar, spelling, or structure; just write from your heart and soul. If you feel stuck or overwhelmed, you can start with some prompts or questions, such as:

- What are my deepest fears about this situation?
- What are my highest aspirations and hopes?
- What do I need to let go of to move forward?
- What actions or steps can I take to align with my purpose?

As you write, allow yourself to express whatever comes up for you without judgment or self-censorship. You can also address Archangel Uriel directly as if you were having a conversation with a wise and compassionate friend. Remember that Uriel is here to help you, to guide you, and to love you unconditionally.

Step 4: Express Your Gratitude

Once you've written down what you wanted to convey, it is important to end with a simple expression of gratitude towards Archangel Uriel. This act of gratitude opens up the connection between the archangel Uriel and the person who is writing the letter.

Step 5: Keep Your Writing Safe

Don't forget to keep your writing in a special place when finished. You may want to read it after a while to see how you have progressed in your journey and the lessons learned or guide yourself through future challenges.

Following these simple steps, you can create a powerful and transformative dialogue with Archangel Uriel through writing. Whether you need comfort, guidance, healing, or inspiration, Uriel is always there for you, ready to support you on your path. Remember that writing is a powerful tool for self-discovery, empowerment, and co-creation with the universe.

The daily rituals and exercises provided in this chapter can help you foster a deeper connection with Uriel and receive his guidance and blessings. As always, be sure to thank him for all he has done for you! May the love of Uriel fill your life with joy, inspiration, and purpose!

Bonus: Correspondences Sheet

Archangel Uriel is known for his incredible ability to help us find our way through challenges and bring clarity to our lives. There are certain correspondences associated with Uriel which can help us better connect and understand his energy. This bonus sheet includes a chart outlining all of the correspondences related to Archangel Uriel. It will serve as a great reference for anyone looking to understand more about this powerful and compassionate archangel. Use this chart as a quick reference to help you connect with Archangel Uriel's energy!

Day Of The Week	Saturday
Hour Of The Day	8 am
Festivals/Feasts Of The Year	1. Feast of St. Michael and All Angels (September 29th) 2. Feast of St. Gabriel (March 24th) 3. Feast of the Nativity of St. John the Baptist (June 24th)
Zodiac Sign And Planet	Leo, the Sun
Angel Number	888

Direction	East
Element	Fire
Colors	Gold, White, and Orange
Symbol/Seal/Sigil	Six-pointed star
Trees, Plants, And Herbs/Oils	Myrrh, Marigold, and Carnation
Crystal(s) And Metal(s)	Citrine, Amber, and Gold

Archangel Uriel is an incredibly powerful archangel who can provide us with the guidance, clarity, and insight we need to move forward in our lives. Correspondences associated with this powerful angel include the colors gold, white, and orange, which are often associated with enlightenment and positivity. Crystals like citrine and amber are also often linked to Uriel's energy, as they connect us with his guidance and bring more light into our lives.

Fire is another element closely associated with Archangel Uriel and carries the energy of transformation, allowing us to become more enlightened and emotionally stable. Similarly, myrrh, marigolds, and carnations can be used to help us connect with Uriel's energy. These plants are often used in healing spells and rituals, helping to bring clarity and understanding into our lives.

The feast of St. Michael and All Angels (September 29th) is also linked to Uriel's energy, so taking the time to honor this day can be a powerful way to connect with him and thank him for his guidance. Meditating with Archangel Uriel's sigil or seal can help us open up to his energy and create a strong connection with him. Calling on Uriel during times of uncertainty or confusion can be a powerful way to gain much-needed insight and understanding. Through his guidance, we can find the courage to move forward and overcome any obstacle in our path.

By aligning ourselves with these spiritual correspondences associated with Archangel Uriel, we can create a strong connection with his energy and invite more understanding, clarity, and enlightenment into our lives.

Conclusion

When it comes to the divine realm, there are few beings as powerful and awe-inspiring as Archangel Uriel. This celestial being is known for the incredible light and love that he brings into the world, spreading joy and positivity wherever he goes. Whether you're seeking guidance, protection, or simply a sense of peace and tranquility, Uriel is there to help you tap into your inner strength and discover your true potential. With his boundless energy and unwavering commitment to goodness, Uriel is a beacon of hope and inspiration for us all. If you're ever feeling lost or alone, just know that Archangel Uriel is watching over you, ready to offer compassion and support whenever you need it most.

In times of uncertainty and confusion, Archangel Uriel shines a light on the path to our truest selves. As the angel of wisdom, clarity, and truth, Uriel helps us see through the fog of doubt and insecurity to find the answers inside us all along. Whether it's uncovering our passion for a new career or realizing the depth of our love for someone special, Uriel's guidance can lead us to fulfilling our deepest desires and dreams.

When we have Archangel Uriel on our side, there's no limit to what we can achieve. With His divine wisdom guiding us, we can trust in our ability to make the right decisions and confidently move forward. Uriel brings a sense of clarity that is reassuring and empowering, allowing us to see situations in a new light and approach them with renewed vigor. Whether facing challenges or pursuing our dreams, Uriel is there to lend us his strength and support.

This guide has explored ways to connect with Archangel Uriel. From creating angelic sacred space and performing solar chakra meditations to using crystals and candles for divination, these rituals and exercises will help you open your heart, mind, and spirit to the presence of this powerful angel. If you're ever feeling overwhelmed or unsure of which direction to take in life, simply call upon Uriel, and you will soon be filled with the strength and courage needed to move forward.

The accompanying Correspondences Sheet with this guide contains helpful symbols and affirmations associated with Archangel Uriel. With these tools, you can deepen your connection to the angelic realm and invoke his powerful presence in times of need. The more you practice, the closer you will become to Uriel and his divine wisdom, enabling you to unlock your potential and lead a life of joy and abundance.

So, let's take this journey with Archangel Uriel and be blessed with his divine energy, wisdom, and guidance!

Part 6: Angel Numbers

Unlock the Secrets of Angels, Divine Messages, Numerology, Synchronicity, and Symbolism

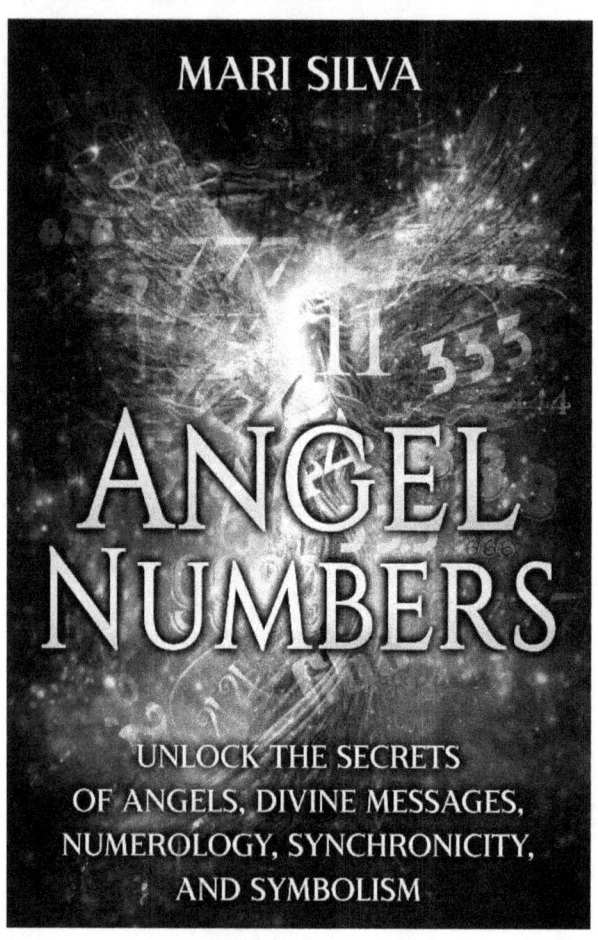

Introduction

Have you ever noticed that the same angel numbers seem to pop up repeatedly and wondered what they meant? Angel numbers are ways through which divine entities try to communicate with humans and offer them support and guidance whenever needed. It's not a coincidence if your eyes repeatedly fall on 333, 444, or other repeated numerical sequences. Each sequence carries a unique meaning that offers insight into certain aspects of your life. Paying attention to angel numbers is a step towards personal growth and development.

In this book, you'll learn all about angel numbers, the secrets of angels, divine messages, numerology, synchronicity, and symbolism. It's an interesting yet informative read that explores the spiritual significance of angel numbers and how they serve as a self-exploratory development practice. It delves into the concept of angel numbers and uncovers the history and origins of this age-old divination technique.

By reading this book, you'll understand the role of various angelic and divine beings and how they communicate with humans through specific signs and symbols. You'll learn about the basics of numerology and the different numerology systems. In this chapter, you'll learn about the most common numerical sequences and their meanings. You'll also understand the role that one's intuition plays when interpreting these sequences.

The book explains how angel signs, like coincidences, bodily sensations, scents, objects, and unexpected occurrences, can manifest. It lists the symbols and sigils of various angels and offers several meditations and prayers that you can try out.

The book also illustrates the difference between the concepts of synchronicity, divine timing, and coincidence. You'll learn what synchronicity is and how it's relevant to today's spiritual practices. You'll understand the universal rules that govern and dictate divine timing and learn how to distinguish between synchronicities and coincidences.

In addition to angel numbers, sequences, and sigils, this guide also explores other angelic correspondences. You'll understand how angels are associated with things like days of the week, hours of the day, zodiac signs, colors, months, and gemstones. You'll find a list that covers the correspondences for the most popular angelic figures.

There's an entire chapter dedicated to the concept of the Law of Attraction that explains how it works and the main philosophical and religious principles on which it is based. You'll find out how angelic correspondences can be used in tandem with the Law of Attraction and learn about several practical exercises, such as meditations and visualization, which can help you put your knowledge into practice. These activities will guide you in activating the Law of Attraction for specific goals.

The book's last chapter serves as a mini directory of daily meditations with which you can practice enhancing your awareness, connect to the angelic realm, and open your third eye and crown chakras. You'll also find grounding techniques and exercises which help with energy cleansing, practices that aid in uncovering synchronicities in the past, and meditations on angel symbols and numbers.

Chapter 1: What Are Angel Numbers?

Do you ever experience a series of weird coincidences where you see certain number sequences everywhere you look? Maybe it's the number 1111 on a digital clock or 333 on license plates and bills. These occurrences may seem like coincidences initially, but when they become more frequent, they could be a sign from the angels. Many spiritual beliefs signal the existence of angel numbers – number sequences that hold spiritual value beyond their numeric meaning. Many people consider them a message from the divine, the universe, and angels. These numbers can appear on clocks, phone numbers, receipts, license plates, and even in dreams. People are divided between firmly believing in the existence of these numbers and being skeptical about the divine presence and messages from the universe. This chapter will be about the belief in angels and how they can communicate with you.

Angelic/Divine Beings

Even if you're not religious, you're probably familiar with angels. Maybe you know them from fiction, movies, or books. They are depicted as divine beings who have wings and special abilities. Angels have been revered in many religions and beliefs since ancient civilizations. And people have always been equally curious and fascinated with the concept of angels. From biblical stories to modern-day accounts, the mere concept of angels has captured the imagination of humans worldwide.

There are so many stories of angel sightings. Some people describe these interactions as a bright light or hearing a heavenly choir during near-death experiences. Others feel a presence over their shoulders looking out for them, offering them guidance and protection. For instance, have you ever had a near-accident experience where you maybe almost stepped in front of an oncoming car but somehow avoided the accident by a second? You never know; this might be the work of your guardian angel.

According to most spiritual traditions, angels are considered to be God's messengers and helpers. They're considered celestial beings of light and love, able to protect and comfort those in need. In some traditions, angels are believed to have individual responsibilities, like looking over humans, delivering God's messages, or overseeing elements or seasons. In Christianity, for instance, there are nine choirs of angels, with the highest rank being Seraphim and the lowest rank being mere angels. Each of these choirs has a specific role in serving God and humanity.

1. The Seraphim

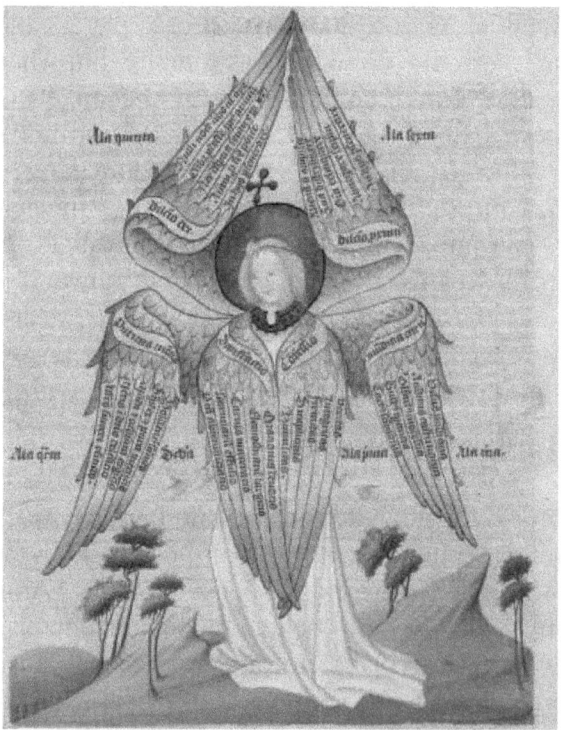

Seraphim are pure light or fire, reflecting their intense love for God.[74]

At the top of the hierarchy of angels are the Seraphim. They are considered pure light or fire; their name translates to "burning ones," reflecting their intense love and devotion to God. According to religious literature, they have six wings; two cover their faces, two cover their feet, and the remaining two are used to fly. These angels are the closest to the divine presence and most likely don't interact with humans.

2. The Cherubim

Next in the hierarchy are the Cherubim. They are believed to be the guardians of God's throne. They are often depicted as having four faces: a human, a lion, an ox, and an eagle, representing their diverse knowledge and wisdom. The Cherubim are known for their understanding of the mysteries of God and their role in protecting His divine presence.

3. The Thrones

The third choir of angels is the Thrones, believed to embody God's justice and authority. They are considered fiery wheels or chariots, which is a representation of their swift and powerful nature. The Thrones are responsible for upholding divine order and maintaining balance in the universe.

4. The Dominions

Next in the hierarchy are the Dominions, who are believed to be the guardians of the cosmos. They oversee the work of the lower ranks of angels and are depicted as holding scepters or orbs, symbolizing their authority and power. The Dominions make sure that the universe functions according to God's will.

5. The Virtues

The Virtues are known for their courage and strength, and they are responsible for maintaining the balance between the spiritual and physical worlds. They are seen as warriors in armor, wielding swords and shields and fighting for God's will. They keep the world in harmony and balance.

6. The Powers

The Powers are responsible for defending humanity against spiritual and physical harm. They are depicted wielding swords or shields, symbolizing their strength and protective nature. The Powers watch over the world and keep humans safe.

7. The Principalities

The Principalities are believed to be the guardians of nations and empires. They are responsible for maintaining order and harmony in the world, and they hold keys or scrolls, symbolizing their role as stewards of governance. The Principalities ensure that nations and empires operate according to God's plan.

8. The Archangels

The Archangels are known for their role as messengers of God, delivering vital messages to humanity. They are often associated with specific tasks, such as healing or protection, and they are responsible for carrying out God's will on Earth.

9. The Angels

Finally, at the lowest rank of the hierarchy are the Angels. They are responsible for carrying out the tasks assigned to them by the higher levels and are often depicted as messengers or helpers. Angels serve God and humanity in various ways, offering humans their love, protection, and guidance.

One common category of angels you might have heard about is the guardian angels. These angels are considered unique to every individual, assigned to every human at birth, and tasked with protecting them throughout life. They watch over you, protect you from harm, both physical and otherwise, and offer you comfort and guidance. They protect you from negative energies and prevent you from making bad decisions in life. Guardians are not limited to a single religion or belief and can be present with every individual, regardless of their belief. Even if you do not want to believe in the existence of actual angels, you could still consider the guidance that comes from angel numbers to be messages from the universe. These divine energies exist beyond the boundaries of space and time, watching over you and guiding you on your spiritual journey. So, while it may seem like a stretch to some people, when you start believing in this concept and manifesting divine guidance, you'll be surprised where this road ends up taking you.

Origins of Angel Numbers

The existence of angel numbers can be traced as far back as the Babylonians and Egyptians. They were of the view that numbers held mystical significance and that they could be used to communicate with the divine. Initially, the Babylonians developed a complicated numerology system related to astrology. They laid the foundation for the idea that each number had a unique vibration corresponding to a specific celestial body. That is when astrology was born, and people's birth dates and locations could provide valuable insight into their life.

On the other hand, the Egyptians believed that they were closely tied to religious beliefs. For instance, the number 7 was especially revered in ancient Egypt because it represented the seven pillars of wisdom and the seven gods of creation. They also believed that the number 42 was a representation of the path to eternal life. These ancient beliefs set the foundation for the connection between numerology and angel numbers.

Over time, this concept became more complex, with more research and religious connections being made to its existence. In particular, Christianity has a lot of references to special numbers and the meanings behind them. For instance, the number 3 is believed to represent the holy trinity, whereas the number 7 is believed to represent perfection or completion. This concept was developed even further during the Middle Ages when numerology was introduced to the world. Both scholars and philosophers were fascinated by the mystical aspects of numbers and their connection to the divine. They truly believed that numbers would help them uncover the universe's secrets.

One of the most famous works on numerology from that period is the "Liber Abaci," written by the Italian mathematician Leonardo Fibonacci in 1202. In it, Fibonacci introduced the concept of the Fibonacci sequence, a series of numbers where each one is the sum of the two preceding numbers. This sequence is found in nature and has been used in architecture, music, and art for centuries. Fibonacci also introduced the concept of Arabic numerals to Europe, revolutionizing mathematics and making calculations easier.

Angel Numbers as a Spiritual Practice

In recent years, the concept and practice of angel numbers have become a fully-fledged spiritual belief, with so many people regularly seeking guidance and insight from the angels. People who have experienced the sightings of angel numbers believe that the more faith you have, the clearer the messages will be. At first, you will surely be skeptical about the whole thing, but once you see it in action and actually make a good life decision following this advice, your belief will only get stronger. Much like tarot and astrology, interpreting angel numbers has become very popular, with more and more people being interested in learning more about it.

Let's consider an example to examine how exactly angel numbers work. Jake is going through a tough time in his life. He just lost his job and is struggling to find a new one. His financial situation has worsened by the day, and he feels like giving up entirely on the job search. One day, as he's walking down the street, he notices the number 888 appearing everywhere he looks. First, he sees it on a billboard ad, then he finds it on his grocery receipt, then a truck's license plate, and on and on. At first, he thinks it's just a coincidence, but after the sightings become frequent, Jake starts researching what this number means. That is when he comes across angel numbers and how they work. Already feeling lost and discouraged, he takes this as a sign that his financial situation would improve if he followed the advice associated with this angel number. Encouraged by this, he does exactly that and soon gets a job offer much better than he expected. This experience proved to be a learning moment for him, and his belief in angel numbers was reinforced by it.

This story offers a glimpse into the power and potential of angel numbers as a spiritual practice. Whether used to receive guidance during difficult times or as a daily practice for spiritual growth and exploration, the interpretation of angel numbers can offer individuals a powerful tool for connecting with the divine and finding guidance and support on their spiritual journey.

Places Where Angel Numbers Can Appear

Have you ever been driving down the road, and a series of numbers on a license plate caught your eye? Maybe you were at the grocery store, and the total on your receipt added up to a repeating sequence of numbers. These are just a couple of examples of how angel numbers can appear in the most unexpected places and how they can be easy to miss if we're not paying attention. Where else can you expect to find these angelic messages? The truth is, they can appear just about anywhere. Some people have reported seeing angel numbers on digital clocks, such as 11:11 or 3:33. Others have seen them on billboards, house numbers, or even in patterns of leaves or clouds. The possibilities are truly endless, but here are some of the most common places:

1. Digital Clocks and Watches

Digital clocks and watches are perhaps the most common place where people see angel numbers. It's not uncommon to glance at your phone, computer, or watch and see repeated numbers. Sometimes, the appearance of angel numbers on digital clocks and watches can be quite bizarre. One woman reported that every time she checked the time on her digital watch, the display showed the number 444. Even when she changed the battery, the watch continued to show 444.

2. License Plates

License plates can be another unexpected location to find angel numbers. Whether driving to work, running errands, or simply taking a stroll around the block, keep an eye out for license plates with repeating or sequential numbers. It may seem like a coincidence, but some people believe that seeing certain numbers on a license plate is a sign from their guardian angels. For example, let's say you've been contemplating a big life decision and keep seeing the number 888 on license plates. You might interpret this as a message from your angels that you're on the right path and that your decision will bring abundance and prosperity into your life.

3. Street Addresses and House Numbers

Another common way people encounter angel numbers is street addresses and house numbers. This is because the numbers used in these addresses are often chosen randomly, yet they can still hold significant meanings for those living there. For example, let's say you're house hunting and come across a property with the address 777. To some, this may simply seem like a nice, easy-to-remember number. But to those who believe in the power of angel numbers, the triple sevens could represent a message from the divine realm. In numerology, 777 is often associated with spiritual awakening, inner wisdom, and good fortune.

4. Receipts

Receipts are a surprising yet common place where people have reported seeing angel numbers. When you get a receipt after a purchase, it's easy to quickly glance at it before throwing it away. However, if you're open to the idea of angel numbers, you might be surprised to see them appear on your receipt. For example, imagine you went to the grocery store and bought a few items for a total of $22.22. You might think nothing of it at first, but if you're paying attention, you'll realize this is a powerful message from your angels. The number 22 is associated with balance and harmony, while the repeated appearance of the number 2 amplifies its significance. This could be a message to focus on finding balance in your life or that everything is working together for your highest good.

5. Phone Numbers

Phone numbers are another place where people may encounter angel numbers. You might receive a call from a number that ends in 1111 or 2222. These repeating digits could be a sign that you should pay attention to the caller's message. Some people even choose phone numbers that contain angel numbers as a way to bring positive energy into their lives. For instance, a person might intentionally choose a phone number that ends in 8888 because they believe it will bring them good luck. In some instances, people have even reported receiving phone calls from numbers that don't seem to exist. One woman repeatedly received calls from a number that ended in 1111. However, she discovered it wasn't a valid number when she tried calling back.

6. Books or Other Printed Materials

Books and other printed materials can also contain hidden messages in the form of angel numbers. For example, imagine you are reading a novel and notice that the page number is 222. This could be interpreted as a sign that the plot is about to take a significant turn or that the character is about to experience a moment of transformation. Similarly, textbooks and self-help books may have certain sections or chapters that are particularly important for the reader to pay attention to. These sections may be marked by the appearance of angel numbers, such as 111 or 555. It's not just the material's content that can contain angel numbers but also anything pertaining to the publication. For example, a book published on 11/11 at 11:11 could hold special significance for the reader.

7. Social Media

In today's digital age, social media has become an integral part of our lives, and it's not surprising that angel numbers can appear there too. Many have reported seeing them while scrolling through Instagram, Facebook, or Twitter. For instance, someone might come across a post with 111 likes or a tweet retweeted 444 times. Others might see the numbers 222 or 555 as the time stamp on a message or notification. Some might even notice a specific number sequence in the follower count of their favorite influencer or brand.

8. Billboards or Advertisements

Ads and billboards can be another interesting place to spot angel numbers. You might notice a billboard while driving or walking down the street. As you look at it, you notice that the phone number or website address contains the sequence of numbers you have seen lately. It could be a combination of 111, 222, or any other number sequence. For example, you might see an ad for a local business with a phone number ending in 333 or a billboard with a website address that includes 444. These numbers can be interpreted as a message from angels urging you to notice the business or its products and services.

Recognizing Angel Numbers

Recognizing angel numbers is the first step in interpreting their message. These numbers may appear to you in many different forms and combinations, and it's essential to be aware of them. Here are some tips to help you recognize and understand angel numbers:

1. **Pay Attention to Repetition:** One of the most common ways in which angel numbers appear is through repetition. If you keep seeing the number 1111 or 2222, it's a clear sign that the angels are trying to communicate with you. Take note of any number sequences that keep appearing to you.

2. **Look for Unusual Number Sequences**: Angel numbers can appear in various number sequences, including triple digits, quadruple digits, or even mixed numbers. Be aware of any number combinations that catch your attention or seem out of the ordinary.

3. **Notice Your Intuition:** Often, your intuition can guide you to recognize angel numbers. If a particular number sequence catches your attention, pay attention to how you feel when you see it. Do you get a feeling of joy or peace? Do you feel like it's a sign from the universe?

4. **Stay Open to Signs:** Angel numbers can appear in many ways, including through dreams, music, and even our daily routines. Keep an open mind and trust that the angels will reach out in a way that is meant for you.

5. **Use Your Inner Guidance**: Ultimately, interpreting angel numbers is a personal journey, and you should trust your intuition and inner guidance. Look within yourself for answers, and let your intuition guide you toward understanding the messages the angels send you.

Angel numbers can be pretty powerful if you believe in them and take the advice they're trying to convey. It doesn't matter if you believe in divine beings or not; you can simply consider angel numbers to be messages from the universe. After all, there's little doubt that there's some universal mystical energy around us, say *karmic energy*, or whatever belief you find reasonable. There's something so undeniably magical about the appearance of certain numbers so frequently that it can't possibly be a simple coincidence. So, the next time you see a repeated sequence, pay attention to it and discover what it means; you never know where it may lead.

Chapter 2: Numerology 101

The concept of angel numbers wasn't the first of its kind. In fact, it all started when philosophers and theorists started to pay attention to the special qualities of numbers. This explains how the concept of numerology – the belief that numbers hold significant meaning – came about; if studied enough, they can reveal the mysteries of the universe. To learn why angel numbers hold such importance, you must first learn about numerology and its associated theories. Essentially, numerology sets the foundation for interpreting the symbolism and unique messages behind angel numbers. Initially, numerology was nothing more than a mathematician pondering the hidden messages behind numbers. It has deep roots in history, with concepts from Greece, Egypt, and China.

This chapter will provide you with a brief introduction to numerology, how it originated, and the different types of numerology systems that have been developed since. Once you've fully grasped numerology, you can move on to understanding and interpreting angel numbers. Unlike other numerology practices focusing on birth information and astrological signs, angel number sequences can appear to anyone at any time.

What Is Numerology?

The universe has a language of its own, one that can speak to you through a series of numbers, symbols, and energies. The communication system consisting of numbers is known as numerology, and it essentially holds the key to unlocking the secrets of the world around you. At its core, numerology studies the link between numbers and their corresponding events. It's a language with perfect synchrony, where everything from your life's patterns to your name's vibrations holds significance. You can find your place in the universe by uncovering the numerical value of words, names, and symbols. That is what numerology is all about. Every person is born with a soul, an eternal and non-physical essence that is imbued with a unique name and energetic symbolism.

The Origins of Numerology

The study of numerology is a tapestry woven with threads of ancient wisdom and timeless insight. Its roots run deep, extending far beyond the introduction of its name and into the very fabric of the universe. While numerology is considered to be a science by most people, it's actually a belief system that has a rich history spanning the entirety of human existence. From the first moment humans started to recognize the powers of numerals and mathematics, the theories and practices of numerology were already likely in motion. Among the first to utilize this concept were the ancient Egyptians. At the time, they weren't aware that the spiritual system they were practicing would be developed into the vast field of numerology. Pythagoras, the great mathematician and theorist, is considered the pioneer of numerology.

The theories by Pythagoras, especially those about numbers and music notes, were considered groundbreaking and essentially led to the development of a direct relationship between the two subjects. Through his mathematical knowledge, Pythagoras could identify people's personality traits based on their birth dates and corresponding vibrational notes. He was a firm believer in the power of numbers and suggested that everything in the universe could be explained by numbers. The principles given by him are still used in modern numerology, which is also known as the Pythagorean Number System.

Pythagoras is considered to be the pioneer of Numerology.[75]

The word "numerology" was only introduced in 1907, but the concept and importance of numbers have been present in all religions and belief systems way before that. Birthdays, anniversaries, and other significant dates hold deep meaning and value for most individuals.

Pythagoras' Teachings on Numerology

While Pythagoras is commonly known for his discovery of the Pythagorean theorem, with which you're probably familiar from high-school mathematics, his contributions to numerology are equally significant. In fact, many consider him to be the inventor of Western numerology. According to Aristotle, Pythagoreans held a mystical reverence for mathematics and believed that all things in the universe were composed of numbers. They saw them not only as means of quantifying the world around them but also as a powerful tool for unlocking deeper truths about the nature of existence. For the Pythagoreans, the study of numerology was not simply an intellectual pursuit but a deeply spiritual one. They believed that by understanding the vibrational energies of numbers, they could gain insight into the hidden forces that govern the universe and that this knowledge could be used to achieve a greater understanding of the self and the world around them.

One of the most important teachings of Pythagoras included the concept of the Divine Triangle, a sacred symbol that would become a cornerstone of numerology. At the heart of the Divine Triangle is the number 3, representing the three aspects of the universe: the physical, the intellectual, and the spiritual. The triangle itself symbolizes harmony and balance, with each of its sides and angles representing different aspects of life. The triangle's base represents the physical world, with its material possessions and earthly pleasures. The left side represents the intellectual world, where your thoughts and ideas take shape. The right side represents the spiritual world, where you connect with your higher self and the divine. Other theories from Pythagoras' teachings will be explained in the Pythagoras' numerology section.

Different Numerology Systems

Numerology is a vast belief system that isn't limited to a single interpretation. In fact, there are multiple types of numerology systems based on how they use numeric values and interpretations to define various aspects of the universe or the individuals residing in said universe. Some of the most well-known numerology systems include:

1. Chaldean Numerology

This ancient numerology system has its roots in Babylonia. It consists of complex mathematical calculations and a unique perspective. Unlike Pythagorean numerology, this system assigns numbers to the vibrations produced by letters instead of simply corresponding to them. According to the teachings of this system, numbers hold a lot more value than just their numeric values. They can correspond to different planets, heavenly bodies, and universal energies associated with life's creation. The Chaldean numerology practitioners consider this practice a spiritual and mystical tool.

Pythagorean numerology, as opposed to Chaldean numerology, uses a more straightforward method of allocating numbers to letters based on where they are located in the alphabet. While the Pythagorean approach may be more straightforward, some numerology practitioners consider Chaldean numerology to be slightly more accurate. Chaldean numerology is distinctive in that it gives letter values of 1 through 8 while reserving the number 9 as "holy." However, if the sum of a name's numerical values is 9, it is retained. Additionally, Chaldean numerology requires practitioners to use the name by which a person is most commonly known rather than their full birth name.

For instance, if the actor Michael Douglas used Chaldean numerology, he would be referred to as "Michael Douglas" instead of "Michael Kirk Douglas," his full birth name.

2. Indian Numerology

Indian numerology, also known as Vedic numerology, is a system of mystical interpretation that assigns numerical values to the letters of the Sanskrit alphabet. This system has been based on the belief that each letter in the Sanskrit alphabet has a unique vibrational energy that can provide deep insights into the spiritual realm and the mysteries of life. In Indian numerology, each letter is assigned a numerical value, ranging from 1 to 9. These numerical values are then used to calculate various aspects of a person's life, such as their personality traits, strengths, weaknesses, and life path. The calculations are usually based on a person's name and date of birth.

One of the key principles of Indian numerology is the idea of karma or the belief that a person's actions in this life are determined by their past lives. You've probably come across the word karmic energy before. According to this principle, a person's name and birth date are not arbitrary or random. Instead, they are calculated by their past karma and the lessons they need to learn in this lifetime. Indian numerology also includes the use of various numerical combinations and patterns, such as the use of repeating numbers, double numbers, and triple numbers. These patterns are believed to hold special significance and can provide insights into a person's spiritual path and destiny.

3. Kabbalistic Numerology

Kabbalistic numerology, or *Hebrew numerology*, provides the mystical interpretation that assigns numerical values to Hebrew letters and words. This system, again centering on corresponding letters and numbers, is based on the belief that every letter in the Hebrew alphabet has a unique vibrational energy and that these energies can be used to gain insights into the universe's secrets. In Kabbalistic numerology, each Hebrew letter is assigned a numerical value, known as its gematria. The gematria of a word or phrase is calculated by adding up the numerical values of its constituent letters. For example, the word "chai" (meaning "life" in Hebrew) has a gematria of 18 because the letters Chet and Yud add up to 18.

Kabbalistic numerology also includes various numerical combinations and patterns, such as the number 72, which is believed to represent the 72 names of God. The practice of combining letters and numbers in this way is known as notarikon. Another aspect of Kabbalistic numerology is the Tree of Life, a symbolic diagram representing the divine flow of energy through the universe. Each of the ten sefirot (or spheres) on the Tree of Life is associated with a specific numerical value and represents a different aspect of divine energy.

Kabbalistic numerology is used more for divination and spiritual direction than anything else. This system is based more on spiritual guidance than numeric logic. In fact, just by looking at the gematria of your name or other significant words and phrases, you can gain helpful insights into your personality. Kabbalistic numerology is also used in the study of the Torah and other Hebrew texts, where numerical patterns and symbolism are believed to hold deep spiritual significance.

4. Chinese Numerology

Chinese numerology has been utilized for over 4,000 years, and it differs significantly from other numerological systems in that the Chinese believe that numbers are either naturally lucky or unlucky. In Eastern culture, luck plays a big role and is linked to the idea of fate. Chinese numerology places a lot of emphasis on a number's sound because they think certain sounds can bring good or bad luck. For instance, the Chinese word for "one" sounds similar to the English word "honor," signifying a person's capacity to overcome obstacles to achieve greater goals. In contrast, the term "four" has the same sound as "death," making the number 4 a bad omen that should be avoided.

Chinese people also believe that there are magical connections in numerical combinations. They contend that there is a link between the 12 rivers that flow in the direction of the Central Kingdom and the 12 blood and air veins that go throughout the body. Acupuncture targets 365 different body parts, corresponding to 365 days of the year.

The Lo Shu Square is the easiest way to use Chinese numerology. This method is based on a rumor that Emperor Yu saw a tortoise with nine perfect squares on its shell near the banks of the Luo River. The original Lo Shu Square is occasionally called the "Magic Square" because, when the numbers are summed up horizontally, vertically, or diagonally, they equal 15. The Lo Shu Square has nine cells, three rows, and three columns. Even numbers go in the corners, with the odd numbers forming a cross in the middle of the vertical and horizontal rows.

Recently, a modernized replica of Lo Shu Square has been created to teach Westerners Chinese numerology. The Hidden Cross, an upgraded form, uses fewer intricate calculations and does not require lunar years. The rows of the Hidden Cross are numbered from 1 to 9, and they are organized from top to bottom as follows: 3-6-9, 2-5-8, and 1-4-7. Understanding the meaning of the squares is necessary to interpret the outcome. The bottom row represents reality, the middle row represents feelings, and the top row represents ideas. From left to right, the columns stand for thinking, volition, and action, respectively.

5. Pythagoras Numerology

Pythagorean numerology is rooted in the work of the Greek mathematician Pythagoras, who believed that numbers were the universe's fundamental building blocks. This ancient practice views numbers as having mystical properties that can reveal much about a person and the world around them. Pythagoras believed that every object has a vibration, and numbers serve as a measure of that energy. The numbers 1 through 9 represent the nine stages of human life, with each number carrying its own symbolic meaning.

Pythagorean numerology has advanced into a complex system that examines a person's complete birth name and date of birth to give insights into their personality traits, motivations, inherent skills, and more. It can also provide valuable guidance on life patterns, timing, and decision-making. Pythagorean numerology has formed the spiritual basis for many secret societies and continues to be used as a tool for personal growth and self-discovery.

How Does It Work?

Modern numerology analyzes a person's full birth name and date to gain insight into their personality traits, strengths, weaknesses, and life patterns. It is based on the Pythagorean system of numerology, which assigns numerical values to letters in the alphabet and uses those values to calculate a person's core numbers. Here are the steps to practice modern numerology:

- In modern numerology, each letter is assigned a numerical value (between 1 and 9) based on its position in the alphabet. For example, A is assigned 1, B is assigned 2, C is assigned 3, and so on.

- Once you assign a numerical value to each letter in your full birth name, add all the values to get your Expression Number. Your Expression Number represents your natural talents, abilities, and tendencies.

- If your Expression Number is a double-digit number, reduce it to a single digit by adding the two digits together. For example, if your Expression Number is 34, add 3 + 4 = 7. Your reduced Expression Number is 7.

- Your Life Path Number is calculated using your date of birth. First, add your birth's day, month, and year together. Then, add the individual digits in the result to get a single-digit number. For example, if you were born on January 1, 1990, you would add 1 + 1 + 1 + 9 + 9 + 0 = 21. Then, you would add 2 + 1 = 3. Your Life Path Number is 3.

- Your Expression Number and Life Path Number represent your core numbers in modern numerology. These numbers can provide insight into your personality traits, strengths, weaknesses, and life patterns. Many online resources can help you interpret your core numbers.

Once you have calculated and interpreted your core numbers, you can use numerology to gain guidance in various areas of your life, like career, relationships, and personal growth. For example, you can use your core numbers to identify your strengths and weaknesses and to make decisions that align with your natural tendencies and desires.

Numerology and Angel Numbers

Numerology and angel numbers are closely connected, as both are based on the concept that numbers carry spiritual energy and can be used to communicate messages from the divine realm. Numerology provides a framework for understanding the meaning behind these angel numbers. They are unique in the sense that they are believed to be direct messages from the divine realm, whereas other esoteric practices in numerology focus more on using numbers to gain insight into a person's personality, life path, and future events. Angel numbers are not meant to provide personal readings or predictions. Rather, they are seen as guidance and support from the spiritual realm. Another difference is that angel numbers are often repetitive sequences of numbers, while other numerology systems may focus on individual numbers or combinations of numbers. For example, Pythagorean numerology assigns meanings to each number from 1 to 9, as well as to double-digit numbers and certain number combinations.

On the other hand, there are various similarities between angel numbers and other forms of numerology. For example, both angel numbers and Pythagorean numerology believe that each number has a unique vibrational energy that can influence our lives. Just as Pythagorean numerology assigns meaning to specific numbers based on their vibrational energy, angel numbers also have specific meanings based on the vibrational energy they carry. Similarly, in Kabbalistic numerology, each letter of the Hebrew alphabet is assigned a numerical value, and words and phrases can be analyzed based on their numerical value. This practice is similar to the interpretation of angel numbers, as both involve analyzing numerical patterns and sequences to gain insight and guidance.

Numerology Exercise

To better understand how the practice of numerology works, there's no better way than to practice it yourself. So, try out this personality analysis exercise to explore your inner self using numerology concepts. Follow these steps:

Step 1: Determine Your Life Path Number

The first step is to calculate your Life Path Number. This is done by adding up all the digits in your birth date and reducing it to a single digit. For example, if you were born on December 25, 1990, you would add 1+2+2+5+1+9+9+0 = 29. Then add 2+9=11. Finally, reduce 11 to a single digit by adding 1+1=2. Therefore, your Life Path Number would be 2.

Step 2: Understand Your Life Path Number

Each Life Path Number has a unique personality profile. For instance, Life Path Number 1 is known for being independent, driven, and ambitious, while Life Path Number 2 is known for being sensitive, intuitive, and nurturing. You can find a detailed description of each Life Path Number's personality traits online or in numerology books.

Step 3: Calculate Your Expression Number

Your Expression Number is derived from your full name. To calculate it, assign a numerical value to each letter in your name using the chart below, then add up the numbers and reduce them to a single digit.

1 2 3 4 5 6 7 8 9
A B C D E F G H I
J K L M N O P Q R
S T U V W X Y Z

For example, if your name is John Doe, you would add 1+6+5+4+6+5 = 32. Then add 3+2 = 5. Therefore, your Expression Number would be 5.

Step 4: Understand Your Expression Number

Just like Life Path Numbers, Expression Numbers have unique characteristics. For example, Expression Number 1 is known for being independent, confident, and innovative, while Expression Number 5 is known for being adaptable, versatile, and adventurous. You can find a detailed description of each Expression Number's personality traits online or in numerology books.

Step 5: Interpret Your numbers

Now that you have your Life Path and Expression Numbers, it's time to interpret them. You can use numerology books and websites or consult a numerology expert to better understand your numbers. You can also use your intuition and reflect on your own experiences to connect with the meanings of your numbers.

Numerology isn't just a belief system. It is a comprehensive spiritual guideline for anyone looking to the universe for guidance. By understanding numerology, you can learn how numbers' symbolic meanings relate to your life. Angel numbers are a specific subset of numerology, and by learning the basics of numerology, you can begin to recognize the significance of these angel numbers and interpret their messages. So, essentially, learning everything you can about numerology is the first step in unlocking the secrets of angel numbers and connecting with the spiritual realm.

Chapter 3: Angel Numbers Interpreted

You likely came across angel numbers at some point and felt that the universe was trying to tell you something. Maybe a number combination kept popping up repeatedly in your life. You will know for sure if you're dealing with angel numbers when the appearance of these numbers starts becoming repetitive and doesn't feel like just a coincidence anymore. Maybe you looked up the meaning of the number combination you kept seeing and came up with an interpretation. But stop right there. Interpreting angel numbers isn't as simple as looking up the meaning of a word you found difficult. Interpreting these divine messages is an art form that needs a delicate balance of intuition and knowledge.

Each angel number has a deep meaning that you need to identify.[76]

Sure, you can look up the meanings of the different numbers and their combinations, but that's just scratching the surface of the deep, deep rabbit hole that is angel numbers. Learning the different meanings of angel number combinations is just the tip of the iceberg, and only when you go beyond this will you fully interpret what they are exactly trying to tell you. The real magic starts happening when you interpret these numbers based on your unique perspective and experiences. Your situation, the context behind your dilemma, and your particular position about a matter all play into the final interpretation of your divine message. This chapter is about helping you learn the art of interpreting angel numbers while considering the factors mentioned above. But first, you should understand the basic meanings of the most commonly seen sequences. Let's start!

1 - Unity

Number one is often seen as the symbol of unity and wholeness. In fact, it has a lot of spiritual significance and is usually taken as a good sign. It's considered the beginning of all things or the starting point from where things emerge. According to many angel number interpretation guides, repeating 1s is representative of divine support. It symbolizes a new phase of self-actualization or the chance for a new beginning. Consider it an opportunity if you encounter this number as an angel number, whether repeated twice, thrice, or four times. It means the energy around you is very conducive and perfect for taking healthy steps forward. Consider this a green light from the universe, and either make a wish, take a risk, plant a seed, set an intention, or shift a pattern. Seeing this pattern should signal that you have your angels' support and that the present is dynamically connected to the future.

For instance, consider a woman named Alice. She has been in a long-term relationship with her partner Bob. Lately, she's been feeling somewhat unsure about their future and wondering if she should continue or move on. Imagine she has been encountering the number sequence 1111 everywhere she goes. It's on license plates, the digital clock, and even her grocery receipt. In her case, this sequence suggests that she should move forward with her relationship. Maybe she needs to shift a pattern or set an intention for the relationship to move to the next step. As another example, consider John, an entrepreneur planning to start a new business. While this is his dream, there are a lot of setbacks and demotivating people all around him who make him doubt if this is the right decision. This is when the angel number sequence 111 starts appearing to him everywhere. In his case, the angel numbers tell him to follow through on his plans.

2 - Finding Balance

In many cultures, the number two is seen as a sign of duality, balance, diplomacy, and harmony. The idea of duality is why 2 is seen as a balanced number. It reflects the balance between opposing forces. Take male and female, yin and yang, light and dark, all opposite pairs associated with the number 2. As an angel number, when it appears in a set of 2, 3, or 4, it could indicate that you're on the right path in an area of your life. It's a confirmation from the angels that you're headed in the right direction and should keep moving forward. Although you might not see results right then, consider this the groundwork you're laying. On the other hand, the appearance of this number could also signal a harmonious partnership, whether romantic, platonic, or professional. So, you should open yourself up to camaraderie, love, and trust whenever you see this angel number.

3 - Creativity and Artistic Expression

The number three indicates believing in yourself, your talents, wisdom, and creativity. Why is this number associated with creativity? Because it's often connected to the three Muses in Greek mythology. These deities were said to inspire art and creativity. This number suggests that you stand your ground and be clear about what you want in life. Apply your unique talents in whatever situation you're in, and you'll be able to get through. The presence of this number, whether in a set of 2, 3, 4, or within a pattern, signifies that you should lean into your special abilities and innate gifts to navigate your circumstances. In response, you'll get all the opportunities and resources needed to move forward.

For instance, assume you're having a tough time in your career. Maybe you've been applying to different jobs only to be rejected or ignored time and time again. Maybe you're starting to feel useless. Now, imagine you start to see the number 333 everywhere. You see it on your alarm clock and on your phone. In this case, the angels are guiding you toward success. This sequence reminds you to keep trying and to apply your unique abilities to your struggles to get successful.

4 - Stability and Structure

As an angel number, it signifies that you should ground yourself or are currently in the process of doing so. After accomplishing this, you may create a long-lasting infrastructure. This might apply to any situation, including a marriage, a home, or a company. If you have the angel number 4, don't hesitate to ask for assistance, especially if you're working on a long-term project that can't be finished independently. This will also assist in building a foundation of trust that will enable you to achieve greater success. Another meaning of 4 as an angel number, especially when it appears as 444, is that angels support you. People frequently see this sequence when they feel low and need some support.

5 - Freedom and Adventure

Five is often associated with the five elements of the universe: air, fire, water, earth, and spirit. It symbolizes the infinite possibilities that come with the combination of the five elements. You could also consider it a symbol of personal freedom and independence. When this number appears as an angel number sequence, it signals a future transformation or transition. Some major changes could be on the horizon, and instead of shying away from the dramatic changes you're going to go through, you should try to embrace the chaos if you have been feeling stuck, stifled, or experiencing a block. Seeing this sequence will shift the scales in your favor. Although, at the moment, it may seem like no changes are taking place within your life, these transformations are most definitely occurring behind the scenes. You might even feel like you have an invisible driving force that's pushing you toward these changes. Seeing a 555 pattern could also signify that you're not alone in whatever change you're going through. This pattern should remind you that, ultimately, you will get through whatever you're facing and come out the other side stronger.

Consider this example, Samantha is a single mother who has been feeling stuck in her dead-end job for years. She's been struggling to make ends meet and provide for her child. One day, she notices the number 555 repeatedly appearing on her clock, phone, and even on her social media feeds. Here, the sequence tells her that transformation and change are coming soon. Motivated by this, she takes it as a sign to take a leap of faith and pursue her dream of starting her own business. With the angels' guidance and her own abilities, she succeeds in achieving her goals.

6 - Unconditional Love

You've probably heard the misconceptions about the number six being associated with the Devil or other evil figures. However, as an angel number, sequence 666 signifies that the angels are supportive and empathetic with your situation. In fact, the number 6 is representative of beauty, balance, and grounding. Its energy is steady and nurturing. For that reason, this angel number should bring you feelings of comfort and relief. If you see it, remember to treat yourself kindly, compassionately, and with understanding. This sequence is also meant to remind you that although things didn't go according to how you planned, with the guidance of angel numbers and divine support, things will work out just fine in the end. You may also see this number if you're trying to bring peace, balance, and stability to an area in your life, whether it's your career, family, or finances. This number also encourages you to give yourself a break and stop working too hard. It could also signal that you need to let go of things that aren't serving you and may be dragging you down.

7 - Trusting Intuition and Spirituality

Everyone knows seven is a lucky number, especially when it appears as an angel number. It is also often connected with your spirituality and might appear when you focus on it or incorporate new practices into your life. Consequently, this number is related to pure divine guidance. It's all about serving the world and honoring the spiritual concept that binds you to the world. When you see this number repeatedly, it can be a sign that you are growing spiritually. It conveys that you should stay on this path. Seeing this number sequence could also be a sign that you may come into good fortune in the future, particularly financially.

8 - Abundance and Manifestation

The number eight is considered to be one of the most divine numbers. It's said to be even luckier than the number seven, especially regarding the financial aspect. Eight is also known as the angel number of abundance, which signals that the universe is going to send you more in terms of career, romance, or health. If you have an abundance of anything in your life, like money, love, or time, spread it around, and you'll likely be rewarded with even more. For people who have a belief in the afterlife, this angel number signals that their loved ones are watching over them and supporting them.

9 - Endings and New Beginnings

Nine is the final digit in numerology and is therefore considered to symbolize the end of a chapter in your life. Life is cyclical, and all things must come to an end. If you witness nine as an angel number sequence, it might mean that a meaningful journey is ending. This could include both good and bad experiences. This number appears to remind you that you should let go of things that have run their course instead of clinging to them. Although it might be difficult initially, you'll soon find out why ending things was important. If you see this angel number, know that this would be a great time to step out of your comfort zone, explore new opportunities, and expand your horizons.

Mirror Numbers

Mirror numbers can be called the Yin and Yang of numerology because they represent the ultimate balance and symmetry between two opposite sides. But what exactly are they? Mirror numbers are number sequences of 3 or 4 numerals that are the same when read backward. For instance, 121, 353, 1001, 1551, etc. See how the sequence remains the same even backward? Why are mirror numbers important? They are a special kind of angel number sequence that symbolizes a connection between the spiritual and physical worlds. They are a reminder that everything is connected and you're a reflection of the world around you.

To interpret mirror numbers, you should refer to the meanings of each one and then come up with a combined interpretation for the sequence. For instance, if you see the number sequence 1001 popping up everywhere, consider the meanings of 1 and 0. The number 1 reflects a chance for new beginnings, while the zero represents wholeness and spirituality. So, maybe this number sequence means that you've been given a new opportunity that you're pursuing by letting your spirituality guide you. Some common mirror number sequences include:

- **01:10** - this sequence suggests you have a blank page for new beginnings, love, or more. You have the chance to start over in an area of your life.

- **02:20** - this sequence points towards a good career or lucrative opportunity in the future.
- **05:50** - this particular mirror number sequence represents adventure.
- **10:01** - this is one of the most magical mirror numbers. If you come across this, make a wish.
- **12:21** - this sequence suggests that you should be more careful and conscious of your actions.
- **13:31** - this particular sequence is a reminder that you should be aware of the opportunities that are all around you.
- **14:41** - this powerful mirror number signals incoming love and passion.
- **15:51** - this sequence suggests that you are at the right place and that you should listen to your intuition and move forward.

Personal Interpretation

Why is personal interpretation so important when it comes to angel numbers? Well, think of it this way: Angel numbers are like snowflakes, and no two interpretations can be exactly alike. How so? The context of the situation matters a lot, and so does the timing of the sighting, the person's mood, and what thoughts are on their mind.

Consider two people who have been seeing the number sequence 444 for a few days in a row. Having just lost his job, the first person is in a state of worry and despair and is feeling hopeless. For this person, the appearance of the number 4 can be a reminder that they will soon achieve stability in their life. It could also be a sign that angels are watching over this person, giving them hope and comfort.

The second person keeps seeing the same number while on vacation in a tropical paradise. They feel relaxed and carefree, so this angel number sequence gently reminds them to stay grounded and focused. In this context, the appearance of the number 4 is a comforting affirmation that they're exactly where they're supposed to be.

The interpretation process for the same sequence can vary. Since this is a deeply personal process, everyone has different interpretations.

Tips for Interpreting Angel Numbers

So, how should you go about interpreting an angel number you've been seeing everywhere? There are some steps you can take to interpret the divine message you're being sent.

1. Focus on Your Thoughts

Before you can move on to discover the meanings of the numbers that appear to you, you need to consider your thoughts first. The meanings of angel number sequences can seem generic and even vague if you don't consider your thoughts and feelings. So, take a moment to reflect on your emotions and what you're thinking. What thoughts are stressing you out, or which emotions have you been feeling the most recently? These are all questions you should ask yourself before you jump into interpreting the meanings of numbers.

2. Consider the Context

The context of a situation is what shapes your interpretation. Suppose you don't consider the situation you're in when you see angel numbers. In that case, the interpretation will be incomplete and pretty much useless. Consider the context, circumstances, and situation you're dealing with. Maybe you're happy with a new relationship or confused about starting one. Maybe you're starting a new project but have doubts about it. Whatever the situation, the angel numbers should guide you through them, and you should therefore consider the link between the numbers and your situation.

3. Consider Combinations

Angel number sequences can appear in double, triple, and four-digit sets. How do their meanings differ? What's the difference between 333 and 3333? Does the meaning change or simply get amplified? Triple digits are power numbers, whereas four digits represent enlightenment and the need for trust. Yes, four-digit sets are more powerful than triple-digit sequences. So, consider this factor before you interpret the meanings of these sequences. You may also encounter a mirror number or number sequences like 2323. This is where you'll have to combine the meanings as discussed previously.

4. Keep a Journal

One of the best ways to interpret angel number sequences is by keeping a journal. Note down all the considerations and answers you come up with. Track any patterns or themes that are consistent with the angel numbers you're seeing. For instance, if you notice you keep seeing angel numbers related to creativity, note down any creative endeavors you're involved in. Write down the context, your thoughts, and anything else you feel is relevant.

5. Trust Your Intuition

Last but not least, trust your gut. Your intuition is a powerful tool, especially when it comes to interpreting angel numbers. If a number sequence speaks to you, consider its meaning and your particular situation. Then, come up with an interpretation that your intuition points towards, even if it doesn't seem like a great idea at the moment.

Interpretation is all about what's inside you, your guiding light, thoughts, feelings, and intuition. Your intuition should play a major role in what your interpretation turns out to be. As Paul Coelho said, "Intuition is really a sudden immersion of the soul into the universal current of life." Trust your intuition and let the universal current of life guide you toward understanding the hidden messages of angel numbers. Remember that the interpretation of angel numbers is a deeply personal process, and it is best to do it on your own. After all, it's unique to every person, and who better to understand you than yourself? So, whether you see double, triple, or four-digit sets, the meaning behind the angel number sequences and combinations will never be black and white.

Chapter 4: Other Signs of Angelic Presence

Angels are all around you, protecting, guiding, and teaching you. They are constantly sending messages, but more often than not, people don't notice the signs and think they are just random occurrences. However, nothing is random. Keep your eyes and heart open, and you will spot the messages you are meant to receive.

Angels are always around you. Once you're aware of the signs, this will become clearer to you."

This chapter covers various angelic signs and symbols and their meanings.

Unexpected Events

You take a day off from work because you must go to the bank. Before you reach your destination, your sister-in-law calls to tell you that your brother has had an accident and that he is in the hospital. You quickly drive there to find that your brother is fine. He only has a couple of bruises and no serious injuries. You are relieved, but it is too late to go to the bank, and you don't know what to do. You look at your phone to find multiple notifications from news apps; there was a shooting at the bank, and nine people were injured. You sit down in shock because you can't believe what happened. This could have been you. You are relieved. Strangely enough, your brother's accident saved your life.

You have probably experienced similar situations where an unexpected event changed your plans, only to find out later it was a blessing. This isn't a mere coincidence; it is the angels' presence in your life protecting you from harm. Sometimes, the angels create unexpected events to push you towards something that will benefit you or away from danger. Remember, angels can't directly interfere with your life since humans have free will. They will only send you symbols, hoping you will decode them and make the right choice.

Coincidences

A coincidence is a series of surprising and meaningful events that don't seem to be connected but are actually related. What seem like insignificant or random events can have a bigger and deeper meaning behind them.

For instance, you got laid off from your job. Even though you never liked it and you always wanted to do something else, you are still upset because you need the work. One day, you are doing your grocery shopping and find a new gym has opened near your home. You decide to join it. You go every day except for Saturdays. One week you get a bad cold and are sick all week. You start to feel better on Saturday, so you go to the gym. There you meet an old college friend. While catching up, you tell them you recently lost your job. Your friend exclaims, "What a coincidence! We have been looking for new people to hire. Why don't you come for an interview?" One week later, you have a new job.

Look at all the coincidences in this story. First, you get laid off, then decide to join the gym, but then you have a cold, so you change your schedule. You then meet an old friend who offers you a job. All of these aren't mere accidents but the work of angels to get you closer to your dream job. Look at your life. You will notice that many small and simple events led you to better things. Trust the process. The angels always have your best interest at heart.

Flashes of Light

Angels are made of light, so it makes sense that they send you flashes or sparkles to inform you of their presence. When one is nearby, you can suddenly see strong light in the corner of your eyes or experience visions of sparkles or shimmers. If you can still see these flashes with your eyes closed, an angel is right by your side. Take a deep breath and be present in the moment. Feel their angelic light around you and let it uplift and heal you.

This light often appears in different colors, depending on the angels communicating with you. It can also signify that the angels are watching over you and protecting you.

Each angel has their own light, but white light is often a symbol of your guardian angel either sending you a message or wanting to get your attention.

Angel Colors

- **Archangel Raphael:** Green
- **Archangel Michael:** Blue
- **Archangel Uriel:** Red
- **Archangel Zadkiel:** Purple
- **Archangel Chamuel:** Pink
- **Archangel Jophiel:** Yellow

Each color can also have a meaning behind it.

- Purple and blue - you are burned out and in need of a break to unwind
- Green symbolizes power
- Orange symbolizes optimism

Disclaimer: Flashes in your vision can result from a health condition. See your doctor whenever you experience this sensation. If there is no medical condition, this can be a sign from your guardian angel.

Bodily Sensations

Physical sensations often occur when an angel is near you. It is a sign of their presence and that they want to communicate with you. You will experience a tingling right above your head in an area called "the crown of the head." That area is connected to the angels' halos. You can also feel a gentle touch on your hand or a slight stroke on your hair, especially when you are sad, depressed, scared, or going through a tough time. The angels will come to comfort you and let you know that you aren't alone and that they will always be here for you. You will also experience these sensations while praying or meditating because, at those moments, your mind is clear, and you can see and feel things on a spiritual level.

As they surround you with their love and positive energy, an angel's presence will bring chills, goosebumps, or a warm feeling. They send you these signals to bring your attention to something, to confirm your thoughts and feelings, or as a sign that you are on your way to something great. For instance, if you experience goosebumps on a date, it can be a sign that this is the right person for you. If you experience chills during a job interview, it means that you will have a future in this place.

Scents

Have you ever experienced a sweet scent or a pleasant fragrance like fruits, flowers, perfume, or your favorite food? The smell will come out of nowhere without any reasonable explanation. This is an angel reaching out to communicate with you. If you notice that the scent is familiar, like the perfume of your late grandfather, it means that the angel is present with his spirit. The angels often approach you with scents that bring warm and loving memories to give you a positive experience.

Coins

Angels send you coins to let you know that your finances are about to improve and that the universe will reward you for all your good deeds. You can find coins in an old jacket, the street, your home, or any other unexpected place. If you find eleven cents, consider

Coins are symbols that the universe is going to reward you for your good deeds.[78]

yourself lucky since it is the most significant angel number. This can mean that something great is about to happen. A coin can also carry other messages, so observe all of its details, like the year and material, and you can find the answers you have been seeking. Whenever you find a coin, be happy, and thank the angels as your life is about to change for the better.

Feathers

White feathers are associated with angels, and they often use them to let you know they are nearby or to get your attention. Whenever you feel lost or alone, your guardian angel will send you a message of love and hope so you know everything will eventually be OK. The angels are aware of your struggles and are listening to your prayers. They understand that you need reassurance and want you to know that they are by your side and will always protect you. If you are struggling and about to give up on something, the feather can be a sign to keep going because things are about to get better.

You will usually find these feathers in random and unexpected places like your home, bag, car, or office.

Messages through People

Sometimes, angels will send you messages through other people who aren't even aware of it. These people can either be your friends, family, or complete strangers, like a waiter at a restaurant. They can tell you something you want to hear, especially when you are struggling with a decision or problem and looking for guidance.

Say you are walking down the street with many thoughts rushing through your head. Suddenly, an elderly lady walks by you and smiles, saying, "You will get through this." You might think that this is a random incident or that this woman is crazy, but it's actually a reassuring message your guardian angel sent to ease your concerns.

The angels can also send you warnings to keep you away from a dangerous path. For instance, you plan to get your cat neutered, and you have already found a vet and reserved an appointment. Your sister visits you a day before the operation and tells you that her neighbor's cat passed away while being spayed because the vet made a mistake. She tells you his name, and you realize it is the same vet who is going to neuter your cat. You quickly cancel the appointment and look for another clinic. The angels send you your sister on that day to warn you against the vet to protect your pet.

Voices

Hearing a loud disembodied voice means that misfortune is coming your way, so you must be careful. For example, you are about to cross the street when you hear a loud voice telling you to stop. You take a step back, and a car quickly drives by. Had you not heard the warning, the car would have hit you.

However, not all these messages are negative. Some can be positive. Many healthcare workers who spend time with patients at the end of their lives have said they heard the words "thank you" multiple times just before their patients die. This can be an angel thanking them for their sacrifice and for helping these people at a critical stage in their lives.

Disclaimer: Hearing voices can also result from a mental health condition. See your doctor whenever you experience this sensation. If there is no medical or mental health condition, this can be a sign from your guardian angel.

Dreams

Angels prefer to appear to people in their dreams since it is the easiest way to reach them, and they can send them all kinds of signs and symbols. When you are awake and see a sign or hear a voice, you may question its validity. However, in the dream world, anything is possible, and people are more receptive to messages. Your guardian angel can warn you of a terrible event in the future, like a plane crash, car accident, or getting sick. You can also receive disturbing premonitions about the future. Knowing that something terrible is about to happen or that you or a loved one can be in danger is disconcerting and can cause you a lot of anxiety. However, the angels don't want you to be troubled. They want you to take all the necessary precautions to protect yourself.

Many survivors of terrible events like plane crashes have stated that they had nightmares before the incident. Pay attention to your dreams and if you have real ones that make you feel awful after you wake up, consider it a warning from the angels, and think carefully before making any decision or taking action.

Uncomfortable Feeling in the Solar Plexus

The solar plexus is the third of the seven chakras and is located in the naval area. The angels use this area of the body to send you warning signs since it is very sensitive, and you can easily feel any change or tingling in it. You can feel discomfort, tightening, nausea, or butterflies. You often experience This gut feeling when something doesn't feel right. Always pay attention to your body and never ignore these sensations. Once you experience something, be vigilant.

Say you have a job interview, and the moment you arrive at the company, you feel a tightening in your stomach. That can signal that this isn't the right place for you. You can also feel queasy or creeped out by certain people. That means they aren't good individuals and don't have your best interest at heart, so you should be careful whenever you are around them.

Don't be scared of these warnings; they are meant to provide guidance and alert you to negative people, places, and events.

Disclaimer: Discomfort or tightening in your chest area or feeling nauseous could be the result of a health condition. See your doctor whenever you experience this sensation. If there is no medical condition, this can be a sign from your guardian angel.

Car Trouble or Delays

Angels often use unexplainable car troubles to get your attention, teach you a lesson, or keep you away from harm. They only want to slow you down for a few minutes or hours until the danger passes. For example, you are on your way to the airport, but your car breaks down, delaying you for twenty minutes. When you arrive, you find that you missed your flight. You are angry and frustrated. However, you discover later that the plane crashed and there are no survivors. Your guardian angel only delayed you to save your life. Don't get angry whenever you miss any opportunity. There is always a hidden meaning or a blessing behind it.

Songs

Angels use recurring songs to reach out to you and send you specific messages. For instance, the radio plays the same song daily on your way to work. Even when you shuffle music on Spotify, you constantly keep getting that one song. If this has ever happened to you, listen carefully to the lyrics and notice the theme, as they can have a meaning behind them. The songs can be reassuring, reaffirm your feelings, or make you feel better, especially if you are going through something. You are in an Uber and considering whether to break up with your boyfriend when the song "Get Another Boyfriend" by the Backstreet Boys plays, and this lyric gets your attention "Now this must come to an end, get another boyfriend." Some lyrics can be straightforward, while others provide a clue relating to your experience.

Temperature

If you feel a change in your body's temperature, you are probably surrounded by angels. You might experience pressure in the back of your neck, feel a tingle on your head, get chills, or feel cold. You might also feel like you are surrounded by a warm light. These sensations shouldn't distress or frighten you and can often feel like a normal experience. You will feel safe because you are in the presence of angels.

Rainbow

Whenever people witness a rainbow, they always feel they are in the presence of something magical. This beautiful natural phenomenon is associated with angels. Your guardian angel can send you a message of love, support, and hope whenever you feel disconnected from the universe or if nothing is going your way. They want to open your eyes to the beauty of nature and remind you that there is so much in life to live for and enjoy. The rainbow is always a symbol of beauty and positivity.

Ringing in Your Right Ear

Angels often communicate with you by making your right ear ring. That is because it is connected to the spirit world. Receiving a message in this ear will surely catch your attention. If the ringing is long and high-pitched, the angels want you to know they are with you and will guide you in all your future endeavors. A short, loud, and sudden ringing is usually a warning. Your guardian angel is worried about you and wants you to reevaluate your life. Perhaps you are about to make a bad decision, and the angels want you to slow down and take your time.

Disclaimer: A ringing in your right ear can result from a health condition. See your doctor whenever you experience this sensation. If there is no medical condition, this can be a sign from your guardian angel.

Clouds

Look up to the sky. There can be a message for you in the clouds. Spend some time in nature, sit silently, and watch the clouds. You can see shapes or symbols like flowers, hearts, or numbers. Those are positive messages sent to encourage and support you. You might find a shape that catches your attention or relates to your current struggles or experience. Say you are considering whether to propose to your girlfriend or not, and you see a heart in the cloud. That indicates that proposing is the right decision.

Direct Messages

Some of the signs can be clear and straightforward and appear in the form of text. Books, billboard signs, ads, or blogs can provide answers to questions you have been pondering. For instance, a book falls from your shelf and opens on a specific page. When you read it, you find that it's a passage that relates to something significant in your life. If you keep seeing the same text in various places, this can be a message worth pondering.

Phone Calls

You are sitting watching TV, and an old high school friend comes to mind. Suddenly, your phone rings, and it is that friend. This isn't a coincidence or a random incident. Your guardian angel has prompted this person to call you because they can give you advice on a current issue, or you just need this person in your life right now.

Pets and Babies

Animals and babies are able to see into the spiritual world. Have you ever seen your pet following around something invisible or your baby smiling for no reason? They are probably looking at an angel.

Animals

Many animals, like dragonflies, butterflies, robins, and hummingbirds, are connected to angels. If you randomly encounter any of them, it can be a message from your guardian angel. Seeing a robin in an unexpected place can mean that the spirit of a loved one is resting in peace and is in a better place.

Strong Intuition

Whenever you are in the presence of an angel, you will feel more alive. Everything around you will look more beautiful and colorful, and your intuition will be heightened. Your gut feeling will always be right, and you will have the ability to feel other people's emotions and empathize with them.

You Aren't Alone

Have you ever felt that you aren't alone and that someone is in the room with you? Perhaps you feel that someone is sitting next to you on the couch or lying beside you in bed. However, this doesn't bother or scare you. An angel's presence will make you feel loved, safe, and warm. You will often experience this sensation when you feel misunderstood, isolated, or stressed. Your guardian angel wants you to know that you are never alone and they are always walking beside you.

You are loved, supported, guided, and never alone. These are the most common messages angels want to convey. Your guardian angel will never give up on you. They will keep sending you symbols and signs to provide assistance in every aspect of your life.

Each symbol they send has a meaning behind it, but only you can decode it. Think of them in the context of your personal experiences, and you will surely find the answers you seek.

Chapter 5: Angelic Symbols and Sigils

Since this book heavily embraces symbolism, the topic of angelic symbols is inevitable. This chapter introduces the symbols and sigils of a variety of angels (putting high emphasis on the Archangels). It also provides several exercises like meditations, prayers, and other forms of spiritual practices that can be used with angelic symbols and sigils.

What Are Angelic Symbols, Signs, and Sigils?

Many people view angelic signs and symbols as a way to identify if and how an angel is communicating with them. However, they can also be quite useful if you want to call on an angel and connect with them. As spiritual beings, angels act as messengers between people and entities on a higher spiritual level. Therefore, they require specific means of communication, a unique language of symbols. Whether you seek their assistance to resolve an issue in your life, comfort, or guidance for moving forward with your life, angelic symbols, and sigils can help you get your message across. Working with angelic symbolism in conjunction with mindfulness exercises and techniques that empower spiritual growth is recommended. Suppose you notice a specific symbol or sign appearing around you. In that case, you can decipher its meaning through meditation, similar mindfulness, and growth-inducing exercises.

Angelic sigils and symbols depict the entity or force associated with them. They are simple patterns made to represent specific intentions or names. The sigil of an Archangel is also viewed as their signature, as these beings specialize in specific forms of assistance they can provide. Not only are the sigils for Archangels derived from letters of names of entities they represent, but they also often look like a monogram.

Symbols Associated with Angels

Here is a list of some well-known angels and their symbols.

Archangel Michael

Archangel Michael is a warrior; many symbols indicate protection and guidance.[79]

As the leader of all Archangels, Michael is depicted as a Warrior of Light. His symbols include:

- **A sword:** It depicts the cutting of bonds from evil and protection from harm. It also expresses strength and courage.
- **Personal items of empowerment:** The angel can guide you on your path to success with many tools. You can use any tool that represents strength, protection, integrity, courage, or success to you.
- **Money:** Financial empowerment and security.
- **Doorways and crossroads:** As the most powerful angel, Michael can shield you and open any door for you.
- **A spear:** This has a similar significance as the sword. It gives you spiritual strength, courage, and protection. It also helps you overcome difficulties or find a new direction in life.
- **Red tape:** This is often depicted on top of the sword or spear but can also appear alone. It spiritually empowers you or your tools.

Archangel Uriel

Often said to be the wisest of all Archangels, Uriel is known for his bright intellect. He can also serve as a source of inspiration, help resolve urgent issues, and empower your magical skills.

Uriel can be symbolized by:

- **Light:** The angel is known as the Prince of Light, and his brightness can illuminate your path toward a happy and fulfilling life. Candlelight is the most well-known symbol of Uriel.
- **A scale:** This item denotes that Uriel can help you resolve dilemmas and find the appropriate answers for difficult moral or spiritual questions.
- **Personal items of joy:** With the right tool, Uriel can help you find joy in life. You can use anything that brings you happiness.
- **Tools for divination:** Being a wise angel, Uriel can provide you with transformative ideas during divination. These can be any tools that help you gain information about the past, present, or future.

- **Tools for spiritual enlightenment:** Items you use for spiritual empowerment can also represent Uriel.
- **A sword:** Sometimes, Uriel is depicted with a sword. It indicates he can help you make urgent decisions and resolve your problems.

Archangel Raphael

The kindest of all angels, Archangel Raphael is an incredibly gentle being who can heal your mind, body, and soul. Also known as the Angel of Providence, he can help you chase away anxiety and depression and overcome despair even during the most trying of times.

Raphael is symbolized by:

- **Items representing self-love:** You can use these items to remind you of your strengths and values.
- **Alabaster jar:** Indicating Raphael's ability to provide healing or relief from traumas affecting you or your loved ones. You can use any type of jar that can hold medicine.
- **Wounded or healed animals:** Raphael is also believed to be kind to animals, and using animals that need healing or have recently healed can be a great way to connect with this angel.
- **Items representing personal safety:** Raphael can help you stay safe during your travels and risky ventures.
- **Donations:** Giving back to the community can also be an excellent way to build a connection to this Archangel.

Archangel Gabriel

The Archangel Gabriel is linked to communication, purity, and the protection of your space. He can help you cleanse your thoughts, emotions, and resulting actions.

Gabriel is symbolized by:

- **A trumpet:** Depicting the divine voice and the messages that carry good news and promise change for the better.
- **Books and literature:** Gabriel is the guardian of your thoughts, words, and behavior. Using the right piece of literature to express your feelings, you can summon him to your aid when you feel hurt, agitated, or confused.

- **Mail, news, and other symbols of communication:** Using these, you can get Gabriel to provide you with some good news in tough times.
- **The four elements:** Linked to transformation and the purity of nature. These are traditionally used for home protection.
- **Mirrors:** They illustrate divine wisdom and a hidden mystery. They are great for self-reflection and discovering your inner power.
- **A lantern:** It empowers spiritual works and helps protect you, your space, and your loved ones. A lantern with a light flickering inside can also depict the heart, the core of a family home that keeps the family together.

Archangel Metatron

Known for his quick thinking ability, the Archangel Metatron is usually symbolized by lightning. This depicts how the angel can guide you when making fast and critical decisions. It can help you get to the core of the matter fast and without risking making a misstep. With this symbol, you will always have the security of Metratron guiding you in the right direction.

Archangel Raziel

As the Archangel associated with magic, Raziel is a source of inspiration for any type of magical or spiritual work. You can use cauldrons, spellbooks, wands, and other tools of magic and symbols to summon Raziel when you feel stuck or don't know how to overcome a challenge in magical or spiritual work. Items or people you find inspiring for your pursuits can also be used to connect with Raziel.

Archangel Sandalphon

This is the Archangel that offers clarity when you're at a crossroads. He can also provide protection from evil spiritual influences. Salphadon is symbolized by:

- **White candles:** They counteract dark energies.
- **Salt:** It can purify your mind, body, soul, and tools from negative energies.
- **Purifying herbs:** They cleanse you and your space from confusing or negative thoughts and influences.

Archangel Jegudiel

Known as the divine Glorifier, Jegudiel is the Archangel of clarity. He is symbolized by:

> **A golden wreath:** Holding this symbol in your right hand, you can summon this angel to gain clarity and see things in a better light.

Working with Angelic Symbols and Sigils

When you work with angels, remember that you might require a different form of assistance at specific times of your life. Archangels have distinctive areas in which they can offer aid, whereas lesser angels might help you in various matters. Your guardian angel might guide you toward a better path, or if they can't help you, they will offer direction to an Archangel.

While your guardian angel can be called on for anything you need – at any time – it is best to invoke an Archangel only when you've got an urgent need and are prepared to make powerful changes in your life. Be clear with your intent when deciding which symbols or sigils to use. The more specific your intention is, the more suitable your choice of symbols will be, and the better an angel will be able to respond in turn.

Whether you use the symbols alongside prayers, meditation, or another spiritually empowering exercise, choose the one that feels right and works for you based on your values.

Arm yourself with patience when using angelic symbols and sigils. For beginners, they rarely will work instantly. In most cases, you'll need lots of practice and repetition. The changes will begin to appear more slowly. Depending on what is best for you at any moment of your life, you might need to wait a significant amount of time until you see the results of your work. However, trust the angels to bring the best possible outcome for you, even if you initially find it confusing.

Angelic Sigils

A sigil is a symbol corresponding to specific angels, although they're typically used to call on higher beings like Archangels. While there are premade sigils, these are designed based on their general meaning and significance to the author. Of course, you can use them to better understand angelic sigils, but making your own will create a more personal connection to the angels. Whether you opt for copying ready-made sigils or creating your own, your first step is to learn how to draw a sigil. Once you master this, you can charge the sigil with the energy of the associated Archangel.

Here is how to create angelic sigils:

1. Take a premade template or create your own. Either way, you'll use the letters of the name of the Archangel you'd like to invoke or the intention that corresponds with the angel.
2. For example, to call on Archangel Michael first, write down the letter M, the first letter of his name. Then repeat until you reach the last letter. Similarly, if you want protection, you start by writing down the letter P.
3. After writing all letters in the intention or name, connect them by drawing lines between them. It's up to you in which format you write the letters or the connecting lines.
4. Once you've connected all of the letters, your sigil is finished.

It's crucial to remember that working with angelic symbols and sigils is highly personal and subjective. A sign that holds significance for one person can be entirely meaningless to another. Trust your intuition and inner guide when interpreting and using angelic symbols and sigils. Also, remember that angels often use distinct symbols to communicate with you at different times, depending on your unique needs and circumstances. It's critical to remain open-minded when working with angelic symbolism. Even the same sign and sigil can have different meanings depending on the circumstances. Sometimes, the significance of a symbol will be more direct. Other times, it will be subtle and open to interpretation. Angelic symbols and sigils can be excellent tools for gaining insight and guidance from angels. The knowledge you gain will aid your spiritual growth and help you navigate your life with ease. By combining these signs with spiritual exercises, you'll learn to trust the angels and yourself more, which will help you overcome any challenge and achieve any goal in life.

How to Use Your Angel Sigil

In most cases, you will need a ritual to prepare your mind to focus on the specific sigil. This involves letting your intent known and calling out an angel's name three times to open the line of communication. Lace your intention with hope and have an open heart, as this helps form an unbreakable link between you and the angel. It creates an organic bond that enables you to work with them freely.

Bringing Angelic Energy into Your Life

As you've seen above, to bring the energy of an Archangel into your life, you must create a sigil by arranging the letters of their name or specialty into an easily visualized symbol. The second step is to imprint the sigil into your subconscious.

Here is how to do it:
1. Gaze into the sigil and repeat its name.
2. Focus on your breathing and keep repeating the sigil's name until it becomes a mantra.

Next, you'll need to connect it to the angel:
1. Draw the sigil on a piece of paper and place it on your altar, surrounding it with crystals, the representation of the angel, and their correspondences.
2. Focusing on the sigil and the angel's name, summon them.

Once you've established the connection between the angel and the sigil, you'll need to repress your conscious memory of the symbol. Make a deliberate effort to forget about it, as sigil work can be influenced by the desires and thoughts of the conscious mind.

Ritual for Better Focus

You can summon an angel by focusing on the sigil and envisioning it being connected to the angel's essence during meditation. You can use their power to empower yourself with better focus during the exercise and gain mental clarity to manifest your intent.

Instructions:
1. On a piece of paper, draw the sigil.
2. Next, light the candles and place them in front of you. Turn off all artificial lights.
3. Place the sigil between the candles.
4. Then, reflect on the meaning it has for you at that moment.
5. Visualize the sigil growing bigger and more brilliant, eventually glowing brighter than the candles around it.
6. Keep the image in front of you until you're comfortable or you gain the mental clarity you need.

Prayers to Archangels

When calling on an Archangel with a prayer, their symbol or sigil can serve as an excellent channeling tool. All you need is a clear intention and an open mind to interpret the messages you'll receive after contacting them.

Instructions:

1. Start by setting clear intentions. Define what you want to obtain by invoking an Archangel; remember, they all have their specialties. For example, call on Archangel Michael if you require spiritual protection and empowerment.
2. The next step is ensuring that you're properly calling on them. If you haven't worked with the angel before, tap into your intuition and see whether you have the correct tools.
3. Once you've defined your intention and know that you're using adequate tools, you can address the angel with the following prayer:

   "Dear (the Archangel you wish to invoke).

   I stand here as your humble follower.

   I ask you to (the angel's specialty).

   Please come to me and send your divine blessings to those I care about."

Meditation Tools

There are several ways you can use angelic symbols and sigils for meditation. Here are some suggestions on what to do when meditating with angelic symbols:

- Express gratitude for the angel's presence in your life and the messages they send you.
- Thank the angel for their guidance and support. Reiterate your trust in their ability to shield and direct you through challenging times.
- Ask for guidance and support if you need it at that specific time.
- Express your desire to deepen your connection with an angel.
- Tap into your intuition to hone in. This will help you trust it more when deciding which symbols and sigils to use or interpreting the ones the angels send you.

- If you are unsure of which action to take after communicating with an angel, use mediation to contact them again to clarify whether they want to make a change, be more present, or take another action.

Instructions:
1. Sit comfortably and take the angelic sigil or symbol into your hands.
2. Focus on taking deep breaths and empty your mind of all thoughts.
3. Visualize an angel (or symbol or sign) in your mind's eye. Imagine them as powerful beings of light.
4. Then, ask them to encircle you with their essence and protection.
5. Remain in this state for as long as you feel comfortable.
6. When you're finished, thank the angel for his presence.

Using Angelic Symbols and Sigils as Charms

Another way to use angelic symbols and sigils is to carry them as talismans or charms. You can wear them as a bracelet, necklace, or earrings or keep them in your pocket. These are all great ways to keep a symbol (and its power) close to your personal space. While most charms and talismans are used for luck and protection, you can also hold them during meditation and other mindfulness exercises. You can empower the symbols and sigils with intent, and looking at the object will remind you of your intention anytime you need it. Charms and talismans can also be displayed in your space. This works great if you need an angel's power to protect your home or workspace or require guidance in matters that concern these spaces. Whether you display them on your altar and use them as a channeling tool to invoke angels or on a table or shelf where you spend a lot of time, they'll remind you of the angel's presence and power.

Clarification Meditation and Prayer

If you are unsure what a specific symbol you've encountered means or which sigils you should use to contact an angel, you can ask the angels themselves. Keep the signs you discover or learn from angels in a journal to track your experiences. Once you understand the meaning of the signs, note them as well in the journal.

Instructions:

1. Sit comfortably and take the chosen sigil or symbol into your hands.
2. Focusing on bringing an angel close to you, address them with the following prayer:

    "Dear angel, I invite you into my hearth and home.

    Please surround me with your love, light, and protection.

    Help me interpret the symbols I encounter and use.

    Guide my intuition to uncover the meaning I need.

    Help me understand them with clarity and wisdom.

    Please bless me with the strength and courage I need

    To follow the instructions, I can gain through the symbols and sigils.

    Help me trust the symbols to lead me toward my purpose.

    Thank you for the support and blessings you've bestowed upon me.

    I trust in your guidance."

3. After reciting the prayer, meditate as long as you need to gain clarity on a specific symbol or sigil.
4. Feel the angel's presence fill you with peace, love, and understanding as you meditate. Feel their guidance and protection.
5. Once you've gained clarity on a symbol, use it according to its meaning to you at that specific time in your life.

Chapter 6: Synchronicity, Divine Timing, and Coincidence

Do you always happen to look at the time when it's 11:11? Perhaps you've seen a specific sequence of numbers multiple times throughout your day. These are known as angel numbers and are believed to be messages from the divine realm. Angel numbers are often associated with synchronicity and divine timing, as they tend to appear during significant moments in life. Some may dismiss them as mere coincidences, but those who believe in the power of angel numbers see them as a sign of guidance and support from the universe.

This chapter will explore the concepts of synchronicity, divine timing, and coincidence. It will examine the history and theory of synchronicity, along with instructions on how to manifest it. It will also discuss the concept of divine timing and its connection with free will versus fate, as well as list various signs which indicate divine timing. Lastly, it will define what a coincidence is, set it apart from synchronicity, and list the various categories of synchronicity with examples. Ultimately, this chapter will help you understand these concepts and how to use them for self-exploration and spiritual growth.

Embracing Synchronicity: Aligning Your Actions with the Universe

Do you ever find yourself experiencing coincidences that seem too perfect to be mere chance? Maybe you were thinking about someone, and then they called you out of the blue. Or, you stumbled on a book that addressed a problem you were struggling with after silently wishing for answers. These meaningful and seemingly impossible coincidences are called synchronicities and are believed to be powerful signs from the universe. This section will explore synchronicity's history, theory, manifestation, and how-tos. With this knowledge, you'll be better equipped to align your actions with the universe and transform your life meaningfully.

History and Theory

Swiss psychiatrist Carl Jung first introduced synchronicity in the 1920s. Jung noticed that certain coincidences were too significant to be explained by chance and believed these events had psychological significance. He coined the term *synchronicity* to describe them and emphasized the importance of paying attention to them as they could reveal deeper insights about the unconscious mind.

Carl Jung introduced the concept of synchronicity.[80]

The theory of synchronicity depends on the concept of the collective unconscious, which is a reservoir of experiences and psychic knowledge shared by all humans. According to Jung, synchronicity occurs when two events, one from the individual's unconscious and another from the collective unconscious, align meaningfully. For instance, an individual struggling to make a decision may encounter a stranger who unknowingly can provide insight into the matter.

Today, synchronicity remains relevant in modern spiritual practices. Meditation, for example, can help individuals increase self-awareness and tap into their unconscious minds for insights. Tarot card reading and astrology are other practices that use the principles of synchronicity to provide guidance and enlightenment. These practices allow individuals to embrace the randomness of life and welcome synchronicities as a means of growth and development.

The power of synchronicity in spiritual practices is not limited to self-discovery alone. Consistently experiencing synchronicities can indicate that an individual is on the right path and can provide reassurance that their goals and objectives are aligned with their purpose. Being open to synchronistic events, even if they seem insignificant, can lead to profound shifts in perspective and greater faith in the universe's ability to guide and support.

Manifestation of Synchronicity

Synchronicity manifests in several ways, including coincidences, telepathy, dreams, and symbols. For example, synchronicity could be experienced when you keep seeing the same sequence of numbers over and over again. Other times, it could appear in your relationships by meeting someone with the same name or birthday. It can even manifest through life-changing events like job opportunities, discovering a newfound passion, or a chance encounter.

Synchronicity can sometimes be as simple as seeing the same number repeatedly or meeting someone with the same name as you. Other times, it can lead to significant discoveries and breakthroughs in your personal and professional life.

Aligning with Synchronicity

Aligning with synchronicity is about cultivating an open mind and heart regarding the universe's signs. When you are open to possibilities and opportunities, the universe sends you synchronistic events that align with your path. You can practice aligning with synchronicity by trusting your intuition, listening to your gut, and paying attention to signs and symbols. Cultivating a daily practice such as meditation or journaling can help you become more self-aware and tuned into the universe's messages.

How to Harness the Power of Synchronicity

To truly take advantage of the power of synchronicity, you must learn to co-create with the universe. This means taking inspired action toward your goals but also allowing the universe to guide you through synchronistic events. You can practice co-creating by setting intentions, clearly defining your goals, and taking action. With this approach, opportunities and synchronicities will begin to appear in your life in no time.

When tuned into the world around you, you'll be more likely to recognize patterns and make connections you may have missed before. You can also try practicing meditation or visualization techniques to help you focus your mind and connect with your intuition. Another essential aspect of synchronicity is being aware of your thoughts and emotions. If you're fixated on negative feelings and beliefs, you'll be more likely to attract negative experiences. On the other hand, if you focus on positivity and abundance, you'll be more open to synchronistic events that bring you happiness and fulfillment.

Benefits of Embracing Synchronicity

Embracing synchronicity has the potential to enhance all aspects of your life. When you begin to pay attention to the subtle cues and follow the signs from the universe, you'll notice that opportunities for personal and professional growth arise more frequently. As a result, life becomes more abundant, and you'll experience fewer struggles. You'll also notice that synchronicity brings people who are aligned with your values and vision into your life, making your relationships more meaningful.

- **Shift Your Perspective:** Embracing synchronicity can help you shift your perspective on life. It can help you see the hidden meaning behind events and circumstances. This shift allows you to stay positive in difficult situations and see the opportunities that come your way. By embracing synchronicity, you learn to see life as a journey filled with wonder, curiosity, and discoveries. You learn to trust that the universe is conspiring to bring you to your highest good.

- **Experience More Positivity and Optimism:** Embracing synchronicity can also bring more positivity and optimism into your life. By seeing the connections between events, you begin to believe that everything happens for a reason. This belief can lead to a more positive attitude toward life. You begin to see challenges as opportunities for growth and learning. You learn to trust that everything will work out in the end. This positivity and optimism can help you attract more positive experiences and people into your life.

- **Lead a Happier and More Fulfilling Life:** By seeing the connections between events and circumstances in your life, you begin to see the bigger picture of your life story. You begin to understand that everything that has happened to you, good or bad, has led you to where you are today. By trusting synchronicity, you can let go of worry and doubt and embrace life's adventures, leading to a greater sense of peace, purpose, and happiness.

- **Connect With Others:** By seeing the connections between events in your life, you begin to see the connections between you and others. You begin to realize that we are all in this together, experiencing similar challenges and triumphs. This can lead to a greater sense of empathy and compassion. By seeing the connections between ourselves and others, we can build more meaningful relationships and create a more compassionate world.

- **Helps you Trust the Universe:** Finally, embracing synchronicity can help you trust the universe. By seeing the connections between events in your life, you begin to trust that everything is happening for a reason. You begin to trust that the universe is working to bring you to your highest good. By trusting the universe, you can let go of worry and doubt and embrace the adventure of life.

The Power of Divine Timing: Understanding Universal Rules and Free Will

Have you ever had a moment when everything seemed to line up perfectly? A moment when you achieved exactly what you always wanted, or an unexpected opportunity appeared that changed your life completely? That is the power of divine timing. It's the universe's way of orchestrating events to perfectly align with your highest good. This section will explore divine timing, the universal rules governing it, and the age-old debate of free will versus fate.

Definition

Divine timing refers to the idea that the universe has a plan for your life and that everything happens when the time is right. It's the belief that nothing in your life happens by chance and that each moment unfolds precisely as it's meant to. Whether meeting the right person at the right time, getting a job offer that changes everything, or simply feeling a sense of flow, it's all part of the universe's plan for you.

Universal Rules of Divine Timing

We've all heard the saying "timing is everything," but have you ever stopped to think about how true that statement is? Many of us have experienced situations where things just seemed to fall into place at the exact right moment or where no matter how much we try to make something happen, it just doesn't seem to be the right time. This is because there are universal rules to divine timing that we all must follow, whether we are aware of them or not. These are the universal rules of divine timing and how you can use them to your advantage in your personal and professional life.

1. **Everything Happens in Its Own Time:** The first rule of divine timing is that everything happens when it is meant to happen. This means that you cannot force or rush anything in your life. If you try to make something happen before it is time, you will only create resistance and push it further away. Instead, trust that the universe has its timeline and that everything will come to fruition when it is supposed to.

2. **Everything Happens for a Reason:** Even the most difficult, painful moments have a purpose that may not be immediately clear. The universe has a way of using these moments to teach us valuable lessons and to help us grow and evolve. Understanding that everything happens for a reason can bring peace and acceptance to difficult times. The key is to try to stay open-minded and trust that the universe always has your best interests.

3. **Everything Is Interconnected:** The universe constantly works to create harmony and balance, so things often fall into place when we least expect it. This is because everything in the universe is interconnected, and when one thing is out of balance, it often leads to something else falling into place. Pay attention to the subtle cues and synchronicities that appear in your life. They could be guiding you toward something bigger. Following the clues can lead you to unexpected opportunities that could completely transform your life.

4. **The Universe Supports Your Desires:** The universe constantly works to bring you closer to your desires, but sometimes that takes time. When you focus on what you want and take action, the universe will support you every step of the way. It's just a matter of trusting in the process and being patient. You will eventually be rewarded with what you seek when you align with your desires.

5. **The Law of Attraction:** This universal law states that what we focus on and think about will eventually come into our lives. This means that if you are constantly worrying and thinking negative thoughts, you will create more of the same in your life. However, staying focused on what you want and keeping your thoughts positive will create the opportunities needed to manifest your desires.

It can be easy to get caught up in comparing our lives to others and feeling like we are not where we are supposed to be. But the truth is that we are all on our unique paths and timeline. Trust that the timing of your life is perfect and that everything is happening as it should. Remember that setbacks and challenges are only temporary and are necessary for growth and learning.

Understanding the Age-Old Debate of Free Will Versus Fate

This debate has been raging for centuries. Philosophers, religious leaders, scientists, and even writers have discussed this age-old argument between determinism and the notion of individual control. But what exactly is free will, and how does it differ from fate?

Free will is the ability to make choices that are not predetermined. It's the notion that we can make decisions that are not influenced by anything but our desires, values, and beliefs. It is often associated with the idea of personal responsibility and the ability to choose our destiny. On the other hand, fate is the belief that our life is predetermined and that there is nothing we can do to change our destiny. This means that no matter how much we try, our life will always follow a set path already laid out for us.

Despite their apparent differences, many philosophers suggest that free will and fate might not be mutually exclusive. For example, the concept of determinism suggests that past experiences and genetic makeup influence our actions and decisions. However, determinists do not necessarily believe that our lives are predetermined. Instead, they suggest that our choices are limited by factors we cannot control, such as environmental factors, social norms, and cultural values.

Another concept that supports the idea of free will and fate coexisting is the notion of compatibilism. Proponents of compatibilism argue that free will and determinism are not mutually exclusive but work together to shape our decisions and actions. They suggest that, even if external factors influence our choices, we can still act freely if we believe that we are making our own decisions based on our desires and beliefs.

Despite the arguments presented by determinists and compatibilists, many people still hold on to the belief in personal control and free will. They believe that they are the sole drivers of their life and that their actions significantly impact the outcome of their lives. These individuals are more likely to take responsibility for their decisions and are less likely to be influenced by external factors.

The debate between free will and fate is complex and cannot be easily or neatly resolved. While some believe life is predetermined, others argue that people can shape their destiny through their choices. While we may never know the answer to this age-old question, what is essential is that we continue to make our own decisions and strive to take control of our lives. After all, in the end, our choices shape who we are and ultimately determine the course of our lives.

Coincidences

Have you ever experienced a moment when something you were thinking about suddenly happened? Or a time when you ran into someone you were just thinking about? These moments are what we call *coincidences*, and they happen to us quite often. At times, these coincidences can be so eerie that they leave us in amazement, wondering if there's a higher force at work. Let's explore the world of coincidences and synchronicities and what they mean.

Definition

Coincidence is a remarkable occurrence of two or more events or circumstances happening simultaneously without any apparent causal connection. Simply put, it's when two things happen simultaneously by chance. Coincidences are often seen as random occurrences, but some people believe in the idea of synchronicities or meaningful coincidences.

The Difference between Coincidences and Synchronicities

Unlike coincidences, Carl Jung believed synchronicities had a deeper meaning or purpose. Synchronistic events are experiences where there is no direct causal relationship between two or more seemingly related events, but they occur together in a way that is meaningful to the person experiencing them. In simpler terms, while coincidences are random occurrences, synchronicity is the universe's way of sending us signs and messages.

Categories of Synchronicities

While synchronicities may seem random, they often fall into distinct categories that can shed light on their deeper meaning. This section will explore three categories of synchronicities, including acausal parallelism, simultaneity, and unfolding.

1. **Acausal Parallelism:** This category of synchronicity involves a meaningful coincidence between two events that have no causal relationship. For example, you may be walking down the street and cross paths with a stranger who happens to be wearing the same shirt as you. While this may seem like a coincidence, it becomes more meaningful if you later discover that you and the stranger share a common interest or hobby. This type of synchronicity suggests that there is a deeper order or intelligence at work in the universe, guiding us towards connections and experiences that are meant to be.

2. **Simultaneity:** This type of synchronicity involves two or more events occurring simultaneously but not causally related. For example, you may be reading a book and come across a passage that mentions a specific song, only to hear that same song playing on the radio moments later. This type of synchronicity often feels like a sign or message from the universe, offering guidance or confirmation of your decision. It can also remind us that everything is connected and that we are part of a larger cosmic dance.

3. **Unfolding:** This category of synchronicity involves a sequence of events that unfolds over time, leading to a meaningful outcome. For example, you may have a series of unrelated dreams or encounters that later merge into a new opportunity or direction in your life. This type of synchronicity can be challenging to recognize at the moment, as it often requires

patience and trust that things are unfolding as they should. However, it can be a powerful reminder to stay open to new experiences and follow the path that feels right, even if it doesn't make sense at the time.

4. **Tone of Voice:** Lastly, synchronicities can also be categorized by the tone or feeling they evoke. For example, they can be upbeat and joyful, signaling a positive shift or alignment in your life. Conversely, they can be sobering or bittersweet, indicating a challenge or lesson that needs to be learned. Being attuned to the tone of synchronicities can help you understand their meaning and interpret the message they hold for you.

Synchronicities are a fascinating and mysterious aspect of human experience, offering a glimpse into the deeper workings of the universe. By exploring the categories of acausal parallelism, simultaneity, unfolding, and tone, we can begin to make sense of these experiences and tap into their wisdom and guidance. Whether you view synchronicities as divine messages or simply random coincidences, they can be a powerful reminder of the interconnectedness and beauty of all things.

Coincidences and synchronicities are fascinating subjects that can't be fully explained. While some people believe these phenomena are random, others see them as meaningful events sent by the universe or a higher power. Whether coincidences or synchronicities, they remind us that we're all connected and that there may be forces beyond our understanding at work behind the scenes. Whatever the case may be, these experiences can bring us moments of joy, inspiration, and awe, and that alone makes them worth noticing. So, next time you encounter a coincidence or synchronicity, take a moment to appreciate the divine timing and see if it might hold a deeper meaning for you.

Chapter 7: Angelic Correspondences

So far, you've learned that angels are associated with numbers, sequences, symbols, and sigils. However, these aren't the only angelic correspondences that exist. Angels can also be linked to other items and concepts, like days of the week, hours of the day, zodiac signs, colors, months, gemstones, and more. This chapter goes over all these correspondences for several angels.

Michael

As the ruler of the Sun, Archangel Michael is associated with Sunday. Due to the Sun's influence, Michael can illuminate your path and inspire you in many aspects of your life. His abilities are also linked to your individual creative spirit. He is a magnificent source of empowerment and a guardian for those aiming to make a difference in the world. If you want to create something unique without compromising your values, Michael can help you with all your creative endeavors.

Flowers, herbs, and trees to use when working with Archangel Michael include angelica, tagetes, blueweed, sunflower, carnation, St John's wort, celandine, saffron, centaury, rowan blossoms, eyebright, peony, goldenseal, orange blossoms, heliotrope, marigold, hibiscus, chamomile, willow, red sandalwood, celandine, bay, cyclamen, calamus root, cowslip, hops, and mistletoe.

In Tarot, Michael is linked to the cards Strength and Judgment. This indicates his vast influence over the development of life. He governs your ambitions and your mental and physical development. Due to the influence of the Judgement card, Michel can greatly help those seeking repentance, fulfillment, or wanting to express righteousness or mercy. He can help you fend off evil influences but will also impart justice on souls when needed.

Other Associations

Hours of the day and night:

- The 1st and 8th hours of the day and the 3rd and 10th hours of the night on Sunday
- The 5th and 12th hours of the day and the 7th hour of the day on Monday.
- The 2nd and 9th hours of the day and the 4th and 11th hours of the night on Tuesday.
- The 6th hour of the day and the 1st and 8th hours of the night on Wednesday.
- The 3rd and 10th hours of the day and the 5th and 12th hours of the night on Thursday.
- The 7th hour of the day and the 2nd and 9th hours of the night on Friday.
- The 4th and 11th hours of the day and the 6th hour of the night on Saturday.

Element and mode: Fire - Fixed.
Season: Summer - Winter.
Month: August.
Metals: Gold.
Color: Yellow, yellowish green, gold, white.
Crystals: Golden topaz, citrine, diamond, clear quartz, opal, and amber.
Animals: Peacock, eagle, lion, griffin, and wolf.
Body part: Spine, heart, arms, and wrist.
Incense: Orange, olibanum, and frankincense.
Harmonious signs: Aries and Sagittarius.

Deities: Demeter, Venus, Vishnu, Selket, and Horus.
Ages ruled: All ages.

Gabriel

The Governor of the Moon, Archangel Gabriel, is associated with Monday. Due to the Moon's influence, this angel can bring increased spiritual awareness and elevate your mystical experiences, whether you're journeying to the spiritual world, astral travel, or doing dreamwork. He can also solidify your intent through prayer and meditation, especially if you're performing these under the moonlight, outside, and close to a body of water. He can help you establish deep spiritual connections in any environment, from work to community to close-knit family. Gabriel can also protect you when traveling across water, against bad weather, or when you feel sorrow. The Moon helps remove self-destructive tendencies and replace them with positivity for the new beginning.

Archangel Gabriel enhances your spiritual awareness.[81]

Flowers, herbs, and trees corresponding to Gabriel are chamomile, houseleek, poppy, moonwort, evening primrose, aloe vera, purslane, passionflower, honesty, watercress, mallow, weeping willow, yellow flag, jasmine, sweet flag, water lily, white lily, comfrey, white rose, lemon balm, lotus, and white poppy.

In Tarot, Archangel Gabriel is associated with The Hanged Man and The Chariot. Both cards indicate that this angel has tremendous influence over destiny, which is also underlined in the Moon's influence on Gabriel's work and abilities. Gabriel can establish the flow of life, whether it's a child from conception to early childhood or finding your purpose and direction in life. Gabriel's connection to the hanged man also alludes to the possible connection to higher spiritual knowledge and psychic abilities.

Other Associations:

Hours of the day and night:

- The 4th and 11th hours of the day and the 6th hour of the night on Sunday.
- The 1st and 8th hours of the day and the 3rd and 10th hours of the night on Monday.
- The 5th and 12th hours of the day and the 7th hour of the night on Tuesday.
- The 2nd and 9th hours of the day and the 4th and 11th hours of the night on Wednesday.
- The 6th hour of the day and the 1st and 8th hours of the night on Thursday.
- The 3rd and 10th hours of the day and the 5th and 12th hours of the night on Friday.
- The 7th hour of the day and the 2nd and 9th hours of the night on Saturday.

Element and mode: Water - Cardinal.

Season: Summer.

Month: January.

Metals: Silver and quicksilver.

Color: Amber and silver.

Crystals: Moonstone, turquoise, pearl, cat's eye, amber, opal, emerald.

Animals: Seagull, crab, turtle, sphinx.

Body part: Stomach, digestive tract, and breast area.

Incense: Jasmine, Onycha, and Myrrh.

Harmonious signs: Taurus, Scorpio, and Pisces.

Deities: Mercury, Apollo, and Khepera.

Ages ruled: 7 years.

Samael

Governing the planet Mars, Samael is associated with Tuesday. He is known for his righteous anger and ability to cleanse away negative influences. He can challenge you to prove that you are worthy of the sacred trust and shouldn't be summoned in inconsequential matters. He also bestows protection when you're feeling vulnerable and eliminates doubts and thoughts of weakness, replacing them with spiritual empowerment to stand against those who abuse power.

Flowers, herbs, and trees to use when working with Samael include gentian, geranium, thistle, gorse, snapdragon, hawthorn, common rue, High John the conqueror, gorse, pennyroyal, wormwood, tiger lily, cowslip, wild rose, chestnut, holly, pine, and sage.

In Tarot, Samael is linked to The Emperor and The Tower cards, which gives this angel an ambivalent quality. On the one hand, Samael is regarded as the angel and harbinger of death and is also said to be a magician. On the other hand, he hints at divine justice, an equally powerful male influence. Together, the two cards can put a lot of pressure on the angel and, in turn, on you.

Other Associations:

Hours of the day and night:

- The 7th hour of the day and the 2nd and 9th hours of the night on Sunday
- The 4th and 11th hours of the day and the 6th hour of the night on Monday
- The 1st and 8th hours of the day and the 3rd and 10th hours of the night on Tuesday

- The 5th and 12th hours of the day and the 7th hour of the night on Wednesday
- The 2nd and 9th hours of the day and the 4th and 11th hours of the night on Thursday
- The 6th hour of the day and the 1st and 8th hours of the night on Friday
- The 3rd and 10th hours of the day and the 5th and 12 hours of the night on Saturday

Element and mode: Fire - Cardinal.
Season: Spring.
Month: December.
Metals: Iron.
Color: Pink, red, white, and scarlet.
Crystals: Diamond, bloodstone, red jasper, ruby, and garnet.
Animals: Magpie, ram, owl, bull, and robin.
Body part: Face, neck, head, brain, and nervous system.
Incense: Dragons blood and allspice.
Harmonious Signs: Leo and Sagittarius.
Deities: Mars, Isis, Minerva, Athena, and Shiva.
Ages: 28-35 years.

Raphael

As the governor of Mercury, Raphael is linked to Wednesday. Due to the influence of this planet, Raphael is known for his protective and healing abilities. He can restore physical, emotional, or spiritual balance, chase away worrisome thoughts, and ground you to nature and the universe. Mercury is the planet of communication; through it, Raphael provides spiritual insights and lessens the negative impact of modern living on spiritual health.

Flowers, herbs, and trees to use to work with this Archangel are caraway, orchid, summer savory, clary sage, gladioli, pimpernel, clover, parsley, lily of the valley, lavender, dill, elecampane, iris, snapdragons, elder, mastic, sandalwood, jasmine, and lavender.

Corresponding to The Fool and The Lovers cards in Tarot, Raphael is the angel of wisdom, healing, and scientific discoveries. With this card,

Raphael can help you discover your true values and defend you against malicious influences. He can also teach you how to manifest your desires, end undesirable processes, or create challenges that will hone your skills and give you a chance to grow spiritually.

Other Correspondences:

Hours of the day and night:

- The 3rd and 10th hours of the day and the 5th and 12th hours of the night on Sunday.
- The 7th hour of the day and the 2nd and 9th hours of the night on Monday.
- The 4th and 11th hours of the day and the 6th hour of the night on Tuesday.
- The 1st and 8th hours of the day and the 3rd and 10th hours of the night on Wednesday.
- The 5th and 12th hours of the day and the 7th hour of the day on Thursday.
- The 2nd and 9th hours of the day and the 4th and 11th hours of the night on Friday.
- The 6th hour of the day and the 1st and 8th hours of the night on Saturday.

Element and mode: Air - Mutable.

Season: Winter - Spring.

Month: April.

Metals: Aluminum and quicksilver.

Color: Orange, white, and yellow.

Crystals: Yellow jasper, citrine, onyx, Iceland spar, topaz, diamond, jade, aquamarine, moss agate, and tourmaline.

Animals: Magpies, finches, and parrots.

Body part: Arms, lungs, and the respiratory system.

Incense: Wormwood, clover, and lavender.

Harmonious Signs: Libra and Aquarius.

Deities: Freya, Frey, Sekhmet, Janus, Bast, Pollux, and Castor.

Ages: 7-14 years.

Sachiel

Ruling over Jupiter, Sachiel is linked to Thursday. This indicates the angel's benevolent nature as he teaches that by giving back, you'll be able to meet your own needs much faster. He can also empower rituals designed to manifest abundant harvests, prosperity, the good of all, and physical and emotional security.

Some flowers, herbs, and trees corresponding to Sachiel are agrimony, wood betony, wood avens, valerian, borage, meadowsweet, cinquefoil, linden, dandelion, hyssop, honeysuckle, willow, heliotrope, elm, carnation, chicory, opium poppy, lilies, lilac, and sage.

In Tarot, Sachiel is paired with The Moon card, also governed by Jupiter. Through this card, the angel can bring you prestige, financial security, and social expansion. It's often a game changer in life and forces you to be patient to persevere in challenging times.

Other Correspondences:

Hours of the day and night:

- The 6th hour of the day and the 1st and 8th hours of the night on Sunday.
- The 3rd and 10th hours of the day and the 5th and 12th hours of the night on Monday.
- The 7th hour of the day and the 2nd and 9th hours of the night on Tuesday.
- The 4th and 11th hours of the day and the 6th hour of the night on Wednesday.
- The 1st and 8th hours of the day and the 3rd and 10th hours of the night on Thursday.
- The 5th and 12th hours of the day and the 7th hour of the night on Friday.
- The 2nd and 9th hours of the day and the 4th and 11th hours of the night on Saturday.

Element and mode: Water - Mutable.

Season: Winter.

Month: February.

Metals: Tin.

Color: Crimson blue, white, and purple.

Crystals: Lapis lazuli, pearl, turquoise, emerald, sapphire, and amethyst.

Animals: Ox, sheep, dolphin, stork, seal, and swan.

Body part: Circulatory system, lymphatic system, pineal glands, body fluids, toes, and feet.

Incense: Sage, ambergris, and sandalwood.

Harmonious Signs: Virgo, Cancer, and Scorpio.

Deities: Neptune, Anubis, Vishnu, Poseidon, and Khepera.

Ages: 55-62 years.

Anael

Governing Venus, Anael, has a strong connection to Friday. As one of the seven angels associated with creation, Anael is known for his pure, altruistic love. Influenced by Venus, Anael can teach you to love people and other beings around you and all creatures in the universe. He can inspire self-forgiveness and help you move on. At the same time, Venus is associated with fertility. Anael can then restore natural balance and help nature thrive.

Flowers, herbs, and trees you can use when working with aneal are almond, aloe vera, violet, apple, calendula, tansy, cherry, rose, cornflower, pansy, cowslip, myrtle, crocus, marshmallow, feverfew, lady's mantle, iris, geranium, heather, goldenrod, walnut, and plum.

Archangel Anael symbolizes love.[82]

In Tarot, Anael is linked to the cards Hierophant and Justice, which influence love, nurturing feelings, children, knowledge, inner power, moral values, and inner self. The two cards help this angel give people hints on the adequate emotional perspective they need in relationships.

Other Correspondences:

Hours of the day and night:

- The 2nd and 9th hours of the day and the 4th and 11th hours of the night on Sunday.
- The 6th hour of the day and the 1st and 8th hours of the night on Monday.
- The 3rd and 10th hours of the day and the 5th and 12th hours of the night on Tuesday.
- The 7th hour of the day and the 2nd and 9th hours of the night on Wednesday.
- The 4th and 11th hours of the day and the 6th hour of the night on Thursday.
- The 1st and 8th hours of the day and the 3rd and 10th hours of the night on Friday.
- The 5th and 12th hours of the day and the 7th hour of the night on Saturday.

Element and mode: Air - Cardinal.

Season: Winter.

Month: December.

Metals: Copper.

Color: Black, emerald green, and royal blue.

Crystals: Lapis lazuli, jade, opal, chrysolite, emerald, and beryl.

Animals: Hare, dove, swan, sparrow, tortoise, and elephant.

Body part: Kidney, lower back, and liver.

Incense: Galbanum.

Season: Winter.

Deities: Vulcan, Ma, Maat, Yama, and Themis.

Ages: 14-21 years.

Cassiel

Cassiel is the Archangel associated with Saturn and Saturday. This alludes to Cassiel's ability as the conservator of strengths and ruler of temperance and solitude. Saturn has great power over investment opportunities. The planet helps the angel bring moderation into people's actions and pushes them to develop patience and the aptitude for contemplation. Cassiel can help reverse bad fortune and conserve your resources in trying times.

Flowers, herbs, and trees corresponding to Cassiel are aconite, skullcap, belladonna, poison hemlock, black nightshade, mullein, bluebell, mandrake, comfrey, henbane, foxglove, hellebore, fumitory, thyme, cypress, and pine.

In Tarot, Cassiel is associated with The World card, indicating power over property, home, and land, but also showing concern over poverty, old age, and long-term illnesses. Cassiel can teach you that you can only receive certain blessings later in life, so you'll have something to look forward to after many years of hard work.

Other Correspondences:

Hours of the day and night:

- The 5th and 12th hours of the day and the 7th hour of the night on Sunday
- The 2nd and 9th hours of the day and the 4th and 11th hours of the night on Monday
- The 6th hour of the day and the 1st and 8th hours of the night on Tuesday
- The 3rd and 10th hours of the day and the 5th and 12th hours of the night on Wednesday
- The 7th hour of the day and the 2nd and 9th hours of the night on Thursday
- The 4th and 11th hours of the day and the 6th hour of the night on Friday
- The 1st and 8th hours of the day and the 3rd and 10th hours of the night on Saturday

Element and mode: Air-Fixed.

Season: Winter.

Month: July.
Metals: Lead and aluminum.
Color: Purple, violet, and sky blue.
Crystals: Malachite, amber, lapis lazuli, aquamarine, garnet, obsidian, and jet.
Animals: Otter, eagle, peacock, and dog.
Body part: Ankles and the circulatory system.
Incense: Galbanum.
Harmonious sign: Leo.
Deities: Juno, Athena, and Nuit.
Ages: 49-56 years.

Angels Associated with the Seasons

Spring

Angels linked to spring are Spugliguel, Amatiel, Milkiel, Core, Carascara, and Commissoros. Milkiel provides the nurturing energy that brings about spring, then Spugliguel takes over as its guardian. The other angels represent rebirth and rejuvenation, creativity, and fun. They can also help plant ideas and establish communication, friendships, and sexual relationships. Spring-ruling angels are also associated with healing, purification, financial matters, harvest, fertility, air, and pastel colors.

Summer

Summer is primarily ruled by Tubiel. Gargatel, Tariel, and Gaviel are also linked to this season. Tubiel is the guardian of small birds and helps them return to their owners. The other angels rule over the Summer, allowing for exponential growth in nature and life. They can help you get inspired with ideas for projects, deepen your relationship or obtain the wealth and wisdom of the universe. They can also nudge you toward the path of love, strength, and partnership. Summer-ruling angels are associated with the fire element and the colors yellow, blue, pink, and green.

Autumn

Torquaret is the angel governing the season, with the angels Guabarel and Tarquam acting as its guardians. Just like the season to which they're linked, these angels rule over harvest, planning for winter months and bringing processes to an end. They can help you sort out ownership over possessions, find new things to study and heal from past traumas. Autumn governing angels are associated with the water elements and the colors orange, yellow, brown, tan, and brown.

Winter

The ruler of the winter season is Attaris, but the angels Cetarari, Amabael, and Archangel Michael also help out. The latter is associated with the snow, while the others ensure rest and relaxation. They can help you lay plans for the following spring, nourish your body, mind, and soul, go over your accomplishments, and find creativity during the coldest season. Winter ruling angels are associated with breaking negative habits, the earth element, magic, and the colors gray, white, red, and green.

Chapter 8: The Law of Attraction

Positivity attracts positive energy, and negativity attracts negative energy. You bring into your life what you send out to the world.

Oprah Winfrey said she used to visualize herself as a successful woman who could make a difference in the world. Jim Carrey also said that before he was famous, he wrote himself a cheque for ten million dollars and dated it Thanksgiving 1995. He expected that he would make this amount of money in five years. Interestingly, in 1995, before Thanksgiving, Jim Carrey's movie Dumb and Dumber was a huge success, and he made ten million dollars.

Oprah Winfrey and Jim Carrey made their dreams a reality with hard work and perseverance. However, the power of belief gave them the push and put them on the right track. They believed that they could, and they did. That was the Law of Attraction at work.

What Is the Law of Attraction?

The law of attraction is one of the seven universal laws, and it is a philosophy that focuses on the power of thought and its impact on people's lives. It suggests that positive thoughts bring good experiences and positive influences, while negative ones attract negativity and bring negative outcomes into people's lives. According to this notion, thoughts are made of vibrational frequencies. If they give off the right frequency, your thoughts are positive, and you will attract good things in your life, like success, happiness, strong relationships, money, and good health. This makes your thoughts extremely powerful since they can influence every area of your life.

Buddha believed that people become what they think.[88]

Buddha believed that people become their thoughts, attracting what they feel and creating what they imagine. Ancient Chinese philosopher Lao Tzu also stressed the significance of thoughts. He said that one should always be aware of them since they become words that eventually influence your actions. Your actions will then become habits that impact your character and who you want to be. Your character will become your future and your destiny. Basically, who you become starts with one thought.

For instance, if you want to lose weight, you must transform your thoughts and believe that you can change your lifestyle, eat healthily, and visualize yourself in perfect shape. This mindset will keep you going, and the positivity will attract more positive changes in your life.

- Your thoughts will focus on losing weight
- You will then tell yourself that you can do it
- This will influence your actions, and you will start working out and eating more healthily
- This lifestyle will become a habit that influences your character, and you will be a fit and healthy person

However, if you keep telling yourself that you won't lose weight, these thoughts will prevent you from taking action, as the negativity will hold you back.

You are like a magnet that is constantly attracting energies and thoughts. Whether you believe in the law of attraction or not, it still governs your life. Similar to gravity, the law of attraction applies to everyone. It doesn't just favor the people who believe in it; it is a fact and one of the strongest powers in the universe.

However, there are many misconceptions about the law of attraction. The most common one is that people often treat it like Aladdin's genie and expect it to make their wishes come true. They think the universe will only give them what they want if they think hard about it. For instance, some people believe that if you think about owning a big house, the universe will give it to you. This isn't how this law works. It requires positive thinking, believing you deserve what you want, and working hard for it. As a result, the universe will open doors for you and provide you with opportunities until you achieve your goals. In other words, just like your thoughts, action is a big part of the law of attraction.

Some people prefer to keep their hopes and dreams to themselves because, deep down, they believe they won't accomplish them. They surrender to the darkness and think they aren't smart, strong, or talented enough to get what they want. If you don't feel comfortable sharing your dreams with others, communicate them to the universe instead. Spread them out with positive energy, and be ready to receive all the blessings you ever wanted.

The law of attraction works using manifestation. Raise your energy and keep it high for as long as you can. Understandably, one can't always be expected to think positively; this isn't realistic. Life can be stressful, and you're bound to encounter things that can upset you or ruin your mood. The point is to keep negative thoughts out of your head and focus on your goal and the life you want to build for yourself.

The History of the Law of Attraction

In 2006, when "The Secret" by Rhonda Byrne was published, everyone was talking about the law of attraction, so it is easy to assume that it is a modern notion. However, it has been around for almost two centuries. Russian author Helena Blavatsky was the first person to coin the phrase "law of attraction" in 1877 in her book "The Secret Doctrine." Although she didn't delve into details or provide any significant information, she introduced the concept and laid the foundation on which many other authors based their work. Helena mentioned that people and their abilities are defined by their thoughts and that they are so powerful that they can shape one's reality. American author Prentice Mulford was the first person to introduce it as a universal law.

In 1907, American author William Walker Atkinson provided more information about the law of attraction in his book "Thinking Vibration or the Law of Attraction in the Thought World." The book was a great success, and many found it very interesting. It was a great inspiration to modern scholars who based their work on Atkinson's writing. He mentioned the concept of vibration in his book, which wasn't popular at the time. He also discussed other notions as well like manifestation, energy, and the principles of thinking.

After Atkinson's work became popular, other writers were fascinated with the concept. In 1910, American writer Wallace Delois Wattles discussed the law of attraction in his book "The Science of Getting Rich." He stressed the idea of the value of thinking in the process of manifestation. He also noted that everything in the universe is made up of energy.

In 1928, American author Napoleon Hill released the book "The Law of Success in 16 Lessons." Hill mentioned the phrase "the law of attraction" multiple times in his book and introduced the concept to a wider audience. In 1986, American author Esther Hicks and her husband, Jerry Hicks, published the insightful book "The Law of Attraction."

However, in 2006, the law of attraction turned from a fascinating concept that authors and philosophers studied and wrote about to a worldwide phenomenon. One can't deny the great contribution Jerry and Esther Hicks made. However, there were people who were skeptical. Although the book was successful among philosophers and scholars, it failed to achieve commercial success.

This all changed with the release of "The Secret." Everyone became curious about the law of attraction and wanted to learn about it. After the book's success, Byrne released a documentary about "The Secret," in which philosophers, authors, and scientists discussed the law of attraction and its meaning. Like the book, the movie was a great success, and millions of people worldwide were interested in and talking about the law of attraction.

Byrne stated in "The Secret" that your thoughts could create anything, you can only succeed if you believe in yourself, and you can manifest your goals with positive thoughts and emotions.

Although the law of attraction was first coined in the 1800s, ancient philosophers like Buddha and Tzu mentioned the idea behind it in many of their writings.

The Principles of the Law of Attraction

One can only understand the law of attraction by learning about its main principles.

Like Attracts Like

Unlike the popular belief that opposites attract, the law of attraction introduces a different theory that like attracts like. That basically means that you attract thoughts similar to yours. This also applies to people. Look at your circle of friends, and you will notice that you often gravitate toward people like you. It is human nature to prefer to surround yourself with people with whom you share common interests and personality traits.

You never have just one negative thought. Once your mind begins thinking negatively, it alters your thought patterns and changes your perspective. For instance, you gain weight and convince yourself that you will never be able to lose it and get in shape. This thought will attract others like "I hate myself," "I am ugly," "no one will love me," "I have never been able to lose weight because I am a failure," etc.

You can only get over the ideas that hold you back by releasing them and replacing them with positive ones. Understand that these negative thoughts aren't realistic or rational. They are just a reflection of your fears and insecurities, but if you face them and apply logical thinking, you will see that they don't hold any merit.

Interestingly, if there is something you lack, you will attract more of that emptiness. For instance, if you are in debt, you will attract more debt. Similarly, you also attract what you don't need. For instance, if you have a job that you are comfortable in, you will be more likely to receive other job offers.

Nature Abhors Clutter

When your brain is cluttered with negative thoughts, there won't be any room for positivity in your life. Eliminate the negativity to free up space to attract positive thoughts and good experiences. If your home is cluttered with things you don't need, it will impact your mental health, and you won't have any room for newer or nicer stuff. Remember, if your brain is cluttered, so will every aspect of your life.

The Present Isn't Always Perfect

Life isn't always easy, and for most people, the present is anything but perfect. There are always wars, diseases, and people dying, besides the stresses you face on a daily basis. Whether it is relationship troubles or a job that sucks the life out of you, there are things that can make it hard to see the good in life.

Most people don't live in the moment. They either let their brains wander to the past and live in regret or are constantly worried about the future. However, there is no point since the past is already gone, and there is nothing you can do to change it, and the future isn't guaranteed. Focus on the present and work on making it perfect.

This point emphasizes that there are always things in the present that can stress you out and make you unhappy. Don't spend your time focusing on the bad things. Instead, improve them and make things easier for yourself. This is better than spending your energy on being miserable and helpless. There will be times when you feel sad, and negative thoughts will definitely creep in at some point, but you are allowed to feel and acknowledge them. Fix what you can, and don't dwell on the things that are out of your control.

Say you are stuck in a dead-end job with a boss who is making your life hard. You can either spend your time complaining or find ways to fix the situation. Either keep sending out resumes while believing that you will find another job or work harder at your current one and better yourself by learning new skills.

Don't waste your energy complaining about your job or boss to your friends and family. Instead, visualize the job of your dreams and talk about it with your loved ones, and you will attract it into your life.

Universal Law

The law of attraction resembles the concept of karma; what goes around comes around. You not only get back the thoughts you release to the universe but also all the good deeds you do. The way you treat others will directly influence your life. Kindness and love attract positive emotions, and people will treat you the same way you treat them. For instance, if you smile at someone, they will smile back at you. When you treat the people below you at work with respect, they will admire and look up to you. However, if you hurt, disrespect, or offend someone, they will respond similarly to you.

Always help those in need; whenever you are in trouble, the universe will send you someone to lend you a helping hand.

Harmony

Your surroundings have a huge impact on your energy. They can influence your thoughts and change your outlook on life. Stay in a positive environment and surround yourself with people who lift you up and influence your thoughts.

Now that you understand the law of attraction and the impact it can have on your life, certain exercises can help you.

Meditation Technique
Instructions:

1. Find a quiet room with no distractions.
2. Sit in a comfortable position.
3. Close your eyes and take a few deep breaths.
4. Focus on the recurring patterns in your life. Spend a few minutes observing them and how often you react to them.
5. Next, turn your attention to the negative thoughts or emotions that result from the recurring themes.
6. Understand the way you deal with these patterns and interpret your life along with the beliefs you hold dear.
7. Ask your higher self to guide you so you can see if your actions are influencing your current situation.
8. Focus your attention on one significant pattern and contemplate all the times its theme was present in your life. Ask yourself what was going on in your life at the time and what your environment looked like?
9. Ponder on your mindset during that time. What were your thoughts and beliefs? How did you feel as a result of your situation? How did your energy and internal reality impact the energy you attracted and the reality you created?
10. How did you express yourself at the time? How did you react to your surroundings and the situation you were facing? How did this pattern end? Were you the one who ended it, or was it an external factor?

11. What lessons did you learn from this experience, and how did you react to them? Did the experience make you any wiser? How can these lessons activate the law of attraction so you can attract positive thoughts, emotions, and experiences in the future?
12. Next, set an intention that you want to heal all the wounds and let go of the old beliefs from your past that have contributed to the negativity. You can say something like, "*I am healing my wounds and releasing my past beliefs and mistakes to free space for love and positivity to enter my life. I am letting go of all the thoughts and emotions that no longer serve me.*"
13. Imagine your guardian angel sending you healing energy and love to heal all your wounds.
14. Feel the healing energy flowing through every part of you and invite the pattern, belief, or person from which you want to heal to appear before you. Now, transfer this energy from your heart to them with the intention of healing their wounds as well.
15. Express your feelings while transferring your energy and ask your higher self for guidance.
16. Now, with love, cut the energetic chord connecting you with the situation or being and watch it as it dissolves.
17. Focus on what energy, thoughts, or emotions you want to manifest or bring into your life right now.
18. Imagine the energy or thoughts as a bright, colorful light bringing you joy, comfort, and excitement. Believe that you are already experiencing these feelings, and notice how your mood will change for the better.
19. Take in everything around you, like the sounds, scents, or feelings, while keeping your eyes closed.
20. Feel the positive thoughts and emotions flowing through you.
21. Express your gratitude for all the blessings the universe has given you.
22. Take a deep breath when the image you created in your imagination looks and feels real.

23. Breathe out while imagining giving energy to your visualization. The air you exhale will give it power and life.
24. Sit with this image for a few minutes and feel how your thoughts and emotions change.
25. After you finish and feel ready to return to the real world, take a long deep breath, release it, and slowly open your eyes.

Visualization
Instructions:
1. Lie in bed and get comfortable.
2. Close your eyes, clear your mind, and relax your body.
3. Feel the mattress against your skin and take in the scent of the room.
4. Focus on the sounds around you, like birds chirping outside, your partner's breathing next to you, or the sound of the wind.
5. Now, visualize all the things you want to attract into your life.

Vision Board
Tools:
- A flat surface
- Objects that represent your goals, like quotes, words, or photos
- Scissors
- Clips or glue
- Printer

Instructions:
1. Set an intention that you want to create a vision board to activate the law of attraction to bring a certain dream into your life, like love or a better career.
2. Set a time frame for the board. This will depend on the goal. For instance, if your goal is to be promoted, the time frame can be one or two years.
3. Decide on the type of vision board you want to create, like a wall grid or a collage. Choose whatever makes you feel happy and comfortable.

4. Prepare your supplies and choose things that motivate you, inspire you, and fill you with positivity whenever you look at them.
5. Create the vision board by pasting the images and quotes together on a collage. You can even write down the quotes or draw the images.
6. After creating the vision board, place it in a location you see every day.

Tips:

- Remember that the law of attraction is all about positivity, so it won't recognize negative statements like "I don't want to be sick anymore," the board will interpret that as "I want to get sick." Keep your words and tone positive. The images and quotes you choose should also be cheerful to attract similar thoughts into your life.
- Choose your words carefully. Don't say, "I want to heal from my sickness," because your energy will focus on the word "sickness." You can say, "I want to heal and be strong and healthy."
- Speak about your goals as if you have already achieved them.

You are what you think, so be aware of where your mind wanders. Remember to remain in the present since it is guaranteed, the future is unknown, and the past isn't relevant anymore.

Although you can't always control negative thoughts, try to be aware of them. Don't fight them. Acknowledge them when they occur, then let them go. Understand that you are stronger than these thoughts and that you have the power to release them.

The law of attraction has been around since the beginning of time. It teaches mankind the significance of thoughts and that you receive what you send to the universe. Keep your thoughts positive and let go of all the negativity impacting your life. Use positive statements when you talk about yourself and your goals. Believe that you can achieve everything you set your mind to and that the universe is guiding you.

Chapter 9: Daily Meditations

Have you ever found yourself bewildered by the seemingly cryptic signs that the universe seems to be throwing your way? Perhaps you've come across repeating number patterns, such as 111 or 333, and been intrigued about their significance? It's all too common to feel disoriented and uncertain when attempting to decipher these messages. But don't worry! Meditation is here to serve as your beacon.

Daily meditation is the key to self-awareness and connecting with your inner self.[84]

This chapter will unveil meditation's profound role in forging an intimate connection with your inner self, fostering emotional stability, and cultivating heightened self-awareness. By delving into specialized exercises, you'll learn how to awaken your third eye chakra, thus demystifying the obscured meanings encoded within those enigmatic angel numbers.

So, if you are in pursuit of understanding and guidance, take a deep breath, let go of any tension, and prepare to embark on a journey of exploration into how meditation can equip you with the keys to unlocking the cosmic code of the universe.

Enhancing Awareness

Cultivating mindfulness carries many advantages, spanning from sharpening focus to mitigating stress and anxiety, all while bolstering overall wellness. In this section, you will find a variety of exercises and meditation practices designed to amplify your consciousness. These will serve as your road map on the exciting expedition towards elevated self-awareness.

- **Mindful Breathing Exercise**

Sit comfortably in a chair or cross-legged on a cushion. Close your eyes and focus on your breath. Inhale deeply through your nose and feel your lungs filling up. Slowly exhale, feeling your stomach deflate.

Continue deep breathing for a few minutes, paying attention to the sensation of the air moving in and out of your body. Every time your mind wanders, bring your attention back to your breath. You can repeat this exercise as many times throughout the day as needed, even if just for a few minutes.

- **Body Scan Meditation**

Lie down in a comfortable position and close your eyes. Slowly scan your body, starting from the top of your head and moving down to your toes. As you focus on each body part, visualize releasing any tension or tightness present. Relax and take deep breaths.

Begin with the crown chakra and focus on that area for a moment before slowly making your way down the other chakras throughout the central line of your body — brow, throat, heart, solar plexus, sacral, and root. Stay with each chakra for a moment and notice what it feels like as you inhale and exhale.

- **Mindful Eating Exercise**

Enjoy a meal or snack in a relaxed environment with minimal distractions. As you eat, pay attention to each bite's texture, flavor, and temperature in your mouth. Notice how the food makes you feel. Mindful eating can help with overindulgent behavior.

- **Walking Meditation**

Find a quiet place to walk, like a garden or a park. Walk slowly and focus on each step, noticing how your feet contact the ground. Focus your mind on your breath to stay present in the moment. You can even take this walking meditation to hallways or paths around your home or workplace, taking a few minutes for yourself to feel the peace moving and breathing bring.

- **Gratitude Meditation**

Sit comfortably and focus on the things or people you appreciate. Begin by taking time to visualize everything you have to be grateful for, from the small things, like a warm cup of coffee, to more significant things, like the people in your life. Try focusing your attention on how these elements make you feel.

Finally, take a few deep breaths, and imagine yourself extending gratitude to the source of these positive experiences. This can be a religious or spiritual figure, the universe, or even a person you are thanking directly.

- **Yoga**

There are numerous yoga styles - beginners may find starting with a restorative practice to be the most approachable. Yoga focuses on bringing awareness to your breath and body, allowing you to relax and center yourself.

These exercises and meditations are just a few examples of how you can focus on increasing awareness. Starting with just one practice and building on it over time can lead to noticeable benefits. With enough patience and dedication, you will improve your focus, reduce anxiety, and live life to the fullest.

Connecting to the Angelic Realm

Connecting to the angelic realm through meditation can be a powerful and transformative experience. This spiritual practice can help you tap into higher consciousness, gain clarity and insight, and feel a deeper connection to the divine.

1. To start, find a quiet, comfortable space where you won't be disturbed. Take a few deep breaths to settle into your body and release any tension or stress. Close your eyes and focus your attention on your breath, feeling the sensation of the air

moving in and out of your body.

2. As you continue to breathe deeply, visualize a bright light surrounding you. This light represents the divine energy that surrounds and protects you. Allow yourself to feel the warmth and love of this light, and let it fill your entire being.

3. Next, imagine a staircase in front of you, leading up into the clouds. This is your gateway to the angelic realm. As you ascend the stairs, feel yourself becoming lighter and more peaceful. With each step, you are moving closer to the divine realm.

4. When you reach the top of the stairs, imagine standing in a beautiful garden filled with flowers, trees, and animals. This is the place where angels and other divine beings reside. Take a moment to look around. Noticing the colors, scents, and sounds of this sacred space.

5. As you continue to breathe deeply, call forth the presence of your guardian angel. Ask for their guidance, love, and support as you connect with the angelic realm. You may feel a warm sensation, a tingling, or a sense of peace as you connect with your angel.

6. Take some time to chat with your angel, asking any questions on your mind. Listen to their voice, which may come to you as a feeling, a thought, or a vision. Trust that they are communicating with you *in the best way for you.*

7. As you connect with your angelic guides, feel yourself becoming more attuned to your intuition and your inner wisdom. Allow yourself to receive any insights or messages that come to you. Know that you are supported and guided by the divine forces.

8. When you feel ready, thank your angels for their guidance and love. Visualize yourself going down the staircase back to the physical realm, feeling grounded and centered. Take a few more deep breaths before opening your eyes.

To deepen your connection with the angelic realm, you may want to consider making meditation a regular practice. Set aside a few minutes daily to connect with your angels and tune into your inner guidance. Over time, you may find that this practice helps you live a more joyful, peaceful, and fulfilling life.

Mediation for Opening Third Eye Chakra

Meditation is a powerful tool for opening the third eye or crown chakra. The third eye chakra is located between the eyebrows and is associated with intuition, spiritual awareness, and psychic abilities. On the other hand, the crown chakra is located at the top of the head and is associated with divine wisdom, unity, and consciousness. Opening these chakras can enhance your spiritual connection with the universe and help you attain a deep sense of inner peace and fulfillment.

1. To begin, find a quiet, peaceful space where you will not be disturbed. You can sit cross-legged on a mat or pillow.
2. Make sure your back is straight and your shoulders are relaxed. You can also choose to sit on a chair, but ensure your feet are planted firmly on the ground. Take a few deep breaths and feel the tension in your body going away as you exhale.
3. Close your eyes and visualize a bright light on your forehead. This light represents your third eye chakra.
4. Focus on this light and imagine it expanding and growing in intensity. Visualize the light shining down and piercing through any blockages or obstacles hindering the awakening of your third eye chakra.
5. As you continue to focus on your third eye chakra, begin to breathe slowly and deeply. Inhale through your nose, hold your breath for a few seconds, and then exhale through your mouth.
6. As you breathe, feel the energy flowing through your body and visualize it reaching your third eye chakra. As you continue to breathe, shift your focus to your crown chakra. Visualize a bright white light at the top of your head. This light represents your crown chakra. Imagine the light growing and expanding, filling your entire body with divine wisdom and spiritual connection.
7. Now, focus on both your third eye chakra and your crown chakra simultaneously. Visualize the energy flowing freely between these two chakras. Imagine the bright light at your third eye chakra merging with the bright white light at your crown chakra, creating a powerful connection between your

spiritual and intuitive self.

8. As you continue to meditate, try to maintain this visualization for at least 10-15 minutes. If your mind wanders, gently bring your focus back to your breath and chakras. You can also incorporate affirmations, such as *"I am connected to my intuition and my divine self"* or *"I trust in the universe to guide me on my path."*

After your meditation, take a few moments to sit with your eyes closed and feel the energy in your body. Visualize the bright light at your third eye chakra and your crown chakra continuing to glow brightly, even as you go about your day.

Opening your third eye or crown chakra through meditation can enhance your spiritual growth and lead to a deeper sense of inner peace and fulfillment. You can awaken these chakras with consistent practice and cultivate a strong connection with your divine self.

Exercises to Open Third Eye Chakra

Opening your third eye or crown chakra can be a transformative experience that can help you tap into your intuition, enhance your spiritual practice, and improve your overall well-being. However, it can also be daunting to undertake such an exercise without proper guidance. Here is how you can open your third eye or crown chakra.

Step 1: Set the Intention

Start by setting the intention to open your third eye or crown chakra. To do this, sit in a quiet and comfortable space where you will not be disturbed. Close your eyes and take a few deep breaths. Imagine yourself surrounded by warm, peaceful, and protective energy. Then, internalize the intention to open your third eye or crown chakra. Repeat to yourself, "I am open and ready to receive universal energy and wisdom."

Step 2: Meditative Breathing

Next, begin with meditative breathing, also known as pranayama. There are many variations of pranayama, but one of the most commonly used techniques is the 4-7-8 breathing method. With this technique, you inhale for four seconds, hold your breath for seven seconds, and exhale for eight seconds. Repeat this for at least five minutes, and focus all of your awareness on your breathing. This will quiet your mind and prepare you for the next step.

Step 3: The Om Chant

The next step is to perform the Om chant. This powerful mantra can activate your third eye and crown chakra. Begin by taking a deep breath, and as you exhale, say the word Om. Repeat this several times, each time visualizing the sound filling your body and mind with positive energy.

Step 4: Forehead Massage

After chanting the Om mantra, gently massage your forehead with your fingers. Place your index and middle fingers between your eyebrows and apply gentle pressure in a circular motion. This will create a sense of warmth and release tension in this area.

Step 5: Visualization

Visualize a bright light in the forehead area. Picture this light expanding with each inhale and contracting with each exhale. Focus all of your attention on this visualization, allowing it to become more vivid and clearer with each breath.

Step 6: Crown Chakra Activation

Place your hands on the crown of your head, and visualize the top of your skull opening up. Picture a bright light shining down on your body and illuminating every cell. Feel this light penetrating your body with warmth, love, and wisdom.

Grounding and Cleansing Mediation

Mediation is a powerful practice that can help you ground yourself and cleanse your energy. It allows you to connect with your inner self and tap into your intuition while also helping you to release any negative or stagnant energy that may be holding you back. To get the most out of your mediation practice, it is important to follow these step-by-step instructions:

Step 1: Find a Quiet Space

The first step in any meditation practice is to find a quiet space to be alone and free from distractions. This could be a dedicated meditation space or a peaceful corner in your bedroom or living room.

Step 2: Set Your Intention

Once you have found your quiet space, take a few moments to set your intention for your meditation practice. This could be a simple goal, such as grounding yourself and clearing your energy, or it could be a more specific intention, such as connecting with your higher self or finding clarity on a specific issue.

Step 3: Get into a Comfortable Position

Next, get into a comfortable position, such as sitting cross-legged on the floor or lying down. Choosing a position that allows you to relax and be comfortable for the duration of your mediation practice is important.

Step 4: Focus on Your Breath

With your eyes closed, begin to focus on your breath. Take a deep inhale through your nose, filling your lungs with air, and then exhale slowly through your mouth. Repeat this deep breathing pattern for several minutes, allowing your body to become more relaxed with each breath.

Step 5: Visualize Roots Growing from Your Feet

To ground yourself, visualize roots growing from your feet and sinking deep into the earth below you. Imagine these roots anchoring you to the ground and providing a sense of stability and security. Take a few moments to focus on this visualization, allowing it to become more vivid in your mind's eye.

Step 6: Scan Your Body for Tension

As you continue to breathe deeply and focus on grounding yourself, scan your body for any areas of tension or discomfort. If you notice any tightness or discomfort, take a few moments to breathe into those areas and release the tension.

Step 7: Visualize a White Light

To cleanse your energy, visualize a bright white light flowing down from the universe and surrounding your body. See this light penetrating every cell and filling you with positive energy and light. As you continue to focus on this visualization, feel yourself becoming lighter and more energized.

Step 8: Release Any Negative Energy

As you visualize the white light surrounding your body, focus on releasing any negative or stagnant energy that may be weighing you down. Imagine it leaving your body and being carried away by the universe, leaving you feeling refreshed and rejuvenated.

Step 9: End with Gratitude

Finally, end your mediation practice by expressing gratitude for the experience. Take a few moments to reflect on how you feel and how your energy has shifted. Express gratitude for your body, mind, and spirit and for the countless blessings in your life.

Mediation is a powerful tool that can help you ground yourself and cleanse your energy. By following these step-by-step instructions, you can create a safe and nurturing space for yourself and tap into the infinite wisdom and energy of the universe. Whether you practice meditation daily or just occasionally, you are sure to experience the profound benefits of this ancient practice. So, take a deep breath, center yourself, and let the magic of meditation transform your life!

Uncovering Synchronicities in the Past

Mediation for uncovering synchronicities in the past can be a powerful tool for finding connections you may have previously overlooked. By meditating on your past experiences and actively seeking out synchronicities, you can gain insight into your innermost thoughts and feelings and ultimately achieve greater self-awareness.

Step 1: Set the Intention

The first step in mediating synchronicities is to set the intention to uncover them. This can involve verbalizing your desire to connect with the universe and gain insight into your past experiences. It is important to approach this process with an open mind and a willingness to be vulnerable.

Step 2: Connect with Your Breath

Once you have set your intention, it is time to begin the meditation process. Start by focusing on your breath and taking slow, deliberate breaths. This can calm your mind and center yourself, allowing you to better connect with your inner thoughts and feelings.

Step 3: Reflect on Your Past

Once you are calm and centered, begin reflecting on your past experiences. Think about significant events or moments in your life that have profoundly impacted you. Try to recall the emotions you felt during these events and any thoughts or beliefs you may have held at the time.

Step 4: Look for Patterns and Connections

As you reflect on your past experiences, start to look for patterns and connections between seemingly unrelated events. Pay attention to any recurring themes or symbols that emerge and any significant coincidences or synchronicities that may have occurred. Write these down in a journal or notebook to help you better analyze and understand these connections later.

Step 5: Interpret the Meaning

Once you have identified these patterns and connections, it is time to interpret their meaning. This can involve exploring your own subconscious thoughts and feelings, as well as seeking out guidance from spiritual sources or professionals. It is important to approach this process with an open mind and a willingness to explore new perspectives and ideas.

Step 6: Take Action

The final step in meditating for synchronicities is to take action based on the insights you have gained. This can involve making changes to your behavior, taking steps towards achieving a specific goal, or simply embracing a new outlook on life. By taking action, you can bring these synchronicities into your conscious awareness and use them as a guide to living a more purposeful and fulfilling life.

Meditating on Angel Symbols or Numbers

One way to practice meditation is by meditating on angel symbols or numbers. Here is how to meditate on angel symbols or numbers.

Step 1: Find a Quiet and Peaceful Place to Meditate

Find a quiet and peaceful place in your home where you can meditate without being disturbed. It could be a room, a corner, or even a specific chair. Make sure that the place is clean, well-ventilated, and comfortable.

Step 2: Use Angel Symbols or Numbers as Your Focus Point

Choose an angel symbol or number that resonates with you. There are different angel symbols and numbers which represent different meanings. For instance, the number 1111 can represent spiritual awakening, while Archangel Michael's symbol represents protection and courage. You can find different angel symbols and their meanings online or in books.

Step 3: Set Your Intention

Before you start meditating, set your intention. Decide what you want to achieve from this meditation. Your intention could be to connect with your guardian angel, receive guidance, or simply relax.

Step 4: Sit Comfortably

Sit in a comfortable position with your back straight. You can sit on a chair or the floor, whichever is more comfortable for you. Rest your hands on your lap, with your palms facing upwards.

Step 5: Close Your Eyes

Close your eyes and take a deep breath. Inhale and then exhale slowly. Repeat this a few times until you feel calm and relaxed.

Step 6: Visualize the Symbol or Number

Visualize the angel symbol or number in your mind's eye. Focus your attention on the symbol or number and allow it to fill your mind with positive energy. If you find it hard to visualize, you can also look at a picture of the angel symbol or number.

Step 7: Repeat a Mantra

Repeat a mantra or phrase corresponding to the angel symbol or number. For example, if you meditate on Archangel Michael's symbol, you can repeat the phrase *"I am safe and protected."* Repeat the mantra or phrase in your mind or out loud as often as you want.

Step 8: Stay Focused

Stay focused on the symbol or number and your intention. If your mind wanders, gently bring your attention back to the symbol or number. Don't worry if you find it hard to stay focused at first; it takes practice.

Step 9: End the Meditation

End the meditation by taking a few deep breaths and gradually returning your awareness to your surroundings. Open your eyes and take a moment to stretch.

Step 10: Reflect on Your Experience

After the meditation, take a moment to reflect on your experience. Did you feel more relaxed? Were there any insights or messages that came to you? This reflection can help you gain more clarity on your intention and how you can improve.

Conclusion

If the angels try to send you a message, you'll suddenly start seeing the same sets of digits every time you look at the time, your bank statement, or an invoice. If you can spot angel numbers everywhere you go, this is a sign that you've been awakened by angels who wish to guide you toward the right path. Interpreting these messages can be challenging if your knowledge of angel numbers, numerology, and synchronicity is limited.

However, now that you've read this book, you should be able to understand the messages that the angels are sending you and know what to do about them. Reading this book should prepare you to work with angel symbolism and provide you with in-depth knowledge about various concepts related to angels and their connection to the universe. You'll find high-value information that you can use to transform your life and take the first steps toward personal growth and development.

This book explores the significance of angel numbers and numerology and how they're age-old spiritual practices. It explains the difference between divine timing, synchronicity, and coincidence and teaches you how to put the Law of Attraction to work. In the first few chapters, you learned about the origins, history, and basics of numerology and how angel numbers differ from other esoteric practices. Most importantly, you can now use your intuition and knowledge to analyze and address different number sequences and patterns.

Understanding the different ways in which angels communicate with people allows you to be more responsive to their messages and attempts to connect with you. With the right safety precautions in mind, you can engage in meditations and prayers that help you get in touch with your angels of choice and work with them to enhance certain aspects of your life.

If you know how to use it, you can use the Law of Attraction to drastically change your life. Understanding this phenomenon and learning about the philosophical and religious principles on which it is based can help you make the most out of using it. This book provides effective exercises and techniques you can use to activate the Law of Attraction.

The last chapter, which offers daily exercises and meditations that you can practice to enhance your awareness, connect to the angelic realm, and open your third eye and crown chakras, serves as a directory that you can always go back to at different points of your life. These practices can support your spiritual endeavors, improve your intuition, and make it easier to connect with the universe.

This book is the perfect opportunity for beginners and seasoned practitioners to enrich their spiritual practices and connect with the angelic realm. While it will take a lot of time, effort, dedication, and practice, reading this book has given you all the knowledge you need to transform your life and tip the universe in your favor.

This guide to angel numbers is an indispensable resource for anyone looking to expand their knowledge in the world of spiritual practices and improve their intuition. It offers a comprehensive understanding of key spiritual concepts that can help you unlock your full potential and lead a more fulfilling life.

Here's another book by Mari Silva that you might like

Your Free Gift
(only available for a limited time)

Thanks for getting this book! If you want to learn more about various spirituality topics, then join Mari Silva's community and get a free guided meditation MP3 for awakening your third eye. This guided meditation mp3 is designed to open and strengthen ones third eye so you can experience a higher state of consciousness. Simply visit the link below the image to get started.

https://spiritualityspot.com/meditation

Or, Scan the QR code!

References

"5 Powerful Signs of Archangel Gabriel Reaching out to You." Www.alittlesparkofjoy.com, 18 Aug. 2021, https://www.alittlesparkofjoy.com/archangel-gabriel/

"5 Tips for Creating a Sacred Space." HuffPost, 19 Apr. 2013, www.huffpost.com/entry/sacred-space_b_3094267.

"6 Types of Spirit Guides & How to Communicate with Them." Mindbodygreen, 23 Jan. 2015, www.mindbodygreen.com/articles/types-of-spirit-guides.

"7 Healing Angels to Call upon for Your Chakras." Soul and Spirit, 18 May 2017, www.soulandspiritmagazine.com/7-angels-call-upon-chakras/.

"7 Shocking Ways Angels Speak to You Every Day." Psych Central, 24 July 2016, https://psychcentral.com/blog/life-goals/2016/07/ways-angels-speak-to-you#2.-Feelings-and-Physical-Sensations-.

"7 Shocking Ways Angels Speak to You Every Day." Psych Central, 24 July 2016, https://psychcentral.com/blog/life-goals/2016/07/ways-angels-speak-to-you#6.-Signs-and-Symbols.

"7 Signs Your Guardian Angel Is Trying to Contact You – Buddha & Karma." Buddhaandkarma.com, https://buddhaandkarma.com/blogs/guide/signs-your-guardian-angel-is-trying-to-contact-you

"10 "Higher Self" Journal Prompts." A Great Mood, 17 Oct. 2022, https://agreatmood.com/higher-self-journal-prompts/#.

"11 Feather Color Meanings: The Significance of Feathers and What They Symbolize." Color Meanings, 22 Aug. 2020, www.color-meanings.com/feather-color-meanings-symbolism/.

"12 Archangels: Their Names, Meanings, Traits, and Their Connection with Zodiac Signs and Birth Dates." WILLOW SOUL, https://willowsoul.com/blogs/angels/12-archangels-names-meanings-traits-zodiac-signs-birth-date

"12 Signs an Angel Messenger Is near - Centre of Excellence." Www.centreofexcellence.com, www.centreofexcellence.com/angel-messenger-12-signs/#.

"A Quick Guide to Chakra Meditation | BetterSleep." Www.bettersleep.com, www.bettersleep.com/blog/a-quick-guide-to-chakra-meditation/.

admin. "The Seven Angels of the Week ★ Angelorum." Angelorum, 16 Dec. 2014, https://angelorum.co/topics/angels/the-seven-angels-of-the-week/

Aletheia. "7 Ways to Connect with Your Spirit Animal." LonerWolf, 6 Feb. 2014, https://lonerwolf.com/spirit-animal/#h-7-ways-to-discover-your-spirit-animal.

Anthony, Kym. "Our 6 Favourite Crystals for Awakening Your Spiritual Self-Awareness!" Luna Tide, 20 Oct. 2021, https://luna-tide.com/blogs/journal/crystals-for-awakening.

"Archangel & Zodiac Signs | a Spiritual Connection - AstroTalk.com." AstroTalk Blog - Online Astrology Consultation with Astrologer, 3 Mar. 2020, https://astrotalk.com/astrology-blog/archangel-and-zodiac-signs/.

"ARCHANGEL GABRIEL and CANCER." Tumblr, www.tumblr.com/whoismyguardianangel/148402320155/archangel-gabriel-and-cancer.

"ARCHANGEL JEREMIEL and SCORPIO." Tumblr, www.tumblr.com/whoismyguardianangel/148402117040/archangel-jeremiel-and-scorpio.

"ARCHANGEL ZADKIEL and GEMINI." Tumblr, www.tumblr.com/whoismyguardianangel/148402350110/archangel-zadkiel-and-gemini.

"Are Auras Real? 16 FAQs about Color, Meaning, More." Healthline, 5 Jan. 2022, www.healthline.com/health/what-is-an-aura#presence-of-colors.

B. A., English. "Acknowledging Guardian Angels in Islam." Learn Religions, www.learnreligions.com/muslim-guardian-angel-prayers-124056.

---. "How Archangels Can Help You Balance Your Life." Learn Religions, www.learnreligions.com/archangels-of-four-directions-124410.

---. "How to Know When Archangel Zadkiel Is Near." Learn Religions, www.learnreligions.com/how-to-recognize-archangel-zadkiel-124287.

---. "How to Recognize Archangel Raziel." Learn Religions, www.learnreligions.com/how-to-recognize-archangel-raziel-124282.

Beckett, John. "6 Ways to Talk to the Gods (and How to Listen for an Answer)." John Beckett, 4 Oct. 2018, www.patheos.com/blogs/johnbeckett/2018/10/6-ways-to-talk-to-the-gods.html.

Benner, Mara. "Learn 5 Ways to Connect with Your Loved Ones in Spirit -." Four Directions Wellness, 27 Oct. 2019, https://fourdirectionswellness.com/2019/10/27/learn-5-ways-to-connect-with-your-loved-ones-in-spirit/

"Higher Self: 3 Effective Ways to Connect to the Guidance Within." Soul Scroll Journals, https://soulscrolljournals.com/blogs/news/higher-self-3-effective-ways-to-connect-to-the-guidance-within

"How Does a Guardian Angel Work?" Catholic Answers, www.catholic.com/magazine/online-edition/how-does-a-guardian-angel-work.

"How to Get to Know Your Guardian Angels + Unlock Their Power." Mindbodygreen, 24 May 2016, www.mindbodygreen.com/articles/how-to-get-to-know-your-guardian-angels.

"How to Recognize Archangel Chamuel." Learn Religions, www.learnreligions.com/how-to-recognize-archangel-chamuel-124273.

"How to Recognize Archangel Michael." Learn Religions, www.learnreligions.com/how-to-recognize-archangel-michael-124278.

"How to Recognize Ariel, Angel of Nature." Learn Religions, www.learnreligions.com/how-to-recognize-archangel-ariel-124271.

"How Your Guardian Angel May Send You Messages through Scents." Learn Religions, www.learnreligions.com/contacting-your-angel-scent-messages-124357.

"LEO and ARCHANGEL RAZIEL." Tumblr, www.tumblr.com/whoismyguardianangel/148402290140/leo-and-archangel-raziel.

McGinley, Karson. "7 Chakra Meditations to Keep You in Balance." Chopra, 3 Feb. 2020, https://chopra.com/articles/7-chakra-meditations-to-keep-you-in-balance

"Meet Archangel Jophiel, Angel of Beauty." Learn Religions, www.learnreligions.com/meet-archangel-jophiel-124094.

Nast, Condé. "Everything You Need to Know about Angel Numbers." Allure, 24 Dec. 2021, www.allure.com/story/what-are-angel-numbers.

Oinam, Goutamkumar. "Mythology about Guardian Gods across the World." Medium, 17 Feb. 2022, medium.com/@goutamkumaroina/mythology-about-guardian-gods-across-the-world-7cf662780198.

"Rapheael, Michael, Gabriel, Uriel: Archangels of the 4 Nature Elements." Learn Religions, www.learnreligions.com/archangels-of-four-elements-in-nature-124411.

Shah, Parita. "The Chopra Center." The Chopra Center, 14 May 2019, https://chopra.com/articles/what-is-a-chakra

Silva, Jorge. "9 Cloud Symbolism & Spiritual Meanings (and Dark Cloud." Angelical Balance, 3 Sept. 2022, www.angelicalbalance.com/spirituality/cloud-symbolism-spiritual-meaning/#9_Cloud_Symbolism_and_Spiritual_Meanings.

"Sugilite Meaning- Physical, Mental, & Spiritual Healing Properties." Tiny Rituals, https://tinyrituals.co/blogs/tiny-rituals/sugilite-meaning

"The Ascended Masters: Who Are They and How Can They Help?" Kaliana Emotional Care, www.kaliana.com/blogs/eatdrinkthink/the-ascended-masters-who-they-are-and-how-they-can-help.

"The Four Bodies - Physical, Emotional, Mental & Spiritual." Goop, 9 Apr. 2015, https://goop.com/wellness/spirituality/the-four-bodies/

The Four Important Archangels. www.divineblessingsforall.com/the-four-important-archangels/.

The Seven Chakras – Vortexes of Power. www.himalayanyogainstitute.com/the-seven-chakras-vortexes-of-power/.

Tran, Dung. "Angel Meditation for Keeping in Touch with Your Angels." Medium, 2 July 2018, medium.com/@dunglongtran/angel-meditation-for-keeping-in-touch-with-your-angels-df2a3b6961d2.

Vaudoise, Mallorie. "A Ritual to Reconnect with Your Ancestors." Spirituality & Health, 24 Nov. 2019, www.spiritualityhealth.com/articles/2019/11/24/a-ritual-to-reconnect-with-your-ancestors.

"Visualizing Your Guardian Angel." Www.beliefnet.com, www.beliefnet.com/faiths/faith-tools/meditation/2007/03/visualizing-your-guardian-angel.aspx.

"Who Is Archangel Michael & 5 Sings of the Great Protector." Www.alittlesparkofjoy.com, 10 May 2021, https://www.alittlesparkofjoy.com/archangel-michael/

"Who Your Guardian Angel Is and What They Do: 10 Things." Holyart.com Blog, 16 May 2018, www.holyart.com/blog/religious-items/who-your-guardian-angel-is-and-what-they-do-10-things-you-should-know/.

Wong, Kenneth. "The 7 Archangels: Names, Meanings and Duties." The Millennial Grind, 5 July 2021, https://millennial-grind.com/the-7-archangels-and-their-roles/

"Yoga and Consciousness: A Meditation to Access Your Highest Self." Healthline, 15 Nov. 2021, www.healthline.com/health/fitness/yoga-and-consciousness#A-meditation-for-consciousness.

Yugay, Irina. "How to Connect with Your Higher Self, according to Spirituality Teachers." Mindvalley Blog, 10 May 2022, https://blog.mindvalley.com/higher-self/

A beginner's guide to 10 types of crystals & how to use each of them. (2021, May 12). Mindbodygreen. https://www.mindbodygreen.com/articles/types-of-crystals

Adele, T. (2023, April 6). Healing crystals: Benefits, uses, and where to buy. Forbes. https://www.forbes.com/health/mind/guide-to-healing-crystals/

Ali, Herman, L., Believe, S., & Wille. (2021, January 15). Archangel Metatron: 7 Ways to Recognize and Connect with Him. A Little Spark of Joy. https://www.alittlesparkofjoy.com/archangel-metatron/

Angelic reiki healing. (n.d.). Naturallygiven.com. https://naturallygiven.com/angelic-reiki-healing-session/

Angelic Reiki. (2021, February 25). Christine Ringrose. https://www.christineringrose.co.uk/treatments/angelic-reiki/

Apollo, A. (2015, November 12). Activate your Pillar of Light. Guardian Alliance. https://guardianalliance.academy/healer/activate-your-pillar-of-light/

Aquarius. Academy ~ ⚛ ~ School of Consciousness. (2018, April 21). Metatron's Cube Heart Meditation. Lightwork. https://medium.com/working-light/metatrons-cube-heart-meditation-5936c241464d

Archangel & Zodiac Signs. (2020, March 3). AstroTalk Blog – Online Astrology Consultation with Astrologer. https://astrotalk.com/astrology-blog/archangel-and-zodiac-signs/

Archangel Metatron Meditation. (2018, February 12). Padre. https://www.guardian-angel-reading.com/blog-of-the-angels/archangel-metatron-meditation/

Archangel Metatron, The Arcahnegl of the Planet Earth – Traditional Magical Correspondences. (n.d.). Archangels-and-Angels.Com. http://www.archangels-and-angels.com/aa_pages/correspondences/angel_planet/archangel_metatron.html

Archangel Metatron. (n.d.). Circleofangels.Nl. https://circleofangels.nl/?page_id=2199

Archangel Metatron: Everything You Need To Know About Him. (2022, October 10). My Today's Horoscope. https://mytodayshoroscope.com/who-is-the-metatron-angel/

Archangel Metatron: Heal your energy. (n.d.). Jennroyster.com. https://www.jennroyster.com/blog/archangel-metatron-heal-your-energy

Archangel Metatron: The Mighty Angel of Judaism. (2021, November 26). OshaeIfa.com. https://en.oshaeifa.com/angelology/archangel-metatron/

Archangel Metatron's cube healing & activation. (2022, August 26). Vince Gowmon. https://www.vincegowmon.com/archangel-metatrons-cube-healing-activation/

Beckler, M. (2011, August 27). New Archangel Metatron meditation. Ask-angels.com. https://www.ask-angels.com/free-angel-messages/new-archangel-metatron-meditation/

Bedosky, L., & Laube, J. (n.d.). Reiki: How this energy healing works and its health benefits. Everydayhealth.com. https://www.everydayhealth.com/reiki/

Bellino, G. Z. (n.d.). From Enoch to metatron. Shulcloud.Com. https://images.shulcloud.com/609/uploads/class_files/Pardes/04aFromEnochtoMetatronSOURCES.pdf

Brown, S. (2019, May 17). Who is Archangel Metatron? And What is The Metatron Cube? The Black Feather Intuitive. https://www.theblackfeatherintuitive.com/archangel-metatron/

Brown, S. (2019, May 17). Who is Archangel Metatron? And What is The Metatron Cube? The Black Feather Intuitive. https://www.theblackfeatherintuitive.com/archangel-metatron/

Brown, S. (2019, May 17). Who is Archangel Metatron? And What is The Metatron Cube? The Black Feather Intuitive. https://www.theblackfeatherintuitive.com/archangel-metatron/

Conscious Vibe. (2022, March 4). Fascinating origin of Metatron's Cube: Meaning & symbolism. The Conscious Vibe. https://theconsciousvibe.com/the-symbolic-meaning-behind-metatrons-cube-sacred-geometry-explained/

CosmicSurfer. (2011, December 17). Michael vs. Metatron (biblical versions). SpaceBattles. https://forums.spacebattles.com/threads/michael-vs-metatron-biblical-versions.210468/

Crawford, H. (2019, December 15). Are you guided by archangel Metatron? Here's compelling 9 signs that you are.... Numerologist.com. https://numerologist.com/spiritual-growth/spiritual-world/9-signs-guided-by-archangel-metatron/

Crystals and archangels: Series intro. (n.d.). Healingcrystals.com. https://www.healingcrystals.com/Crystals_and_Archangels__Series_Intro_Articles_1789.html

Crystals for spiritual healing. (2022, January 20). Moonrise Crystals. https://moonrisecrystals.com/crystals-spiritual-healing/

Desy, P. L. (2015, January 25). 5 traditional Usui reiki symbols and their meanings. Learn Religions. https://www.learnreligions.com/usui-reiki-symbols-1731682

Discover the folklore of gemstone magic and crystal healing. (2021, December 28). The Creative Cottage. https://thecreativecottage.net/healing-properties-of-gemstones/

Dublin, A. (2023, April 26). Metatron: the most Powerful Angel in the Celestial Hierarchy. The Grimoires Corner.

https://www.thegrimoirescorner.com/2023/04/metatron-most-powerful-angel-in.html

Enlightenment, V. A. P. (2017, June 26). 7 The Chariot – Archangel Metatron – Angel Tarot Cards. DREAM WEAVER. https://enlightment1.wordpress.com/2017/06/26/7-the-chariot-archangel-metatron-angel-tarot-cards/

Get guidance from archangel Metatron and the number 11. (n.d.). Pandagossips.com. https://pandagossips.com/posts/6442

Heart, A. L. (n.d.). Archangel Metatron –. Angel Light Heart Blog. https://angeltherapycoach.wordpress.com/tag/archangel-metatron/

Hopler, W. (2012, April 18). How to recognize archangel metatron. Learn Religions. https://www.learnreligions.com/how-to-recognize-archangel-metatron-124277

Hopler, W. (2013, January 1). Archangel Metatron's cube in sacred geometry. Learn Religions. https://www.learnreligions.com/archangel-metatrons-cube-in-sacred-geometry-124293

Hopler, W. (n.d.). How to Recognize Archangel Metatron. Learn Religions. https://www.learnreligions.com/how-to-recognize-archangel-metatron-124277

Hughes, D. (2022, May 4). What is angelic reiki? Divine Escape. https://www.divineescape.co.uk/post/what-is-angelic-reiki

Insight Network, Inc. (n.d.). Daily Multidimensional Clearing With Archangel Metatron. Insighttimer.Com. https://insighttimer.com/kristintaylorintuitive/guided-meditations/multidimensional-general-clearing-meditation-and-connection-to-archangel-metatron-life-upgrade-psychic-clearing-and-protection-cutting-cords-highest-good-activation

Insight Network, Inc. (n.d.). Divine Alignment With Archangel Metatron. Insighttimer.Com. https://insighttimer.com/kristintaylorintuitive/guided-meditations/divine-alignment-with-archangel-metatron-life-upgrade-energy-clearing-psychic-clearing-and-protection-deep-spiritual-cleansing

Insight Network, Inc. (n.d.). Pillar Of Light. Insighttimer.Com. https://insighttimer.com/awakenedlife/guided-meditations/pillar-of-light-meditation

Judgement Tarot Card Meanings. (2011, December 22). Biddy Tarot. https://www.biddytarot.com/tarot-card-meanings/major-arcana/judgement/

Lazzerini, E. (2022, February 10). Archangel crystals & angel healing stones revealed. Ethan Lazzerini. https://www.ethanlazzerini.com/archangel-crystals/

Lewis, B. (2022, November 15). The meaning of Metatron's cube: Definition and origin – GFL. Galactic Federation Of Light.

https://www.galacticfederationoflight.com/blogs/consciousness/what-is-meaning-metatrons-cube-sacred-geometry

Linda. (2020, April 3). Pillar of Light Meditation. Thought Change. https://thoughtchange.com/pausing-to-discover-yourself/

lucifall. (2010, August 21). The Fool and Temperance and The High Priestess and The Pargod. Tarot Forum. https://www.tarotforum.net/threads/the-fool-and-temperance-and-the-high-priestess-and-the-pargod.145106/

Maggie. (2022, November 25). Metatron: Make an altar to the archangel of understanding. Spiru. https://spiru.com/metatron-make-an-altar-to-the-archangel-of-understanding/

Maloney, J. (2022, June 15). Personal and Planetary Ascension. Spirituality+Health. https://www.spiritualityhealth.com/personal-and-planetary-ascension

Manolo. (2022, October 14). Archangel Metatron: Everything You Need To Know. Better Numerology. https://www.betternumerology.com/archangel-metatron-everything-you-need-to-know/

Manolo. (2022a, January 1). Archangel Colors: The 7 divine rays of light. Better Numerology. https://www.betternumerology.com/archangel-colors/

Manolo. (2022b, October 14). Archangel Metatron: Everything you need to know. Better Numerology. https://www.betternumerology.com/archangel-metatron-everything-you-need-to-know/

Marshall, L. (2022, October 23). Reiki symbols: Meaning and drawings of each. Drawings Of. https://drawingsof.com/reiki-symbols/

Metatron Significance & Facts. (n.d.). Study.Com. https://study.com/academy/lesson/metatron-significance-facts-archangel.html

Metatron. (2015, December 23). ZAYAT AROMA. https://www.zayataroma.com/en/oils/metatron

Metatron. (n.d.). Angelology Wiki. https://angelology.fandom.com/wiki/Metatron

Metatron's cube: What it means in sacred geometry. (2023, March 15). WikiHow. https://www.wikihow.com/Metatron%27s-Cube

myspiritualshenanigans. (2020, May 30). 10 Stages Of Spiritual Awakening & Tips To Master Spiritual Growth. My Spiritual Shenanigans. https://myspiritualshenanigans.blog/stages-of-a-spiritual-awakening/

Newman, T. (2017, September 6). Reiki: What is it, and are there benefits? Medicalnewstoday.com. https://www.medicalnewstoday.com/articles/308772

Oracle, D. ~. A. (2013, August 7). Archangel Metatron ~ The Dreamer. Archangel Oracle. https://archangeloracle.com/2013/08/07/archangel-metatron-the-dreamer/

Rand, W. (2006, March 1). Knowing which Reiki techniques to use. Reiki. https://www.reiki.org/articles/knowing-which-reiki-techniques-use

Reddit – dive into anything. (n.d.). Reddit.com. https://www.reddit.com/r/Soulnexus/comments/gctn3b/my_amazing_meditation_experience_with_archangel/

Reiki symbols & their meanings: Everything you need to know. (2018, May 8). Mindbodygreen. https://www.mindbodygreen.com/articles/reiki-symbols-meanings

Roots, A. (n.d.). Connecting with Archangels. Angelic Roots. https://www.angelicroots.com/products/connecting-with-archangels-archangel-metatron-rainbow-tourmaline-moss-agate-and-garnet

Salow, S. (2022, May 18). How to Activate Your Pillar of Light & Why It's Essential. SYLVIA SALOW. https://sylviasalow.com/2022/05/18/activate-your-pillar-of-light/

Sievert, M. (n.d.). No title. Joynumber.com. https://joynumber.com/archangel-metatron/

Sinclair, G. (2019, December 18). 11 signs you're being guided by archangel metatron. Awareness Act. https://awarenessact.com/11-signs-youre-being-guided-by-archangel-metatron/

Spiritual. (2015, November 27). Angel Hierarchy – The Three Spheres Of Heaven. Spiritual Experience.

Stardust, L. (2020, December 22). The 10 most common types of crystals—and what they're used for. Oprah Daily. https://www.oprahdaily.com/life/a35045011/types-of-crystals/

Stewart, T. (2021, September 5). How to use crystals & stones for spirituality (ultimate beginner guide). Whimsy Soul. https://whimsysoul.com/how-to-use-crystals-stones-for-spirituality-ultimate-beginner-guide/

Support, W. W. a. (2020, March 30). How to Cut Cords with the Angels. Caroline Palmy. https://carolinepalmy.com/how-to-cut-cords-with-the-angels/

The benefits of crystal therapy – and why we think it rocks! (2016, May 4). Devonshire Dome. https://www.devonshiredome.co.uk/news/the-benefits-of-crystal-therapy-and-why-we-think-it-rocks/

The Fool Tarot Card Meanings. (2011, December 23). Biddy Tarot. https://www.biddytarot.com/tarot-card-meanings/major-arcana/fool/

The Ultimate 10 Step Guide To Cutting Cords Forever. (2020, June 26). Georgie G Deyn. https://www.georgiegdeyn.com/ultimate-10-step-guide-to-cutting-cords-forever/

victoriaGB. (2022, November 3). Cord Cutting Meditation. Gabbybernstein.Com. https://gabbybernstein.com/cut-the-cord/

Who is Archangel Metatron? The angel of the Akashic Records, Soul Ascension and 5D – Angel Readings, Angel Healings, Psychic Medium. (2022, March 18). Angel Readings, Angel Healings, Psychic Medium. https://archangelwisdom.com/who-is-archangel-metatron/

Wille. (2021, January 15). Archangel metatron: 7 ways to recognize and connect with him. A Little Spark of Joy. https://www.alittlesparkofjoy.com/archangel-metatron/

Zhelyazkov, Y. (2023, March 13). What is Metatron's cube symbol and why is it significant? Symbol Sage. https://symbolsage.com/metatron-cube-symbolism

(N.d.-a). Questionsonislam.com. https://questionsonislam.com/question/what-are-duties-mikail-michael-did-he-see-and-talk-prophet-pbuh

(N.d.-b). Chabad.org. https://www.chabad.org/library/article_cdo/aid/3825092/jewish/What-Are-Archangels.htm

11 Steps To Connect With Archangel Michael. (2019, July 11). Georgie G Deyn. https://www.georgiegdeyn.com/11-steps-connect-archangel-michael/

5 Easy Ways. (2022, April 22). The Quantum Lab. https://www.newworldblueprints.com/how-to-communicate-with-archangel-michael/

6 Undeniable Signs Archangel Michael is Connecting to You – Angel Readings, Angel Healings, Psychic Medium. (2021, October 4). Angel Readings, Angel Healings, Psychic Medium. https://archangelwisdom.com/6-undeniable-signs-archangel-michael-is-connecting-to-you/

7 Angelic Morning Rituals. (2015, April 15). Angelorum. https://angelorum.co/topics/angels/7-morning-rituals-to-infuse-your-day-with-angelic-energy/

7 Signs Archangel Michael Could Be Your Personal Healer. (2021, January 15). Archangel Secrets. https://www.archangelsecrets.com/7-signs-st-michael-the-archangel-healer/

888 Angel Number and Angel Michael. (2020, July 9). AskAstrology.

A Daily Angel Routine – New Age. (n.d.). Bellaonline.Com. http://www.bellaonline.com/articles/art38477.asp

Angel, A. (n.d.). Archangel Michael. Circleofangels.Nl. https://circleofangels.nl/?page_id=2038

Angels and essential oils. (2017, April 3). S.O.N.C.E. https://spiritualyopeningnowtocosmicenergy.wordpress.com/angels-and-essential-oils/

Archangel Michael – He who is like God Angel. (2021, March 16). Unifycosmos.com. https://unifycosmos.com/archangel-michael/

Archangel Michael, Archangel of the Sun – Traditional Magical Correspondences. (n.d.). Archangels-and-Angels.Com. http://www.archangels-and-angels.com/aa_pages/correspondences/angel_planet/archangel_michael.html

Archangel Michael. (n.d.). Angelwingsart.Co.Uk. https://www.angelwingsart.co.uk/archangel-michael.php

Archangelic Flower Correspondences. (2022, August 8). Angelorum. https://angelorum.co/angels-2/angel-mystic-monday/archangelic-flower-correspondences/

Askinosie, H. (2016, February 5). 8 ways to use crystals in your everyday routine. Mindbodygreen. https://www.mindbodygreen.com/articles/how-to-use-crystals-everyday

August. (2020, August 30). Scientific facts about wearing gemstones – Hubert jewelry – fine diamonds and gemstones. Hubertjewelry.com. https://hubertjewelry.com/scientific-facts-about-wearing-gemstones/

Brandstatter, T. (2013, May 25). Guardian angels in the orthodox faith. Synonym.com; Synonym. https://classroom.synonym.com/guardian-angels-in-the-orthodox-faith-12087290.html

Brown, S. (2018, September 7). Who is Archangel Michael? Overcome fear with the Archangel of Courage. The Black Feather Intuitive. https://www.theblackfeatherintuitive.com/who-is-archangel-michael-the-archangel-of-courage/

Catholic Online. (n.d.). St. Michael the Archangel. Catholic Online. https://www.catholic.org/saints/saint.php?saint_id=308

Cheryl. (2017, October 25). 4 Ways to Connect with Archangel Michael (It's Easier than you Think!). Intuitive Journey. https://intuitivejourney.com/connect-archangel-michael/

Connect to Angels with Angel Mantras & the Power of Intention – Angel Readings, Angel Healings, Psychic Medium. (2021, September 6). Angel Readings, Angel Healings, Psychic Medium. https://archangelwisdom.com/connect-to-angels-angel-mantras/

Cotton, I. (2015, October 21). Think on these things: Book of Daniel's Michael is Jesus. Today In BC

Crystals to help connect with archangel Michael. (n.d.). Healingcrystals.com. https://www.healingcrystals.com/Crystals_to_Help_Connect_with_Archangel_Michael_Articles_1790.html

Dagny. (2016, September 3). Writing to Archangel Michael. Reiki Rays. https://reikirays.com/33506/writing-archangel-michael/

Deyn, G. G. (2019, July 11). 11 steps to connect with Archangel Michael. Georgie G Deyn.

https://www.georgiegdeyn.com/11-steps-connect-archangel-michael/

Elias, A. A. (2021, April 4). Hadith on Mikaeel: Michael has not laughed since Hell was created. Daily Hadith Online. https://www.abuaminaelias.com/dailyhadithonline/2021/04/04/mikaeel-laughing/

Helen West, R. D. (2019, September 30). What are essential oils, and do they work? Healthline. https://www.healthline.com/nutrition/what-are-essential-oils

Hope - The Angel Writer. (2020, February 18). 6 Signs Archangel Michael Is Visiting You —. The Angel Writer. https://www.theangelwriter.com/blog/signs-archangel-michael

Hopler, W. (2011, May 20). Meet Archangel Michael, leader of all angels. Learn Religions. https://www.learnreligions.com/meet-archangel-michael-leader-of-angels-124715

Hopler, W. (2012a, January 1). Do you have your own guardian angel? Learn Religions. https://www.learnreligions.com/your-own-guardian-angel-123820

Hopler, W. (2012b, March 21). Archangels: God's leading angels. Learn Religions. https://www.learnreligions.com/archangels-gods-leading-angels-123898

Hopler, W. (2012c, May 1). Archangel Michael will lead the fight against Satan during end times. Learn Religions. https://www.learnreligions.com/bible-angels-archangel-michael-124047

Hopler, W. (2012d, May 1). How to recognize archangel Michael. Learn Religions. https://www.learnreligions.com/how-to-recognize-archangel-michael-124278

Hopler, W. (n.d.). How to Recognize Archangel Michael. Learn Religions. https://www.learnreligions.com/how-to-recognize-archangel-michael-124278

Hopler, W. (n.d.). How to Recognize Archangel Michael. Learn Religions. https://www.learnreligions.com/how-to-recognize-archangel-michael-124278

Hughes, L. (2019, March 1). What are healing crystals, and do they actually work? Oprah Daily. https://www.oprahdaily.com/life/health/a26559820/healing-crystals/

Hunter, M. G. (2022, November 11). Who is the archangel, Michael? Earth and Altar. https://earthandaltarmag.com/posts/who-is-the-archangel-michael

Incredible Personal Encounters with Saint Michael. (n.d.). Original Botanica. https://originalbotanica.com/blog/saint-michael-personal-encounter-stories

Insight Network, Inc. (n.d.). 21-Day Spiritual Cleansing With Archangel Michael. Insighttimer.Com. https://insighttimer.com/meditativeawakening/guided-meditations/21-day-spiritual-cleansing-with-archangel-michael

Insight Network, Inc. (n.d.). Archangel Michael Protection Meditation. Insighttimer.Com. https://insighttimer.com/gusferreira/guided-meditations/archangel-michael-protection-meditation

Insight Network, Inc. (n.d.). The Shield Of Michael Guided Visualisation. Insighttimer.Com. https://insighttimer.com/stevenobel/guided-meditations/the-shield-of-michael-meditation

ireneblais. (n.d.). Archangel Michael... – Angel Feathers Energy. Angelfeathersenergy.Ca. https://angelfeathersenergy.ca/2017/09/06/archangel-michael/

Khepri, V. A. P. by. (2012, August 19). Archangel Michael: How to Invoke His Help & Protection. The Magickal-Musings of Nefer Khepri, PhD. https://magickalmusings.blog/2012/08/19/archangel-michael-how-to-invoke-his-help-protection/

Khepri, V. A. P. by. (2015, May 15). Spiritual House Cleansing with Archangel Saint Michael. The Magickal-Musings of Nefer Khepri, PhD. https://magickalmusings.blog/2015/05/15/spiritual-house-cleansing-with-archangel-saint-michael/

Kranz, J. (2013, November 7). 7 biblical facts about Michael the archangel. OverviewBible. https://overviewbible.com/michael-archangel/

Lmhc, L. H. (1488904367000). Why Archangel Michael is the Ultimate Career Counselor. Linkedin.com. https://www.linkedin.com/pulse/why-archangel-michael-ultimate-career-counselor-lisa-hutchison-lmhc/

Lucey, C. (2022, April 6). Who is the Archangel Michael? Christianity.com. https://www.christianity.com/wiki/angels-and-demons/who-is-the-archangel-michael.html

Lundal, J. A. (2021, February 13). 7 Signs Archangel Michael Is Close. Spirit Miracle. https://www.spiritmiracle.com/signs-archangel-michael/

MacDougal, C. (2019, August 15). Crystals: The science behind the spiritual. ĀTHR Beauty. https://athrbeauty.com/blogs/goodvibesbeauty/crystals-the-science-the-spiritual

Malaikah. (n.d.). BBC. https://www.bbc.co.uk/bitesize/guides/z43pfcw/revision/3

Marie, T. (2019, January 17). How to use healing crystals & summon the Archangels you need most. YourTango. https://www.yourtango.com/experts/angellady-terriemarie/how-to-use-healing-crystals-to-connect-with-archangels-based-on-their-meanings

Michael the archangel. (2019, February 11). The Spiritual Life. https://slife.org/archangel-michael/

Michael, Wille, & Mary. (2021, May 10). Who Is Archangel Michael & 5 Sings of the Great Protector. A Little Spark of Joy.

https://www.alittlesparkofjoy.com/archangel-michael/

Miller, F. P., Vandome, A. F., & McBrewster, J. (Eds.). (2010). Archangel Michael: Roman Catholic traditions and views. Alphascript Publishing.

Miller, F. P., Vandome, A. F., & McBrewster, J. (Eds.). (2010). Archangel Michael: Roman Catholic traditions and views. Alphascript Publishing.

Mishra, D. P. (2023, February 9). Angel Number 36 – A Complete Guide to Angel Number 36 Meaning and Significance. EAstroHelp. https://www.eastrohelp.com/blog/angel-number-36-meaning/

Murray, B., & March, B. (2017, September 5). A beginner's guide to crystals. Harper's BAZAAR. https://www.harpersbazaar.com/uk/beauty/fitness-wellbeing/a43244/crystal-healing-beginners-guide/

pakosloski. (2020, October 8). Prayer to St. Michael for protection against spiritual enemies. Aleteia — Catholic Spirituality, Lifestyle, World News, and Culture. https://aleteia.org/2020/10/08/prayer-to-st-michael-for-protection-against-spiritual-enemies/

Payment, D. (2017, May 11). Archangel Michael Protective Holy Water. Dar Payment – The Official Site of Psychic Medium, Author, and Spiritual Teacher Dar Payment. https://darpayment.com/archangel-michael-protective-holy-water/

Payment, D. (2017, November 3). Archangel Michael Room Purification Salt Recipe. Dar Payment – The Official Site of Psychic Medium, Author, and Spiritual Teacher Dar Payment. https://darpayment.com/archangel-michael-room-purification-salt-recipe/

Payment, D. (2020, February 3). All About Archangel Michael. Dar Payment – The Official Site of Psychic Medium, Author, and Spiritual Teacher Dar Payment. https://darpayment.com/all-about-archangel-michael/

Payment, D. (2020, February 3). All About Archangel Michael. Dar Payment – The Official Site of Psychic Medium, Author, and Spiritual Teacher Dar Payment. https://darpayment.com/all-about-archangel-michael/

Payment, D. (2022, May 27). Using Essential Oils to connect with angels. Dar Payment – The Official Site of Psychic Medium, Author, and Spiritual Teacher Dar Payment. https://darpayment.com/using-essential-oils-to-connect-with-angels/

Plant, R. (2021, March 10). Michael Name Meaning. Verywell Family. https://www.verywellfamily.com/michael-name-meaning-5115812

Richardson, T. C., & Richardson, T. C. (n.d.). 5 ways Archangel Michael has your back – beliefnet. Beliefnet.com. https://www.beliefnet.com/inspiration/angels/5-ways-archangel-michael-has-your-back.aspx

Rose, M. (2022, December 8). StyleCaster. StyleCaster. https://stylecaster.com/how-to-use-protection-magic/

Rue. (2010, May 28). Protection Charm Charged With The Fire of Saint Michael the Archangel — Rue's Kitchen. Rue's Kitchen. https://www.rueskitchen.com/articles/protection-charm-charged-with-the-fire-of-saint-michael-the.html

Saint Michael's Day Rituals for Abundance and Protection. (n.d.). Original Botanica. https://originalbotanica.com/blog/saint-michaels-day-rituals-abundance-protection

Spiritual. (2016, January 18). Sigil Of Archangel Michael - How To Create It. Spiritual Experience

Stefan. (2021, April 25). Archangel Michael in the Reiki Session. Reiki Rays. https://reikirays.com/87365/archangel-michael-in-the-reiki-session/

The Archangel Michael—Who Is He? (n.d.). JW.ORG. https://www.jw.org/en/bible-teachings/questions/archangel-michael/

The Crystal Garden, South Florida's home for the holistic community. (n.d.). The Crystal Garden. https://thecrystalgarden.com/category/angels/

The Editors of Encyclopedia Britannica. (2020). Mīkāl. In Encyclopedia Britannica.

The Editors of Encyclopedia Britannica. (2022). Michael. In Encyclopedia Britannica.

The Editors of Encyclopedia Britannica. (2022). Michael. In Encyclopedia Britannica.

The word Michael mentioned in Quran. (2019, February 10). The Last Dialogue. https://www.thelastdialogue.org/article/the-word-michael-mentioned-in-quran/

View Archive →. (2023, April 11). Sigil of Archangel Michael: Meaning and Origin. Malevus. https://malevus.com/sigil-of-archangel-michael/

Waters, R. (2016, November 3). Crystals for the Archangels. Carpe Diem With Remi. https://www.carpediemwithremi.com.au/blogs/news/crystals-for-the-archangels

Webster, R. (2004, November 1). Contacting the Archangel Michael. Llewellyn Worldwide. https://www.llewellyn.com/journal/article/732

Webster, R. (2022, June 13). 7 ways to connect with archangels. Llewellyn Worldwide. https://www.llewellyn.com/journal/article/3023

Webster, R. (2022, June 13). 7 Ways to Connect with Archangels. Llewellyn Worldwide. https://www.llewellyn.com/journal/article/3023

Who is Saint Michael? (2019, December 23). Saint Michael's College. https://www.smcvt.edu/about-smc/who-is-saint-michael/

Wille. (2021, May 10). Who is Archangel Michael & 5 sings of the great protector. A Little Spark of Joy.

https://www.alittlesparkofjoy.com/archangel-michael

Barker, M. (2006). The Angel Raphael in the Book of Tobit. In M. Bredin (Ed.), Studies in the Book of Tobit. A&C Black.

Barnes, W. H. (1993). Archangels. In M. D. Coogan & B. M. Metzger (Eds.), The Oxford Companion to the Bible. Oxford University Press.

Coogan, M. D. (1993). Raphael. In M. D. Coogan & B. M. Metzger (Eds.), The Oxford Companion to the Bible. Oxford University Press.

Cresswell, J. (2011). Archangels. In J. Cresswell (Ed.), The Watkins Dictionary of Angels. Duncan Baird Publishers.

Cyr, M. D. (1987). The Archangel Raphael: Narrative Authority in Milton's War in Heaven. The Journal of Narrative Technique.

Esler, P. F. (2017). God's Court and Courtiers in the Book of the Watchers. Wipf and Stock Publishers.

Grabbe, L. (2003). Tobit. In J.D.G Dunn (Ed.), Eerdmans Commentary on the Bible. Eerdmans.

Grossman, M.L. (2011). Angels. In M.L Grossman (Ed.), The Oxford Dictionary of the Jewish Religion. Oxford University Press.

Laptas, M. (2016). Archangel Raphael as protector, demon tamer, guide, and healer. Some aspects of the Archangel's activities in Nubian painting. In Aegyptus et Nubia Christiana. The Wlodzimierz Godlewski jubilee volume on the occasion of his 70th birthday. Wydawnictwa Uniwersytetu Warszawskiego.

Lasota, M. (2003). Archangel Raphael. iUniverse.

LaSota, M., & Sternberg, H. (2007). Hope, help, healing with archangel Raphael and the angels. iUniverse.

Mach, M.(1999). Raphael. In K.Van der Toorn, B.Becking, & P.W.Van der Horst(Eds.), Dictionary of Deities and Demons in the Bible. Eerdmans.

Meier, S.A.(1999). Angel I. In K.Van der Toorn, B.Becking, & P.W.Van der Horst(Eds.), Dictionary of Deities and Demons in the Bible. Eerdmans.

Schaller, B.(1999). Enoch. In G.W.Bromiley(Ed.), The Encyclopedia of Christianity(Vol 2), Eerdmans.

Soll, W.(2000). Raphael. In D.N.Freedman&A.C.Myers(Eds.), Eerdmans Dictionary of the Bible. Eerdmans.

Van Henten, J.W.(1999). Archangel. In K.Van der Toorn, B.Becking, & P.W.Van der Horst(Eds.), Dictionary of Deities and Demons in the Bible. Eerdmans.

Virtue, D. (2011). Archangels 101: How to Connect Closely with Archangels Michael, Raphael, Gabriel, Uriel, and Others for Healing, Protection, and Guidance. Hay House Incorporated.

Virtue, D. (2010). The Healing Miracles of Archangel Raphael. Hay House, Inc.

Webster, R. (2012). Raphael: Communicating with the Archangel for Healing & Creativity. Llewellyn Worldwide

Brown, S. (2017, September 20). Who is Archangel Uriel? The Black Feather Intuitive. https://www.theblackfeatherintuitive.com/archangel-uriel/

Hopler, W. (2011, June 5). Meet Archangel Uriel, angel of wisdom. Learn Religions. https://www.learnreligions.com/meet-archangel-uriel-angel-of-wisdom-124717

Jensen, E. (2022, January 4). Archangel Uriel - angel of truth spiritual symbolism. IPublishing. https://www.ipublishing.co.in/archangel-uriel

Kalu, M. (2021, January 11). Who is the archangel, Uriel? Christianity.com. https://www.christianity.com/wiki/angels-and-demons/who-is-the-archangel-uriel.html

Varnell, J. R. (2016). Uriel. Createspace Independent Publishing Platform.

What is the role of the archangel Uriel in human life? (2020, April 20). Andija Store. https://andija.com/useful-articles/what-is-the-role-of-the-archangel-uriel-in-human-life/

Wille. (2021, January 15). Who is Archangel Uriel? The Angel of Truth. A Little Spark of Joy. https://www.alittlesparkofjoy.com/archangel-uriel

– H. (2019, May 13). Being visited by Angels? Here are 14 Angel signs that you are! The Angel Writer. https://www.theangelwriter.com/blog/angel-signs

(N.d.-a). Psychicsource.com. https://www.psychicsource.com/numerology

(N.d.-b). T2conline.com. https://t2conline.com/the-history-of-numerology/

(N.d.-c). Instyle.com. https://www.instyle.com/lifestyle/astrology/numerology

12 signs an angel messenger is near - centre of excellence. (2019, March 18). Centreofexcellence.com. https://www.centreofexcellence.com/angel-messenger-12-signs/

18 signs you're experiencing A synchronicity (and not just coincidence). (2022, December 23). Mindbodygreen. https://www.mindbodygreen.com/articles/synchronicities

Allard, S. (2020, May 12). The beauty of synchronicity. Divineknowing.com. https://www.divineknowing.com/blog/the-beauty-of-synchronicity/

Angel Correspondences. (n.d.). Tripod.Com. https://athena523.tripod.com/angelcorres.htm

Angelic Correspondences in the Tarot. (2015, July 8). Angelorum. https://angelorum.co/topics/divination/angelic-messages-and-correspondences-in-the-tarot/

Angelic Correspondences. (1970, January 1). SpellsOfMagic. https://www.spellsofmagic.com/coven_ritual.html?ritual=152&coven=108

Archangelic Flower Correspondences. (2022, August 8). Angelorum. https://angelorum.co/angels-2/angel-mystic-monday/archangelic-flower-correspondences/

Aúgusta, J. (2023, February 17). Where can you see angel numbers? Ministry of Numerology. https://ministryofnumerology.com/where-can-you-see-angel-numbers/

Aymen. (2011, July 26). Angelic Correspondences. Spiritual.Com.Au. https://spiritual.com.au/2011/07/angelic-correspondences/

Beck, M. (2016, August 11). Martha beck: How to tell when the universe is sending you signs. Oprah.com. https://www.oprah.com/inspiration/martha-beck-how-to-tell-when-the-universe-is-sending-you-signs

Blair, S. (2022, May 30). What are angel numbers? A guide to the phenomenon and why it may occur. RUSSH; RUSSH Magazine. https://www.russh.com/what-are-angel-numbers/

Blanchard, T. (2021, December 3). 7 signs of divine timing working in your life. Outofstress.com. https://www.outofstress.com/signs-divine-timing-is-working/

Bose, S. D. (2022, September 8). When Jim Carrey wrote himself a $10 million cheque. Far Out Magazine. https://faroutmagazine.co.uk/jim-carrey-wrote-himself-10-million-cheque/

Bronzeman. (n.d.). Method of invoking angels, by Sigil Ritual proven to be effective. Opera.News. https://gh.opera.news/gh/en/religion/c9b4f2070eb6c478ad6dff37c26471fb

Canfield, J. (2021, September 8). A complete guide to using the law of Attraction. Jack Canfield. https://jackcanfield.com/blog/using-the-law-of-attraction/

Cheung, N. (2017, November 17). Signs of an angel watching over you. Woot & Hammy. https://wootandhammy.com/blogs/news/angel-signs-watching-over-you-guardian-angel-numbers

Debutify, & Tarot, A. (2021, August 3). What Are Angel Sigils? Apollo Tarot. https://apollotarot.com/blogs/insights/what-are-angel-sigils

Eatough, E. (n.d.). What is the law of attraction, and can you use it to change your life? Betterup.com. https://www.betterup.com/blog/what-is-law-of-attraction

Estrada, J. (2021, April 8). No, it's not just a coincidence—here's how to spot and decode spiritual synchronicities. Well+Good. https://www.wellandgood.com/what-does-synchronicity-mean-spiritually/

Glitch Digital. (2021, June 23). Jim carrey's law of attraction and visualization tips. Influencive. https://www.influencive.com/jim-carreys-law-of-attraction-and-visualization-tips/

Graf, S. (2012, July 15). How to meditate on the third eye for better intuition. WikiHow. https://www.wikihow.com/Meditate-on-the-Third-Eye

Günel, S. (2020, May 29). How to manifest your wildest dreams: A beginner's guide to the law of attraction. Mind Cafe. https://medium.com/mind-cafe/how-to-manifest-your-wildest-dreams-a-beginners-guide-to-the-law-of-attraction-b82ca96e7fc9

Henry Cornelius Agrippa. (n.d.). Umich.Edu. https://quod.lib.umich.edu/e/eebo/A26562.0001.001/1:13.19?rgn=div2;view=fulltext

History of Numerology – Kabbalah, Chaldean, Pythagorean, Chinese, Angelic Numerology. (2021, June 4). MyPandit. https://www.mypandit.com/numerology/history/

Hurst, K. (2019, June 5). Law Of Attraction history: Discovering the secret origins. The Law Of Attraction; Cosmic Media LLC. https://thelawofattraction.com/history-law-attraction-uncovered/

Hurst, K. (2023, March 7). 14 warning signs from angels - look out for these symbols. The Law Of Attraction; Cosmic Media LLC. https://thelawofattraction.com/angel-signs-symbols/

JABAMIAH. (n.d.). Symbolikon - Visual Library of Worldwide Ancient Symbols. https://symbolikon.com/downloads/jabamiah-angel/

KatrinaKoltes. (2020, October 15). Ask The Angels - Angelic Sigils and Keys. Katrina Koltes. https://katrinakoltes.com/ask-the-angels-angelic-sigils-and-keys/

Kelly, A. (2021, December 24). A guide to angel numbers and what they mean. Allure. https://www.allure.com/story/what-are-angel-numbers

Kirsten, C. (2022, May 16). Who invented angel numbers? The truth behind numerology origins! Typically, Topical. https://typicallytopical.com/who-invented-angel-numbers/

Kurt. (2017, July 4). Finding your centre: Grounding meditation techniques. Earthing Canada. https://earthingcanada.ca/blog/grounding-meditation-techniques/

Law of Attraction visualization. (2022, October 13). Selfpause. https://selfpause.com/law-of-attraction/law-of-attraction-visualization-how-to-activate-the-law-of-attraction-through-visualization/

Lou. (2022, May 13). 9 common angel symbols and signs from your angels. A Little Spark of Joy. https://www.alittlesparkofjoy.com/angel-symbols/

Louise, E. (2020, February 14). Synchronicity and signs from the Universe that you shouldn't ignore. Through the Phases. https://www.throughthephases.com/synchronicity-signs-from-universe/

Marissa. (2021, January 1). 10 powerful vision board ideas to master the law of attraction. A to Zen Life. https://atozenlife.com/vision-board-ideas/

Meaningful coincidences, serendipity, and synchronicity. (n.d.). Psychology Today.

https://www.psychologytoday.com/intl/blog/connecting-coincidence/202101/meaningful-coincidences-serendipity-and-synchronicity

Miedaner, T. (2015, February 25). 3 laws of Attraction: Like Attracts Like, Nature Abhors a Vacuum, The Present is Always Perfect. Lifecoach.com. https://www.lifecoach.com/articles/laws-of-attraction/3-laws-attraction-the-present-is-always-perfect/

Moore, J. D. (2016, July 24). 7 shocking ways angels speak to you every day. Psych Central. https://psychcentral.com/blog/life-goals/2016/07/ways-angels-speak-to-you

Moore, J. D. (2016, July 24). 7 shocking ways angels speak to you every day. Psych Central. https://psychcentral.com/blog/life-goals/2016/07/ways-angels-speak-to-you

O., T. (2021, October 15). Mirror hours: what are they trying to tell you? WeMystic. https://www.wemystic.com/mirror-hours/

Parlak, M. (2022, December 25). Deep spiritual meaning of mirrored numbers. Gemset. https://gemset.net/deep-spiritual-meaning-of-mirrored-numbers/

Paxton, P. (2022, February 15). Law of Attraction: History and overview - mind altar - medium. Mind Altar. https://medium.com/mind-altar/law-of-attraction-history-a-80bc52daa925

Powers, S., Barkataki, S., & Marglin, A. T. to. (2021, June 15). Everything you need to know about the solar plexus (navel) chakra. Yoga Journal. https://www.yogajournal.com/yoga-101/chakras-yoga-for-beginners/intro-third-navel-chakra/

Quinn, J. (2023, January 10). What do angel numbers mean, and why do you see them everywhere? Reader's Digest. https://www.rd.com/article/angel-numbers-meaning/

Rebecca Joy Stanborough, M. F. A. (2020, November 13). What is vibrational energy? Healthline. https://www.healthline.com/health/vibrational-energy

San, D., & Ph, F. D. (n.d.). Angels As Spiritual Guides. Digitalcommons.nl.edu. https://digitalcommons.nl.edu/cgi/viewcontent.cgi?article=1054&context=faculty_publications#:~:text=These%20spiritual%20beings%20are%20thought,different%20times%20in%20their%20life.

Sappington, T. (2020, September 10). The spirit world: Angels. The Gospel Coalition. https://www.thegospelcoalition.org/essay/the-spirit-world-angels/

Scott, E. (2007, February 18). What is the law of attraction? Verywell Mind. https://www.verywellmind.com/understanding-and-using-the-law-of-attraction-3144808

Sendef, G. (2016, September 26). 5 common ways angels bring you guidance and messages. Change Your Thoughts; Steven Aitchison.

https://www.stevenaitchison.co.uk/5-common-ways-angels-bring-guidance-messages/

Siegel, J. (2022, May 4). Your angel number: What it means and how to discover it. WikiHow. https://www.wikihow.com/Find-My-Angel-Number

Sipress, J. (2021, July 21). Everything you need to know about angel numbers. Cosmopolitan. https://www.cosmopolitan.com/lifestyle/a37079416/angel-numbers-numerology/

Spiegelhalter, D. (2012, April 26). Coincidences: What are the chances of them happening? BBC. https://www.bbc.com/future/article/20120426-what-a-coincidence

Stokes, V. (2021, May 6). How to open your third eye chakra for spiritual awakening. Healthline. https://www.healthline.com/health/mind-body/how-to-open-your-third-eye

Tamara. (2022, October 29). 7 beautiful angel signs and symbols of love and support. Tamara Like Camera; Tamara. https://tamaracamerablog.com/7-beautiful-angel-signs-and-symbols-of-love-and-support/

Taphorn, S., & Taphorn, S. (n.d.). 5 warning signs from the angels. Beliefnet.com. https://www.beliefnet.com/inspiration/angels/5-warning-signs-from-the-angels.aspx

The law of attraction, simplified: A primer on this spiritual concept. (2020, April 24). Mindbodygreen. https://www.mindbodygreen.com/articles/the-law-of-attraction-simplified-what-it-is-and-how-to-use-it

Thorp, T. (2018, August 2). A meditation guide to activate the Law Of Attraction & love. Chopra. https://chopra.com/articles/a-meditation-guide-to-activate-the-law-of-attraction-love

Thorp, T. (2019, February 4). Guided meditation: Ground yourself using the Earth element. Chopra. https://chopra.com/articles/guided-meditation-ground-yourself-using-the-earth-element

Wang, C. (2022, September 5). The Sigil of Archangel Michael: What Is It and How to Use It? Buddha & Karma. https://buddhaandkarma.com/blogs/guide/what-is-the-sigil-of-archangel-michael-meaning

What is the Law of Attraction & how does it work? (2023, March 7). The Law Of Attraction; Cosmic Media LLC. https://thelawofattraction.com/what-is-the-law-of-attraction/

White, L., & White, L. (n.d.). 7 common ways angels bring you guidance and messages. Beliefnet.com. https://www.beliefnet.com/inspiration/angels/galleries/7-common-ways-angels-bring-you-guidance-and-messages.aspx

Why certain numbers keep showing up in your life + what to do when you see them. (2017, May 26). Mindbodygreen. https://www.mindbodygreen.com/articles/angel-number-sequences-and-what-they-mean-for-you

Wille. (2021, December 28). Angel number 7777 - A call for spirituality and meditation. A Little Spark of Joy. https://www.alittlesparkofjoy.com/angel-number-7777/

Wille. (2022, January 18). What are angel colors and what do they mean? A Little Spark of Joy. https://www.alittlesparkofjoy.com/angel-colors/

Young, A. (2019, November 7). Learn numerology: An easy-to-understand beginners guide. Subconscious Servant. https://subconsciousservant.com/learn-numerology

Image Sources

[1] https://unsplash.com/photos/DRgrzQQsJDA?utm_source=unsplash&utm_medium=referral&utm_content=creditShareLink

[2] https://pixabay.com/images/id-5628622/

[3] https://www.pexels.com/photo/close-up-photo-of-caution-signage-4447140/

[4] https://commons.wikimedia.org/wiki/File:Four_elements_representation.svg

[5] https://unsplash.com/photos/HfGEtmnRwuE?utm_source=unsplash&utm_medium=referral&utm_content=creditShareLink

[6] https://pixabay.com/images/id-1836875/

[7] https://pixabay.com/images/id-3777403/

[8] Nordwest, CC BY-SA 4.0 <https://creativecommons.org/licenses/by-sa/4.0>, via Wikimedia Commons https://commons.wikimedia.org/wiki/File:Buddha_in_Meditation_2023-05-11-22.jpg

[9] https://commons.wikimedia.org/wiki/File:Ganesha_Basohli_miniature_circa_1730_Dubost_p73.jpg

[10] Andrewrabbott, CC BY-SA 4.0 <https://creativecommons.org/licenses/by-sa/4.0>, via Wikimedia Commons: https://commons.wikimedia.org/wiki/File:West_window,_St_Michael_and_All_Angels%27_Church,_Somerton.jpg

[11] https://www.pexels.com/photo/woman-wearing-white-sleeveless-lace-shirt-935985/

[12] Photo by Marcus Aurelius: https://www.pexels.com/photo/woman-practicing-yoga-6787217/

[13] https://www.pexels.com/photo/texture-wall-white-colors-1843717/

[14] https://unsplash.com/photos/eB1ziPSixIQ?utm_source=unsplash&utm_medium=referral&utm_content=creditShareLink

[15] https://unsplash.com/photos/z4n8CGRuzOA?utm_source=unsplash&utm_medium=referral&utm_content=creditShareLink

[16] https://unsplash.com/photos/dVRD8E3XUGs?utm_source=unsplash&utm_medium=referral&utm_content=creditShareLink

[17] https://unsplash.com/photos/Ar6eXpQaCwk?utm_source=unsplash&utm_medium=referral&utm_content=creditShareLink

[18] https://unsplash.com/photos/OxHPDs4WV8Y?utm_source=unsplash&utm_medium=referral&utm_content=creditShareLink

[19] https://commons.wikimedia.org/wiki/File:Metatrons_cube.svg

[20] Tomruen, CC BY-SA 4.0 <https://creativecommons.org/licenses/by-sa/4.0>, via Wikimedia Commons: https://commons.wikimedia.org/wiki/File:Stellated_octahedron_stellation_plane.png

[21] Tomruen, CC BY-SA 4.0 <https://creativecommons.org/licenses/by-sa/4.0>, via Wikimedia Commons: https://commons.wikimedia.org/wiki/File:Tetrakis_hexahedron_cubic.png

[22] Tomruen, CC BY-SA 4.0 <https://creativecommons.org/licenses/by-sa/4.0>, via Wikimedia Commons: https://commons.wikimedia.org/wiki/File:Octahedron_orange.png

[23] Ancella Simoes from Atlanta, CC BY 2.0 <https://creativecommons.org/licenses/by/2.0>, via Wikimedia Commons: https://commons.wikimedia.org/wiki/File:Origami_Isosahedron_(Design_by_Heinz_Strobl)_(3595750701).jpg

[24] DTR, CC BY-SA 3.0 <http://creativecommons.org/licenses/by-sa/3.0/>, via Wikimedia Commons: https://commons.wikimedia.org/wiki/File:Dodecahedron.svg

[25] Derrellwilliams, CC BY-SA 4.0 <https://creativecommons.org/licenses/by-sa/4.0>, via Wikimedia Commons: https://commons.wikimedia.org/wiki/File:Light_pillar_in_winter.jpg

[26] https://commons.wikimedia.org/wiki/File:Cho-Ku-Rei_(Reiki_Symbol).svg

[27] Stephen Buck The Reiki Sangha, CC BY-SA 4.0 <https://creativecommons.org/licenses/by-sa/4.0>, via Wikimedia Commons: https://commons.wikimedia.org/wiki/File:Seiheiki.jpg

[28] Stephen Buck The Reiki Sangha, CC BY-SA 4.0 <https://creativecommons.org/licenses/by-sa/4.0>, via Wikimedia Commons: https://commons.wikimedia.org/wiki/File:Honshazeshonen.jpg

[29] Stephen Buck The Reiki Sangha, CC BY-SA 4.0 <https://creativecommons.org/licenses/by-sa/4.0>, via Wikimedia Commons: https://commons.wikimedia.org/wiki/File:Daikomyo.jpg

[30] Juan Camilo Guerrero, CC BY-SA 4.0 <https://creativecommons.org/licenses/by-sa/4.0>, via Wikimedia Commons: https://commons.wikimedia.org/wiki/File:Raku_Symbol.jpg

[31] https://unsplash.com/photos/jLWLxX6i3R8?utm_source=unsplash&utm_medium=referral&utm_content=creditShareLink

[32] https://unsplash.com/photos/WKkTwwBILec?utm_source=unsplash&utm_medium=referral&utm_content=creditShareLink

[33] Rama, CC BY-SA 3.0 FR <https://creativecommons.org/licenses/by-sa/3.0/fr/deed.en>, via Wikimedia Commons: https://commons.wikimedia.org/wiki/File:Tourmaline-MCG_79448-P41.50859-black.jpg

[34] https://unsplash.com/photos/vxf-uurQ5rY?utm_source=unsplash&utm_medium=referral&utm_content=creditShareLink

35 https://unsplash.com/photos/ppmiXmhHHyc?utm_source=unsplash&utm_medium=referral&utm_content=creditShareLink

36 https://unsplash.com/photos/CrO6G4it4lY?utm_source=unsplash&utm_medium=referral&utm_content=creditShareLink

37 https://unsplash.com/photos/IQXhLIoBA8g?utm_source=unsplash&utm_medium=referral&utm_content=creditShareLink

38 *JJ Harrison (https://www.jjharrison.com.au/), CC BY-SA 4.0 <https://creativecommons.org/licenses/by-sa/4.0>, via Wikimedia Commons: https://commons.wikimedia.org/wiki/File:Rhodochrosite_on_Matrix_-_Peru.jpg*

39 *No machine-readable author provided. Adam Ognisty assumed (based on copyright claims)., CC BY 3.0 <https://creativecommons.org/licenses/by/3.0>, via Wikimedia Commons: https://commons.wikimedia.org/wiki/File:1Lapis_lazuli.jpeg*

40 *Rob Lavinsky, iRocks.com – CC-BY-SA-3.0, CC BY-SA 3.0 <https://creativecommons.org/licenses/by-sa/3.0>, via Wikimedia Commons: https://commons.wikimedia.org/wiki/File:Chrysocolla-230109.jpg*

41 https://unsplash.com/photos/7NGU2YqBue8?utm_source=unsplash&utm_medium=referral&utm_content=creditShareLink

42 https://unsplash.com/photos/x5hyhMBjR3M?utm_source=unsplash&utm_medium=referral&utm_content=creditShareLink

43 *Bielpincet, CC BY-SA 3.0 <https://creativecommons.org/licenses/by-sa/3.0>, via Wikimedia Commons https://commons.wikimedia.org/wiki/File:Icon_of_Archangel_Michael_in_Cathedral_in_the_name_of_Archangel_Michael.jpg*

44 https://unsplash.com/photos/lYMbHxtntRo

45 https://unsplash.com/photos/y02jEX_B0O0

46 https://unsplash.com/photos/M-xaOaCzy_M

47 https://pixabay.com/es/photos/miguel-san-miguel-arc%C3%A1ngel-5764009/

48 https://unsplash.com/photos/HK1BuoReZmM

49 https://unsplash.com/photos/Tlcy2YCFwlg

50 https://www.needpix.com/photo/892366/symbol-wind-rose-nautica-free-vector-graphics

51 https://www.pexels.com/photo/white-and-gray-stone-on-brown-wooden-table-3610752/

52 https://www.pexels.com/photo/two-clear-glass-bottles-with-liquids-672051/

53 https://pixabay.com/es/illustrations/arc%C3%A1ngel-rafael-arc%C3%A1ngel-angel-7964678/

54 *Saint Raphael the Archangel. Colour lithograph. Raphael (Archangel). Work ID: gza6qtuq, Creative Commons Attribution (CC BY 4.0) <https://creativecommons.org/licenses/by/4.0/> https://www.lookandlearn.com/history-images/YW032933VEL/Saint-Raphael-the-Archangel*

55 https://unsplash.com/photos/AsahNlC0VhQ

56 https://unsplash.com/photos/ReEqHw2GyeI

57 https://www.pexels.com/photo/grayscale-photo-of-feather-1320724/

58 https://www.pexels.com/photo/man-and-woman-near-grass-field-1415131/

59 https://pxhere.com/en/photo/910362

60 https://unsplash.com/photos/r6_xcsNg0kw

61 Stephen Buck The Reiki Sangha, CC BY-SA 2.0 <https://creativecommons.org/licenses/by-sa/2.0>, via Wikimedia Commons https://commons.wikimedia.org/wiki/File:Chokurei.jpg

62 L orlando, CC BY-SA 4.0 <https://creativecommons.org/licenses/by-sa/4.0>, via Wikimedia Commons https://commons.wikimedia.org/wiki/File:Sei_He_Ki.jpg

63 Stephen Buck The Reiki Sangha, CC BY-SA 4.0 <https://creativecommons.org/licenses/by-sa/4.0>, via Wikimedia Commons https://commons.wikimedia.org/wiki/File:Honshazeshonen.jpg

64 https://unsplash.com/photos/yn7R3DLA-ik

65 Andrewrabbott, CC BY-SA 4.0 <https://creativecommons.org/licenses/by-sa/4.0>, via Wikimedia Commons: https://commons.wikimedia.org/wiki/File:Angelic_Hierarchy_in_Christianity,_St_Michael_and_All_Angels%27,_Somerton.jpg

66 https://commons.wikimedia.org/wiki/File:Image_of_Uriel_the_Archangel,_Cairo.jpg

67 https://www.pexels.com/photo/orange-flame-635926/

68 https://commons.wikimedia.org/wiki/File:Ottobeuren_basilika_ottobeuren_altar_of_the_guardian_angel_006.JPG

69 https://pixabay.com/images/id-7182133/

70 https://unsplash.com/photos/vs-PjCh5goo?utm_source=unsplash&utm_medium=referral&utm_content=creditShareLink

71 https://unsplash.com/photos/rUc9hVE-L-E?utm_source=unsplash&utm_medium=referral&utm_content=creditShareLink

72 https://unsplash.com/photos/bGxyxfqeq34?utm_source=unsplash&utm_medium=referral&utm_content=creditShareLink

73 https://unsplash.com/photos/WvDYdXDzkhs?utm_source=unsplash&utm_medium=referral&utm_content=creditShareLink

74 https://picryl.com/media/postilla-in-prophetas-ubu-hs-252-f043v-moralisacio-seraph-3655d7

75 See page for author, CC BY 4.0 <https://creativecommons.org/licenses/by/4.0>, via Wikimedia Commons https://commons.wikimedia.org/wiki/File:Pythagoras._Etching_by_F._L._D._Ciartres_after_(C._V.)._Wellcome_V0004826.jpg

76 https://www.publicdomainpictures.net/en/view-image.php?image=339272&picture=numbers-and-digits

77 https://creazilla.com/nodes/1712425-guardian-angel-wing-sky-illustration

78 https://unsplash.com/photos/close-up-photo-of-assorted-coins-NeTPASr-bmQ?utm_content=creditShareLink&utm_medium=referral&utm_source=unsplash Photo by Josh Appel on Unsplash

79 https://www.wallpaperflare.com/angel-soldier-archangel-michael-archangel-michael-combative-wallpaper-etybt

⁸⁰ https://picryl.com/media/eth-bib-jung-carl-gustav-1875-1961-portrait-portr-14163-cropped-c7875d

⁸¹ https://commons.wikimedia.org/wiki/File:Archangel_Gabriel;_The_Virgin_Annunciate_MET_ep1975.1.120c.bw.R.jpg

⁸² https://commons.wikimedia.org/wiki/File:Anael_como_el_regente_de_la_Luna.jpg

⁸³ https://pixabay.com/es/illustrations/buda-zen-meditaci%C3%B3n-4264589/

⁸⁴ Amila Tennakoon, CC BY 2.0 <https://creativecommons.org/licenses/by/2.0>, via Wikimedia Commons https://upload.wikimedia.org/wikipedia/commons/7/7e/Meditation_in_a_yoga_asana.jpg